MARTIN PUGH

'We Danced All Night'

A Social History of Britain
Between the Wars

VINTAGE BOOKS
London

Published by Vintage 2009

4 6 8 10 9 7 5

First published in Great Britain by The Bodley Head in 2008

Vintage
Random House, 20 Vauxhall Bridge Road,
London SW1V 2SA

www.vintage-books.co.uk

Addresses for companies within The Random House Group Limited
can be found at: www.randomhouse.co.uk/offices.htm

The Random House Group Limited Reg. No. 954009

A CIP catalogue record for this book
is available from the British Library

ISBN 9781844139231

The Random House Group Limited supports The Forest Stewardship Council
(FSC®), the leading international forest certification organisation. Our books
carrying the FSC label are printed on FSC® certified paper. FSC is the only
forest certification scheme endorsed by the leading environmental organisations,
including Greenpeace. Our paper procurement policy can be found at
www.randomhouse.co.uk/environment

Printed and bound by
CPI Group (UK) Ltd, Croydon, CR0 4YY

CN 941
=
AN 300867

'The great success of Martin Pugh's sparkling new volume is to set the familiar events of the 1920s and 1930s in their proper context and to connect them to longer-term patterns of change . . . this is social history with a human face . . . this is one those rare books that deserves a wide audience, but which will also be required reading for specialists'
BBC History Magazine

'An extraordinary book [that] reveals how modern society was born between the wars . . . comprehensive, often astonishing'
Daily Express

'It succeeds in bringing out both the strangeness and the familiarity of this odd period of history . . . allows us to see a version of ourselves in the culture of the Twenties and Thirties in a way we simply cannot when we look at the elusive Edwardians'
Daily Telegraph

'A lively, tactile history of inter-war Britain'
Sunday Times

'A fascinating, detailed look at how we lived during the inter-war years'
Daily Mail

Contents

Preface and Acknowledgements

Demarcated by the tragedy of the Great War on one side and the looming threat of the Second World War on the other, the 1920s and 1930s boast a coherent identity enjoyed by few twenty-year periods of history. It has been seen in fairly stark terms. Interwar social history has often been portrayed in a light-hearted way as the 'Roaring Twenties', and not entirely wrongly, for, after the privations of wartime many British people were keen to seize any opportunities for leisure and self-indulgence. But at the other end of the spectrum the political history of the period, heavily coloured by economics, presents a gloomy picture of a society dogged by mass unemployment and class divisions, punctuated by protests such as the General Strike and the hunger marches, and dominated by uncaring right-wing governments. The British Left, out of power for most of the period, scored a belated victory in writing the history of the interwar period as one of poverty, failure and reaction. In effect our impressions have been heavily influenced by some celebrated pieces of contemporary literature ranging from novels to autobiographies to ostensibly factual accounts including Walter Greenwood's *Love on the Dole* (1933), Vera Brittain's *Testament of Youth* (1933), George Orwell's *The Road to Wigan Pier* (1937), and Ellen Wilkinson's *The Town That Was Murdered* (1939). However, the combination of political bias and the literary skills of their authors make them dubious sources for social historians. Orwell's famous Left Book Club volume is more a piece of journalistic embellishment than the kind of sober account he was originally commissioned to write. Brittain's moving story is not entirely consistent with the diary she wrote at the time. Moreover, her personal account of the Lost Generation of the Great War has created pitfalls for later students. Quite recently, indeed, it has helped generate Virginia Nicholson's

Singled Out: How Two Million Women Survived without Men after the First World War (2007), a notable example of a book based on a myth: that a generation of women was condemned to spinsterhood by the casualties of the war. In fact, as the current volume shows, interwar British women by no means lacked husbands; despite contemporary fears, *more* of them got married than had before 1914, and by the 1930s the institution of marriage was reaching its heyday in this country.

The present volume reflects the drastic revisionism achieved by modern research on the 1920s and 1930s. The British economy was never as badly affected by the depression as those of the United States or Germany, unemployment was never as high, and the loss of output much less. Nor was depression a continuous feature of the period – there were growth phases in 1919–20, 1922–8 and 1934–7. More importantly for our social history, we now recognise that in Britain, as all over the world, this was a bad time for producers in industry and agriculture but a good one for *consumers* because of the steady fall in prices. As most people managed to retain their employment, the rising real value of their wages made possible the boom in housing, consumption of minor luxuries, motoring, holidays and leisure activities that became characteristic of the era. Indeed, the society of obsessive consumers and shoppers that the British have now become owes its origins to the interwar period. Admittedly the process was interrupted by the Second World War and consequent austerity but it soon reasserted itself. Above all, the dedication to housing in general and to home-ownership in particular that came to dominate British politics and the economy by the later twentieth century finds its proximate origins between the wars. Despite this, no one would attempt to depict the period as an 'age of improvement' as is routinely done for the mid-Victorian era when poverty was far grimmer and more widespread. The explanation is that contemporary Victorians, or some of them, devoutly believed that theirs was an era of progress, and their optimism was not seriously deflated until later in the century and in the First World War. By contrast, the expectations of improvement raised by reform during the Edwardian period were dashed after 1914, leading to a prolonged mood of disillusionment and an underlying fear of national decline.

In writing the current volume I have tried to aim somewhere between two admirable earlier works. As long ago as 1940 Robert

Graves and Alan Hodge published *The Long Week-End*, an exuberant, entertaining and impressionistic account whose chaotic nature was accentuated by the absence of an index and of any organising theme. The book is still well worth reading although they were too close to events to have much perspective on the period. At the other end of the spectrum John Stevenson's 1984 volume in the Pelican British Social History, *British Society 1914–45*, is scholarly, judicious and well-organised and has been deservedly widely used.

But in addition to differences in tone and structure the present volume differs in several respects from earlier works, even those published in the 1980s. With a frankness one could not get away with today, Graves and Hodge admitted that 'events in London and its environs are here treated in disproportion to events elsewhere. But this could not be helped.' Today we recognise that Britain is not quite the homogeneous little country that the metropolitan Establishment has traditionally assumed her to be. England is once again a country of *regions*, while the United Kingdom is actually a *multi-national* state comprising four nations. Thus, where Graves and Hodge saw the re-emergence of the Loch Ness Monster in 1930 as a joke, we see it for what it tells us about English attitudes towards Scotland. The 1920s was the stage when, under pressure from the sharp post-war decline of their industrial economies, the Welsh and Scots began to lose their confidence in Union with England and to develop their modern expressions of nationalism.

The content of social history has also changed significantly in recent years. For example, whereas the treatment of women by Graves and Hodge was inadequate and flippant, they form a central element in the present volume, appearing in every chapter as well as in a separate assessment of their changing role and status in society. Hence the title of the book, which is taken from Barbara Cartland's *We Danced All Night* (1970). Cartland's early life encapsulated some of the major themes of the period. At eighteen she emerged from the Great War, in which her father had died, financially strapped, but picked herself up by taking paid work and also threw herself into a life of leisure and pleasure after the privations of wartime. Keen on marriage, but rather slow to get married, she produced three children and was divorced. Cartland reminds us that the interwar period was a complex phase for women. While women made formal political advances as voters and MPs, they experienced a sharp reaction against Edwardian feminism, and by the 1930s the women's movement had begun to suffer an organisational decline that was not reversed until the 1960s. The economic pattern was equally mixed. While mass unemployment accentuated all kinds of prejudices and political obstacles to female employment, underlying structural changes in the economy enabled women to maintain their overall position in the labour force.

The writing of this book has also made me reflect on major aspects of our modern history that tend to be neglected, notably motoring and aviation. These subjects have largely been the province of enthusiasts or military specialists, rather than mainstream historical writing. Yet the motor car and the aeroplane were not only increasingly important in economic and political terms, they began to make a major impact on our behaviour and our thinking between the wars. Some of the defining characteristics of the British people were revealed in their approach to motoring and aviation. Both appealed strongly to the buccaneering, anarchic element in the national character, something that sits awkwardly with the British self-image as a phlegmatic, law-abiding people. In many ways the trend during the interwar period was towards an increasingly calm and domesticated society as people devoted more time to the home, family and marriage, in the process retreating from some of the vulgar Victorian forms of leisure. We have been subject to so much ill-informed propaganda about 'Victorian values' that it is not generally recognised that several of the classic vices of Victorian society – alcoholism and prostitution – were in serious decline in this period, so much so that by 1930 the total prison population of England and Wales stood at a little over 11,000 and governments were busily closing down prisons. Taking a long-term view, the 1920s and 1930s represented a calm interlude between the violent crime of the Victorian era and trends since the Second World War. But despite this, interwar newspapers filled their pages with alarmist accounts of the 'crime wave' afflicting Britain, the difference being that their readers accepted it as entertainment and interwar politicians were less intimidated by them than they are today.

Finally, in writing this book I have made no attempt to produce a social history with the politics left out. Political connections feature in every chapter, though I hope not intrusively, because explanation is otherwise difficult. Although the war ended in November 1918, events enabled Lloyd George to extend the wartime coalition into four years of peace. In the process he experienced a reaction against high wartime taxation, conscription and interventionism, but on the other hand he managed to perpetuate some of the remarkable state controls, notably on the sale and production of alcohol and on the rents charged by private landlords, which had long-term consequences for British social life. War also gave a boost to some of the unfinished business of the Edwardian era, notably public investment in housing, re-afforestation and the wider ownership of land.

However, the disintegration of the coalition in 1922 restored the country to a state of *three*-party politics in which the Conservatives, contrary to expectations, became the dominant element. Conservatives, albeit often as part of a coalition, were in office for the entire interwar period except for nine months in 1924 and for two-and-a-half years from 1929 to 1931. In fact, from 1914 to 1945 Britain enjoyed coalition governments for twenty-one years and single-party rule for less than eleven. It was of considerable relevance to British social history that the massive extension of the parliamentary vote to over twenty-one million people, including 8.4 million women, in 1918 produced nothing like the revolutionary changes widely expected and feared; indeed, it probably contributed to the relative stability of society between the wars. Of course, many contemporaries detected an alarming pattern of subversion including the Bolshevik Revolution of 1917, the expansion of trade unionism, the formation of a British Communist Party in 1920, the Zinoviev Letter of 1924 and the General Strike of 1926. But the main political trend was the steady, though not spectacular, rise of the Labour Party, which formed a government for the first time in 1924, and its incorporation into the conventional pattern of politics. The collapse of Ramsay MacDonald's second government in 1931 has made the economic and political crisis of that year the major turning-point in interwar history. But from the perspective of social history this is not so obvious. The 1930s was in fact a calmer decade than the turbulent 1920s, and the social trends already established were accentuated rather than checked. The dominance of the National Government from 1931 until it was fatally discredited by the fiasco of the Norwegian Campaign in May 1940 has contributed to received accounts of the decade as one of reaction when it really saw significant social progress. Political accounts naturally emphasise the poor tactics of the Labour Left, weak leadership, and failed causes like the hunger marches and Popular Front. However, to right-wing observers the Left, though out of power, came to dominate the literary, intellectual and cultural world during the 1930s. Indeed, most of the building blocks that transformed the Labour Party from a sectional to a national party and generated the electoral landslide of 1945 were in place by the late 1930s; revival was both delayed and enhanced by the impact of the Second World War.

Despite the revisionist work that has been done on interwar Britain I had not appreciated how strong was the case for a new general account of the period until my agent, Andrew Lownie, made the suggestion to me. I am very grateful to him and to my editors at the Bodley Head, Will Sulkin and Jörg Hensgen, who make publishing so enjoyable. I would also like to thank Fred Millican of the West Newcastle Local Studies and Picture History Collection for making available the photographs of the Byron Terrace Peace Tea (1919), the Violet Street charabanc trip (1922), and the Centre Street Silver Jubilee Party (1935). The image of the Belisha Beacon is reproduced courtesy of Getty Images. For permission to make quotations from accounts of the period, acknowledgements are also due to John Julius Norwich for *The Duff Cooper Diaries* (2006); Eland Publishing for William Woodruff's *The Road to Nab End* (2000); Little Brown Book Group for William Woodruff's *Beyond Nab End* (2003); Bryan Magee for *Clouds of Glory: A Hoxton Childhood* (2003); The Random House Group, on behalf of Laurie Lee, for *Cider with Rosie* (1959); HarperCollins for Carol Thatcher's *Below the Parapet: The Biography of Denis Thatcher* (1996); and Weidenfeld and Nicolson, a division of the Orion Publishing Group, for Paul Johnson's *The Vanished Landscape: A 1930s Childhood in the Potteries* (2004).

I

'Will never really came home': The Impact of the Great War

At eleven o'clock on the morning of 11 November 1918 the church bells were rung at the village of Enstone in Oxfordshire to celebrate the news that an armistice had been signed and that the Great War was consequently over. The job was not well done. As the regular ringers were either in the army or dead, a 'scratch' team assembled. 'Thee never heerd such a pandemonium in your life', recalled one of them, 'more like ringing in a new scare than ringing the old war out.'[1] Having done their best the bell-ringers walked the five miles to Chipping Norton in search of a celebratory beer, but on arrival found none to be had and the town in darkness for lack of paraffin to light the lamps. Elsewhere, though, things were livelier. In neighbouring Gloucestershire Laurie Lee's mother returned from Stroud 'with excited tales of its madness, of how strangers had stopped and kissed each other in the streets and climbed statues shouting [peace].'[2] The closer to the heart of the Empire the wilder the celebrations became. Motoring home with Lady Diana Manners, Duff Cooper wrote: 'As we got nearer London we saw flags flying . . . all London was in uproar – singing, cheering, waving flags. [But] in spite of real delight I couldn't resist a feeling of profound melancholy, looking at all the crowds of silly, cheering people and thinking of the dead.'[3] After consoling themselves with dinner at the Ritz they went home, still feeling gloomy, where Diana 'broke down and sobbed'.

Duff Cooper, who had spent much of the war working as a civil servant, had escaped the worst material privations of wartime, though this left him even more exposed to the emotional impact of losing friends and contemporaries. But for the crowds he saw flocking to Trafalgar Square the Great War, as it became known, had created fresh opportunities and novel experiences as well as inflicting hardships and tragedies upon them. Young men had seized the chance to see exotic foreign countries; older men had emerged from retirement to plough the land and boost scarce food supplies; young women had abandoned the monotony of domestic service for the comparative freedom and high pay of employment in munitions factories and on trams; and young ladies suddenly found there were no chaperones available to monitor their path to matrimony.

This combination of greater personal freedom and higher disposable incomes for many ordinary people provoked widespread complaints about a decline of moral standards in Britain during and immediately after the war. But, as always, moral standards were whatever middle-aged, middle-class men said they were. In the fluid situation created during the war by the disruption of families and migration in search of employment, the elderly saw young people behaving badly, men feared that women were emulating their own behaviour, and the higher social classes thought the workers were taking advantage of the scarcity of their labour. Of course, the picture painted by the pessimists was not entirely imagination. They were correct in thinking that British social life was beginning to change rapidly if only in terms of the commercialisation of entertainment and fashion. By 1919 conservatives feared that British society was being swamped by American cultural influences ranging from cocktails to jazz, cinema, lipstick, face powder and bobbed hair. Younger women were abandoning their traditional whalebone corsets and relishing the freedom of movement this gave them: 'men don't dance with you if you're all laced up'. But the discarded corset seemed symbolic of a wider rejection of the proper goals of British womanhood.

The war had detached thousands of young people from their homes for the first time and gathered them together, the men in military camps and the girls in munitions factories. Not surprisingly, when the opportunity offered they were to be seen 'canoodling' in parks and other public places where they were harassed by vigilance patrols designed to deter any un-English displays of affection between the sexes. But the situation was too emotional to be subject to such controls. Young men, about to depart for the front, knew that their first girlfriend might well be their last. In the factories girls sometimes incorporated love letters, including their names and addresses, within boxes of munitions destined to be opened by unknown soldiers who might get in touch when home on leave. Meanwhile, cinemas offered the best opportunities for the sexes to meet in the dark and in comparative privacy. There, too, patrols organised by the new women police and other busybodies attempted to preserve decorum; but they were rowing against the tide. In May 1915, just nine months after the first of Lord Kitchener's volunteers had departed for Flanders, the pessimists who had warned about falling moral standards seemed to have been vindicated by the birth of thousands of illegitimate children. Hastily dubbed 'War Babies' by the patriotic press, these children were soon regarded even in official circles as a contribution to replacing the manpower that Britain was now losing in the profligate offensives on the Western Front. It was not long before opinion leaders were complaining that too few babies were being born rather than too many.

Indeed, the arrival of peace was attended by fresh fears that marriage, and thus the population, was now threatened by the shortage of husbands and by the effects of female emancipation. As a result of the war the number of British women exceeded men by 1.9 million, and 'Our Surplus Girls', as the *Daily Mail* called them, were thought to be so 'desexed and masculinised' as to be unfit for or uninterested in marriage and motherhood. Thirsting for a romantic marriage to focus the minds of the young on the delights of matrimony, the newspapers hailed the wedding of Duff Cooper and Lady Diana Manners, a daughter of the Duke of Rutland, in May 1919. The *Daily Sketch* had devoted its entire front page to the announcement of their engagement and photographs of the happy couple. The event was portrayed as a triumph of love over social class, for Duff, a relatively impecunious civil servant, was not what the Duke had in mind for a son-in-law. When news of their engagement broke, Duff noted: 'terrible scenes appear to have taken place at Arlington Street – the Duchess in a great state.'[4] As it would have seemed vulgar to mention his lack of money, the Duchess contented herself with denouncing Duff's character, his drunkenness and his friends, finally insisting that 'she had rather Diana had had cancer than was married to me'.

As if to prove that moral standards had not, in fact, changed at this level of society, Duff waited only a few months after his marriage before embarking on an affair with Diana Capel: 'intrigue of this sort has a fatal fascination' he admitted.[5] He rounded off 1919 in style when he was introduced to an actress, Cathleen Nesbit, at a fancy dress ball and promptly made 'frantic love' to her. 'I experienced a wish to kiss her feet, having admired them when bare in the part of Perdita. She obligingly removed her stocking.'[6] Meanwhile, Lady Diana stoically upheld the rules of the game, as understood in upper-class circles, by putting up with his behaviour.

Yet behind the gaiety, exuberance and irresponsibility of post-war social life lurked a pervasive undercurrent of pessimism, the inevitable consequence of the devastating human impact of four years of mass war. Officially the British forces suffered around 750,000 deaths during the war, though the figure almost certainly understated the casualties as many men died of their injuries during peacetime. Although this total was not large by comparison with French and Russian losses, Britain had experienced nothing on this scale since the French and Napoleonic wars had ended at Waterloo in 1815. For four and a half years families had endured the lengthening columns in their local newspapers announcing the names of the dead. In households that received few letters the arrival of the post meant only one thing: 'Morning after morning you'd dread to see the postman going to the doors, because the postman used to come round with the notices "killed" or "missing" you know.'[7] The best a family could hope for was an unofficial letter from a man's immediate officer that followed a standard pattern, telling them he had been a good soldier, was popular with his comrades and had died without pain; this was rarely true but it gave some comfort. For years after the declaration of peace, the war continued to announce itself through the ex-soldiers disabled by their injuries, men racked by coughs from being gassed in the trenches, and survivors too shell-shocked and demoralised to adjust to civilian life. To the young William Woodruff in Blackburn it came as a shock when he realised that his neighbour, 'the gibbering idiot', had been a soldier like his father: 'On fine days Mrs Beatty put Mr Beatty outside the front door to air. He lay on a long patched wicker bed on wheels on the narrow pavement, inches away from the street, jabbering and drooling at passersby ... His eyes were like a blind man's, they looked directly ahead but didn't see. The carters called and waved their whips at him. "Up and at 'em" he shouted back.'[8]

Before long the casualties began to be characterised as Britain's 'Lost Generation', the cream of the race who would have become leaders in all walks of life during the 1920s and 1930s. Research into the statistics confirms that the casualty rates were especially high among junior officers who were first out of the trenches and were drawn disproportionately from the upper and upper-middle classes. As a result the highest in the land shared their grief with the humblest families. The prime minister, H. H. Asquith, lost his talented eldest son, Raymond. Both sons of the Opposition leader, Andrew Bonar Law, were killed. Rudyard Kipling never recovered from the death of his only son. In 1915 Lord and Lady Desborough suffered the loss of their elder sons, Billy, and the poet, Julian Grenfell, only to lose their third son, Ivo, in a motoring accident in 1926. 'When I think of Oxford now I see nothing but ghosts', wrote Duff Cooper after Billy Grenfell's death in 1915.[9] Large numbers of MPs had served in the armed forces including Neil Primrose, MP for Wisbech and younger son of Lord Rosebery, who was killed fighting the Turks in Gaza. Admittedly, for politicians war service was sometimes a useful career move. After losing his Cabinet post at the Admiralty in 1915 Winston Churchill concluded: 'I do not feel in times like these able to remain in well-paid inactivity', and he opted to return to his original career in the army. Characteristically Churchill suggested he should be made a general at once, but settled for being a major, later promoted to colonel, in the Grenadier Guards!

Yet before the British people had come to terms with their losses in battle they were overtaken by what was, in fact, a greater disaster to human life in the shape of the so-called 'Spanish influenza epidemic' that struck the country during the winter of 1918–19. This misnomer arose in June 1918 when *The Times* reported on 'a mysterious sickness now prevalent in Spain'. The explanation is that as a neutral country Spain reported more widely on the outbreaks than other states and thus became linked to them. The influenza was also reported in Germany where it was supposed to have been caused by the poor diet involving too many turnips. In fact there had been outbreaks among the Allied troops at Etaples late in 1916 and at Aldershot barracks early in 1917. In both cases soldiers already weakened by gas attacks who were living in close proximity to wild or domestic birds were vulnerable, and about half of those infected died. However, the rate of infection was low and the outbreaks were contained.

The real influenza pandemic originated among birds in the Far East and mutated into something highly contagious but less deadly than the earlier outbreaks. As a result approximately half the world's population caught it but only a fraction of them died, amounting to an estimated twenty-six million people. In Britain the influenza was reported to be spreading across the country by July 1918 and soon turned into an epidemic as victims collapsed in the streets. 'In Hull it began on a glorious summer's day, 1 July,' recalled a local doctor, Maurice Jacobs. 'Robust young men and women who had been to work only a day or two before were stricken low . . . Many were already in a state of coma and at the point of death.'[10] Jacobs, who found it impossible to visit all the patients demanding attention, admitted that his chief contribution was to sign a death certificate, thereby saving the victim's family from the horror of attending a coroner's inquest. For a time most schools and many factories closed down for lack of staff. 'The church bells never stopped tolling; the undertakers were busy day and night', recalled William Woodruff. When his mother, sister and grandmother all went down with it the family almost collapsed but for 'a good Samaritan woman who walked in off the street. She had seen us in the morning, a dejected group of children huddled in the doorway; we were still there in the late afternoon . . . the stranger went in and took care of everything.'[11] The worst of it was that no one knew what to do; the virus was not identified until 1933. Meanwhile frantic people rushed to chemists to buy up supplies of cinnamon, quinine and even snuff which were all claimed to be cures. In the event the outbreak lasted for eighteen months, resulting in the death of 230,000 British people.

These deaths, coming on top of the war casualties, left most families in a state of mourning by 1919 despite the organisation of 'Peace Day' celebrations in the summer. Things were more difficult for the bereaved because many of them had no grave to act as a focus for their grief. The Imperial War Graves Commission decided that the mass casualties made it impossible to repatriate the bodies and, of course, many were never recovered. Instead they built permanent cemeteries in or near to the main battlefields. However, for grieving families these were of limited use, and as a result they took their own initiatives by creating local war memorials. This movement had begun as early as the autumn of 1916 in the wake of the disastrous Somme campaign when local communities began raising funds to build shrines to commemorate the dead of their town or village. These shrines were so localised that they seemed tantamount to gravestones; in one parish in Bethnal Green, for example, eighteen shrines were erected recording

1,506 names.[12] Typically they comprised a triptych with space for the names of the fallen, some shelving to place flowers, a calvary and a Union Jack displayed on a central panel.

It has sometimes been assumed that the loss of life during and after the war led more people to turn to their religion for consolation and to help them rationalise what had happened. However, although the religiosity shown by the recruits in the early months of the war had created an impression that a religious revival was taking place, disillusionment soon set in. By 1919 many clergymen admitted that, even in rural districts, many of their former churchgoers had lapsed. Woodruff's vicar took his father to task for not attending church: 'Do you believe in God, Will?' he asked. 'I did until the war,' his father replied. 'Tha'd be surprised if tha'd seen what Ah've seen.'[13]

It is easy to misread the relationship between the war and the churches because bishops and clergymen were usually keen to involve themselves in the organisation of war memorials, to dedicate them and to give the war a Christian rationale. Many had been belligerent exponents of the Allied cause. A. F. Winnington-Ingram, the Bishop of London, dedicated one shrine with the words: 'This nation had never done a more Christ-like thing than when it went to war on August 1914 . . . the world had been redeemed again by the precious blood shed on the side of righteousness.'[14] However, many ex-soldiers felt sick of hearing this kind of patriotic rhetoric from civilians who, they felt, had no real idea what the war had been like. In effect the churches had turned themselves into instruments of the state and their clergy into recruiting sergeants; and in the 1920s they found it difficult to establish their distance from the state, not least because clergymen often joined in puritanical attacks on the leisure activities and looser moral behaviour of young people. Not surprisingly, church attendance, which had reached a peak of around eight million during the Edwardian period, including Anglican, Nonconformist and Roman Catholic churches, went into a sharp decline during the war. This was followed by a partial recovery in the 1920s, but by the 1930s the decline resumed. The churches never really recovered from the role they had played as agents of official propaganda during the Great War.

In a sense clergymen were victims, along with other symbols of authority, of a resurgence of scepticism and disillusionment that set in during 1919 once the mood of patriotism and relief over the declaration of peace had worn off. 'Like so many of her generation', wrote William Woodruff, 'my mother blamed the war for everything . . . She was convinced it had changed father for the worse . . . "My Will never really came home again," she grieved.'[15] Disillusionment manifested itself in the reluctance of ordinary citizens to follow the self-appointed leaders of their community even at the very local level. In Andrew Purves's remote village of Linton in the Scottish Borders the entire adult population enjoyed the Victory Picnic in 1919 but the mood changed when they went on to discuss the erection of a war memorial. A heated argument developed before the villagers eventually agreed on a site and a design for a memorial to honour the twenty war heroes of the parish.[16] At Slad in Gloucestershire Laurie Lee recalled Peace Day as 'a day of magical transformations, of tears and dusky sunlight, of bands, processions and buns by the cartload'. But authority was anxious to get the villagers back under control by summoning them to the squire's house where 'on the steps of the manor stood the wet-eyed Squire, already in tears at the sight of us. His mother, in a speech from a basket chair, mentioned the Glory of God, the Empire, us, and said we wasn't to touch the flowers.'[17] Such accounts, with their note of dissent and scepticism, give a more authentic impression of the post-war mood than the more formal records of committees set up to organise peace celebrations and war memorials.

Behind the impressive public displays of patriotism and national unity, many families privately distanced themselves from the war. Their sense of alienation was accelerated by the onset of post-war unemployment. One Bristol man who had joined up, aged sixteen, and was wounded three times, later commented: 'After all that trouble, when we got discharged they gave us six months' money at twenty-six shillings a week, an' when that six months was up – finished, nothing. An' that was how they treated the First World War soldiers . . . They soon forgot you . . . Bitter? I should say I was.'[18] In William Woodruff's family his father's action in rushing off to volunteer, leaving behind a wife and three children, was viewed as *recklessness* rather than the act of a patriot. 'Father was a gormless creature', commented his daughter, Brenda, 'He didn't foresee anything because he never thought about anything.'[19] After serving three years as a private, Woodruff Senior was gassed at the third battle of Ypres in 1917 but, as a great athlete, he had managed to sprint away from the advancing cloud of gas, been picked up quickly and treated. However, the experience left him with a hacking cough and he returned home a disillusioned man.

Post-war disillusionment led some people to be diverted from orthodox forms of Christianity into alternatives such as Second Adventism. For anyone afflicted by pessimism as a result of the war, Adventism held an obvious appeal. The conflict had left people in many countries susceptible to all kinds of apocalyptic predictions that appeared to be borne out during the 1920s by the collapse of political institutions, the disruption of the Western economy and the undermining of moral values. For proof of the Second Coming Adventists pointed to natural phenomena, including the increase in storms, earthquakes and volcanic eruptions. They also interpreted several of the political trends of the 1920s, notably the reconstruction of the Roman Empire by Mussolini and the return of Jews to Palestine, as preconditions for the return of Christ to earth. The Reverend F. B. Meyer, a prolific writer on biblical prophecy, succeeded in attracting a prominent new recruit to the cause in the person of Christabel Pankhurst who published five volumes of Adventist literature between 1923 and 1940 and addressed large gatherings in Britain and the United States.

In their dissatisfaction with conventional religion many people, particularly women, found comfort and consolation in spiritualism. Once thought of as a Victorian-Edwardian phenomenon, spiritualism experienced a major resurgence throughout the interwar period because it offered grieving people the chance of renewed contact with dead relatives. British popular culture was already receptive to accounts of supernatural sightings, but the war had gone much further in establishing the credibility of supernatural intervention in human affairs by generating accounts of mysterious figures appearing on the battlefield and tending the wounded before inexplicably disappearing. The most famous example originated with a popular writer, Arthur Machen, who wrote a piece in the *Evening News*, 29 September 1914, about the 'Angel of Mons'. Subsequently his story took on a life of its own as people insisted that an army of angels had appeared in the sky to assist the British troops resisting the German advance.

After 1918 the widespread interest in supernatural phenomena of all kinds led to a fashion for seances, Ouija boards and table-turning parties. In 1920 two Yorkshire girls claimed to have seen fairies at the bottom of their garden – and produced photographs to prove it. It was a sign of the times that the novelist, Sir Arthur Conan Doyle, travelled to Yorkshire to investigate their claims and wrote a book entitled *The Coming of the Fairies*. Indeed, spiritualism gained greatly from the endorsement of prominent figures including the Duchess of York, whose brother, Fergus, had died in the war, Oliver Lodge, the physicist, Hannen Swaffer, a Fleet Street journalist, and Conan Doyle who had lost several relations in the war and actively proselytised for the cause. In September 1919 he attended a seance at Portsmouth where the Welsh medium, Evan Powell, put him in touch with his dead brother via a Red Indian spirit named Black Hawk. Dismissing the 'decadent Christianity of today' Conan Doyle argued that spiritualism offered a vision of 'an etheric heaven where friends are reunited and the dead of this world survive in, as a rule, a far higher state of society'. Explaining that God chose and inspired messengers to bring fresh knowledge to the world he had created, he insisted: 'we can break through the barrier of death . . . those who have lived in this world have not changed either their form or their characters, but only their vibrations.'[20] Mediums usually transmitted information to the effect that dead relatives were experiencing a life that mirrored that on earth, continuing to eat, work, and even enjoy themselves with whisky and cigars.

Although these fanciful depictions of the afterlife coincided with what many people wanted to believe, they provoked predictable derision from the sceptics. 'I always knew the living talked rot,' snorted Margot Asquith, 'but it's nothing to the nonsense the dead talk!' In 1917 Duff Cooper, grieving for the death of a contemporary, had attended an afternoon seance with a medium who told him that the spirit of a young man was standing beside him. This seemed a good guess for 1917 and Duff 'came away very sceptical of the whole business'.[21] Inevitably the spiritualists became a target for satire. In Richmal Crompton's *William's Happy Days* (1930) William encountered a Mrs Porter who was mourning her dog who, she said, had 'crossed over last week'. 'Crossed over?' replied a puzzled William. 'I thought you meant from Oxford to Cambridge or from Lib'ral to Conservative, or something like that.'

However, the mention of spiritualism in a children's book was probably symptomatic of how familiar a phenomenon it had become by this time. Spiritualism had already weathered a good deal of criticism before 1914, and after the war people were so desperate for comfort that they were prepared to be convinced. Nor did the movement decline as people came to terms with their losses. The number of registered spiritualist societies increased from 145 in 1914 to 309 in 1919 and 500 by 1932.[22] It was claimed that by this time 100,000 home seance circles were operating in Britain, and well-known mediums attracted up to 9,000 people to the Albert Hall to hear them communicating with the dead. This was achieved in the face of continual disparagement cast on spiritualists by the Anglican and Catholic churches. Admitting that the Church had been too cautious about satisfying people's desire to pray for their dead, some clergymen tried to restate the Christian sense of life after death, and in 1937 they even felt obliged to institute an investigation into why their members were still drifting towards spiritualism.[23] But while Anglican clergymen often felt inclined to compromise with the needs of their flock, the Catholic Church stuck rigidly to its view, condemning spiritualism as dangerous and suggesting that psychic phenomena were inspired by demonic spirits. From time to time mediums were prosecuted as frauds. A Perthshire medium, Helen Duncan, was denounced as a witch by Presbyterian ministers, prosecuted in 1933 and 1944 and eventually given nine months in prison. In 1932 the *Daily Mail* castigated a popular medium, Mrs Louise Meurig Morris, as a fraud who had been found out. When she sued, the allegations were not upheld but the judge ruled in favour of the *Mail* on the grounds of fair comment.[24] However, spiritualists remained largely unconcerned by these attacks because they created martyrs for the cause.

Scepticism towards the churches was all of a piece with wider attitudes towards authority in the aftermath of the war. Part of the explanation for this mood is that civilians had done comparatively well as a result of full employment and rising wages during the latter stages of the war, and, as a result, had been gripped by rising expectations by 1918. But although they had cash in their pockets, not enough goods were available to spend it on, especially as food was still rationed. This resulted in consumers snapping up anything that became available. In London Arthur Harding saw people buying up watches, furs and, above all, pianos. 'They all wanted a piano. Pianos was [*sic*] eighty guineas, half a crown a week or five shillings a week.'[25] But by 1920, when many people had lost their jobs, payments on these pianos lapsed and one originally costing £80 could be bought for as little as £10.

Although the vast majority of people had shown complete loyalty to the national cause, after 1918 this gave way to an undercurrent of anger, provoked by the huge profits made through the inflation of food prices during the war and the feather-bedding of businesses by generous government orders. The discontent manifested itself in a rising tide of strikes that began in 1917 and continued until 1921 when it was finally turned by the onset of mass unemployment. However, this mood had had little opportunity to express itself politically because the general election, which was due in December 1915, had been repeatedly postponed by Parliament. *Punch* mocked the idea of a wartime election in a cartoon portraying the British troops erecting posters above their trenches: 'SORRY FRITZ – NO FIGHTING TODAY. WE'RE HAVING AN ELECTION'. Lloyd George, who became prime minister in December 1916, felt tempted to silence his critics in Parliament by appealing to the voters for a mandate to finish the war, but just as he had started to plan one the Armistice was declared. He then took a calculated risk by holding the election just a month later in December 1918 while his popularity as 'The Man Who Won The War' was still very high. As a result the election took place while the patriotic emotions aroused by wartime were at their height. Audiences became impatient with well-meant speeches about proposals to build 'Homes For Heroes' and interrupted candidates with demands to 'Hang the Kaiser' and 'Make Germany Pay'. Many candidates gave way to this mood of anti-German hysteria, or actively cultivated it. In a notorious speech at Cambridge Sir Eric Geddes promised his audience: 'We will squeeze Germany like a lemon. We will squeeze her until you can hear the pips squeak.' However, despite these incidents the election was more subdued than usual because the party organisations had been disrupted and because several million voters were still abroad. Special arrangements were introduced to allow the 3.9 million naval and military electors to participate either by postal ballot if in France or Flanders, or by appointing proxies if they were further afield. In the event only fifty-seven per cent of electors voted – compared with over eighty per cent before 1914 – many of the non-voters being servicemen who had other things on their mind, notably surviving until they got home again.

By January 1919 tension was mounting among the two million men still in the armed forces who were naturally anxious to be demobilised. Apart from a desire to return to their families, they felt they had missed out on the high wages and plentiful employment enjoyed by civilians for the last four years. Morale in the army was now so low that mutinies began to break out. On 30 January 5,000 troops in camp at Calais demanded to be sent home at once. Field Marshal Haig suppressed the revolt and announced his intention of trying the ringleaders by court martial and having them shot. A pedestrian general, Haig was also a foolish politician, for such action was almost calculated to turn the discontent among the troops into a revolutionary situation at home. Fortunately, the new Secretary of State for War, Winston Churchill, warned him: 'I do not consider that the infliction of the death penalty would be justifiable', and Haig, though very offended, backed down.

The men's frustration had been exacerbated by news that the War Cabinet had decided to demobilise the men by releasing them as and when employers offered them jobs. This seemed unfair as it meant that men who had already spent four years in the forces might have to remain even longer. Fortunately Churchill scrapped this scheme and decided on the immediate release of anyone over forty and those who had enlisted before 1916.[26] He, at least, understood the need to be fair and to conciliate the men for fear that discontented soldiers might combine with striking workers at home to create a real threat to law and order. But the situation remained volatile throughout 1919. By November most servicemen had returned home, though 353,000 of them were unemployed despite the general policy of giving preference to them when filling vacancies and expelling women from jobs that had been filled by men in peacetime. The brief boom of 1919–20 encouraged workers to demand higher wages and to strike if employers resisted. As a result the number of working days lost in strikes reached 5.8 million in 1918, 35 million in 1919, 26 million in 1920 and 85 million in 1921 largely because the miners struck in that year. Many of these disputes were settled quickly because, encouraged by the government, the employers made concessions.

For a short time the authorities felt apprehensive that the trade unions, whose membership had increased from 4.1 million in 1914 to 8.3 million by 1920, might be influenced by the subversive doctrines emanating from Russia whose new Bolshevik regime was dedicated to exporting the revolution across Europe. The formation of the Communist Party of Great Britain in 1920 was not a very significant development, as it transpired, but at the time it was taken seriously especially as the Bolsheviks were known to be paying subsidies to foment strikes and chaos in Britain. The government was shaken when the police went on strike in 1919, and they were not entirely confident that they could rely on the troops to keep order when faced by workingmen. At the War Office Churchill received weekly reports on the political attitude of the troops. The commanders warned that the men did not want to be used as strike-breakers or as 'blacklegs', and were unwilling to be sent to Russia to help the anti-revolutionary forces there.[27] The most dangerous incident occurred at Glasgow in January 1919 where, for two weeks, troops and tanks were stationed in the city centre to control the general strike that took place there. Suddenly conscious that strikes among electricity, coal and railway workers could paralyse the entire economy, the government began to organise an emergency system for implementation whenever industrial militancy threatened to reduce the country to chaos. It was against this background that many politicians welcomed Mussolini's coup in 1922 as the first evidence that the onward march of the Bolshevik Revolution had been checked.

These signs of authoritarianism represented a partial reaction against the earlier concessions made by the political leaders towards the end of the war. They had been reassured by the loyalty and patriotism shown by the majority of the population and sought ways of consolidating the political system. In 1917 a new order, the OBE, had been created specifically to recognise the contribution made by civilians to the war effort. By 1922 OBEs had been awarded to no fewer than 22,000 people, thereby giving rise to the disparaging cry 'Lloyd George Knew My Father'. But the politicians displayed even more confidence in 1918 by increasing the parliamentary vote from just under 8 million before the war to over 21 million including 8.4 million women. Parliament had been close to enacting similar reforms in 1914 but the war had removed much of the controversy from the issue. This new electorate was notable for including many more young people than before, a large working-class majority, and a female element that comprised forty per cent of the total; on all three counts it looked like a risk when peace came and the new electors had to be consulted.

Parliament also recognised the material needs of the new voters in 1920 by extending the limited existing scheme of unemployment insurance to cover twelve million workers, by creating a Ministry of Health for the first time, and by passing a Housing Act designed to give effect to Lloyd George's promise to build homes fit for heroes to live in. Up to a point the politicians had accepted that the agenda of politics had to change, not only because of the expansion of the electorate and the rise of the Labour Party, but because of the impact wartime experience had made on many upper- and middle-class men. Those who had served as junior officers were often deeply affected by the sacrifices made by their men who had left lives of hardship and poverty to serve their country. After 1918 they did not want to let them down, and were angered by early indications that these men were going to be thrown into unemployment. For some this took the form of individual friendships. In 1919 when Siegfried Sassoon met John Law, an ex-miner from South Wales who had been his servant in the 25th Royal Welch Fusiliers, he was deeply moved by his difficulties in settling back into civilian life; he gave Law money several times during the 1920s and sent him food parcels bought at Harrods.[28] Sassoon was not simply a philanthropist; as a result of his experiences he had adopted socialist and pacifist views, he wrote anti-war poetry, and supported anti-war candidates such as Philip Snowden and Ramsay MacDonald at the 1918 election. His 'wilful defiance of military authority' almost led to a court-martial, but the army decided to declare him unfit for active service instead. Such deviant attitudes in an upper-class war hero – Sassoon had won the Military Cross – were naturally disturbing to the authorities.

In fact, the war had politicised many men of his generation and his class, making rebels and critics of people whose background suggested that they ought to be pillars of the Establishment. Sir Archibald Sinclair, who was twenty-four in 1914, had joined the army as a professional in 1910 and should have been less affected than the volunteers, but 'he hates every hour of [the war] with a profound loathing' as his fellow officer, Churchill, put it. Sinclair, who was elected a Liberal MP in 1922, became a prominent opponent of appeasement. Anthony Eden, who enlisted at eighteen, had won the Military Cross for carrying his wounded sergeant across no-man's-land under enemy fire at Ploegsteert in 1917. Subsequently Eden rejected a career as a diplomat 'forever handing round teacups in Teheran' as he put it. He stood for Parliament in 1922 and got elected in 1923 as a progressive Tory. Harold Macmillan, who was twenty in 1914, was wounded three times in the war and almost died as a result. Subsequently he found his purpose in life by becoming MP for Stockton-on-Tees in 1924, a northern constituency suffering from unemployment that confirmed him as a left-wing rebel Conservative. Most dramatic was the career of Sir Oswald Mosley who was already in the army when war broke out and served for a time in the Royal Flying Corps. Mosley plunged immediately into parliament in 1918 advocating 'socialistic imperialism'. An interventionist Conservative, he felt angry at what he saw as the betrayal of the troops by the old men who retained their grip on power, bungled the peace settlement and failed to respond to the social consequences of the war. Throughout his career he consistently advocated policies designed to defeat unemployment. It was this that led him to join Labour in 1924 and become a fascist in 1932. Although this evolution made him appear an extremist, Mosley was actually typical of men from his class and his generation in the emotive way he reacted to the war and its aftermath.

As this suggests, the euphoria surrounding Britain's victory in 1918 proved to be short-lived. In 1911 Norman Angell, one of the opponents of war with Germany, had published a book entitled *The Great Illusion*, in which he argued that regardless of the military outcome of a European war, all the participants would suffer badly from its *economic* consequences. In the summer of 1920, when the post-war boom collapsed, inaugurating two decades of mass unemployment, it began to seem that Angell had been right. Britain, previously the world's biggest investor, had emerged from the war owing £1,150 million to the United States. Her national debt had increased from £650 million to £8,000 million, and servicing the debt consumed a quarter of all government expenditure in 1920. Income tax had been raised to the dizzy heights of six shillings in the pound by 1919, and although it was subsequently reduced, it remained well above Edwardian levels. The key to economic recovery, and thus to a reduction in unemployment, was widely believed to involve restoring the level of international trade and recapturing Britain's export markets. However, as most countries hastily erected tariff barriers against imports this appeared an impossible objective. Even though world trade did increase during the 1920s, Britain found it very difficult to recapture her previous share, leaving her staple industries handicapped by overcapacity and much of their workforce apparently doomed to unemployment.

In these circumstances the fruits of Britain's victory began to appear elusive. It was no great comfort that the war had left the British Empire at the peak of its territorial extent as a result of the mandated African territories acquired from Germany. On the contrary, she lacked the resources to manage and defend her sparsely populated and vulnerable possessions, now increasingly unstable as a result of the development of nationalist movements. But, as always, the Empire took second place to domestic and financial pressures; these dictated a drastic reduction in the size of the British Army from four million in 1918 to 370,000 by the end of 1920 and 200,000 by 1924, comparable to the pre-1914 level. War had also had a disruptive effect on imperial sentiment. The Australians, who had suffered a much higher casualty rate, emerged full of anger at the incompetence of the British generals who had led them. 800,000 Indian troops had seen for themselves that Britain was far from being the dominant world power she appeared to be in India, but was one of four or five more or less equal powers. For the British themselves war had shaken their confidence in the role of the Royal Navy; there had been no great naval battles apart from Jutland and the engagements that did occur demonstrated how vulnerable Britain's ships were to attack by mines and submarines. In the next war, dominated, it was presumed, by air power, the British Isles was going to be very vulnerable. In the light of such thinking the post-victory optimism rapidly gave way to an uneasy feeling that Britain was now on the retreat, and it was increasingly obvious who had overtaken her. In the words of the authors of the famous spoof on history textbooks, *1066 and All That,* in 1930: 'America was thus clearly top nation and History came to a.'[29] In a characteristically English fashion they were deploying humour to make a serious point.

On the surface these underlying reservations about the outcome of the Great War were obscured by the instigation of a regular com-memoration designed to unite the nation. George V instigated the first anniversary of the Armistice in 1919 with a two-minute silence. The idea was immediately taken up in the City of London, large crowds gathering in the area between the Mansion House, the Bank of

England and the Royal Exchange. People stood, men bared their heads and the traffic stopped: 'those two minutes silence seemed to last for so long I thought they would never end', one schoolboy remembered.[30] The commemoration had been intended as a unique event, but it became so firmly established in the public imagination that it was repeated each year. In November 1920 the unveiling of the Cenotaph in Whitehall, designed by Edwin Lutyens, gave the country the central focus it needed for the annual ceremony. In 1923, when Armistice Day fell on a Sunday, it was immediately recognised that this enabled many more people to participate and helped to maintain the sombre and reverent tone rather than the celebratory note of the early days. The day thus became 'Remembrance Sunday' in subsequent years.

However, reactions were more complicated and ambiguous than is suggested by the successful inauguration of the annual Armistice Day. Some ex-servicemen who still felt uncomfortable about what seemed a display of triumphalism and militarism were beginning to feel let down by the society that had sent them to war. They preferred to retreat into Old Comrades Clubs for sing-songs and reminiscences. The sale of poppies, which was instituted by the British Legion in 1921, represented an effort to show respect for the dead and to help the living. But it was challenged by sales of white poppies organised by the Women's Co-operative Guild and other anti-war groups to mark their rejection of what they saw as the nationalistic tone of the official commemoration. They argued that men had been asked to fight in order to crush the militarism that had caused the war and asked when governments were going to live up to their promises about 'The War to End War' as characterised in official propaganda.

It is easily forgotten how awkward – and unusual in the context of other European countries – any discussion about British objectives in the Great War was. Only in Italy, who had entered the war late and reluctantly, did people question whether the sacrifices were really justified by the outcome. Although Britons had responded to the cry to fight 'For King and Country' and to defend 'Gallant little Belgium', the rationale for Britain's entry into war in 1914 was not, in fact, widely understood, though it was perfectly sound. This was because there had been no direct threat to the British Isles or to British overseas territory. On the contrary, the case for participation consisted in the need to preserve France as a great power in the face of German aggression for fear that her defeat would leave Britain, her trade routes and the Empire vulnerable to a Continental superpower. But the case could hardly be put in these terms at the time; the British were not going to volunteer to fight to restore Alsace and Lorraine to France. During the 1920s, however, as the implications began to sink in, the war provoked a bitter reaction against the French who were widely accused of trying to drag Britain into another war as they had done in 1914. By adopting a policy of disarmament governments implicitly validated the critics' diagnosis that the First World War had been caused by the arms race with Germany. By 1920 British defence expenditure had been slashed from £600 million to £300 million, and by 1922 it had fallen to £110 million, the level at which it remained until 1935. None of this meant that the British had become a nation of pacifists. For most of the 1920s people simply wanted to forget the war and place their faith in an alternative means of settling international disputes – the League of Nations. Over 400,000 people joined the League of Nations Union, a pressure group designed to ensure that British governments did not revert to their old habits of secret diplomacy, deals with dictators and frantic attempts to out-build the armies and navies of their rivals. For the next decade this offered the element of hope and idealism that checked the scepticism generated by the horrors of the Great War.

2

'A Babylonian touch':
British Food Between the Wars

For the Edwardian generation plentiful supplies of food at rock-bottom prices, made possible by huge imports from all over the world, were simply taken for granted. Cheap food underpinned Britain's entire industrial and political system by relieving pressure on manufacturers for higher wages and by popularising governments pledged to maintain free trade. Since the 1870s improvements in transport by sea and by transcontinental railway had flooded Europe with grain from the prairies of the United States and Canada, thereby reducing the price of bread by half. In 1880 the arrival of the *Strathleven* from Australia with a cargo of frozen meat, still largely edible, marked another turning point. To the cans of imported corned beef Britain now added frozen carcasses of beef, mutton, lamb and pork from Argentina, Australia, New Zealand and the United States; the effect had been to reduce meat prices by nearly half. Meanwhile expanded cultivation of sugar in Australia and the West Indies, and new tea plantations in Assam and Ceylon made other staple British food items cheaper too. The falling cost of living enabled many families to divert the money saved on bread to more expensive and unusual food items. In this way the modern British diet came into being during the thirty years before 1914.

However, the Great War posed a dire threat to a society highly dependent on overseas supplies. Even before the German submarines began to decimate merchant shipping, food-hoarding by merchants and panic-buying by consumers had created shortages and pushed up prices. In this situation the manufacturers attempted to exploit the patriotism of their customers. Nestlé, whose products were hit by their heavy reliance on imported sugar, piously claimed that the patriotic housewife would continue to buy as much as usual because this would maintain production levels and thus sustain employment. The makers of Horlicks Malted Milk Tablets urged women: 'Send a flask to YOUR soldier.' Oxo ran advertisements depicting British bulls impatiently queuing up to help the war effort by being turned into Oxo cubes. The suppliers of Perrier saw a fine opportunity to destroy the traditional popularity of German mineral waters: 'At the present time, thanks to the iron grasp of the British and French fleets, Perrier is being shipped as usual. The Battle Cry of the Allies: A Fight to the Finish in War and Trade.'

Meanwhile, government propaganda urged wealthy patriots to buy expensive food such as asparagus, leaving cheaper items for the workers. They also began to buy food on world markets in order to release it with a view to checking rising prices, imposed targets on farmers to compensate for falling wheat imports, and in 1917 they introduced a rationing system, though bread and potatoes were excluded from it; by 1918 the housewife was required to register with her retailer even for her weekly tea allowance of two ounces. Both the Food Department and the National Food Economy League embarked upon propaganda campaigns designed to educate housewives to select the most nutritious food and to make economical use of scarce resources: 'Waste is at all times folly, but in such a time as this it is unpatriotic.' Women were encouraged to save on fuel by taking advantage of the new National Kitchens where meals were cooked communally, and to display the 'Pledge Card' in their windows: 'In honour bound we adopt the national scale of voluntary rations.' Middle-class wives, experiencing a sudden shortage of domestic servants, may not have appreciated the irony in official advice that attempted to be uplifting rather than censorious about their cooking: 'The British fighting line shifts and extends, and now *you* are in it . . . it is in *your* larder, *your* kitchen and *your* dining room. Every meal *you* serve is now literally a battle.' In fact, the most effective initiative for encouraging housewives in the better use of food probably lay in the foundation of the Women's Institutes in 1915. Otherwise the official propaganda made little impression, though rationing was appreciated as a fairer way of sharing out scarce resources.

The conservatism of British consumers in dietary matters was most evident in their reactions to innovations in bread. By Victorian times the British had become addicted to white bread, regardless of the fact that the whiteness was achieved by roller-milling, which removed

most of the wheatgerm and bran, and even by bleaching the flour with
noxious chemicals such as nitrogen peroxide. Long before 1914 the
British had taken to scorning brown or 'black bread' as something
eaten by the very poor and by Germans. Despite the invention of
Hovis in 1892, by 1900 ninety-five per cent of all loaves eaten in Britain
were white.[1] In 1909 the Bread Reform League had launched 'Standard
Bread', produced with flour containing eighty per cent of the wheatgerm, with the support of the *Daily Mail* which informed readers that
it was eagerly consumed by the royal family! Opponents sabotaged the
new loaf by suggesting that wood shavings and sacking were
incorporated with the flour.

However, during wartime shortages of American grain forced the
government to impose controls on millers and bakers. Not only were
they to retain most of the wheatgerm, but they were required to
stretch the flour by incorporating a variety of substances including
other grains, soya, potato and bean flour. The resulting 'War Bread', a
greyish, unappetising product which sagged miserably in warm
weather, proved highly unpopular; and at the end of hostilities the
public promptly reverted to its traditional white loaf. Only the food
scientists regarded these wartime experiments as an advance for
nutritional standards.

Not surprisingly, the end of the war saw a vociferous demand for a
return to pre-war eating habits in Britain. The extra income earned
through full employment and new work for women had boosted
family incomes, thereby creating a huge unsatisfied demand for more,
and more appealing, consumables. In his parents' corner shop in
Salford, Robert Roberts noted that weekly takings had risen from
about £7 to £45 by 1918. But their customers, who now had money to
spend, were dissatisfied with the limited items on offer. One housewife
'airily enquired when we were going to stock "summat worth
chewing". "Such as what?" asked my father, sour-faced. "Tins o'
lobster!" she suggested, "Or them big jars o' pickled gherkins!"'[2]

This rising mood of discontent among consumers dictated a speedy
return to the traditional British diet and to the resumption of free trade.
Imports of tea rose from £366 million in 1918 to £494 million in 1919;
and, with Brooke Bond and others increasing supplies by establishing
new plantations in Kenya and Nyasaland in the 1920s, prices fell. From
seven pounds of tea per head in 1914 consumption rose to nearly nine

pounds by 1925. The period from 1913 to 1934 also saw a significant rise in the consumption of items such as fruit (eighty-eight per cent), vegetables (sixty-four per cent), eggs (forty-six per cent) and milk (fifty-five per cent), which considerably improved the popular diet. Only the cheapest foods were an exception to this pattern; potato consumption, for example, remained stable and bread consumption fell because as real incomes increased families diverted expenditure to more expensive and novel items.

Despite this trend, there remained ample scope for improvement. 'I was vaguely aware that Authority regarded the popular English diet as unhealthy', recalled Paul Johnson.[3] In fact, throughout the Victorian and Edwardian periods housewives had been the target of well-meant propaganda about making better use of cheap, nourishing vegetables rather than relatively expensive items such as meat. During the 1920s and 1930s they were bombarded by campaigns to 'Eat More Fruit', 'Drink More Milk' and support 'Empire Shopping Week'. But they appeared unresponsive to official advice. A survey by Sir William Crawford, 'The People's Food', in 1936 reported that in the highest social class sixty-six per cent declared themselves 'not interested' in diet and nutrition, and as many as eighty-nine per cent at the bottom of the social scale.[4]

Despite this negative response it would be a mistake to assume that British attitudes towards food did not change between the wars. While very conservative about food in many ways, the British had already shown themselves ready to adapt. By 1900 all levels of society had come to copy the French habit of serving food in separate courses as opposed to the English tradition of putting everything, whether sweet or savoury, on the table at once. Since the 1870s chips had acquired respectability in their French form: *pommes de terre* à la mode. Even crisps, which also originated in France, were adopted by Britons as an essential element in their diet during the 1920s; by 1928 they bought a million packets annually, each containing the much loved, but damp, blue twists of salt. For their part the French poured scorn on authentic British favourites such as the Christmas Pudding – 'an indigestible and bizarre mixture'![5]

In fact, tastes in food were determined by several factors including tradition, gender, social status, price, availability and even cooking equipment. During the Victorian period many poor families, lacking the means for anything but the simplest cooking, were obliged to rely on a frying pan, held over an open fire, for all their needs or simply to eat their food cold. The British desire for red meat was strongly under-pinned by habit and social status. While brown bread and vegetables were seen as the food of the poor, meat signified a higher standing. It was the aim of every respectable family to enjoy at least a midday dinner comprising meat and potatoes; and among the middle classes this formula was usually repeated in the evening. Traditionally bacon had been the meat most commonly consumed because it could be eaten cold, it kept longer than fresh meat and a little went a long way in flavouring cooked dishes. But popular aspirations were represented in illustrations of John Bull, the archetypal, stout Englishman sup-posedly nourished on a diet of beef and beer. To modern eyes John Bull appears dangerously obese, but to contemporaries he was the epitome of the fit, healthy Englishman. This deep-seated prejudice in favour of meat gained force, if anything, in the 1920s and 1930s if only because falling prices made its purchase easier. Though there was a vogue for vegetarianism and health food shops, most people regarded this as eccentric at best and dangerous at worst. In India the British inter-preted the vegetarian diet of Hindus as the root cause of their physical weakness; by contrast, red meat was the essential food of the active, virile Englishman. Pictures of an apparently emaciated M. K. Gandhi, the best-known vegetarian and pacifist of the period, appeared to confirm this view. Similar popular prejudices helped to sustain the role of alcohol despite the fall in consumption after the war. It was still widely accepted that a manual worker must drink beer at regular intervals during the working day, and at every meal, in order to maintain his strength and energy; in any case, to abstain from beer consumption was to cast some reflection upon one's manhood.

Yet despite the popular myth about the British diet of red meat, many families, especially in rural areas, lived on vegetarian meals for half the week, buying a joint on Sundays which they eked out for several days. In Laurie Lee's isolated Gloucestershire village, Slad, the nine-strong household relied heavily on bread and lentil stews in the early 1920s: 'Eight to ten loaves came to the house every day, and they never grew dry. We tore them to pieces with their crusts still warm, and their monotony was brightened by the objects we found in them – string, nails, paper, and once a mouse; for those were the days of happy-go-lucky baking.' At his home in the Scottish Borders Andrew Purves took a scone to school each day with a can of tea or milk; the evening meal involved potatoes, Welsh rarebit and a milk pudding, with porridge (made with treacle when the cow ran dry) eaten later at supper time. Purves's family consumed boiled and minced meat regularly on Saturdays and Sundays, but meat was not plentiful except during brief periods following the slaughter of the family pig.[6]

Another staple element in the British diet, fish and chips, reached a peak between the wars. Though fried fish had been sold in the East End from the 1830s onwards, the idea of combining it with chips is thought to have originated with John Rouse in Oldham in the 1860s. The original rationale involved buying up cheap end-of-the-day stocks from fishmongers because they would have gone bad by next morning. It was the Victorian railway system that accelerated the spread of the dish all over the country; every day the proprietors of Fishy Moore's in Coventry, one of the oldest known fish and chip shops, and as far from the sea as was possible, travelled by train to Skegness to buy fresh North Sea cod. When Harry Ramsden opened his famous shop at Guiseley near Leeds in 1928 consumption had already reached its peak in the North, but it continued to grow rapidly in the South and the Midlands such that by the late 1920s the National Federation of Fish Friers estimated the number of fish and chip shops in Britain at 30–35,000.

Fish friers traditionally attracted criticism on account of their poor hygiene and the offensive smell of the cotton seed oil, dripping or lard they used for cooking. As late as 1932 health inspectors complained about friers who never used potato peelers 'but just scrub the potatoes and leave all the diseased parts of them to go into the pans with the rest. The customer picks them out.'[7] Others condemned fish and chips as a convenience food resorted to by lazy or ignorant housewives. Yet this was misplaced criticism. During the Victorian era fish and chips had played a major part in improving the nutrition of poor people. Cooked in batter the fish retained its food value, while potatoes supplied a high proportion of all the vitamins and minerals consumed. It remained good value between the wars. In Hoxton, in London's East End, Bryan Magee's family ate fish and chips once a week, paying threepence for cod, or twopence for 'rock salmon', and one penny for chips.[8] Without this meal most working-class families would simply not have eaten fresh fish apart from those who enjoyed the cheap herrings that were landed in huge quantities in Scotland and along the North-East coast.

Less advantageous from the nutritional point of view was the enduring British love affair with sugar. With the exception of the Danes, Britons consumed more sugar than any people on earth. Already by the 1890s their weekly intake stood at fifteen ounces per head, but it continued rising to seventeen ounces by 1937, higher than dieticians considered healthy in all social classes. Sugar was consumed in endless cups of tea, in puddings, in jam, in sweets and in chocolate. Even reputable jam-manufacturers used only forty-five pounds of fruit in one hundred pounds of jam, and they complained of being undercut by cheap imports in which the fruit constituted just ten per cent, the rest comprising sugar and water.[9]

From an early age most British people became addicted to the regular consumption of sweets, which were basically concoctions of sugar, colourings and flavourings. By the Edwardian period many of the enduring favourites were already established including the 'wine gums' marketed by the teetotaller, Charles Riley Maynard, in 1909, and William Wrigley's Doublemint Chewing Gum. But the post-war period saw some major innovations. At the end of the war Bassett's relaunched the Unclaimed Babies, as they were sinisterly known to the Victorians, as Peace Babies, better-known to later generations as Jelly Babies. By the 1930s new chocolate sweets, such as Mars Bars and Milky Way priced at one penny, were appearing, and in 1937 Rowntree's launched their much loved Chocolate Beans, better known as Smarties. Other interwar favourites such as Pontefract Cakes and Liquorice Allsorts were also manufactured by Bassett's. Invented in Sheffield but made at nearby Pontefract, where the liquorice plants were traditionally cultivated, liquorice sweets could be formed into innumerable shapes. For interwar children the combination of liquorice sticks and sherbert created a much-loved ritual graphically evoked by Laurie Lee in his account of village life: 'Sucked gently, the sherbert merely dusted the tongue; too hard and you choked with sweet powders; or if you blew back through the tube the sherbert bag burst and you disappeared in a blizzard of sugar. Sucking and blowing, coughing and weeping, we scuffled our way down the lane.'[10]

On the positive side sugar had been the means of boosting fruit consumption, in the form of jam, since the late Victorian period when Chivers, Blackwell and Wilkins Tiptree took advantage of cheap imported sugar and new supplies of soft fruit from farmers who were switching from wheat to market gardening. During the war British troops had been so generously supplied with big tins of plum and apple jam that they sometimes threw them into the German trenches. Jam was largely eaten in sandwiches, though in polite circles such as Paul Johnson's Tunstall in the Potteries it was regarded as the meanest filling; there mothers were heard to criticise their neighbours by saying: 'she's a jam sandwich woman'.[11]

But fresh fruit was another matter. The further down the social scale one went the less was consumed; indeed many people considered fruit unhealthy especially for children. Between the wars plums and apples were cheap and widely available, but in Bryan Magee's East End home: 'At sit-down meals we never had fresh fruit; it had to be either stewed or tinned'.[12] Yet fruit consumption certainly increased in this period largely on the strength of bananas, already imported from Jamaica and becoming very popular. Annual imports rose from just over one million bunches in 1900 to eleven million by 1924, raising the annual consumption per head from nine to thirty bananas. As a result of the steady fall in price bananas soon came to be regarded as the fruit for poor people, another example of the close link between food and status in British society. At least the example of bananas suggests that British people were less conservative in their attitudes and more willing to vary their diet if they could afford to do so. Yet food consumption continued to reflect habit rather than simply income. Even Paul Johnson's middle-class family ate peaches, pineapples and apricots only from tins, just as the working classes did; and they never had grapes and oranges except at Christmas. He remembered imported grapefruit as 'one of the choicest novelties of the Thirties'; served halved, generously sugared and with a crystallised cherry in the centre, grapefruit was 'a Babylonian touch'.[13]

Although British diets benefited from buoyant supplies of imported food after the war, the main force for change lay in commercial and technological developments. The traditional practice whereby farmers transported their produce to market towns and sold directly to millers and butchers had steadily given way to a system based on middlemen who took over the distribution and processing of food. The spread of railway branch lines in the late Victorian era and of motor vehicles in the Edwardian period accelerated this development. As a result inter-war Britain witnessed a major shift from a multiplicity of local suppliers to a concentration in fewer hands, so much so that certain sectors became dominated by one or two large companies, notably Tate & Lyle (moving towards a monopoly in sugar), Spillers (flour milling), United Dairies and the Co-operative Wholesale Society (milk), Vesteys and Union Cold Storage (meat), Lever Brothers (soap) and Unilever (which incorporated Chivers, Home and Colonial, Liptons and Allied Suppliers). However, there was still plenty of competition among the suppliers of tea including John Sumner, who marketed Typhoo, Liptons, Brooke Bond, Lyons, Twinings, Hornimans and Ridgways. Birmingham, the home of Typhoo, boasted no fewer than sixty local tea merchants in the 1900s, and by 1934 the number had actually increased to sixty-six.

A notable feature of the 1920s and 1930s was the vogue for tinned and canned food. Experiments with canning corned beef, salmon and condensed milk during the late nineteenth century had familiarised consumers with the technique. However, as the process had not yet been perfected the contents of tins often suffered from an unpleasant metallic tang which made some people feel nauseous. The mass distribution of tinned meat and jam to the troops during the war may not have helped to win consumers round. On the other hand, for Britons struggling to conjure up an English dinner party in remote parts of the Empire, cans offered a lifeline. In India this proved attractive for those who were anxious to avoid a wholesale adoption of 'native' eating habits. When the Viceroy, Lord Reading, visited the princely state of Bahawalpur in the 1920s he was fed an 'English' dinner comprising soup, tinned pâté, tinned salmon in white sauce, roast game, caramel custard, Kemps bottled coffee and a savoury on toast.[14]

During the interwar period most British families became heavily dependent on the canned products marketed by Heinz and Crosse and Blackwell, notably peas, beans, ham, meat loaf, pilchards, peaches, pears and pineapples. Consumption of canned fruit increased from 3 pounds per head around the turn of the century to 10.2 pounds by 1924. Other items became available in jars; for example in 1928 Baxters, the Scottish preserve makers, spotted an opportunity by buying up a glut of summer beetroot and bottling it as 'baby beet', a new line that appealed to the British taste for pickled food. Admittedly this fondness for tins and cans provoked a sharp reaction in some quarters. Lord Lymington, one of the leaders of English Mistery and English Array, extremist pressure groups that sought to restore the feudal system, condemned the fashion for tins and even the use of pasteurised milk as a cause of physical degeneracy; Lymington also claimed that processed food attracted foreign imports which were ruining the small farmer. However, most consumers were too keen on obtaining cheap and convenient food to be susceptible to such criticism.

Of course, processed brands were already familiar before 1914 mostly in the form of cheap substitutes for fresh food including margarine, condensed milk, and fish and meat pastes. But the interwar years saw a huge increase in sales of cheap convenience items including jellies from Rowntree's and Chivers, custard powder from Bird's, spreads such as Marmite, Bovril and Vitamite, and night-time drinks including Horlicks, Ovaltine and Bourneville Chocolate. In 1932 Nestlé introduced their 'instant' coffee which proved popular among the majority of the population who did not know what coffee actually tasted like. It was also in these years that those families who lacked a servant to stand laboriously stirring the lumps from their porridge each morning resorted to Quick Quaker Oats. But from America came a greater threat to this traditional British breakfast favourite. In 1902 Will Kellogg first marketed Corn Flakes, the result of squeezing wheat dough between rollers, toasting it, and adding a little malt flavouring. The bland, crunchy, cardboard flakes did not reach Britain until 1924 when Kellogg employed teams of unemployed men and Boy Scouts to give away millions of samples of Corn Flakes and, later, Rice Krispies. For families already accustomed to cold food these cereals offered a quick and easy breakfast. Kellogg's, who sold over a million packets annually in Britain by 1936, found it worthwhile to open a factory in Manchester in 1938.

The fashion for selling food in packeted and branded form, rather than loose, had developed in the nineteenth century partly as a means of giving the housewife a guarantee that her purchase was not adulterated; the pioneering sector was tea which produced famous brand names such as Mazawatte, Typhoo and Kardomah tea. After 1918 the marketing of brand names stimulated some costly advertising campaigns, in the process generating several famous commercial slogans such as 'Everybody Drinks Typhoo'. Horlicks Malted Milk was recommended for anyone suffering from 'Night Starvation'; and the makers of Bovril ('Don't get tired – drink Bovril') suggested rather bizarrely that all the successful men in history from Julius Caesar to Cecil Rhodes had benefited from it! Perhaps the most celebrated and influential commercial promotion was that associated with Guinness whose manufacturers employed John Gilroy, the in-house artist for S. H. Benson, a pioneering British advertising agency, from the early 1930s onwards. Newspapers and hoardings carried the slogans 'Guinness is good for you', 'Guinness for Strength' and, from 1935 onwards, 'My Goodness, My Guinness' depicting sea lions, kangaroos, pelicans, giraffes and other animals carrying a pint and pursued by an irate zookeeper.

In the case of milk commercial interests joined forces with the government to achieve a major advance in consumption from 1.8 pints per head weekly in the early 1900s to 2.8 pints by 1937. Traditionally poorer people largely avoided fresh milk because it was expensive, would not keep long, and was of dubious quality, being much watered down on its way from the cow to the consumer. Instead they opted for condensed milk which lasted well but was full of sugar. However, the spread of railways and refrigeration now brought fresh rural supplies into the towns. Even so, the urban cow was a great survivor. As a boy in Hoxton in the 1930s Bryan Magee was sent down the road with a jug to find a Mrs Jenkins sitting behind a little window ladling out milk for one penny one farthing a pint from a solitary cow kept in her yard.[15] However, as such traditional supplies were invariably unhygienic the Ministry of Health required the pasteurisation of milk in 1922 as a means of preventing the spread of tuberculosis from the dairy herds. Consumption was also boosted by the introduction of doorstep deliveries by the big commercial dairies. Even so, the consumer ran the risk of fraud because at this time milk bottles were topped with corks that could be removed and replaced by the roundsman. In evidence to the Food Council in 1926 some roundsmen admitted that they gave their customers short measure and sold the surplus milk for up to thirty shillings a week.[16]

From 1932 onwards the establishment of the Milk Marketing Board gave customers stable prices and reliable quality, though the 'Drink

More Milk' campaign was designed to help struggling farmers as much as the consumer. Later in the decade some of the local authority maternity clinics offered free milk to expectant mothers, though this did not become general policy until the Second World War. Meanwhile commercial interests complemented the official efforts by pioneering the new milk bars. According to Paul Johnson their arrival caused great excitement: 'Hast 'eard? They've gorra milk bar in Buzlum [Burslem, Stoke-on-Trent].' He described it as 'a brand new art deco set-up with plenty of chromium, glass and bright colours – apple-green, cherry red and ivory white – with waitresses in high caps behind the bar at which you sat on important stools.'[17] For children a visit was evidently a novel, sophisticated and extravagant experience. 'I sipped and sipped like an old don savouring ancient port. Outside, I recall, the Salvation Army band played. As part of their campaign against demon drink they saw the milk bar as an ally.' Johnson's account suggests that the milk bars probably marked a real breakthrough by making milk fashionable with the younger generation for the first time.

Milk bars were only one of many businesses that attracted customers to Britain's high streets in this period. In the towns most women went shopping every morning. For many of them this formed a major part of their social lives; but the daily trip was also a necessity because they had no means of keeping perishable food and they wanted to cook at midday. Even a middle-class housewife like E. M. Delafield numbered the lack of refrigeration among her many domestic tribulations: 'Cook says the mutton has *gone*, and will I speak to the butcher, there being no excuse [in] weather like this.'[18] In towns housewives bought from open-air market stalls, from barrows bearing fruit and vegetables, and from a range of small specialist food shops. For the hard-up housewife good tactics dictated shopping towards the end of the day, especially on Saturdays when butchers invariably reduced their prices because they knew the remaining meat would not be fit for sale by Monday. The really poor waited until the market stalls were closing down when children were allowed to scavenge for anything that had been discarded or left on the ground.

The major challenge to this form of shopping was the spread of chain stores such as Liptons, Home and Colonial, The International Stores, David Greig and Sainsbury. In these shops customers were treated to displays of butter decked out in the national flags of England,

Holland, Denmark, New Zealand, Ireland and France to mark its origin:

> The assistants all wore straw hats, and I loved to see one of them take two grooved wooden paddles to an immense block of butter and slash a great chunk out of it, and then slap the chunk around between the paddles, weighing it every few seconds and knocking bits off the edges until it was a dapper little square half pound.[19]

For the middle-class housewife some of these stores maintained much of the ritual of the traditional grocer:

> At the Home and Colonial my mother would sit on a high wooden stool at the counter, while the assistant (always male) in a spotless white apron down to his feet and a white cap, got her purchases. Each was carefully spooned out with a silver shovel from huge bins in heraldic jars, weighed on a vast brass scale, then packaged into neat white or brown paper parcels, tied with string and made up with astonishing dexterity.[20]

The climax of this ceremony came when the customer paid: 'bill and money were loaded into a mechanical device which was shot by wires into the cashier's pulpit high in the shop, to the ringing of a bell. The cashier (always a woman) returned the change in the same device which shot down onto the counter, ting-a-ling!'

However, these grocers faced stiff competition from the Co-operative Society which reached its peak between the wars. By 1939 it controlled twenty-five per cent of all milk distribution, forty per cent of the retail trade in butter and twenty per cent of tea and sugar. The appeal of the Co-op lay in its guarantee of pure, unadulterated food at low prices and in the dividend it offered to its customers. But the drawback was that the Co-op did not give credit. For this reason the poorest families continued to rely on local corner shops where prices were higher but where they could buy on tick when funds ran out towards the end of the week. Naturally the spread of the Co-op was not without its critics. Bryan Magee's grandparents disapproved of his mother for patronising the Co-op because they felt it put small shopkeepers out of business, but 'she was undeterred because she said she wanted the dividend and was damned if she was going to cut off her nose to spite her face'.[21]

Traditional shopkeepers also resented the spread of the 'multiples', chain stores and 'combines' including Woolworths, Marks & Spencer, Boots and Timothy Whites. Liptons had over 600 shops by 1929 and Vesteys ran 2,000 Dewhurst butchers by 1939. However, seen in context the multiples seem less of a threat. Britain still boasted 80,000 grocers, 40,000 butchers, 30,000 bakers and 30,000 greengrocers, and small shops dominated the sale of fish, fruit, vegetables and bread. On the other hand, they were less responsible for their own goods and increasingly reduced to selling branded goods at prices set by the wholesalers, manufacturers and refiners. Small shopkeepers were also extremely vulnerable if they allowed too much credit to their customers, and went bankrupt because they could not pay their suppliers. In the 1930s their grievances were exploited by the British Union of Fascists who attacked the chain stores on the grounds that they were owned by foreigners, sold non-British goods produced by cheap labour, undercut the small shopkeepers, and squeezed producers into giving big discounts for bulk purchases; the fascists condemned Woolworths as American, Marks & Spencer and Montagu Burton as Jewish, and the Vestey Meat Trust for dealing in Argentine beef. They proposed to defend small shopkeepers by restricting the big stores to selling one type of product, by limiting the number of licences so as to minimise competition among retailers, and by closing down any combine deemed to be too alien.[22] On the whole, however, there was sufficient purchasing power in the 1930s to sustain the small shops as well as the chain stores and the Co-operatives.

These controversies are a reminder that in spite of the general fall in the cost of food between the wars, price and supply remained politically sensitive issues throughout the period, and governments took care to keep the mass of consumers happy. 'The food question ultimately decided the issue for this war', Lloyd George had claimed; though exaggerating he had been influenced by the realisation that the collapse of morale in Germany and Italy at crucial stages in the struggle reflected the impact of deteriorating supplies of food on both soldiers and civilians. Even though Britain had coped relatively well, the introduction of conscription had revealed the effects of poor diet on the health of her population, thereby making governments more receptive to scientific advice about the importance of nutrition after 1918. Yet post-war governments found themselves caught between, on the one hand, farmers complaining about collapsing prices, and on the other hand, workingmen and trade unions angry about wartime food profiteering.

It was for this reason that they felt obliged to extend rationing into peacetime, and in the case of meat, butter and sugar it was not abandoned until October 1919. Not until March 1921, when the Ministry of Food was finally wound up, was there good reason to feel optimistic about food supplies. Wartime had seen a major extension of the cultivated area and in the early 1920s men were keen to move into agriculture. More importantly, the international markets were awash with food. During the 1920s and 1930s between ten and fifteen food ships docked every day at British ports conveying some twenty-two million tons of food and feed for livestock. By pushing the cost of living down, and thus helping to take the edge off popular discontent, falling prices were of crucial importance in promoting the relative stability of British society during the prolonged depression of the interwar period. Even in the worst of the slump prices fell faster than money wages, thereby boosting real disposable incomes for most people. In the process they found that some of the relatively expensive food items had become affordable: fresh milk at threepence a pint and eggs at one shilling a dozen, for example. Britain drew even more heavily on imports from foreign and empire markets. Canada, Australia and Argentina increased their acreage of wheat; New Zealand exported more butter, lamb and mutton; Denmark raised her surplus of eggs, bacon and butter; and new tea plantations covered the highlands of Kenya and Nyasaland. As a result, between 1911 and 1936 British imports of butter almost doubled and imports of meat rose by fifty per cent.

Yet because the British people took cheap food for granted, the authorities could never afford to relax their efforts. In 1921 voters punished the Coalition Government when the Minister for Agriculture, Sir Arthur Griffith-Boscawen, had to fight a by-election at Dudley. The Labour Party attacked him for granting guaranteed prices to wheat farmers and for failing to lift the embargo on imports of store cattle from Canada – both of which pushed up the cost of living. Griffith-Boscawen lost his seat and his ministerial career as a result.

Even stronger evidence of popular feeling came at the extraordinary general election of 1923. Stanley Baldwin, the prime minister, called the election to obtain a mandate to abandon free trade and introduce 'Protectionism'. This meant charging tariffs on imports, a policy that was expected to help British manufacturers, and thus reduce unemployment, but would also make food more expensive. As a result the election became a referendum on protectionism and food prices. The *Daily News*, a free trade supporter, invited voters to sing to the tune of 'Yes, We Have No Bananas', which was all the rage at the time:

> No, we won't have Protection,
> We won't have Protection today.
> 'Twould rush up the prices
> And squeeze us like vices
> And we'd have to pay, pay, pay.

In the event Baldwin's heavy defeat was widely ascribed to the newly enfranchised women who voted against higher food prices.

Subsequently, Baldwin approached food in a very circumspect way when he returned to office. In January 1925 a Royal Commission on Food was established to take evidence from housewives complaining about rising prices, and from indignant manufacturers and wholesalers who felt they had been put in the firing line unfairly. Criticism focussed on the fixing of prices to maintain profits. This was certainly practised in several sectors. For example, the Tea Associations for India and Ceylon tried to regulate the amount of tea coming up for auction and their spokesmen talked up shortages with a view to inflating prices. In 1933 they signed an 'International Tea Agreement' which was designed to stabilise prices by setting quotas.[23] In their evidence to the Royal Commission the Master Bakers Protection Society claimed that imports of flour by the Russians were pushing up their costs and they felt they were entitled to a halfpenny rise on the ten pence charged for a standard loaf.[24] However, accusations that the millers and bakers were colluding to maintain prices rumbled on into 1926. When the Food Council inspected the books of the millers it forced them to concede that flour costs indicated a price of 9½d. a loaf rather than the 10d. charged; but they countered that the agreements with the bakers enabled them to avoid sharp price fluctuations caused by following the cost of flour.[25] Lord Vestey was also subjected to accusations that his and other combines kept the price of Australian and Argentine meat artificially high. But Vestey blamed the butchers for making excessive profits from low-cost supplies: 'I have no doubt that hundreds of tons of imported meat are sold as English', he claimed.[26] There was no obvious way of resolving these issues, although the publicity probably put retailers on the defensive.

Meanwhile, the government attempted to appease all parties in 1926 by establishing the Empire Marketing Board whose task was to boost food imports from the empire. Protectionists really wanted to impose tariffs on foreign imports with exemptions for anything imported from the British Empire. But as dearer food was obviously unpopular they opted for a propaganda campaign designed to stimulate empire trade by educating public opinion. To this end the board organised 'Empire Shopping Weeks', poster campaigns, shop-window displays, films, radio broadcasts, exhibitions and material for use in schools. The posters focussed on specific territories, itemised the products they sent to Britain and urged housewives to 'Buy Empire Goods' and to 'Ask Is It British?' In December 1926 consumers were urged to 'Have An Empire Xmas Pudding' using Canadian flour, South African raisins, Australian sultanas, currants and demerara sugar, English or Scots suet, eggs and apples, Indian spices and Jamaican rum. In 1927 it published the recipe for 'The King's Empire Christmas Pudding'. Yet despite its efforts the Empire Marketing Board failed to make more than a marginal impact on food imports from the Empire; on the whole British consumers bought the cheapest food available without being too particular where it came from. In 1932 the board was abolished.

In that year the National Government initiated policies that made the board redundant. By freely importing food from all over the world post-1918 governments had largely satisfied consumers, but they had antagonised landowners and agriculturists who accused them of being under the thumb of big business and the City of London financiers who made profits by investing in foreign food producers, flooding the domestic market with cheap imports and ruining British farmers in the process; the critics especially objected when governments offered credits to countries like Russia and Argentina to export food to Britain. The National Government took advantage of the economic crisis that had brought it to power to find a way out of these difficulties. It used the Agricultural Marketing Act of 1931 to impose quotas on food imports, offered subsidies to British farmers, and established marketing boards for milk, potatoes, pigs, wheat, sugar and hops to buy their produce at guaranteed prices. It also decided to abandon Britain's historic commitment to free trade by levying tariffs on all imports. However, preferential terms were offered for Empire products; empire tea, for example, paid a levy of twopence compared with four pence on foreign tea. As a result, by 1937 two-thirds of all food imports originated in the Empire.

These initiatives went some way to keeping all the interested parties, consumers, farmers, manufacturers and imperialists, content. However, by 1939 Britain remained as highly dependent on imported food as she had ever been. It is startling to note, for example, that just two per cent of the onions consumed in Britain were grown at home. Some seventy-six per cent of cheese, eighty-eight per cent of flour, eighty-two per cent of sugar, fifty-five per cent of meat and forty per cent of eggs came from abroad. As a result, the outbreak of war found Britain with a population that was better fed but even more vulnerable to attacks on merchant shipping than it had been in 1914.

3

'Mr Can and Mr Can't':
Health and Medicine

Between the wars Britain was a society obsessed with its bowels. Constipation attracted avid discussion both among the professionals and the lay public, and children were freely dosed with syrup of figs, milk of magnesia and castor oil – the last was much favoured by Mussolini as a remedy for his political opponents! Thousands of people routinely tried to alleviate 'the furred colon' and to 'Tone up your system' by taking Bile Beans, and housewives bought Eno's Salts for 'Mr Can and Mr Can't'. Even Brooke Bond tea and breakfast cereals were promoted on the strength of their laxative qualities: 'Eat [Corn Flakes] every day and never miss a day!' as a 1939 Kellogg's advertisement put it.

And where commerce led, science was not far behind. Sir Arbuthnot Lane, one of the most eminent and controversial interwar doctors, insisted on a daily motion as the foundation of good health for his patients; he regarded sluggish bowels as the cause of 'internal poisoning' as manifested in a wide range of complaints including migraine, lethargy, indigestion, halitosis, poor complexion, depression, problems in childbirth, sexual frigidity and impotence. Faced with an overloaded colon, Sir Arbuthnot immediately prescribed paraffin as a lubricant before removing the entire organ from his patients, a practice that attracted extensive criticism from the medical establishment at the time.

However, only the wealthy could afford Lane's radical remedies. Among much of the British population the tradition of self-prescription and folk remedies, complemented by patent medicines bought at the chemist's, remained very strong. In her Devonshire village E. M. Delafield was overwhelmed by the vicar's wife's remedies for colds, coughs and sore throats: 'cinnamon, Vapex, gargling with glycerine of thymol, blackcurrant tea, onion broth, Friar's Balsam, linseed poultices, thermogene wool, nasal douching and hot milk last thing at night'. In rural Lincolnshire sufferers from whooping cough were still advised to go down to the sea when the tide was going out, cough into it and 'the tide will take your cough with it'. Nor was this a purely rural phenomenon. In Salford mediums tried to cure varicose veins by means of herbs and the laying on of hands.[1] Cuts and abrasions, unless very serious, were routinely dealt with. In Tunstall (Stoke-on-Trent) Paul Johnson suffered at the hands of his barber, Mr Greasley, who had not mastered his electric clippers and drew blood from his customers. This was immediately treated by 'dabbing the wound with an agonising swab of iodine, the universal medicament and antiseptic'.[2]

In fact, when families felt the need for more professional help their immediate recourse was to the local druggist or chemist who was usually happy to treat a wide range of symptoms including dental and eye problems. It seemed cheaper and quicker to purchase the patent medicines they sold rather than take the risks of visiting doctors and hospitals, especially as advertisements for these remedies routinely assured patrons that 'the doctor' recommended them to his patients, to the intense irritation of the medical profession. As late as 1937 a single edition of *Woman's Own* included advertisements for Beechams Pills, Bile Beans and assorted tablets and powders designed to cure piles, varicose veins, gastric ulcers, constipation, anaemia, neuritis, depression, indigestion, weak nerves, liver and kidney troubles, lumbago, rheumatism and period pains. This catalogue of ailments, incidentally, painted a graphic picture of the poor health of British women between the wars.

Not surprisingly, medical treatment was the scene of stiff competition between GPs and druggists, not to mention an army of untrained midwives, herbalists, osteopaths and bone-setters. After the war osteopaths became very popular with the public for treating wounded soldiers. The most prominent, Herbert Barker, was even awarded a knighthood in 1922 after a petition to the prime minister; but as he was not a trained doctor this recognition was interpreted as a rebuff to the General Medical Council. Barker's success provoked further controversy in 1925 because of his anaesthetist, Dr F. W. Axham, who had been struck off the medical register in 1911 for his work with osteopaths. If Barker was fit to be knighted, why was Axham left in disgrace? A number of prominent sympathisers, including G. B. Shaw, who denounced the GMC as 'a trade union of the worst kind', agitated for his reinstatement, but Axham died before any decision had been made.[3]

In the eyes of many conventional doctors the war had boosted another enemy and charlatan: the psychoanalyst. In fact, the methods of Sigmund Freud and his disciples had become familiar during the Edwardian period, but during the war they became much more widely used in treating shell-shocked patients in hospitals established at Craiglockhart near Edinburgh and Maghull near Liverpool. As in all academic disputes the protagonists exaggerated the differences between them; few professional psychologists were entirely Freudian in their approach. Conversely, many conventional doctors such as Bertrand Dawson, later eminent as a royal doctor, had spent time in France and became aware of the impact of battle stress or 'soldier's heart'. Dawson, who supported the establishment of centres to study and treat these problems, became convinced that 'diseases of invasion' would steadily recede in importance and be replaced by 'diseases of stress'. During the 1920s psychoanalysis became rather fashionable because of its wider application in treating nervous breakdown especially among lonely and wealthy women who appreciated doctors who were willing to listen, and even encouraged them to talk freely about their private emotions; this was a novel contrast with the abrupt and high-handed approach adopted by many eminent medics. However, orthodox medicine covered the Freudians with abuse. In 1925 the BMA urged an enquiry into the practitioners of psychoanalysis, accusing them of teaching that 'there was only one thing in our lives and that was sex'. Psychoanalysis was condemned by its critics as being too risky because patients could end up feeling degraded and liable to attempt suicide.[4] In their attack the doctors won support from clergymen who, also seeing psychology as a professional threat to their authority, condemned it for encouraging sex obsession and free sexual expression rather than self-control; as one put it, the 'dustbin of the mind' was best left undisturbed. The impact of these learned disputes is unknown, but the novel methods certainly became popular with the comparatively few people who could afford the treatment. 'We are all psychoanalysts now', commented the *Daily News* in 1922. In the aftermath of a war in which the emotions had been bottled up the idea of dropping one's inhibitions, obeying one's sexual urges and emancipating oneself from neuroses by releasing dangerous feelings appealed to the contemporary thinking.

Not that the medical profession was fighting a losing battle. Orthodox, professional treatment gradually won greater acceptance during the early twentieth century; but changes of attitude were hampered by the expense and by the ineffectiveness of conventional medicine. Many ordinary people still considered money spent on doctors as a waste and the advice they gave routinely to women – rest, put your feet up and eat nourishing food – as largely impractical. Consequently they managed with minimal medical assistance. In his isolated Gloucestershire village Laurie Lee experienced the whole gamut of boyhood illnesses in the early 1920s: 'For a year I lay prone to successive invasions . . . diphtheria, whooping cough, pleurisy, double pneumonia and congestion of the bleeding lungs.' His parents evidently regarded all this fatalistically as something beyond their control: 'Those were the days when children faded quickly, when there was little to be done, should the lungs be affected, but to burn coal-tar and pray . . . In those cold valley cottages, with their dripping walls, damp beds and oozing floors, a child could sicken and die in a year.'[5] However, the steady reduction in child mortality rates through medical intervention gradually undermined this fatalism. As a child in Blackburn William Woodruff suffered for years from an inability to pass water properly; but his parents ignored his complaints. However, once their GP found out he undertook immediate surgery in the Woodruffs' home: 'Fearful, I climbed onto the kitchen table over which my mother had spread a clean sheet . . . A gauze cup was placed over my nose and mouth. "Give him a whiff," said [Dr] Grieves to his aid. "All over in a tick," he said to me reassuringly.'[6] William came to, dazed from the chloroform and endured 'a week or two of agony'; but he was fully cured and consequently less sceptical about professional medicine than his parents.

Resistance to hospitalisation was even more deeply rooted because, as Woodruff recalled, 'father believed that if he ever entered a hospital he would die'. When Woodruff Senior collapsed at work the doctor detected appendicitis, a favourite diagnosis in this period, and recommended immediate surgery: 'he was bundled into the ambulance and despatched to the Royal Infirmary. But Mr Woodruff never arrived. Somewhere en route he managed to persuade the ambulance driver, who was a mate of his, to take him home. His mate had great difficulty explaining the empty ambulance when he got to the infirmary.'[7] Meanwhile Mr Woodruff took to his bed, resorted to folk remedies and survived, thereby demonstrating that stomach pains were frequently diagnosed incorrectly, and, no doubt, proving to his own satisfaction that self-help was as good as doctors' medicine.

To some extent fear of hospitals lay in their connection to the Poor Law authorities. For example, St Leonards's in Hoxton had begun life as a huge, intimidating workhouse which made the transition to municipal hospital in 1930, when the workhouse was closed down; but among the local East Enders who were treated there its history was not easily forgotten.[8] In any case, fear of hospitals was perfectly rational. They were the source of the puerperal fever that killed thousands of women in childbirth at home. During the war many voluntary hospitals closed their outpatient departments and some of their wards, so as to divert resources to the war effort, with no detrimental effects on the domestic population. In fact, in the absence of doctors civilians lived longer and infant mortality rates continued to improve, the result of higher family incomes, food rationing and reduced consumption of alcohol during the war years.

Indeed, some doctors privately conceded that patients were justified in taking a sceptical attitude towards their prescriptions. One interwar GP admitted: 'Well, you used your placebos. We had a lot. White aspirin, green aspirin and blue ones. We had a mixture of lactose, you know, milk sugar which was dissolved. Some put some stuff in to give it a horrible taste, some didn't.'[9] On the occasions when William Woodruff's family were persuaded to resort to a professional cure he was dispatched to Dr Grieves's surgery for a sixpenny bottle of medicine: 'I knew if I'd got the right bottle by the colour. Coughs and chest problems were treated with a blue liquid (if goose grease and a home-made concoction of lemon, glycerine and cod liver oil had failed). Aches in the head, eyes, ears and nose were dosed with yellow; joint troubles with red; those in the belly – there being no response to the usual doses of prune and fig juice – with a black, tar-like substance.'[10] Nor, despite their dislike for herbalists, were GPs averse to using similar remedies. 'We had every drug from every plant and every weed that grew', explained one doctor. 'We made them in the surgery – your mixtures, your concoctions, your infusions.'[11]

In fairness doctors often recognised that there was little they could do for their patients. 'Remember,' warned one experienced GP, 'ninety per cent of your patients will get better whether you treat them or not . . . seven to eight per cent will require some skill and two per cent will die anyway.'[12] For example, in cases of pneumonia 'you treated the patient because you couldn't treat the disease'. This meant giving them strychnine, camphor and oil as a stimulus to the heart, combined with morphine injections to help them sleep; the doctor hoped this would keep them going and build up their strength. Faced with congestive heart failure one doctor felt he could do practically nothing, but the remedy for 'these old girls, I remember, was digitalis washed down with champagne'.[13]

Yet despite the well-founded cynicism about medical treatment, interwar Britain was steadily becoming a healthier society. Average life expectancy for men improved from fifty-two to sixty-one between 1910 and 1938, and for women from fifty-five to sixty-six years. To a large extent this reflected the long-term effects of improved diet, sanitation and housing, and a succession of state innovations during the Edwardian period including medical inspection of schoolchildren (1907), old-age pensions (1908), maternity benefits (1911), expansion of TB sanatoria (1911) and health insurance (1911). The First World War helped to accelerate this improvement in several ways. Doctors noticed the poor standard of physical fitness among the volunteers examined for the armed forces. Forty-one per cent of military-aged men were pronounced unfit for service, one in nine were 'chronic invalids with a precarious hold' and only a third were found fit and healthy. Subsequently many doctors took the opportunity to promote national health in the widest sense, campaigning for better diets, presenting a scientific rationale for nutrition, and devising precise criteria for improvement. A soldier, for example, was considered to require 3,500 calories a day. In the early 1920s Sir Arbuthnot Lane started campaigning about poor diet which he saw as a cause of cancer. The recent discovery of vitamins aroused wider public interest in his theories, though few people felt inclined to alter their diet. In 1924 Lane was censured by the BMA ethics committee for discussing these issues at a press conference because it looked like advertising on his part.

Characteristically, Lane resigned from the BMA to carry on with his propaganda to promote the consumption of wholemeal bread, fruit and vegetables as well as more exposure to sunlight, another fashionable notion that was regarded as suspect by the medical establishment.

However, diet was increasingly taken seriously even in conventional circles. In 1933 the BMA itself instituted an enquiry to determine the weekly expenditure on food necessary to maintain health and working capacity; their conclusion – five shillings a head – implied that ten per cent of the British population was undernourished. When Sir John Boyd Orr constructed a diet designed to promote optimum health in 1936 he concluded that the bottom ten per cent of people suffered a diet that was inadequate in every respect, that is in calories, protein, fat, calcium, iron, phosphorus and vitamins A and C. The diet of the next twenty per cent was judged adequate only in fat and protein. In effect, the professionals were now saying that although British people were not starving, their unhealthy diet left masses of them a prey to ailments such as rickets, anaemia, tuberculosis and dental caries, to take the more obvious examples.

By far the most striking evidence of the beneficial effect of diet lay in infant mortality rates. In 1900 there had been 142 deaths for every 1,000 births up to twelve months. But the total fell steadily to 110 in 1910, 82 in 1920, 68 in 1930 and 55 by 1938, though this was still considerably higher than the rate in comparable countries such as the United States and Australia. It also varied regionally from 47 in the South-East in 1935 to 68 in the North and 76 in Scotland. Significantly, infant mortality had continued to improve during wartime. This was largely due to the modest allowances paid directly to mothers, in the absence of male breadwinners, which was channelled to their families. This success inspired the idea known to contemporaries as 'endowment of motherhood', a reform that was championed by the Independent MP, Eleanor Rathbone, and was finally enacted as 'Family Allowances' in 1946. Meanwhile the government had started to subsidise local clinics for mothers in 1914. This policy was greatly extended by the 1918 Maternity and Child Welfare Act which required local authorities to appoint welfare committees and instituted grants to establish the clinics. By 1938 3,580 infant welfare clinics and 1,795 natal clinics were in operation in England and Wales. Many local authorities provided milk, cod liver oil, iron and vitamin products cheaply or free to mothers and infants. In combination with the general increase in food consumption these policies eventually made a major impact on health and fitness; in London, for example, twelve-year-old boys were found to be, on average, three inches taller and eleven pounds heavier by 1939 than their fathers had been twenty years earlier.

But how far were improvements in health and longevity due to advances in scientific knowledge and medical practice? One GP who qualified in 1928 privately admitted 'there was practically no difference in medical knowledge in 1928 than there was when my father qualified in 1897'.[14] Yet this seems unduly cynical. The nineteenth century had seen the introduction of several more or less effective remedies, if not cures, including aspirin, introduced in 1896, quinine for malaria, digitalis to stimulate the heart, colchicum for gout, amyl nitrite for angina and opium as a pain reliever. Admittedly many diseases were still beyond a cure, and as a result, the successful doctor was often the one who cultivated a good bedside manner and eased the discomfort of his patients. Hence the growing emphasis on sedatives and quick-acting painkillers, notably morphine, heroin (1898), barbitone (1903) and phenobarbitone (1912). For this relief patients were so grateful that the doctor's problem was to stop them becoming addicted. Yet paying patients were hard to refuse. When Lady Diana Manners became highly distressed by the rows she was having with her parents, Duff Cooper noted that 'after dinner [she] had an injection of morphine to help her in the fight'. But a fortnight later: 'we had a quarrel because Diana wished for morphine which I refused'.[15] In July 1919 she broke her leg, and in September Duff recorded that 'the chief trouble . . . is to cure Diana of taking morphine. She has been having it ever since her accident and now cannot do without it. Every evening there is a scene until she gets it.'[16]

After 1918 medical treatment improved significantly in many respects. As a result of the destructive effects of high-explosive shells during the war doctors acquired extensive practice with lung and brain surgery, plastic and reconstructive surgery on shattered limbs, and with experiments with blood transfusions and the establishment of blood and plasma banks. By the 1930s battle casualties were able to receive stored blood in the operating theatres. The mass transfer of troops to France had also promoted better treatment of venereal diseases, including the use of Salvarsan for syphilis. Other significant advances in the treatment of major diseases included insulin for diabetes in 1922, immunisation against diphtheria in the 1930s, and sulphonamides for treating pneumonia and puerperal fever from 1935 onwards.

Along with alcoholism and tuberculosis, syphilis had long been one of Britain's most crippling and widespread diseases. If untreated it resulted in general paralysis and insanity, but it also spread to unborn children with the result that entire families suffered from congenital blindness, deafness, idiocy and malformations. After 1910 Salvarsan gradually replaced mercury, the traditional treatment, which was both ineffective and dangerous. During the war the army distributed condoms to the troops as a prophylactic and local authorities were required to establish clinics to treat the disease. However, it was not until 1922 that the GMC altered the regulations so that medical students were routinely taught about venereal diseases for the first time.

Tuberculosis, or consumption of the lungs, remained a major problem in interwar Britain, though the total number of deaths fell from 51,000 in 1910 to 27,000 in 1938. TB also caused prolonged disablement of wage-earners in the prime of life and turned entire families into invalids. As it flourished where poor, damp housing conditions prevailed, the steady clearance of overcrowded housing in the 1920s and 1930s helped to reduce the spread. But the cause lay in milk supplies. Forty per cent of cows and up to thirteen per cent of raw milk samples included the tubercule bacilli, leading to contamination of milk collected in bulk. To counter this the Ministry of Health required suppliers to label milk as pasteurised in 1922, though pasteurisation was still not compulsory.

As yet there was no cure for TB, the main treatment being good food, sunlight, fresh air and rest. State investment in TB sanatoria increased the number of beds available from 8,000 in 1911 to 25,000 by 1930. Meanwhile the BCG vaccine was being developed but it did not come into general use until after the Second World War.

The application of new scientific ideas and best practice was hindered by the separation between general practice and specialism or consultancy in Britain; GPs were effectively excluded from surgery, were unable to attend their patients in hospital and remained rather isolated from scientific advances. This traditional pattern had been entrenched by the 1911 National Insurance Act which weighted the health system heavily towards GPs rather than specialists. In 1920, when the government consulted Lord Dawson about the organisation of health provision, he again recommended that the service should continue to be divided between primary care, that is, general practitioners, and secondary health centres, that is, district general hospitals.

Moreover, those doctors who were open to new medical techniques often had to contend with the conservatism of their profession and its bias against 'theoretical' work. As late as 1918 one eminent doctor, Sir James Mackenzie, pronounced that 'laboratory training *unfits* a man for his work as a physician', a commonly held view at the time.[17] Nor did doctors always take as much notice of their patients as was desirable. One exception to this was Thomas Horder who became noted for his keen observation at the bedside combined with laboratory investigation; but senior colleagues criticised him for spending too much time at the patient's bedside. He became famous for 'Horder's Box', a device containing a folding microscope, syringes, needles and tubes of broth and agar that were used for preparing cultures at the bedside. Fortunately Horder managed to overcome the prejudice against his methods when he made his breakthrough with a successful diagnosis for King Edward VII; as a result he went on to treat a succession of royal patients, but this route was open only to a few doctors.

It is easy to forget how handicapped interwar doctors were in dealing with many serious ailments. As they had no antibiotics, infections spread quickly through patients' bodies and lingered far longer than they would today. Although Alexander Fleming was experimenting with penicillin by 1928, it did not become available until 1941. Consequently an operation remained a very dangerous procedure, though doctors resorted to it with increasing enthusiasm in this period. Indeed they regarded surgery as the solution to a wide range of problems. Why was this? Partly because the discovery of X-rays in 1895 enabled them to monitor the interior of the body. Also, the application of chloroform to the patient made operations far easier, for it not only eased the patient's pain but gave the surgeon extra time, thus making difficult operations feasible. Chloroform had become fashionable since 1853 when it was administered to Queen Victoria during the birth of Prince Leopold; she subsequently insisted on having it. However, it left patients suffering from vomiting for days afterwards. By the twentieth century the usual procedure was to give morphine first to knock the patients out, and then apply chloroform, though this was difficult because of the danger that the patients would suffocate or struggle violently on becoming unconscious; as a result they usually had to be strapped to the bed. Medical techniques also improved. Sir Arbuthnot Lane made his reputation as a skilled pioneer of aseptic surgery by developing long instruments that allowed the surgeon to work without touching the tissues and to undertake surgery that had previously been very dangerous for the patient. Lane also required co-operation from his nursing staff in ensuring that the operating areas were kept sterile.

Despite this, recovery from an operation was often extremely slow. In 1921 when the archaeologist of Tutankhamun fame, Howard Carter, underwent an abdominal operation to remove his gall bladder, he spent six weeks in hospital in Leeds and a further six weeks recuperating.[18] In November 1929 King George V became seriously ill with a streptococcal infection of the chest which soon affected two-thirds of his lung according to the X-rays. But as the doctors could not see where the cause lay there was little they could do to stop the spread of the infection. By 12 December septicaemia had set in and the King became unconscious. More by inspiration than science Bertrand Dawson found the site of the original abscess, plunged his needle in and drew off sixteen ounces of fluid. The surgeons then operated, drained the abscess and removed a rib. But not until February 1930 did they send the King off to Bognor to recuperate. Four days later they allowed him to start smoking again![19]

Nevertheless, interwar medics were notably gung-ho in their resort to surgery, as, it must be said, were some of their patients. Any pain in the stomach was apt to be diagnosed, often incorrectly, as appendicitis, followed by removal of the offending organ. Wealthy people routinely had their appendix out before departing for a long sea voyage so as to avoid spoiling the holiday. Even more fashionable was the removal of children's tonsils, a quick operation usually conducted at home using ether or chloroform. Many GPs seemed to consider this as simply routine. 'On Sunday morning it was tonsil morning', commented one enthusiast.[20] According to Bryan Magee having his tonsils out was 'one of the high points of my medical history'. Unfortunately he 'woke up during the operation (I think they gave the merest whiff of anaesthetic to small children for an operation that was expected to last only a couple of minutes) and it was a nightmarish experience'.[21] From such accounts it seems that doctors underestimated or simply ignored the effects of surgery on their patients.

The mass removal of organs such as tonsils, now considered to have been unnecessary, reflected a fashionable view in the medical profession, associated with Sir Arbuthnot Lane and his 'Theory of Focal Sepsis'. According to his theory, trouble in one part of the body spread infection to all parts; rapid recovery therefore lay in identifying the source of any infection and then whipping out the affected part immediately. This sometimes led to drastic interventions; as late as 1937, for example, a woman who developed puerperal fever following her confinement at home had her leg amputated to stop the spread of the fever.

When it came to women the medical profession relied on a modicum of science generously tempered by prejudice and ignorance. Many doctors remained uncomfortable both about female sexuality and about women as a threat to their profession. During the Victorian and Edwardian periods several leading doctors had used scientific authority to undermine the case for giving votes to women, arguing that they were physically and emotionally unfit for a political role and that their functions as mothers would be damaged by involvement in politics. This mentality survived female enfranchisement in 1918 and 1928. In the 1930s Sir Arbuthnot Lane was cited in press reports on 'Are Women Overdoing Sport?' in which he issued warnings to the effect that 'a craze for athletics is sweeping over women . . . Any excess in this direction is bound to have a serious effect on the motherhood of the nation.'[22] Lane commended Italy for curtailing female participation in the Olympic Games. His blinkered attitude towards women was fully reflected in his treatment of one of his society patients, Lady Diana Cooper, who went in fear of breast cancer. Lane dismissed her concerns and advised that having a baby would do her more good than anything else! 'He hoped we did not use preventives', reported her husband.[23] At this time old-fashioned GPs were still known to lecture young wives that it was their duty to populate the Empire and to refuse to advise them on contraception, and up to 1930 the BMA opposed the provision of information on birth control even to married women. Wives who consulted their doctors about sexual diseases faced similar obstructionism. Doctors who knew perfectly well that husbands had contracted venereal disease from prostitutes usually withheld the information from their wives on the basis that nothing should interfere between a man and the exercise of his conjugal rights. Even sympathetic doctors sometimes confessed to being unable to give women effective advice about sexual matters because of their own ignorance. In the late 1920s when Sylvia Pankhurst was examining the whole question of prenatal care she was surprised to discover that obstetrics was neglected in the training of doctors, being crammed into a brief period at the end of their course, and thus leaving them with little practice in delivering babies.

The results of these failings had long been obvious in the high rates of maternal mortality in Britain. Against the generally improving trend the maternal mortality rate increased from 4.83 per 1,000 births in 1923 to 5.94 in 1933, though it fell back to 3.35 by 1939. There was in fact a marked correlation between medical intervention and maternal mortality. This was partly because doctors used instruments for delivery, which midwives did not, and also because they often came from hospitals, and even mortuaries, to the delivering rooms, thereby infecting mothers with puerperal fever when they were at their most vulnerable; once infected a mother usually died within hours. In Germany it had been found that if medics washed their hands and their instruments in chlorinated lime solution this materially reduced mortality rates; but best practice was slow to spread. In fact, where a birth involved no complications a mother was usually best advised to rely on an experienced midwife, even an untrained one. In the absence of universal knowledge about birth control methods, 'midwives' also continued to be responsible for enabling thousands of women to obtain illegal miscarriages and abortions throughout the interwar period.

The shocking maternal mortality statistics provoked the interwar feminist organisations into pushing the neglect of women's health further up the political agenda. In 1933 they established the Women's Health Committee Inquiry, which investigated the health of some 1,250 married women, and published the findings in 1939 as *Working-Class Wives: Their Health and Conditions*. Strikingly, most of the women understated the seriousness of their condition and seemed grateful for any interval of good health between illnesses. The study identified the high incidence of certain ailments, notably anaemia (which affected no fewer than 588 of the 1,250 women), headaches, constipation with haemorrhoids, rheumatism, gynaecological problems of various kinds, decayed teeth, varicose veins (exacerbated by excessive childbirth and standing up all day), ulcerated legs, phlebitis and white leg. Only thirty-one per cent of the women claimed to enjoy good health; a further twenty-two per cent claimed indifferent health, which meant suffering only one or two serious ailments; fifteen per cent were in bad health, which meant they had numerous major and minor problems; and thirty-one per cent were in a grave condition – they never felt fit and well.[24] An example from the 'indifferent' category was a 38-year-old Cardiff woman with eight children who admitted to suffering from decayed teeth, bronchitis every winter and a prolapsed uterus ever since her second pregnancy. She never had treatment for the bronchitis or the prolapsed uterus, but still described herself as fit and well.[25]

Part of the explanation for the poor health of these women lay in their poverty and consequent reluctance to seek professional medical treatment. The study found a 47-year-old Sheffield housewife and mother of seven who had suffered from rheumatism since an operation for gallstones, backache, headaches and toothaches. 'For none of these does she consult anyone. She owes her private doctor for the last five years' attendance, including the last confinement, £14, which she pays off in 1s. weekly instalments'.[26] As few of the women were insured they had no access to the panel doctor who treated their husbands and had to make other arrangements; but they invariably put the rest of the family before their own health. The working-class wives in the sample had an average of 4.5 births which was twice the average by this time, and to that extent their health reflected the problems of an older generation of women. For younger wives things had improved partly because they were having fewer children and partly because of the provision of antenatal care by local authority clinics. Also, by the 1930s more mothers were receiving professional care at childbirth because of the gradual demise of the tradition of giving birth at home. As late as 1927 only twenty-seven per cent of births took place in hospitals, but major improvements in the provision of beds and in the standard of treatment had increased this to thirty-five per cent by 1937.

Female patients were, of course, only the most obvious victims of a profession that was still bedevilled by a confusion of amateur and professional practitioners. To some extent this was symptomatic of a wider scepticism towards formal training and professionalism still common in British society. For example, it was not until 1902 that the Midwives Act made it illegal to practise as a midwife in Britain without being trained. Doctors themselves had been unenthusiastic about this reform because they saw themselves as being in competition with midwives. Yet, as many doctors were inadequately trained in obstetrics, there was a continuing demand even for untrained midwives, and, as most births still took place in the home, midwives continued with their work without attracting attention. Things did, however, improve after the 1936 Midwives Act which imposed an obligation on local authorities to train and employ midwives.

Similarly, the medical profession had always been cool towards training for nurses because they were likely to offer a cheaper service especially in rural areas. Despite the campaign for compulsory training, which had been waged for over forty years, successive governments had evaded the issue. Florence Nightingale, who regarded character as far more important for nurses than formal qualifications, proved to be a major hindrance to professionalisation right up to her death in 1910. Eventually the pressures created by the war tipped the debate in favour of reform. Even in military hospitals there was only one trained nurse to every sixteen beds. Moreover, the huge influx of untrained women into nursing – around 180,000 VAD nurses in military and auxiliary hospitals – united the existing professionals who felt that their status was being undermined by the newcomers and feared becoming unemployed after the war. Eventually in 1920 the government required all nurses to be registered and trained, though existing untrained ones were allowed to register and continue to practise. Not until 1925, when 4,000 new nurses joined the profession, did a regular system of state examinations for nurses begin.

Doctors themselves had effectively established their professional status back in 1858 by means of the Medical Act which created a single medical register and set up the General Medical Council to oversee the training and licensing of doctors. Subsequently the profession had been energetic in ousting competitors and in excluding women, at least until comparatively recently. Female doctors numbered only 477 in 1914, a total that rose slowly to 1,253 by 1921 and to 2,810 by 1931. This was not a large number among the 61,000 doctors, one for every 800 people, who were at work by 1939. At this time a medical training cost around £1,000, after which the young doctor required £2,000–3,000 to buy into a GP practice.[27] As the banks saw them as a good risk, the money could be borrowed, but the young doctor was faced with paying off his debts over fifteen to twenty years.

For patients themselves the provision of medical treatment varied widely according to their income. As many as five grades of patients can be identified in Britain during the 1920s and 1930s. At the bottom of the pile were the very poor who had to obtain a note from the local relieving officer entitling them to free treatment on the parish. Slightly better off were the members of a variety of working men's clubs and Friendly Societies including the Forresters and the Oddfellows. In return for paying anything from one to threepence a week they received treatment from a doctor to whom the club paid an annual retainer. The largest group comprised those people insured under the 1911 National Insurance Act, around twelve million in 1913, fifteen million in 1921 and twenty million by 1938. They were entitled to free treatment from a panel doctor as well as sickness benefit. By 1939 over two-thirds of all doctors had joined the scheme. The flaw lay in the fact that health insurance covered insured employees not their dependents. In 1937 health insurance was extended to include employed youngsters aged fourteen to sixteen, but this still left millions of women and young children excluded. The fourth category comprised the 'poor private' patients, including both working-class and middle class people who simply paid the doctor's fees or used a hospital outpatient department. They often ran up big debts that had to be paid off over many years. Finally there were the well-off private patients who were admitted to the front door of the surgery – the others entered at the scruffy back entrance – and waited in a pleasant dining room. They comprised about ten per cent of a typical GP practice but generated half its income. There were other gaps in the system too. As dental care was entirely a matter of private provision, teeth were widely neglected and dental decay became a massive problem. Faced with failing eyesight poor people usually visited Woolworths and other department stores for do-it-yourself treatment; they tested their own eyes and bought the pair of glasses that seemed to improve their vision most.

It is fair to say that the unfairness of this system was recognised by GPs, many of whom helped to mitigate its effects themselves. For example, in the 1920s a visit and a bottle of medicine typically cost three shillings and sixpence, but affluent patients would be charged ten shillings and sixpence for exactly the same. In Blackburn William Woodruff noted that 'Everybody admired Dr Grieves not least because he sometimes forgot to send bills. House visits, when he remembered to charge, were two shillings and sixpence.' One Lincolnshire GP explained that the agricultural labourers earned only twenty-eight shillings a week: 'You couldn't charge people on that.'[28] In effect, these doctors were redistributing income from their wealthy clients for the benefit of the poor.

At the other end of the spectrum a handful of fashionable medics who dealt only or largely with rich patients in plush private practices acquired reputations that were based on their medical skills but often enhanced by their opinionated stance and by their high-handed behaviour. Sir Arbuthnot Lane, who received his knighthood in 1913, was a classic example of a doctor whose eminence enabled him to defy the medical establishment and campaign for his ideas. Thomas Horder, immune from attack by virtue of his role as doctor to George V, George VI and Elizabeth II, became a knight in 1918, a baronet in 1923 and a peer in 1933. Bertrand Dawson, who had been appointed physician extraordinary to Edward VII in 1906 and also served George V, was appointed Lord Dawson of Penn in 1920 and raised to a viscountcy in 1936. Both Dawson and Horder defied conventional medical opinion, notably by supporting birth control. But reputation was easily abused. Sir Bernard Spilsbury, who had attained prominence by appearing for the Crown in the prosecution of Dr Crippen in 1911, was regularly called as a witness in headline-making trials. He became notorious in 1925 when giving evidence against one John Thorne who had been charged with strangling his mistress. The defence produced a series of medical witnesses who testified that the lady had been strangled by the pressure of a cord consistent with having hanged herself. But Sir Bernard insisted that she had been manually strangled, and the court, as was usual, preferred to believe him. As a result both the bar and the press complained that the courts were attaching too much importance to Spilsbury's opinions at the expense of rival authorities.[29]

Bertrand Dawson, who was consulted by the government in 1918 about the new Ministry of Health and in 1920 about the structure of the health services, became arguably the most politically influential doctor of the period. Dawson was at the bedside of George V on 20 January 1936 when, in the early evening, he took the decision to scribble a bulletin on the back of a menu card: 'The King's life is moving peacefully towards its close.' Dawson was able to state this with some confidence. As the King's heart failed he had been moving in and out of consciousness for several days. But he continued to read *The Times*, signed official papers and reportedly enquired 'How is the Empire?' His reluctance to die made things complicated for the government and the rest of the royal family. Eventually Lord Dawson, apparently untroubled by his recent opposition to voluntary euthanasia in the House of Lords, ensured a peaceful and timely end for the King by injecting three-quarters of a grain of morphine and a grain of cocaine into his jugular vein. The timing was carefully calculated so as to enable the London newspapers to lead with the news of the King's death next morning.

Despite their useful role in challenging the assumptions of the more obdurate members of the profession, eminent doctors also represented a major hindrance to reform of the system. Although significant gaps in provision remained, a high proportion of people were receiving primary care by the 1930s. The major weakness lay in the chaotic arrangements for secondary care. By 1939 Britain had around 3,000 hospitals of three different types. The Poor Law infirmaries established in the nineteenth century provided 80,000 beds, the municipal hospitals, run by the bigger local authorities and financed from the rates, provided 74,000, and the voluntary hospitals, which were charitable institutions relying on donations and fees from patients, provided 56,000. The whole system was badly in need of reorganisation and rationalisation. But little was done except that in 1928 local authorities were empowered to take over the Poor Law hospitals. Few did so for lack of resources.

The major obstacle to reform lay in the voluntary hospitals and their resistance to being merged into a comprehensive state system. Yet their growing inability to finance medical treatment was creating problems, leading some to close wards. As a result they began to demand funding from the Exchequer while trying to retain their independence. During wartime the voluntary hospitals had drifted away from their original function – treatment of the poor – by admitting middle-class patients; increasingly they sought to resolve their financial problems by charging these patients and turning away poorer people. Unfortunately, although Dawson had urged the integration of the voluntary hospitals into a national scheme in 1920, they enjoyed influential patronage, not least from George V who told the Health Minister, Christopher Addison, of his opposition to any change; he regarded any state intervention as socialism. The King persuaded all the members of the royal family, apart from the Prince of Wales, who thought he was misguided, to help him raise funds to support the voluntary hospitals. He made a personal contribution by shooting more pheasants than usual to be sold at £3 a brace. Although the King's pheasants can have made little material impact, his intervention helped to delay serious reform. But the responsibility lay largely with the eminent doctors who resisted any mergers out of a general prejudice against state regulation. Most of them upheld Victorian thinking about the value of local and voluntary effort, even in the face of growing evidence that the existing arrangements were no longer adequate. But their obduracy also reflected the self-interest of men who had been enriched by private practice involving the treatment of a minority of the population and who intensely disliked the prospect that they might become absorbed into a state salaried medical service; even Dawson considered this to be tantamount to Communism. It took the strain placed on Britain's hospital system by the Second World War to sweep away this accumulated resistance and thereby prepare the ground for radical change in the 1940s.

4

'Where the air's like wine': The Origins of the Property-Owning Democracy

Around midnight on a cold, starry Friday in 1929 the Woodruff family quietly quit their home in Griffin Street, Blackburn, piling their three beds and bedding, assorted 'pisspots', four broken chairs and stools, a bench, a rough table, some orange boxes, peg rugs, and pots and pans on to a flat-topped handcart. For an hour Mr Woodruff pulled the cart through the cobbled streets while the boys ran behind to see that nothing fell off until they arrived at a new house in Livingstone Road on the edge of the town. They celebrated with hot tea: 'We hugged one another at our triumph. "We've done it," we laughed.'[1] The Woodruffs had executed a classic midnight flit. Along with their meagre furniture they had made sure to take their 'clean' rent book which was a useful means of obtaining loans from moneylenders and doing business with pawnbrokers. On Saturday afternoons the rent collector appeared in Griffin Street looking for seven shillings and sixpence: 'a burly, red-faced chap who burst into the house from the street. He never knocked, he never took off his cap, he rarely spoke. If you said the roof leaked . . . he'd give a grunt and leave. Complaints got us nowhere.'[2] Not surprisingly, none of the Woodruffs' neighbours told the rent collector where they had gone, owing a week's rent, and the police simply ignored midnight flits.

This episode speaks volumes for the attitudes and aspirations of millions of British people between the wars, particularly their fear and dislike of landlords and rent collectors, and the appeal of improved housing in semi-rural locations. In convincing her reluctant husband of the need to move Mrs Woodruff had emphasised that the new property enjoyed front and back gardens: 'Just think, Will, a proper garden, and views of the fields and hills.' Close behind came the amenities: 'There's an indoor petty, one that flushes, and a bathroom . . . think of that, Will – a whole room to wash in!' Worn out by the impossibility of keeping damp, draughty, dust-laden Victorian houses clean and comfortable, women placed improved housing high among their aspirations in the 1920s. But for Mrs Woodruff one further ambition remained as yet beyond reach. ' "Oh," said mother, striking further fear into father's heart, "wouldn't it be luvly if this was really ours." After which she gave a long sigh.'[3]

The Woodruff family's move from one rented home to another represented a very modest part of a much wider revolution in housing in interwar Britain that was to have immediate effects on leisure and family life but also profound consequences for the British economy and the political agenda for decades to come. As the urban slums were cleared and four million new houses constructed during the 1920s and 1930s, ordinary people began to enjoy domestic amenities previously associated with the wealthy. In the process the appearance of much of the country, especially London and the South-East, changed. Before 1914 houses for middle- and working-class families had usually been built at about forty to the acre in terraces with backyards; now the fashion was for semi-detached and detached homes at twelve to the acre with gardens front and back. Interwar Britain also saw a major shift in housing tenure; as private rented accommodation dwindled it was replaced by what now seems a characteristically British obsession with owner-occupation.

Before 1914 housing had been a relatively stagnant sector of the economy; Britain's Industrial Revolution had largely passed it by, leaving unchanged the traditional methods of building and the system for financing the construction of houses. Despite the initiatives of a few entrepreneurs, the industry operated on a small scale. Anyone with a little spare money found it attractive to invest in a few terraced houses with a view to living off the income from rent. But such landlords were often widows or retired people who had insufficient resources to maintain their property in good repair; as a result much of the housing stock deteriorated during the nineteenth century. The rising burden of rates in the late Victorian period hit small householders hard and led many to regard housing generally as a dwindling asset. Also, many town houses had been built on leasehold, and consequently reverted to the ownership of the ground landlord on the expiry of the term. In view of these weaknesses in the housing industry it is not surprising that urban-dwellers suffered from overcrowding; before the war overcrowding affected eighteen per cent of all properties in London, thirty-one per cent in Newcastle and fifty-five per cent in Glasgow.

In this situation the industry stood in need of a major stimulus. But in the absence of technological innovations costs remained high in a business that was very labour intensive. Some contemporaries argued that as the development of industry and the growth of the urban population had inflated the price of land the state should force more land onto the market by taxing site values. Nor was investment either by small builders, building societies or governments adequate to the task. In fact shortages had been exacerbated during the late Victorian period because local authorities began to clear some of the worst slums without replacing them. State regulation impinged more on the design of new building schemes than on their construction. In 1909 the traditional back-to-back houses had been banned but existing terraces remained narrow and deep, deficient in light and fresh air. Here and there initiatives had been taken by enlightened entrepreneurs who constructed high-quality homes in attractive villages or garden suburbs for their employees. But the model set by Sir William Lever's Port Sunlight and the Cadbury family's Bourneville was not widely followed. Perhaps more influential was Ebenezer Howard's Garden City Movement which pioneered a new community at Letchworth in Hertfordshire, home to 9,000 people by 1914. The Edwardian garden suburbs at Hampstead and Golders Green represented modified versions of Howard's ideas for lower-density housing and less uniformity.

However, it was the First World War that eventually set the Victorian system on the path to oblivion by triggering an explosion of popular discontent. Before 1914 Britain's housing shortage was officially estimated at 120,000, but by 1918 it had risen to 300,000 as a result of deterioration and the suspension of building activity; subsequent estimates have put it at around 600,000. By 1915 thousands of workers had left home to take employment in munitions, thereby exacerbating local shortages of accommodation and allowing landlords to raise their rents substantially. This provoked an angry wave of rent strikes in cities such as Glasgow, Liverpool and Birmingham.

Already an unpopular group, the private landlords rapidly lost what little sympathy they had enjoyed. Governments were so anxious to retain the co-operation of the labour force in boosting munitions output that they imposed drastic and unprecedented rent controls in 1915. No increase on the rent charged in August 1914 was permitted on houses with a rateable value of £26 or £30 in Scotland and £35 in London. Nor were landlords permitted to evict tenants except for failing to pay the rent.

Despite subsequent infringements, these rent restrictions were never entirely abandoned during the interwar period. This was remarkable because, in effect, the policy reduced the value of privately owned property. Even the Conservatives, who dominated government during the period, accepted the necessity for controls, though they modified them in 1923 and 1933. As a result the private rented sector went into a prolonged decline from which it never really recovered. Before the war it had provided ninety per cent of British housing; by 1938 the total had fallen to fifty-eight per cent and it continued to decline thereafter. In effect the war, combined with the enfranchisement of adult men and women in 1918 and 1928, had forced housing up the agenda. Although state intervention was by no means a complete answer to the problem, it was adopted initially by the wartime premier, David Lloyd George, and subsequently by the Labour Party. 'What is our task?', Lloyd George had asked the electors of Wolverhampton during the 'Coupon Election' in November 1918: 'To make Britain a fit country for heroes to live in.' The Housing Act of 1919, pioneered by Dr Christopher Addison, was designed to put this promise into practice.

Hitherto local authorities had cleared slums on health grounds in the hope that private enterprise and philanthropists would build replacement homes. But this never happened on the scale required, and most municipal councils felt reluctant to step in because of the costs involved. During the Edwardian period only 5 per cent of newly built houses were constructed by local authorities with government grants, representing only 0.5 per cent of the housing stock. Now the 1919 Act required them to survey the housing needs in their areas and draw up plans to meet the shortage. The Exchequer offered subsidies towards the cost of building them. Labour councillors, who were being elected in growing numbers from 1919 onwards, were especially keen to implement the new policy. The party's journal, *The Labour Woman*, reflected an awareness of the pressures arising from poor housing conditions and the lack of facilities; it reported on a scheme run by Fulham Council in 1920 offering 'Bag Wash' facilities whereby housewives could wash twenty-eight pounds of clothes for one shilling and nine pence in municipal launderette machines, a boon to women with inadequate hot water and no drying facilities in cramped homes.[4] The hopelessness of the task faced by many housewives was graphically recorded by William Woodruff when he lodged at The Cut in Stratford in 1933 where 'the cracked walls were held together by layers of bulging wallpaper'. He felt his landlady's idea of housekeeping was not very ambitious: 'The kitchen sink was always covered with grime. The bugs, which dropped down the walls with the noise of grains of sand, were worse, though in fairness, she would have had to burn the house down to defeat them.'[5]

Housing was one of the few issues on which governments actually sought the opinion of women, a recognition of their new influence as forty per cent of parliamentary voters after 1918. As a result the post-war 'council houses' were built to very high standards which some critics considered a waste of money. Women wanted extra bedrooms, indoor lavatories, a hot water supply, separate parlours, and gardens rather than yards. For Bryan Magee, growing up in 1930s Hoxton, the absence of some of these facilities loomed large: 'Because we had no indoor lavatory, the use of chamber pots was part of our everyday life, and I took them for granted. There were always two under each bed upstairs . . . they were referred to as "the po" . . . and were the first focus of repression I can remember. I was supposed to try hard not to use the po, and to use it only when I had to, and to crap in it only when I *absolutely* had to.' In his Stratford lodgings William Woodruff would 'come back from the foundry at the end of the day to find his room-mate's window shut and the stench of the unemptied pisspot under the bed unbearable'.[6]

Women's views were fed into the report of a committee under the Liberal MP, Sir John Tudor Walters, who was influenced by the garden city movement; his report set the framework for local authority developments between the wars involving spacious, low-density developments and semi-detached or short-terrace houses including one or two living rooms, three bedrooms and separate kitchens and bathrooms. Tudor Walters set a new higher standard of municipal housing provision which effectively obliged private builders to improve their quality too, though their houses were usually less well constructed and had smaller rooms than council houses. Much controversy was aroused by the provision of a 'parlour' or front room. For many working-class families this was visible proof of respectability; but as it was usually set aside to receive visitors or hold occasional celebrations the room was little used. For this reason parlours were widely seen as unnecessary and by the later 1920s Tudor Walters houses, which had initially extended to over 1,000 square feet, had diminished to around 620.

Unfortunately, the open-ended subsidies offered in 1919 soon proved to be a heavy commitment. After 1918 Britain suffered an acute shortage of skilled bricklayers as a result of war deaths and slow demobilisation; and builders found it more profitable to construct commercial buildings rather than council houses. Consequently the price of small homes that had cost £250 in 1914 rose briefly to £900 after 1918. The Addison Act soon fell victim to post-war demands to lower income tax and to reduce government expenditure. When the Act was suspended in 1921 only 170,000 homes had been built, though eventually 213,000 were completed, well short of Lloyd George's promise to create 'Homes for Heroes'. However, the 1919 Act was neither a failure nor a temporary expedient, for it reflected the aspirations of millions of people to better living conditions. In the new mass democracy no government could afford to ignore this. In 1924 Addison's policy was revived by John Wheatley, the Health Minister in the first Labour government; enjoying a subsidy of £9 per house some 520,000 homes were constructed under Wheatley's legislation. Arthur Greenwood's 1930 Housing Act extended subsidies to 700,000 houses built by local authorities between 1931 and 1939, and also accelerated slum clearance with the result that four out of five existing slum-dwellers had been rehoused by 1939.

Although council housing generated controversy between Labour and the Conservatives, their differences were not fundamental. Conservative governments changed the emphasis by introducing subsidies for private house-building in 1923, by chipping away at rent controls and by abolishing subsidies for council building in 1933, though not for slum clearance. But they accepted that building for sale would never solve the housing problem, just as Labour conceded that council housing was only a partial answer. As a result rented council accommodation, which was a negligible element before 1914, comprised eleven per cent of housing stock by 1938 and reached twenty-four per cent by 1961. In the process big municipalities with large resources changed the appearance of urban Britain by constructing huge estates at such places as Longbridge (Birmingham), Kirkby (Liverpool) and Quarry Hill (Leeds). Between the wars thirty-one per cent of all new housing in Britain was in the public sector, and in Scotland as much as seventy per cent.

However, even such extensive building could never resolve the problem if only because the financial constraints on councils meant that they charged rents around fourteen to sixteen shillings a week which was manageable only for better paid, skilled workers. In theory as the higher paid vacated private property poorer families moved in, leaving the slums to be cleared. In fact after 1930 local authorities were obliged to rehouse slum-clearance families and therefore to set rents at lower levels for those in greatest need; Liverpool for example, offered flats at ten and sixpence weekly in the 1930s. By this time all the big municipalities achieved economies of scale by constructing five-storey blocks of flats modelled on Continental patterns; though of high quality they were less attractive to tenants.

Despite municipal building, the real revolution in interwar housing lay in a dramatic rise in owner-occupation which covered thirty-five per cent of all British homes by 1938 and forty-two per cent by 1961. It is often forgotten that before 1914 barely ten per cent of housing was owner-occupied, according to official estimates, and even this figure is probably an exaggeration. In effect, thousands of middle-class people who could well have afforded to buy their homes chose not to do so. During the Victorian-Edwardian era this was often quite rational. Houses were not the financial asset they became in the twentieth century. Renting seemed more sensible and economical for families that began with a modest home and then periodically moved into larger accommodation as additional children, nurseries, governesses and servants expanded their requirements; they avoided the expense and trouble of buying and selling each time.

In fact, in late Victorian times, the aspiration to home ownership was more characteristic of skilled manual workers and lower-middle-class employees on modest incomes for whom it offered visible proof of status and respectability. Families higher up the social scale were sufficiently secure to dispense with this. The social aspiration to home ownership helps to explain the original location of many of the early Victorian building societies: Leeds Permanent, Halifax Permanent, Bradford and Bingley. Originating as expressions of the self-help strategy, the societies had been the chief vehicle for expanding home ownership; but they remained marginal.

During the war, when building largely ceased, the societies strengthened their finances by investing in National Bonds and in companies made highly profitable by the war. After 1918 they were strongly placed to satisfy popular demand among newly married couples anxious to establish separate households. As it no longer seemed economic to invest in rented accommodation, landlords were often willing to sell their property, indeed by 1938 1.4 million of the 5.3 million pre-war houses had been sold, often to sitting tenants. Building societies also enjoyed assistance from governments in the shape of tax concessions. From 1916 tax on their investments was deducted at the rate of three shillings in the pound compared to a standard rate of five shillings, thus making it more attractive to invest with them rather than in rented property. The societies were also exempted from the wartime Corporation Profits Tax until its abolition in 1925. In this way, the combination of social and financial pressures generated a major expansion of building societies after the war. The Co-operative Building Society's membership rose from 6,600 in 1918 to 73,000 by 1930 and its staff from 17 to 150.[7] The two largest societies, the Halifax Permanent and Halifax Equitable, enjoyed assets of £6 million and £2 million in 1918 and £33 million and £14 million by 1928 when they amalgamated; by 1939 they had £128 million.[8] Whereas in 1910 building societies had advanced just £9 million on mortgages, by 1925 the total increased to £49 million and reached £140 million in the peak year, 1936.[9] By 1925 the 1,088 societies had 1,125,000 members, and, though they remained strongest in Lancashire, Yorkshire, Durham and Northumberland, their branch offices were spreading rapidly across London and the Home Counties.

Although post-war economic factors accelerated the trend, there are indications that the ideal of home ownership was already spreading among the middle classes in the Edwardian period, especially in the

London suburbs. 'Ilford, albeit of mushroom growth, has a pretty conceit of itself', wrote one observer in 1907 who noted that the aspiration of its residents was to live on the more respectable side of the railway line: 'its street vistas are beautifully monotonous; every front garden is a replica of its neighbour; while the names of the thoroughfares have a poetry and distinction that will be found hard to beat elsewhere'.[10] This was a foretaste of the condescending attitudes often adopted towards the new housing of the interwar years. But there is no doubt that the commercial interests exploited aspirations to social climbing; one 1909 advertisement argued: 'it is greatly to a purchaser's advantage to purchase a house in a district where [home ownership] prevails, because the future respectability and stability of that district is assured. When a district has a majority of individual owners in it, a far greater interest is taken in local government and needless or reckless expenditure is avoided.' In the 1930s building firms liked to refer to 'properties of a definite class' and emphasised 'the need to keep the estate select'.[11] Between 1900 and 1914 new suburbs spread across North London in Ilford, Walthamstow, Wood Green, Edmonton, Wanstead, Enfield, Palmer's Green, New Southgate and Hendon. South of the river building focussed on Wimbledon, Raynes Park, Streatham, Croydon, Barnes, Merton and Morden. These were still largely terraced houses with a narrow sixteen- to twenty-foot frontage relying on a back extension for the kitchen. Priced from £250–350 leasehold and £350–450 freehold, they were bought by clerks and skilled workers for whom the extension and electrification of the metropolitan railways and tramways made it possible to live so far from their places of work.

After the war politicians of all kinds found it expedient to encourage this trend. They had expanded the electorate from eight million to twenty-one million at a time when revolutionary doctrines from abroad seemed likely to appeal to the unpropertied mass of the British people. Consequently politicians anxiously looked for ways of stabilising the political and social system. While they could not undo their political reforms they hoped to redefine the role of the voter in terms of his commitment to the system rather than his desire to change it. As Lord Burnham put it: 'the love of home is believed to be among the leading qualities of British citizenship'.[12] For Conservatives, threatened by the moral challenge posed by socialism and by attacks

on capitalism following wartime profiteering and post-war unemployment, it was imperative to identify some means of extending the
benefits of private ownership more widely through society. This idea
was famously articulated by the MP, Noel Skelton, in a 1924 pamphlet
on *Constructive Conservatism* in which he coined the phrase 'property-
owning democracy'; the aim was to stabilise the new mass democracy
by building bridges between labour and capital, and housing offered
the most practical and popular method of doing this.

However, home ownership was far more than simply a
Conservative tactic. It won enthusiastic endorsement on the Left too.
During the 1920s and 1930s the Halifax Building Society recruited a
succession of ministers for its annual meetings including Austen
Chamberlain and Sir Kingsley Wood (Conservatives), Viscount Sankey
and Arthur Greenwood (Labour), and J. E. B. Seeley and Sir Hilton
Young (Liberal). Jimmy Thomas, a leading Labour figure, commended
the money invested in building societies as a triumph for working-class
organisation: 'It's an escape from the ruinous cost of renting and from
dependency and insecurity of the landlord system. It promotes the
formation of a body of independent, thrifty and law-abiding citizens.'[13]
As Ramsay MacDonald himself pointed out, building societies gave the
worker an incentive to save and to help his fellow men at the same
time, so there could be no ethical objection to his investment.[14] By the
late 1920s three-quarters of building society loans were for sums of £500
or less, clear evidence that they were catering to families on
comparatively low incomes. Another indication of the working-class
footing in home ownership is that by 1938 thirty-seven per cent of
Abbey Road borrowers were described as 'wage-earners'.

But even without encouragement from politicians many families in
interwar Britain readily saw the economic advantages of buying their
own homes. House prices fell by around sixty per cent between the
1920s and 1930s, partly as a result of huge increases in supply of new
homes, leaving construction companies keenly competing for
customers. Progress was slow immediately after the war, but in 1923
Neville Chamberlain tried to revive the building trade by offering a
subsidy of £6 per house to private builders; local authorities were also
allowed to lend up to ninety per cent for the purchase of houses valued
at up to £1,500. This in turn put pressure on landlords who increasingly
experienced difficulty in finding tenants unless they kept rents down.

Housing also benefited from a steady fall in the cost of building materials, including bricks, cement and paint, during the 1920s. In view of the acute shortage of wood in Britain the introduction of cheap steel window frames in 1919 proved highly advantageous. At Maldon in Essex the firm of Valentine Crittall mass-produced the metal frames that remain today as visible evidence of 1930s houses. Even more important were the extensive sales of land during the 1920s which depressed prices to the benefit of builders. By the mid 1920s land could be acquired for £100 an acre in Croydon and for as little as £40 in Dorking. This led local authorities and private builders to scramble for cheap plots, no longer worth cultivating, on the edge of towns and along new main roads, such as the North Circular and the Kingston bypass, as sites for new housing estates. The result was the much-criticised 'ribbon development' that disfigured much of South-East England.

The housing boom of the 1930s was also accelerated by the cheap-money policy adopted by the National Government following the financial crash of 1931. This greatly stimulated home ownership by effectively cutting interest rates, which had been around 6 per cent in the 1920s, to 4.5 per cent after 1932. The building societies, which operated on the basis of maintaining a 1.5 per cent difference between the rate paid to their investors and the rate charged to their borrowers, found no difficulty in passing on the gains to customers.[15]

These economic trends brought ownership within the reach of thousands of families for the first time. After the brief peak in the immediate aftermath of war prices fell steeply. By the mid 1920s small bungalows could be purchased for £225 or less, 'non-parlour' houses for £340–450, and three-bedroom 'parlour' houses for around £500–600 in London. By the 1930s the three-bedroom, two-living-room semi-detached was down to £450, three-bedroomed detached houses were available at £775, and an imposing detached property could be bought for £1,450.[16] Property became more affordable not only because of the fall in interest rates but because building societies eased their terms. During the 1930s a typical £450 semi-detached home could be purchased with a deposit of just £25 and weekly repayments of fourteen or fifteen shillings. Whereas in the 1920s the repayment period had usually been fifteen years, it was extended to twenty-five years during the 1930s, lowering weekly repayments to as little as ten to thirteen shillings. This put a mortgage within reach of families with a regular income of £4 or even £3. Building societies worked on the basis that total outgoings on housing, including rates, ought not to exceed a quarter of income. Not surprisingly this calculation was endorsed by the builders; in 1936, for example, Costain advertised their three-bedroom semi-detached 'Arcadia' homes in Elm Park for payments of thirteen shillings as suitable for anyone with an income of £3. 15s. a week. By this time the oversupply of new houses had left firms increasingly anxious to find buyers, but, in any case, houses had become markedly more affordable than they had been in the Victorian era and than they were to be later in the twentieth century. As a result the number of families paying mortgages reached 554,000 by 1928 and 1.4 million by 1937.

Although much of the industry remained small-scale and reliant on traditional labour-intensive methods, the interwar years saw the emergence of several major speculative building firms including Richard Costain, John Laing, New Ideal Homesteads (Leo Meyer), Frank Taylor of Taylor Woodrow, and George Wimpey. By the 1930s demand was such that banks and building societies were very willing to advance loans to them, and even to small builders who routinely obtained supplies from builders' merchants on credit. They correctly identified a large demand for modern, easily managed homes among young couples with small families who could not afford servants. Nonetheless, as speculative builders they were apt to oversupply the market; the peak for private building came in 1934 when they constructed 287,000 houses but this fell back to 250,000 in the later 1930s. As a result builders took to establishing bureaux at the London railway stations and advertised heavily in order to tempt aspiring homeowners further into what they marketed as the countryside. They offered metropolitan purchasers homes 'built round a farm', 'long vistas of green fields' and, rather improbably for the Home Counties, 'Devon at your door'. Customers were invited to live 'amid the fairyland of Surrey' (Tattenham Corner) and to hear 'the nightingale singing at Carshalton'. One advertiser was even moved to verse:

> Live in Ruislip where the air's like wine,
> It's less than half an hour on the Piccadilly Line.

Contemporary critics, however, regarded the mundane delights of the new housing in Finchley, Hendon, Harrow, Wandsworth, Sutton and Beckenham with more scorn than admiration. They derided the spread of 'Tudorbethan' semi-detached housing as the product of unimaginative architecture and an inadequate planning system that allowed ribbon development along all the main roads. Osbert Lancaster variously satirised contemporary design as 'Wimbledon Transitional', 'Stockbroker's Tudor' and 'Bypass Variegated'. In his memorable lines, written in 1937, Sir John Betjeman added his condemnation:

> Come friendly bombs and fall on Slough!
> It isn't fit for humans now,
> There isn't grass to graze a cow,
> Swarm over, Death!

By decking their houses with pitched roofs and beams, the critics argued, architects were merely giving a shallow impression of Tudor and Stuart styles. Their gardens front and back were a waste of space, designed to pander to the myth of the Englishman as a country gentleman returning to his roots. What they had created were dreary suburbs that lacked the advantages of either town or country life.

These attacks were not without some foundation. Although Welwyn Garden City in Hertfordshire and the south Manchester suburb of Wythenshawe were conceived as garden suburbs, interwar planners and builders largely ignored the ideas of the garden city movement. Local authorities constructed schools in the new housing estates but otherwise made little effort to provide services or to ensure that new developments involved a balance of homes, offices and industrial sites. This condemned most men to lengthy journeys 'straphanging' on crowded trains and motor buses into town centres each day. 'Two hours spent every day is a terrible waste of time and nervous energy', as one critic put it in 1937.[17] Admittedly plots were often set aside for shops, public houses and even cinemas, but they remained vacant for years; this was sometimes in deference to the view that residential districts should be kept 'select' or simply from pressure to preserve custom for the existing shopkeepers in town centres.

For their part speculative builders concentrated on land adjacent to the new arterial roads in Essex, Hertfordshire, Middlesex and Surrey where costs were minimal. Few facilities were required beyond occasional petrol stations and large pubs, known as 'road houses', also built in mock-Tudor style. The resulting elongated suburbs were not checked until 1935 when Parliament passed the Ribbon Development Act. As they acquired sites behind the main roads the builders simply crammed in as many houses as possible, which meant creating a cul-de-sac to fill every awkward corner and ignoring whatever natural features the land might possess. At most they added lines of trees along the frontages and monotonous rows of privet hedges. In the 1920s the roads, invariably named 'Rise', 'Way', 'Gardens' or 'Drive' in an attempt to create a rural ambience, were constructed of gravel, flint or granite chips over hard core with footpaths of clinker or hard core. But under pressure from traffic and the weather they soon deteriorated into mud in winter and dust in summer, though it was sometimes ten years before the local council 'adopted' them. During the 1930s it became more common to construct concrete roads first so as to improve access for the builders themselves.

Contemporary critics also accused speculative builders of 'jerry-building'. They cited the use of light roof frames of cheap timber and a lack of felt or boarding beneath which left them vulnerable to driving snow and rain. However, by the 1930s quality had improved. In an effort to reduce costs builders adopted the mass-produced Fletton brick in 1925, often covering it with fashionable pebble-dash or roughcast. The nine-inch brickwork typical of the 1920s had become eleven inches by the 1930s and cavity walls were used even in the cheapest houses.

Despite this, the new homes were not an improvement in all respects. Rooms were generally smaller than in the 1920s council houses, and kitchens in particular were very small. Many new homes retained a traditional range heated by coal in the living room and relied on a back boiler for hot water. However, the builders knew their market; coal was still a cheaper means of heating than gas. If their houses small they were 'specially designed to meet the requirements of a small family not wishing to incur the worry and expense of keeping a servant'. Nor did the architecture provoke much complaint from the residents. In fact, speculative builders made minimal use of architects, preferring to retain and reuse standard plans or go by rule of thumb. The only real architectural innovation was the so-called 'modern' style involving smooth white walls, flat roofs (for sunbathing), and large steel-framed windows (for more light). Much favoured for lidos, the modern style enjoyed a brief éclat in the early 1930s and was adopted for all the houses at the 1934 Ideal Home Exhibition. But though popular with sun-worshippers it quickly ceased to be fashionable.

The truth was that although builders attracted scorn for pandering to rural illusions by decorating their houses with gables, pitched roofs, lattice windows, half-timber, leaded lights and cosy porches, they satis-fied a real demand for a vaguely traditionalist style; the sophisticated critics were a poor guide to popular taste. Nor, regardless of aesthetic considerations, were the new owner-occupiers mistaken in regarding the semi-detached suburban homes as a material improvement on most existing housing. Brighter, more comfortable and easier to keep clean, they came with an array of fittings including basins, baths, tiles, airing cupboards and electric points previously regarded as luxury items.

Above all, families appreciated having an indoor lavatory and a bathroom that rendered the laborious bath-filling ritual obsolete. 'Saturday night was bath-night, at least as far as the children were concerned', recalled Bryan Magee, 'A zinc bath would be carried into the kitchen from the yard and set on the hearthrug in front of the fire. Water was boiled up in every available utensil simultaneously. My sister, being a girl, was given the clean water, and I would clamber into it the moment she got out so as to catch it while it was still warm.'[18] But while waiting for their weekly bath, as Paul Johnson recalled, many people smelt: 'In the Potteries I doubt if one in ten working-class families had a bathroom'. As they could not afford dry-cleaning, their clothes received only an occasional wash in hot water boiled in a kettle on the kitchen fire; consequently, 'a shirt had to last a week, a vest (all wore them) a fortnight or a month'.[19] In fact, at all levels of society standards of personal cleanliness were lower than today. Even in the spacious homes of the upper classes, where servants carried water upstairs, the erratic hot water supply and the scarcity of bathrooms made proper baths a comparatively infrequent event. During the 1930s St John's College, Cambridge, somehow managed with just 6 baths for the needs of 450 students. Faced with complaints from the unwashed, one of the tutors responded indignantly: 'What's all this fuss about baths? Terms only last eight weeks, you know!'

Crucially, the interwar building boom coincided with a major innovation: the extension of electricity supply. Before 1914 Britain had neglected investment in the industry with the result that only two per cent of households were wired for electricity by 1910; most of the suppliers were small-scale companies selling electricity at high cost. The national interest required a state enterprise to achieve the economies of scale that would reduce prices for all. In 1919 the government divided the country into districts under a Joint Electricity Authority with responsibility for extending supply, and it allocated £20 million for investment. In 1926 it created the Central Electricity Generating Board which owned and operated the National Grid with powers to raise capital on ordinary commercial lines and a responsibility to establish interconnected lines covering the whole country. Hailed in the press as 'Cheap Electricity For All' the new policy meant that by 1939 seventy-five per cent of all homes were wired for electricity.[20] Initially, however, many housewives felt nervous of this novel form of power and became the target of propaganda of all kinds. Wilfred Randall wrote a pamphlet entitled The Romance of Electricity. The Labour Woman used its 'Housewife' column to persuade women that cooking and ironing would be much easier by electricity, though it complained that the cost of installation was too high for most workers.[21] In 1924 Caroline Haslett even established a pressure group, the Electrical Association for Women, which sponsored travelling exhibitions and cookery classes to reassure nervous housewives.

At twelve to the acre the new semi-detached houses also attracted criticism for wasting space. But this, too, reflected a widespread and distinctively English desire for self-contained homes surrounded by gardens rather than the more communal style of living in blocks of flats and apartments close to city centres which was favoured on the Continent and in Scotland. 'One assumption that I absorbed in my childhood, I believe from my mother,' wrote Bryan Magee, 'was that a flat was not a proper home . . . only if you occupied all the premises of a building was it your home . . . if you shared it with other families it was almost as if you were camping, passing through.'[22] Between the wars this attitude fostered an increasingly privatised, family-centred style of life, focussed on home decoration and improvement, gardening (even for those who did not really like gardening) and other leisure activities. The classic expression of this spirit was the annual Daily Mail

Ideal Home Exhibition which had begun in 1908. During the 1920s all four railway groups offered excursions to the exhibition from almost every station in the country. 'It has by now become a national event, an academy where the year's masterpieces in gardens and in homes are displayed and the fashions in the domestic arts are originated', boasted the *Mail* in 1926.[23] In that year the desire for novelty was bizarrely expressed by the Rubber Growers' Association who built a rubber house equipped with domestic fittings including furniture, curtains and flowers all made of rubber.[24] More typical were the nine full-sized and furnished model homes, in mock-Tudor style, crammed with labour-saving devices designed to eliminate unnecessary labour on the part of servantless housewives. 'Do you remember the antiquated Victorian furniture and appliances that still survived in the all-in-a-row houses built before the first exhibition?' asked the *Mail*'s reporter. Condemning the 'dust-harbouring corners and crevices so prolific that sheer domestic drudgery lasted until long after the disgracefully inefficient gas-bracket had been lighted for the night', he concluded 'if you were a housewife in those days you will never forget it'.[25]

By 1938 the Ideal Home Exhibition was attracting 600,000 visitors. A major feature was the twelve to fifteen gardens reached via winding paths but designed to appear as one huge garden containing pools, waterfalls, rockeries and shrubberies. Interwar Britain saw a fashion for 'natural', as opposed to 'grand', gardening as reflected in the popularity of rock gardens and woodland dells planted with rhododendrons, azaleas and camellias. The influence of the artist and plantswoman, Gertrude Jekyll, was especially strong in both large and modest British gardens. At her home in Munstead Wood, near Godalming, Jekyll had employed the mixture of annuals, perennials, shrubs and trees traditionally seen in English cottage gardens with wide borders dominated by informal drifts of plants. The colours flowed into one another creating the impression that the garden merged into the surrounding countryside. A similar emphasis on informality, native plants and mixed borders was developed at Great Dixter in East Sussex, another famous garden started in 1910 by Nathaniel Lloyd and Edwin Lutyens. They divided the garden into irregular outdoor 'rooms' separated by walls, hedges and topiary, a strategy also adopted by Lawrence Johnston at Hidcote in Gloucestershire, a garden where one compartment led into the next, ending in woodland and eventually a vista of the countryside beyond. Perhaps the most celebrated interwar garden of this kind was at Sissinghurst Castle in Kent where Vita Sackville-West and Harold Nicolson created ten distinct garden rooms. They, too, departed from formality by mixing plants; the rose garden, for example, was softened with clematis, alliums and delphiniums to create the Romantic and traditional ambience that came to be thought of as the essence of the English approach to gardening.

To reproduce these ideas in the typical long but narrow, semi-detached garden composed of badly drained London clay mixed with builder's rubble was a formidable task. But in back gardens, which were often from 80–200 feet deep, it was possible to create several separate areas including rectangular lawns and mixed borders leading towards a 'woodland' and thence to the country beyond. In plots usually twenty to forty feet wide the borders were invariably too narrow to achieve the effect Gertrude Jekyll aimed for, but the relaxed English blend of annuals, perennials and shrubs authentically reflected her ideas.

The combination of gardening, suburban housing and owner-occupation underlines the distinctiveness of the interwar housing revolution in Britain. Despite being the first society to undergo an industrial revolution and to embark upon urbanisation in the later eighteenth century, the English had evidently retained a strong desire for a lifestyle characterised by separate homes, domestication, privacy and direct access to gardens. No doubt the retreat into suburbanisation involved a certain amount of self-delusion on the part of homeowners. Privacy was inevitably limited in small semi-detached houses. And the extent to which town-dwellers really wanted to escape to country life was very limited. Many residents actually preferred houses on the busy main roads because of the availability of regular transport; for them suburban life created a vicarious sense of living in the country without its many drawbacks. Yet allowing for all the qualifications, it is impossible to exaggerate the centrality enjoyed by housing in British life between the wars; in particular owner-occupation was elevated into a great moral good and almost a patriotic objective in these years. In 1934 the Co-operative Permanent Building Society celebrated its first fifty years by publishing a triumphal volume entitled *Brick Upon Brick*. Far from being merely a survey of commercial success, the book waxed lyrical about 'England Our England', the happy amalgam of peoples and races, and the talented individuals who had served the country down the centuries. Above all, it argued that 'England has derived much of her strength from the institution of the family'; hence the need to maintain that institution by steadily improving family housing.[26] This was not mere rhetoric. Whereas between 1870 and 1900 investment in housing amounted to about eighteen per cent of gross domestic product, by the 1930s the figure had risen to thirty-three per cent. This was symptomatic of a sustained long-term shift in national priorities and individual aspirations in Britain. The extensive damage done to the housing stock during the Second World War further accentuated the importance of housing in general and home ownership in particular during the post-1945 period. By the 1950s political parties measured their popularity by the fluctuations in the mortgage rate, and political reputations were made on the basis of meeting increasingly ambitious building targets. This emphasis was also to have a distorting effect on the economy in that the resources diverted into housing to satisfy the British obsession with home ownership might have been better applied to industries that were suffering from inadequate investment; by the end of the century the housing market had become the tail that wagged the dog.

5

Wigan Pier Revisited: Work, Unemployment and Class Conflict

During the first week of November 1922 dozens of contingents of unemployed workers marched out of Glasgow, Newcastle, Barrow-in-Furness, Manchester, Rotherham, Sheffield, Walsall, Coventry, Southampton, Plymouth and other towns en route for London where a demonstration in Hyde Park and a rally in Trafalgar Square was planned. There they intended to put their demands for work or maintenance before the prime minister. On the way the men were lodged in workhouses and subsisted on a diet comprising tea, bread with cheese or jam, and bully beef. On reaching Rugby they were so fed up with bully beef that they solemnly buried a tin of it in the cemetery:

> Ashes to ashes, dust to dust,
> Goodbye bully, our bellies you've bust.

The only luxuries available to the men during the march were a choice of a shave and haircut, a packet of cigarettes, some stamps or repair of their boots, funded by donations from sympathisers collected en route.

By 17 November 2,000 of the marchers had reached the North London suburbs. As they passed through Barnet and Finchley 'muffled plutocrats in motor cars eyed us with casual indifference through the fog', as one of the contingent put it.[1] Unfortunately, political circumstances had changed since the march was planned. On 19 October a new crisis had erupted when the Conservative MPs, meeting at the Carlton Club, voted emphatically to sever their party from Lloyd George's Coalition Government. The prime minister resigned immediately and a new Conservative government was formed by Andrew Bonar Law. As the new administration was determined to hold a quick general election, the hunger marchers found themselves on the road during two weeks of the election campaign, and they arrived in London two days after polling day. As a result they faced, not a vulnerable coalition tottering under scandal and controversy, but a government bolstered by a fresh mandate and disclaiming responsibility for the unemployment that had brought the men to London. This frustrating experience was to be repeated throughout the interwar years as the victims of the slump tried to pressurise well-entrenched governments.

These 'hunger marches' originated in the autumn of 1920 when a demonstration of unemployed men, supported by fifteen London mayors, marched to Trafalgar Square and Downing Street to demand action by Lloyd George's Coalition Government to provide work or relief from the slump that had recently hit the economy. The organisation and national co-ordination urgently required by the protest movement was subsequently provided by the National Unemployed Workers Movement (NUWM) led by two Communists, Wal Hannington and Harry McShane; at its peak the movement mobilised 50,000 members. The marches helped to create an indelible image of interwar Britain as a time of economic depression, mass unemployment, poverty and inequality. For subsequent generations this reputation was memorably captured by Walter Greenwood's novel, *Love on the Dole* (1933), and two Left Book Club volumes, *The Road to Wigan Pier* (1937) by George Orwell and *The Town That Was Murdered* (1939) by Ellen Wilkinson. Perhaps the best-known episode of the entire period, apart from the Abdication, was the Jarrow Crusade of 1936.

The protests were all symptoms of the dramatic collapse of Britain's Victorian manufacturing economy after 1918. During the Edwardian years the great nineteenth-century staples – coal, cotton, shipbuilding, iron and steel – had enjoyed a final boom, although less because of their own efficiency than because the rapid growth of other economies had created a temporary demand for British goods. The war stimulated the market for the products of Britain's heavy industries even further, thereby creating full employment for a few years. The arrival of peace released a pent-up demand for consumer goods previously in short supply and thus caused a brief boom in 1919–20. But entrepreneurs had invested rashly and oversupplied the market. As a result, by the summer of 1920 domestic demand had collapsed and foreign markets wanted fewer British goods. During wartime America, India and Japan had expanded their output of textiles, hitherto Britain's largest single export sector, leaving far less scope for selling cotton goods abroad. The erection of tariff barriers by most countries after 1918 made things even worse for a country like Britain heavily dependent on exports and on a buoyant level of world trade for indirect earnings. As a result, between 1920 and 1921 unemployment leapt to two million, or seventeen per cent of the insured labour force, a level literally unknown before 1914.

Every interwar government sincerely believed that it could best tackle unemployment by restoring the export markets for Britain's staple industries. This, however, was largely a delusion because Britain no longer enjoyed the ability to stimulate world demand or to restore free trade; and the one power capable of doing so, the United States, chose to adopt a suicidal policy of withdrawing behind her tariffs, calling in her debts and letting the slump run its course. Meanwhile, as Britain's new democracy seemed unlikely to tolerate poverty and unemployment for long, governments felt it politic to offer assistance to men thrown out of work by forces beyond their control. Since 1911 Britain had operated an unemployment insurance scheme, pioneered by Lloyd George, covering 2.5 million workers. Based on contributions by workers, employers and the state, the scheme relied on a self-financing fund capable of paying benefits to insured men for a limited number of weeks each year. In 1920 this scheme was extended to include twenty million workers. However, as this coincided with the onset of mass unemployment the fund quickly ran into deficit and had to be subsidised by the Exchequer. In any case, once men suffered *long-term* unemployment they lost their entitlement to benefits.

Their alternative was the rather discredited Victorian Poor Law system to which around 450,000 people applied annually for support during the 1920s. As the Poor Law Guardians were elected they often proved sympathetic and did their best to make reasonable payments to families with no breadwinner. However, as this meant raising the poor rate it provoked a hostile reaction from Westminster governments who usually regarded local democracy as subversive. Controversy focussed on the borough of Poplar where the Guardians, led by the local mayor, George Lansbury, paid above the minimum wage rates and refused to apply a family means test; they also demanded an equalisation of rate income to help the less well-endowed authorities, who had to spend most, and organised passive resistance to the precepts paid to the LCC. In 1921 Lansbury and his fellow Guardians were prosecuted and imprisoned. After a time the government relented, released them and equalised the rates. But the problem kept reappearing, so much so that in 1926 the minister, Neville Chamberlain, empowered himself to suspend offending Guardians in West Ham, Chester-le-Street and Bedwellty for paying excessive relief. By 1929 Chamberlain had decided to transfer Poor Law functions to Public Assistance Committees (PACs), which were county council committees. But as they, too, proved unduly generous for ministers they were replaced in 1934 by the Unemployment Assistance Boards (UABs) whose job was to apply a uniform, national scale of payments and thus remove local discretion entirely.

Despite the bitterness and controversy aroused by these innovations, the benefits paid did represent some improvement. For a family of five the rates rose from twenty-three shillings in 1922 to twenty-nine shillings in 1931 and thirty-six shillings in 1937. These payments were vulnerable during the financial crisis of 1931 when the government imposed a ten per cent cut in unemployment benefits, thereby saving the Exchequer £26 million up to April 1934, when it was cancelled. In view of the fall in prices these payments meant extra purchasing power, though they still left many families struggling with poverty and thousands of children suffering from malnourishment. The 1937 payment of thirty-six shillings, for example, may be set against the calculation made by S. B. Rowntree that forty-three shillings was the minimum needed to keep a family of five above the poverty line. The predicament of many families was highlighted in 1937 when the NUWM published case studies collected from doctors and councillors as *The Housewives' Minimum*. One typical example ran: 'Mrs D. A. of Liverpool, who is a widow. There are five in the family including four children aged seventeen, fourteen, eleven and seven. One child is a cripple. They have no gas-stove or oven in the house . . . Cooking utensils consist of one small kettle, one frying pan in a very bad condition, one saucepan with no lid and a hole in the side . . . only two lead spoons, two dessertspoons and one knife – fingers are used for eating most of the time. There are three cups without handles . . . they cannot all drink tea at the same time . . . there are only two beds, two sheets, one flannelette blanket, three pillow-cases and one bolster. The deficiency in bed covering has to be made up by using old coats. This woman receives 36s. to keep a family of five. The rent for one living room and a boxroom is 5s. The weekly check for clothing the family is 3s., burial club 9d., coal 3s. 6d.'[2]

However, the benefit system provoked resentment less because of the rates paid than because it seemed calculated to exclude people. From 1921 onwards applicants were required to demonstrate that they were 'genuinely seeking work' even though the committees were under no obligation to show that work was actually available locally. As a result 1.7 million applicants were refused benefits, largely on these grounds, between 1925 and 1928 alone. Claimants also felt they were treated with insolence by the clerks who interrogated them, though as the latter were under pressure to detect abuses, friction was difficult to avoid. 'They treat you like a lump of dirt they do', complained one applicant. 'I see a navvy reach across the counter and shake one of them by the collar the other day. The rest of us felt like cheering.'[3] The rule was deliberately used to deter women in the belief that they ought to be at home looking after their families rather than taking jobs needed by men; to this end it became common practice, especially among local authorities, to sack women as soon as they got married. In addition, almost any woman who refused employment as a domestic servant was liable to be denied benefits. As a result the number of women officially unemployed stood at 500,000 in January 1921, but fell to 370,000 a year later, an indication that many women had simply stopped registering. In 1931 an Anomalies Act imposed more stringent terms on married women who wished to draw unemployment benefits, and as a result in the first three months forty-eight per cent of women's claims were rejected compared with four per cent of men's; 180,000 wives failed to qualify in the following year even though they had made contributions.

Much the most bitterly disliked deterrent was the Household Means Test, introduced in 1931, which meant that the assessment for one family member could be reduced if others were working. 'For the first time within mortal memory the government and the nation has set out on a definite deliberate campaign to make the poor poorer', as G. K. Chesterton put it in 1931.[4] The Trades Union Congress published examples of the impact of the means test. In a family of four living in Wigan the unemployed father's benefit was cut from twenty-three shillings to ten shillings a week because his two sons earned between them thirty-one shillings.[5] In this way the means test sometimes had the effect of splitting families by encouraging sons and daughters to leave home, and even of encouraging people to inform on the domestic situation of their neighbours. Some of the PACs even made a point of asking mothers whether they were breast-feeding their babies, as this could be used as further grounds for reducing their allowances.[6] The government admitted that during 1931–3 – the height of the slump – the effect of means testing had been to lower overall payments by nearly £28 million.[7]

Long-term unemployment and the means test were the chief targets of the six National Hunger Marches that began in the autumn of 1922. Although the economy partially revived after the slump of 1920–1, economic growth remained sluggish and by the end of the decade it appeared that Britain was stuck with an irreducible minimum of over a million unemployed workers. Faced with this problem, the government's key policies – revaluing the pound in 1925 and trying to curtail expenditure on social welfare – actually made things worse. As a result, by 1928 the NUWM decided to organise the second hunger march, followed by others in 1930, 1932, 1934 and 1936. Although these marches were monitored by the intelligence services for signs of subversion and violence, they were remarkably orderly and moderate. In October 1932 William Woodruff and his friends joined the crowd in Blackburn's town square to give a send-off to the local contingent. 'We're going to tell t'King that we need work and food', one of the marchers told them with a touching naivety. 'Once 'e knows what's 'appening in Lancashire, matters will be put right, there's no doubt.'[8] The local organisers doled out bread, mashed potatoes and tea as men arrived from the nearby towns. A month later they returned to Blackburn thinner than before and wearing worn-out boots. They claimed they had been shunned by the Labour Party, refused an audience with Ramsay MacDonald, the prime minister, and run down by mounted police in London. The petition, bearing a million signatures, had been prepared for Parliament but was seized by the police. Despite the public sympathy the marchers aroused, they lacked effective political leadership. Many Labour politicians suffered from an obsessive fear that organisations like Hannington's were being manipulated by Communists trying to gain influence within the Labour Movement. But contemporaries like Woodruff dismissed such fears: 'Despite all the talk of hunger marchers being nothing but Communist riff-raff, these men were a good-natured, law-abiding lot. I doubt there was a revolutionary among them.'[9] The truth was that the failure of the conventional politicians and the decline of the trade union movement left a large vacuum among workingmen which the Communists helped to fill. Men joined up for want of any alternative.

The protest movement reached its peak in the autumn of 1936, the year of the Jarrow Crusade. In fact, Jarrow was one of four more or less simultaneous marches including the sixth National Hunger March, the National League for the Blind March, and the Scottish Veterans March. But although the National Hunger March made a greater impact at the time, it is the Jarrow Crusade that has left its mark on interwar history. Largely created by the shipbuilding yards of the Victorian entrepreneur, Sir Charles Mark Palmer, the town of Jarrow, on the south bank of the Tyne, was unusually dependent on a single, vulnerable industry. Britain had so much excess capacity in shipbuilding that in 1929 the National Shipbuilders Security scrapped no fewer than thirty-eight yards. In Jarrow the last ship, the destroyer, HMS *Duchess*, was launched in 1932, and next year Palmers called in the receivers.

The march was organised with the immediate object of winning a new steelworks for the town. 1,200 men volunteered to make the journey but the number was restricted to just 200 so as to maintain control. It was therefore easy to find replacements when someone dropped out at the last minute; the organisers pulled in Billy Beattie who had no time to ask his wife but left a note on the mantelpiece to let her know where he had gone.[10] On 5 October the marchers, four abreast, headed by David Riley, a bowler-hatted town councillor, and carrying the banner 'Jarrow Crusade', left town with the blessing of the Bishop of Jarrow, the mayor and the town clerk; they also took two doctors, a barber, an ambulance, a kitchen and a petition signed by 12,000 people.[11]

The figurehead was Jarrow's recently elected MP, Ellen Wilkinson, described as 'an undersized, fiery red-headed agitator'. As an ex-Communist and a feminist, Wilkinson was *persona non grata* with the Labour establishment; but her stirring speeches belied a willingness to compromise and a determination to ensure that the protest stayed respectable and non-partisan. 'Remember,' the mayor told them, 'you are going to London for Jarrow and we depend on you to maintain the credit of the town.' In this spirit the organisers banned alcohol on the march. Eight out of ten marchers were married men, half were ex-servicemen, many wore their British Legion badges, and some had been unemployed for fifteen years. The oldest, George Smith, had served in the Boer War as well as the First World War in which four of his brothers had died.[12] One man, Fred Harris, was understood to have been excluded from the march on account of his 'Communistic beliefs', but although Special Branch carefully monitored the marchers, as was usual on such occasions, it found nothing of any significance; there were reckoned to be exactly eight members of the Communist Party in the whole of Jarrow and neighbouring Hebburn at this time! The Metropolitan Police were also keen to stop the march being filmed for fear that this would generate too much sympathy; but *Movietone News* simply defied them. In fact, even unsympathetic journalists found the march endearing because it had acquired a stray black dog called Paddy at the outset. At Harrogate the RSPCA bought Paddy a licence, and dog-lovers from all over the country wrote in offering to adopt him when he had reached London.[13]

With Paddy and Ellen Wilkinson at their head the marchers left behind Chester-le-Street and Darlington to reach what they expected to be the more politically hostile towns of Northallerton, Ripon and Harrogate in North Yorkshire. However, the men were welcomed by enthusiastic crowds, by Anglican and Methodist clergymen and by local Conservative politicians in many places. They were invariably fed with ham sandwiches and tea, though Leeds treated them to a lavish roast-beef dinner. As a result the men put on weight despite walking anything from eleven to seventeen miles each day. One marcher was seen to remove the ham from his sandwiches and put it in an envelope to post back to his family.[14] Meanwhile back in Jarrow the UAB announced that the men's families would not receive payments during their absence.

At last marchers arrived at Marble Arch at the end of their 291-mile journey on Saturday 31 October. But what had they achieved? On Sunday Wilkinson told a rally in Hyde Park that 'Jarrow as a town has been murdered . . . I do not wonder that the cabinet does not want to see us. It does not want anyone to tell the truth about these black areas in the North, in Scotland and in South Wales that have been left to rot.' Already there was a tacit admission of failure in her words. The Cabinet pompously rebuffed demands for a meeting with the hunger marchers: 'In a country governed by a parliamentary system where every adult has a vote . . . processions to London cannot claim to have any constitutional influence on policy.' The anticlimax came in the next week when the petition was presented to parliament while the marchers were packed onboard a steamboat on the Thames to prevent them making a scene in the House of Commons. Later they were invited to take tea in the members' dining room by Sir Nicholas Grattan Doyle. 'We got turned down. We got a cup of tea', Billy McShane summed it up. 'When we got turned down in the House of Commons, that was it. You knew you were finished.'[15] On 5 November the men left King's Cross on a special train except for one who was in hospital and another who had found a job as a baker's assistant. Jarrow effectively marked the end of the interwar hunger marches.

McShane's verdict, which stands in contrast to the importance attributed by later generations to the Jarrow Crusade, was understandable. The marchers had raised a modest £1,567 towards their costs including just £680 donated by the general public.[16] While the Sunday newspapers printed large photographs of the march, they did little to promote the cause; even as sympathetic a newspaper as the *News Chronicle* had reported the start and the finish of the march but only three times in between. The Hyde Park rally attracted only 3,000 people according to the police, though supporters claimed many more. At a political level its impact was defused by the announcement by a businessman and MP, Sir John Jarvis, who colluded with ministers, of plans to build a new steel tubes mill in Jarrow. In the circumstances this looked like a solution but when the plant eventually opened in December 1937 it employed just 200 men. In fact the National Government, which had been returned to power in 1935 by a large majority, was fairly secure and was never seriously embarrassed by the protests of the unemployed during 1936; although it lost several seats at by-elections, the defeats were ascribed more to defence and appeasement than to domestic issues.

Despite this, the National Government handled the treatment of the unemployed with some care. It had attempted to introduce new, lower benefits but suspended them in the face of protests in January 1935 because it contemplated holding an election later that year. When the new scales were eventually introduced in November 1936 they were more generous. Ministers would have been more vulnerable if they had been effectively challenged by their political opponents. At the time the non-political character of the Jarrow Crusade was regarded as a tactical advantage; but in reality the flaw lay in the fact that it was not sufficiently political. The Labour leaders did their best to keep the march at arms length and tried to stop local Labour parties helping the marchers. In the process they threw away opportunities to mobilise a wider coalition against the National Government. Significantly, Jarrow coincided not only with other marches but with several other controversies that aroused strong passions. While the men were on the road Labour's annual conference debated British policy over the Spanish Civil War, but it tamely accepted the official policy of neutrality as General Franco's troops, armed by the fascist powers, advanced on Madrid. Nor did the party want anything to do with the volunteers now joining the International Brigades forming to support the Republican cause; it consistently dismissed attempts to establish a Popular Front to oppose appeasement and steered clear of the mobilisation of opponents of fascism at the Battle of Cable Street to stop Mosley's Blackshirts marching through London's East End in October 1936. Most alarming for the Cabinet was the Abdication crisis that reached its climax in November and December of that year. As William Woodruff had seen, many workers had a touching faith in the sympathy Edward VIII had been showing for their plight and welcomed his implied criticisms of official policy on the depressed areas. One of the reasons for forcing him off the throne was to avert the threat of an alliance between the King and the unemployed. Fortunately for the Cabinet the Labour leaders unhesitatingly supported them over the royal marriage. This concatenation of controversies in 1936 underline the extent to which the potential for a wide alliance existed among anti-government forces but was never realised because of the caution and conservatism of the official opposition. As a result the hunger marchers remained too marginalised to be able to capitalise effectively on public sympathy for their cause.

In any case, sympathy was complicated by fear. The hunger

marches were, after all, conspicuously working-class expressions of discontent in a period when economic failure appeared to have exacerbated social class antagonisms within British society. While the war had raised expectations for some, it had also created insecurity for many: manual workers angry about profiteering and state regulation of labour, ex-officers struggling to maintain a middle-class lifestyle on inadequate incomes as clerks and insurance salesmen, small shop-keepers undercut by the chain stores, farmers bankrupted by falling prices, landowners caught by death duties. Despite a slight redis-tribution of income since the Edwardian period, Britain remained a very unequal society roughly divided between the eighty per cent defined as manual working class by their occupation, fifteen per cent middle class, and five per cent upper class. While millions of people survived on a typical weekly wage of around £3. 10s., and many on less, great fortunes were still being amassed, especially in urban property, finance and consumer goods industries. When the brewer, Edward Guinness (the Earl of Iveagh), died in 1927 he left £13.6 million, and the linoleum manufacturer, James Williamson, who became Lord Ashton, left £10.5 million. However, while such disparities in wealth and income suggest the potential for conflict between the classes, they have to be set against the evidence of social harmony and the wide-spread material improvements during the 1920s and 1930s. Whereas in 1914 the top one per cent of the population possessed sixty-nine per cent of the wealth, its share had fallen to sixty per cent in the 1920s and to fifty-five per cent by the 1930s. This gradual flattening of the pyramid reflected the growth of modest income-earners in the middle ranks of British society.

Contrary to received opinion, class relations were probably worse during the 1920s than in the 1930s by which time things had settled down and material improvements were taking the edge off popular grievances. In the immediate aftermath of the war middle- and upper-class people feared that the contrast between poverty and wealth, combined with the sudden insecurity in employment, was bound to promote conflict, leading to violence and chaos, especially as it was being encouraged by sinister external forces, notably Bolsheviks and Jews, bent on manipulating British workers and subsidising subversive actions. By way of proof the pessimists pointed to the huge increase in trade union membership up to 1920, the wave of strikes during 1919–21, the Zinoviev Letter of 1924, supposedly an instruction from the president of the Communist International to unleash a class war in Britain, and above all the General Strike of 1926.

In this context middle-class people felt increasingly conscious of representing a single, embattled interest during the early 1920s. Alarmist articles appeared entitled 'The Crushing of the Middle Classes', arguing that 'between the two governing and opposing extremes of capital and labour, the centre or great middle class is in for a bad time . . . in politics we do not count – we are the taxpayers.'[17] 1919 saw the formation of a Middle Class Union and 1920 produced campaigns by the Anti-Waste League designed to defend taxpayers from extravagant state expenditure used for the benefit of the organised working class. Income tax, which had reached six shillings in the pound by 1919, was vociferously attacked as a burden on the middle class. Small landlords felt aggrieved by government controls on rents that left them with property that yielded insufficient income but was not worth selling. Those who relied on incomes from what were usually safe investments in stock in railways, tram and gas companies, and banks had been hit by wartime inflation. This middle-class sense of vulnerability was enhanced by the post-war shortage of domestic servants. In a *Punch* cartoon of 1926 the lady of the household asked her butler: 'What is the cause of the servant problem?' 'Well, Madam,' he replied, 'you're going down and we're coming up.' More precisely, women increasingly refused to work as domestics and those that did so left their jobs much more readily than before 1914.

However, this defensiveness did not last. Once the middle classes had asserted themselves politically the post-war scaremongering subsided. Income tax was slashed in 1923 and 1924 and was down to four shillings by 1926, though even this was well above the standard rate in the Edwardian period. Before 1914 barely a million people had been eligible for income tax, but wartime wage inflation had swept large numbers into the tax net. However, subsequently governments lifted many of them out by introducing allowances or 'abatements' in respect of dependent children. This meant that by 1929 a married man with two children and £400 per annum paid no income tax at all, and one on £500 paid only £8 tax.[18] In fact, middle-class people, defined by annual incomes between £250 and £1,000, paid a lower proportion of their incomes in taxes than those below and above them in the social scale. In addition, middle-class employees suffered far less from unemployment between the wars; in 1931, for example, unemployment stood at only five to six per cent in non-manual occupations. Seen in this perspective, the interwar period proved to be a very comfortable one for most middle-class families as their growing real income allowed them to take advantage of the wider range of consumer goods and services. As a result, by the 1930s middle-class attitudes towards those below them in the social scale were rather more relaxed than they had been in the 1920s. One of the by-products of this shift was a body of sympathetic middle-class writing that played a large part in creating the traditional view of the decade as one of suffering for the workers. An extreme expression of this sentiment was *The Road to Wigan Pier* (1937) in which the upper middle class George Orwell recorded his feelings of guilt and admiration towards men for whom hard physical labour was routine. On venturing down a coal mine Orwell wrote:

> You crawl through the last line of pit props and see opposite you a shiny black wall three or four feet high. This is the coal face . . . You cannot see very far because the fog of coal dust throws back the beam of your lamp, but you can see on either side of you the line of half-naked kneeling men, one to every four or five yards, driving their shovels under the fallen coal . . . They really do look like iron – hammered iron statues – under the smooth coat of coal dust which clings to them from head to foot. It is only when you see miners down the mine and naked that you realise what splendid men they are.[19]

In fact, by the 1930s domestic revolution was definitely off the agenda. But this outcome would have seemed improbable to many people during the 1920s faced by what appeared to be an inexorable advance of the workers. The turning point came in the General Strike of 1926 which was widely expected to paralyse the economy and destroy the Baldwin government or force it to capitulate to the demands of the unions. When the strike began William Woodruff's family 'sat in silence in our kitchen, holding their breath, waiting for the revolution to begin'.[20] Before long mass violence broke out especially in the North, in Glasgow and in the London docks and south of the Thames.[21] However, this was not typical and the violence was not organised; the unions advised their members to avoid clashes and to co-operate with the movement of essential supplies. The authorities also exercised restraint particularly in the use they made of troops who were employed judiciously to escort food convoys but not placed in positions in which they might have to fire on strikers. As a result, despite the involvement of three million strikers and many more supporters, no one was killed during the nine-day strike. 'Our dear old country can be well proud of itself,' wrote the King in his diary, 'it shows what a wonderful people we are.'[22] Of course, things would have deteriorated if it had lasted longer than nine days.

Despite the solid backing given to the strike, it would be an exaggeration to claim that it mobilised a united working class in support of the miners. At the most only fifty-five per cent of working-men belonged to trade unions; and since its peak in 1920 union membership had fallen back from eight to five million, leaving large sections of the working population outside direct union influence and often equivocal towards industrial action. In the Scottish Borders Andrew Purves noted that farm workers felt sympathetic to the strikers but did not feel personally affected. 'Dive ye no see that the miners are fightin' a fight for 'ou?' demanded one militant. But not everyone was convinced, arguing that 'townsfolk were quite happy to exist on cheap food dumped from abroad, no matter what the effect that had on agriculture and those employed therein'.[23] Even in urban areas some working-class communities lacked a common political culture. In poor districts where unionism was weak the population was often more individualistic than class conscious. In London's East End, for example, Arthur Harding was too cynical and detached to feel much loyalty to the strike: 'In our language these strikers were what we called mugs . . . We didn't much mind which side we helped as long as it brought us in money.'[24] In this spirit of opportunism Harding helped to distribute the TUC news-sheet, *The British Worker,* but he also accepted £1 a day to protect food convoys leaving the London docks! Similarly, communities reacted differently towards unemployment. Bryan Magee left a telling account of his mother who was originally from the North-East but lived in London. One of her brothers back in Newcastle was on the dole: 'my mother openly declared contempt for him, repeatedly saying that anyone could get a job if he really tried, and that Fred was just a layabout, a parasite'.[25]

Such divisions often reflected the gulf between skilled workingmen who insisted on sticking to their trade, even if this meant periodical unemployment, and the more flexible approach adopted by unskilled, casual labourers who were in the habit of chasing temporary jobs as the opportunity arose.

The General Strike was also revealing about working-class politics. Despite alarmist right-wing propaganda, the union leaders had no desire to use a general strike to overthrow parliamentary government. On the contrary, they were wedded to the system, they financed the Labour Party and they subsidised union officials to stand as parliamentary candidates. Any sense of alienation from the system had been largely dispelled by experience during wartime when Labour politicians entered Cabinet for the first time and the state had involved organised labour in scores of official committees dealing with working-class interests. After 1918 the Labour leaders believed that once they had won a parliamentary majority, which was now clearly within reach, the British system of government could be made to work for them; they enthusiastically endorsed the monarchy and the Empire and even abandoned earlier plans to abolish the hereditary element in the House of Lords. Consequently the apparent polarisation of British politics between one party representing capital and wealth and the other representing the workers proved far less significant than the party rhetoric suggested. Although Labour posed as the working-class party it freely recruited men and women from upper-class Conservative backgrounds and it never promoted a soak-the-rich policy. Meanwhile, although Tory propaganda attempted to frighten the middle-class voters by painting Labour as a tool of subversives, Stanley Baldwin frankly endorsed the party as the legitimate alternative government. By endorsing the same values and the same institutions the two parties effectively frustrated the emergence of class antagonism in British politics.

However, the caution of the political leaders is only part of the explanation for the absence of revolutionary politics in interwar Britain. It is striking to see how manual workers rationalised their situation amid what was, after all, the worst and most protracted economic depression anyone had experienced. A minority adopted a socialist analysis of their society in the sense that they interpreted the depression as symptomatic of the climax – and imminent collapse – of the capitalist system. Yet most workers simply took it for granted that slumps occurred from time to time, caused perhaps by wars or by foreigners, and that everyone suffered from them to some extent. As the period wore on they became increasingly sceptical about whether a realistic alternative existed. By 1931 the disillusioning experience of two brief Labour governments seemed to demonstrate that no one had a plausible answer to the mass unemployment that had affected the entire world. During the 1930s this encouraged a mood of fatalism rather than one of radicalism in the manufacturing districts. At the age of fourteen William Woodruff left school in the depressed textile town of Blackburn, and, along with almost all his contemporaries, took a dead-end job as an errand boy, acquired no training and lived in hopes that eventually trade would pick up and create employment for him in the cotton mills; he understood that this was what his father hoped for too.[26] In short, his station in society was static and determined by forces beyond his control. The only real alternative, which Woodruff took eventually, was to leave home to find work in London. Significantly, no one saw education as a way out. Secondary schools sent their pupils on to manual jobs, the grammar schools channelled middle-class children into clerical employment, and the public schools prepared students for professional occupations. The system largely sustained the traditional separation of classes in Britain.

Yet if education offered no route to a higher station in life, there were other ways of achieving mobility between the classes. This is less apparent if society is examined through the experience and attitudes of *men* who were often committed to an occupation and to the group loyalties that it engendered. Women, by contrast, were often influential in promoting social mobility from one generation to the next. This was because working women, by virtue of their occupations, were more frequently in contact with the people and the values of higher social classes than their husbands and were also less likely to be members of trade unions and thus to be influenced by class solidarity. In particular, their experience as domestic servants endowed many women with the ideas and the behaviour of middle-class society, and as a result they sometimes married into slightly higher social groups, passing on to their children a more positive attitude to education and ambitions to rise in the social scale. Sometimes, social climbing provoked friction between husbands and wives as in the family of

D. H. Lawrence. His mother, Lydia Beardsall, who had married a Nottinghamshire miner, had attempted to become a pupil-teacher, though she was forced to abandon her aim to work in the lace industry. This left her keen to find a vicarious escape by encouraging her children to seek education and non-manual occupations.

However, between the wars only a minority of people regarded schoolteaching as worth taking up even though it marked a definite advance into the ranks of the middle class for working-class males. Employment as a shop assistant, traditionally regarded as a social advance, offered insufficient income or status to bestow middle-class status; and, in any case, during the 1930s the number of men working in this capacity went into decline as they were replaced by women. For working-class families a far more appealing escape route lay in sport and the stage, where lack of education was not an obstacle, as Gracie Fields's migration from Rochdale to the Isle of Capri demonstrated. For talented boys sport, especially football and boxing, offered a means to modest wealth, though even the most successful continued to retain their working-class affiliations. By contrast, the police force, which usually recruited men from working-class backgrounds, effectively separated them from their community, involved them in the value system of the higher social classes, and gave them some of the advantages of a profession.

In Victorian times the idea of social mobility had been more realistic largely because it was possible for men to set up small businesses, say, as buyers of tea, with minimal capital, and to became self-made businessmen by ploughing their profits back. However, by the twentieth century this was less feasible because of the need for far more initial capital and because improvements in communications had destroyed local markets and given advantages to large companies who bought in bulk and undercut the prices of small traders. With the exception of small builders the number of self-employed artisans declined steadily as their role became redundant or was filled by larger enterprises. To this extent social mobility became more difficult and class lines more rigid in the twentieth century.

Despite theses trends working-class families continued to find entrepreneurialism in the shape of a small shop very attractive. Shop-keeping had the advantage that the business could be run initially by a wife while her husband retained his job until the shop became secure.

In the long run successful shopkeepers could certainly rise in the social scale; they were influential figures because they supplied credit to their communities and they often became elected as municipal councillors. Even so, it was a dubious and risky strategy. Many small shops either failed entirely or struggled along on minimal profits, especially during the 1920s and 1930s when they faced severe competition from the Co-operatives and the chain stores.

An important exception to this pattern was the fish and chip shop which became a favourite option because it made use of housewives' skills and could be developed by selling pies, cooked meat and tripe. After the war a fish and chip shop could be bought for as little as £150. This proved attractive to discharged soldiers some of whom set themselves up with a grant from the Ministry of Pensions in the brief boom of 1919–20. Later, the onset of long-term unemployment drove families to use their savings to enter the fish and chip trade. In this sector they were not vulnerable to big business. Indeed, a fish and chip shop could be viable on the basis of a very local market comprising 400–600 people, though 2,000 was more typical.[28] Not surprisingly, as many as 70,000 people were employed directly in the trade by the 1930s and a further 200,000 indirectly in supplying the ingredients and transport.[29]

However, even in the fish trade the influx of families looking for an alternative to the dole drove prices down and forced some out of business in the depressed areas. Deflation and stiff competition made the interwar period a difficult one for the retail trade and small businesses generally; and as many people were struggling against costly loans and bankruptcy to avoid slipping down the social scale as were clawing their way up it. An easier route for those with some educational qualifications lay in the expansion of employment in commercial institutions such as building societies, banks and insurance and in local authority offices where modestly paid but more secure white-collar jobs could be had. By 1931 white-collar employment comprised twenty-three per cent of total employment in Britain by comparison with eighteen per cent in 1911.

On the other hand, the vast majority of British people remained where they were in the social scale and evidently accepted the status quo or at least resigned themselves to it. Though divided by income and living standards, they shared many things with members of other classes. Traditionally certain sports had united people in a common enthusiasm, notably horse racing and boxing which enjoyed upper class and even royal patronage but were keenly followed by the working class. Between the wars the annual Oxford and Cambridge Boat Race was another popular event among workers who adopted one of the teams despite having not the remotest connection with the universities involved. Weeks before the event vendors walked the streets of the East End selling light and dark blue favours, and on the big day entire communities followed the race or bet on the outcome.[30] By following sport, cinema and politics thousands of people who lived lives of hardship obtained a vicarious pleasure in linking themselves to the lives of successful, powerful and glamorous people, thereby mitigating any sense of alienation or antagonism they might otherwise have developed towards them.

This was, however, less true in other sports, notably football, which middle-class Victorians had attempted to use as a means of social control over the behaviour of the lower orders. By the 1920s such efforts had clearly failed and football had become a notably proletarian sport dominated by professional players rather than the gentlemanly amateurs who had pioneered the modern game. Cricket was more complicated. On the one hand its enthusiasts saw it as a game that brought men of different classes together in common endeavour. Yet it was in cricket that the divide between amateur, that is unpaid, upper-class players, and professionals, that is paid working-class men, had been sharpest. Cricket operated something akin to a caste system at county level where amateurs and professionals were required to enter the field by different gates. Yorkshire, more democratic than most, had abolished this practice in 1902, but it lingered in the county clubs of southern England where the gentleman still dominated. During the 1920s and 1930s scorecards continued to demarcate the players by printing their initials before the names of amateurs and after the names of professionals.[31]

In so far as class distinctions became less marked between the wars the main agent of change lay in the spread of consumerism especially during the 1930s. There is certainly evidence that the combination of rising real incomes and energetic marketing encouraged middle and working-class families to spend their income on the same minor luxuries and on similar leisure activities and to entertain common aspirations in terms of home ownership. Popular branded and tinned products were sold to both classes. Fish and chips, previously not quite respectable, moved upmarket, being offered to a middle-class clientele in restaurants and department stores; in the 1930s Harry Ramsden's welcomed patrons with wall-to-wall carpet, leaded windows, chandeliers and music.

Fashion, especially for women, was another important dimension to consumerism. The use of cosmetics, especially lipstick, face powder, rouge and eyebrow paint, became routine among women in all classes in this period. They were observed delving into their handbags for a mirror and compact to avoid having a shiny nose. 'Ladies now do not hesitate to powder their noses not only in public places but at one's private dining table', complained a *Times* correspondent. Critics interpreted the resort to make-up as another symptom of the American influence on British society, helping to promote an egalitarian spirit at least to the extent of extending cheap luxuries to people on modest incomes. By taking advantage of the cheap but fashionable clothes manufactured from rayon and artificial silk young working women managed to emulate film stars, and, as a new colour or style was launched each year by the fashion industry, they found it possible to follow the dress of the wealthy for the first time. This pattern was accelerated by the spread of department stores, a form of shopping that had begun with Fenwick of Newcastle upon Tyne in the 1890s and was copied by Selfridges a decade later. Offering customers the 'democratisation of luxury', department stores made it easy for people of all sorts to shop, or simply to wander around inspecting their goods, by clearly pricing the items and thus allowing them to decide whether they could afford to buy.

In some ways the most significant indication of common values lay in the aspiration to better housing and in particular to home ownership. During the late Victorian period few people in any class owned their own homes, and ownership was associated with improving working-class families. But the aspiration to home ownership moved up the scale as it became adopted by thousands of middle-class people after the First World War. But by the 1930s, as the price of new houses fell sharply, mortgages became affordable for many working-class families who, in the process, acquired a common interest with people higher in the social scale. The authorities were fully alive to the political importance of the spread of a property-owning democracy as is evident from the language used by the Minister for Health in 1925. He praised the building-society movement for 'building up a new class in the community – a class that has a stake in the country . . . and is bound to comprise good citizens and good neighbours'.[32]

No doubt the effects of these commercial changes in softening class divisions can be exaggerated, for consumerism created an illusion of equality that left the reality largely intact. Although people in all sections of society spent more on luxuries, their patterns of expenditure continued to reflect class distinctions in many ways. For example, when shopping for food the poorest housewives still used corner shops because there they could get credit, better off working-class families relied on the Co-operative Stores, and middle-class women were more likely to patronise specialist shops and family grocers who delivered purchases to the door. The general enthusiasm for holidays reflected similar distinctions. The poorest could afford day trips to downmarket resorts such as Blackpool, the better off might take a week or two at Bournemouth or Torquay, and for the wealthy the traditional escape to villas in Italy or the South of France was now supplemented by more exotic holiday locations marketed by Thomas Cook. In effect, then, class remained a very pronounced feature of British life between the wars, but it generated less conflict than might have been expected largely because the benefits of economic change were being distributed more widely than before.

This is not the perspective in which the 1920s and 1930s have traditionally been seen. However, the earlier focus on economic depression, mass unemployment and the means test in contemporary writing by Orwell, Wilkinson, Greenwood and others has been superseded by a revisionist analysis of the period that emphasises the material gains and plays down the impact of the slump. In effect, the traditional view exaggerated the scale of the slump and misrepresented its social effects. As measured in terms of unemployment and lost output the slump was much less severe in Britain than in the United States and Germany. Even in the worst periods the majority of people kept their jobs. Moreover, because prices actually fell faster than wages in Britain, the real value of incomes increased, on one calculation by seventeen per cent between 1924 and 1935, thereby allowing a sense of prosperity to take the edge off social discontent. The major exception to this was coal miners whose wages were sharply reduced after 1926. But generally consumers benefited from a period of almost continuous deflation. Without this the boom in consumer goods, housing, motor cars and holidays would hardly have been possible.

Modern perspectives on the interwar period also take greater account of the fact that it was not one of *continuous* depression. After the brief boom in 1919–20 had collapsed into a sharp slump in 1920–21 there was a period of partial recovery. As a result by 1929 unemployment had fallen back to 1.1 million or 10.4 per cent; it then deteriorated up to 1933 reaching 3 million or 22 per cent. But during 1934 another limited recovery set in which lasted to 1937 when unemployment had returned to 10.8 per cent, reflecting a 46 per cent increase in industrial output between 1932 and 1937. These fluctuations reflected the fortunes of different sectors of the economy. Although heavy manufacturing, coal and textiles emerged severely handicapped after 1918, the war stimulated other industries, notably chemicals, electrical goods, motor vehicles and aviation in which Britain had previously lagged behind her competitors. The creation of the National Electricity Grid brought huge benefits both for consumers and for industrialists who now enjoyed more freedom to locate industry away from the traditional manufacturing areas. In any case the generation of new employment was due less to manufacturing than to sectors such as housing which required extra labour and had an indirect effect in generating a demand for bricks, pipes, paint and glass. Above all, the new employment in the offices of both private commercial businesses and in local and central government departments signified that Britain had entered a period of painful readjustment; she was evolving steadily away from the manufacturing economy of her Victorian heyday to the service economy of the twentieth century.

This more optimistic view of Britain's economic recovery implies a redefinition of the interwar depression as essentially a regional problem arising from the original Industrial Revolution which had left her manufacturing and extractive trades heavily concentrated in the North of England, South Wales and central Scotland. This was apparent as early as 1921 when unemployment nationally stood at 17 per cent but reached 27 per cent in engineering and 36 per cent in ship-building. It had further social implications in that the jobs lost in the depression were largely men's jobs, except in textiles where women formed a high proportion of the labour force. This was reflected in stark regional variations. In 1932, for example, London and South-East England reported 13.7 per cent unemployed, while the northern counties recorded 27 per cent. At a local level the disparities were much greater. In 1934 unemployment reached 50 per cent in Bishop Auckland, 57 per cent in Jarrow, 61 per cent in Maryport (Cumberland), and sixty-seven per cent in Merthyr Tydfil. In the same year it stood at just 3.9 per cent in St Albans in Hertfordshire.

The relocation of industry to the South and Midlands inevitably meant that the depressed areas were much slower to recover when the economy picked up. This condemned many workers to long periods of unemployment; in 1934 the 148,000 people out of work in the Tyneside and north Durham area included over 9,000 who had been unemployed for five years, 18,500 for four years, 41,000 for three years and 63,000 for two years.[33] Eventually these stubborn pockets forced the government to adopt a regional strategy for the first time. In 1934 commissioners were appointed to investigate four 'Distressed Areas' comprising four million people: south-east Wales, west-central Scotland, west Cumberland, and Tyneside-north Durham. The most visible signs of this initiative were the new trading estates which were designed to create a more diverse economy by attracting light industry. At the Team Valley trading estate near Gateshead thirty factories had been built by 1939. However, the impact of the Distressed Areas policy proved fairly limited partly because the commissioners lacked sufficient powers and resources. Initially the government allocated just £2 million expenditure, a very modest figure when compared with the £26 million used to subsidise agriculture during 1932–4. In 1939 only seventeen per cent of new factories opened in these districts by comparison with forty per cent in Greater London.

To some extent the social impact of the depression was mitigated by extensive migrations of people into the more buoyant economies of the Midlands, London and the South-East, largely comprising young men who joined relations or friends already living in these areas. Hence the large concentrations of Welsh people, for example, in Oxford, Slough, Hayes and Southall. The construction of an aluminium rolling mill at Banbury in Oxfordshire attracted so many migrants from the depressed Lancashire textile belt that it became known as Little Rochdale.

The migration seems to have been largely a matter of individual initiative. Only one in five people used labour exchanges to find work. The traditional practice of boys following their fathers after leaving school, or relying on personal and family contacts to tip them off about vacancies or 'speak for' them to foremen and employers still prevailed. When William Woodruff left Blackburn to find work in London in 1933 he went equipped with a letter from the manager of a brickworks in Darwen to an acquaintance who ran a foundry, and, despite grumbling, gave him a job. At his lodgings in Bow he found that no fewer than six members of the household had jobs with the local council simply as a result of the political influence of their landlady following a Labour victory in the local elections: 'Nobody threw a fit of conscience about it.'[34]

Those who lacked connections often tramped the streets hoping to pick up a job; one contemporary estimated that unemployed men in South London were spending four to five hours a day in this exhausting and usually futile search.[35] In fact, for men whose normal life was emphatically work-centred this regular daily routine became a kind of substitute for employment. Alternatively they spent their days culti-vating allotments and gardens, where they constructed huts cynically described as 'country cottages', or visiting public libraries to read the newspapers, to rest and to escape the cold. Even there they were sometimes harassed by bureaucracy as Paul Johnson noticed in Stoke: 'The reading room of the public lending library was thus a winter garden of rest for them. But of course they fell asleep and Miss Cartlich, who regularly visited it to detect sleepers, would then wake them up and escort them off the premises, if necessary taking a hand to their collar. "Out, out, out!" she would say, "I'll have no men here snoring in my reading room." '[36]

By one means or another a million workers moved from the North and Wales between the wars, representing four per cent of the labour force. The question is: was this a large number or a small one? It is tempting to assume that if the British workforce had been more mobile unemployment would have fallen much more significantly. It is possible that the availability of the dole reduced the incentive to leave home in search of work and thereby limited the extent of migration. However, this is not entirely plausible because the payments, representing only half an average wage, were enough to keep a family from starvation but still on the edge of poverty – hardly generous enough to have had a major effect on behaviour. But other factors may have played a part. Residual suspicion towards the labour exchanges, which were widely known as 'the dole house', made some workers reluctant to seek professional advice about the availability of employment in other parts of the country. Adolescents recently out of school found it easy to obtain temporary, low-paid jobs as errand boys, shop assistants or bookie's runners, even in depressed areas. It was usually a little later as single men in their twenties that they were likely to migrate. However, older men had less incentive, especially if they were skilled workers, because a high proportion of the new jobs available in the South offered unskilled work at low rates. In any case, the employers often preferred to recruit women or young workers for light production-line employment because they were more amenable, less likely to be union members and would accept low wages. In effect, there was not always a good match between the jobs lost in traditional industry and those created in the South. At least by remaining at home workers continued to benefit from the lower cost of living and from the informal support system offered by friends and relations in the same predicament as themselves. They feared becoming vulnerable and isolated in an unfamiliar part of the country.

In this perspective the reluctance of many unemployed workers to leave home is not so puzzling and not necessarily irrational. Ultimately migration was limited by the extent to which the expanding industries of the Midlands and the South managed to generate extra employment. Yet even in the later 1930s, after a period of growth, the recovery appeared fragile and partial; it was far from certain that Britain had really left the slump behind. In December 1937 Board of Trade returns showed a rise of 166,000 in unemployment over the previous month, bringing the total to 1,665,000; in four months it had increased by 350,000. Optimistic activity in the building industry leading to an oversupply of new houses was partly responsible for this contraction. As a result by 1938 there were indications that Britain was heading back into a slump. From 10.8 per cent in 1937 unemployment rose to 12.9 per cent during that year, causing fresh social tensions in the process.

The results were obvious to shoppers in London's Oxford Street, five days before Christmas 1938, who were shocked to see a hundred unemployed men carrying yellow placards and shouting 'Work or bread' and 'We want extra winter allowances'.[37] As the snow fell they reached Oxford Circus where they lay down four abreast in the road, stopping the traffic for fifteen minutes. Police lifted the men off the road and eventually they marched off to Regent Street and Piccadilly Circus. Two days later a hundred unemployed men sat down at the Ritz and demanded afternoon tea; throughout January and February they regularly invaded restaurants in Piccadilly and Regent Street and interrupted functions at the Savoy and Grosvenor House. These stunts won publicity for the unemployed and maintained the familiar pattern of non-violent protest, but whether they made much political impact is unclear.

By this time the plight of the unemployed began to be overtaken by popular reactions to the arrival of Jewish refugees escaping persecution in Nazi Germany. 'BRITAIN BECOMES DUMP FOR NAZI EXILES' proclaimed the newspaper headlines. In fact, by 1939 Britain had admitted only 70,000 refugees, a fraction of those trying to flee. But ministers shared the popular belief that Germany's Jews had probably brought their troubles on themselves, and were fearful that the shortage of employment in Britain would give new wind to fascist propaganda. The British Union of Fascists ran scare stories along the lines of 'Refugees to Have Your Boys' Jobs', hoping to capitalise on popular resentment towards the Jews for supposedly embroiling Britain in another war with Germany.[38] In the event the Jewish refugees created new businesses and employment. But at the time they appeared likely to compete with indigenous workers for scarce jobs. The hostility towards them reflected an underlying fear that Britain's recovery remained insecure and that the depression might well return. Unemployment had never dropped below ten per cent since 1920. It was still at eleven per cent when war broke out again in 1939 although last-minute rearmament was helping to reduce it. But it took the Second World War to push unemployment below the ten per cent mark at last. Indeed, by 1941 the country was officially reported to be suffering from a shortage of two million workers. In this way things had finally come full circle since the boom conditions created by the Great War.

6

Screwneck Webb and Jimmy Spinks:
Crime, Violence and the Police

To judge from the reports in the newspapers interwar Britain was a society in the grip of violent crime of all kinds. During January 1925 the front pages of the best-selling Sunday newspaper, the *News of the World,* was dominated by a catalogue of British crime stories: 'How Did Elsie Cameron Die?'; 'Lady Artist's Fate'; 'Girl with Two Lovers'; 'Butler Driven Mad by Jealousy'; 'Craving for Neat Spirits'; 'Hooley's Confessions'; 'Gloated Over Exploits: Jewel Thief Gives Gems to Woman'; 'Riddle of Lost Typist'. As these headlines suggest, women figured prominently despite the fact that most crime was committed by men in their teens and twenties. In 1925 the press dwelt lovingly on the case of Emma Smithers, a twenty-year-old cook who had posed as the wife of Edward Wall, a butler aged thirty-seven, but also cultivated the attentions of a rival to whom she agreed to become engaged. According to the coroner Wall 'fell into a state of frenzy, as men sometimes do – even over worthless women'.[1] He then resorted to a cut-throat razor – a weapon routinely carried by the majority of men in the 1920s – gashed his own throat and died. 'Do you think it was playing the game?' Smithers was asked at the inquest. 'I know it was not but I have paid the price,' she replied bitterly.

Apart from war and the royal family, these lurid tales of morality, violence and crime sold newspapers more effectively than anything else, and judges complained regularly, though unsuccessfully, about the publication of photographs of the leading suspects in the press even before identity parades had been held. The newspapers of the 1920s and 1930s approached crime as a matter of popular entertainment and as a stimulus to circulation, as they still do today, rather than with a view to offering a balanced picture of society. As a result, Britain had been subject to regular panics about the crime wave supposedly sweeping the country throughout the Victorian period. In fact, the official statistics depicted a sober trend of falling crime from the mid nineteenth century down to 1914. The end of the war saw a predictable upsurge of fears about a fresh crime wave unleashed by the four-year conflict. Some attributed it to the brutalising effect of a war that had left former soldiers with a callous attitude towards life. Others interpreted it as the consequence of allowing the young to get out of hand during wartime. Certainly there seemed to be abundant evidence that something had gone seriously wrong. During 1919 and 1920 Britain experienced a wave of strikes, looting and riots. Right-wing critics attributed this to subversive influences on the workers, while to the Liberal Left the war had undermined the belief in progress and civilised values. The brutality seemed to enjoy official sanction in the violent foreign policy pursued by the government in India, Egypt, Iraq, Russia and, above all, in Ireland where a civil war raged. While the IRA assassinated British officers, the notorious Black and Tans recruited by the British authorities were known to torture, shoot and mutilate their prisoners. However, many politicians refused to believe that the troops were capable of such atrocities and the Secretary of State, Sir Hamar Greenwood, praised them as 'the cream of the ex-servicemen'. The notorious Amritsar Massacre of 1919 when 400 Indians were shot on the order of General Reginald Dyer also provoked dismay and controversy. Winston Churchill denounced his action as 'absolutely foreign to the British way of doing things', but others argued that Dyer had simply nipped a revolution in the bud by prompt intervention.

Despite all these manifestations of violence and disorder, it was not long before the traditional view reasserted itself to the effect that the British were essentially a non-violent and law-abiding people who simply harboured a small 'criminal class' in their midst, reinforced by recruits from abroad and by alien influences. As the idea of a 'criminal class' reminds us, the lawmakers and the law-enforcers habitually defined criminality in terms of misbehaviour among the lower classes. This was slightly at odds with the presentation of crime by the newspapers whose readers enormously enjoyed reading about the misdemeanors of their social superiors. Middle- and upper-class crime was different in that it usually involved fraud, corruption and dishonourable moral conduct rather than larceny and violence. In March 1925 the *News of the World* regaled readers with the case of a 33-

year-old divorcee, Mrs Adelaide Lubbock, the granddaughter of the fourteenth Earl of Eglinton, who sued a Francis Greswolde-Williams for breach of promise. A wealthy fifty-year-old, Greswolde-Williams was described as ex-master of Ledbury Hounds and the owner of estates in Worcestershire and East Africa. Mrs Lubbock emerged with £500 in damages.[2]

Tales about the fraudsters operating in well-to-do circles were so popular that the press had no reservations about digging up old cases. For example, in 1925 the confessions of Ernest Terah Hooley – 'The Greatest Scoundrel I Ever Met' – made excellent copy.[3] Hooley had swindled various members of the aristocracy out of large sums as far back as the 1890s. More topical was the notorious former MP, Horatio Bottomley, who, among other irregularities, had used his journal, *John Bull*, to raise £650,000 in Victory Bonds during the war. Bottomley coolly proceeded to pocket the proceeds, but in 1922 he was eventually prosecuted and sentenced to seven years for embezzlement. In 1933 justice arrived belatedly at the door of Maundy Gregory, a notorious honours tout who had sold titles during Lloyd George's premiership. Selling honours had not been an offence until 1925 and Gregory, who was the first to be prosecuted, got off lightly with two months in prison and a £50 fine because of the intervention of J. C. C. Davidson, Conservative Party chairman, who persuaded him to plead guilty and thus keep the names of scores of prominent people out of court. In return money was quietly raised among his corruptees to settle Gregory in a flat in Paris with a generous annual pension of £2,000. This largely deprived the press of an opportunity to attack the Establishment and helped the authorities to bury the scandal.

After peers and politicians there was nothing better than a clergyman caught in the act. One such provided the classic scandal of interwar Britain from 1932 to 1937. During this period readers followed the roller-coaster fortunes of the Reverend Harold Davidson, a 57-year-old former actor, who had been rector of Stiffkey (pronounced 'Stewkey') in Norfolk for twenty-six years. During the 1920s Davidson actually spent his weekdays in London as a chaplain in West End theatreland where he became known as the 'Prostitutes' Padre'. He later claimed to have helped 500 women in this period. But in 1932 the Bishop of Norwich appointed a firm of private detectives to investigate Davidson's 'slackness', leading to a twenty-five-day trial at the Great

Hall at Westminster. In fact no reliable evidence of wrongdoing was produced but a bogus photograph showing Davidson with a semi-nude woman, probably arranged by some newspapers, was enough for him to be found guilty, and he was defrocked. Subsequently Davidson protested his innocence and tried to raise money towards his costs by joining a freak show at Blackpool.

These cases of errant clergymen, embezzling MPs and two-timing cooks are among the highlights but they scarcely present a balanced perspective on interwar crime in Britain. According to the official record Britons committed 149 crimes per 1,000 population in 1901, 269 in 1911, 273 in 1921 and 399 in 1931. Owing to the Second World War we have no comparable figures for 1941. But by 1951 Britain was recording 1,299 crimes per 1,000. Despite the modest increases in overall crime statistics, this hardly suggests that interwar fears about crime waves were justified. On the contrary, by comparison with early Victorian Britain and post-1945 Britain, this was a relatively stable and law-abiding period. Governments actually managed to close down twenty-four of the fifty local prisons during the 1920s and 1930s. Several types of offences that had dominated the Victorian crime scene appear to have diminished, notably drunkenness, prostitution and murder. For example, convictions for drunkenness fell dramatically from 161,000 in 1910 to 95,000 in 1920 and 53,000 by 1930. As a result the prison population in England and Wales diminished from 20,904 in 1910 to just 11,346 in 1930.

Admittedly, crime statistics are notoriously unreliable partly because many crimes involving violence are never officially recorded and also because of fluctuations in the activity of the police in response to the pressures put upon them. For example, the police felt obliged to devote more of their efforts to dealing with motoring offences, so much so that by the mid 1920s this one aspect of crime was placing excessive demands on police time and clogging up the magistrates courts. Indeed, any generalisation about the reputation of the British as a law-abiding people must be heavily qualified by their attitude towards motoring offences which increased from 55,000 in 1910 to 475,000 by 1938. During the Edwardian period motoring had brought many 'law-abiding' citizens into conflict with the law for the first time in their lives, and they reacted by denouncing the injustice of prose-cuting them on what they saw as dubious evidence sometimes based on the testimony of a single constable. As a result they sometimes counter-sued policemen with giving false evidence about speeding, and even accused them of insolence. After 1918 the feud between police and motorists was renewed. For their part the police complained that rules, such as the 20 m.p.h. speed limit prevailing in the 1920s, were almost universally disregarded, and proved very difficult to enforce. One chief constable pointed out that 'the majority of motor car owners care little or nothing for a fine of £5, some having told me that they pay between £1,000 and £2,000 for their machines and that the cost of keeping them up is in some cases £500 a year'.[4] Although behaviour gradually improved, assisted by the construction of better roads and the introduction of safety devices, the horrendous number of road casualties during the 1930s underlined the reluctance of most British drivers to accept that the law applied to them.

Of course the bulk of crimes committed between the wars – around three-quarters of the total – involved theft and burglary; these categories were responsible for much of the increase in recorded crime between the wars. Was this a reflection of mass unemployment and social distress during the period? Some authorities dispute this on the grounds that the large rise in crime during the post-1945 era was associated more with affluence than with hardship. On the other hand, one wonders why theft was more common in winter than in summer if it was not connected with social distress. Given that so much of the rise in interwar offences involved casual and petty acts of theft committed by young men, as opposed to organised and violent crime, it is very difficult to explain the trend except in terms of the large numbers of young unemployed men left hanging around Britain's towns.

This view is certainly corroborated by accounts of communities where much of the population lived permanently on the edge and was consequently always susceptible to opportunistic, low-level crime. For example, in his description of his life in 1930s Hoxton Bryan Magee pointed out that poverty and crime had always been closely associated because of the shortage of reliable employment for men in the area. In effect, many men were constantly on the lookout for short-term opportunities to earn extra money by means of a whole spectrum of activities ranging from the legitimate to the illegal: odd-jobbing, doing favours for friends, acting as a lookout, being a bookie's runner, prostitution, storing stolen goods, and stealing. Hoxton became a focus for dubious activities especially receiving stolen goods from all over London.[5] For the regular criminals it was crucial to recruit people to help them in transporting the goods and to obtain the co-operation of respectable local businessmen in storing them. For these services they received protection money on an ad hoc basis.

As low-level activity of this kind lacked drama it usually escaped the attention of the press. By dwelling heavily on serious violence their accounts often gave the impression that murder was a routine part of interwar life. In his novel *Coming Up for Air* (1939), George Orwell described Mrs Bowling happily following the murders in her Sunday newspapers regardless of whether they were new or old ones: 'I think Mother thought of the world outside Lower Binfield chiefly as a place where murders were committed.'[6] Their reports have the flavour of the Agatha Christie novels that were becoming popular in the 1920s. A classic English, interwar murder occurred in 1922 in the idyllic little town of Hay-on-Wye. There a Major Herbert Armstrong travelled up to London to purchase an arsenic-based weedkiller which he subsequently used to poison his wife who had recently made a will leaving him all her money. Evidently emboldened by his success, the major then made the mistake of dispatching a box of arsenic-filled chocolates to the local solicitor who was demanding settlement of a bill for £500.

Agatha Christie was, of course, right about one thing: murder was still largely a family affair. And, despite all the lurid reports about the use of guns, razors and coshes by criminal gangs, murder went into a decline in Britain between the wars. Whereas seventy people were committed to trial for murder each year during the Edwardian period, and seventy-two each year during the 1940s and 1950s, only fifty-six were tried annually between 1931 and 1938. A conviction still carried the death penalty. Between 1910 and 1919 120 men and women were hanged for murder in England and Wales, 141 between 1920 and 1929, and only 83 between 1930 and 1939. Many murderers got off on charges of manslaughter because juries were persuaded that the accused had been provoked in some way. But the downward trend is largely explained by a growing readiness on the part of judges and juries to interpret cases of murder in terms of insanity and unfitness to plead. In 1922 controversy was aroused by the case of Robert True whose plea of insanity in a murder trial was supported by psychiatric evidence but was rejected by the jury and the Court of Appeal. However, the Home Secretary reprieved True despite protests from those who believed he should hang. Similar thinking influenced the enactment of the Infanticide Act of 1922 which provided that a mother who killed a 'newly born' child should be acquitted of murder and charged with manslaughter. Further modifications in 1938 made it rare for a woman in this position to be indicted of murder on the grounds that her mental balance was apt to be upset by birth or the aftermath. By the 1930s some forty-seven per cent of all murder cases were being dealt with in terms of insanity or unfitness to plead. By this time there was a feeling that it was wrong to impose the death penalty unless the case was very clear-cut.

Despite this, most British people appear to have regarded capital punishment as a necessary deterrent to murderers even though a number of Continental and American states had by now abolished it with no detrimental results. In Britain a campaign for abolition had been running sporadically since the 1830s but made little impact. However, the debate was revived in the aftermath of the war partly by the new opposition to capital punishment in the Labour Party. Wider concern was also stimulated by several sensational trials leading to controversial executions, notably that of Emma Thompson. She was hanged in 1923, along with her lover, for the murder of her husband. The facts were not in doubt. Mr Thompson had been stabbed by the lover; but Emma had played no part in the killing except to seek medical assistance. By this time comparatively few women were executed: two between 1920 and 1929 and three between 1930 and 1939. Those that were had usually aroused the moral disapproval of judge and jury. In effect, Emma Thompson was hanged as much for her adultery as for her involvement in her husband's death. However, in Holloway Prison the governor and the chaplain were badly affected by Thompson's execution, while the executioner subsequently resigned his post and committed suicide. Partly as a result of the unease aroused by the Thompson case, the National Council for the Abolition of the Death Penalty was founded in 1925, and there was a parliamentary debate and a select committee on the subject in 1929–30. However, the only reform to emerge from this was the removal of the death penalty for desertion and cowardice in 1930. Majority opinion held that capital punishment was the only means of restraining the mass of murderers of foreign origin – 'a crowd of polyglot undesirables' – who supposedly threatened British society. Despite the predominantly domestic nature of murder, the comments made by judges in this period suggest that they, too, continued to see it as the product of 'the methods of the gangster and the gunman' which were imported from the United States and from Continental Europe.

Indeed, it remained an article of faith that Britain was a relatively non-violent society. The Victorians had always regarded the peoples of the Continent as turbulent and excitable and thus in need of authoritarian systems and firm policing methods. By contrast, in Britain order was best maintained through the influence of the 'gentleman', by fostering deferential attitudes among the masses and by diverting the violence that came naturally to men into rough sports subject to strict rules. The drift towards extremist and violent political regimes in Europe between the wars only accentuated these assumptions. In 1941 even George Orwell, a notable critic of British society, insisted that Britons were essentially a gentle, pacific people. After all, they were famous for standing quietly in queues, they never committed political murders, and they allowed their police to go unarmed except for truncheons; the Italians actually coined a phrase – *il bobby inglese* – to describe British police practice.

Before dismissing such views as complacent, one should note that crimes of violence increased by a mere one per cent in the whole period between 1920 and 1948. Admittedly a great deal of violent crime went unreported and thus unrecorded, notably street fights between men, wife-beating and violence on children by teachers and parents. In towns male-on-male violence, often associated with drinking, was simply taken for granted. There was still a code of honour to the effect that arguments could be settled quickly by fist fights on the street and that no one would press charges subsequently. Consequently the evidence exists, if at all, only in the neglected records of hospital accident and emergency departments.

The other major form of violence between the wars was domestic. There is some evidence that during the nineteenth century the courts had become less tolerant towards wife-beating, and the law became more severe towards violent husbands. On the other hand, among juries traditional attitudes survived quite strongly after the First World War; many held that a husband had some right to beat his wife, especially if she fell short in the performance of her domestic duties or if she allowed her affections to wander. In 1924 the Police Code was revised to read: 'Police should not interfere in domestic quarrels, unless there is reason to fear that violence is likely to result . . . Beware of being overzealous or meddlesome.' In practice the police adopted an even more relaxed attitude. As a young constable in London in 1935 Edward Lyscom came across a husband who had 'battered his wife with a frying pan' in the early hours, but he declined to arrest him and suggested she take out a summons for common assault. Later, when dealing with a husband and wife who were fighting in the back of a taxi, Lyscom intervened to pull him off. Thereupon the couple joined forces to attack him, the wife biting his finger badly. On arrival at the scene Lyscom's sergeant took a philosophical view: 'Look boy, you may be developing into a useful copper, but you haven't learned about women. She doesn't mind a belting from her old man, but she won't stand for a copper pinching him for it.'[7] As a rule no one intervened in marital disputes unless things got unusually serious. At an incident in Hoxton neighbours became alarmed by the sound of screaming when a local rough, Screwneck Webb, was beating his wife so badly they thought he might kill her. They called the police who attempted an arrest. But Screwneck Webb promptly knocked off the constable's helmet while his wife slipped off her metal-tipped shoe and began to hit him over the head with it.[8]

Despite these examples, wives suffered badly from violence fuelled by alcohol. Moreover, it usually proved difficult for the female victims of male attacks to obtain justice from the courts, partly for lack of evidence, but partly for lack of sympathy towards battered wives. In January 1926 Sarah Ward applied to magistrates in Chesterfield for a maintenance order against her husband of twenty years. He had taken to coming home drunk, beating her with his fists and dragging her along the ground. Yet the magistrates dismissed her application; she had no witnesses and her injuries were presumably insufficient evidence.[9] Bryan Magee recounted the case of Jimmy Spinks, a noted East End bareknuckle fighter with a criminal record, who got into a row with his girlfriend when drunk; in the course of the argument he grabbed a heavy mirror, smashed it over her head and killed her. In a drunken panic and covered in blood, Spinks ran off and tried to board a bus, but the conductor refused to let him on. Despite this trail of incriminating evidence, witnesses subsequently refused to say they had seen Spinks; some friends swore he was elsewhere at the time of the killing, and it became impossible to link him directly to the crime.[10] In Spinks's case there was clearly an element of intimidation. But juries commonly reflected the popular prejudice towards women who were badly treated by their husbands and displayed a marked understanding towards the men. This was often shown by treating a wife's murder as manslaughter. During the 1920s this prejudice was even accentuated by reforms in the law that allowed wives to obtain separation and maintenance orders from violent or absentee husbands; the courts considered that women resorted too easily to such options, and that they should accept their lot rather than break up their homes.

Toleration of marital treatment of wives does underline the assumption that interwar society generated more violence than was readily admitted, and that in some ways the British were reluctant to recognise how integral crime was to their culture. This of course was not unique to the interwar period; there is always a certain gulf between the makers and the enforcers of the law, on the one hand, and the attitudes taken by ordinary citizens, on the other. It is notoriously true that certain types of offences are not widely recognised and their perpetrators suffer little or no ostracism. In working-class communities street fighting, domestic violence and receiving stolen goods were too much part of the daily routine to attract much criticism. Higher up the social scale rioting and destruction of property by undergraduate students was invariably interpreted as mere high spirits. For their part the hard-pressed middle classes commonly practised tax evasion and broke the motoring laws; after 1918 one notable wartime tax-dodger, Sir William Vestey, had even been raised to the peerage by Lloyd George. Between the wars the thousands of respectable citizens who were caught for motoring offences regarded themselves less as a danger to society than as the victims of interference by a bureaucratic state. Those who had ridden horses and driven motors during the Edwardian period naturally saw the imposition of speed limits and compulsory driving tests as officious and unnecessary. As late as 1939, for example, Lady Helen Adare insisted on being driven around by her maid, Sullivan, who had not only not passed a driving test but was thought certain to fail one. However, as a pillar of the community Lady Helen evidently thought minor bureaucrats were easily dealt with. She therefore equipped Sullivan with an envelope containing £2 to hand to the senior examiner at her driving test together with a letter in which she assured him that the maid would be confined to quiet roads until she improved! For this Lady Helen was fined fifty guineas with ten guineas costs.

Such complications were apt to arise wherever the state was seen to interfere unreasonably with the pleasures of its citizens. So much so that official attempts to criminalise activity seen as unexceptionable by ordinary people proved counterproductive. This was notoriously the experience of the United States in imposing an absolute prohibition on alcohol in 1919, a policy that not only failed to stamp out drinking but drove it underground, thereby fuelling a major expansion of the criminal underworld. Later in the century British governments were to make an equally disastrous mistake by trying to suppress drugs and in the process multiplying their use and creating vast profits for criminals. Between the wars similar problems arose through attempts to tackle gambling. While bets could be placed at racecourses, it was illegal to place cash bets on horses anywhere else. Under the 1906 Street Betting Act anyone found loitering to take bets or making one could be fined £10 for a first offence, £20 for a second and £50 or six months in prison for a third. Alternatively, punters could have a credit account with a bookmaker, but this option was simply not available to most people. As a result millions of men placed cash bets illegally every day through a huge network of bookie's runners who lingered at regular pitches on street corners, in public houses, barbers, factory gates and labour exchanges. As a result Britain became a nation of illegal gamblers. Although the police were largely unable to suppress this activity, they had to be seen to be doing something about it. They therefore took to arresting bookmakers who refused to pay them and allowed those who did to carry on as usual. In this way the police became an integral part of a nationwide protection racket.

However, gambling sustained more serious crime too; with an annual turnover estimated between £350 million and £450 million it was Britain's second largest industry after the building trade. Inevitably the huge profits attracted organised criminals. Throughout the interwar period the gambling world was dominated by criminal gangs run by bosses who operated openly from public houses such as the Yorkshire Grey in Clerkenwell and the Admiral Keppel at Hoxton.

Many people in authority were simply in denial about this situation, arguing that organised crime scarcely existed in Britain and, to the extent that it did, it was the product of foreign influences. This chimed in neatly with contemporary Hollywood impressions about gang violence in America. No doubt Britain saw nothing on the scale of American lawlessness, but in some of the major cities a similar phenomenon was in evidence. Glasgow enjoyed a dubious reputation for violent gang culture propagated by such books as *No Mean City* published by Alexander McArthur and H. Kingsley Long in 1935. Contemporaries saw this as symptomatic of the social stress caused by unemployment, loss of respect for authority and the breakdown of family values. But it also reflected the importance of violence in the lives of young men for whom fighting had long been an integral aspect of male pride. Gang warfare was also a symptom of the survival of sectarian loyalties on Clydeside. In Glasgow Billy Fullerton ran the Bridgeton Billy Boys, reputedly 800 strong, who enjoyed regular battles with Catholic gangs known as the Norman Conks. These gangs operated on the basis of rackets and intimidation. They were too large and too well integrated into local communities for the police to be able to suppress them, though during the 1930s they gradually brought the situation under control by the use of better intelligence, radios and motor cars.

For the criminal gangs the profits of horse racing were too tempting to resist. At racecourses, where the bookies were vulnerable owing to the large sums of cash they accumulated, the gangs found it comparatively easy to extract protection money despite the police presence. They became known as 'razor gangs' for obvious reasons; the use of a razor to slash opponents across the face was preferred as a more effective deterrent than guns and coshes – it disfigured but was less likely to result in a fatality. Up to the early 1920s the dominant gang was led by Billy Kimber and based in Birmingham, hence the 'Birmingham Boys'. But towards the end of the war a rival emerged based at the Yorkshire Grey in Clerkenwell under Darby Sabini and his five brothers. The rival gangs regularly fought pitched battles. Eventually, however, the Sabinis decided to cultivate the police by notifying them about the battles so that they could arrest members of the Birmingham Boys and ignore the Sabinis. By 1924 with half his members in prison, Billy Kimber agreed to confine his activities to the

Midlands and the North, leaving the rest of the country to the Sabinis. Even so, the violence continued because several smaller gangs continued to operate in places such as the Elephant and Castle throughout the period. In June 1936 the Sabinis, now led by 'Harry Boy' Sabini, repeated their tactics at a fight with the Hoxton gang under Jimmy Spinks at Brighton races.[11] Spinks ended up with five years' penal servitude. Meanwhile the author, Graham Greene, studied the trial evidence on the 'Battle of Brighton' and used it as the basis for his novel, *Brighton Rock*, in which he renamed Spinks as Pinkie.

In view of their involvement in interwar crime the police escaped remarkably lightly. Expenditure on policing increased from £7 million in 1914 to £18 million by 1920, a sign that those in authority were becoming apprehensive about the behaviour of the lower classes, fearful of subversive influences from abroad and alarmed by challenges to private property. In this situation the police became politically vulnerable, not least because the evidence for their effectiveness in containing crime and catching criminals was not very compelling. The annual average number of persons convicted of offences of all kinds in Britain increased from 55,000 during 1910–14 to 75,000 during 1935–9, a rise of nearly fifty per cent. But in the context of a 300 per cent increase in the total number of offences committed this was hardly impressive.

In effect the police regarded their job as one of containment, focussing on certain notorious districts like the East End of London and on serious, violent crimes. This meant that routine, low-level crime – petty thieving, burglary, drunkenness, domestic violence, prostitution – could be regarded as normal and thus tolerated. In so far as serious crime was solved this was done less by detection and more by paying for information. Among the army of criminals there were plenty willing to become informers and to keep the police in touch with the movements of the key figures. But this inevitably fostered close and venal relations between the police and the criminal community, and in the worst cases led the police themselves to become involved in organised crime.

Admittedly any attempts to reform the police were inhibited by the fact that at this time Britain had no fewer than 190 separate police forces each enjoying almost complete operative autonomy. As a result many of them lacked proper resources and skills and failed to co-operate with each other. For the government the most alarming symptom of this unregulated system was the participation of the police in the great wave of strikes that hit Britain during 1919–20. This dissatisfaction led to the appointment of the Desborough Committee and to several reforms in 1919–20 including the introduction of standard pay and conditions of service, common codes of discipline, the establishment of the Police Federation and a ban on strikes. During the 1920s recruits joined the force on weekly wages of £3 10s. rising to £4 after ten years. As a regular income for a workingman this was reasonable, but it was low enough to leave the police susceptible to the temptation to boost earnings by corrupt dealings with criminals. This was especially so when the police became the victims of pay cuts during periods of financial retrenchment in 1922 and in 1931–5.

The British had by no means lost their ingrained prejudice against having a centrally controlled national police force which was traditionally seen as inimical to a liberal state; and the Home Secretary was often obliged to admit that he lacked powers over the force. Thus, despite the recommendation of the Desborough Committee that no force should cover a population below 100,000, very limited progress was made in rationalising the structure. Even though half the cost of policing was borne by national government after 1921, Home Secretaries remained reluctant to put pressure on local forces to improve efficiency or to enforce amalgamations on the smaller forces. As a result, by 1932 there were still fourteen forces staffed by twenty-five or even fewer men and serving populations of 20,000 or under. On the other hand, chief constables did become increasingly responsive to direction from the Home Office between the wars. In 1935 Sir Hugh Trenchard established the Hendon Police College in order to generate officer material for police forces throughout the country. This was an important symptom of the trend towards a federal structure that gradually replaced the old pattern of independent forces.

Popular attitudes towards the police varied widely from those who regarded the bobby on the beat as a reassuring figure to those who resented police interference and saw them as a weapon used by the powerful and privileged to keep the lower orders in their place. 'For us they had a stigma', recalled William Woodruff. 'We distrusted them because they defended the rich.'[12] The 1920s certainly saw widespread criticism of the police for a range of reasons: 'third degree' methods, bribing people to give false evidence to secure convictions, undue severity towards motorists, unnecessary interference with public pleasures, and political bias. Between the wars the wide range of 'political dissidents' including strikers, pacifists, Communists and fascists became a major target of the law and order system, but they considerably complicated the work of the police and stretched their resources. In 1933 Sir Vernon Kell admitted that surveillance undertaken by MI5 focussed largely on the Communists, and he claimed he would need extra funds to cover the fascists adequately.[13]

The police also became the victims of shifts in moral attitudes. A prolonged controversy engendered by overzealous policing erupted in April 1928 over an encounter between a Miss Irene Savidge and an elderly former MP, Sir Leo Money, in Hyde Park. A rather chaste kiss was spotted by an alert constable whose report led to a charge of indecent behaviour against the pair. This was dismissed by the magistrates. Subsequently, however, the Director of Public Prosecutions, Sir Archibald Bodkin, authorised the police to take Miss Savidge in to Scotland Yard for prolonged interrogations. This action provoked a debate in Parliament and led to the appointment of a tribunal which rapped the police over the knuckles for conducting arbitrary interrogation. According to Lord Balfour of Burleigh the public wanted the police to be guardians of law and order, not 'to try to be censors of public morals'.

One of the enduring British myths was the kindly bobby alone on the beat. Beat patrolling was indeed a routine feature of police work in this period, though it was never a very effective means of tackling crime. Unfortunately, it exposed the police to physical attack in hostile districts where crowds could gather quickly and set upon isolated constables if they tried to make an arrest. Officers of the Metropolitan Police suffered 2,421 recorded cases of assault and injury, affecting twelve per cent of the total force, between 1920 and 1927. However, whether this should simply be interpreted as symptomatic of popular hostility is not clear. The truth is that many officers liked to get their retaliation in first; when out on the beat in urban areas they used the opportunity for a quiet assault on anyone they suspected of committing a crime for which they had no convincing evidence. In effect a charge of 'assault' was an easy method of making an arrest. They invariably got away with it because the magistrates chose to believe their accounts and reject the evidence given by members of the public; not surprisingly, successful prosecutions of police officers committing assault were virtually unknown.

On the other hand, the antagonism between police and public is easily exaggerated. Ordinary officers largely reflected the prejudices of the society from which they were recruited. Accustomed to street violence, they resorted to it themselves without inhibition. As working-class authoritarians they looked with suspicion on political dissidents and nonconformists of all kinds. They were usually anti-Semitic and prejudiced against women. Moreover, local communities evidently managed to find an accommodation with their policemen by acting as paid informers and by co-operating with them at the expense of rivals. Even a hardened criminal like Arthur Harding, who was repeatedly jailed, sometimes for offences of which he claimed to be innocent, developed a sound working relationship with them. This often involved making a modest payment of 2s. 6d. to 10s. to a constable for turning a blind eye to illegal gambling: 'You changed your position according to the type of policeman who was on [duty]'. Harding also supplied bogus witnesses to corroborate the police version of events. Things grew more complicated when the local officers were subject to external inspection designed to ascertain whether they were tackling illegal betting and making appropriate arrests. For this they required volunteers, who were paid anything from £2 to £5, to get arrested. According to Harding 'they'd come round quite polite and say, "Albert, stick a man up tomorrow, we're having a raid" . . . They'd stand in the street and then the plain-clothes men would take them in, and charge them with illegal betting. That way the bookmaker wouldn't have a record against him. It was all part of the game.'[14] Sometimes such deceptions were so routine and so elaborate that someone of standing had to be appointed to ensure that everyone got paid for their efforts in thwarting the law: 'Jimmy Smith was the man who straightened up the police. The street bookies gave him the money to share out among the different sergeants and inspectors . . . the police trusted him and the bookies trusted him.'[15]

After the war the work of the police was greatly complicated not only by motoring but by public order problems and the violence associated with political activity. By 1920 trade union membership had doubled to over eight million since 1914 and the post-war years saw an explosion of strikes involving the loss of eighty-five million working days in 1921. The Emergency Powers Act of 1920, which sanctioned the use of troops to protect food and fuel supplies, exacerbated union fears that the machinery of the state was being strengthened to crush industrial action. This put the police in an exposed position between the authorities and their local communities; and the rise of the Labour Party meant that their actions were increasingly likely to be taken up by MPs in questions in Parliament and letters to the Home Secretary.

The friction thus generated should be seen in the context of a strong tradition that regarded political violence as essentially alien to British society. This view gained credibility between the wars as states such as Italy, Spain and Germany abandoned liberal democracy and fascist movements seized power, ran private armies and used the state machinery to subdue their political opponents. Despite this, the traditional view was an unduly rosy one. In the 1920s most British people were familiar with violent behaviour as a routine element in election campaigns. They remembered the suffragette militancy of 1912–14, the emergence of private armies among Unionists and Nationalists in Ireland before the war, the civil war in Ireland during 1920 and the assassination of an MP, Sir Henry Wilson, by the IRA on the doorstep of his London home in June 1922.

Admittedly, the traditional drink-fuelled rowdyism and intimidation associated with Victorian elections was now in decline. Significantly the general election of 1918 was the first to be held on a single day; previously voting had been extended over several weeks to allow the police to transfer their limited resources to the most disturbed districts. On the other hand, while elections became more subdued affairs, violence remained a lively tradition in many areas where political meetings were routinely broken up, platforms stormed by opponents and candidates hired boxers and criminals for personal protection during election campaigns. At the 1924 election Arthur Harding, recently released from prison, was employed as a bodyguard by Major Nathan, the Liberal candidate in Whitechapel, 'to see that nobody attacked him or knocked him about'.[16] According to Harding, the Labour Party used dockers to break up rival meetings, and so he organised the Irishmen to counter them. Clement Attlee, Labour MP for Limehouse, claimed that his meetings were regularly disrupted by the Communists. Above all, the Conservatives felt that they were the victims of physical attack by both Labour and Communist opponents.

In fact all parties traditionally organised what were euphemistically called 'stewards' to throw hecklers out of their meetings. The police took the view that it was their own responsibility to keep order – quite correctly because under legislation passed in 1908 the police had no right to enter an indoor meeting unless violence had broken out, and the organisers enjoyed the right to eject anyone who interrupted provided that they did not use excessive force. Such practices continued during the 1920s. Among the more notorious stewards was the eighteen-year-old William Joyce who was employed in October 1924 by Jack Lazarus, the Conservative candidate in North Lambeth. At the conclusion of one of his rallies left-wing opponents made the usual rush on the candidate's platform hoping to seize the Union Jack. In the ensuing melee Joyce was slashed across his face with a razor, leaving him with a livid scar stretching from his ear to his mouth.

In this situation the early fascist organisations that appeared in Britain from 1923 onwards, were appreciated for supplying stewards to maintain order at Conservative rallies. Moreover, the fascists' adoption of paramilitary methods was far less alien to the British tradition than is usually supposed. Although it had been an offence to drill men since 1819, the law was completely ignored by the Home Office and the police.[17] Consequently no one hindered the British Fascists or the National Fascisti when they put men into uniform during the 1920s, armed them and drilled them as, in effect, private political armies.[18] They justified their methods on the basis that Britain was under threat from revolutionary movements financed by the Soviet Union, and that in the expected crisis the fascists would be ready to assist the government in defeating them. Remarkably such considerations encouraged some ministers to turn a blind eye to what the fascists were doing. Sir John Gilmour confessed his admiration for their disciplined military organisation in 1924 and recognised that 'the forces of the Crown may require substantial help in the future'.[19]

Many contemporaries believed that just such a crisis was looming during the later months of 1925 as the country came under threat of a general strike. In September the government announced the formation of a semi-private body called the Organisation for the Maintenance of Supplies which would mobilise volunteers during the emergency. But the fascists interpreted this as an invitation to recruit their own vigilantes to break the strike.[20] For volunteers it was often difficult to distinguish between unauthorised activity and the official system. Harding recalled: 'There was a colonel at the Guildhall who was employing tough guys to stop strikers interfering with the food convoys. The rougher, the more hooligan they was [sic], the better . . . [he] paid good wages – a pound a day.'[21]

In the event the General Strike, which lasted just nine days in May 1926, passed into legend for its non-violent character. One American journalist wrote that he had seen 'more fighting in one night of a local steel strike in Pittsburgh, than there has been in all England this week'. Yet such complacent impressions are not entirely borne out by the reports arriving daily from the official organisation in the provinces. Particularly in Leeds, Newcastle, Glasgow, in the East End and south of the river in London mobs sometimes including thousands of people rioted and stoned buses and trams. At Preston a mob 5,000 strong attacked a police station to obtain the release of a man arrested for throwing a missile at a bus; it took two hours of fighting, repeated baton charges and reinforcements before the angry crowd finally dispersed.[22] It is, however, fair to note that in the context of several million people who participated in the strike the violence was much less than might have been expected. This was partly due to restraint on the part of the TUC. Many strikers accepted that the troops and the police were only doing their job; by contrast they resented the OMS and other volunteers who they saw as politically motivated and as strike-breakers.

With the General Strike over political violence diminished for several years until the emergence of the British Union of Fascists under Sir Oswald Mosley in 1932. At Black House in the King's Road, Chelsea, the BUF ran what was, in effect, a barracks where an elite body of fascists were trained in martial arts so that they could protect the movement in street fighting and keep control at indoor meetings. Officially the fascists took pride in using their fists rather than weapons, and headquarters claimed to authorise nothing except rubber truncheons. Yet fascists were often caught carrying guns without licences, and local branches were known to instruct their men in the use of knives, knuckledusters, corrugated rubber truncheons filled with shot, potatoes stuck with razor blades and breastplates studded with pins. In May 1940 when Mosley was arrested the police confiscated a Walther automatic pistol and truncheons, and later at his farm in Buckinghamshire they discovered nine other guns including rifles, pistols and revolvers, as well as ammunition, truncheons and swordsticks.[23]

The controversy over fascist violence reached a climax as a result of the treatment of hecklers at a huge BUF rally at Olympia in June 1934. Members of the audience reported that spotlights had been focussed on the hecklers who were then set upon by Blackshirt stewards, dragged outside, and kicked and pummelled before being thrown into the street covered in blood. 'It will be a matter of surprise to us if there were no fatal injuries', wrote three of the MPs present.[24] In fact, these methods were not as novel as the critics claimed. Olympia attracted controversy because it was an unusually big rally, because many politicians turned up and because many now wanted to burst the fascist bubble by drawing attention to their brutality. Yet reactions were much more mixed than might have been expected. When the House of Commons debated fascist tactics at Olympia in June many MPs frankly defended Mosley's methods on the grounds that the violence had been exaggerated and was, in any case, justified by Communist attempts to disrupt the rally. Earl Winterton dismissed the complaints, insisting that any injuries had been sustained 'in the good old-fashioned way by the use of a fist'.[25] His remarks underline the point that fist fighting was still widely approved as a very manly, British way of settling arguments. A Scottish member, F. A. Macquisten, blandly observed that no one had been seriously injured: 'Almost a score of people got black eyes and that sort of thing. Why, they would get more than that in the Cowcaddens in Glasgow on a Saturday night.'[26] Such relaxed responses were not eccentric. The police themselves merely reported that thirty people had been ejected from Olympia 'with a certain amount of violence', and Hammersmith Police Station recorded that the rally passed off 'without any serious violence'.[27] These remarks tell us a good deal about attitudes towards political violence at least in British cities at this time. The rowdy traditions of the Victorian-Edwardian era had not yet died out. From the perspective of the Metropolitan Police the ejection of around 50 hecklers in an audience of some 12,000 people seemed quite modest, and the injuries sustained were not unusual in their dealings with working-class communities.

Despite the outrage expressed over fascist methods in 1934 the

National Government declined to take any action until late in 1936 when the Public Order Act was hastily introduced. This was the result of the disorder arising out of a long-running campaign of anti-Semitism by the BUF in the East End which absorbed a high proportion of Metropolitan Police resources. The climax of this period was the notorious Battle of Cable Street on 4 October 1936 when 50,000 anti-fascists blocked the route of a BUF march through Jewish areas of the East End and many more waited along the route. After prolonged conflict between the police and the anti-fascists, the 3,000 BUF members eventually accepted police advice to withdraw and were escorted back to the Embankment before dispersing.

Although the Public Order Act banned political uniforms and gave the police additional powers to stop or divert marches, it had little effect on fascist activities. At indoor meetings they continued to eject hecklers violently and a police presence was exceptional. At dozens of small street meetings the violence was over before the police arrived. In Hoxton the Blackshirts actually employed extra 'minders' to beat up the interruptors. These were local roughs accustomed to such work at the racecourses. For them casual employment offered by Fascist organisations was simply a useful addition to earnings: '"The Black-shirts want a dozen people in Dalston, Sunday morning – seven-and-six. Who's on?" And that was how it worked . . . for the minders it was money for jam.'[28] Things were more complicated at big open-air rallies and marches which attracted opposition and thus placed the police in an awkward position. Many on the Left accused the police of being biased in favour of the fascists. This is true to the extent that they admired the fascists' discipline and usually refused to intervene when left-wing hecklers were being beaten up. But once the police had given permission for a fascist meeting to be held outdoors at a specific place or had changed the route of a fascist march they were obliged to be present to keep the opposing sides apart so as to prevent fighting. In effect, the police found themselves, as at Cable Street, fighting with the anti-fascists and protecting the smaller numbers of fascists from the mass of demonstrators.

The persistence of political violence throughout the interwar years puts a different perspective on the British view of themselves as a notably non-violent people. By doing its best to ignore fascist rowdy-ism in the hope that it would simply go away, the National

Government subscribed to the myth. This was just one symptom of the wider perception of British society as essentially orderly and peaceful. As violence and crime was concentrated in a limited number of urban districts it was possible to see it as an aberration in the broader picture; and the increasing publicity given to events in Nationalist Spain, Nazi Germany and Fascist Italy during the later 1930s lent further credibility to the received view of Britain as a country set apart from, and even immune to, the disorder inherent in the societies of Continental Europe.

7

'The Best Job of All':
Marriage and Divorce

On 17 April 1939 two 25-year-old women, Heather Jenner and Mary Oliver, opened Britain's first marriage bureau in Bond Street. Their qualifications were not obvious. 'Both Miss Jenner and Miss Oliver have decided not to be tempted to the altar by even the most eligible lonely bachelors among their clients', reported the *Daily Mail*.[1] As they had been refused a licence by the London County Council in 1938 it was clearly incumbent on the proprietors to demonstrate their respectability. Oliver was the daughter of a country parson and Jenner the daughter of a brigadier general; both had been presented at court. On the first day they were overwhelmed with 250 applications by letter, by telephone and in person, from wealthy widows to lonely planters, country gentlemen and retired officers: 'I never thought so many people in social circles would seek assistance', commented Miss Oliver.[2] Half the applicants were men who paid five guineas initially and twenty on the day of their wedding; by contrast women were charged according to their means, often as little as ten shillings. The men, who were more likely to call in person at the bureau, were by no means all elderly. One shy young insurance clerk, so the ladies told journalists, said he could not meet the kind of girl he wanted to marry; she had to be young, pretty, domesticated ('all the men insist on that'), blonde and interested in sports.

Jenner and Oliver may have been amateurs, but they were shrewd, for marriage was a flourishing business in the 1930s. This would have surprised many observers of British society in the immediate post-war period. To contemporaries it seemed only too obvious that in taking the lives of 740,000 British men the Great War had deprived a generation of young women of husbands; it had indeed left the country with an excess of 1.9 million women over men. In her celebrated autobiography, *Testament of Youth*, Vera Brittain was to paint a compelling picture of the devastating personal effects of the death of her brother, Edward, and her friend, Roland Leighton, in the trenches. The press, resounding with lamentations about 'Our Surplus Girls', endeavoured to resurrect Victorian schemes to promote female emigration to the colonies to find eligible young men.

Yet a shortage of husbands was only the start of the problem. Seduced by wartime employment and by the newly won vote, young women, so it was claimed, had seen visions of themselves as free, self-reliant individuals and thus become distracted from their proper role in life: marriage and motherhood. Hence the attacks launched by the *Daily Mail* and the *Daily Express* on 'flappers', young girls whose devotion to leisure, entertainment and emancipation was leading them to avoid altogether the responsibilities of marriage. Social change, so the argument ran, was even producing a physical alteration in Britain's women. 'Many of our young women have become de-sexed and masculinised', wrote Arabella Kenealy, 'with short hair, skirts little longer than kilts, narrow hips, insignificant breasts, there has arrived a confident, active, game-loving, capable human being who shuns the servitude of household occupations.'[3] As the young Barbara Cartland, already establishing herself as an authority on women and relationships, put it, with small breasts and narrow hips the younger generation would produce unhealthy babies – if they produced them at all: 'scientifically a woman only attains her full development after giving birth to a child'.[4] In a typically gloomy book entitled *The Twilight of Parenthood* (1934), Enid Charles condemned the upper classes for encouraging the poor to copy their habit of restricting family size, and warned that on current trends the population of England and Wales would decline from 45 million to a mere 6 million in 200 years.

It is not difficult to account for such apocalyptic prophecies. Since the late-Victorian period the authorities had been concerned about a slight but unmistakable trend towards the postponement of marriage. This partly explained the steady decline in the birth rate from 35 per 1,000 population in the 1870s to 24 by 1914. After a brief recovery around 1920–1 the birth rate resumed its downward path. For a great industrial, military and imperial nation this fall seemed a sure recipe for national decline. To contemporaries the remedy appeared obvious: all women must marry and bear three children. But how to bring about this happy state of affairs?

Throughout the 1920s and 1930s the rapidly expanding women's magazines devoted themselves to promoting marriage in general and the idea of romantic love in particular. Hailing marriage as 'The Best Job of All', *My Weekly* solemnly debated the question 'Should a girl propose?' The answer seemed to be 'yes' on the grounds that so many of the soldiers returning from war were too broken in health or in spirits to do their duty.[5] Reluctantly accepting that single women increasingly sought paid employment, *Woman's Own* suggested that certain types of work were acceptable as a prelude to marriage, not just because they required relevant skills but because they offered opportunities to catch husbands. These included nurse, library assistant and private secretary, which was commended as 'a short cut to a prosperous marriage', and above all, telephonist because 'many a man falls in love with a voice'![6] As if this was not enough, the magazine painted a stark picture of the fate awaiting the woman who was misguided enough to devote herself to a career and remain single; she would inevitably become a lonely, neurotic individual: 'you have only to go into a restaurant and note the strained, dissatisfied look on the face of a woman feeding alone'.[7]

This propaganda continued through the 1930s. Yet long before that stage it had become apparent that the pessimists had frightened themselves unnecessarily into seeing a great crisis for marriage in post-war Britain. The explanation is not hard to find. Far from being a new phenomenon, the existence of a substantial minority of unmarried women had been a pronounced feature of Victorian and Edwardian society. Although critics blamed the influence of feminism for this, there had long been an imbalance in favour of women in the population. This was partly due to higher infant mortality rates among boys, as is still the case today, but largely to massive emigration, sometimes running to 250,000 annually, before 1914. Of the emigrants two-thirds were men, mostly of marriageable age. Hence the schemes to promote female emigration and the tradition in the higher social classes for dispatching unmarried girls to India, accompanied by suitable female relatives, to dig out husbands, a tradition derisively known as 'the fishing fleet'. E. M. Forster found this practice a useful device in his novel, *A Passage to India*, in 1924. However, emigration was interrupted by the war, and after 1918 it never returned to its former levels. As a result, between the wars more marriageable young men were being retained at home; and despite the personal tragedies caused by the killing fields of Flanders, on the whole British women were not deprived of husbands.

There are also grounds for thinking that the trauma of wartime made many people of both sexes more determined to seek the security and reassurance that marriage offered. Men were often thought to have become especially anxious to marry. Barbara Cartland, who was eighteen when the war ended, felt that they returned home in need of wives and quickly became emotional when frustrated. By her own account Miss Cartland was a major cause of the frustration. She recalled being propositioned for the first time in 1919 by a 45-year-old colonel on the Isle of Wight. Viscount Elmley, a more suitable eighteen-year-old, also proposed, but she felt reluctant: 'He was awfully uncouth. He had a sort of thing . . . he used to shake occasionally when he was frightened . . . he would attack chauffeurs when he went out to lunch . . . [and] when I kissed him it was horrible.'[8] These skirmishes were but two of no fewer than forty-nine proposals that Barbara Cartland claimed to have received up to 1927 when she finally accepted one. Nor was she quite as untypical as one might suppose. Although marriage rates among women dipped slightly during wartime and the early 1920s, this proved to be temporary, and in 1930 they began to rise sharply. Even in the 1920s a higher proportion of women in their teens and twenties were getting married than had before 1914, an indication of the underlying trend; by 1931 average ages for marriage had fallen to twenty-five for women and twenty-seven for men. The proportion of people marrying by the age of forty-nine in England and Wales shows an increase among men from eighty-eight per cent around 1900 to ninety-two to ninety-three per cent by the 1920s and 1930s, and for women from eighty-one per cent in 1900 to eighty-three to eighty-four by the 1920s and 1930s.[9] It is now clear that the interwar period marked the beginning of a long-term trend towards a more heavily married society that continued after the Second World War and was not finally checked until the 1970s.

This outcome seems surprising in view of the widespread economic hardship experienced in the 1920s and 1930s; one assumes that prolonged unemployment would have encouraged many people to postpone marriage in hope of better times. Of course, we now know that even during the slump, standards of living improved for many people, and, for whatever reason, the young felt sufficiently optimistic to embark on married life. This was the underlying message of the famous novel by Walter Greenwood, *Love on the Dole*, published in 1933. Although set in the context of chronic unemployment and its demoralising effects, the book nonetheless showed that love triumphed over even the greatest of difficulties in the end. In earlier periods working-class parents had been inclined to exert their authority by delaying the marriage of both sons and daughters as long as they contributed their earnings to the family income.[10] However, the trend towards younger marriage between the wars suggests that parental control may have been weakening. In any case, by the 1930s there was good reason for wage-earning children to move out of the parental home so as to avoid disqualifying their fathers from receiving benefits under the means test which took account of the entire family's income. In Blackburn, where his family relied on a low income from work in the cotton mills, William Woodruff recalled the circumstances of two marriages in his family. When his sister, Brenda, married, no attempt was made to seek her father's permission: 'members of the working class rarely did. The couple just said they'd made up their mind.' Woodruff's account of the marriage of his other sister, Jenny, underlines that, even where income was desperately low, marriage was not regarded in rational, economic terms; it acquired its own momentum as an important display of consumption and status. 'Of course, mother was the driving force. She insisted on new clothes for every member of the family. Father's suit lasted him the rest of his life.' The bride was equipped with a white dress, veil and lilies of the valley, while the groom was forced into a hired frock coat and striped trousers: 'nobody would have guessed he was a painter's apprentice'. After church the family returned for a wedding breakfast of ham, tongue and trifle, before escorting the newly-weds to the railway station in a shower of confetti and streamers. 'It must have taken father a long time to pay for that wedding', wrote Woodruff. 'He must have spent the family's savings on it and gone into debt.' But his wife insisted that 'everybody is entitled to go mad once. [She] saw that the wedding got into the paper. She kept asking father to read [the report] to her over and over again.'[11]

Higher up the social scale there is more evidence of parental control over marriage, though even in the aristocracy the traditional arranged marriage designed to cement family alliances or to bolster shaky finances had long been under challenge. Among Jenner's and Oliver's clients in 1939 was one titled lady seeking a wife for her son who enjoyed an annual income of £2,500; though this was substantial she wanted him to marry a woman with enough money to enable him to live up to the title when he inherited it.[12] This may have been a desperate case. On the whole the upper classes continued to rely on elaborate 'coming out' seasons and presentations at court for young debutantes. Each year the ritual began with tea parties and lunches for the mothers and debutantes at which they traded the names of useful men to invite to dances; it was not necessary to know them personally as long as someone thought them respectable. As all the hostesses kept lists of suitable bachelors, once on one list a man could expect to be invited to practically every function during the season. Despite this, however, there were never enough available men. Some were reluctant to attend so many glittering but deadly occasions. Hostilities commenced with a dinner, followed by a dance and supper, and would end around 3.00 a.m. with bacon and eggs. Meanwhile, the girls' chaperones often grew tired and left early.

Although large sums were spent on these events, many girls underwent three or four seasons without finding husbands. There is impressionistic evidence that between the wars some girls became increasingly disenchanted with the immaturity of upper-class youths and their inability to handle women. 'Please, *please*, find me an intelligent, reliable man of about forty to marry me,' one debutante wrote to Jenner and Oliver. 'I am tired of the bright young men I meet.'[13] A recurrent problem was engaging in conversation with the bachelors for any length of time. The girls were under instructions that they must talk at all costs – but in so doing they had to avoid acquiring a reputation for being intelligent or clever for fear of putting off the superficial, brainless young men. One governess remarked approvingly, 'You see, Laura is intelligent enough to hide her intelligence.' According to the Duchess of Westminster, 'two good subjects if you are stuck for conversation are ghosts and the royal family'. Moreover, with all their social experience the girls seem to have been unable to assess the marital material they were taking on. In 1927 Barbara

Cartland finally became engaged to Alexander McCorquodale who was rich and handsome and promised her a house in Mayfair and a Rolls-Royce. But he turned out to be a drunkard and an adulterer who spent most of his time at his club. They did not sleep together before marriage, but later Barbara said that if she had done so she would have had second thoughts about him.[14] Admittedly, most upper-class women seem to have taken these hazards in their stride.

At all events, once the war was over society threw itself enthusiastically into the celebration of marriage once again. The first big society wedding was that between Lady Diana Manners and Duff Cooper in June 1919 which took place, as society weddings usually did, at St Margaret's, Westminster, where huge crowds turned out to greet them. The marriage caught the popular imagination as a union between a war hero and a duke's daughter. It also offered reassuring evidence that female emancipation and domesticity were compatible. Lady Diana had been a VAD during the war, and later she accepted work as an actress and a journalist as Duff needed money to help him launch his political career. Moreover, despite Duff's perennial infidelity, the marriage proved to be a success – by the standards of the day at least.

1922 saw a similar but more spectacular wedding between Edwina Ashley, who was the granddaughter of the wealthy Sir Ernest Cassel, and Dickie Mountbatten, the son of the former Prince Louis of Battenburg, now Marquess of Milford Haven. At Brook House in Park Lane crowds gathered despite the July drizzle to see the bride leave for St Margaret's. This interest was not surprising as the event had been the subject of eager speculation for weeks. Gossip columnists endlessly discussed the bride's huge trousseau including 'Miss Ashley's exquisite lingerie': slips and knickers in old rose, deep mauve and yellow ochre adorned with lace, each set folded into perfumed satin pads and embroidered with E and M intertwined. A week before the wedding the manufacturers, Savigny and David, displayed the underwear at their Dover Street offices where, to the horror of Queen Mary, the press and public were invited to inspect them.[15]

Meanwhile at Brook House the servants mounted a vast display of the wedding presents and detectives had to be hired to guard the jewellery. The gifts included a diamond pendant from Queen Alexandra, an assortment of tiaras, rings, brooches, bracelets, clocks, silver candlesticks, gold wine coolers, innumerable cufflinks, diamond waistcoat buttons, a silver inkstand, shooting sticks, a telescope, an aneroid barometer, a cut-glass bottle containing River Jordan water, books on Nelson and naval battles and other works by Kipling and Captain Marryat. Contributions for the honeymoon comprised maps of Europe, travel rugs, leather cushions, dressing cases, silver picnic kettles, a portable egg-boiler and a dance gramophone. The Mountbattens' more original friends sent home-made presents such as knitted shooting sticks and home-made lampshades, while the former prime minister, H. H. Asquith, presented a copy of his book, *Occasional Addresses*. Edwina thoughtfully presented her husband with a Rolls-Royce purchased, second-hand, from the Prince of Wales.

Thus equipped, Dickie and Edwina drove down from London to start their honeymoon with a four-day stay at Broadlands, the Ashleys' estate in Hampshire. But their privacy was short-lived. The bells of Romsey Abbey announced their arrival; next day Edwina's father and stepmother turned up; and photographs surreptitiously taken of the couple appeared in the newspapers. After five days spent visiting relations in the county, they returned to London en route for Paris. Edwina, who liked to live dangerously, had wanted to spend a week in Paris 'going to the most awful places we can find'. But they soon moved on to Spain to see King Alfonso, reluctantly staying at big hotels because of fears that Edwina's jewellery was attracting burglars. Finally, they travelled to Germany to dig up some of Dickie's ancestors before coming home in September.

Rather less was known about the other famous post-war marriage, that between Albert, Duke of York, and Lady Elizabeth Bowes-Lyon, in 1923. Like the Mountbattens' this was a marriage between a rather insecure man and a strong-minded woman – a common pattern in aristocratic circles. At the time this was not obvious as Lady Elizabeth hid her determination beneath an outward show of conventional femininity that endeared her to the public. The Duke himself symbolised his generation of men in his slightly desperate search for a wife; indeed, he appears to have been rejected several times by Lady Elizabeth. Of course, such intimate details were not supposed to become public knowledge. King George V and Queen Mary were reportedly horrified when the bride granted an interview to an enterprising journalist from the *Star* who called at the Earl of Strathclyde's home in Bruton Street to offer congratulations on the engagement. But the King had little to fear. The reporter was obviously charmed: 'the bride is very petite and has a magnetic personality', he wrote.[16]

The marriage proved to be immensely popular not least because it symbolised the aspirations of millions of ordinary British people between the wars. With their two daughters, Elizabeth and Margaret, the Duke and Duchess of York appeared the very model of tranquil domesticity. Faced with a husband handicapped by a terrible stutter and troubled by doubts about his ability to perform his public functions especially after ascending to the throne in 1936, the Duchess was seen to play a crucial role as his support and comforter. In this way the royal marriage conformed to conventional thinking. Yet at the same time it was modern: a love match rather than the traditional arranged marriage with a foreign princess. It was hardly surprising that the public believed that the Duke's elder brother, the Prince of Wales, was entitled to the same good fortune when he became enmeshed in his complicated relationship with Mrs Wallis Simpson.

However, Wallis Simpson was a divorced woman whose second husband was still alive. Admittedly, adultery was generally accepted as routine among the British upper classes: the anger towards Edward VIII was not provoked by his behaviour but by his failure to be discreet about it. 'No woman should expect to be the only woman in her husband's life', observed Margot Asquith. 'I not only encouraged [H. H. Asquith's] female friends, but posted his letters to them if I found them in my front hall.' The only qualification was that one must keep out of the divorce courts and the newspapers. In this spirit society tolerated a variety of relationships involving married people provided that certain decencies were observed. It was well-established practice among the upper classes to indulge in purely platonic affairs once a wife had become bored with her marriage and had done her duty by providing several children. Nancy, Viscountess Astor, who had married Waldorf in 1904, devoted herself largely to her role as a political hostess and as an MP after 1919. While Waldorf was not especially interested in sex, Nancy frankly disliked it, and she indulged in several safe, platonic affairs, notably with Philip Kerr, Lord Lothian, who shared her enthusiasm for appeasement. Such relationships gave her the intimacy and emotional support of an affair without the risks and the physical complications.

By far the most remarkable such relationship between the wars was that between Edith, Marchioness of Londonderry, and Ramsay MacDonald, the first Labour prime minister. Their affair began in 1924 when they sat together at a dinner at Buckingham Palace. An inveterate hostess and networker, Edith was also gushing, attractive and neglected by her husband. MacDonald, who had never recovered from the death of his wife in 1911, was, for all his political success, a lonely figure and easily flattered. They shared a love of Scotland where both had been brought up. Soon a flirtatious correspondence developed. Edith asked for MacDonald's private address and invited him to 'come and see me sometimes if you're not too busy. I should so much like to see you.' She would write: 'Bless you – all my love is yours', while he replied: 'My Dear, you were very beautiful, and I loved you'.[17] To modern ears these endearments are suggestive, but at the time the language was simply conventional between friends. Things appeared more serious when they stayed at Windsor Castle where he visited the Marchioness's bedroom every night to talk from 11.30 until 2.00 the next morning. The elderly MacDonald may have enjoyed the frisson of this nocturnal prowling through the corridors of the castle, but it seems to have amounted to no more than a sentimental friendship. As the 1930s wore on Edith began to find him a nuisance but she never abandoned the relationship. While the affair damaged MacDonald within the Labour Party, Edith herself attracted no criticism, indeed from one perspective she was playing a proper wifely role as a hostess in promoting her husband's career; as leader of the National Government MacDonald made Londonderry a minister at a time when his own party leaders regarded him as unsuitable material.

Yet MacDonald's liaisons with titled ladies paled into insignificance beside the Olympic-class adulterers of the interwar period: Duff Cooper, David Lloyd George, Sir Oswald Mosley and Lord Londonderry himself. Duff Cooper demonstrated how easy it was for a public person to be a serial philanderer without ever causing scandal or damaging his career. 'If [he] saw a woman who attracted him, he laid siege with every device, and his success rate was very high.'[18] Passionate, charming and chivalrous, Cooper reportedly embarked on his first marital affair during his honeymoon in Venice; he loved the chase, the secret assignations, the love-letters and the challenge of juggling three or four flirtations simultaneously. He got off lightly because his abandoned lovers never resented him. Also, he always returned to his wife, Diana, who was not especially interested in sex and tolerated his philanderings: 'I don't mind adultery', she said, 'I'm not a jealous nature.' Not surprisingly Duff appreciated her attitude: 'She is the only person who is worth making love to, who understands the game and how to play it', he once said.[19]

By contrast, Lloyd George stood outside the upper-class school of adultery. His affair with his secretary, Frances Stevenson, which had begun in 1913, had taken on every appearance of domesticity by the interwar period. While his wife, Margaret, remained largely in North Wales maintaining his constituency links, Frances lived in Surrey where Lloyd George ran his alternative household. An intelligent, emancipated woman, Frances Stevenson had a degree from Royal Holloway College, shared his fascination for politics and was delighted to be invited to act as his secretary-cum-mistress. For a senior politician casual sex posed few risks in this period, but Lloyd George had chosen something different: a permanent relationship that lasted for thirty years until his death. In effect Lloyd George had two wives rather than one wife and a mistress. As his secretary Frances was able to see him regularly without the necessity for clandestine meetings, though things occasionally grew complicated when Mrs Lloyd George entered by the front door as Frances hurriedly left by the back door. By this time Margaret was aware of the situation, but evidently acquiesced because she had the life she wanted and did not wish to share her husband's exhausting metropolitan lifestyle. As a result there was no real risk of the divorce that would have ruined him. Ironically, what damaged Lloyd George eventually was his decision to *marry* Frances after Margaret's death; as so often, the English, and Welsh, felt happier with an adulterous relationship to which they could turn a blind eye.

By contrast with Lloyd George, Charles Vane-Tempest-Stewart, 7th Marquess of Londonderry, came from one of Britain's grandest and wealthiest families. Six feet tall and rakishly thin, he always appeared to be looking down his nose. After a brief career as Air Minister Londonderry acquired a dubious reputation as a pro-Nazi. He managed to live out an Edwardian lifestyle between the wars before it all came crashing down around him in the Second World War. In 1899 he asked his new wife, Edith: 'What is the difference between a March hare and a beautiful woman? One is mad as a hatter, of course, the other is had as a matter of course.' During their engagement he indulged in an affair with Sybil, Lady Westmorland. But Edith, upholding upper-class stoicism, uttered no word of protest: 'Myself, I don't care because I know it is all nonsense . . . Darling you know I don't mind one little bit.'[20] Charley Londonderry's other conquests included Fanny Ward, an American actress known as 'the Eternal Flapper', whom he made pregnant, Consuelo Vanderbilt, an American heiress married to his cousin, the Duke of Marlborough, and Eloise, another American who was the wife of the Earl of Ancaster. During the war he had the cheek to enclose his letters to Eloise to Edith with the request: 'You might send the enclosed to Eloise . . . Put a stamp on and just send it off. That would be very sweet and dear of you.'[21] In his arrogance Charley assumed that all the women in his life would be understanding about his liaisons, and when things became fraught he complained – to Edith of all people – 'Why can they never make the best of things?' Edith, like Diana Cooper, never issued an ultimatum and always forgave her husband: 'I want you so much that I do not mind what you do.' She was so much in love that she found it easier to find excuses for him: 'I don't blame you because the women hunt you to death. You are so beautiful.' [22]

As a public figure Londonderry was never damaged by his behaviour because he played by the rules. By contrast, Sir Oswald Mosley, in many ways very similar, did overstep the mark. The product of a Staffordshire gentry family, Mosley had served in the army and the Royal Flying Corps and emerged from the war a glamorous figure much in demand by the leading political hostesses. Cheerfully describing his pursuit of married women as 'flushing the covers', Mosley had complete contempt for what he regarded as middle-class notions of moral behaviour. When he met his wife, Lady Cynthia Curzon, in 1919 Mosley undertook to give up his philandering to concentrate on his political career. He claimed to have told Cynthia about all his other women when they married; but on being challenged about this he admitted: 'well, all except her stepmother and her sister'.[23] In fact the only restraint on Mosley's moral conduct was the Labour Party which he joined in 1924. Recognising that in the puritanical atmosphere of his new party he could not expect to get away with affairs with the wives of his colleagues, Mosley decided to confine his philandering to the upper classes: 'Vote Labour – Sleep Tory' as he put it.

However, things got out of control in the spring of 1932 when he met the 21-year-old Diana Mitford, the wife of Bryan Guinness. Keen to escape from a boring marriage, Diana responded eagerly to overtures from the handsome, confident, dynamic Mosley. But they disregarded the rules of the game. As a married man Mosley already had his own flat in Ebury Street, but to facilitate his visits Diana moved out of her marital home into a flat only five minutes away in Eaton Square. She proceeded to seek a divorce from the compliant Bryan who agreed to offer false evidence of his own infidelity to save her from a court appearance. To make matters worse, although Lady Cynthia died in 1933, Mosley did not marry Diana until 1936 in the home of Joseph Goebbels in Berlin. 'Tom Mosley is a cad and a wrong un', as Stanley Baldwin put it. In the eyes of his critics Mosley's willingness to flout conventional moral codes was all of a piece with his opportunism in deserting both the Conservative and Labour parties for fascism.

Yet these examples of brazen male infidelity cannot obscure the fact that this emancipated era produced several notable female adulterers too. Lady Dorothy Macmillan, a daughter of the Duke of Devonshire, had married a junior officer, Harold Macmillan, in April 1920. This was another union between a masterful, aristocratic woman and a bookish, bourgeois man who was still shattered by his war wounds and entirely lacking the self-confidence he displayed later in life. Macmillan, whose previous knowledge of women was almost nil, admitted to being frightened by the female sex. After some years of marital bliss the outgoing and highly sexed Lady Dorothy grew tired of Harold's devoted love; their marriage seemed too bourgeois and his dogged career as MP for Stockton became boring. In 1929 she seduced Robert Boothby, the raffish, good-looking Tory MP for East Aberdeenshire. Widely tipped as a future prime minister, Boothby was a far more exciting figure than Harold, and he was much more interested in sex.

However, even Boothby found Lady Dorothy rather a handful both literally and metaphorically: 'She never suffered a pang of remorse . . . absolutely none about me or Harold.'[24] Whenever the unmarried Boothby met a potential wife she forced him to break the engagement, at least until 1935 when he finally married her cousin. But their affair, which became widely known in society circles, continued until

Dorothy's death in 1966, severely damaging Boothby's political career in the process. During this period Lady Dorothy barely maintained appearances. 'I am faithful to Bob', she insisted. She managed a double life, running Harold's household but spending as much time with Boothby as possible. It was widely believed that her daughter, born in 1930, was Boothby's child and that by acknowledging this she was trying to push her husband into a divorce. For his part Harold considered divorce but shrank from the prospect of losing his wife and so settled for a celibate life. 'She filled my life', he explained, 'I thought in everything I did of her . . . I told her I'd never let her go.' [25] His stoicism and determination to maintain his marriage created nothing but sympathy and admiration for him.

By sticking to one lover Lady Dorothy Macmillan was comparatively restrained. No such inhibitions troubled Edwina Mountbatten. After her glamorous marriage in 1922 she, too, quickly became bored, especially as Dickie's career in the navy took him away from home for long periods. Meanwhile Edwina consoled herself with dozens of admirers, known as 'ginks' in the private slang of the Mountbatten circle, who were attractive, unattached men ready to escort her to parties in the absence of her husband; by keeping several of them in tow at once she indicated that she was not available. For his part, Dickie regarded Edwina's friendships as unwise but innocent.[26] However, the marriage soon began to collapse. With nothing to do except enjoy herself and spend money Edwina went in search of men who possessed the sexual drive and self-assurance her husband seemed to lack.

From early 1925 she plunged into a series of serious affairs, beginning with Hugh, Lord Molyneux, and she and Dickie largely abandoned physical relations with one another. Hot on the heels of Molyneux came Laddie Sanford who was constantly to be seen going in and out of Brook House until the early hours; even when Dickie was at home Laddie was entertained there, and he clearly became aware of the relationship. From the late 1920s to the 1930s Edwina enjoyed relationships with Mike Wardell, Larry Gray, Gray Phillips and his brother Ted 'Bunny' Phillips. But as Edwina proved unable to confine herself to one lover at a time, things sometimes grew com-plicated; on one occasion a flustered servant at Brook House reported that he had shown Lord Molyneux into the morning room, and Mr Sanford into the library: 'but where should I put the other gentleman?' Although Edwina was not especially discreet, her great wealth and a largely respectful press enabled her to avoid serious scandal. She was rumoured to be involved with Douglas Fairbanks, and in 1932 the *People*'s gossip columnist ran a story suggesting that a lady who was easily identifiable as Edwina was having an affair with Paul Robeson, the black American actor. She sued and cleared her name. Meanwhile the Mountbattens decided to stay together as a matter of convenience; this preserved his career and reputation while she agreed not to complain about his absences in the navy!

Although the Londonderrys and Mountbattens remained resolutely hostile to divorce, other sections of British society were less willing and less able to sustain marriages that had ceased to work. As a result the period saw two successful attempts to change the divorce law in 1923 and 1937. In the immediate post-war years all the feminist pressure groups identified the equalisation of the law on divorce between men and women as a key target. However, the subject had rarely been discussed by Parliament. Before 1857 divorce was obtainable only by a complex and expensive three-stage process: first a couple sought a separation from the Church courts, then the husband prosecuted the adulterer for damages, and finally a private bill was put through Parliament. Not surprisingly, the entire period from the Reformation to 1857 saw only 300 divorces in Britain. The 1857 Matrimonial Causes Act excluded the Church and allowed a husband to divorce his wife for adultery; but a wife could not obtain a divorce without proving adultery plus a further offence.

Despite the proposals made by a Royal Commission in 1909 no further change was made until 1923 when two Liberal backbenchers, Major C. F. Entwhistle and Isaac Foot – governments refused to touch the issue – introduced a simple bill to enable a woman to obtain a divorce on grounds of adultery alone. Arguing that this would remove an anomaly, they pointed out that even the Church of England now accepted the general principle of equal treatment between the sexes. The chief opponent, the anti-feminist MP, Dennis Herbert, warned against making divorce too easy. Revealing his unspoken male assumptions, he demanded: 'Is there any man in this House who is the father of a son and a daughter who would regard the sin of adultery on the part of his son as being as severe as the sin of adultery on the part of his daughter?'[27] But when Herbert claimed that divorce did not ruin a man's reputation as it did a woman's, members interrupted to shout: 'It should do.' There was little serious opposition and the House approved the bill by 231 votes to 27.

Despite this, English law still recognised sexual misconduct as the only sufficient grounds for divorce; a husband might have any number of vices, but without proof of adultery his wife would be unable to get rid of him. It was not until 1937 that an Independent MP, A. P. Herbert, presented a Matrimonial Causes Bill designed to allow alternative grounds, notably desertion for three years, cruelty, habitual drunkenness, incurable insanity, non-consummation, rape, sodomy, bestiality and venereal disease. As is obvious from this catalogue, the beneficiaries of this legislation were overwhelmingly women. As things stood couples whose marriage had broken down were unable to escape from it except by proving adultery by one partner. This frequently led people either to commit adultery or to perjure themselves in court. Solicitors routinely arranged things by booking a hotel room for the husband and paying a chambermaid to certify his presence there to convince the courts that misconduct had taken place. In 1922 when the scientist J. B. S. Haldane wanted to marry an already married woman he enlisted a private detective (who was already employed by the husband!), and informed him of the hotel, including the room number, in which he intended to commit adultery. Duff Cooper recorded how a friend of his organised his divorce by adjourning to a flat he had booked at the Savoy where he was to meet a woman he had never seen before and spend the night with her accompanied by a detective who would collect the 'evidence'. In the event, 'I gathered that after a great deal of champagne he had contrived to commit the necessary crime in very deed.'[28] In effect, as A. P. Herbert observed, the law promoted immorality: 'we are rapidly reaching a situation in which no stigma whatever will attach to a public confession of adultery'.[29]

This was the strategy adopted in connection with one of the most crucial divorces of the interwar period – that of Mr Ernest Simpson in 1936. As the compliant husband of Wallis Simpson he provided the necessary evidence of a night spent at a hotel with another woman despite the fact that, as far as is known, the only adultery committed was by his wife with the Prince of Wales. However, even this routine deception held dangers, for collusion between the parties was a bar to divorce. Also, as Simpson's case resulted in a provisional separation, they had to wait another six months for the full divorce to be granted. If any evidence arose during that time that the supposedly innocent party had also committed adultery this would have upset the whole thing. The law required one guilty party and one innocent party; as Lord Chief Justice Hewart put it: 'if one of two married persons is guilty of misconduct there may properly be divorce, while if both are guilty they must continue to abide in the holy estate of matrimony'. Eventually Mrs Simpson did obtain her divorce, but for six months it remained in doubt whether the then Duke of Windsor would be able to marry her.

Although A. P. Herbert's bill was passed in 1937 and came into operation in 1938, it was noticeable that only ninety MPs turned out to vote on the second-reading division. This probably reflected their embarrassment and fear of provoking criticism in their constituencies. At a personal level divorce was, after all, a sensitive subject for many MPs and peers. However, at least one sitting member, Robert Boothby, managed to escape apparently unscathed. He had eventually married Diana Cavendish in 1935, but, unable to shake off Lady Dorothy Macmillan, he divorced her shortly afterwards. However, Boothby's constituents seemed to tolerate his action, which suggests that public hostility to divorce may have been exaggerated.

However, among members of the Establishment Robert Boothby and Lady Dorothy were not typical. Many people seem to have felt that a stigma attached to divorce. When the brilliant scientist, J. B. S. Haldane, was cited as co-respondent in a divorce case in 1926, the Senate of Cambridge University promptly sacked him from his post as Reader in biochemistry.[30] Agatha Christie discovered that as a divorcee she was barred from accompanying her daughter when she was presented at court. In 1934 when one of Lady Londonderry's daughters wanted to marry a divorced man whose wife was still alive, she regarded the idea as a social disaster: 'he offers her a soiled life', she commented bitterly.[31] When her daughter defied her views, the Londonderrys boycotted the wedding. As an MP from 1919 onwards Nancy Astor initially refused to support legislation for divorce reform despite the fact that she had taken advantage of American law to divorce her first husband. Astor was embarrassed because her correspondence as an MP included letters from women trapped in unhappy marriages who assumed that she would help them.[32] Under pressure she reluctantly voted for the 1923 bill but she prevaricated over any further reforms.

Astor's correspondence suggests that lower down the social scale attitudes were less rigid. Many women wanted a divorce but were deterred by the costs rather than by disapproval. Quite apart from the expense, women faced a barrage of anti-divorce propaganda in the magazines they read. This reflected the belief that if a woman's first object in life was to catch a man, her second aim was to keep him. To this end *Woman's Own* presented features on cosmetics and beauty as 'Looks Do Count After Marriage'. Writers never tired of warning wives not to let themselves go: 'He will notice – none quicker – if you cease to be the attractive, alluring girl he married. Resolve – early in your married life – never to get slack about your appearance.'[33] From this it followed that wives had a responsibility to shore up the institution of marriage by resisting the resort to divorce if things went wrong, and to help a man to avoid the temptation of flirtatious girls who they described as 'vamps'. Women were considered guilty if anything went wrong in their marriage because 'the happily married man has no more inclination to have affairs with any other woman than his wife desires other men'.[34] Barbara Hedworth bluntly told wives: 'Dress for your husband. After all, he pays the bills, and he is the one to please!' Conceding that husbands were susceptible, she insisted: 'Stop to think how often these lapses on the part of a devoted husband are due to the fact that their wives refuse to dress up for them . . . really it was your face, the physical charm of you which first made you attractive and winsome to the man.' In particular Hedworth regarded slippers as symptoms of wifely neglect: 'the wife who greets her spouse in this slovenly type of footwear deserves all she gets'.[35]

A woman's strategy, according to Barbara Cartland, should be to indulge her husband and pander to his selfishness. Laura Sayle reminded women that men needed their sense of freedom, and should therefore be encouraged to feel as though they were still bachelors: 'when you come to think about it the average man gets a fairly raw deal out of marriage in comparison to what he puts into it'.[36] Real women, so the argument ran, happily surrendered their own freedom for 'the spiritual security of someone to look after us', and consequently they should be prepared to put up with a good deal of difficulty in married life because 'a bad husband is better than no husband'.[37]

Yet in the face of all this advice some women were obviously tempted by divorce, including Barbara Cartland herself; and *Woman's Own* tried to stem the trend with articles entitled 'Dragooned into Divorce' and 'I wish I hadn't divorced my husband'. It argued that women should not be misled by relatives and friends into punishing errant males by resorting to the law; rather they were advised to take an understanding view of male psychology: 'Men get these attacks like kiddies get measles . . . Let him have his fling and he'll come back a thousand times more in love with you than ever.'[38] The magazines also employed moral blackmail by reminding women that they were indulging themselves at the expense of their children who would inevitably suffer from the absence of their father, an argument employed by those MPs who opposed the 1937 divorce reform bill.

How far attitudes about marriage and divorce were influenced by Christian thinking on the subject is unclear. Some people certainly believed that the marriage vows – 'till death us do part' – were to be taken literally. However, this exaggerates the real influence of the Church and overlooks the fact that the churches were themselves divided. Only the Catholic Church opposed divorce without reservation. The Nonconformists, on the other hand, accepted the legal reforms of 1923 and 1937. The Church of England, while hostile to divorce in principle, compromised as always. In 1935 Convocation registered a protest at current practice that made divorce by consent quite easy for those who were sufficiently wealthy, and, as a result, A. P. Herbert was able to claim that he had Anglican support for his bill in 1937.

Attitudes also varied according to social class. As we have seen, many of the upper classes took a remarkably relaxed view of marital infidelity but saw divorce as shameful. As marriage was still regarded as the only career open to girls at this level of society they were taught to make the best of it. It is usually believed that working-class communities also saw divorce as a disgrace and as a mark of failure for a woman, though views were probably coloured by the expense it entailed as much as by the morality. In fact, while the 1937 reform did not increase the total number of divorces very greatly, it did alter the grounds of divorce such that by the 1950s twenty-three per cent of all divorces were obtained on grounds of cruelty, many brought by working-class wives against drunken and violent husbands.

Between the wars contemporaries thought that it was among middle-class people that divorce was becoming more acceptable. This may be partly because some middle-class women saw better opportunities for employment and thus for an independent life. Certainly several of the prominent divorcees of the period had empowered themselves by means of successful careers. For example, in 1928 Gracie Fields had married the comedian and theatrical manager, Archie Pitt, who was ten years her senior. Describing the marriage as 'a star-spangled humiliation', she sued for divorce in April 1939 claiming that she had left him in 1932 due to her unhappiness and had had no communications since.[39] When her petition was heard in July Archie was alleged, on evidence supplied by Gracie's private detective and a chambermaid (who had been paid), to have been unfaithful with his secretary at a hotel in Hastings in October 1938. Gracie, now forty-one, was awarded a decree nisi and costs although she was herself conducting an open relationship with one Monty Banks, which was not mentioned in court.

The perils of divorce were even better illustrated by one of the least expected divorcees of the interwar period: Barbara Cartland. To judge from her own copious writings she should have been prepared to endure marital infidelity to preserve her marriage to Alexander McCorquodale. But she discovered that he was a serial adulterer after finding love letters from married women in his desk, including plans to abduct her daughter, Raine. But when Cartland sued for divorce in 1933 McCorquodale counter-sued on the grounds that his cousin, Hugh, had made daytime visits to Barbara's bedroom. This was doubly difficult for Barbara since she had little money; but Sir Patrick Hastings QC agreed to take her case without a fee. She explained in court that as a writer she used her bedroom as a place of work; she received guests there; she called everyone 'darling', kissed everyone and plied all her visitors with cocktails![40] Luckily for her the judge, Lord Merrivale, advised the jury that this was normal behaviour for a literary lady; and the jury took only fifteen minutes to find in her favour! Wisely Cartland then waited for three years before marrying Hugh McCorquodale to whom she remained married for twenty-eight years.

Then there was the strange case of Agatha Christie. After marrying Colonel Archie Christie in 1914 at the age of twenty-four, Agatha gave every appearance of being a conventional woman. Her mother had advised her that in the early stages of marriage she should be careful not to neglect her husband or afford him any opportunity for finding other women.[41] However, like many ex-soldiers, Archie found it difficult to settle into civilian life again in the 1920s. As he managed to earn only a modest salary in the City, they could afford no more than a small flat. Yet Agatha was obliged to behave as a lady of leisure, employing a maid and a nurse; this was partly a matter of social status and also a necessary boost to Archie's vulnerable male pride.[42] In 1926 Archie told her he no longer loved her and admitted to an affair. By this time Agatha was thirty-six, an established author and much more self-confident. But she did not proceed immediately to a divorce. In December 1926 she left home and disappeared for eleven days. After abandoning her car at the roadside near Guildford Agatha made her way to Harrogate where she checked into the Hydropathic Hotel as 'Miss Neele'. Contrary to speculation that she had been so distracted by grief as to be losing her mind, she knew exactly what she was doing. The point was to cause the maximum embarrassment: Neele was the name of Archie's lover. In this way she put the affair into the news-papers and aroused suspicions that Archie had murdered her. Eventually Agatha divorced him in 1928, obtained custody of their daughter and returned to her writing. As a divorcee in her late thirties she was pleasantly surprised to find that men were ready to flirt with her. At forty she started a new phase of life by marrying the archaeologist, Max Mallowan, who was fourteen years her junior.

However, despite these divorces by successful career women, the legislation of the interwar period did not revolutionise divorce in Britain. Admittedly the 1923 Act seems to have encouraged more women to come forward; by 1924 wives comprised sixty-two per cent of those seeking a divorce compared with forty-one per cent in 1921. But for many people the chief inhibiting factor continued to be the financial implications of being divorced and, more immediately, the cost of obtaining one. Before the war only a quarter of petitioners were from working-class couples, and the Royal Commission of 1909 recommended that they should enjoy the same opportunities as middle-class people. Until 1926 there was provision for legal aid – known as the Poor

Persons Procedure – for anyone whose annual income fell below £50. Even so, in the 1930s a divorce cost around £50, or £100 or more if contested, a deterrent for many people. Also, some people experienced difficulty in finding solicitors willing to accept cases; some firms avoided matrimonial work because they felt it detracted from their standing and even disliked workingmen appearing at their offices.

Wives were often deterred by the arrangements for maintenance after a separation. Before 1920 a wife could be awarded up to £2 a week for her and her children; the 1920 Married Women (Maintenance) Act introduced payments of up to ten shillings per child, and the 1925 Guardianship of Infants Act raised this to £1 maximum. However, for families whose income was already barely sufficient, the enforcement of a maintenance order proved very problematical. In 1923, for example, for every one hundred orders made, forty-six men were subsequently imprisoned for default; by the early 1930s they comprised seven per cent of the entire prison population – clear evidence that desperate men were not deterred from defaulting even by prison.

However, divorce did become more easily available for other reasons. Until 1920 all divorce cases were heard at the High Court in London, but by 1918, when five times as many petitions were heard as before the war, the pressure had become too great. Consequently, cases were heard at the Assize Courts from 1922 onwards, and the system was fully decentralised by 1926, reducing costs in the process. One beneficiary was Wallis Simpson who obtained her decree nisi at Ipswich in 1936.

Despite this, the increase in divorces was modest. During the early 1920s the annual total ran at 2,800 for England and Wales, rising to over 4,000 in the later 1920s and early 1930s. Put another way, a mere two per cent of marriages contracted in 1926 ended in divorce after twenty years, and only six per cent of those contracted in 1936. Such figures make interwar Britain look like a golden age for marriage at least in terms of its stability. In earlier periods of history marriage had been cut short by the death of one partner after a few years; but growing longevity meant that it lasted much longer and was thus increasingly exposed to the chance of breakdown. It was not the liberalisation of the law but wider social change that eventually made divorce much more common in Britain. The disruption to relationships caused by the Second World War greatly increased the divorce rate during the late

1940s, but the total diminished to 32,000 annually in the early 1950s and 27,000 in the late 1950s.

While recognising the deterrents to wives who contemplated divorce, one should not overlook the positive changes that made married life more attractive than it had been. Although the lot of married women appears hard from late twentieth-century perspectives, for younger women the relevant comparison was with the experience of their own mothers. There are grounds for thinking that between the wars many women began to experience a more companionable relationship with their husbands. One indication of their aspirations was the popular response to the little book, *Married Love*, published by Marie Stopes in 1918. Stopes painted a very positive picture of the married relationship, emphasising particularly that couples should aim to enjoy their physical relationship without the constant fear of pregnancy that had dominated the lives of their parents. Those women who married between the wars had, on average, fewer than half the babies produced by their Victorian predecessors. As a result, women completed their families, on average, by the age of twenty-eight, their lives were not dominated by endless childbirth and child-rearing, and their health improved.

This crucial change was complemented by other trends that assumed especial significance for women. The construction of new higher-standard housing and slum clearance made a considerable impact on those who spent a high proportion of their lives in the home. Improvements in leisure activities such as the spread of the wireless was a boon to many housewives. Increasingly, too, husbands and wives spent time together either on home decoration and gardening, or on going out together to the pub and the cinema, where previously men were more likely to disappear with other male friends. While this does not mean that husbands became more domesticated in the sense of sharing household duties with their wives, it does indicate that their marriages were gradually becoming more companionate and more satisfactory for their wives.

Among younger couples relations moved a long way from the Victorian patriarchal marriage towards a more equal partnership between the wars. Jennie Lee, a miner's daughter who attended university, worked as a teacher and got elected as MP for North Lanark in 1929–31, continued to pursue her political career despite marrying

Aneurin Bevan in 1934. Although they lived together from 1933 onwards, Jennie never became Nye's housekeeper: 'I was as helpless as an old-fashioned male', she claimed. Once married she employed a girl for housework, and a boy for the gardening, and her mother moved in to cook for them. Nye was heard to say that he had to marry Jennie in order to get his mother-in-law.[43] Of course, theirs was not an approved form of marriage: in the eyes of Bevan's family he needed a proper wife; Jennie had no children, was regarded as promiscuous, and flaunted her independence. Although he liked children, they seem to have accepted that their two careers would have made motherhood too complicated; but she never contemplated abandoning her political ambitions to promote his: 'I'm not his secretary', she would say. Later in life Nye told her approvingly 'you are my sister', meaning his friend as well as lover; while she evidently agreed: 'To Nye I was friend and mistress – never wife. The very word offended me.'[44] Neither had wanted a conventional marriage; on the one hand they valued highly their privacy as a couple, but on the other, they placed little importance on sexual fidelity.

Another untypical but perhaps more indicative marriage was that between Vera Brittain and George Catlin in 1924. Though ostensibly concentrating on establishing herself as a writer in the post-war years, Vera entertained conventional aspirations to marriage and mother-hood. After several years living with Winifred Holtby, also a novelist, she accepted Catlin's proposal on the slender basis of a correspondence lasting a year and a mere five days spent together in June 1924. From the start it was understood that both partners would pursue their careers, he as an academic at Cornell University and she as novelist and journalist. However, after spending a year with him in America, Vera decided to return to Britain for the autumn-winter of 1926 with a view to returning for the spring-summer of 1927.

This did not mean their marriage was over, simply that Vera was having it on her own terms. She lived mainly in Britain, had children in 1927 and 1930, and joined George in his university vacations.[45] Vera refused to accept that a woman must either sacrifice her career for a life of domesticity or forget marriage to concentrate on her own work: 'Few people appear as yet to understand how wicked is this alternative.' She insisted that the dilemma could be solved as long as marriage was not regarded as 'a day by day, hour by hour, unbroken and unbreakable association'. Writing in 1928 she advocated a 'semi-detached' marriage. Admittedly Catlin found what he called 'this strange equal comradeship' hard to adjust to, especially as he felt that Vera's reputation damaged his own political career. However, their marriage was not simply the product of Vera's idiosyncrasy; it was symptomatic of a wider shift away from the unequal Victorian-Edwardian style of marriage towards a looser partnership. Between the wars few women managed to combine marriage, motherhood and employment as successfully as she did, but in the long run many more would aspire to do so.

8

'Abnormalities of the brain': Sex, Sexuality and Gender Confusion

Before 1914 the discussion of sexuality in Britain was largely confined to small groups of intellectuals, socialists and feminists including G. B. Shaw, Bertrand and Dora Russell, Edward Carpenter, author of *The Intermediate Sex*, and Havelock Ellis, author of *The Psychology of Sex*. Arousing wider public interest was difficult – and dangerous. Anyone caught publishing literature on birth control, for example, ran the risk of being prosecuted for obscenity. Scotland Yard kept a watch on the pressure group, the Legitimacy League, which campaigned to reform the law on marriage, divorce and bastardy, on the assumption that anyone with unconventional opinions on sex must also harbour politically subversive notions such as anarchy. Undeterred, Edward Carpenter and Laurence Housman founded the British Society for the Study of Sex Psychology in July 1914 to promote a more rational or 'scientific' approach and, in particular, to educate the public about female sexuality, birth control, homosexuality and the factors influencing sexuality. However, although active during the 1920s, when it became the British Sexological Society, it recruited only about 250 members. In these circles feminists such as Stella Browne, Dora Marsden and Dora Russell challenged the assumption that women were sexually passive, and advocated freedom for women to choose whether to become pregnant by adopting birth control. But they were not typical of pre-war British feminists, most of whom feared that to remove the prospect of conception from sex would merely encourage men to make demands upon women; the aim, in their view, should be to get men to live up to the higher standards of women by exercising restraint in sexual matters.

Victorian attitudes were also challenged by the followers of Freud who helped to make it easier, even fashionable, to discuss sex and promoted the view that it should be accepted without guilt as a central aspect of human existence. However, critics accused 'Freudians' of being obsessed with sex and encouraging the uninhibited pursuit of sexual desires. Although Freud's methods were adopted by psychologists in treating shell-shocked patients during and after the war, knowledge about his ideas was very limited even in the 1920s.

In fact, the only group that had any success in making interest in sexual issues respectable in this period was the Eugenics Society, founded in 1907. This was because it reflected a wide concern in Victorian-Edwardian society about the deterioration of the population, and it succeeded in popularising the idea that the national interest could be served by selective breeding and by preventing reproduction by the 'feeble-minded' and the racially impure. Evidence from the census showed that during the 1870s some middle-class couples had begun to practise birth control, a trend that stimulated fears that the most intelligent and enterprising section of the population was now dwindling. As a result eugenics became fashionable in smart circles. One actress famously wrote to George Bernard Shaw suggesting they should have a baby because the combination of her looks and his intelligence would produce a perfect specimen. Shaw replied: 'But what if it had *my* looks and *your* intelligence?'

As a remedy for national decline eugenics attracted support from Fabian socialists like Sidney Webb, reformers like William Beveridge and Conservative politicians like A. J. Balfour. As they saw it the state had a duty to ensure that thrifty, industrious and intelligent people produced children and that the feeble, ignorant and dissolute did not. Eugenicists were encouraged in 1909 when Lloyd George introduced income tax allowances for middle-class earners with children under sixteen and by the maternity benefit in his 1911 National Insurance Act. However, some favoured more drastic methods such as the compulsory sterilisation of anyone held to be suffering hereditary defects. Not surprisingly, the cause of eugenics was hopelessly handicapped by the patronising attitude adopted by its adherents towards the behaviour of ordinary men and women; in effect they aspired to regulate sexual behaviour. As a result, even in the 1920s the Eugenics Society had only 1,200 members and it proved more of a hindrance to the general adoption of birth control than a help.

The eugenicists were overtaken by the Great War which had the effect of stimulating a wider discussion about sex and immorality in Britain. Authority was alarmed by the sight of thousands of young men gathering at barracks and training centres and young working girls with money in their pockets looking for a good time. 'The girlhood of the country was thrown off balance [by] the crowds of khaki-clad men who were gathering together to fight for King and Country', complained the *Church Family News* in 1915. 'This unfortunately in many instances was expressed by foolish, giddy, irresponsible conduct'.[1] In particular the sight of young men and women canoodling in parks and in darkened cinemas was interpreted as proof of immoral conduct. As a result, during 1915 patrols of women police were instituted in these areas, though to little effect. More drastic measures were adopted in places where large numbers of young people gathered; in Cardiff, for example, women were banned from public houses and the streets after seven each evening, and in Grantham women were restricted to their homes from eight in the evening to seven the next morning.

The moralists felt vindicated when, nine months after the outbreak of war, it emerged that the departing volunteers had left thousands of unmarried mothers behind them. Opinion was divided about this, however. Patriots welcomed the 'War Babies' as a contribution to the national effort; and the newly formed National Council for the Unmarried Mother campaigned for allowances to be paid by the state and maintenance collected from the fathers. But the older generation felt that youth was getting out of hand as the war disrupted the normal controls over their behaviour.

In this situation the army tried to help by instituting a mass distribution of condoms to the troops departing for the front. 'In this new experience', warned Lord Kitchener, 'you may find temptations both in wine and women. You must entirely resist both temptations, and while treating all women with perfect courtesy, you should avoid any intimacy.' In effect, as the authorities took it for granted that the men would visit French brothels, condoms were simply a prophylactic against venereal disease which was a massive and persistent problem in the British Army. In the event one soldier in five returned home suffering from VD. At least their experience abroad had important post-war consequences for thousands of young husbands who had familiarised themselves with one method of contraception. However, although the mass manufacture of condoms reduced the price, many men were reluctant to pay for them. Also, as condoms were still associated with illicit sex, not all men were willing to admit to being familiar with them to their wives and girlfriends.

War experience may have been more significant in changing the aspirations of young women many of whom left employment in which they were rather isolated to work in huge factories. In these conditions information about pregnancy and methods of birth control spread much more rapidly. As a result, after 1918 when young women abandoned employment for domesticity, they seemed keen on getting married but equally determined to avoid the life of endless childbirth that their mothers had endured. In the 1920s young wives were known to attend local maternity clinics for advice about birth control without telling their disapproving mothers-in-law and grandmothers.

As in many areas of life there was now a divergence in attitude between the generations. For example, older people felt very unsettled about the gender confusion supposedly caused by the war. Women had abandoned their normal role, not only by taking industrial jobs usually done by men, but by donning uniforms in the Women's Legion, Women's Volunteer Reserve, Women's Land Army, Women Police Volunteers, Women's Army Auxiliary Corps, Women's Royal Naval Service and Women's Royal Air Force. Many men, especially those who had not served in the forces, interpreted these uniforms as a reproach to their masculinity. One husband refused to allow his wife to join the WRAF, saying: 'Madam, my wife is a truly feminine woman!' Lady Londonderry noticed that when she wore her Women's Legion uniform porters squeezed her out of lifts, and she was once told to use the tradesmen's entrance by a maid who explained: 'I thought you was one of them 'orrible army women!' As a result the 1920s saw a sharp reaction against what Charlotte Haldane called 'the war-working type of women – aping the cropped hair, the great booted feet and grim jaw, the uniform, and if possible the medals of the military man'.[2]

Respectable society found proof of its fears in the revelations about the life of Valerie Arkell-Smith during the 1920s. In the course of her wartime work as a VAD, when she drove ambulances in France and worked at a remount depot in Bristol, she had discovered that it suited her to dress as a man and to be treated as one. Arkell-Smith hated women's clothes – 'these horrid things' – and quickly saw that it was easier to get a job if people took her for a man. She married a businessman, Harold Arkell-Smith, but in 1923 she left him for a Miss Hayward. The two women eloped to Brighton – naturally – where they checked in at the Grand Hotel. Valerie married Miss Hayward at St Peter's Church and they lived in Hove where she found work as an actor in male parts. For the next six years she masqueraded variously as Sir Victor Barker, Captain Barker and Ivor Gauntlet. Subsequently Valerie parted from her wife but lived with another woman as man and wife in Rupert Street, Soho. While there she joined the National Fascisti in 1926–7. Once again, the uniform was part of the attraction: 'I am quite certain', she wrote, 'that they never suspected my sex. Believe me, a pair of trousers makes a wonderful difference to matters of this kind.'[3] In fact the discovery of Valerie Arkell-Smith's real sex arose through her repeated appearances in court, though for some time court searches failed to uncover the truth. Eventually after becoming involved in bankruptcy proceedings while working at the Regent Palace Hotel in Piccadilly she was detained at Brixton for contempt of court; as a result she was transferred to the women's prison at Holloway and eventually prosecuted for making a false declaration on a marriage certificate.

The notoriety of the Arkell-Smith case merely underlined the warnings already issued to women against attempting to compete with or imitate men. In *Feminism and Sex Extinction* (1920), Arabella Kenealy advocated a return to femininity and conventional behaviour before it was too late. For contemporaries it was not just that the 'masculine' girl would be unable or unwilling to have a large family; as girls became boyish they undermined masculinity, encouraging the emergence of the passive, languid, effeminate male. 'Men must look to their laurels', pronounced Kenealy, 'for truly these weak-chinned, neurotic young men of the rising generation are no match for the heavy-jawed, sinewy, resolute young women Feminism's aims and methods are giving us.'[4]

Such fears help to explain the intolerance towards unconventional sexual behaviour during the 1920s and in particular the growing concern about 'sexual inversion' in both sexes. For the first time politicians began to denounce lesbianism in Parliament. During the Victorian and Edwardian periods society had largely failed even to recognise the idea; in 1885 when Parliament was amending the punishments for homosexual behaviour, Queen Victoria had reportedly told Gladstone that no reference should be made to women in the legislation on the grounds that as sex between females was a physical impossibility it was unwise to put ideas into people's heads. However, this attitude made it comparatively easy for unmarried women to live together without attracting hostile comment. Society was more inclined to make fun of unmarried suffragettes such as the composer, Dame Ethel Smyth, who was routinely satirised for her masculine style comprising a severe tweed suit, battered hat and cigarette. In fact, Smyth was an unapologetic lesbian: 'from the first my most ardent sentiments were bestowed on members of my own sex', she wrote.[5] Between the wars she continued to engage in passionate relationships with women, Virginia Woolf being one of her targets.

However, post-war society was much less tolerant of lesbian relationships because they were now identified as a threat. Consequently, when MPs debated the Criminal Law Amendment Bill in 1921 they voted by 148 to 53 to criminalise sexual acts between women. F. A. Macquisten urged the House to 'do its best to stamp out an evil which is capable of sapping the highest and best in civilisation'. Sir Ernest Wild reported that asylum doctors had assured him that institutions were 'largely peopled by nymphomaniacs and people who indulge in this vice'. Lt Col Moore-Brabazon, who opposed the amendment on lesbians, insisted that the cause lay in 'abnormalities of the brain' and argued that the only solutions were to ignore it, to lock up lesbians as lunatics, or to impose the death penalty on them.[6] In the event the proposal was rejected by the House of Lords on the grounds that the publicity would simply make lesbianism seem glamorous to young women presently ignorant of it.

However, the debate underlined how much more difficult it was for women who wished to live together in the hostile moral climate of the early 1920s. In political circles the outrage of middle-class people towards what they saw as the moral laxity among both upper and working classes was articulated by Sir William Joynson-Hicks, a puritanical and reactionary figure who served as Home Secretary from 1924 to 1929. One of Joynson-Hicks's targets was the novelist, Radclyffe Hall, a lesbian who adopted men's suits and the cropped hairstyle and liked to be addressed as 'John'. She had a relationship with Una Troubridge, the wife of Admiral Troubridge, who advised her to seek treatment for her 'nerves'; a fashionable doctor recommended psychoanalysis which helped her to realise that she was a lesbian.

In 1928 Radclyffe Hall published *The Well of Loneliness* which told the story of a masculine woman and a feminine woman struggling to find happiness in a hostile environment. Apart from kissing, the novel described no physical activity and only briefly suggested a love scene with the words: 'and that night they were not divided'. But although Radclyffe Hall was already a successful novelist, her book was rejected by four publishers before Jonathan Cape accepted it. However, Joynson-Hicks, fearful of the depraving effect the novel would have on young readers, was keen to ban it. As 4,000 copies had sold almost immediately, the Home Secretary and the Lord Chancellor demanded that Cape withdraw it, threatening to prosecute for obscenity; ministers felt confident that a prosecution would succeed as they had already obtained the agreement of the Bow Street magistrates! Eventually the publishers backed down but the text was smuggled to France where an English edition was printed. In October 1928 300 of these copies were seized by customs at Dover, and in November the magistrates ordered all copies destroyed on the grounds that Radclyffe Hall 'had not stigmatised this [lesbian] relationship as being in any way blameworthy'.

Inevitably the heavy-handed action of the government publicised the cause of lesbians, and also inspired the author, Compton Mackenzie, to write *Extraordinary Women*, a humorous story about lesbians living on an island in the Mediterranean. When MPs complained that this was pornography, the Director of Public Prosecutions, Sir Archibald Bodkin, read the book and admitted it indicated 'a wider spread of the disease than would have been thought possible and . . . curiosity might lead to practice'. However, Bodkin advised against prosecution because, unlike Hall, Compton Mackenzie made fun of lesbianism rather than defending it.

Not surprisingly, most female homosexuals kept a low profile between the wars. The wealthier ones met privately in certain nightclubs, and provided they did not draw attention to themselves by their masculine dress, they largely escaped attention. The novelist, Vita Sackville-West, famous for her garden at Sissinghurst in Kent, was a passionate lesbian who remained feminine in appearance. Vita was already in love with a woman in 1913 when Harold Nicolson, the diplomat and MP, proposed to her: 'It is a wild person you are going to marry', she told him. Despite this warning there was only one real crisis in their marriage in January 1921 when Vita eloped with Violet Trefusis from Dover, hotly pursued by Violet's husband and her father, George Keppel. Mr Keppel had approached Scotland Yard who had the ports watched in an effort to prevent the couple leaving the country. Eventually all the parties, including Harold, met up at Amiens to arrange the return to England.

In fact the marriage not only survived but was regarded by Vita and Harold as a great success. 'Vita is absolutely devoted to Harold', commented her mother, 'but there is nothing sexual between them . . . she is not in the least jealous of him and willingly allows him to relieve himself with anyone.'[7] Vita saw nothing shocking in the fact that Harold was attracted to men. Treating sex in an entirely matter-of-fact way, they were unfaithful by mutual agreement. Aware that most people would have regarded their behaviour as scandalous, they felt no guilt: 'I don't want to boast', wrote Vita, 'but we *are* alive, aren't we?' Ultimately the relationship survived because their wealth enabled Harold and Vita to lead separate but married lives.

Male homosexuals had to be more careful as they ran the risk of blackmail and imprisonment. Somerset Maugham, who was promiscuously homosexual during the 1920s, accepted advice to go to France, a move that turned into permanent exile. Quentin Crisp, conspicuous by his long red or purple hair and flamboyantly camp style, regularly got beaten up in the streets of London during the 1930s. This, however, was exceptional; men were able to find partners in bathhouses and hotels without difficulty. Moreover, the enforcement of the law was very erratic as the police rarely entered private houses and usually relied on public complaints or second-hand information before taking action. When they felt under pressure to secure more convictions the police patrolled public places including Hyde Park, Piccadilly and Charing Cross or sent decoys to public lavatories to entrap homosexuals. However, as entrapment was an incitement to crime it came under severe criticism from the magistrates in the 1920s and the number of arrests had fallen sharply by the end of the decade.

For homosexuals like Harold Nicolson, who were discreet and deliberately confined their relationships to circles in which it was accepted as routine, the risks were slight; Nicolson calculated that by limiting his partners to men from his own social class he minimised the dangers of exposure. Many of the famous poets and novelists of the 1920s including Stephen Spender, Christopher Isherwood, Siegfried Sassoon and E. M. Forster, regarded romantic friendships between boys as routine and encountered no great problems with their sexuality as adults. At Oxford Spender had associated with a group of young men 'for many of whom homosexuality was an almost fashionable phase, if not a matter of sexual identity'. He claimed it was unnecessary to give oneself a label or make a choice; sexuality was regarded as a symptom of the modernisation that was influencing literature and signifying a break with convention in all aspects of life. Like a number of soldiers Sassoon found that his wartime service in the army had 'given a certain legitimacy to his love of men', but it was not until the end of 1918 that he felt able to express it openly; then his love affair with another soldier helped him to forget the horrors he had witnessed in the war.[8]

On the other hand, some men experienced a real crisis over their sexuality during the 1920s. The pessimists who declaimed against the degeneracy of British manhood could point to young men like Oliver Baldwin, the son of prime minister, Stanley Baldwin. Always a rebel, Oliver Baldwin had a traumatic time during the war, first in France in 1917–18, and subsequently as a soldier in the Armenian Army fighting against Turks and Russians in 1920–1, both of whom imprisoned him. He returned to Britain shattered, found his family sceptical about his account of his experiences, and claimed to be suicidal for a time.[9] Baldwin's alienation from his family may have been exacerbated by his homosexuality. It also manifested itself in his politics, for he blamed his father's generation for betraying his own in the war and joined the Labour Party in 1923, even becoming a Labour MP in 1929. Not surprisingly, for Baldwin's critics his political subversion and his moral 'perversion' were symptomatic of the perils facing British youth in the 1920s.

The lives of older men were just as easily wrecked by their sexuality. Lewis Harcourt, a former Cabinet minister and now a viscount, was married with four children. But in February 1922 he was found dead in his bedroom in Brook Street, having taken an overdose of a sleeping draught. This was widely interpreted as suicide, though this view was rejected by the coroner, following accusations of sexual impropriety against him by a young man; similar allegations had been made against Harcourt previously.

There was more certainty about the cause of the ruin of William Lygon, 7th Earl Beauchamp, in 1931. Apparently a happily married man, Beauchamp was a senior figure in the Liberal Party and held public posts in the royal household, as Lord Lieutenant of Gloucestershire, Warden of the Cinque Ports and Chancellor of London University. However, Beauchamp had 'a persistent weakness for footmen' as one contemporary put it; and he behaved very indiscreetly. He was observed at the baths at the Elephant and Castle 'in the act with a boy'.[10] This made Beauchamp vulnerable to his enemies, notably his brother-in-law, the Duke of Westminster, who informed his wife and tried to pressurise his children into testifying against him. Westminster also denounced him to a startled King George V who reportedly replied: 'Why, I thought people like that always shot themselves!' Beauchamp, who contemplated suicide, was obliged to resign from the royal household and to relinquish his public offices, and when Westminster pressed for a warrant to be issued against him, he went into exile in France.[11] In 1936 when Beauchamp's wife died he attempted to return to Britain, but his friends kept him on-board ship at Dover for fear that he would be arrested. Beauchamp died in 1938 and his misfortunes later inspired Evelyn Waugh to write *Brideshead Revisited*.

In this context homosexuals understandably regarded Britain as a repressive and narrow-minded society. By contrast, Stephen Spender, Christopher Isherwood and the painter, Francis Bacon, were delighted by the uninhibited sexuality they found in Hamburg and Berlin, at least under the Weimar Republic. 'Germany's the only place for sex', as one of Spender's characters put it. All the same, they were not deterred from pursuing affairs at home, and, unlike Nicolson, saw no need to confine themselves to a narrow circle. Indeed, they actively sought young working-class men on the grounds that 'sex would have been impossible between two Englishmen of our class', in Spender's words.[12] For Spender and Isherwood this meant experiencing enjoyable sexual adventures with a whiff of danger but little emotional involvement. In parts of London where barracks, docks, hostels and hotels concentrated large numbers of single men, young working-class men traditionally conducted 'trade' with middle-class men for payment. They did not regard engaging in casual sex in this way as incompatible with their masculinity, seeing it simply as an acceptable phase in the years before marriage.[13] Discreet homosexual activity in these areas was not too risky, but most of the writers and intellectuals steered clear of public protests over the treatment of homosexuals and the suppression of novels such as *The Well of Loneliness*.

This was especially true of the uninhibitedly camp Noël Coward whose plays and revues came to be regarded by contemporaries as symptomatic of the degeneracy of the 1920s. After his first involvement with another man in 1914 at the age of fourteen, Coward enjoyed a series of affairs notably with actors including Louis Hayward and Alan Webb in the 1930s, and with John 'Jack' Wilson, an American stockbroker who became his personal manager. He also enjoyed flirtatious relationships with men such as Dickie Mountbatten to whom he wrote letters peppered with 'Dear dainty darling' and 'Love and kisses, bosun Coward'. But he took care to confine himself to circles that were fairly tolerant including the theatre, the cinema, the political establishment and royalty. On a visit to Venice in 1934 Coward was invited on-board ship by Admiral of the Fleet, Sir Dudley Pound, along with Ivor Novello, Douglas Fairbanks and Lady Castlerosse to whom the admiral had rashly given an open guest list. 'Noël, I have a dreadful feeling we've asked too many queers,' Lady Castlerosse confided. 'If we take care of the pansies,' quipped Coward, 'the Pounds will take care of themselves.'[14]

However, Noël Coward's greatest triumph was what he called his 'little dalliance' during 1923 to 1925 with Prince George, better known as the Duke of Kent. The blue-eyed, athletic Prince had a taste for adventure; he drank heavily, experimented with cocaine and was exuberantly bisexual, being especially interested in black women and young men. 'I was told no one – of either sex – was safe with him in a taxi', as one acquaintance put it.[15] Though well known in smart circles, the Duke's affair with Coward was relatively safe. But he cast his net much wider, and in 1932 the royal officials were obliged to spend a substantial sum of money to retrieve his letters to a male lover in Paris. Eventually the Duke covered his tracks by making a conventional royal marriage to Princess Marina in 1934.

However, for all his cultivated camp image Coward remained very circumspect about his sexuality, partly because he was aware of the downfall of Oscar Wilde a generation earlier, and because of the danger of blackmail. He also disapproved of public displays of homosexuality; essentially Edwardian in his outlook, he believed that homosexuals had a responsibility to their friends to be discreet. And though he wrote about homosexuals – in his 1926 play *Semi-Monde* the main characters were lesbians and homosexuals – he avoided writing about homosexual love. As a result, though some of his work remained unperformed during his lifetime, he never became embroiled in controversy in the manner of Radclyffe Hall.

In the context of this flourishing world of alternative sex, official concerns about conventional relations, the birth rate and the population in the post-war period are readily comprehensible. After the war authority correctly sensed that many British citizens were trying to evade traditional restraints and to take control of their lives in sexual matters. Whereas only nineteen per cent of women who married before 1904 had experienced pre-marital sex, thirty-nine per cent of those who married during 1915–25 had done so, and forty-three per cent of those who married during 1924–34. Did this signify a decline in moral standards? One consequence of the more relaxed relationships was a reduction in prostitution which had been a ubiquitous feature of Victorian society. After 1918 prostitutes became less visible, more discreet, and catered to a more limited clientele of older or better-off men.

Despite signs of greater sexual freedom, however, most women lacked any education about sex and childbirth and received little or no information from their parents. In 1915 Frances Stevenson visited a well-educated college friend who told her she had been 'brought up in such ignorance of the world that on her marriage day she knew absolutely nothing of what was expected from a wife to her husband. The consequence was that she was frightened and unhappy.' One domestic servant recalled: 'sex was really out of it . . . right up to the time that my first daughter was born I had an idea they cut you open to get the baby away . . . [the doctor] said "No, the baby would come out where it went in," you know, that kind of thing, and I think that frightened me even more at the time.'[16] Not surprisingly, even in 1938–9 thirty per cent of all women conceived their first child before marriage, and among those under twenty as many as forty-two per cent. This evidence makes the widely endorsed and characteristically

British belief in the importance of pre-marital chastity look rather dubious. In any case, it had always involved double standards in the sense that both sexes regarded chastity as more important for women than for men who were assumed to need the experience or simply to be unable to control themselves. Working-class men in particular were regarded as sexually incontinent, which is why army regiments traditionally maintained their own supply of women for the troops both at home and in the colonies. Double standards were commonly justified on the basis that for women sex was not very important as they did not experience the passion and pleasure that was natural to men. Once married, women usually accepted sex as their duty and considered themselves unusual, or even unnatural, if they enjoyed it. Wives were known to boast about a husband who 'doesn't bother me very much'.

For interwar governments the most worrying evidence of a weakening of traditional behaviour came from the census which showed an inexorable, long-term decline in the birth rate dating from the 1870s; there were 24 births per 1,000 population in 1914, around 20 in 1922–3, and only 16 in 1930. By the late 1920s British women produced on average 2.2 babies by comparison with 5–6 in the Victorian period. The remarkable thing is that this quiet social revolution was accomplished by millions of ordinary couples in the face of hostility or obstructionism from politicians, the churches, the medical profession and the press.

Of course, the trend to smaller families was not unique to Britain. A similar pattern in other Western countries accompanied the shift from rural to urban societies, the decline in infant mortality rates and the realisation that, due to compulsory education, children were no longer an economic asset to their parents. In France, where falling birth rates had preceded those in other countries, interwar governments feared that their manpower was falling dangerously behind that of Germany. The USSR awarded gold medals of Soviet Motherhood to mothers of ten children. In Italy Mussolini was desperate to reverse the falling birth rate by keeping the population in rural areas. The Nazis dismissed married women from employment, offered loans and tax relief for large families, and even imposed extra taxes on childless couples. Despite this the German birth rate fell from thirty-eight in the 1870s to fifteen by 1932, rising to twenty by 1939 because more people were marrying; but average family size continued to decline.

Even in Britain a variety of inducements were employed to promote child-rearing. In January 1919 the *News of the World* offered free willow-pattern tea-trays to 'every proud mother of ten children . . . useful for taking up mother's cup of morning tea'! By 1921 the National Baby Week Council, which had been started during the war, boasted over a million members and 1,000 local committees; it organised baby shows, pram parades, slide lectures and welfare exhibitions. Under the 1918 Maternity and Child Welfare Act governments invested considerable money in local authority clinics for mothers and children with the result that by 1937 fifty-four per cent of mothers attended one. During the 1930s free milk was distributed to children and pregnant women, and efforts were made to persuade mothers to give birth in hospital; between 1927 and 1937 the proportion doing so rose from fifteen to twenty-five per cent. In his 1935 Budget Neville Chamberlain increased the married man's tax allowance and raised allowances in respect of all second and subsequent children: 'I must say that I look upon the con-tinued diminution of the birth rate in this country with considerable apprehension', commented the Chancellor. 'I have a feeling that the time may not be far distant when the countries of the British Empire will be crying out for more citizens of the right breed, and when we in this country shall not be able to supply the demand.'[17]

Yet British women seemed reluctant to follow Chamberlain's appeal to become breeding machines to populate the Empire. The reason seems obvious: the appalling effects of repeated childbirth on their health. This had been highlighted in 1915 when the Women's Co-operative Guild published *Maternity: Letters from Working Women*, a compilation of harrowing first-hand accounts showing how frequent pregnancy caused high infant mortality rates and ruined the health of mothers.

While most politicians remained out of touch, the public mood was brilliantly caught by Marie Stopes in her famous book, *Married Love*, published in March 1918; after six reprints in 1918 alone, the book had sold 400,000 copies by 1923 and a million by 1939. Yet despite its reputation *Married Love* was far from being a manual on birth control. Stopes, who had been trying to find a publisher since 1915, had been advised to publish it in France. Some contemporaries found her use of terms such as 'orgasm' and 'ejaculation' distasteful, and endorsed the Victorian view of contraception as a form of self-abuse on the grounds that it encouraged mutual masturbation. Moreover, the political climate of the 1920s remained hostile, as a health visitor, E. S. Daniels, found in 1922 when she was sacked for giving advice about birth control to her clients. In the early 1920s the Home Office considered banning advertisements for contraceptives and all birth control literature. Rose Witcop and Guy Aldred were prosecuted for obscenity when they circulated a pamphlet on the subject in 1923. Marie Stopes found that several newspapers, including The Times and the Morning Post, refused to accept advertisements for a meeting she organised at the Queen's Hall in London to promote birth control in 1921.

In this repressive context Stopes's tactics were shrewd. She conceived her book as a panegyric on marriage as a patriotic duty: 'More than ever to-day are happy homes needed. It is my hope that this book may serve the state by adding to their numbers. Its object is to increase the joys of marriage, and to show how much sorrow may be avoided.'[18] In Married Love she held out a vision of a more satisfying and loving relationship by removing the element of fear from sexual pleasure. One woman wrote to her to say: 'I am so afraid of conception that I cannot bear for my husband to even speak fondly to me or even put his hand on my shoulder for fear he wants his rights. It is two months since I last allowed him intercourse.'[19] Thousands of letters in this vein arrived in Stopes's post from women who were anxious to be able to enjoy physical relations with their husbands. 'It seems incredible now that this book was such an eye-opener', wrote the novelist, Naomi Mitchison, one of its many enthusiastic readers.[20]

Sophisticated critics such as Bertrand and Dora Russell professed to find Marie Stopes's language overly sentimental and her advice unduly cautious. But her book served a wider purpose. Stopes argued that by deliberately spacing pregnancies each couple would safeguard the woman's health and ensure the survival of more babies; the present haphazard approach to conception did not really serve the national interest. This helped her to disarm critics who assumed that the spread of birth control throughout society would weaken Britain as an industrial and imperial power by reducing her manpower. Many politicians had simply not thought of the idea in such rational terms before. Stopes also helped to remove the stigma attached to birth control and to make the whole subject respectable. She wisely avoided the critical and negative tone adopted by eugenicists who invariably made couples feel guilty for overbreeding. Instead Stopes took an entirely positive view of marriage and of sex within marriage. It was in this sense, rather than at a practical level, that her book represented a breakthrough for birth control.

Marie Stopes's achievement was all the more remarkable because she was not quite what she appeared to be. Though taken as a scientific expert, her degree and her doctorate from London University were in botany; but she was not a doctor of medicine. Though in some ways Stopes seemed an emancipated young woman – she had supported the suffragettes, became a highly educated professional and retained her maiden name after marriage – her Victorian upbringing had taught her that ladies were innocent and pure. Through reading Edward Carpenter's *Love's Coming of Age* (1896) she had come to see Victorian prudery as foolish and to believe that the purpose of sex for women was pleasure, not simply procreation. But at the age of thirty-one she still knew very little about human sex. Stopes had also been influenced by eugenics, as became apparent later in life when she disapproved of her son's girlfriend because she wore glasses – a sure sign of degeneracy! Fortunately she kept eugenics out of her writing.

Marie Stopes met Reginald Ruggles Gates in January 1911; a week later he proposed, she accepted and they married in March. It proved to be a disastrous mistake. The marriage was unconsummated; but for the first year she apparently had no idea that there was anything unusual about it. Five years later when they divorced Stopes was still a virgin but had an intense desire to have children.[21] This was the immediate background to the writing of *Married Love* in 1918. 'In my own marriage', she wrote, 'I paid such a terrible price for sex-ignorance that I feel knowledge gained at such a cost should be placed at the service of humanity.'

Consequently, for all its success, *Married Love* was of limited practical use. To some extent Stopes compensated for its deficiencies in her second volume, *Wise Parenthood*, in which she explained the application of rubber caps and soluble quinine pessaries by women. She discussed the use of the sheath but did not recommend it 'for normal healthy people'. She also condemned coitus interruptus as placing too much strain on both partners. This rather patchy advice by the most widely read advocate of contraception only deepens the mystery: we know that many couples practised birth control during the 1920s and 1930s but we are not entirely sure how they did it. That large numbers of people urgently sought better information and assistance is beyond doubt, for when Stopes opened her first clinic in Holloway 20,000 women turned up for advice in the first 3 months. Their doctors often told them that another pregnancy could be fatal to their health but hardly ever explained how this was to be avoided.

Anecdotal evidence suggests that the higher social classes had practised various methods of birth control for a long time. After the necessary heir had been produced couples avoided the issue by retreating to separate bedrooms, and husbands resorted to mistresses, prostitutes or extramarital affairs. When Cynthia Mosley had her first child in 1921 Margot Asquith was so worried by the effect on her health that she impressed on her the need to avoid becoming pregnant again for several years; drawing on her own experience (two live births and three stillbirths) with former prime minister, H. H. Asquith, Margot enthused: 'Henry always withdrew in time; such a noble man!' How far Sir Oswald co-operated is unknown, but it was two years before Cynthia had her second baby. In 1927 when Edwina Mountbatten's sister, Mary, was about to depart on her honeymoon there was a panic when it was discovered she had forgotten her douche, but Edwina managed to smuggle it into the motor car as the couple waved goodbye.[22]

As far as is known the most common methods of birth control in Britain were abstention from sex, withdrawal and the safe period. Although rubber sheaths, known as 'male appliances', had become increasingly available since the late nineteenth century, they were largely used in the context of extramarital sex. By the late-1920s the first latex condoms, marketed as 'Dreadnoughts' presumably to foster a sense of pride and patriotism among their users, had been introduced; by 1935 the London Rubber Company was manufacturing two million annually. But the packets costs two or three shillings which was not cheap for workingmen. However, attempts to make their sale illegal were frustrated and in 1925 pharmacists were finally allowed to give customers advice about their use.

However, the greatest obstacle was still medical ignorance. Even Marie Stopes, who disapproved of the method, believed that the safe period was the middle of the month when conception was, in fact, most likely to take place. Traditionally birth control had been regarded as a man's responsibility, but increasingly women now took the initiative. Wives commonly resorted to prolonged breastfeeding, the safe period and a range of pessaries, sponges and douches to avoid pregnancy. Discreet advertisements in the women's magazines testified to the demand for these appliances among the middle classes. But desperate working-class wives frequently had recourse to abortion and self-induced miscarriages. In addition to taking the traditional herbal remedies, including penny royal and raspberry leaf, they resorted to laxatives, gin, hot baths and violent exercise, frequently in combination. It is impossible to know how many abortions took place in interwar Britain, though a government committee estimated 40,000 to 66,000 in 1939. Some contemporaries reckoned that a fifth of all pregnancies ended in abortion which suggests that among working-class women it may have been the most common single method of birth control. Certainly when Marie Stopes opened her clinic she was deluged with requests to assist with abortions from women who were unaware that it was a criminal offence or were simply too desperate to care. Miscarriages and abortions were usually performed in the women's own homes not by backstreet abortionists. One East End boy graphically described his mother's successful efforts: 'By means of gin, quinine, jumping down the stairs and similar traditional methods, she managed to abort . . . The foetus, raw and bloody-looking, "came away" to flop on the floor when she was in the kitchen.'[23] In their predicament the women received no assistance from doctors who felt unable to risk an abortion to safeguard a woman's health, even after the 1929 Life Preservation Act which made it unlawful to terminate a pregnancy except to preserve the life of the mother. Although the Abortion Law Reform Association was founded in 1936, it gathered very little support in this period.

Unfortunately, all the effective methods of birth control involved complications and drawbacks. According to the contemporary survey by Margery Spring Rice, even in the late 1930s only a minority of couples who practised birth control used condoms.[24] Some men flatly refused to use them, while others believed sex should be free once they were married. There were also doubts about their effectiveness. Rumour had it that Catholic pharmacists made holes in their condoms and that the government had required manufacturers to include a certain proportion of defective ones so as to stop the population declining! Although women increasingly favoured the cervical cap, they faced conflicting advice about it. Stopes encouraged women to fit it themselves, but it was widely thought that a doctor's help was needed; doctors also argued that she was wrong in advising that the cap could be left in place for several days or even weeks at a time.[25] In view of these difficulties it seems probable that the trend towards smaller families was achieved largely by the increasing use of traditional methods, however ineffective, due to changing attitudes and aspirations, rather than by the application of any novel methods.

Moreover the spread of birth control through society between the wars was limited because lower down the social scale the less effective methods, notably withdrawal, were more commonly adopted. High fertility rates persisted among the families of unskilled manual workers, partly for lack of knowledge and advice, but also because conventional ideas about gender roles survived more strongly. However, behaviour varied even within working-class communities. In Lancashire, where a higher proportion of women traditionally worked in textile mills where they exchanged information, birth control was relatively common; by contrast in mining and agricultural districts, where there was much less opportunity for women to find employment outside the home, family size remained considerably higher.

Even those couples who were keen to limit family size were, to a large extent, on their own. From 1918 onwards governments possessed an ideal means of extending advice to married women through the maternity and child welfare clinics. But for more than a decade after the war every minister for health flatly refused to allow the clinics to give advice on birth control on the grounds that this would be an illegal use of funds as it had not been specified in the Act. This, of course, was a convenient excuse by politicians anxious to avoid controversy. In the Labour Party middle-class feminists pressed repeatedly for a change of policy, but the men who controlled the conference agenda largely managed to exclude birth control from the programme on the grounds that it was not a political question. The truth was that Labour feared antagonising the Catholics who formed a major part of its vote in some regions. In 1926 when the House of Commons voted by two to one against allowing the local authority clinics to give contraceptive advice, only one woman MP, Ellen Wilkinson, voted in favour. Nancy Astor, who found the whole subject embarrassing both personally and politically, resisted pressure to support the proposal: 'Please don't think I am in favour of wholesale knowledge of the methods of birth control', she protested. Astor also opposed the unrestricted sale of contraceptives and refused to become a vice president of the National Birth Control Council. In effect she upheld the Victorian view that these innovations would lower moral standards by encouraging women to behave more like men in sexual matters.

As so often the politicians found it convenient to take refuge behind 'science'. Although, as the census demonstrated, many doctors privately practised birth control, they condemned it in public. Throughout the 1920s the British Medical Association stuck to this position, though the royal physician, Lord Dawson of Penn, spoke out in its favour. Many gynaecologists declared birth control to be physiologically harmful to women and one even claimed to have diagnosed a new complaint called 'Malthusian uterus' caused by contraception. Even those GPs who were sympathetic felt embarrassed by their own ignorance on the subject, the result of the exclusion of instruction about birth control from training courses by the medical schools in the period up to the Second World War. In this situation the small but growing number of female doctors also failed to play a constructive role. Some of them were simply embarrassed by their inability to give the help that female patients expected; but others adopted the traditional feminist argument to the effect that the fear of pregnancy helped to deter husbands from making excessive sexual demands on their wives.

Added to these obstacles was the moral disapproval exerted by the churches. Many Christians held that sex was justified only when procreation was the aim, and that abstinence was consequently the only acceptable method of birth control. In 1908 the Church of England officially pronounced contraception wrong on social, moral and theological grounds, a position it reaffirmed in 1924. Naturally Anglicans were divided, however. While the Bishop of Exeter warned that it would weaken the race, as the French had discovered, the Archbishop of York, William Temple, admitted in 1929 that 'the traditional attitude of the Church on this question is unwarrantable'. Catholics adopted a more censorious view, often regarding contraception as only marginally less abhorrent than abortion. The Catholic clergy not only preached against the practice, but even intervened in elections. In 1935 when Edith Summerskill, who was herself a doctor and an advocate of birth control, stood in Bury in Lancashire, the local clergy delivered an ultimatum to her to recant her views or they would urge Catholics to vote against her; she refused to do so and was heavily defeated.[26]

On the other hand, many Christians paid lip service to the advice issued by their clergy. Although the Catholic Church made people feel guilty about birth control, it often failed to change their behaviour even in Spain and Italy where birth rates continued to fall rapidly. In 1925 when a clinic was opened in Manchester, local Catholics organised protest meetings but this only had the effect of encouraging Catholic women to attend.[27] On Merseyside Catholic wives were known to practise self-induced miscarriage on the basis that this was acceptable because it was not actually contraception.

Eventually most of the religious, medical and political authorities retreated from their official opposition because they realised that they were being ignored and becoming discredited as a result. In 1923 *Married Love* was turned into a film called *Masie's Marriage* with a view to popularising the idea of the small, planned family to a wider audience. T. P. O'Connor, the Catholic chairman of the British Board of Film Censors was eager to stop the circulation of *Masie's Marriage*, but he found few grounds for doing so, and after no fewer than four viewings the film was granted an 'A' certificate. O'Connor banned the use of Stopes's name or *Married Love* in the film, but cinema proprietors circumvented this by referring to them in their promotional material.

To some extent official obstructionists were undermined by the establishment of voluntary birth control clinics by Marie Stopes in Holloway in 1921, in Walworth in 1922, in Kensington in 1924 and Manchester in 1925. By the end of the decade nearly twenty clinics were operating. However, after the 1929 Local Government Act some local authorities began to frustrate government policy by opening clinics or by using existing hospitals to give advice to women in defiance of Ministry of Health prohibitions. Self-interest also weakened medical resistance as doctors realised that they were losing female patients through their obduracy over birth control. Some GPs actually began to approach the voluntary clinics for help in advising their own patients. Finally, in 1930 the BMA backed down at least to the extent of accepting that birth control advice was justified for women whose health was endangered by further pregnancies. In the same year the Church of England, meeting at Lambeth, also abandoned its outright opposition.

Meanwhile Arthur Greenwood, the Health Minister, suddenly decided that he did not have the power to prevent local authorities supplying information about birth control after all; however, he consigned this concession to a memorandum which was not circulated for eight months! Eventually it was leaked and publicised by Stopes. In effect Greenwood neatly sidestepped the controversy by putting the local authorities in the firing line: they were permitted, but not required, to offer assistance on birth control and consequently many of them avoided doing so. In fact, by 1937 only 95 of 423 councils had implemented the new policy, although by this time seventy voluntary clinics were operating. Even so, advice was available only to married women for whom further pregnancies would be detrimental to health, though from 1937 the service was extended to all women attending post-natal clinics.

In this way the politicians continued to avoid taking a lead on the issue, leaving matters to local councils and to pressure groups such as the National Birth Control Council which adopted a new name, Family Planning Association, in 1939. As a result family planning was denied the resources it really required. Yet despite so many obstacles, British men and women had achieved substantially smaller families by 1939 and in the process proved the post-war prophets of doom and the demographic experts wrong. The effects of the continuing fall in the birth rate were balanced by a steady rise in the number of people getting married, by an increase in the proportion of women who had at least one child and by continuing improvements in infant mortality rates. The combined effect was that the British population increased by 3.8 million between the census of 1921 and that of 1941. If Britain's position as a great power was vulnerable in 1939 it was not because of the spread of birth control.

9

'Keep Young and Beautiful':
Women, Domesticity and
Feminism

During the war many working women had embarked on a revolution in fashion that greatly reduced the weight and restrictions imposed on them by their clothing. Initially shorter skirts – a response to the need to economise on material – had been a convenient sign of one's patriotism; but by the early 1920s younger British women regarded their choice of clothes as an outward expression of their new-found freedom. For some women the raised hemlines – just above the knee by 1925–6 – were a cause for embarrassment. A pre-war visit to a tattooist with her husband had left Edith Londonderry with a left leg embellished by a snake that wriggled up from her ankle and disappeared naughtily beneath her skirt.[1] Lord Londonderry, more conservative, had opted to have his regimental badge tattooed on his forearm. But Edith's snake was now exposed to the world, though some observers assumed that she was trying out a new fashion in stockings.

However, most fashion-conscious women had no hesitation in taking full advantage of the changes that replaced the Edwardian 'hourglass' shape with the 'tubular look'. This involved wearing straight dresses without an obvious waistline, discarding whalebone corsets and starched cotton petticoats, and buying the lighter under-wear that was designed to flatten, rather than accentuate, the bosom. The traditional heavy wool stockings gave way to lighter fabrics including silk and, later, cheap, artificial, flesh-coloured rayon and nylon; the new materials did not last long but this was seen as advantageous because it allowed women to opt for the latest fashions. Meanwhile, hair had already become shorter because women working in munitions and on farms did not have time for the elaborate grooming required by long hair. After 1918 the favoured style included the 'bob' and the 'shingle', followed in 1926 by the 'Eton crop'. The overall result was the boyish figure for young women that provoked so much concern among traditionalists. In Birmingham some employers started a 'morality crusade' to stop waitresses wearing short skirts. High-heeled shoes were condemned by doctors on the grounds that a woman who used them would, in time, displace her uterus and become unable to give birth. Even the innocuous woollen jersey, now known as the jumper or the pullover, was the first item of clothing to become interchangeable between men and women and, as such, was seen as a dangerous symptom of gender confusion. Admittedly, by 1930 a reaction had set in as the boyish look gave way to a revived femininity, encouraged by the new Duchess of York. The lavish use of cosmetics distinguished the sexes more clearly. Dresses involved more flowery chiffon, frills, ruffles, bows and padding to accentuate the shoulders. Hats, often in Victorian colours such as violet and plum, became encumbered once again with feathers and brooches.

But despite this, women were doing their best to retain their slimline figures. 'Seventy pretty, bare-legged City girls wearing as little as possible were led by two resigned-looking policemen into Hyde Park'.[2] Thus ran one newspaper account of the first annual demonstration, in 1930, of one of the iconic movements of the interwar period: the Women's League of Health and Beauty. Known initially as the Build the Body Beautiful League, the organisation had been founded by a 47-year-old widow, Mrs Mary Bagot Stack, known as Mollie. After the death of her husband in the war she set about supporting herself and her daughter by offering classes in what later became the Bagot Stack Health School involving dancing, callisthenics and remedial exercise. It was a select group; her clients included ladies Ursula and Isobel Manners, daughters of the Duke of Rutland. But by 1930 she had decided to move downmarket to something pitched at business girls and housewives: 'side by side will be a countess and a char-woman'. For only sixpence per class and two shillings and sixpence annual subscription members pledged to devote fifteen minutes every day to healthy activity including walking, running, sports and indoor exercises. Mrs Bagot Stack believed that 'women are the natural Race Builders of the world', and the Bagot Stack Stretch and Swing Exercises were intended to ensure that a woman's body could take the strain of childbearing. She claimed that the lonely businesswoman who joined the League would be so revitalised that she would find a boyfriend dazzled by her vitality and beauty. On the other hand, Bagot Stack was realistic enough to accept that 'the modern girl no longer regards wife-and-motherhood as her only career', and her ideal was to make women 'so beautiful they are an inspiration rather than a temptation'.[3]

The undoubted success of the Women's League of Health and Beauty was symptomatic of a wider fashion for walking, sunbathing, dieting and slimming between the wars. But Mrs Bagot Stack kept ahead of her competitors by some eye-catching publicity for the League. She issued gramophone records of music and exercise instructions, and dressed her girls in a standard uniform comprising black satin knickers and sleeveless white blouses, a little daring for the time but appealing to the press who eagerly covered the annual Hyde Park demonstrations and the League's indoor performances at the Albert Hall and Olympia, not to mention the Coronation Pageant at Wembley Stadium in 1937. Audiences watched up to 5,000 girls going through their paces on these occasions.

Mrs Bagot Stack had also shrewdly groomed her daughter, Prunella, who, at nineteen, was hailed by the *Daily Mail* as 'the most physically perfect girl in the world', as her successor. Journalists routinely went into raptures over Prunella: 'nothing more exquisite could be imagined than her beauty and her glamour – beyond the dreams of Hollywood'. Even an isolated cynic described her as 'a radiant, strapping, 23-year-old Nordic with excellent teeth and a rather too thin upper lip'.[4] The League's penchant for leader-worship made one member admit 'It puts me in mind of the Nazis'. But the League was generally regarded as an acceptable British counter-strategy to the Germanic obsession with fitness. In 1938 Prunella duly captivated the public by her marriage to Lord David Douglas-Hamilton, boxer, pilot, Scots landowner and son of the Duke of Hamilton. The League hired trains to Glasgow where 10,000 excited women and girls besieged the cathedral to see what the *Sunday Chronicle* dubbed 'The Strangest Society Wedding in Britain: Royalty, Typists, Boxers to See "Perfect Girl" Wed'.[5]

With 170,000 members the Women's League of Health and Beauty was in touch not only with contemporary leisure patterns but also with female aspirations. In the aftermath of the war many women experienced the desire to return to femininity and marriage and were encouraged in this direction by powerful commercial pressures now mobilising to promote the domestic ideal. The message was relentlessly propagated in the popular songs of the period:

> Keep young and beautiful.
> It's your duty to be beautiful.
> Keep young and beautiful – if you want to be loved.

An even more pervasive influence in the lives of millions of British women were the magazines marketed specifically for them. Women's magazines were far from new; *Home Chat* started in 1895 and *My Weekly* in 1910. But by the 1930s there were over fifty titles on sale including *Peg's Paper* (1919), *Good Housekeeping*, which arrived in Britain from America in 1922, and other 1920s titles such as *Women and Home*, *My Home*, *Modern Woman* and *Wife and Home*. By the 1930s the latest introductions were able to take advantage of technological advances in the form of printing by colour-gravure to offer a more glamorous read for younger women: *Woman's Own* (1932), *Woman's Illustrated* (1936) and *Woman* (1937). *Woman* quickly established itself as the market leader with a circulation reaching a million by 1940.

These magazines prospered on the basis of a standard formula comprising romantic fiction, marriage-and-husband tips, fashion, health and beauty, babycare, cookery, knitting patterns, dress-making, gardening and flower arrangement. In the aftermath of the war they increasingly emphasised household management especially for middle-class readers now struggling to find or to afford domestic servants. In the mid-Atlantic phraseology adopted by *Woman's Own* in 1932, 'any girl worth her salt wants to be the best housewife ever – and then some'.[6] Most magazines also relied increasingly on sheer escapism by offering housewives a peep into the lives of glamorous women, especially film stars and royalty. In 1923 they identified their ideal of English womanhood in Lady Elizabeth Bowes-Lyon, shortly to become Duchess of York: petite, charming, motherly and above all a vital support for her husband in his arduous public role. In fact the royal family became an irresistible source of copy for magazines keen to boost circulation; in 1937 *Woman* put Queen Elizabeth, as she had now become, on the cover of its first edition and repeated the tactic regularly thereafter. They were also prepared to recognise women such as Gracie Fields and Mary Pickford who achieved fame as film stars. But they were less comfortable with women who succeeded in unconventional roles by emulating men including 'Fabulous' Fay Taylour, the racing driver, Gertrude Ederle, the first woman to swim the English Channel in 1926, and the female pilots, Lady Heath and Lady Bailey who flew the London to Cape Town route, and, most famously, Amy Johnson with her solo flight to Australia in 1930. They also ignored the political pioneers such as Nancy Astor, the first woman to sit in Parliament in 1919, and Margaret Bondfield, the first Cabinet minister in 1929, as well as the younger MPs such as Ellen Wilkinson, Jennie Lee and Megan Lloyd George; the fact that many female MPs remained unmarried no doubt made them seem unsuitable role models. Admittedly, interwar governments were just as reluctant to recognise female achievement. On 1 January 1926 the *Daily Graphic*, complaining that the New Year's Honours List contained only one woman, urged the prime minister to 'break the dull monotony of masculine monopoly. Have the women of England, then, done nothing to warrant their being honoured with the town clerks, councillors and others? . . . No one believes it.'

Although women's magazines had originally been pitched more at a middle-class readership, their huge sales figures suggest they were widely bought by working-class wives between the wars. But how far these publications simply reflected contemporary ideas and how far they actually influenced women is difficult to say. Although the proprietors saw their publications primarily in commercial terms, they seem to have followed an agenda designed to confine women to lives of domesticity and to deter them from taking advantage of the wider opportunities now available to them. Several of their male writers – Godfrey Winn, Beverley Nicolls, Lord Birkenhead – were patronising at best and misogynist at worst. However, these were only token men, for the magazines offered a vehicle for career women as journalists and even as editors. Perhaps the most striking was the young Barbara Cartland. She was born in 1904 into a family dogged by financial problems that made it difficult to maintain the upper-class lifestyle to which they had been accustomed. The death of Barbara's father in 1918 only exacerbated things. For a girl in such a position everything – according to the later Cartland at least – pointed to making an early marriage to a suitably well endowed and well-connected man. Far from it, the young Barbara turned herself into a career girl in the 1920s first by writing gossip columns for newspapers and subsequently by setting herself up as an authority on motherhood – of which she had no experience. Meanwhile Barbara devoted herself to having a good time and delayed marriage until 1927; in 1932 she sued for divorce, remarried, but did not become a mother until 1937.

Editorial chairs were also occupied by several successful women including Alice Head at *Good Housekeeping* and Mary Grieve at *Woman*. Head, who had always aspired to become a journalist, started as a typist for *Country Life*, moving up as secretary and contributor; each day she bought her lunch for one shilling at Lyons or the ABC like thousands of other young 'business women'.[7] After moving to several other magazines she arrived at *Good Housekeeping* in 1922. Its American proprietor, William Randolph Hearst, who regarded her very highly, made Head a managing director and she reputedly became the highest paid woman in Britain. Mary Grieve's first job was at *Nursing Mirror*. By 1925 she earned £3. 5s. a week. She gained experience in several posts in Glasgow before returning to London in 1936, aged thirty, to work for Odhams on the staff of *Mother*. Grieve later admitted 'it had not yet dawned on me that for many years knitting would be one of my main editorial preoccupations . . . it continued to be the biggest single circulation raiser in the women's press.'[8]

Both Grieve and Head regarded themselves as emancipated women in that they took advantage of what had been achieved by women in the recent past but did not see it as their duty to campaign for further reforms or equal rights. Yet they were conscious of the criticism levelled at them by feminists and felt obliged to offer a defence of their role. Launching *Woman* in 1937 Margaret Lane admitted that the suffragist generation regarded them as regressive, but: 'That is not entirely true nor entirely fair. We are trying to do something which is as difficult, in its way, as the things which they achieved. We are trying to blend our old world with our new. Trying to be citizens and women at the same time. Wage-earners and sweethearts. Less aggressive feminists than independently feminine. It is a difficult balance to strike.'[9] Certainly these 'business women' were helping to redefine the idea of female emancipation by living the lives of independent, self-supporting women. But whether they used their journals to find a new balance between feminism and femininity as Lane claimed seems doubtful in view of the heavy bias towards domestic themes in their pages. *Good Housekeeping* was a partial exception at least in the early 1920s when it carried articles by Frances Stevenson on 'My Work at Number 10 Downing Street', and other feminists such as Rebecca West, Millicent Fawcett and Lady Rhondda, and politicians including Margaret Bondfield MP, Margaret Wintringham MP and Violet Bonham Carter.

However, on the whole the magazines took little or no notice of feminist issues except in so far as they urged women that it would be a mistake to take advantage of reforms in the law on divorce. When the first 'Evelyn Home' advised one unhappily married wife to spend a weekend with her lover, her copy was promptly censored and she herself was replaced![10] *Woman* recognised women's employment as legitimate only in so far as it could be a *preparation* for marriage not as a career in itself. It had no interest in lifting its readers' aspirations to anything wider except by means of escapist stories. Ultimately the female editors justified themselves on the basis that they printed what the market wanted in their magazines, though in practice this often meant they tried to avoid offending anyone. According to Mary Grieve, *Woman*'s proprietors felt obliged to rewrite the 'agony aunt' page for Irish editions because of objections from Catholics. When the monthly *Everywoman* printed an article on birth control William Temple, the Archbishop of Canterbury, immediately complained to Odhams Press. Lord Southwood, the proprietor, backed down, saying 'While we must be up to date . . . we must not be too much in advance . . . when the schools put this subject in their curriculum, it will be time for us to deal with it in our paper.'[11] As many of the readers were by this time practising birth control, Southwood was clearly content to follow social change at a considerable distance.

As though aware of the unconventional roles young women had played during wartime the magazines made determined efforts to encourage them to take pride in being good 'home-makers'. It was the special mission of *Good Housekeeping*, for example, to try to elevate housekeeping to the status of a profession. 'We are on the threshold of a great feminine awakening', declared the enthusiastic editors in their first edition. 'Apathy and levity are alike giving place to a wholesome and intelligent interest in the affairs of life, and above all the home.'[12]

In reality what they offered was less a new departure than improved competence in the performance of women's traditional skills. Readers of *Good Housekeeping* received a correspondence course in managing their resources, improving their cookery and needlework, and especially taking full advantage of the new mechanical household aids which were regularly tested by the Good Housekeeping Institute.

Some women, driven reluctantly back into domesticity, may have found it flattering to be told that their role was important enough to deserve proper training. At a more practical level the idea appealed to middle-class wives who were increasingly obliged to manage without the plentiful supply of domestic servants their mothers had enjoyed. During the 1890s around 1.7 million women had been engaged as domestic servants, but thereafter there was a gradual decline accelerated by the First World War when 400,000 servants left their jobs. Girls who had previously been resigned to leaving their homes in the countryside after the age of fourteen to become resident maids in urban households were lured into munitions. Not only were the wages much higher, but the conditions seemed far better. In industry working hours were strictly defined so that a girl was not perpetually at the employer's beck and call. Also, factory work often involved sitting down, not running upstairs carrying coal and water all day. Harold Begbie's book, *Life Without Servants* (1916 and 1930), and Randall Phillips' *The Servantless House* (1922) were unmistakable signs that Britain's 'servant problem' had arrived. Even though many young women returned reluctantly to domestic service after the war, they were more ready to quit and resented the poor conditions. For all its humorous tone E. M. Delafield's *The Diary of a Provincial Lady* (1930) underlined how stressful some housewives now found the management and retention of servants: 'porridge is slightly burnt . . . Robert suggests ringing for Cook, and I have greatest difficulty in persuading him that this course [would be] utterly disastrous . . . Arrival of William and Angela at half past three. [I] should like to hurry up tea, but feel that servants would be annoyed . . . Ethel brings in cocoa, but [I] can tell from the way she puts down the tray that she thinks it an unreasonable requirement, and will quite likely give notice tomorrow . . . Ethel as I anticipated gives notice. Cook says this is so unsettling, she thinks she had better go too. Despair invades me. Write five letters to Registry Offices.'[13] For their part servants found their lives unreasonably hard especially when working in small households; typically they rose at 6.30 to clean the grates, set fresh fires, take up early morning tea, cook breakfasts and scrub the steps, all before breakfast. Many complained about insulting treatment by their employers who sometimes weighed out their food in small portions to stop them eating too much. Margaret Powell once handed a letter to her employer who reprimanded her: 'Langley, never, never, never on any occasion ever hand me anything in your bare hands, always use a silver salver.'[14]

In the early 1920s any sign of independence on the part of young women provoked outrage among the newspapers whose proprietors evidently felt they should accept 'proper and natural employment' as servants rather than competing for jobs with men or languishing on unemployment benefits. They complained bitterly about young munitionettes who had used their high wages to indulge in luxury goods. In December 1918 the *Daily Chronicle* sent a reporter to the labour exchange in Acton where girls previously employed making shells at the Park Royal factory were registering. Under the headline 'Unemployed In Fur Coats', he described the 'young girls with elaborately curled hair' who were rejecting jobs as general domestics and as cooks 'at tempting wages'.[15] It is a measure of the seriousness with which the 'servant problem' was regarded that the government appointed a committee on the recruitment and retention of domestic servants. The issue was widely discussed by leading female politicians including not only Conservatives such as the Duchess of Atholl and Lady Londonderry, who used the Women's Legion to encourage women to return to service, but also Labour figures including Susan Lawrence and Marion Phillips, as well as the Women's Co-operative Guild, the Fabian Women and Labour Party Women's organisations. Lawrence urged that the most effective change would be a minimum wage and a maximum week. It was agreed that employers ought to stop referring to servants by their Christian names, which seemed patronising, and use surnames instead.

Whether because of these efforts or simply because of the prolonged depression, many women did return reluctantly to domestic service, the total reaching 1.6 million by 1931. But according to the magazines an alternative was available to the modern woman. Appliances like vacuum cleaners, so the argument ran, saved time and helped housewives achieve a higher standard of household management. This seems plausible in that middle-class women had begun to discover how much hard and heavy work it took to run even a modest-sized home. Laundry day involved heating large quantities of water, a laborious process of washing and rinsing the clothes in a large tub or boiler, followed by running them through a mangle before pegging them out to dry on the washing line. Bryan Magee described how much his mother appreciated the arrival of washing powders in the 1930s. Previously she did her laundry with 'unmanageable blocks of green soap'. Even dish-washing was complicated before the intro- duction of washing liquid; his family put all their leftover bits of toilet soap into a gauze-metal cage with a handle which had to be whisked around in the hot water to create a lather.[16]

Rising real wages enabled some families to take advantage of the mechanical aids. But they spread slowly; by 1931 1.3 million electric cookers, 400,000 vacuum cleaners, 220,000 fridges and 60,000 washing machines were in use in Britain. From the housewife's perspective there were many reasons to be sceptical despite the enthusiasm of the women's magazines. Dishwashers were not very effective at this time. Most women still used coal-fired ranges for cooking because coal was cheap and the new anthracite offered a cleaner fuel. Refrigerators seemed unnecessary for a generation of housewives accustomed to shopping for food every day. Vacuum cleaners were simply too expensive.

More fundamentally, claims about the labour-saving advantages of the appliances were seriously flawed. An early edition of *Good Housekeeping* urged readers 'there should be no drudgery in the house. There must be time to think, to read, to enjoy life.' To this end it printed helpful articles such as the one by Viscountess Gladstone, whose own domestic experience must have been slight, on 'The Model Housewife'. She recommended that housewives drew up a proper budget each week, did the laundry at home, made their own furniture polish, emulated French housewives by buying all their food themselves so as to avoid waste, and bought seasonal food which could then be used for jam and bottling.[17] Not much time for leisurely reading in this scheme. Revealingly, Viscountess Gladstone's best tip was to be kind to servants as that way one could get the best out of them! The truth was that just as, later in the century, computers turned

The scene in Whitehall on 11 November 1918 when news of the Armistice was received.

Residents of Byron Terrace, Newcastle-upon-Tyne, celebrate with a 'Peace Tea' in the summer of 1919.

Women pack poppies for sale on the first 'Poppy Day', November 1921.

A row of miners' cottages in South Wales, 1931.

High-quality, low-density 1920s municipal housing at Curtis Road, Liverpool, built under the 1919 Housing Act.

A fine example of inter-war 'Tudorbethan' style: the Railway Hotel, Edgware, 1931.

A lady bus conductor, about to surrender her job to a man, says good-bye to a colleague during demobilisation, 1919.

Unemployed men queue outside a Labour Exchange in 1922, marshalled by policemen.

(*Left*) Miners play cards during the six-month coal strike that followed the General Strike in 1926. (*Above*) Sam Needham on the Jarrow March, October 1936, with 'Paddy', the marchers' adopted dog.

ed by Roderick Kedward (*centre*), angry farmers protest about tithes at Westwell, Kent, 1935.

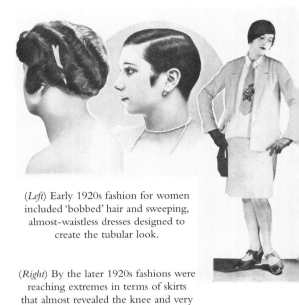

(*Left*) Early 1920s fashion for women included 'bobbed' hair and sweeping, almost–waistless dresses designed to create the tubular look.

(*Right*) By the later 1920s fashions were reaching extremes in terms of skirts that almost revealed the knee and very short hair cuts, including the 'Shingle' (*top left*) and the 'Eton Crop' (*top right*).

A parade of the latest bathing costumes and wraps at Southport, Lancashire, May 1928.

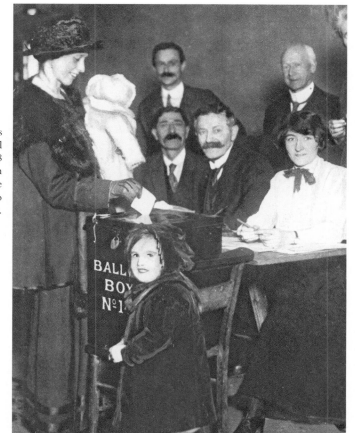

A woman votes in the general election of 1918 when women over thirty were allowed to do so for the first time.

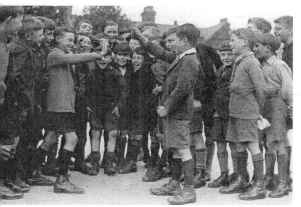

London schoolboys gather to play conkers, October 1926.

(*Top*) During the 1920s children were chased away by police and park attendants for trying to bathe naked in the Serpentine.

Scouts of all nations gather for the Scout Jamboree at Arrowe Park, near Birkenhead, July 1929.

A party of children on the first leg of their journey to Australia in 1932, apparently unaware of what awaits them.

professionals unconsciously into secretaries, so, between the wars, domestic appliances enabled middle-class housewives to become domestic servants without quite realising the fact. In the process they may have raised their standards of housekeeping, but without reducing the burdens or the time involved.

The pressure put on women to cultivate their domestic skills underlines the anxiety of the post-war Establishment to minimise any threat to the position of men in the shrinking labour market. During the war women had undertaken male jobs in engineering, trams and agriculture as well as banking, commerce and administration. According to Board of Trade statistics the number of women in paid employment rose from 3.27 million when war broke out to 4.93 million in 1918, though they took no account of the 400,000 reduction in domestic servants; this left a net increase of 1.2 million working women. Yet there was no revolution in attitudes towards women's employment; in fact, by the summer of 1918 a backlash had already developed. Newspapers that had recently lauded 'our gallant girls' for driving trams now denounced them as 'pin money girls'. Under the Restoration of Pre-war Practices Act those who had been employed in munitions were obliged to leave, with the result that one year after the Armistice 775,000 women had lost their jobs. According to the prevailing wisdom it was unpatriotic for a woman to retain any job that might be required for a man returning from the forces. In January 1919 the Glasgow Govan labour exchange reported that 900 local munitionettes were now out of work, but 'no local demand exists for women's labour except in domestic service which is very unpopular'.[18]

When the post-war boom collapsed abruptly in the summer of 1920 women were forced even more into a defensive position from which they never really recovered until 1940 when another national manpower shortage brought them back again in large numbers. In 1933 Sir Herbert Austin, the motor manufacturer, spoke for many when he declared that all women should be sacked as an effective means of solving the unemployment problem. It is especially shocking that someone like Austin, who had been MP for Birmingham (King's Norton), could get away with such remarks at a time when women comprised fifty-two per cent of the electorate. All the political parties treated women as though their interests lay entirely in the cost of living, housing and welfare, and as though unemployment concerned them only indirectly through their husbands. Nor were there many protests by those who had lost their jobs after 1918. In November that year some 6,000 women, recently made redundant by Woolwich Arsenal, demonstrated at the House of Commons with posters: 'Shall Peace Bring Us Starvation?' But this was exceptional. Most young women seemed content to abandon employment and even welcomed the break, partly because they expected it to be temporary.

As a result of a contracting economy and official hostility women were pushed out of the labour market for lengthy periods. By 1921 half a million women were registered unemployed, but, as many had abandoned attempts to register, this was an underestimate. They suffered from the steady decline of the textile industry which traditionally employed a high proportion of female workers. But others became victims of discriminatory policies such as the marriage bar, widely operated by local authorities who simply sacked female employees, notably teachers, nurses, doctors and cleaners, as soon as they married. In 1921 St Pancras Borough Council outraged feminists by dismissing Dr Miall Smith, an assistant medical officer. This appeared to contravene the 1919 Sex Disqualification (Removal) Act which stated that 'a person shall not be disqualified by sex or marriage from being appointed to or holding any civil or judicial office or post'. However, following legal advice the feminist organisations concluded that it was not worth pursuing a case for wrongful dismissal; the new legislation was a broken reed already.[19] Meanwhile the number of women teachers fell from 187,000 in 1921 to 181,000 in 1931; the decline would have been steeper had not some married women managed to conceal their status from the employers. It was a similar story in central government where four per cent of female civil servants were expelled from their jobs each year.

Faced with this attack on their role, women received little support from the trade unions despite having a substantial footing in the movement. By 1918 the unions had 1.2 million female members representing fifteen to sixteen per cent of the total. However, women paid lower union membership subscriptions and received lesser benefits. The only leading woman to emerge from a union background was Margaret Bondfield who became an MP in 1923. But Bondfield rose precisely because she was not seen as a threat by the men who dominated the organisation and its policies. Even Susan Lawrence, a middle-class Labour MP, respected the prevailing male priorities, accepted that married women should be dismissed from their jobs and that female workers should be paid as though they were single while men were paid on the basis that they had a wife and dependents to support.[20] This claim was exploded by the Independent MP, Eleanor Rathbone, in an analysis in 1921 showing that among men over twenty only thirty-nine per cent actually had dependent children under sixteen. Wage discrimination against women also ignored the fact that many women whose husbands had died in the war or were too disabled to work, were now obliged to work to support their families. However, trade unionists adopted the idea of the 'family wage', that is, a wage sufficient to enable a man to support his family, thus making it unnecessary for his wife to take a job outside the home. The same logic made the unions active in promoting 'protective legislation' which was supposedly designed to safeguard the health or morals of female employees, but was merely a euphemism for excluding them from male employment. In 1920 Parliament banned women from working at night, which excluded them from the printing trade; they were barred from the paint industry because the lead was poisonous; and in 1937 they were subjected to a maximum forty-eight-hour week which made it complicated for employers to retain them.

In the context of economic depression and legal discrimination, it is surprising that overall women held their ground in employment between the wars. As a proportion of the British labour force women comprised 29.6 per cent in 1911, 29.5 per cent in 1921 and 29.8 per cent by 1931. In effect, the losses were being balanced by structural changes in the economy that boosted women's opportunities. In particular, the rapid expansion of secretarial and administrative employment in offices created a sustained demand for female workers. And during the 1930s manufacturing industry sought to fill light, unskilled production-line jobs with women and young people on the assumption that they would accept low pay and were less likely to be unionised. Even the Sex Disqualification (Removal) Act made a marginal contribution in opening up several of the professions to women. By 1935 116 women were practising as solicitors and 79 as barristers. Women doctors also increased from 477 in 1914 to 2,810 by 1931, nearly all as GPs because the men who controlled the highly paid hospital consultancies reserved these posts for themselves.

These gains and losses left women's employment looking fairly stable in that the proportion of women in paid employment stood at thirty-five per cent in 1911, thirty-three per cent in 1921 and thirty-four in 1931. But this conceals significant changes in the composition of the female labour force between the wars. It included fewer widows, probably as a result of the introduction of widows' pensions in 1925. There was also a slight but significant rise in the proportion who were married, from fourteen to sixteen per cent between 1921 and 1931, representing ten per cent of all married women. In some cases they had been driven to work by prolonged periods of unemployment by their husbands. But as this represented the start of a long-term trend towards employment among wives, it suggests that attitudes had begun to change. Among working-class women it was traditionally assumed that they would work outside the home in their teens and twenties but give it up as soon as they married. This continued to be broadly true; the female labour force was young, some sixty-nine per cent being under thirty-five. However, now that women were having fewer children their families were complete much earlier in life, leaving them with greater opportunities to return to employment.

Finally, it became more widely accepted after the war that it was proper for single women to seek careers. This was not recognised by the interwar women novelists who largely continued to write Victorian-Edwardian stories about the fate of spinsters confined to the family home as unpaid companions for elderly relatives. In fact, well over ninety per cent of unmarried women enjoyed paid employment by the 1930s. The explanation may be that middle-class families became less willing to support their daughters after the financial strains of wartime and the post-war period, or simply that they assumed that their chances of marriage had been reduced.

Lower down the social scale employment opportunities had important implications for young 'working girls'. Traditionally parents indulged their sons because of the contribution they made to family income and allowed them far more leisure time than their daughters. But the balance had shifted. By the 1930s not only was women's work expanding in shops, offices and factories, but it was often more secure than male employment in industry. Some mothers encouraged their daughters to take advantage of this brief period between school and marriage to enjoy their leisure time and indulge in minor luxuries, even though they continued to deduct money for board from their wages. As a result a generation of young women emerged who were significantly more independent than the pre-war generation and who became prominent as consumers of leisure, clothes and cosmetics.

Despite this, there was more continuity than change in working-class attitudes towards employment. Oral studies of women in several Lancashire towns, where women's employment was traditionally at a high level, underline that the majority continued to regard paid work as a necessity but a purely temporary one. Their goal was to marry a man with a sufficiently well paid, regular job to make it unnecessary for them to work. For them emancipation consisted in being able to move away from employment by their mid or late twenties, not to develop a career as it was for middle-class feminists. Conversely, respectable workingmen often felt that it reflected badly on them if their wives were obliged to take jobs, hence they found periods of prolonged unemployment especially demoralising. The good husband was also expected to turn over his weekly wage packet to his wife without the intervention of a prolonged visit to the pub. According to one woman 'the man passed over the money . . . I mean in those days the wages were so poor that really the man didn't get a right lot out of it.'[21] In such cases the wife actually handed him some pocket money for tobacco, beer and betting, as she did to her wage-earning children. In this sense the working-class housewife often enjoyed a position of considerable power within her sphere. She managed the family's money and made crucial decisions about expenditure, making sure that they kept out of debt and could always pay the rent. When things got tough she would discreetly visit the pawnbroker or obtain credit from local shopkeepers. Either way her financial skills were largely responsible for maintaining the reputation of a respectable family.

By contrast middle-class women often suffered more acutely from prejudice and discrimination, and even those who were successfully fighting their way out of domesticity via education continued to be harassed and patronised by man-made rules. Despite the Sex Disqualification (Removal) Act, women continued to face entrenched prejudice at the older institutions. Although a college for women had been founded at Girton as long ago as 1869, Cambridge remained reluctant to award degrees to its female students; indeed, the university refused to admit them as full members until 1948. Though the war had disrupted the provision of chaperones for unmarried girls, a female undergraduate at Lady Margaret Hall, Oxford, was not yet permitted to join a man on a bicycle ride unless she had the Principal's permission and was accompanied by two women. In this hostile context it is not surprising that middle-class women often took a far more positive view of employment as an escape route than their working-class sisters. 'Work has been the twentieth century's great gift to women', proclaimed Vera Brittain in *Time and Tide* in 1927. 'It is dignified work which puts her upon the same level as men.' After embarking on a career as author and journalist after the war, Brittain married, but she was soon repelled by the conventional wifely role: 'to have to "get tea", make beds, to be called on, return calls, be a "Faculty Wife", be called "Mrs Catlin" – God! How I hated it.'[22] By the age of thirty-three, however, she felt she understood how to manage husband, children and career: 'my great object', she wrote, 'is to prove that work and maternity are not mutually exclusive'.[23]

However, Vera Brittain was a little ahead of her time, and her remarks help us to understand why the feminist movement encountered difficulty in extending its appeal to the mass of ordinary women during the interwar years. Many women, while taking advantage of the vote and other feminist achievements, seemed reluctant to follow them any further. 'The fierce feminist is an old-fashioned figure, unsympathetically remembered by all but a very few', as *Woman* put it in its first issue in 1937. Writing in the feminist journal, *Time and Tide*, E. M. Delafield satirised the survivors of Edwardian suffragism by creating a 'Miss Pankerton' who dressed eccentrically, smoked publicly and sat astride the arm of her sofa to deliver lectures: 'Miss P becomes personal and says that I strike her as a woman whose life has never known fulfilment . . . she goes on to ask accusingly whether I realise I have no *right* to let myself become a domestic beast of burden with no interest beyond the nursery and the kitchen . . . Miss P finally departs saying that she is determined to scrape all the barnacles off me before she has finished with me.'[24] Delafield effectively made the point that it was difficult to campaign for further reforms for women without at the same time appearing to patronise or disparage women who followed a conventional route in life.

For their part younger women who adopted a positive view of marriage and the male sex were inclined to dismiss their critics as women who had failed. Portraying a meeting with a group of distinguished feminists E. M. Delafield wrote: 'Lady B waves her hand and declares That may be all very well, but if they had got *husbands* they wouldn't *be* Feminists!'[25] These exchanges reflected a growing gulf between the generations. Most leading feminists, who had been born in the late-Victorian period or even earlier, found the current trends repugnant, especially female fashion and liberated behaviour. They disparaged the flappers, not just for being irresponsible, but for dressing up to please men. Emmeline Pankhurst, who objected to 'the modern abbreviated styles in women's gowns . . . and too much rouge and lip paint', explained that 'we wanted to preserve as enfranchised women that modesty and delicacy which have been held to be our adornment'. To many of her generation the relaxed view about sex and birth control seemed a betrayal because, by removing the constraints on personal behaviour, it effectively lowered women to the level of men.[26] Nor were her daughters any more comfortable with contemporary trends. Sylvia eloquently disparaged 'the emancipation of today [which] displays itself mostly in cigarettes and shorts . . . painted lips and nails and [the] return of trailing skirts and other absurdities of dress which betoken the slave-woman's sex appeal rather than the free woman's intelligent companionship'.[27]

On the other hand, some post-war feminists were very alive to the need to adapt their movement and widen its agenda so as to appeal more widely to women who had never participated in the struggle for the vote. Eleanor Rathbone, who became president of the National Union of Societies for Equal Citizenship – formerly the National Union of Societies for Women's Suffrage – in 1920, pioneered the 'New Feminism'. Meanwhile, the more traditional 'equal rights' organisations such as the Women's Freedom League continued much as before, while several new pressure groups emerged including the Women's Citizens Association (1917), the Six Point Group (1921) and the Open Door Council (1926). Lady Rhondda also launched *Time and Tide* as a feminist journal in 1920, giving a platform to feminist writers including Rebecca West, Vera Brittain, Winifred Holtby, Virginia Woolf, Elizabeth Robins, Rose Macaulay and Cicely Hamilton. 'New Feminists' and 'equal rights' feminists shared a wide range of objectives including equal voting rights, equal pay, equal rights of guardianship, divorce law reform, the opening of the professions and Civil Service,

the equal moral standard, equal access to the honours list and separate
taxation for married women. During the 1920s, while the momentum
achieved by female vote in 1918 remained strong, the movement
extracted a good deal of women's legislation from Parliament. However, by 1928 Rathbone and the New Feminists had committed NUSEC
to a new agenda that included family allowances, provision of birth
control and opposition to protective legislation. This represented a
bold and realistic attempt to work with social change and, in effect, to
accept that most women aspired to marriage and motherhood.
However, many equal rights feminists regarded family allowances and
birth control as involving too great a compromise with conventional
ideas about women's roles and a concession to what Winifred Holtby
called the 'boring obsession with sex'; to them this seemed a betrayal
of Edwardian feminism.

However, it proved difficult for feminists of either sort to sustain the
momentum. The militant methods that had kept women in the
forefront in the Edwardian period seemed inappropriate now that they
had the vote. The Six Point Group maintained the suffragette tradition
to the extent of publishing a 'blacklist' of MPs who had the worst
record on women's legislation with encouragement to vote against
them at the elections of 1922, 1923 and 1924. But most of the former
militants became diverted from the cause. Emmeline Pankhurst spent
much of her time in Canada and pointedly declined an invitation to
take the lead in the campaign for equal suffrage. Christabel toyed
briefly with becoming an MP in 1918 but abandoned it, devoted herself
to preaching the Second Coming of Christ in the United States, and
even renounced the vote as 'a devalued currency'. Some ex-
suffragettes ended up in surprising roles. Flora Drummond founded
the Women's Guild of Empire, Mary Allen devoted herself to
promoting the women's police even to the extent of dressing up in
uniforms she was not entitled to wear, while several, including Mary
Richardson, famous for her attack on the 'Rokeby Venus', eventually
joined the British Union of Fascists after 1932.

Meanwhile, many of the younger feminists, such as Vera Brittain,
became active, not in explicitly feminist organisations, but in other
progressive causes such as the League of Nations Union, on the basis
that peace and disarmament were an integral part of feminism; they
agreed with Virginia Woolf that 'the war was an inevitable outcome of

male chauvinism'.[28] Feminists were also torn over female participation in party politics: was this an efficacious way of promoting women's interests now that they had the vote, or did it simply enable politicians to make use of women's voluntary work without granting them real power? There were good grounds for scepticism. After 1918 all three parties made strenuous efforts to enrol female members, to give them representation on party committees and to train female organisers. But as women constituted over half the electorate after 1929 there was obviously a large element of self-interest in this. They reserved their safe seats in Parliament for men, so that the number of women MPs between the wars reached only 15 at the maximum in 1931, representing 2.4 per cent of those elected. Moreover, while politicians willingly granted health-and-welfare reforms to women, they made few concessions to feminist demands. This caused acute controversy in the Labour Party which refused to adopt family allowances because the unions feared this would lead to lower wages for men, or to support birth control for fear of offending Catholic voters. As a result some feminists argued that women were deceived if they expected collaboration with men to change anything. 'I am an old-fashioned feminist', commented Rebecca West in 1924, 'I believe in the sex war.'[29] Even the moderate feminists in NUSEC believed that it was essential to maintain independent women's pressure groups rather than be swallowed up by male-dominated organisations.

At all events, the 1930s proved to be a barren decade for women's reforms despite women's formal entry into the political system. 'Today the battle we thought won is going badly against us', wrote Cicely Hamilton in 1935, 'we are retreating where once we advanced.'[30] While women won only a toehold in Parliament, the feminist organisations lost members heavily as their older supporters died or left public life. But why were they not replaced by members of the younger generation? In effect the younger women had redefined feminism in terms of making a career rather than campaigning for further change. In her famous address to female students at Cambridge in 1928, published as *A Room of One's Own* in 1929, Virginia Woolf recognised this: 'may I also remind you that most of the professions have been open to you for close on ten years now? . . . there must at this moment be some 2,000 women capable of earning £500 a year in one way or another, you will agree that the excuse of lack of opportunity, training, employment, leisure and money no longer holds good.'[31]

This emphasis on employment crystallised the generation gap among interwar women. Vera Brittain, born in 1893, showed her feminism in her pursuit of university education and a career, but was also conventionally feminine in her attention to dress and her determination to become a wife and mother. She joined the Six Point Group in 1922, but left it and devoted more time to the League of Nations Union and the Labour Party. 'One happily married wife and mother is worth more to feminism than a dozen gifted and eloquent spinsters', she wrote.[32] Inevitably, to the older feminists Brittain and her generation appeared to have retreated into collaboration with a male-dominated system. But for their part the younger women regarded their Edwardian counterparts as privileged ladies with the time and money to spend sitting on endless committees for feminist pressure groups. They believed they were promoting feminism by pursuing independence through regular employment, which simply left far less time for campaigning. This generational gap became even more obvious in the lives of some of the emancipated, interwar women such as Jennie Lee, born in 1904, and Barbara Castle, born in 1911. They attended university, embarked on political careers and felt free to enjoy affairs on the same basis as men; both married but had no children and continued to pursue their ambitions in the public sphere. Significantly, neither Castle nor Lee became much involved in women's campaigns or organisations until much later in life.

However, while the overtly feminist organisations struggled between the wars, other women's groups flourished by appealing to popular tastes, but without simply surrendering to Victorian notions of womanhood. The Women's Co-operative Guild, which dated back to 1883, aimed to mobilise working-class housewives, to push their interests up the political agenda, and to equip them with practical skills to engage in public work. The guild's membership rose from 31,000 in 1914 to 67,000 by 1931. Its success lay in its role as a mouthpiece for married women closely attuned to an age of consumerism; it aspired to awaken the housewife to the 'basket power' she wielded as the person who spent the nation's wages each week. Though linked with the Labour Party through the Co-operative Movement, the guild explicitly rejected the masculine assumption that labour and production were the basis for a better society. Instead it urged consumption as an efficacious weapon for change, arguing that an alternative to capitalist society could be achieved through the spread of the co-operative system and the distribution of its profits. Nor did the guild hesitate to adopt controversial issues such as divorce reform, family allowances, birth control and even the legalisation of abortion, as opposed to the health-and-welfare topics that were easily acceptable to a male-dominated movement.

The 1920s and 1930s also witnessed the dramatic rise of the Women's Institutes whose membership reached 318,000 by 1937. The jam-and-Jerusalem jokes gave a misleading impression of their significance. In fact the WIs trod a careful line between feminism and citizenship, on the one hand, and femininity and domesticity on the other. They managed to take women outside their homes and involve them in a wide range of activities without directly challenging conventional thinking about gender roles. Today it is usually forgotten that in the 1920s many men regarded the WIs with suspicion. One organiser was surprised to find her meeting to form a WI in a Sussex village attended largely by local men; when she returned a fortnight later she found it full of women who had received their husbands' approval in the interval. But many women joined in defiance of their husbands; in one such case a Yorkshireman, when asked how he felt subsequently, admitted: 'I think she's a deal easier to live with now.'[33]

Yet the men's misgivings were justified in the sense that the Women's Institute also had a political side. WIs were designed to be run democratically without bias towards class, sect or party. 'We have elected five ladies, five women and one schoolteacher', as one WI president proudly reported.[34] The annual gathering of up to 5,000 delegates, known as the Countrywomen's Parliament, made repre-sentations to ministers on topics including rural libraries, telephones and water supplies, cheap electricity, milk for children, cinema censorship, women police and the provision of midwives and infant welfare centres. In 1929 their success encouraged NUSEC to extend the WI formula into more urban districts by founding the Townswomen's Guilds which had recruited 54,000 women by 1939. On the other hand, political work was potentially divisive. No fewer than 600 WIs joined the League of Nations Union, with encouragement from the national executive, but they felt obliged to avoid campaigns for peace and disarmament for fear of being accused of pacifism. Although their national leaders included well-known feminists such as Lady Denman, Margaret Wintringham, Mary Stocks and Dame Margery Corbett Ashby, their ideas were diluted at the local level where the WIs ensured their popularity and avoided controversy by sticking to housewifely activities and interests. Though to a later generation this seemed to fall short of the feminist ambitions of the Edwardian period, it represented a logical advance from women's enfranchisement in 1918 by extending female participation in the public life of the nation.

10

'The mills were our destiny': Childhood, Youth and Education

In July 1926 the Duke and Duchess of York left London for Glamis Castle in Angus. On the sleeper to Scotland they were accompanied by Glen, their golden retriever, but their three-month-old daughter, Princess Elizabeth, was not with them as she had been dispatched with her nanny the day before. The royal couple undertook a much longer excursion to Australia starting in January 1927. During their six-month absence Elizabeth, now eight months old and ready for her first words and her first steps in life, remained at home, and while they were in Australia no communications passed between them. On their return the Princess failed to recognise her parents.

The Duke and Duchess of York were not unfeeling towards their children, indeed the Duchess felt unhappy about leaving them, but their behaviour was typical both of people in the circle in which they moved, and also of the era in which they lived. Lower down the social scale parents felt a similar need to minimise direct contact with young children, and, in the absence of older siblings to amuse or supervise them, they were often left to fend for themselves. Working-class children normally spent much of their life outdoors wandering the streets: 'my mother sent me out every day to get me from under her feet', recalled one East Ender. 'Soon after I could run I did a lot of my growing up on the street.'[1] When he was three his parents decided that he was capable of crossing roads and allowed him to go where he liked. This was also true of middle-class families. Paul Johnson, who routinely took himself off to the local park, admitted: 'It amazes me now, looking back, how free my life as a small boy was, how little supervised and how confident my parents were that I would come to no harm . . . I was never molested. Nor did I know, or hear, of any child who was. Crime played no part in our lives.'[2]

The persistence of traditional ideas about bringing up children was particularly marked among upper- and upper-middle-class families who relied heavily on nannies, few of whom were trained in the rearing of children. Parental priorities were well illustrated by Edwina Mountbatten when she gave birth in February 1923 and promptly handed over the baby to a nanny. Lots of visitors arrived, not to see the baby but to see Edwina who was concentrating hard on restoring her appearance with a view to returning to her social round. In March she travelled to the Riviera leaving the baby with relatives in Dorset.[3] The overriding aim of the upper classes was to arrange things so that young children did not disrupt their social life The messy side was handled entirely by nurses and nannies, and, as they grew older, the boys were packed off to boarding schools and the girls handed over to governesses. Virtually all adults at this level of society had been brought up by nannies; when very young they were presented to their parents for half an hour each evening after being fed and washed, but otherwise many of them saw little of their parents until well into their teens. In the case of Winston Churchill his nanny, Mrs Everest, was a beloved figure who gave him the affection he felt he was denied by his parents; but at the other extreme Lord Curzon had suffered physical abuse and psychological torment from a sadistic nanny that left him scarred for life. In the 1920s the new thinking about child psychology made very little impression at this level of society. On the whole parents seemed unconcerned about a strict and even violent regime, in fact if it erred on the side of severity so much the better. This reflected a deep-rooted belief that children were naturally evil. Consequently any indulgence or liberality would only encourage their worst propensities; they had to be disciplined and guided towards a useful life as adults.

It is worth emphasising that in the context of attitudes in other European societies the British approach to children and childhood was distinctive. Visitors from abroad were surprised by the severe treatment of children, not least the habit of sending them away from home to be educated; it was as though the English did not like children very much. Education in boarding schools proved especially disruptive of family life for those whose careers kept them in the colonies. In India British children enjoyed an early upbringing in the hands of affectionate and indulgent native nurses, but as soon as they were deemed old enough to require education they embarked for England.

Wondering why their parents had left them, they invariably found the atmosphere of England cold, both literally and emotionally, and endured lives divided between terms at spartan boarding schools and holidays being shunted between unwelcoming relatives, unapproachable guardians and grim boarding houses. They often spent many years without even seeing their parents back in India and emerged emotionally scarred for life. Although this practice continued between the wars, the availability of good English schools in India made it less necessary. Moreover, attitudes were changing slowly; when Lord Lumley became Governor of Bombay in 1937, for example, his wife explained that they would never have accepted the post if they had had to leave their children behind.

Yet their plight was nothing by comparison with the thousands of children who, from a mixture of misguided philanthropy and blatant imperialism, were dispatched to populate the empty parts of the Empire. In official circles children had long been regarded primarily as national assets whose transfer to Australia, Canada and South Africa represented a useful piece of social engineering. Anglican and Catholic organisations as well as Dr Barnardo's and the Salvation Army actively recruited children from orphanages, from Poor Law institutions and from poor homes where parents were deemed unable to look after them. Some parents signed papers agreeing to let them go without realising that they would lose contact forever. In fact most of the children were not orphans at all, but the organisations frequently told them that their parents had died and that they had no family; their birth certificates were destroyed and sometimes their names were changed; in later life the organisations even withheld the records that proved they had relations living in Britain.

Although the religious and philanthropic groups responsible for the trade in children believed they were rescuing them from lives of destitution and immorality, they made little or no attempt to ascertain what really happened to them once they left the country. At best they were used as cheap labour on farms in Canada, the girls becoming unpaid domestic servants. At worst, and this was a feature of Australian experience, they were treated with cruelty and were sexually abused. During the 1920s questions were raised in Britain about the treatment of these 'children of the Empire', and in 1924 a junior minister, Margaret Bondfield, visited Canada to investigate. But

Bondfield, an old-fashioned imperialist who had no desire to rock the boat, merely advised that the export of children should be encouraged. Although some of the children eventually prospered after escaping from their original placements, they were traumatised by their separation from home and family, and many felt that they never recovered emotionally from the ordeal. The practice appears extraordinarily callous in the light of rosy modern perceptions about the Victorian family and the superior parenting skills of the nineteenth century. These, of course, are myths. In fact, Victorian families, both working class and middle class, were routinely split up in times of economic difficulty, and the children dispersed to relations, neighbours and institutions, often for many years. Exporting children to the Empire was only a variation on the traditional theme. It is not, then, surprising that the practice continued into the 1950s.

Despite the evidence of continuity there is a presumption that attitudes towards children changed after the First World War. Yet in some respects this was clearly not so. Traditional moral ideas about their propensity for evil were even accentuated by fears about post-war violence and the rise of 'juvenile delinquency' that seemed to justify severe treatment of the young. Nor did the view of children as small adults, as yet untrained, disappear quickly; they remained potential assets, not just to the state, but more immediately to their families. Indeed, in an era of economic depression the need to put them to useful work to boost family income as soon as possible remained strong, and it fortified the traditional English prejudice against compulsory schooling.

On the other hand, there is abundant evidence that society was increasingly willing to recognise childhood as a distinct stage in human development. To some extent this was an indirect result of the growing concern of the Edwardian state about the health and training of the young; this had resulted in a succession of interventionist measures that impinged upon the role played by parents including provision of school meals, medical inspection of schoolchildren, the 1908 Children's Act which allowed them to be taken into care, the idea of 'child abuse', and the introduction of child welfare clinics in 1914. During the 1920s the concept of childhood became fashionable as a result of the extensive writing about childcare in the women's magazines and the *Parents' Magazine*, which sold 100,000 copies; advice was also offered by a succession of supposedly scientific authorities including Sigmund Freud, Cyril Burt, an advisor to the LCC, and Dr Frederick Truby King, author of the *Mothercare Manual* (1923). Truby King, who urged parents to instil regularity of habits as the foundation of all-round obedience, was especially keen on rigid potty-training and the suppression of thumb-sucking and masturbation; he recommended the use of hand and leg splints on stubborn children. Not surprisingly, by the 1930s much of the advice of these professional childcare experts was already being revised because it was found to be damaging to children!

It was of greater practical significance that by the 1920s more children survived and fewer were being born. Interwar children were thus more likely to grow up in a family with only one or two siblings in contrast to their pre-war counterparts. As a result their parents enjoyed greater opportunities to spend time with them and indulge them. Their homes were less crowded and more likely to become the centre of leisure activities involving all family members. During the 1930s the nation was also given a much-publicised example of the ideal family in the shape of the Duke and Duchess of York and their two daughters, Elizabeth and Margaret Rose, who were regularly depicted as a family at leisure, playing in the garden or having tea together. This had not been done before. To some extent the new pattern reflected the influence of the Duchess who had had the benefit of a warm and relaxed childhood life in Scotland and was naturally taken aback by the cold, dysfunctional family into which she had married. She even gave expression to her view during the Second World War when the royal family refused to follow many wealthy people who were dispatching their children to the United States for safety: 'The children can't go without me. I can't leave the King and of course the King won't go.' Although several thousand children were sent across the Atlantic, the sinking of the *City of Benares* in 1940, when hundreds of children were drowned, put an end to the practice. Similar thinking led the government to evacuate millions of children to the countryside at the outbreak of war, but many were unhappy there and before long their parents brought them home again.

One unmistakable symptom of society's recognition of childhood was the marketing of clothes expressly designed for children during the 1920s; previously they simply wore smaller versions of adult styles or discarded clothes. It was also becoming normal to give pocket money. At age nine the middle class Paul Johnson received threepence a week, while working-class families were more likely to give a halfpenny a time sometimes on a daily basis; this was a useful amount as it bought an ounce of sweets or a comic.[4] These sums could be supplemented by gifts from visitors and relations, and by running errands. Johnson lovingly recalled the vast range of sweets sold loose, mostly at a farthing a time, at Mrs Keely's shop in Tunstall, Stoke-on-Trent:

> Acid drops, pear-drops, Mint Imperials, aniseed balls, bulls-eyes, lavender lozenges, banana glories, gobstoppers, raspberry shapes – all sucking sweets guaranteed to last longest. There were Pontefract Cakes, Liquorice Allsorts, and dolly mixtures, bootlaces and girdles, also Brazils (expensive and not recommended), honey nuts, coconut ice, walnut chocs and sugared almonds, marzipan marvels, Broken Chunks (cheap but of inferior chocolate), various caramels, wrapped and unwrapped, Treacle Sweets, treacle toffee, in slabs broken by a silver hammer, and various other jaw-breakers. Brands like Quality Street, let alone Cadbury's Roses, were too expensive, as were all boxed chocolates like Milk Tray or Black Magic, then new. But there were halfpenny wrapped chocolate bars from Fry's and a penny Turkish Delight.[5]

Magazines for boys, such as *Gem* and *Magnet*, had appeared in the late Victorian period but between the wars commercial publishers, led by the Dundee firm of D. C. Thomson, calculated that the market had by no means been satisfied; they published *Champion*, *Wizard*, *Hotspur*, *Rover* and *Skipper*, to be followed in the 1930s by the new 'comics', *Dandy* and *Beano*. There was also a growing range of toys and games including Hornby model train sets, Meccano, which adopted the famous red and green colours in 1926, Monopoly, ironically popularised by the stock-market crash of 1929, pogo sticks (a feature of the 1920s), yo-yos, which enjoyed one of their periodical crazes in the 1930s, Diabolo, which involved catching a spinning bobbin on a string, plasticine, snakes and ladders, jigsaw puzzles (much favoured by the royal family), dice, shove ha'penny, dart boards, pea-shooters, penknives, guns, bows and arrows, kites, roller skates, skipping ropes and scooters; finally interwar Britain was a golden age for marbles which went under special names such as Corkscrews, Popeyes, Swirls and Rainbows. However, this catalogue gives an exaggerated impression in that only a few of these toys would have been available to most children and in rural districts children usually made their own amusements. One country boy remembered: 'Toys and other playthings were practically unknown and we didn't play ball games . . . Much of our play was centred on the occupations of our fathers.'[6]

Yet despite these signs of indulgence, British society continued to be greatly exercised by the need to discipline and control errant children so as to check the emergence of 'juvenile delinquency'. In their sedate, middle-class household Paul Johnson's parents regularly paraded models of good behaviour before him: 'Shirley Temple [the child prodigy film star] never complains abut her food and always smiles at table', they told him. 'Princess Margaret Rose is never late for meals. Princess Margaret Rose has clean hands at all times.'[7] Many years later when Johnson met the Princess he recounted this view of her as a paragon: 'Well,' she replied, 'I *was* very well behaved then.'

Some parents, feeling in need of outside help to instil discipline and to work off the excess energy of their children, enrolled them in one of the many youth movements whose membership suggests that they were very popular; they included the Boy Scouts and Girl Guides with over 400,000 members by 1938, the Boys' Brigade with 96,000 in 1934, the boys' club movement with 126,000, and smaller numbers enrolled by the Kibbo Kift, founded in 1920, and the Woodcraft Folk, founded in 1925. However, the organisations that had been founded in the Victorian era experienced difficulty in coming to terms with interwar youth culture. The Church Lads' Brigade went into a steep decline and was absorbed by the Boys' Brigade in 1926. But even the Boys' Brigade took a dim view of cinema, smoking, drinking and gambling, even to the extent of urging members to take a pledge of abstinence. One of its captains warned that British youth was growing up 'caring nothing for military virtues of sacrifice, discipline [and] hardihood . . . soaked in the luxury of the cinema and the glittering excitement of the sweepstake.'[8] Not surprisingly, although some boys enjoyed the uniforms and drilling, the brigade began to encounter strong anti-militarist resistance in regions like the North-East and South Wales where they had previously recruited well. Some working-class parents refused to allow their sons to join a movement that looked like a recruiting agency for the army, and the Boys' Brigade found itself the target of jeering, mockery and even stone-throwing:

> 'Ere comes the Boys' Brigade,
> All smovered in marmalade,
> A tuppenny 'a'penny pillbox,
> An' 'alf a yard of braid.[9]

It tried to defuse criticism by cutting its ties with the War Office Cadet Scheme, refusing affiliations with the Territorials and abandoning the use of dummy rifles for drill. In fact, only a minority of youngsters ever joined the youth movements, partly because they disliked their associations with the military and with the churches, but largely because the competition offered by commercial leisure activities was now so attractive.

Of course, for the pessimists the reluctance of the young to learn discipline by joining these organisations proved that the moral panic that followed closely on the end of the war was justified. But although authority blamed the war and the disruption of family life for the emergence of street gangs and youthful petty crime, these phenomena were no more than a continuation of Edwardian behaviour. As always, most crime was committed by young males aged between ten and twenty-nine. The number of juveniles charged with offences rose from 12,000 in 1910 to over 29,000 by 1938, though many petty acts committed by young children went unrecorded. 'In our wild escapades we rarely ran foul of the police', wrote William Woodruff. He and his friends would rush through a market snatching items from bins of fruit and vegetables: 'It wasn't as easy as you might think. I had to run, jump, hang on to the bin, reach down in the half-dark, fill my pockets and make my escape before a rod descended across the seat of my pants.'[10] In Hoxton Bryan Magee and friends worked in pairs, one distracting the stallholder while the other grabbed something from the other side of the counter.[11] Boys were also attracted to the dockyards where they could sometimes pilfer exotic consignments of oranges and other tropical fruit.

For boys petty offences such as pilfering sweets and fruit, slipping into cinemas or climbing into football grounds without paying, and rushing the ticket barriers at railway stations, were often a means of relieving boredom, responding to dares by their mates or maintaining control of a gang. However, they could also be a reaction to economic hardship. In the case of a large family without a male breadwinner the oldest boy often felt obliged to help his mother stretch her meagre resources – and without feeling any guilt about the methods adopted: 'Being the eldest boy, I was the one that kept the family going. I did a bit of pilfering when I was small, never thinking that it was wrong.'[12] Children commonly resorted to a multitude of expedients varying from the legitimate to the illegal. For example, sea coal was traditionally collected on the beaches, but it was also stolen from pitheads and yards especially during strikes; day-old buns could be bought cheaply from bakers, but if broken biscuits were not on sale whole ones could be knocked off the counter and broken up; damaged fruit could be collected at the close of market day, but it might also be deliberately knocked on to the ground; wild berries and mushrooms were freely available in the countryside, but apples and vegetables were also taken from farmers' fields. One ingenious idea adopted by some children involved laying a halfpenny coin on the railway track to be flattened, retrieved and then used as a penny in the gas meter.[13] Hard-up parents usually connived at these activities when presented with the results. After all, they themselves executed 'moonlight flits' to new homes without paying the last week's rent; and they were responsible for the petty pilfering at places of work, a practice commonly ignored by employers as a legitimate perk or a means of supplementing low wages.

Higher up the social scale responses towards adolescent misdemeanours were also rather relaxed, largely because upper-class delinquency was not generally recognised as crime at all. Throughout the interwar years university students maintained the tradition of misrule, frequently resulting in violent clashes with the police. At their annual rag in November 1934, for example, Cambridge students fought a 'battle' on Market Hill resulting in thirty-five of them appearing before the magistrates; seven were charged with assaulting the police, four with obstruction and three with resisting arrest.[5] Another regular occasion for horseplay and attacks on property was the University Boat Race when thousands of students congregated at Piccadilly Circus before spending the evening rampaging through the West End theatres smashing the stalls. Yet the police were tolerant of 'playful', that is, not malicious, violence of this kind when committed by young gentlemen. Even the hapless theatre managers resigned themselves to the practice on the understanding that the universities would compensate them for the damage.

In view of the loud complaints about juvenile delinquency in the 1920s and the upward trend in the number of offences, it comes as a surprise to find that the treatment of young offenders developed in a consistently liberal direction throughout the period; this was a recognition that 'tough' Victorian methods had simply not worked. The change dated from the 1908 Children's Act which made provision for separate courts to handle offenders under sixteen. But the development of a juvenile justice system also went hand in hand with the appointment of women as JPs which began in 1919. The new idea was to create juvenile courts as a domestic space in which male and female magistrates could perform their 'natural' gendered roles as parents; women were assumed to have special knowledge of children's delinquencies and therefore to be able to make a distinct contribution. The policy culminated in the 1933 Children and Young Persons Act which was based on the idea of reforming offenders by getting them into education and training and using non-custodial sentences for those under seventeen. The Act required a panel of justices to handle juvenile cases in each petty sessional division and the inclusion of women in every juvenile court so as to replicate a traditional family. Fewer offenders aged seventeen to twenty-one were to be sent to prison and more to borstal or probation where they would receive training. As a result the number receiving custodial sentences fell from fifty-three per cent in 1901 to forty-five per cent in 1931 and sixteen per cent by 1951.

To most Continentals the traditional enthusiasm for corporal punishments, in the form of birching, whipping and flogging, for young offenders – known as *le vice anglais* – seemed indicative of a masochistic streak in the British national character. However, although scares about juvenile delinquency led to increased use of the birch during wartime, after 1918 magistrates increasingly condemned the practice on the grounds that it had none of the beneficial effects claimed for it; they argued that eighty per cent of those birched reoffended whereas probation reduced the rate. The JPs were now advised to study psychological and medical reports on young offenders and in so doing they became familiar with the views of academics such as Cyril Burt, the author of *The Young Offender* (1925). As a result the birching of young offenders fell sharply during the post-war years from some 3,759 orders made in 1918 to only 365 in 1926. In some areas the practice virtually died out. In January 1938 when a fifteen-year-old boy was sentenced to receive twelve strokes for housebreaking at Leicester there was an outcry because this had not been done for twenty years; the police could not even find a birch or, indeed, anyone who was used to using one. However, it would be a mistake to conclude from the trend in official policy that the use of violence on children diminished significantly. Corporal punishment continued to be routinely adopted both in schools and by parents. In 1932 Parliament rejected a government bill designed to abolish it, and the Second World War delayed the ending of corporal punishment by the courts until 1948.

On the whole interwar society was less concerned about youthful rowdyism and criminality than about the propensity for self-indulgence. As the majority of children left school at fourteen and did not marry until their mid twenties, they enjoyed a lengthy period in which they were usually earning money and thus able to take advantage of the leisure opportunities now available to them. Through their expenditure on clothes, dances, cigarettes, the cinema and sports adolescents marked their passage from childhood to adulthood. The 1920s and 1930s presented the younger generation, for the first time, with the opportunity to turn the pursuit of leisure into a major object of life, and in so doing helped to lay the foundations of the consumer society that Britain was to become later in the twentieth century.

However, by comparison with the post-1945 era youth culture and consumerism was modest, partly because wages were low but also because adolescents and young adults remained subject to effective restraints. They lived in the parental home where their spare time and their money were usually regulated. Especially in rural areas, where families were apt to stay under the same roof, parental influence remained strong. Andrew Purves worked as a shepherd in the Scottish Borders from 1926 onwards. But as he was employed jointly with his father their monthly pay arrived in a lump sum for the household not in individual packets. As was still common, his mother handled the money, retaining something for the children's board and passing on to Andrew an agreed sum for his personal needs. 'I never bothered my head about money when I was young', he admitted.[14] This practice continued until he finally left home in 1944 – when he was thirty-two years old.

In towns parental control was not so easy to maintain because the young enjoyed more temptations in the shape of leisure activities and more opportunities to pursue an independent lifestyle. During the depression the young were often better placed than their elders to obtain employment because employers knew they would work for lower wages; this, however, only exacerbated the tension between the generations where the male head of household was unemployed but remained determined to retain his control of the family. As a result, the start of wage-earning did not always mark a clear divide between dependent childhood and independent adulthood. However, where the wages brought in by sons and daughters formed a vital part of family income some concessions were likely to be made to them. One thirteen-year-old girl obtained a job at the skating rink in Barrow-in-Furness earning eighteen shillings at a time when her father earned only twenty-one shillings as a labourer. This enhanced her status within the family; her mother released her from household duties and made a point of feeding her poached eggs for tea every day: 'I'm not going to kill the goose that lays the golden eggs.'[15] But the most important concession for most teenagers was the freedom to go out in the evenings and return late. For girls cinema attendance usually meant they stayed out until eleven at night, and they found it especially irritating if fathers made difficulty about this or came down the street to ensure they were on their way home. One girl dealt with this difficulty by returning home by a different route, leaving her frustrated father to waste his time before eventually finding her at home; he abandoned his practice as a result.[16]

On the face of it parental control of adolescents was strongly under-pinned by the work ethic; working-class children grew up to regard work as an intrinsic moral good in addition to being a necessity if the family was to be saved from poverty. However, among girls especially the work ethic was heavily qualified by the influence of an alternative, and to some extent conflicting, ideal: marriage. For most working-class girls employment represented no more than a temporary expedient, taking second place to their ambition to marry a man whose wages would enable them to stay at home and abandon paid work. This aspiration often caused tension if a working girl found it difficult to save towards her marriage as a result of tight parental control of her income. One Preston girl who earned twenty-seven shillings in the local textile mill was allowed only one shilling by her mother; she resented this and retaliated by getting married at eighteen.[17] In this way excessive parental control effectively pushed girls towards early marriage because they understandably saw this as the means to freedom and a new status in the community.

It was inevitable that friction would arise between the generations during the 1920s partly because unemployment among older, skilled men undermined their self-confidence, and also because, after weathering the privations of wartime, they resented what seemed like self-indulgence on the part of sons and daughters who were taking advantage of a more varied and exciting social life than they had had. J. B. Priestley cast a curmudgeonly eye on the young of Bradford for indulging in the practice of 'promenading on Sunday nights'. He admitted that the young adopted it because they were denied indoor entertainment such as the cinema on Sundays. 'They have, of course, to get on with their mating', he ungraciously conceded, 'but they could easily do it in a much more civilised fashion than this of monkey-parading.'[18] In fact weekend promenading up to ten o'clock was widely accepted in provincial towns as an opportunity for both sexes to catch one another's eye: '[the boys] would keep turning round and sometimes . . . they would come and ask us to go in the park'.[19] Most parents reasoned that as promenading took place in public there was a measure of control over their behaviour.

Much the best opportunity for meeting members of the opposite sex was afforded by dances where a high proportion of young people found their lifelong partners. Parents usually regarded dances as preferable to clandestine meetings which carried the danger of illicit sexual relations. This is why dances organised by the churches filled an important place in interwar social life. The organisers calculated that if young people socialised under Church auspices they would meet people of the same denomination and under conditions in which nothing untoward was likely to occur.[20] At one church dance held regularly in Barrow the vicar usually sat on the door: 'If he didn't like the way you were dancing he told you so . . . I can remember one lad getting into trouble one night because he was holding a lass round her bottom.'[21] However, even this control failed to satisfy some critics, especially those in the Nonconformist community who condemned all dances organised for the young because of the moral dangers involved; their disapproval only had the effect of encouraging young people to abandon the Nonconformist churches and transfer their allegiance, at least nominally, to the Church of England.

Encounters at dances led to lasting relationships usually character-ised as 'courting' in the language of the time. But courting could be a prolonged and frustrating period that commonly lasted for years. It was not unknown for two years to elapse before a boy was even invited into his girlfriend's home.[22] Parents had an obvious financial motive in slowing the development of the relationship to a snail's pace, but this had to be balanced against their fear of provoking premarital sexual relations if matters were unduly prolonged. Even couples who were in a regular relationship were usually separated early each evening: 'We used to go into the parlour when Reg and I were courting and about half past nine they used to give Reg a cup of tea and m'dad would get the alarm clock off the mantelpiece and wind it; he was ready for bed and that was a good hint for Reg to go.'[23] It is telling that in this case the girl felt that her parents 'weren't terribly strict'.

Perhaps surprisingly, this picture of adult regulation of the social lives and sexual behaviour of the young was more representative of urban than of rural areas. In the absence of sophisticated or organised leisure activities in the countryside, children traditionally found their own amusements away from the home and this habit seems to have carried over into adolescence. Whereas contemporary accounts of growing up in industrial towns suggest that sex outside marriage was almost universally condemned and a pregnancy was regarded as a disgrace, in the countryside sexual experimentation before marriage was something of a tradition. As a result the illegitimacy rates, which were stable at around four to five per cent nationally, were often twice as high in rural districts. As Laurie Lee recalled, teenage canoodling caused little comment: 'very little in the village was either secret or shocking . . . early sex-games were formal exercises . . . if anyone saw us they laughed their heads off'.[24] As a result of this relaxed attitude sexual transgressions rarely came to the attention of the police or the magistrates: 'The village neither approved nor disapproved, but neither did it complain to authority.'[25] In effect, the relative isolation of the village community meant that when a baby was born to an unmarried mother it was usually absorbed into her family without too much fuss being made about its origins.

In the long term the major formative influence on attitudes towards children lay in the development of the educational system. Back in 1880 when elementary schooling became compulsory it provoked complaints from parents, though the abolition of fees in 1891 helped to pacify them. The gradual extension of the length of education and the creation of colleges for girls in the late Victorian period, gradually undermined traditional notions about children as assets to the family, so much so that by the turn of the century they had become a burden. Hence the desire to take them out of school as soon as legally permitted. In rural districts scepticism about the value of schooling still led to children being withheld to help with harvesting and other activities. In the Scottish Borders, for example, holidays were usually extended through August to enable boys to work as beaters, thereby earning five shillings a day, a substantial sum that helped to buy their boots and winter clothes.[26]

Yet despite the controversy aroused by schooling, interwar Britain was still a very undereducated society. The foundation of the system was the elementary school. A majority of children spent their entire school life there, never received secondary education and left at twelve or thirteen if they had reached the prescribed standard. The 1918 Education Act raised the leaving age to fourteen and proposed to extend secondary education. However, the expenditure cuts recommended in 1921 by the Geddes Committee effectively frustrated these aims, partly because they reduced Exchequer grants to local authorities and partly because the voluntary, that is Catholic and Anglican, schools could not meet the higher costs and refused to allow more local authority control. In the financial crisis of 1931 teachers' already modest salaries were cut, so much so that even their pupils noticed that although their teachers wore suits, it was 'the very same, very cheap suit every day, bagging and shiny at the joints'.[27] They routinely taught classes comprising forty, fifty or even sixty pupils with minimal classroom facilities. In his elementary school in Roxburgh-shire Andrew Purves used slates, which were cleaned by breathing or spitting on them and rubbing them with dusters, and jotters with lead pencils: 'only serious work such as composition and tests were done with ink'.[28] All the books, slates, jotters and other items had to be bought by the parents from the headmaster. In his school in Tweedsmuir Andrew Lorimer noticed that there was only one row of books, all of them presented by the philanthropist, Andrew Carnegie, not supplied by the county council.[29]

Since the late Victorian period academics had been attempting to improve society's understanding of childhood and psychologists such as Cyril Burt were keen to turn teaching into a scientific profession. By 1900 educational experts were making use of intelligence tests attempting to explain how children learned and how they acquired fluency in their own native language. Yet despite these advances interwar teaching methods and the school curriculum were determined by fixed assumptions about children. For example, it was still usual to compel left-handed children to write with their right hand, a practice that caused a psychological condition known as 'misplaced sinister'. This often resulted in the children developing a serious stammer, a condition that was much more common among left-handed children, Albert, Duke of York, the future King George VI, being a notable example. When Paul Johnson's parents discovered he was left-handed they accepted it: 'Leonardo da Vinci was left-handed. So was Michelangelo,' said his father, 'so you're in good company little Paul.'[30] But few parents were so enlightened.

Some schools also made energetic, but usually futile, attempts to eradicate local and regional dialects and accents with the aim of promoting a standard, middle-class form of speech. In his Hoxton school Bryan Magee's teachers went to absurd lengths to achieve upper class Cockney pronunciation: 'We mustn't say *cross*, which we all did, we must say *craws*. We mustn't say *off*, we must say *awf*. [The teacher] had a special thing about *often* . . . not only must we pronounce the first bit *awf*, we mustn't pronounce the *t* at all, so we had to say *orphan*'.[31] He concluded that in Hoxton these efforts were like baling out the Atlantic with a teaspoon!

Most contemporary accounts of classroom teaching suggest that the teachers' main aim was simply to keep order; and the best way of doing that was learning by rote: 'the whole class chanting in unison what was on the blackboard, over and over again, day in day out. We enjoyed this because it meant we spent most of the day shouting, all at once.'[32] Admittedly these accounts should not be taken at face value, for those who developed literary talents later in life made things sound grimmer than they were. 'Through the dead hours of the morning, through the long afternoons, we chanted away at our tables', wrote Laurie Lee. 'Twelve-inches-one-foot, three-feet-make-a-yard, fourteen-pounds-make a-stone. We absorbed these figures as primal truths declared by some ultimate power. We asked no questions; we didn't hear what we said; yet neither did we ever forget it.'[33] In fact many pupils acknowledged that they learnt a lot. 'I certainly received a good grounding in the three Rs, history and geography, along with a deep appreciation of music', wrote Andrew Purves.[34] Andrew Lorimer learnt screeds of poetry especially Scott's *Marmion*, some Robert Burns and *Lochinvar*. He also learnt music by singing songs such as the 'Rowan Tree', 'Scots Wha Hae', and the 'Canadian Boat Song'.[35] Magee's musical repertoire included Handel's 'Wherever You Walk', Schubert's 'Who is Sylvia?', 'D'ye Ken John Peel', 'There's a Tavern in the Town', 'Early One Morning' and 'Sweet Lass of Richmond Hill'.[3] Even he admitted that within twelve months he had a grasp of the multiplication tables, the Ten Commandments and the Sermon on the Mount: 'I can think of no other way in which I would have taken them in so thoroughly at that age.' However, he often felt perplexed by religion. He sang 'There is a green hill far away, Without a city wall', but 'it always struck me as a peculiar thing to say'; and, 'I never had the remotest idea what "Hallowed be thy name" meant or "Thy kingdom come".'[37]

Most teachers backed up their learning-by-rote methods by a routine resort to corporal punishment. Laurie Lee's graphic account must stand for many from this period: 'Each morning was war without declaration; no one knew who would catch it next. We stood to attention, half-crippled in our desks, till Miss B walked in, whacked the walls with a ruler, and fixed us with her squinting eye. "Good a-morning, children!" . . . scarcely had we bellowed the last Amen than Crabby coiled, uncoiled, and sprang, and knocked some poor boy sideways.'[38] Admittedly, most pupils made light of the routine violence: 'In a locked draw in the Master's desk lurked the dreaded tawse, [but] it was quick and carried little disgrace.'[39] Andrew Lorimer's view is replicated by Bryan Magee whose teachers employed 'a continuous flow of light and perfunctory assault. They saw their main task as keeping order, and thought hitting us the only way of doing it . . . It was all over in five seconds . . . we took it in our stride.'[40]

Unfortunately, the physical violence often had a psychological side to it. Andrew Purves described his teacher, Mr Hislop, as 'a good teacher, strict disciplinarian and pretty handy with the tawse. His worst fault in the schoolroom was his cutting sarcasm and habit of ridiculing pupils in front of the class . . . he had a habit also of picking on the backward scholars and thrashing them for their failures'.[41]

It is all too easy for historians to interpret pupils' understandable antagonism towards their teachers as indicative of a complete rejection of education and even as a revolt against the imposition of middle-class values upon them. Certainly pupils sometimes rebelled by refusing to accept punishment, usually by grabbing the cane and breaking it, occasionally by attacking the teacher, and even by organising strikes. Parents objected to certain practices including the removal of boys' trousers for caning and making girls hold their petticoats above their heads. This pressure led many local authorities to impose regulations designed to limit the use of corporal punishment during the 1930s. However, it is a mistake to view interwar practice from the perspective of a later era. On the whole parents did *not* object to corporal punishment. Indeed, Bryan Magee found that when he told them he had been smacked at school they showed no sympathy or disapproval of the teachers but cross-questioned him about what he had done to deserve punishment.[42] As a result he stopped telling them about it. The explanation is that both generations had grown up in a society in which violence was accepted as routine. 'Most of us were hit by our parents as a normal thing,' as Magee recognised. Children expected to become the targets not only of teachers and parents but of other children: 'as a street kid I was fairly violent myself, involved in fights every day as a matter of course'.[43]

Despite their flaws the elementary schools guaranteed a basic education. The real problem, as contemporaries increasingly recognised, lay in Britain's failure to provide secondary education for the majority of children; only 9.5 per cent of those leaving elementary school went on to secondary schools. In 1926 the Hadow Report recommended raising the school-leaving age to fifteen and making a clear break at the age of eleven when all children were to go on either to 'modern' or to 'academic', that is, grammar, schools. Some progress was made in that by 1938 two-thirds of children received education in the modern schools up to the age of fourteen. The alternative route involved gaining the School Certificate which had been instituted in 1917 as a passport to white collar and professional careers and to the universities. The grammar and high schools prepared pupils for this stage, and, as more such schools were built in the 1920s while the birth rate declined, it became easier to get in. However, they charged fees. Since 1907 a quarter of the places at grant-aided schools were supposed to be awarded free of fees to children who passed an examination at eleven, but in practice many of them failed to offer these free places.

In any case many parents, especially fathers, retained a deep-rooted prejudice against extended education in any shape. Robert Roberts left a graphic picture of his Salford father's reaction, just after the end of the war, to the idea of allowing his children to receive anything beyond the compulsory education: 'he had let it be known that *he* wasn't bringing up his lads to be "stool-arsed Jacks – sitting all their days in some bloody office. They're going to do a man's job – engineering!" '[44] Working-class parents had to weigh the cost of uniforms, fares, satchels and hockey sticks, not to mention the inconvenience of homework in homes with no spare room, against the loss of earnings; they knew that fourteen- and fifteen-year-olds were almost certain to get jobs, even in the depression, because employers did not have to pay National Insurance contributions for them. One compromise involved sending just one child in the family, usually a younger one, to the grammar school, and making the rest leave at fourteen to start earning a living. Some children relieved their parents of an awkward decision by deliberately failing the examination. But in other families the issue caused prolonged arguments. William Woodruff's sister, Brenda, got her name in the local newspaper for winning top marks in the examination in Lancashire and thus earning a place at grammar school in Preston ten miles away. Yet, despite the scholarship, her parents carefully considered whether they could afford to buy her shoes, instead of clogs. '"Well, we can borrow money to buy shoes, or we can leave her where she is," father said finally. "We might be making a fuss about nothing, Maggie. It's not good to put big ideas into young people's heads. What use is there in this learning when she could be doing real work?" '[45] Brenda did not go to Preston. According to William his father never encouraged the children to try to better themselves by education: 'the mills were our destiny . . . and each should be satisfied with his station'. As a result of such attitudes, half of all the free places offered during the 1930s were declined; fewer working-class children reached grammar schools than had done during the 1920s. On several occasions legislation designed to extend secondary education to sixteen was introduced but by 1939 nothing had been enacted; the Board of Education lacked the necessary clout to push the reform through at a time when free secondary education was not a priority for governments.

On the other hand, the educational experience of girls proved to be more positive than the prevailing ideas suggested. Girls responded enthusiastically to teachers who lifted their sights by introducing them to classic literature and widening their vocabulary. Admittedly, the curriculum had been biased towards domestic subjects since the 1880s when governments became concerned that young women were not being properly trained to run households and rear healthy children. During the 1920s and 1930s girls were required to spend two afternoons each week on cookery alone, and some authorities arranged another afternoon in maternity centres and infant welfare clinics: 'we aim to make the modern girl a little housewife when she leaves school', as one headmistress put it in 1939.[46]

However, many girls regarded domestic education as a waste of time and many teachers actively discouraged them from going into domestic service after they left. Moreover, those girls who managed to enter secondary schools – about 500,000 by 1936 – discovered that they were islands of subversion flourishing in the face of the prevailing back-to-home-and-duty mentality of the post-war period. The secondaries formed autonomous, single-sex institutions run by women for the benefit of women and offered a curriculum modelled on that provided for boys. The staff, who generally had little time for domestic training, focussed on an academic education calculated to produce a new generation of career women. In 1920 a committee appointed by the Board of Education to consider whether girls should have a different curriculum to that for boys recommended that the sexes were not very different academically or psychologically; the committee even warned that it would be unwise to try to restrict girls because 'experience suggests that the division of work between the sexes has changed frequently in the past, and the range of employment followed by women is likely on the whole to increase'.[47] The real problem arose when the girls left secondary school and encountered prejudice towards their career aspirations. Some of them proceeded by taking two-year teacher-training courses, others by enrolling in local authority classes in shorthand and typing, and a few by studying for university degrees. Their entry into the provincial university colleges was now clear, and they were even eligible to take degrees at Oxford from 1920 onwards, though Cambridge held out until 1948.

However, the total number of students in higher education institutions, including teacher-training colleges, rose from 52,000 in 1920–1 to just 68,000 by 1938–9; within this total university students increased from 42,000 to 50,000 between 1924 and 1938, representing less than two per cent of all nineteen-year-olds. This was lower than the proportion in any other European country. The modest increase was largely the result of several new 'red-brick' university colleges that awarded London University degrees at Exeter, Southampton, Nottingham, Hull, Leicester and Reading. Like the Scottish universities they admitted more working-class students who lived at home, and they offered courses relevant to the regional economy. Unhappily, as the red-bricks aspired to become more like Oxford and Cambridge, in time they became steadily divorced from their local communities.

On the whole, however, entry was confined to a very narrow section of society simply because of the costs involved; in 1939 seventy-seven per cent of Oxford's students came from public schools, for example. To overcome the financial hurdles required great determination. At school in Cornwall the future historian, A. L. Rowse, was flattered to be told that his headmaster 'had it in mind that I should go up to Oxford'. But he could not even see his way to attending the nearest university college at Exeter: 'my people hadn't the money even for that'.[48] Calculating that a minimum of £200 was required for one year at university, Rowse spent several years accumulating no fewer than three scholarships of £60, £80 and £60, thus enabling him to enter Christ Church in 1923.

Even middle-class families were deterred by the expense rather than by any academic obstacles. 'It was a damned sight easier to get in in those days', commented Denis Thatcher, explaining his own failure to attend a university. 'Effectively what you needed was money. My father hadn't got the money and I think he thought it wouldn't do me any good.'[49] Sons and daughters of professional men were likely to encounter less resistance, though even in these families girls' aspirations to university education were commonly regarded as inappropriate, and, as a result, they usually found it simpler to settle for a teacher-training college. Katharine Chorley was the daughter of a prosperous lawyer who became an MP in 1900. At this point he abruptly announced that Cambridge was 'off' because he required her to act as an unpaid assistant to him: 'At twenty-one I had no effective free choice in the direction of my own affairs!'[50] After the war Chorley determined to attempt the entrance examination for Newnham College, but as she worked as a driver for a doctor she had to fit in her history reading surreptitiously while he visited patients: 'I used to fish Bryce's *Holy Roman Empire* from under the seat and replace the book hastily as he emerged lest I should be seen engaged with a "heavy" book.'[51]

While some students struggled against prejudice and costs to enter a university, many of the upper- and upper-middle-class candidates who entered from public schools adopted a very relaxed view of their studies. The three years spent at university were simply a pleasant, if expensive, prelude to adult life in which the only serious activity was sport, especially rowing, cricket and athletics. Even among the non-sporting students it was still common to leave without taking a degree; Evelyn Waugh, who described his life as 'idle, dissolute and extravagant', and John Betjeman quit Oxford in 1924 and 1925 respectively before completing the course. Lionel Hedges, a Kent cricketer and Oxford blue, was irritated when, one morning before a cricket match, a 'seedy-looking, middle-aged gentleman' called on him. As Hedges failed to recognise the man he assumed he was a reporter, and abruptly turned him away saying 'I have nothing to say to you.' It transpired that his visitor was his academic tutor.[52] This offhand attitude towards academic work was reciprocated among employers, who, by and large, did not expect or particularly want to recruit graduates; indeed, of the 554,000 people who entered upon employment in Britain in 1934 only 13,000 came from universities. Only in the recruitment of administrators for the remoter parts of the Empire was a university background seen as an advantage, though even there the selection boards showed as much interest in candidates' sporting record as in their academic achievements; sportsmen were so frequently employed to administer the Sudan that it became known as 'the land of Blacks ruled by Blues'![53]

This elitist university system had dire implications for the British economy. Like the schools, universities failed to exploit the talents of large numbers of young men and women and thus generate the skilled and sophisticated labour force required by an advanced economy. It was not until the 1950s that the idea of a positive relationship between economic performance and investment in education became fashionable. At the end of the 1930s the combination of traditional prejudice against schooling, financial disincentives and political apathy had left British education in a backward condition by comparison with other Western countries. In effect, after the largely abortive Education Act of 1918 no major reform was introduced for a quarter of a century. In 1938 another official investigation, the Spens Report, urged the adoption of a school-leaving age of sixteen and free secondary education for all, but the outbreak of war the following year put paid to any chance of implementing its proposals until the question was eventually revived by the 'Butler' Act of 1944.

II

'Reminiscent of Negro orgies': Leisure Between the Wars

Victorian society had seen a protracted struggle between the majority of workingmen, who were keen to win extra spare time in which to enjoy themselves, and an evangelical minority who regarded idleness as evil and leisure as an opportunity for improvement. Improvement manifested itself in the foundation of art galleries, museums, libraries and parks, in the imposition of rules and codes of conduct on rough sports like football and boxing, in visits to the seaside for the health-giving properties of seawater and the 'ozone', and in the promotion of temperance hotels, gardening and charitable work. But although ordinary people went along with this, they routinely took extra leisure simply by failing to turn up for work on Mondays after a weekend of heavy drinking. This led employers to put holidays on to a more formal and regular basis. However, in the long run the combination of additional free time, an increase in purchasing power among the mass of consumers and the development of commercial interests had the effect of putting leisure activities largely beyond the control of the improvers in British society.

This process was well under way before 1914. The late Victorian period had seen the introduction of bank holidays and half-day holidays on Saturdays. Employers increasingly closed their factories and released workers for a week's unpaid leave during the summer. During the First World War the government created extra daylight in the summer by introducing Daylight Saving in 1916; and society enjoyed a dramatic increase in the number of cinemas as well as the import of leisure activities from America including new dances, jazz music and cocktail parties. All this laid the foundation for the emergence of a leisure-oriented society in Britain during the 1920s and 1930s. While the falling cost of living boosted spending power, average weekly working hours fell from fifty-four to forty-eight, and commercial interests invested heavily in a range of innovations including football pools, dance halls, luxurious cinemas and holiday camps. The Victorian work ethic had by no means disappeared, but increasingly British people regarded work as the means to a life of leisure and pleasure, not an end in itself. On the other hand, the improvers could take some comfort from the knowledge that interwar leisure was not all dissipation, idleness and irresponsibility. There was, for example, less emphasis on heavy drinking and more interest in domesticated forms of leisure such as gardening, home improvement and family outings.

By 1918 the privations and strains of wartime, both emotional and material, had generated a huge pent-up demand for popular entertainment especially among the young. In the early 1920s this desire manifested itself in the craze for dances and nightclubs at all levels of society. The patronage of wealthy and fashionable people helped to deter efforts by those in authority to suppress them. Edwina and Dickie Mountbatten, for example, spent most evenings at a nightclub, revue, play or dinner, often a combination. They enjoyed something smart like the Embassy Club in Bond Street where the Prince of Wales could be seen on Thursdays, reclining on his own sofa, and the Duke of Kent arrived accompanied by partners of either sex. Slightly less respectable was the Grafton Galleries which boasted a Negro band but closed at two in the morning and required guests to wear gloves while dancing. Edwina's favourite, the Kit-Kat Club, opened in the Haymarket where one could dine for fifteen shillings a head, a considerable sum in 1925. There, 400 people crowded on to the dance floor, cheek to cheek in the heat: 'a novel ventilation system made it possible to breathe'. But Edwina, who had a taste for the low life, also enjoyed visits to Rectors Club in a cellar in the Tottenham Court Road.[1] Venturing further afield the smart metropolitan set drove out to the banks of the Thames at Maidenhead for a night at Murray's, a club owned by the racketeer, Jack May. The glamour of Murray's was enhanced by the celebrities who turned up, everyone from Lady Diana Manners, the society beauty and film star, to Georges Carpentier, the world light-heavyweight boxing champion. 'Cocaine was what people came to Jack May's club for' claimed one contemporary. 'It was slipped to you in packets, very quickly, when you coughed up the loot.'[2]

However, politicians and the police condemned the nightclubs as responsible for encouraging all kinds of immoral and illegal behaviour, and, to make things worse, the patronage of well-connected men and women endowed them with glamour in the eyes of the rest of society. By 1918 London alone boasted 8,000 nightclubs, and 11,000 by 1925. Between 1924 and 1929 a new, puritanical Home Secretary, Sir William Joynson-Hicks, endeavoured to take things in hand, strongly supported by Lord Byng, the commissioner of the Metropolitan Police; both men were obsessed with destroying London's nightclubs. Greeting a deputation from the Bishop of London and the Council for the Promotion of Public Morality in February 1925, Joynson-Hicks denounced the clubs as 'a blot on the life of London'; but he recognised that it would be difficult to do anything about them because the police did not have the power to enter and were often unable to obtain enough evidence. The police could, of course, try to enter by posing as customers, but 'England does not love a spy', as the Home Secretary put it.³ As a result, only sixty-five clubs were prosecuted between 1924 and 1929, chiefly for selling alcohol out of hours. Joynson-Hicks wanted to have a list of approved nightclubs – opening from six in the evening until after one in the morning – to institute regular police inspection and to close down illegal ones.

Meanwhile attempts to control the clubs generated a good deal of titillating material for the newspapers. One raid was reported as: 'COLOURED MAN'S CLUB . . . Black men and white girls mingling in a bacchanalian setting'.⁴ At 2 a.m. on 30 November 1924 police had entered the Erskine Club in Whitfield Street where whisky, gin, champagne, beer and stout were on sale and most of the customers appeared drunk. They prosecuted the owner, Uriah Erskine, for selling intoxicating liquor without a licence and after hours. Erskine ran a restaurant on the ground floor but closed it at midnight and moved his customers upstairs to the club where dancing took place. On arrival the police found the door locked but they forced their way in to find fifty people, a jazz band including 'men of colour', and white women aged eighteen to twenty-five. According to evidence given by the police, 'the dancing was most objectionable from the suggestive movements'; they reported seeing men and women caressing one another and a white woman sitting on a black man's knees. It was this that really caused the outrage rather than the drink offences for which the owner was prosecuted.

Modest clubs of this kind operating in dingy accommodation and lacking prominent patrons were comparatively easy targets. Other proprietors proved more adept at manipulating the system. Joynson-Hicks played cat and mouse with a Mrs Kate Meyrick who ran Proctor's Club at 43 Gerrard Street in Soho. After a raid in July 1924 she was fined and her club was struck off the register for twelve months. Undeterred, Mrs Meyrick continued to operate an unregistered club and earned six months in prison for selling intoxicants. Following each release she celebrated by throwing a champagne party. After reopening again as the Cecil Club Mrs Meyrick apparently survived for four years without being raided. Eventually it transpired that she had been in collusion with a Sergeant George Goddard who tipped her off whenever her premises were being watched.[5] She was accused of bribing Goddard with sums of £260 and £155, which she denied, although several £10 notes drawn from her daughter's account were found in Goddard's possession; he had some £12,000 in his own account. This proved sufficient to convict both of them.

Of course, the main attraction of nightclubs – dancing – was freely available without running any risks. Indeed, the craze for dancing soon became the symbol of the 'Roaring Twenties'. It had been stimulated by the arrival of American troops in Britain in 1917 bringing jazz and ragtime bands with them. By 1914 London was already familiar with the foxtrot, but peacetime saw a wave of novel, and, to their critics, erotic, dances including the tango, the jogtrot, the shimmy, the Missouri Walk, the Vampire, the Black Bottom and, above all, the Charleston which was indignantly denounced by the *Daily Mail* as 'reminiscent only of Negro orgies'. When the renowned Hammersmith Palais de Dance, noted for American-style jazz bands, opened in 1919 one irate clergyman exclaimed that 'the morals of the pigsty would be respectable in comparison'.

Why were British reactions so extreme? By comparison with the sedate waltzes and the German and Austrian oompah bands to which the Edwardians were accustomed, jazz music seemed very disordered and the dancing undisciplined and suggestive. Modern music epitomised the threat of moral decline, especially in combination with the new fashions worn for dancing, notably the truncated styles adopted by women which seemed embarrassingly similar to male clothing. In the 1930s similar complaints were made about the jitterbug, a dance for fast swing music in which the partners could improvise as long as they kept time with the music. Even the Lambeth Walk, a very English dance, initially attracted criticism for vulgarity, but its respectability was assured when it became known that the Duke and Duchess of Kent enjoyed it.

In any case, the critics were soon swept aside by the apparently insatiable popular demand for dances and by the entrepreneurs who built chains of dance halls across Britain. Along with the pub and the cinema dancing formed the basis of mass entertainment between the wars. For an entrance fee of one or two shillings a dance offered several hours of entertainment. Famous bands led by Roy Fox, Ray Noble and Lew Stone won a following that spanned the entire social spectrum. By 1926 even the BBC had its own house band, the London Radio Dance Band, and in the 1930s it devoted several hours to light dance music every evening. Dancing also gained respectability from its popularity with women who would attend in groups, dancing together until approached by the boys. Women were especially attracted by 'Tea Dances' held in the afternoons and by the dance floors now being installed by smart restaurants.

At a more modest level village halls and church halls organised regular dances; indeed, in a provincial town anything up to a dozen would take place on Saturday nights. In Blackburn William Woodruff attended church-hall dances each Saturday, partly for the hot tea and meat pies that were liberally dispensed: 'To escape from the murky darkness of the streets into the lighted dance halls was the highlight of my week . . . To see the mill girls prettied up with their curled hair and white dresses, and all the boys in their tight-fitting suits, raised my spirits . . . It was so intimate and intense that there was no room for wallflowers.'[6] Along with his sisters and their boyfriends Woodruff also danced at home in the cramped front room when friends brought a banjo or a concertina. There he learnt the Charleston and the Black Bottom, stepping out into the street when it grew too hot indoors.[7] These modest local hops and impromptu front-room dances offer a corrective to the exaggerated claims made by self-appointed opinion-leaders about the degeneracy of the new dances. Dancing was indeed a craze, but one that acted as a safety valve after the privations of wartime and the new strains imposed on ordinary British people by the slump.

Yet for all their popularity dances could never displace the casual, day-to-day leisure patterns based around less energetic activities such as smoking, drinking and gambling. Smoking had established itself as a key part of British social life during the Victorian period, especially cigars and pipe-smoking among men. Gradually, from the 1880s onwards the cigarette had ousted the pipe in popularity; it was less trouble, more sociable, and offered a more glamorous and woman-friendly form of smoking. 'A cigarette is the perfect type of a perfect pleasure', wrote Oscar Wilde. 'It is exquisite, and it leaves one unsatisfied. What more can one want?' Its success was sealed by the invention of a machine capable of mass-producing cigarettes by James T. Bonsack in 1883 which reduced the price and widened the market.

In Britain smoking enjoyed its heyday during the 1920s and 1930s. 'The atmosphere I grew up in was thick with cigarette smoke and I took it for granted in the way most people then did', wrote Bryan Magee. 'As soon as two friends met, one would offer the other a cigarette . . . There was something universal about smoking that is difficult to convey now.'[8] He was right; by the 1930s eighty per cent of men and forty-one per cent of women smoked. Although an Anti-tobacco Society had been founded as long ago as 1853, it had never made the impact of the campaigns against alcohol consumption, and it was not until the 1950s that the effects of smoking on health were established. Between the wars there was virtually no campaign against smoking, and even children were not discouraged. King George V, normally a very strict father, gave his sons cigarettes at sixteen; he himself had smoked as a teenager. [9] In Bryan Magee's boyhood home 'adults would sit around in smoke playing cards for hours with a great deal of coughing and smarting eyes'. He took it for granted that 'as a small boy [I] should be constantly sent out to buy cigarettes'.[10] In fact, boys happily performed this service because the packets contained picture cards in sets of thirty featuring motor cars, film stars, foot-ballers and boxers. Magee and his friends would circulate the markets asking 'Hey, Mister, got any cigarette pictures?'[11] This was shrewd marketing by the manufacturers because collecting appealed strongly to boys of all ages. To take up smoking was widely regarded as an initiation into adulthood and thus accepted by most parents as soon as a boy started earning wages which for many was at fourteen. During wartime the comparatively high wages earned by young boys helped to increase smoking and to enshrine the habit as a rite of passage into adulthood. Although the Children's Act of 1908 had made it illegal to sell tobacco to anyone under sixteen and policemen were empowered to confiscate cigarettes from children in public places, it is doubtful that the law was strictly enforced; the 1908 Act was widely resented as state interference with individual freedom and there was no question of tightening it up.

Between the wars smoking crossed the boundaries of age, social class and gender as the manufacturers multiplied their brands and invested in extravagant advertising campaigns. In the 1930s the cheapest cigarettes cost twopence for five and the middle range sixpence for ten. Among the most successful were WD and H. O. Wills (Woodbine, Goldflake and Capstan), Player's (Navy Cut), Gallagher (Park Drive) and Carreras (Black Cat). Stiff competition led to huge expenditure on advertising, to the profit of the newspapers, rising from £30 million a year in the 1920s to a peak of £60 million in 1937. Many firms favoured patriotic-imperial themes, notably the Navy Cut famously marketed by Player's but copied by most manufacturers. More surprisingly, advertising campaigns also tapped into the fashion for health and fitness; they dwelt on the health-giving properties of smoking if only by depicting active sportsmen on their packets. Some were more explicit. Carreras claimed that the cork tip on their Craven A was 'made specially to prevent sore throats'. Kensitas suggested that smoking checked overeating: 'when tempted to overindulge . . . say "No thanks, I'll smoke a Kensitas instead." '[12] The manufacturers also continued to exploit the traditional link between smoking and masculinity especially for pipes: 'The Everyday Sign of Manhood'. They depicted women coquettishly confiding 'I like to see a man SMOKE A PIPE. Won't you?'[13] Yet it was widely, if tacitly, recognised that smoking often signified masculine weakness, for many men who had adopted it during the war to steady their nerves, resorted to it in the 1920s to boost their self-confidence or simply to relieve boredom.

The manufacturers were surprised to discover that there was no need to market cigarettes especially for women as they largely smoked the same brands as men. During the Edwardian period cigarettes had become firmly established as a symbol of emancipation and equality among women; some suffragettes deliberately smoked in public to make the point but they gave up once the novelty had worn off. By

1918, when smoking became associated with flappers, even the women's colleges had lifted their ban on cigarettes. Eleanor Rathbone, a prominent feminist and MP, was constantly seen puffing on her Turkish cigarettes, but by this time the habit no longer provoked comment.[14] Smoking among women was perfectly acceptable, although some medics were unable to refrain from giving them advice on the subject. In 1922 a Dr Greenwood urged women to adopt pipes rather than cigarettes: 'His opinion, revolutionary as it may seem, is shared by the whole medical profession', reported the Daily Chronicle.[15] The rationale for this view was that 'pipe-smoking . . . is healthy smoking because only tobacco is burned – no paper. Also the pipe smoker is more moderate in his consumption – gives him satisfaction more quickly than cigarettes.' Above all, the doctor believed the pipe to be soothing and conducive to reflection and calm judgement: 'these are the very qualities so many modern women lack'. This comment tells us as much about the mentality of medics as about the state of medical science in 1922. Meanwhile Hollywood was exercising its influence by offering images of glamorous and fashionable women including Mae West, Marlene Dietrich and Tallulah Bankhead perpetually lighting up; it has been calculated that around a third of its heroines were shown smoking in American films, and hardly any of the villains.[16]

Interwar Britons were also addicted to several other substances now regarded as harmful. Snuff, for example, which remained very popular, was available in up to a dozen different types in most tobacconists. Among the drugs opium had traditionally been administered in liquid form mixed with sugar and spices to keep babies quiet; one such brand, Daffy's Elixir, was still sold in the 1930s. Cocaine had been widely used in the Victorian and Edwardian periods, often in tonic wines combined with ethanol which acted as a solvent to extract cocaine from the leaves of the plant. It was taken as a pick-me-up by many successful people, notably authors such as Sir Arthur Conan Doyle, Mrs Humphry Ward and Robert Louis Stevenson, and the explorers Ernest Shackleton and Captain Scott. In 1916 Harrods offered a special kit, including cocaine, to send to soldiers at the front. Not surprisingly, cocaine remained fashionable as a means of relieving depression between the wars, especially among show-business stars such as Cole Porter and Tallulah Bankhead. When challenged on whether cocaine was habit-forming Tallulah famously replied: 'Of course not! I ought to

know. I've been using it for years.' It was not until after the Second
World War that society abandoned its relaxed approach to drugs.

Like smoking, alcoholic drink had become a staple item in British
leisure activities. However, drink was also a key indicator of changes
in behaviour during the interwar period in the sense that less alcohol
was consumed and, to some extent, drinking lost its disreputable
associations. Although drinking habits varied widely, convivial consumption of alcohol in pubs, clubs, restaurants and homes remained
common to people of all ages and social classes. In the 1920s the new
Duchess of York, Lady Elizabeth Bowes-Lyon, enthusiastically adopted
cocktails, as did many fashionable young people; but in the royal
family the very term 'cocktails' was prohibited as being 'too
American'. Instead Lady Elizabeth enjoyed what she called 'drinkie-
poos', usually involving a couple of large measures of gin and
Dubonnet before lunch and a brace of dry martinis before dinner. In
middle-class circles sedate cocktail parties now became fashionable.
Meanwhile in the East End pubs entire families spent happy evenings
singing favourite songs including 'Nellie Dean' and 'Lily of Laguna' in
a 'slow, blearily sentimental, almost lachrymose' style. Before going
home they rallied themselves by linking arms in concentric circles and
performing a high-stepping prance into the centre and out again,
making 'an unbelievable noise, stamping and cheering after each
verse'.[17]

For decades alcoholic overindulgence among the working classes
had been the target of temperance reformers, a tradition that had not
entirely disappeared by the 1920s. In Blackburn William Woodruff's
family was shaken and embarrassed when his sister, Brenda, joined the
Salvation Army at seventeen and decided to 'launch a holy war against
drink'. This involved picketing the local pub, the Griffin, at the end of
the street, selling the Salvation Army newspaper, the War Cry, and
persuading locals to take the pledge of abstinence. However, as
Woodruff recognised, the temperance tradition was now fading fast:
'The pub was one of the few places where the workers could relax.
Drink meant conviviality and friendship. For some it meant oblivion
from a bleak existence.'[18]

While working-class drinking had attracted criticism, in the past
drunkenness among prominent people had usually been tolerated;
however, between the wars politicians like Winston Churchill, who

regularly overindulged in brandy and champagne, exposed themselves increasingly to disapproval. The political career of F. E. Smith (Lord Birkenhead) was effectively terminated by drink. Birkenhead claimed that alcohol never damaged his intellectual faculties and was an essential part of his masculinity, so much so that he considered himself insulted if anyone gave him a *glass* of wine – he always demanded the bottle. But by 1922 his habit of appearing half-drunk on election platforms was attracting complaints from members of local Conservative associations. When he turned up at an Oxford-Cambridge athletics match in 1928 the students, no doubt mischievously, asked him to give a speech; they propped him up with a glass in one hand and a cigar in the other and happily watched him slide under the table. These public exhibitions eventually led Stanley Baldwin to exclude Birkenhead from the Cabinet as too much of an embarrassment.

On the other hand, by the 1920s it was also becoming a drawback for a politician to go too far in the opposite direction. Nancy Astor, the first woman to enter Parliament in 1919, was a staunch advocate of temperance. But as an American she was naturally suspected of wanting to foist the disastrous experiment with Prohibition on to Britain. In 1922 the brewers put a shot across her bows by running a candidate against her at Plymouth who slashed her majority. As a result the most that Astor could risk was to introduce a bill designed to ban the sale of alcohol to anyone under eighteen.

Despite this, by the 1920s drink no longer aroused the controversy it had provoked in Victorian England and, as a result, pro-temperance MPs like Nancy Astor appeared distinctly eccentric. Attitudes and behaviour related to drinking had changed significantly. There had, in fact, been a steady reduction in the production of beer since the 1880s, and even the pre-war output of thirty-five million barrels had fallen to twenty-four million by 1931. This suggests that in the long run consumers were diverting their expenditure to other forms of consumption and entertainment at the expense of the pub and alcohol. In the process the number of convictions for drunkenness fell by two-thirds between 1910 and 1930. Although this was a gradual trend it had been accelerated during the First World War. In 1915 the newly appointed Munitions Minister, Lloyd George, became convinced that the output of munitions was seriously hindered because workers turned up under the influence of alcohol or did not turn up at all on

Mondays. The politicians toyed with the idea of taking the manufacture of drink under state control, and to this end they launched an experiment with state-owned breweries at Carlisle, Enfield Lock and Cromarty. However, by 1921 these had been abolished except at Carlisle whose residents cheerfully imbibed nationalised beer for the next forty years. In the emergency the authorities took risks with the drinking classes that they would never have contemplated in peacetime. They established a Central Control Board that simply shut down many pubs. By 1917 the board had reduced annual beer production by ten million barrels to twenty-six million. It also lowered the alcoholic strength of both beers and spirits. Above all Britain's opening hours, which had traditionally run from 5 a.m. to midnight in London and 6 a.m. to eleven elsewhere, were drastically curtailed; by 1915 the pubs closed at ten each evening. On top of all this alcohol became much more expensive because the duty was raised from eight to fifty shillings a barrel on beer and from fifteen to thirty shillings a gallon on spirits. As with income tax the price never returned to Edwardian levels – nor did the alcoholic content.

Although peace brought an expected surge in beer consumption this was not sustained beyond 1919. The average consumption of beer per head that had been twenty-six to twenty-seven gallons back in 1900, and nineteen to twenty gallons in 1919, had fallen to thirteen to fourteen gallons by the 1930s, despite increases in the real value of wages. This trend was not the result of temperance propaganda – only ten per cent of men and twenty per cent of women abstained in the 1930s – nor of mass unemployment; it reflected changes in attitudes and in behaviour. Young people were increasingly likely to be found in cinemas or dance halls rather than the pub. Many pubs remained a masculine domain in which 'Gentlemen Only' signs appeared above the vault and the taproom while a small corner or 'snug' was set aside for women. However, they became less exclusively male. During the 1920s wives increasingly accompanied their husbands to pubs even if they separated on arrival; and younger women acquired the habit of going with their boyfriends which usually meant a lower level of drinking per head.

However, the extent of change is easily exaggerated, and traditional habits survived especially in urban districts. As a GP in the Gorbals during the 1920s Dr John Stone witnessed the effects of the consumption of 'Red Biddy', a lethal concoction of cheap red wine and methylated spirits. Once consumers had been knocked out by this potion his only option was to pump their stomachs as quickly as possible.[19] At the Admiral Keppel in the Hoxton Road in the East End the bar was regularly full of women in mid morning, when the men were mostly at work. They left their prams outside: 'usually one or other of the babies in the street would be yelling, and a steady succession of women emerged from the pub, drink in hand . . . and gave the baby a drink from her glass to tranquillise it, and [went] back into the pub'.[20] This picture of mid-morning mothers captured a pattern of behaviour that had its roots in the pre-1914 era but was increasingly untypical between the wars. Within working-class communities drinking habits were a key indicator of distinctions between the families that were respectable and those that were not. Only in the poorest slum areas were mothers and wives likely to loom so large among the patrons of the local pub. Migration to the new housing in estates and in suburbs dissolved the traditional drink culture, and led working-class families to adopt a lifestyle closer to that of the middle classes. Consequently, by 1938 half of all expenditure on alcohol was made at off-licences for consumption at home. As the population left for the suburbs the brewing companies seized the opportunity to build more attractive pubs along the new arterial roads stretching away from town centres and to discard the old spit-and-sawdust image. These pubs or 'roadhouses' were much larger – the layout was supposed to make it easy for the police to circulate – and rather characterless according to the critics who derided the style as 'Brewer's Tudor'. But they were lighter, brighter, more woman-friendly, and came equipped with cocktail bars and enough seats to make standing at the bar unnecessary. As a result the magistrates were more likely to look kindly on applications for licences, a material consideration in a period of declining consumption. For despite the brewers' efforts the total number of pubs in Britain fell from 99,500 in 1905 to 77,500 in 1935. Some council estates remained largely destitute of local watering holes. In one especially badly served south London estate 30,000 people relied on a single pub, the Downham Tavern.[21]

The reforms and innovations of the post-1914 period left Britain's drinkers paying a minimum of five pence or sixpence a pint for mild and seven pence for bitter, which was double the pre-war price, sixpence a shot for gin and rum and seven pence for whisky. The higher duty caused a steep fall in consumption of spirits in working-class communities, so much so that the Mass Observation survey of Bolton in 1938 found that four in seven pubs sold no spirits at all.[22] It was confidently predicted during the 1920s that the drinking classes would not tolerate paying higher prices for weaker drinks. And with some reason, for at a time when prices generally were falling, alcohol became dearer with the result that total expenditure on drink fell from £426 million in 1920 to £306 million in 1938. Meanwhile, the brewers struggled to rationalise production and lower costs by a series of mergers and takeovers that reduced the number of breweries from 3,650 in 1914 to 885 by 1939.[23] They also tried to arrest the trend by advertising campaigns claiming 'Guinness is Good for You', 'Younger's Beer – Just What the Doctor Ordered', and, rather wordily, 'Bass gives an edge to your appetite and promotes good digestion'. Questioned by Mass Observation in the 1930s, drinkers loyally protested that beer promoted their health, though this was merely a variation on the traditional belief that a manual worker must drink at intervals throughout the day to keep his strength up. Nor did the government do much to help. Legislation passed in 1921 left most of the wartime restrictions in place. Opening hours were limited to eight a day, or nine in London, which was half the pre-war total, pubs being closed before eleven in the morning, for two hours in the afternoon, and at ten in the evening, or eleven in London. In April 1939 George Read, the landlord of the Robin Hood at Kettering, was prosecuted for selling beyond 10 p.m. when police spotted one customer drinking a glass of beer, topped with froth, at 10.20. Representatives from the breweries testified that beer drawn from the cask lost its head within two minutes, but 'expert' witnesses and several sympathetic landlords argued that, if drawn with short, sharp pulls into a clean glass, beer could keep its head for half an hour – putting Mr Read conveniently in the clear![24] Sadly, when the case went to the King's Bench Division the Lord Chief Justice upheld the decision of the local magistrates and found him guilty.

Such infringements of the law could not obscure the lasting change that had come about in British drinking habits as a result of wartime restrictions, price rises, commercial investment in alternative leisure and shifts of attitude among the younger generation. In the process the aims of the Victorian temperance lobby had been achieved at least to the extent of curtailing some of the worst aspects of drinking. Without straying into the quagmire of Prohibition, Britain was acquiring more moderate drinking habits and the pubs were becoming more respectable than they had been before 1914.

Among the young, and among women generally, the cinema offered serious competition to the pub. Moving pictures had appeared as early as the 1890s, but during the Edwardian period and the First World War thousands of cinemas opened, many of them in former music halls. By 1914 3,000 cinemas operated, rising to 5,000 by 1939. Bolton, with a population of 180,000, boasted 14, and suburban Middlesex had 82 in 1920 and no fewer than 138 by 1939. This expansion represented a huge investment in new cinemas designed to attract customers away from the old 'fleapits' and 'bug huts' of pre-war days. The other boost came with the arrival of the 'talkies' in 1927. Sceptics warned that they would be a brief novelty because the American accents would prove off-putting to British audiences. But this proved to be a complete misconception. In May 1929 when Al Johnson sang 'Sonny Boy' in *The Singing Fool* at the Stoll Picture Theatre in Newcastle upon Tyne, the film ran to packed houses for ten weeks and, according to the local newspaper, he 'kept Newcastle weeping for weeks'. In fact the only hitch with the talkies was a technical one arising from the frequent breaks in the film. When this happened it was so difficult to re-synchronise the film and the sound that projectionists were paid a bonus if they managed to get through a week without a break.[25]

By 1939 23 million people attended a cinema each week, many going several times, and some 990 million tickets were sold in the year. The success is not difficult to explain. Cinema offered entertainment at very modest prices. A Saturday morning matinee cost as little as twopence or threepence; afternoon seats could be had for sixpence, and evening ones for a shilling. By the 1930s cinemas were offering reduced prices for the unemployed, eighty per cent of whom attended every week. This was a bargain considering that the typical programme might last up to three hours and included a main film, a B feature, a newsreel and a cartoon or 'short'.

Customers also appreciated the taste of comfort and luxury in the new cinemas with their wall-to-wall carpeting, plush seats, coffee lounges, marble staircases and ladies powder rooms painted pink and lined with mirrors. Built at a cost of anything from £50,000 to £100,000 the supercinemas could seat from 1,000 to 2,000 people and were usually situated at suburban sites with good access by road, Tube or bus. Interwar cinemas were typically called Odeon, Gaumont and Astoria, though some proprietors, hoping to foster a feeling of opulence, favoured Ritz, Regal, Rex, Paramount, Essoldo, Embassy and Ambassador. Inside the decor was carefully calculated to suggest a smart, modernist ambience by means of the art-deco style, or to create an exotic illusion by using Mexican motifs, the Spanish hacienda style or Egyptian temple decoration. The Egyptian mode became fashionable after November 1922 when the archaeologist, Howard Carter, and his patron, Lord Caernarvon, discovered the 3,300-year-old tomb of Tutankhamun in the Valley of the Kings. Their exploit captured the popular imagination not least because of the curse that was supposed to fall upon those responsible for disturbing the dead King's tomb. Only a few months after the discovery Caernarvon suffered a fatal illness, as did several other members of his team, though Carter survived until 1939.

The popularity of cinema was also attributable to the fascination and hero worship aroused by its leading stars, especially as several of them had been catapulted to fame and fortune from very humble origins. Emerging from a life of poverty Charlie Chaplin had served his apprenticeship as a music-hall performer before being spotted by an American film company in 1912. By 1914 Chaplin could demand $1,000 for a week's work, and he earned $12,800 by 1916.[26] During wartime miracles were freely attributed to his films by wounded soldiers who laughed so much at his screen antics that they got up and walked without using their crutches. Gracie Fields, who made a similar progress from industrial Rochdale, personified the fantasies of thousands of mill girls. She made her first film, *Sally in our Alley*, in 1931 followed by seven more until 1937 when she was signed up by Twentieth Century Fox to make four films for a fee of £200,000. At a time when most British actresses were stilted and wooden Gracie Fields was natural and spontaneous; she combined the talents of a comic actress with a bubbly personality and a remarkable singing range that included opera, ballards, hymns and comic songs. It is some indication of her status as a national icon that, following an illness in 1934, Gracie Fields arranged with the BBC to broadcast her message of gratitude to the nation; and in the House of Commons Sir Samuel Hoare announced the termination of the debate early so that members would not miss it.

Inevitably some contemporaries detected a moral downside in the popularity of cinemas among the young. During the war critics complained that 'the darkness encourages indecency'. But such fears were soon swept aside. Cinema actually proved to be a potent force in drawing people away from the heavy drinking, rowdyism and violence associated with traditional leisure activities towards a respectable and domesticated pattern of mass entertainment. Critics also condemned the cinema as a vehicle for imposing vulgar American culture on British society. However, such complaints made little headway against the strong preferences for American films among British audiences who regarded British ones as too tame. British fascists launched outspoken attacks on Hollywood because they considered it a tool of Jewish propaganda. 'One of the first duties of Fascism,' proclaimed A. K. Chesterton, 'will be to recapture the British cinema for the British nation.' But, as so often, the fascist case was undermined by the Nazis who derided Charlie Chaplin as 'a little Jewish acrobat' and banned his films. Chaplin famously responded by satirising Hitler in *The Great Dictator*: 'I did this for the Jews of the world', he said.[27]

It is worth remembering that a majority of the cinema audience in this period was female. This represented a novel development because up to this time the very concept of women's leisure had scarcely been recognised. Most women were tied to the home, they usually denied themselves pleasures for the benefit of the rest of the family, and, in so far as they enjoyed 'leisure' activities at all, these involved sewing, knitting and entertaining. For middle-class women especially the combination of smaller families and more easily managed homes left them with spare time which they filled with bridge, tennis, dancing, gardening, motoring and lunching with friends. Less affluent women, especially those who were reluctant to visit pubs, happily attended cinemas with friends, family and boyfriends, often several times a week. While the dance hall provided the best way of meeting boyfriends, when they began courting an evening at the cinema offered an ideal means of developing intimacy in the relationship to the extent of kissing and fondling but stopping short of sex. In this way leisure activities for millions of British women centred around cinema, dancing, women's magazines, shopping expeditions to the big department stores and a visit to a Lyons Corner House or ABC where they could eat in comfortable surroundings but at modest prices. In 1933 William Woodruff ventured into the Lyons Corner House at Marble Arch where he was 'overwhelmed by the lights and the glitter'. Slightly intimidated by the gold chairs and a starched tablecloth that almost touched the floor, he found he could only afford tea and a bun; this he consumed 'crumb by crumb', and then repeated his order as he enjoyed listening to Harry Roy's famous band so much.[28]

Despite these new opportunities, women continued to spend much of their time labouring at home; but the home itself became a major focus for leisure thanks to several innovations. For the wealthy the telephone was now becoming available; from a mere 122 telephones in 1910 Britain had 980 by 1920, 1,996 by 1930 and 3,339 by 1940. Of far wider significance for women was the radio or 'wireless', available initially in the form of 'cat's whiskers' or crystal set receivers and later as battery-powered models. The cheapest sets cost £2. 10s. in the 1920s, falling to 30s. in the 1930s, plus a 10s. licence. The number of licence-holders increased from 36,000 in 1922 to an astonishing 8.8 million by 1939. Women provided the largest audience for radio simply because they spent so much time at home listening while they did their housework. It opened up wider interests not just in music, but in drama, literature, history and health, thereby lifting horizons that had been restricted and leaving women better informed than men in some respects.

The wireless also had a formative effect in creating leisure for the *family* as opposed to the individuals within it. Many contemporaries recalled how, every evening, the whole family sat round the wireless in their kitchen listening to it. Each night the BBC, which had its own in-house Radio Dance Band by 1926, offered light music programmes such as *Band Wagon*, *Monday Night at Eight* and *Music Hall*. On Sundays when Sir John Reith insisted on a menu of uplifting programmes, listeners tuned in to Radio Luxembourg and other foreign stations for more light music. Previously most families had relied on wind-up gramophones for their musical entertainment. But during the 1930s the gramophone was fashionably combined with the wireless in the shape of the radiogram, a large, highly polished wooden item of furniture that could be plugged into the mains. Though decorative fixtures, radiograms suffered from faulty electronic connections that produced a red glow and caused consternation among householders who still found electricity alarming. When this happened in the Magee household his mother, fearing that 'the whole thing was about to go up in flames and burn the house down', threw a large basin of water over it.[29] Surprisingly the radiogram continued to function once it had dried out.

While radio, cinema, dances, smoking and drinking formed the routine elements of British social life, many families increasingly aspired to the more expensive option of an occasional week's holiday away from home. A luxury in 1914, by the end of the 1930s holidays had become the expectation for millions of people. Fifteen million enjoyed a holiday away from home by 1939, though for most of them this was attained only by careful saving because they had to forgo their week's wages. Only 1.5 million employees were entitled to a paid holiday in 1925, rising to 4 million by 1937. Consequently holidays usually had to be managed on a modest scale. For East Enders it might involve hop-picking in Kent or day trips by charabanc to Southend and Clacton on the Essex coast or Margate and Ramsgate in Kent. In Hoxton the departure of an open-decked, forty-seater charabanc from the Admiral Keppel public house, after the men had fortified themselves with a pint, was a festive occasion: 'when it moved off the men emptied their pockets of coppers which they threw to the waiting children – crowds waited for this and a great cheer went up'.[30]

To take a family to the seaside for a week, however, required careful budgeting. In Blackburn the Woodruffs chose Wakes Week when the mills traditionally shut down, for an excursion by train to Blackpool. They filled the family's sole suitcase, not with clothes, but with food. 'As the price of food at Blackpool was too high, we took bread, oats, a large can of Lyle's Syrup, margarine, cans of milk, fish and pineapple chunks, tea, sugar, eggs marked with our name, a jar of jam, a jar of piccalilli relish, salt and sauce.'[31] They also took the week's rent to spend, but left two shillings on the mantelpiece 'to pay for iron rations when we returned broke'. Before reaching the station they noticed something dripping from the case: '"It's the bloody syrup," father exploded, and the offending item was thrown into the gutter.' On arrival at Blackpool the children were instructed by their parents to rush past the ticket barrier: 'If you're caught, act daft,' their father advised.[32] At their lodging house the Woodruffs shared a single bedroom and had the use of a large room where they and the other families prepared and ate their food.

Clearly a week's holiday represented a struggle for a working-class family. By the late 1930s the cost of a week for two adults and two children was put at £10, a substantial sum when the weekly wage was around £3. 10s. Abortive legislation to give workers a week's compulsory paid holiday was introduced in 1925, 1929 and 1936, and by this time it had become a central aim of the trade union movement. Although governments evaded the issue, employers were increasingly sympathetic to the idea, regarding paid holidays as a sound investment that effectively paid for itself in terms of improved productivity. As a result paid holidays were increasingly being achieved through collective bargaining. Eventually in 1937, when the government was convinced the proposal was no longer controversial, they appointed a committee whose recommendations led to the 1938 Holidays With Pay Act. By June 1939, when eleven million employees were entitled to a week's paid holiday each year, most British workers had come to it as their right.

For the new holidaymakers the chief destinations were the South coast (Brighton, Eastbourne, Bournemouth, Worthing and Bognor), the South-West (Weston-super-Mare, Weymouth, Torquay, Ilfracombe, Newquay and Penzance), Kent (Ramsgate, Margate and Broadstairs), Essex (Southend, Clacton and Frinton-on-Sea), the East coast (Scarborough, Skegness, Filey and Bridlington), Lancashire (Blackpool, Southport and Morecambe) and North Wales (Llandudno, Rhyl and Prestatyn). While vulgar Blackpool and raffish Brighton pulled in huge numbers, each region boasted a more sedate resort for the middle classes. Bournemouth maintained a ban on slot machines on the pier, while Eastbourne claimed it 'does not despise the day tripper so heartily as she once did'. Some resorts actually offered distinct social zones; Scarborough, for example, reassured visitors that she had 'natural barriers which separate her classes of visitors'.[33]

But what were the holidaymakers to do once they arrived? The days when seawater was recommended as a cure for gout were long gone. By the 1930s seaside resorts felt obliged to invest up to £4 million a year improving their facilities, building piers, fairgrounds, 'pleasure beaches', lidos, bandstands, cinemas, dance halls, ballrooms and floral halls. In addition to the famous illuminations that began in 1925 Blackpool offered the Winter Gardens, the Pleasure Beach and the Golden Mile with scores of peep shows and freak shows including 'The

Elephantine Woman', a crucifixion, and a honeymoon couple who starved in a glass case by day but fed on fish and chips at night when the visitors had gone home. In 1932 a Mr Luke Gannon exhibited the Reverend Davidson, notorious as the defrocked Rector of Stiffkey, fasting in a barrel on Central Beach at Blackpool. On the first day alone 10,000 people paid twopence a head for a glimpse at him. Gannon was sued for causing a public nuisance and Davidson for attempted suicide; but the Reverend, who had become a popular figure by this time, was found not guilty and successfully sued for damages! He then reverted to his original career by joining a circus at the age of sixty-two and decamped to Skegness where, in July 1937, he appeared in a cage with two lions. One lion, named Freddy, grabbed Davidson who was rescued but died two days later.

These bizarre attractions helped to compensate for the fact that the sun and the sea could both be elusive at British resorts. On arrival at Weston-super-Mare Laurie Lee's villagers gazed hopefully around: 'But we saw no sign of the sea. We saw a vast blue sky and an infinity of mud stretching away to the shadows of Wales.'[34] It hardly mattered. Where once ailing visitors had come searching for seawater, medical opinion now endorsed sunshine as an aid to health. During the 1920s the old idea that a pale skin indicated gentility was rejected in favour of the cult of the suntan; and most resorts accordingly published their sunshine statistics. British builders adopted the fashion by introducing the sun and its rays into the stained-glass windows and the garden gates of semi-detached houses all over the country. However, Britons who wanted to acquire a tan exposed only limited areas of their bodies. In keeping with its risqué reputation, Brighton offered the only beach where men were allowed to bare their chests. Admittedly, shorts grew shorter and narrow straps replaced sleeves, but much of the torso remained covered. Women's bathing suits also shrank as it became fashionable to 'show as much of yourself as possible' in the words of *Picture Post*. The height of fashion was represented by Jantzen's 1929 figure-hugging, one-piece costume with its narrow straps and scooped-out back.

The cult of the sun, bathing and the healthy outdoor life culminated in the building of lidos all over Britain, including at many inland towns, during the 1930s. With their sweeping, modernist lines lidos suggested luxurious cruise liners or aerodromes. Rather oddly they were often sited on the seafront or even jutting into the sea and were filled with seawater. The explanation is that many municipalities charged bathers for huts and cubicles and even for erecting tents on the beach. They could be fined for changing beneath towels, a practice known as 'mackintosh bathing', and they were banned from entering the sea if the weather was rough. In view of these restrictions it must have seemed simpler and more comfortable to use the lidos instead.

Meanwhile the proprietor of an amusement park, one William Butlin, had spotted that many families found traditional boarding houses uncomfortable and unattractive. His alternative, the first Butlin's holiday camp, was opened by Amy Johnson at Easter 1936 on the northern edge of Skegness on the Lincolnshire coast. Certain practical obstacles had first to be overcome. At Butlin's invitation the local council inspected arrangements for sewage disposal for the 1,500 people who were expected to generate a 'Daily Dry Weather Flow' of 15,000 gallons.[35] The sewage was treated at a disposal works before being pumped into the sea on the ebb tide.

Butlin was not the first in the field; during the 1920s some rather austere and regimented holiday camps had been pioneered by Lever Brothers and the Co-operative Society for their employees and by the Workers Travel Association; but Butlin was the most successful. He offered 'A week's holiday for a week's wages', though at £3 per person for full board at the height of the season the deal was beyond the reach of most people. However, the price included everything offered by the major resorts including bathing pools, boating, dance halls, orchestras, sports grounds, billiards, table tennis and physical culture classes. A typical menu comprised: porridge, prunes, bacon and eggs, marmalade, tea and coffee at breakfast; roast pork, stuffed veal, vegetables, jam roll and cheese for lunch; cakes, preserves, brown and white bread and butter for tea; and beef or mutton with pickles, custard pudding, bread and cheese for supper. This proved appealing to lower-middle-class families, partly because they wanted to be in control of their expenditure for the week, and because it offered them a mixture of community activities and the privacy of their individual timber-and-concrete chalets. Butlin expanded by building further camps at Hayling Island, Seaton, Clacton and Filey, where 100,000 visitors a year took their holidays by 1939.

Amid the fun and frolics some of the British also upheld the more sober Victorian traditions of holidaymaking. The vogue for healthy athleticism and love of the countryside encouraged enthusiastic bands of ramblers, hikers and cyclists to explore the remoter parts of Britain. In the 1930s a new bicycle could be purchased for £5, often paid in weekly instalments. The Cyclists Touring Club and the National Cyclists' Union, representing 3,500 local clubs, boasted nearly 60,000 members by 1938. It was also in 1930 that the 23-year-old Alfred Wainwright, later famous as the author of guides for walkers, made his first visit to the Lake District fells. He described the experience as 'magic, a revelation so unexpected that I stood transfixed, unable to believe my eyes'. Wainwright eventually contrived to get within easy reach of Lakeland by moving to a job in Kendal where the fells offered him an element of romance that was missing from an otherwise boring life and a loveless marriage.

However, at this time remote rural districts offered little accommodation for walkers. British visitors to Germany returned with accounts not only of the Nazi cult of physical fitness but of the building of *Jugendherbergen* in the countryside. A handful of youth hostels had already been created by the Trampers Guilds and the Holiday Fellowships in the Lake District, the Pennines, the Cheviots and North Wales, and in 1930 they merged to form the Youth Hostels Association under the presidency of the historian, G. M. Trevelyan. They offered ramblers a bed at one shilling a night along with cheap meals and cooking facilities. By 1939 297 hostels had been opened, with another 100 in Scotland and Ireland, enrolling 83,000 members.

Meanwhile, wealthier and less active people looked abroad for their holidays. After the restrictions imposed on foreign travel by four and a half years of warfare the return of peace saw something like a mass exodus. By 1930 a million Britons took holidays on the Continent. Traditionally British families rented villas on the French Riviera or in Italy to benefit from the mild winters, but this habit increasingly gave way to summers spent soaking up the sun. The 1920s and 1930s were also the heyday of the luxury cruise liners plying the transatlantic routes to New York and the West Indies or taking in the Mediterranean ports. By 1933 175,000 Britons were embarking on cruises each year, but only a minority were first-class passengers. Previously the main business for these ships had been the cheaply priced 'steerage class', but after 1918 tighter immigration laws curtailed this custom. Shipping companies therefore expanded the market by creating 'Tourist Third Class' which was within the means of middle-class people keen to visit exotic parts for the first time. Cunard, White Star Line and French Line boasted fleets of romantically named 'floating cities' including *Mauretania*, *Aquitania*, *France*, *Majestic*, *Olympic* and *Berengaria*. After the war they acquired new ships in the shape of redundant destroyers which they converted to cruising, and vessels handed over by Germany as reparations payments which had to be renamed. But on Clydeside, Tyneside and Merseyside luxurious new liners were launched: *Isle de France*, *Normandie*, *Franconia* and *Queen Mary*. They were a source of national pride and a welcome guarantee of employment for thousands of skilled workers. In 1934 the *Queen Mary* was launched with support from Gracie Fields who sang 'Land of Hope and Glory'. In the past shipowners had contrived to create a country-house atmosphere on board by using heavy wood panelling; but the new vessels strove for a lighter, modern ambience using art-deco decoration and much glass, metal and Formica, as well as air conditioning and bedside telephones. Among the passengers in first class a tourist might encounter Walt Disney, Alfred Hitchcock, Marlene Dietrich and even the Duke of Windsor who liked to stand on deck hitting golf balls into the sea. In the last days of peace the new *Queen Elizabeth* was ready to join this fleet, but by 1939 the end of an era was already in sight. Once again, cruising was suspended for six years of international war, and after 1945 the liners, increasingly faced with competition from air travel, rapidly lost their brief appeal to the modern-minded holidaymaker.

12

Yellow Earl and Silver Ghost: Motoring and Interwar Society

On 17 August 1896 Bridgett Driscoll, a Croydon housewife, was on her way to a folk-dancing display at the Crystal Palace when she was hit by a motor car. Witnesses described it as 'coming at a great rate – as fast as a bicycle'. Two minutes later Mrs Driscoll was dead, the first victim of the new fashion for motoring in Britain. As yet, however, the fashion had not spread far, for motor cars were not only expensive and unreliable but were a source of amusement to some, and an object of suspicion for many people. Only a few months before Mrs Driscoll's death Parliament had repealed the Locomotive Act of 1865 – better known as the 'Red Flag Act' – which imposed speed limits of four miles per hour in the country and two miles per hour in towns, and required that 'at least three persons shall be employed to drive or conduct such a locomotive' one of whom had to walk not less than sixty yards in front 'and shall carry a red flag constantly displayed'.

Historians and contemporaries agree that this legislation held up the development of the British motor industry for thirty years. It did, however, have some compensating effect in diverting resources and inventiveness into the manufacture of bicycles which enjoyed a boom in the 1890s. Several of the entrepreneurs later famous for motor cars began as cycling enthusiasts, notably William Morris, and some of the companies, including Rover, Humber and Dunlop had started as bicycle-makers.

Meanwhile, however, the Germans began producing their Benz and Daimler motors and the French their Peugeot-Levassors during the 1880s and 1890s. Consequently, the early British motoring enthusiasts acquired their vehicles abroad, or, in the case of Harry J. Lawson, bought up all the foreign patents they could. It was Lawson who organised the first London to Brighton Run, known as the

'Emancipation Run', to celebrate the repeal of the Red Flag Act in 1896. Although fifty-eight vehicles were due to race, only thirty-three managed to start. The mechanics, mostly French, laboured for up to half an hour with the starter handles before they could get the engines to fire, 'making a noise like a number of field guns going off'. The crews then jumped in hastily before the engine died, wrapped themselves cosily in rugs, and chugged off down the road. Only ten vehicles made it to Brighton.

Not surprisingly, it seemed far from obvious to most Edwardians that the new invention was going to transform their lives. Up to 1914 the motorist remained a figure of fun lampooned by music-hall entertainers and mocked by *Punch* cartoonists because his vehicle broke down every few miles. The survival of the motor car in these years lay in the hands of a collection of enthusiasts, eccentrics, entrepreneurs and engineers. Among them the titled motorists, including Lord Rosebery, the Duke of Westminster, the Earl of Derby and the Prince of Wales, helped to make motoring a fashionable and viable activity. The Earl of Macclesfield loaned William Morris £4,000 in 1912 and a further £25,000 in shares in 1919.[1] Dunlop put Earl de la Warr on the board – an established means of lending respectability to untried companies. Hugh Lowther, 5th Earl of Lonsdale, who became known as the Yellow Earl on account of his love for the colour, subordinated his passion for horses and hunting to concentrate on motors and racing. As the first president of the Automobile Association in 1910 Lowther made it adopt yellow as its official colour, and in May 1922 he attended the wedding of Princess Mary in a Daimler strikingly painted in primrose and black. Lord Montagu of Beaulieu, who began acquiring motors in 1896, became the first MP to use one in an election campaign in 1900; in 1903 he founded the *Car Illustrated* and was employed as motoring correspondent by *The Times* from 1921 to 1929. The Hon. Charles Rolls, son of Lord Llangattock, started selling expensive motor cars to peers and princes in 1902. When he met the engineer, Henry Royce, in 1904 Rolls agreed to buy all his output. Their motors, marketed as Rolls-Royce, were ten, fifteen, twenty or thirty horsepower machines selling at prices ranging from £395 to £890. As early as 1906 they dubbed their Silver Ghost 'the best motor car in the world'.

Between the wars even these aristocratic motorists were eclipsed by the Indian princes. Bhupinder Singh, Maharaja of Patialia, was Rolls-Royce's best customer, owning twenty-seven of their models among a collection of over a hundred vehicles. Jay Singh, Maharaja of Alwar, always specified a blue finish and no leather for his purchases. His pride was a 1924 Lanchester, part car and part royal coach, with two seats in front and a throne at the back with room for two postillions. When he tired of his cars Jay Singh had them buried with full honours in the hills around his palace in Rajasthan. However, although the patronage of peers and princes was flattering to the manufacturers, their demands for customised motor cars encouraged British producers to concentrate too much on expensive, prestigious vehicles rather than on cheap, mass-produced ones.

In this period upper-class men commonly regarded the motor car as their 'horseless carriage'. As Siegfried Sassoon admitted in 1924 'it is a substitute for my hunter, much less trouble than a horse and much more mobile'.[2] However, the cost of buying and maintaining a motor car quickly made it the symbol of Edwardian plutocrats, newly rich men who attracted criticism for their vulgar and irresponsible ways. They were satirised as Toad of Toad Hall in Kenneth Grahame's *Wind in the Willows* (1908). But Grahame's caricature simply reflected the behaviour of drivers who provoked a good deal of class antagonism by their display of ostentatious wealth, by forcing pedestrians off the road and by routinely ignoring the speed limit which had been raised to fourteen miles per hour in 1896 and to an alarming twenty in 1903. Traditionalists warned that motoring threatened to shorten the relaxed country-house weekend and would compete with riding and fox hunting; the smell put the hounds off the scent, the noise frightened the horses, and as a result some hunt committees banned members from arriving at the meet by car. Country-dwellers, who generally regarded motor cars as a dangerous intrusion, encouraged children to throw stones at them and to line the roads with tacks and glass to cause punctures. S. F. Edge of the Dunlop Company admitted: 'on more than one occasion I have had drivers of horse-drawn vehicles slash at me with their whips as I have passed them on the road. I have had stones hurled at my head and broken glass bottles deliberately placed in front of motor tricycles . . . In London one was bombarded by jeers and insults from practically every bus-driver and cab-driver one met.'[3] To complete their sense of being a persecuted minority

motorists became a political target when the government, in the shape
of the Chancellor, David Lloyd George, dragged them into the famous
'People's Budget' in 1909. Casting around for ways of financing the
new old-age pensions and building dreadnoughts for the navy, Lloyd
George hit upon the idea of a licence for motor cars and a duty of four
pence per gallon on petrol. As there were so few drivers at this time his
innovations were a brilliant means of focussing extra taxes on the
conspicuously wealthy, as well as endowing future chancellors with a
huge new source of revenue.

However, while the flamboyant motorists attracted public hostility,
the prosaic but equally determined pioneer manufacturers began to
turn out larger numbers of British models. In many cases they moved
into motor cars from an existing engineering business. Henry Royce,
the son of an impoverished Lincoln miller, had been apprenticed to the
Great Northern Railway, and worked in tool-making in Leeds and in
electronic cranes in Manchester before setting up independently. An
obsessive genius, Royce subsisted on a diet of sandwiches and sausages
cooked on the works boiler. In the charming young aristocrat, Charles
Rolls, he found a partner who was ostensibly very different but who
shared his fascination for tinkering with engines.

The bowler-hatted Herbert Austin, who had also completed an
engineering apprenticeship, was originally employed by the Wolsey
Sheep Shearing Machine Company. Austin produced the first four-
wheel vehicle for Wolsey in 1899, but in December 1905 he launched
the Austin Motor Company at Longbridge. By 1914 he employed 2,300
men and produced 1,500 vehicles a year. William Morris, originally
apprenticed to a cycle-repairer in Oxford, set up his own repair
business at his parents' house with capital of just £4. By stages he
started to assemble bicycles from parts ordered from the Midlands,
moved into his own workshop in Oxford High Street, and in 1909
established the Morris Garage to sell, hire and repair motor cars. When
Morris began to manufacture motors in 1912 he adopted the American
practice: buying in the parts and assembling them to his own design
and specification, thereby reducing the capital required. His first car,
the Morris Oxford, described by *Autocar* as 'a two-seater torpedo', was
cheap, easily maintained and aimed at a popular market; by 1913 he was
making 1,300 a year.

By 1914 nearly 400 British motor manufacturers had appeared, but only 113 were still in business. In contrast to Morris, most of them were unwilling or unable to make large numbers of vehicles efficiently; they preferred to produce a wide range of customised motors in small numbers but at high prices. However, profitability lay in focussing on a few models in the manner of Henry Ford whose eight-horsepower Model A became available in Britain in 1904 priced at £195. In 1911 Ford began production at Trafford Park in Manchester, using the first assembly line in British manufacturing industry.

However, the First World War transformed the scale of the industry in Britain and also changed the image of motoring from a hobby for wealthy eccentrics into an economic asset for Britain. Initially the war diverted British manufacturers into the production of armoured cars, ambulances and other equipment required by the army. Rolls-Royce models were fitted with armour plating and turrets on which machine guns could be mounted. Adapting his hobby to patriotic purposes, the Duke of Westminster acquired twelve armour-plated Rolls-Royces for service on the Western Front and in East Africa. Meanwhile the economic blockade with Germany greatly stimulated the industry after 1915 when the government imposed a 33.3 per cent tariff on imports. Although seen as a temporary infringement of free trade designed to raise revenue, this duty was extended after the war, leaving the British motor industry heavily protected for the next fifty years. Though obviously welcome at the time, the tariff caused long-term damage by effectively feather-bedding British manufacturers against competition.

With the arrival of peacetime motoring really took off in Britain. From just 132,000 in 1914 the number of private cars reached 1,056,000 by 1930 and 1,477,000 by 1935. Total vehicles, including taxis, motor buses, motor bicycles and tractors licensed for roads, amounted to 2,287,000 by 1930. By 1936 two million people relied on the industry for employment; measured by work and wages it was the second largest industry in the country. In two far-sighted letters to *The Times* in 1919 Lord Montagu of Beaulieu argued that, with the leading powers gathered at Versailles for the peace negotiations, the time had come to reach an international agreement about the future of motoring: 'we need rules for the road as for the sea'. [4] In particular Montagu questioned whether the British habit of driving on the left of the road with the driver on the right side of his vehicle – the opposite to that adopted in most countries – was wise; it would be in the interests of British manufacturers to follow a uniform practice. But the politicians were not listening.

Meanwhile, for many contemporaries the car was ceasing to be a luxury for the wealthy and becoming a necessity for ordinary people. Men in particular, falling victim to fashion and consumerism, found that motoring absorbed a good deal of their time and money. Like a later generation of computer-owners they were easily persuaded that, having bought their first car, the next thing to do was to buy a higher performance model which they did not actually need. Ownership of a motor car commonly formed a central part of male emotional and social life; it helped men to define themselves and acquire some sense of purpose. 'The temptation of talking about cars, when one has a car, is quite irresistible', admitted Aldous Huxley, 'I am ruthlessly prepared to bore the non-motorist by talking interminably of this delightful subject.'[5]

On the other hand, there was a great deal of exaggeration and commercial hype behind these attempts to talk up the significance of the motor car. *Mayfair Magazine* was a little premature in 1912 when it claimed that the horse would soon be seen only in the Zoological Gardens; there were still two and a half times as many horses as tractors in use in the 1930s. Even in London's East End cars were a comparative rarity: 'the perpetual background noise of my childhood was the sound of horse-drawn vehicles passing by' recalled Bryan Magee. During the 1930s almost everything was still delivered by horse including coal and milk.[6] Also, as J. B. Priestley observed in his journeys round Britain, cars were far less in evidence in the North than in the affluent South-East. In fact, as late as 1938 only one person in fifteen owned a car, though many others used motor buses and coaches. Although the Society of Motor Manufacturers and Traders claimed in 1926 that one could run a car on a minimum of £450 a year, this was considered optimistic and was, in any case, beyond the means of many people. A less expensive alternative was the motorbike. Sales increased from 115,000 in 1919 to 724,000 by 1930, a popular purchase for young men whose girlfriends perched on what was cheerfully called the 'flapper bracket'.

Nonetheless the optimists were correct in claiming that motor cars were becoming increasingly affordable; the average factory price, which had been £308 in 1912, was down to £259 by 1924 and £130 by 1935. This was the inevitable result of the huge increase in output; British production alone rose from 34,000 vehicles per annum in 1913 to 212,000 in 1928 and 445,000 in 1938. A major contributor to this expansion was the Austin Seven, launched in 1922 and variously known as the 'Baby Car' and the 'Mighty Miniature', though music-hall comics rudely dismissed it as the 'Bed Pan' and a 'motorised pram'. But Herbert Austin shrewdly described it as 'a decent car for the man who, at present, can only afford a motorcycle and sidecar, yet has the ambition to became a motorist'. Denis Thatcher recalled: 'My first car was a minute Austin Seven. I paid £5 for it, buying it off a mate.'[7] As the registration number began EMM, Thatcher called it 'Little Emma', an example of motorly endearment that was common among interwar drivers. With a top speed of fifty-two miles per house the Austin Seven did fifty miles per gallon and sold for £165 new; it was very reliable if not the cheapest small car on the market.

William Morris marketed his motors much more aggressively. 'The one object in life of many makers seems to be to make the thing the public *cannot* buy', he argued. 'The one object in my life has been to make the thing they *can* buy.' Morris had a habit of slashing his prices just before the Motor Show each autumn. The Morris Cowley, originally priced at £465, had been reduced to £299 by 1921 and to £225 by 1922. He followed up with the famous Morris Minor in 1928 and the Morris Eight in 1935. By 1930 Morris and Austin together accounted for two-thirds of all British cars. Ford, a dominant manufacturer before the war, had lost sales after 1918. But in 1928 Henry Ford acquired a 600 acre marshland site at Dagenham in Essex in the hope of reviving his fortunes. From 1932 onwards the new Ford Eight, priced at just £120, rolled off the production lines. As a result of this revival, Morris, Austin and Ford together commanded around sixty per cent of the market in the 1930s.

Aspiring motorists were also tempted by falling maintenance costs after the war. In 1922 Captain E. de Normanville, the *Daily Chronicle*'s motoring correspondent, urged motorists to take advantage of this; for example, a set of five Dunlop tyres recently selling for £40 could now be bought for £29.[8] But drivers were more concerned about the costs imposed on them by the government. In 1928 some 925,000 of them signed an AA petition asking the government to put the tax on petrol rather than on horsepower. However, the politicians regarded it as fairer to make the more powerful cars bear higher licence charges; they also knew that this policy boosted domestic manufacturers by placing the high-horsepower American imports under a disadvantage. By 1939 motorists paid tax at fifteen shillings per horsepower. At that time a gallon of petrol cost one shilling and sevenpence halfpenny of which ninepence, or almost half, went in tax.[9] Motoring correspondents advised that costs could be kept down by driving carefully: 'Speed costs money. It is extravagant on petrol, on oil, on tyres and it accelerates to an alarming extent wear and depreciation.'[10] Tests on a typical ten horsepower family car showed that it ran for twenty-five miles a gallon when driven at sixty miles per hour but for forty-four miles when driven at thirty miles per hour.

However, the careful driver was a rare phenomenon in this period. As a result, although motoring became much less exclusive after the war, it continued to be regarded as an antisocial activity in many quarters. Although the speed limit had been set at twenty miles per hour few drivers took much notice of it, provoking a litany of complaints from pedestrians about 'road hogs', noise and excessive speed, not to mention the horrendous casualties. During the early 1920s fatal accidents ran at 2,500 a year and non-fatal ones at 62,000, and this total steadily increased so that in 1930 alone over 7,000 people died on British roads and 150,000 were injured. In comparison, in 2004, with 33 million vehicles on the roads, only 3,221 were killed and 31,130 injured. Taking the interwar period as a whole the total casualties included 120,000 fatalities and 1.5 million injuries, making motoring comparable to fighting a war. Perhaps the most famous victim was the 46-year-old T. E. Lawrence whose motorcycle swerved when overtaking two cyclists on 13 May 1935; he clipped one of their wheels, was thrown over the handlebars and fractured his skull.

Yet for many years governments took little action, perhaps because they listened to the vociferous motorists' pressure groups whose members frankly resented any suggestion that the law ought to apply to them. The Automobile Club, formed by Frederick Simons in 1897, which eventually became the RAC, upheld the pre-war gentlemanly tradition. Much more energetic and anti-Establishment in character was the AA, founded in 1905 by Charles Jarrott. The original members, who felt angry about what they saw as government neglect and police persecution of the motorist, gave the organisation a distinctly subversive role. Taking advantage of the general election in December 1918 the AA pressurised MPs and candidates with a view to obtaining 'logical and adequate legislation in the matter of modern road transport in all its branches'.[11] In particular it demanded the extensive reconstruction of roads that had been built for horse-drawn vehicles, better fuel supplies 'at a reasonable price' and lower taxation on motorists. The AA also reminded politicians that at a time of economic uncertainty the motor industry was in a position to create large numbers of skilled jobs in manufacturing and maintenance.

But the AA's *enragés* went well beyond political campaigning. They organised patrols to warn drivers about the speed traps set by what they saw as overzealous police. Faced with widespread disregard for the law, police constables had taken to hiding in bushes and climbing trees, armed with stopwatches, ready to pounce on the motorist exceeding the speed limits. The AA published maps to show the favourite sites for police ambushes. Such tactics prompted Sir Edward Troup of the Home Office to compare the AA with 'an association of burglars employing scouts to warn them which houses are and which houses are not watched by the police'.[12] For their part the patrolmen warned drivers that a police trap was in the vicinity by abstaining from giving their usual salute to AA members. The police countered by booking the scouts for obstruction and reminding them that it was illegal to issue warnings if a crime was being committed. They also attempted to fool the scouts by setting fake speed traps in the shape of a deliberately half-hidden constable if they saw a car that they thought might be speeding.

In fairness, the AA's patrolmen, smartly attired in cap, collar and tie, knee breeches and red rosettes, played a constructive role too. They offered a support system to drivers whose vehicles had broken down, and they erected road signs long before the local authorities undertook the responsibility. Recognising that in the absence of petrol stations motorists routinely risked running out of fuel, the AA established the first petrol station at Aldermaston in Berkshire in 1919; it withdrew from the business once the commercial interests had created a network. Not surprisingly, 725,000 appreciative motorists had joined the organisation by 1939.

None of this, however, significantly reduced the danger and

inconvenience caused by bad drivers and defective vehicles. Even T. E. Lawrence, usually afraid of nothing, was traumatised after spending five minutes as a passenger with Siegfried Sassoon who drove his car as though setting his horse at a very high fence. On his first solo drive Sassoon ran into a dog cart, and next day he knocked down a cyclist. He never gave signals, always blamed other drivers for his innumerable accidents and apparently remained oblivious to the dangers he posed to other road users.[13]

With people like Sassoon on the loose Britain's five to six million cycle-owners were especially vulnerable, though their spokesmen objected to the introduction of cycle tracks which made their journeys safer. In 1926 when the House of Commons tried to help cyclists by voting to make it compulsory to carry a reflector at the rear, Captain W. Brass MP, observed: 'I am told that the best reflector is a pair of pink silk stockings, but we cannot ask every woman cyclist to promise to wear silk stockings.'[14] His facetious tone was indicative of the fact that road accidents were not taken seriously as yet. Meanwhile, cyclists sometimes retaliated against motorists by riding four abreast down the centre of the road. On one occasion in 1934 the Prince of Wales was involved in such an incident. When he jumped out of his car to remonstrate one cyclist told him he used the middle of the road primarily to annoy the idle rich!

Why was British society so complacent about the huge volume of road accidents? Part of the explanation is that motoring was widely regarded, less as a mundane matter of transport, than as a very physical *sport* like boxing, horse racing and hunting, in which serious accidents were to be expected. The same was true of aviation. Also, motoring still retained much of its original upper-class ambience during the 1920s. The arrogance shown by wealthy and powerful men towards pedestrians and cyclists, who were presumed to come from the lower classes, was epitomised by Lt Col J. T. C. Moore-Brabazon, an early motorist and aviator, who, in a speech in Parliament, dismissed road accidents by saying: 'Over 6,000 people commit suicide every year and nobody makes a fuss about that.' Indeed, motoring enthusiasts increasingly blamed pedestrians for causing accidents, so much so that several MPs urged the government to introduce an offence of 'dangerous walking'! Admittedly, not all motorists were unsympathetic. In June 1926 Miss Jessie Betts of Uxbridge was knocked off her bicycle at Cowley in Middlesex en route to Iver in Buckinghamshire. She got an additional shock when the King and Queen alighted from the motor car full of concern for her. They wanted to summon a doctor but Betts insisted she was only bruised and was more concerned about the damage to her vehicle: 'Never mind the bicycle so long as you are not hurt,' said the King.[15]

It was indicative of official complacency and the influence of the powerful road lobby that interwar governments did their best to avoid regulating motoring. The AA and the RAC consistently opposed the speed limit, pedestrian crossings, driving tests and indeed anything that appeared likely to interfere with the enjoyment of the motorist. In 1930 the Transport Minister, Herbert Morrison, actually abolished the thirty miles per hour speed limit for light cars, though it was reintroduced in built-up areas in 1934. Admittedly the 1930 Road Traffic Act made careless driving an offence that could be punished by disqualification, and it also introduced the Highway Code. However, this had no force in law, offering, in Morrison's words, 'a code of good manners to be observed by all courteous and considerate persons'.

Motoring enthusiasts rationalised the road safety issue by arguing that accidents were caused by a small minority of 'road hogs', which was a complete delusion. As a result driving offences were not always taken seriously by the courts. Some magistrates took the view that a guilty driver had merely committed an error of judgement rather than a criminal offence. One judge told a driver who was convicted for manslaughter and sentenced to three months: 'It is no reflection on you morally to go to prison.' Conversely, motorists considered themselves harshly treated especially by benches of magistrates to which, to their intense annoyance, women were now being appointed. Certainly the treatment varied a good deal. Fines for a simple offence such as passing traffic lights could be anything from ten to twenty shillings, and motorists summonsed for obstruction were fined anything from fifteen shillings to forty shillings.[16] When standard rules were drawn up for the London courts in 1939 the AA expressed the hope that the magistrates would show some discretion by imposing fines according to the means of the offenders.

Unhappily for the cause of road safety the politicians themselves failed to set a good example by respecting the law. In May 1924 Viscount Curzon MP was summonsed for exceeding the twenty miles per hour speed limit by driving at thirty-two miles per hour at Chiswick. But Curzon, who had already acquired twenty-one convictions for motoring offences since 1908, showed little remorse or embarrassment: 'the car had four wheel brakes and could be pulled up very quickly,' he told the magistrates. [17] Unimpressed, they fined him £20 and suspended his licence for six months. In fact the manufacturers were slow to fit adequate brakes in the early 1920s. Commenting on this in 1924 the *Daily Mail* assured readers: 'four wheel brakes have proved their value and have come to stay'; but they were not standard even on expensive models. Not until 1926 was the latest Rolls-Royce equipped with four wheel brakes, for example.[18] In any case, private motorists seemed unaware that their brakes would not last forever and ought to be tested periodically. As late as 1930 tests showed that eight per cent of all vehicles were in a dangerous condition with the brakes often completely out of balance so that they skidded violently on wet and greasy surfaces.[19]

Winston Churchill adopted the same high-handed attitude when he was stopped by police in January 1926 driving his car from Millbank to Whitehall. At the new roundabout – then known as a 'gyratory' or 'merry-go-round' – at Parliament Square Churchill was confronted by Constable George Spraggs who told him he was going in the wrong direction! But as Churchill simply refused to be interrupted or corrected a heated argument quickly developed. Ignoring advice to drive in a clockwise direction, 'Mr Churchill persisted and the constable took Mr Churchill's name and address. The car was then allowed to go on.'[20] Although a summons should have been issued, Scotland Yard apparently declined to take further action against the Chancellor of the Exchequer. Wilfred Ashley, who was Transport Minister at the time, cheerfully explained that the merry-go-round 'is a delightful institution that the Police Commissioner and I have started in order to make a Brighter London'. Parliament Square had been selected because he wanted to make MPs aware of the ministry's work: 'All I am afraid of', Ashley burbled, 'is that sometimes traffic in the inner ring won't get out at all and that cars may have to go round and round until their petrol is exhausted, and then they will have to be regarded as derelicts [laughter].'[21]

Given this light-hearted approach, it is not surprising that the behaviour of motorists was slow to improve. Viscount Curzon, who had succeeded as Earl Howe in 1929, was fined so many times for excessive speed that eventually a magistrate advised him to take up motor racing, which he did in 1928 at the age of forty-four. Although he achieved some fame in this role, the reckless Earl also suffered seven accidents. In 1937 he broke six ribs in a crash which left him within an inch of his life. While he spent seventeen days in hospital at Weybridge, his stoical, 23-year-old wife told the *Daily Mirror*: 'I have been wondering whether this will be the end of my husband's racing career. These terrific speeds terrify me, but I would never dream of asking him to give up. His heart is too much in it.'[22]

Despite the dangers it created and the controversies it provoked, it cannot be denied that the motor car became an object of fascination for growing numbers of British people who saw it as another symbol of the 'Roaring Twenties'. Journalists waxed lyrical about 'The Magic of Modern Cars' and freely described them as instruments of civilisation. Though increasingly common, motor cars were still enough of a novelty for small boys to gather along major roads watching for the distant cloud of dust that heralded the approach of a vehicle. Above all, the greater availability of motor transport helped to change people's economic and social lives. It accelerated the trend towards living in the suburbs, begun earlier by the railways; it encouraged ordinary people to enjoy cheap seaside holidays by means of motor buses and coaches; and it began to open up remoter regions including the Lake District, Wales and Scotland to tourists. 'The chief end of my car', commented Rudyard Kipling, 'is the discovery of England. The car is a time machine on which one can slip from one century to another'.[23] At a more practical level tours of discovery were facilitated by maps such as the *Daily Mail Road Map of London and South-East England*, published in 1926 at four miles and one mile to the inch; priced at three shillings they sold out quickly. The AA printed a book on *Scotland for the Motorist*, describing the car as 'a magic carpet' for the discovery of new lands – language that spoke volumes about the insularity of the southern English. There were plenty of guide books written in similar vein such as the popular series by H. V. Morton: *In Search of England*, *In Search of Scotland* and *In Search of Wales*. But the car really did help to open up their country to ordinary British people for the first time, not simply by helping them to enjoy the beauty and tranquillity of the countryside, but by stimulating an interest in history and archaeology. For example, whereas in 1901 just 4,000 people visited Stonehenge each year, by 1929 100,000 did so. Among other things this concern for Britain's heritage laid the foundations for the later success of the National Trust.

Not that recreational travel was all sober and improving. During the early 1920s thousands took short excursions by charabanc in which the journey was the most enjoyable part of the holiday. An open vehicle with a hood at the back, the charabanc could seat up to thirty passengers in rows. By the mid 1920s padded seats, pneumatic tyres and an enclosed all-weather protection offered greater comfort for long journeys. The conductor had to cling to the running board from which precarious position he collected the fares. The passengers enjoyed this experience because, in contrast to travel by train, they were in control of things; they could stop the charabanc to take on more beer at frequent intervals and make as much noise as they wished.

Naturally contemporary sceptics found plenty of scope for criticising the fashion for motoring. Instead of appreciating the peace of the countryside, they claimed, most motorists happily endured the bumper-to-bumper conditions on the main roads. But main roads seemed preferable to many drivers who feared that their vehicles would be damaged by the potholes in rural lanes, and that they would not be able to find petrol stations. Critics also condemned the growth of 'shanty towns' in Essex and along the Sussex coast as the worst consequence of the motor car. In the mid 1930s Laurie Lee described the 'shabby shoreline suburbia' now creating a continuously built-up coastline around Worthing. Meanwhile, following the introduction of articulated lorries in 1919, the railways had lost a quarter of their goods traffic to road transport by the mid 1930s. With no thought of a co-ordinated transport policy, governments simply allowed the market to dictate the pace of expansion and decline regardless of the long-term consequences.

Then there were the supposed moral effects. Cars featured prominently in novels such as Evelyn Waugh's *Vile Bodies*, and in films in which the motor-car chase became a favourite climax. Fashionable stars like Rudolph Valentino were invariably photographed getting into or out of motor cars. For the romantically inclined but socially inept young man an invitation to a girl to take a ride in his car was an unembarrassing way of starting an affair. One could become bolder, without being too explicit, by suggesting a trip to Brighton, on the basis that 'all men learnt that Brighton meant sex' as one contemporary put it.[24] Certainly the town had come down in the world since the days of the Prince Regent, so much so that by the 1930s its clientele had more in common with Blackpool. In his 1939 novel, *Brighton Rock*, Graham Greene captured the shabby, seedy atmosphere of the place in his depiction of the youths and petty criminals who gathered there.

For many women the motor car offered a new sense of freedom and independence comparable to that ushered in by the 'safety bicycle' in the 1890s. Even before 1914 the suffragettes had regarded it as an expression of emancipation as well as a practical means of transporting Emmeline Pankhurst to provincial rallies. They made a point of employing female chauffeurs, Muriel Thompson, Vera Holme, Charlotte Marsh and Aileen Preston, the last being the first woman to qualify for the AA's Certificate in Driving. A similar spirit of adventure mixed with feminism led many young women to drive ambulances in the First Aid and Nursing Yeomanry during the war where they gained practical skills in car maintenance. 'I positively dreamt of carburettors, magnetos and how to change tyres', recalled one of the drivers, Pat Beauchamp.[25]

Against this background it is not surprising that women were quick to appreciate the opportunities that a driving licence brought them during the 1920s. The young Agatha Christie, restricted by her marriage, described motoring as a revelation because of the freedom it gave her to go wherever she wanted: 'I don't think anything has given me more pleasure, more joy of achievement, than my dear bottle-nosed Morris Cowley', she enthused.[26] The wartime spirit of adventurous motoring was upheld by interwar female racing drivers, notably 'Fabulous' Fay Taylour, and by the Hon. Mrs Victor Bruce. Mrs Bruce, who usually drove with a string of pearls swinging round her neck, claimed the dubious distinction of being the first woman to be fined for speeding and the first to ride a motorbike. In 1927 she carried off the Ladies Cup at the Monte Carlo Rally and drove all the way to the Arctic Circle and back, having an audience with the King of Denmark en route. In 1929 Mrs Bruce won the record for the greatest non-stop run by a single motorist by driving for twenty-four hours at an average speed of ninety miles per hour.

These escapades certainly won headlines for female motorists, but probably made less impact on the average middle-class driver than innovations designed to improve the safety and comfort of women drivers. The manufacturers, seeing no advantage in promoting motoring as an expression of feminism, took some trouble to make their vehicles manageable for the less technically minded woman, notably by introducing the self-starter, widely known as the 'ladies' aid', which spared drivers the laborious task of cranking their engines into life, not to mention the pneumatic tyre which gave passengers a smoother ride over Britain's potholed roads than the solid tyres endured by Edwardian drivers. Women's magazines helpfully advised readers on alterations in their dress style to enable them to get in and out of cars without embarrassment. And the makers of the Lanchester guaranteed women a really smooth ride: 'at fifty miles per hour you can knit comfortably!'

Yet despite these concessions to femininity, men interpreted women's encroachment into motoring as another worrying sign of gender confusion. In 1934 the *Aeroplane* quoted with approval a typical waspish comment: 'The woman driver is generally content with half the road, but she always wants the middle half!'[27] However, as always, gender prejudice was qualified by social class. Men freely conceded that a woman who was good with horses would probably make a decent driver! Certainly upper- and middle-class ladies took to the motor car with enthusiasm. *Eve: The Ladies Pictorial*, a light-hearted magazine dedicated to encouraging leisured women to get out more, printed a regular feature on 'Eve and Her Car', accompanied by photographs of titled ladies at the wheel, and collected the usual complaints about the tax burden borne by motorists.

Yet, despite the male complaints, it is far from clear that men and women differed much in their approach to driving; aristocratic women seem to have been just as reckless as their male relations. When the Duff Coopers were given a car by Lord Beaverbrook in 1919 Duff reported: 'Today [Diana] drove it into a milk cart in Stafford Street, upset the cart and flooded the street.' Soon after this, as they drove out of Beccles in Norfolk, Lady Diana looked down to arrange their belongings and forgot to steer: 'before we knew what had happened the car was on its side in a ditch'. They climbed out of the window and summoned help.[28] Edwina Mountbatten, who notoriously refused to allow her chauffeur to drive at all, regularly dented her Rolls, bumped other vehicles and crashed into shopfronts, leading to a stream of insurance claims. In one incident in 1922 her headlights dazzled another driver who swerved into her car, ripping off the running board of the Rolls; but Edwina calmly wired Dickie: 'All well. Car very little damaged'.[29] In 1923 she tipped the car into a ditch, was caught speeding at thirty-four miles per hour over a crossroads and was prosecuted for dangerous driving. Unabashed, Edwina complained that the car was too slow for her needs and sold it for a faster model!

In fairness to Britain's drivers it should be remembered that they laboured under major disadvantages during these years: they had to cope with dangerous, narrow and uneven roads designed for horse-drawn traffic, and the majority of them had never been properly trained to drive a car in the first place. Fearful of antagonising influential people or the taxpayers, interwar governments proved reluctant to tackle these problems. Most existing roads comprised a mixture of clay, rubble, mortar and stone that disintegrated into loose dust or greasy mud under the pressure of motor traffic. It was for this reason that many 1920s drivers regularly laid up their vehicles for the winter, waiting for Easter as the signal to emerge for the new season's motoring.[30] During the 1920s local authorities gradually began spraying tar over the main roads, thereby greatly reducing the clouds of dust and dirt that so annoyed pedestrians and left a thick coat on the faces and clothes of drivers. However, differences in local authority spending meant that road quality varied a good deal; the Great North Road, for example, came under the jurisdiction of no fewer than seventy-two authorities. Moreover, post-war governments, anxious to cut taxation and expenditure, largely contented themselves with widening some existing roads rather than building expensive new ones.

One exception to this was the Great West Road, which opened in May 1925, an eight-mile stretch from Chiswick High Road near Kew Bridge through Brentford, Heston and Isleworth to the main Staines road at Bedfont. It was opened to a great fanfare by King George and Queen Mary who drove along it amid cheering crowds.[31] 'This master-piece of road engineering', as the News of the World described it, was fifty feet wide, bordered by avenues of plane, chestnut, beech, lime and Norway Maple trees; it had foundations of twelve-inch consolidated hard core under nine inches of Portland cement, reinforced with a steel fabric and topped with two inches of rock asphalt. The road cost £1 million and was expected to last twenty to thirty years with minimal repairs. However, many motorists considered the new arterial roads now extending around London to be dangerous, especially when wet. In 1924 Charles Grey, who was pressing the MP, Moore-Brabazon, to launch an agitation, complained about his drive from Hounslow Heath to Brent: 'I cannot hold her straight at anything above thirty miles per hour on one of these roads when it is wet'.[32] He also claimed that 'it is practically impossible to tell where one is going on a dark wet night. The only possible way of keeping a course on them is to hug the edge and steer by the curbstones.'

However, the costs of providing adequate lighting as well as building new roads deterred most governments during the 1920s. Back in 1910 it had been agreed with Lloyd George that the money raised by his car licences and petrol tax would go into the Road Fund and thus finance improvements in Britain's roads. But when Churchill became Chancellor in 1924 he flatly refused to be bound by this agreement. In fact he raided the Road Fund for general revenue purposes, justifying his action on the basis that motoring was merely a rich man's pleasure and thus not a priority for the national Exchequer! Churchill's behaviour provoked another AA petition signed by 350,000 angry motorists in 1926, but he blithely ignored the complaints and used up all the money in the Road Fund. This proved to be a liability for the government in 1928 and 1929 when Lloyd George produced his dramatic Keynesian programme, 'We Can Conquer Unemployment', which relied on massive road-building schemes, funded by the state, designed to get the unemployed back into work and stimulate the economy. However, although the government was defeated in 1929, its successors continued to be cautious about investing in roads. As late as 1939, for example, the Great North Road, one of the country's major routes, boasted not a single mile of dual carriageway along the entire 276 miles from London to Newcastle upon Tyne. In contrast to Germany, Britain had built no motorways by the time war broke out in September of that year.

As for Britain's drivers, they remained, for the most part, ignorant about their vehicles and content to take to the wheel without any formal training or testing. Writing in the *Daily Mail* in 1930 the motoring correspondent, Captain Woolf Barnato, emphasised the need for proficiency in basic skills such as changing gear. 'By shifting to a lower gear before a corner', he wrote, 'you will be able to accelerate round it better than if you were in top.'[33] Barnato also advised on overtaking a car that was sitting in the middle of the road – a common cause of accidents. 'Never run up too close behind a car you wish to pass,' he warned,' because then your vision of the oncoming traffic is obscured. Pull out a hundred yards away from it and then, if you decide it is safe to pass, put your foot down hard. Blow your horn. The other motorist will then pull in and let you by without hindrance.'[34]

For the government's part, the only conditions it imposed on drivers involved a declaration of physical fitness introduced by Herbert Morrison in 1930.[35] Before applying for a licence the driver had to obtain a certificate from a doctor, though the only absolute dis-qualifications were extremely defective eyesight, a heart condition or 'nervous trouble' likely to cause loss of control. The driver was supposed to be capable of reading a car's number plate at thirty-five yards in ordinary light.

Until the mid 1930s this was about as far as the politicians were prepared to go. Reforming British motoring habits was simply too intimidating a task for the lowly Ministry of Transport which had only been created in 1919. The first politician to grasp that this ministry could be the means of advancing a career was Leslie Hore-Belisha who entered office in June 1934. An ebullient and energetic man whose rivals accused him of being too fond of publicity and spoke of him privately in anti-Semitic terms, Hore-Belisha deserves credit as the first minister to get to grips with British motoring in a comprehensive way. Recognising that the public had to be made more traffic conscious, he started a campaign in January 1935 to reduce the 'mass murder on the roads' by initiating an inquiry into the causes of fatal accidents; he required the chief constables to submit comments on the conduct of both drivers and pedestrians at road crossings which were to form the basis for future policy.[36] Subsequently he drew up a curriculum of road safety for use in schools: 'we have realised that we must begin in schools', he told the National Safety Congress in 1935.[37]

As long ago as 1927 authorities such as Leeds and Wolverhampton had introduced 'traffic control robots', better known as traffic lights. Their example spread to other towns, but pedestrians were confused by the lights and drivers largely ignored them! Some towns also devised pedestrian crossings, but they, too, were never clear to drivers. It was to introduce greater clarity that the new minister pioneered the innovation that made his name: the Belisha beacon, an unmistakable orange globe sitting atop a black and white striped pole at black and white zebra crossings. Yet even they were of limited use in the evenings as the ministry claimed it could not afford to have them illuminated. However, the beacons, which were sold as pencils and as miniature cigarette holders, quickly became familiar items in the urban landscape. On the other hand, during the first four months 3,000 of the 15,000 beacons in London were attacked by vandals.

To launch the scheme Hore-Belisha, keen to demonstrate the advantages for pedestrians, visited a pedestrian crossing in Camden Town, where for his pains he was almost knocked down by a passing sports car! No doubt the publicity-conscious minister felt this a price worth paying. But his experience only underlined the point that pedestrians still did not enjoy right of way. The courts refused compensation to anyone who was knocked down on a crossing if he had stepped out abruptly or if he had hesitated for a few moments, leaving it unclear whether he wanted to cross![38] Hore-Belisha's work was complemented by initiatives taken by several local authorities. Croydon, for example, experimented with new safety signs erected in the High Street warning: 'SAFETY FIRST, 4 KILLED, 127 INJURED IN DECEMBER 1934'. These were illuminated at night and amended each month to record any improvement in the local accident rate.[39]

To mollify aggrieved non-drivers Hore-Belisha revised the Highway Code, added new roundabouts and road signs to prevent crashes, imposed silence zones in London from 11.30 at night when all hooting was banned, and introduced 'courtesy cops' whose role was to use microphones to warn drivers politely if a minor offence was being committed. But he also recognised the need to give something back to motorists who saw themselves as a heavily taxed and persecuted minority. In February 1935 he decided to remove the maintenance of trunk roads from local authorities because they were too important to be left to the vagaries of local rates, and he instituted a programme of road construction to which all highway authorities were asked to submit schemes. Another concession was the introduction of a thirty miles per hour speed limit in March 1935 that did not apply to the thirty-eight newly constructed bypass and arterial roads in the London Traffic Area.[40]

Above all Hore-Belisha felt it necessary to conciliate motorists in view of his determination to require all new drivers, and those who had acquired a licence since April 1934, to pass a driving test. In some quarters the test was frankly regarded as an interference with the rights of freeborn Englishmen. When the idea, already in use elsewhere, had been aired in the Edwardian period, Lord Balfour of Burleigh had insisted: 'we in this country are not accustomed to be governed quite in the same way as the French people'.[41] Even in 1935 the policy took some political courage. Tests were to start on 1 April 1935, conducted by 200 officials who had been selected from 34,000 applicants.[42] A charge of 7s. 6d. per test meant that the scheme would be self-supporting. Drivers were required to demonstrate 'proof of capacity to manipulate a motor car and knowledge of the Highway Code'.[43] At the end of May Hore-Belisha noted that of the 33,824 people so far tested 3,045 had failed even though the test was 'of an elementary kind'. This, he said, gave some indication of 'the perfectly needless risk to the public safety that was previously run'.[44]

Before long these innovations had turned Hore-Belisha into a national figure; promoted to the Cabinet in 1936, he became Secretary of State for War in 1937. Yet for all his efforts Hore-Belisha managed to reduce the annual road deaths by only 800; this was an achievement but still left the total number of fatalities at around 6,500 a year, and there were only slight falls in subsequent years. It would be a long time before driving standards and road safety improved significantly. At a time when the British thought of themselves as a notably well behaved and law-abiding people, motoring had exposed the stubborn strain of recklessness, bordering on anarchism, deep within the national character.

13

'Cider With Rosie':
The Countryside Between the Wars

In many ways the countryside of interwar Britain looked much as it had done for centuries. The South, Midlands and West were dominated by small fields divided by miles of hedgerows punctuated at intervals by tall, stately elms, the most distinctive trees of lowland England. This network of hedges, combined with the availability of arable fields that retained stubble and fallen grain through the winter, sustained large populations of birds, especially yellow hammers, skylarks, partridges, linnets, corncrakes and song thrushes that were to become scarce when farming practice changed after the Second World War.

Two post-war innovations, however, began to alter the landscape. In 1919 the Forestry Commission was established with a view to redressing the acute shortage of timber Britain had suffered during the war. Taking advantage of cheap, infertile upland areas, it had acquired a million acres by 1939, mostly in the North, Wales and Scotland; there its huge plantations effected a lasting alteration by blanketing the countryside with Sitka spruce, Norway spruce and Scots pine. The Forestry Commission was quick to recognise the threat posed to its plantations by another invader, the grey squirrel, or 'tree rat' as its critics described it; spreading rapidly after being introduced at Henbury Park in Cheshire, the grey was officially pronounced a pest in 1930. In 1932 the commission offered a bounty of 2½d. for every squirrel tail brought in; this created some extra income but the scheme was dropped during the war, reintroduced in the 1950s and abandoned again in 1957.

Another controversial intrusion into the rural picture came from water companies who were, in effect, local authorities at this time. In the autumn of 1930 Manchester Corporation began work on thirty miles of tunnels and eighty-seven miles of aqueducts designed to enable water to flow the sixty-seven miles from Haweswater in the eastern Lake District to Manchester. This involved flooding the village of Mardale Green and expanding the existing lake from two to ten miles in length.[1] 'Mardale is still a noble valley. But man works with such clumsy hands!' wrote the hillwalker, Alfred Wainwright, some years later. 'Gone for ever are the quiet wooded bays and shingly shores that nature had fashioned so sweetly in the Haweswater of old; how aggressively ugly is the tidemark of the new Haweswater!' Wainwright fixed his sights on Manchester again when criticising the social effects of converting another Lakeland valley, Thirlmere, into a reservoir: 'Hidden away in the depths of the Thirlmere plantations are many reminders of the community life here before Manchester condemned the area to a slow death and an everlasting silence.'[2]

With these exceptions, however, the appearance of rural Britain displayed more continuity than change between the two world wars. Most farmers continued to practise mixed agriculture, though with a bias towards arable cultivation in the drier eastern counties and a concentration on livestock in the wetter pastures of the West. Farm animals reflected many more regional variations than today. Traditional pig breeds were still much in evidence, notably Essex Saddlebacks in the eastern counties, the Yorkshire Large White in the North, the Gloucester Old Spot in the West Country, and the Berkshire in central England. Herds of cattle were less dominated by the ubiquitous Friesian and more by local preferences for Dairy Shorthorns, Red Devons, Ayrshires, Herefords and Aberdeen Angus. Above all, despite the use of 25,000 tractors, steam engines for ploughing, self-binders and reaper-binders on farms, the role of the horse was only gradually being eroded. No fewer than 668,000 horses still worked on British farms in 1939, mainly shire horses but with Clydesdales and Suffolk Punches in some areas. The change to mechanisation proved slow because many fields were still too small or irregular and thus better handled by horses. Also, the depression in agriculture deterred investment in expensive equipment that tied up farmers' capital. Although the contract system, which enabled machinery to be hired out for a few days at a time, helped to spread the new technology, it was not until the 1950s that British farms became fully mechanised.

As a result of the survival of working horses blacksmiths and saddlers continued to flourish. And even when the business generated by horses diminished, blacksmiths continued to be occupied supplying and repairing agricultural implements, wrought iron and even wheelbarrows. So, too, was a wide range of ancient crafts: wheelwrights and iron foundry men who produced plough shares, sickles, grates and iron rods to shore up houses, as well as crafts dependent on local woods and reed beds such as thatchers, coppicers and hedgers, and the makers of hurdles, besom brooms, chairs, hurdles, hoops, hayrakes and pitchforks.

Yet while the countryside remained a place of work for some, it was increasingly a source of leisure for others. Although the countryside is often seen primarily in terms of agriculture, for those who did not live and work there it appealed more to the aesthetic than the material side of life; for nature-lovers, ramblers, artists, holidaymakers and others bent on escaping from urban life the countryside represented something to be enjoyed for itself rather than for its contribution to the national economy. Something of the exuberant response of town-dwellers to the countryside was captured by William Woodruff's expedition from Blackburn to the Forest of Bowland in 1933:

> Not even the cramp in our legs could stop us from appreciating the beauty of the Trough of Bowland on a clear day . . . we marvelled at the great vistas, at the seeming limitless expanse of the high moors and the windy fells – ridge after ridge with not a sign of human habitation . . . we heard the curlew's lonely cry and the tumble of streams. We smelled the lemon-scented gorse . . . this was the Lancashire I would remember when choice and fate had carried me far away.[3]

Although this perspective originated much earlier in the nineteenth century, during the 1920s and 1930s it became increasingly characteristic, not least because agriculture seemed to have become increasingly marginal to the British economy.

As long ago as the 1840s Britain had decisively opted for becoming an urban-industrial society that relied heavily upon imported food because her rapidly growing population could not be fed cheaply from domestic resources. By 1911 only 1.38 million people were still employed in agriculture. In the 1920s the industry generated just four per cent of national income. Many of those who depended on agriculture felt badly let down because the Great War appeared to have checked the decline of the industry. North American wheat supplies were interrupted by submarine attacks and the closure of the Dardanelles alone cut off thirty-five per cent of grain previously imported from Turkey, Russia and Romania. Consequently, by 1916 when the cost of food had risen by sixty-eight per cent, the country faced a crisis. This forced the government to intervene with guaranteed prices for farmers and minimum wages for labourers; under the Corn Production Act quotas were imposed on farmers; retired ploughmen returned to work and in 1917 the Women's Land Army recruited thousands of extra workers. As a result between 1916 and 1918 the cultivated area of England and Wales expanded by 1.86 million acres; and by the end of the war British agriculture was capable of feeding the population for 155 days a year by comparison with 125 in 1914.

However, this statistic cut both ways. On the one hand the expansion led many people to feel optimistic about the future of agriculture. On the other hand it meant that even with the extra output the country was bound to rely heavily on foreign food supplies; once the crisis was over governments inevitably reverted to traditional policies and dismantled the wartime controls. But for a year or two high prices attracted men into farming; in 1920, for example, food prices were still around three times the 1913 levels. In any case back-to-the-land was very much a matter of unfinished business for the politicians. Lloyd George's Land Campaign had been interrupted by the outbreak of war, but he returned to it in 1919 with the first of several Smallholdings Acts which were designed to make 45,000 acres in England and 20,000 acres in Wales available for returning servicemen; eventually 24,000 of them were settled on the new government holdings.

Meanwhile, in the immediate aftermath of war the better-off farmers were busy buying motor cars – dubbed 'war memorials' by the cynics – and ditching their old carts and carriages. Many tenant farmers felt tempted to buy land now that so much was coming on to the market as a result of the high wartime casualty rates that had left landowning families struggling to pay death duties. By March 1919 500,000 acres were up for sale and, as the sales continued until 1922, prices soon fell substantially. In the process a quiet social revolution occurred in the countryside: whereas in 1914 only eleven per cent of land had been owner-occupied, by 1927 thirty-six per cent was under owner-occupation.

However, the bubble of optimism collapsed as abruptly as it did in manufacturing. In the summer of 1920 the Corn Production Act was repealed and by June 1921 the government had abandoned minimum prices and wage controls, leaving agriculture to face the vagaries of the world economy once again. During 1920–1 wheat prices fell from over £4 a quarter to around £2; ewes that fetched £7 in 1920 were down to £1. 10s. by 1932, the worst year of the entire period; store cattle prices fell by a half and wool prices dropped by a third leading some farmers to store several seasons' fleeces in the hope of an eventual upturn. Yet despite some fluctuations and measures of state intervention later in the 1930s, things never fully recovered and profits proved elusive for most farmers until the outbreak of another war in 1939 rescued them from their dilemma. Those who had acquired land when prices were high were left handicapped by heavy mortgages and bank loans; having gambled on prices remaining high they felt let down. Of course, those who bought land later had got what seemed to be a bargain. Within a few years land that had fetched £24 an acre was being sold for £10; and by the 1930s good arable land in Norfolk could be had for as little as £5 an acre. But this was little comfort if the owners could not make profits. Bankruptcies among farmers ran at around 400 a year in the 1920s and reached 600 by 1932. As a result the total acreage under cultivation shrank during the 1930s as arable land especially was neglected and allowed to revert to scrub and weeds. This produced alarmist newspaper headlines along the lines of: 'GREATEST CRISIS OF THE ENGLISH COUNTRYSIDE'.[4] Reports suggested that in Norfolk, Lincoln-shire and the Cotswolds crops were being left unharvested or simply turned over to pigs because they commanded such poor prices. During the 1920s, it was claimed, the numbers working on the land had dwindled by 130,000 and 2 million acres were no longer ploughed. In his account of a journey through Norfolk, between Watton and Thetford, in 1927 S. L. Bensusan observed 'an area of desolation . . . it did not seem rightly to belong to England, it recalled to me in part the backlands of Ontario and the bare plains of Manitoba before the settlers came'.[5] Admittedly he was describing one of the worst-affected regions and the least innovative. Some farmers prospered by cultivating sugar beet, which now attracted subsidies as a result of the sugar shortages during the war. Others also gave up cereals in favour of egg and poultry production or became market gardeners growing fruit and flowers for the urban markets that were now well served by road and railway transport.[6] But even in these sectors imports ensured that prices were kept competitive.

Farmers also felt handicapped by the growing role of middlemen. For example, although the extension of road transport helped them to market their produce, not everyone was able to take advantage. Those who lived near to large towns could use their own motor-vans to convey perishable food and sell it directly. But more commonly transport fell into the hands of large combines such as the dairy companies who bought the farmers' milk but squeezed their profits to vanishing point. They resented receiving only 6–7d. a gallon for milk that retailed at 2s. in the 1920s.[7]

To add to their grievances farmers laboured under an increasing burden of regulation and interference designed to raise standards of health and hygiene on their farms. The outbreaks of foot-and-mouth disease that occurred routinely during the 1920s were dealt with by slaughtering infected cattle and any suspected of being diseased. In the worst years there were 1,500 to 2,000 separate outbreaks spread over 25 counties in England, Wales and Scotland, and the total number of animals slaughtered increased from 3,500 in 1919 to 125,000 by 1925.[8] This pattern suggests that the slaughter policy was not very effective in controlling foot and mouth, but as movement of livestock was less rapid and extensive than it became later in the century, the disease spread more slowly.

Dairy farmers felt particularly under pressure to provide clean milk supplies. Older workers remembered the days when they had milked the cows manually and dipped their hands into the milk pails when they became too dry. But by the 1920s mechanical milking using clean equipment had become more common. Farmers were irritated by pressure to pasteurise all their milk, by visits from the inspectors who took samples to test for TB, and by the new fashion for sterilising milk so as to remove all danger of contamination.[9] The Clean Milk Societies that sprang up during the 1920s and organised Clean Milk Competitions reported that only thirty-six per cent of all samples met the requirements for clean milk.[10] 'I have kept cows for fifty years and I never took notice of all these newfangled notions', complained one dairyman. 'I brought up my children on the milk, and the village had it too, and nobody ever made a complaint. Why can't the government mind its own business and leave us to mind ours?'[11] Yet farmers benefited from both the official regulations and the commercial innovations that gave greater confidence to consumers. For example, when distributors such as Express Dairies started putting milk into bottles, instead of selling it loose, they bore the extra cost of one penny per quart.[12]

In effect farmers wanted state support in the shape of subsidies and controls on imports but otherwise demanded to be left alone. Throughout the 1920s the powers-that-be remained largely deaf to their pleas, but during the 1929–31 Labour government the minister, Christopher Addison, drew up a bold new scheme which was subsequently adopted by the National Government as the 1931 Agricultural Marketing Act. Under this scheme farmers benefited from quotas on imports, subsidies to encourage production, and new marketing boards for milk, pigs, wheat and sugar beet that bought up their output at guaranteed prices. This gave protection to inefficient producers and boosted output. However, the additional bureaucracy continued to irritate and confuse many farmers. In April 1939 the Milk Marketing Board summoned one sixty-year-old farmer, Jellis, of Oakley in Bedfordshire, to London, alleging that he had understated both the quantity of milk sold by retail and the number of his cows on several occasions. 'Record books? Never have kept 'em and never will', responded an indignant Jellis. Brandishing his stick in the faces of the board, he shouted: 'We work seventeen or eighteen hours a day and I am an Englishman to the backbone. We are nothing but slaves under the Milk Marketing Board.'[13] He was fined £5. Yet Jellis was far from untypical, for the board was beset by complaints not only about the bureaucracy but about the prices paid which were considered so low as to make dairying uneconomic. In 1939 this led to a 'strike' by about one in twenty milk producers and retailers who attempted to upset the scheme by refusing to complete the forms and records required. Despite this the board claimed it was receiving the forms more punctually than ever even from 'rebels' and that the strike was fizzling out.[14] As proof of growing consumer confidence in the purity of the product it pointed to the increase in milk sales of 1.6 million gallons in the year from March 1938.

These exchanges are a reminder that although urban Britain is traditionally seen as the seat of protest between the wars, disaffection was equally pronounced in rural areas. After the sudden collapse of wartime prosperity the farming community spent almost the entire period nursing a sense of grievance. This was partly because it felt it had been marginalised from the mainstream of British life by the urban workers who had gained influence through trade unions and the Labour Party. The agriculturalists' anger was exacerbated by the apparent failure of their natural political allies to protect them. Ever since the 1870s when agriculture had come under severe competition from abroad, Conservative governments had been reluctant to help farmers because electoral expediency now pointed to cultivating the suburban and urban voters who saw cheap food as a priority. After the war the party was even less likely to take risks. In 1923 Andrew Bonar Law, the Tory leader, flatly rejected demands for agricultural subsidies, arguing that 'in every business you had to take the good with the bad. Farmers had had a good time during the war.'[15]

It was in order to make the voice of agriculture better heard that the National Farmers Union had been established in 1908. It claimed 76,000 members by 1920 and 131,000 by 1939. However the NFU leadership was somewhat out of touch with the opinions of small farmers; as a result it was never sure of its tactics and became the target for rebellion by its own members. During 1920–2 the disaffection among farmers was so great that many of them wanted the NFU to seek direct representation in Parliament. It compromised by giving support to a few candidates in 1922 but dropped the whole idea in favour of tacit co-operation with the Conservatives.[16] In effect the NFU became absorbed into the official system but without gaining any obvious influence as a result. In the 1930s when the new marketing boards were proposed it initially opposed them, but then changed its mind. In the event, local branches, recognising the benefits, usually demanded an extension of the board system although they complained that the NFU's representatives had failed to get high enough agreed prices.[17] West Country livestock farmers felt especially irritated by the failure of the NFU to persuade the government to establish a marketing board for cattle.

In fact, the more the NFU was seen as an apologist for official policy, the more it was bypassed by farmers militant enough to organise their own protests. Their anger was ignited by the issue of tithes. Originally known as 'Queen Anne's Bounty', tithes were originally a ten per cent levy on produce used for the maintenance of Church of England clergymen, but commuted to cash payments. Since 1836 tithe-owners had had the legal right to distrain for payment, but by the 1930s tithe was widely regarded as an archaic and unjustified imposition on hard-pressed farmers. Many new owners had been unaware that they were becoming liable for tithe on buying their land, and they bitterly resented having to pay it to the Church and to wealthy Oxford and Cambridge colleges.

As a result a 'tithe war' broke out in the early 1930s, especially in East Anglia and Kent, led by Roderick Kedward, a farmer, Nonconformist minister and Liberal MP for Ashford. It came to a head in 1935 when effigies of Cosmo Lang, Archbishop of Canterbury, were burned at protest meetings. Clashes occurred when bailiffs turned up at farms to seize moveable items, including livestock, to be auctioned off to pay the debts. The most famous incidents occurred at Ringshall in Suffolk in August 1933, at Wortham in Suffolk in February 1934, where a farmer faced a demand for £565, and at Westwood in Kent in 1935 where bailiffs sought £69-worth of goods. Acting with the consent of the farmers, the protesters obstructed the bailiffs by felling trees to block access roads, digging ditches and even running electric fences around farms. On several occasions teams of Blackshirts from the British Union of Fascists arrived to assist the obstruction and busloads of police had to be mobilised to keep order and make arrests.

Meanwhile reports and photographs printed in sympathetic national newspapers such as the *News Chronicle* publicised the issue and portrayed the protesters largely as respectable people driven to desperate measures. As a result, hundreds of cases of non-payment flooded into the county courts. Even the nineteen Blackshirts arrested at Wortham in 1934 were discharged when brought to court. 'I am told you are good fellows and I hope you will remain good fellows, realising how badly advised you were in this matter', the judge told them.[18] The protracted struggle damaged the Church, and added to the existing troubles faced by the National Government with agriculture. Ministers were fully aware that the fascist leader, Sir Oswald Mosley, was devoting much of his time to well attended and enthusiastic meetings in market towns all over England at this time. BUF propaganda relentlessly attacked the government for promoting huge imports of cheap eggs, beef, lamb, bacon, fruit and grain from Russia and Argentina as well as from the Empire. It alleged that the politicians were merely tools of City of London financiers who made profits by investing in foreign producers who undercut the prices of British farmers. Hoping to defuse the issue the government established a Royal Commission whose report led to legislation in 1936 designed to extinguish tithe over a forty-year period by means of a redemption scheme. However, as distraint sales continued to be enforced against non-payers the controversy rumbled on for many years.

Rural disaffection also manifested itself in the early organic movement. At this time organicists were usually struggling landowner-farmers drawn from within the rural community including Rolf Gardiner, Lady Eve Balfour, Viscount Lymington, Captain George Pitt Rivers, Henry Williamson and Jorian Jenks. They believed that the soil should be treated as a living entity not as a means for conveying chemicals, and its fertility maintained by composting vegetable waste. With its belief in the moral superiority of rural life and the decadence of urban society the movement was inspired by the back-to-the-land campaigns of the pre-war period. One of the pioneers was Balfour Gardiner who acquired Gore Farm in Dorset in 1924 where his nephew, Rolf Gardiner, created a back-to-the-land community based on the principles of organic cultivation, self-government and the revival of English folk customs. Organicists also reacted against the growing stranglehold of the big commercial interests; they condemned the consumption of tinned, canned and processed food, white bread, and sterilised and pasteurised milk over healthier, more natural products.

Although only a small minority, the organicists were far from being eccentrics or outsiders, for at this time many farmers were unconsciously organic to the extent of being less reliant on chemicals; the really destructive chemicals like derris and DDT were not to come into general use until after 1945.[19] The enthusiasts recognised that the decline of soil fertility had become a serious problem as a result of intensive cultivation during the war and the subsequent neglect of arable land by farmers desperate to reduce their costs. The development of dust bowls in the American Midwest in this period made their fears all the more compelling. On the other hand, the involvement of prominent organicists such as Lord Lymington in fascist organisations gave the movement a reputation for extremism, though this was not the only reason for its failure to become more than a fringe movement. Most country-dwellers were keen to take advantage of modernisation, cheap tinned food and commercial innovations rather than to resist them. As a result the main development of the movement was delayed until the Second World War. In 1941 Rolf Gardiner founded Kinship in Husbandry, in 1943 Lady Eve Balfour published *The Living Soil* and in 1945 the Soil Association came into being.

Amid the mass of writing that romanticised the English countryside and disparaged urban life it is easy to overlook the determination of many ordinary people who had grown up in villages to take the escape route into towns during the 1920s and 1930s. A careful reading of contemporary accounts often reveals a distinctly ambiguous attitude to the country. In *Cider With Rosie*, drawn from his childhood experiences in Slad, an isolated Gloucestershire village several miles from Stroud, Laurie Lee painted what, at first sight, seems an enchanting picture. In the summer of 1918 his large but fatherless family went to live in 'a cottage that stood in a half-acre of garden on a steep bank above a lake; a cottage with three floors and a cellar and a treasure in the walls, with a pump and apple trees, syringa [lilac] and strawberries, rooks in the chimneys, frogs in the cellar, mushrooms on the ceiling, and all for three and sixpence a week'.[20]

In fact, it was a grim life for most of the inhabitants. Rural housing was much slower to improve than that in towns, especially as hard-pressed landlords felt reluctant to invest in tied cottages. Many homes suffered badly from damp as Laurie Lee's references to frogs and mushrooms suggests. As late as 1939 a quarter of English parishes still had no piped water supply. They were also the last areas to receive electricity; only 35,000 of the 400,000 farms had been connected to the national grid by 1939. Country-dwellers also suffered a poorer diet than town-dwellers partly because of low incomes but also because they enjoyed less access to the retail outlets that offered competitive prices. In 1936 a survey of Cuckfield Rural District Council area in Sussex found that although there was almost no unemployment, the agricultural labourers were the worst fed group of workers. Of the 304 children no fewer than 99 suffered from subnormal nutrition. In the lowest-income families the weekly expenditure on food ran at around two to three shillings per head by comparison with the British Medical Association's view that five shillings was the necessary minimum. In Cuckfield the residents consumed one-third of a pint of milk daily, well below the national average, forty-four per cent bought no fish and forty-five per cent no fresh fruit.[21] The diet was much healthier on farms in the Scottish Borders where Andrew Purves, a shepherd, recalled that it was usual for farm workers to keep a pig and a cow, receive an allocation of potatoes and cultivate a garden.[22]

Nonetheless, wherever they lived agricultural labourers suffered from low wages. During the war the minimum wage had been set at twenty-five shillings; but the National Agricultural Labourers' Union took advantage of the shortage of skilled men to push wages much higher, increasing its membership from 9,000 to 170,000 by 1919. However, following the abandonment of wage controls and the collapse of prices farmers began to reduce their labour force; as agricultural labourers had not been included in the National Insurance scheme in 1920 they were left without benefits and forced to rely on the Poor Law authorities when unemployed. After reaching thirty-seven shillings in 1921 the pay for agricultural labourers fell to twenty-nine shillings in 1922 and twenty-four shillings in 1923. Some men went on strike, especially in Norfolk, a well-unionised county. This led Ramsay MacDonald to intervene to fix minimum wages at twenty-five shillings for a fifty-hour week, and in 1924 the Wages Boards were reinstated. As a result average wages rose to twenty-eight shillings in East Anglia and to 36 shillings in the North. By the late 1930s the average agricultural wage stood at thirty-five shillings, a real improvement in view of the fall in the cost of living since 1921; but unskilled workers in industry got fifty-three shillings and skilled men twice as much. As a result men continued to leave the land. During the Victorian era this had been the pattern in the North and Midlands where alternative employment was available, but now similar migrations occurred in the southern counties. Workers left the villages of Oxfordshire for employment at the Morris Cowley works in Oxford and the MG plant at Abingdon, rural Berkshire for Reading and the booming trading estate at Slough, and Buckinghamshire to work for Hoover and the furniture factories at High Wycombe.

Indeed, the underlying story of *Cider With Rosie* was the process of opening up isolated villages as a result of improved transport and better prospects after 1918. Laurie Lee described the coming of the motor-bus to Slad as 'the end of a thousand years'. Admittedly, the migration went in both directions. Motor cars enabled middle-class people to live in villages and rural towns and commute to work. As a result small market towns such as Dorking in Surrey and Beaconsfield in Buckinghamshire developed into prosperous suburban centres for those who worked in London. Regular road transport also helped to revolutionise the limited social life of remote villages by putting cinemas and dances within reach, not to mention trips by motor-bus to places hitherto unknown. At his home near Wooler in north Northumberland Andrew Purves joined his local choir on their annual excursions by hired bus to Roker (Sunderland), Loch Lomond, Edinburgh, Keswick and the Lakes, and Barnard Castle in County Durham.[23] In Laurie Lee's Slad the prospect of a one-day outing to the seaside by charabanc was a major event in the early 1920s: 'we had saved up for months to be worthy of it', he wrote. The entire village piled into five charabancs for the trip to Weston-super-Mare: 'mothers with pig-buckets stuffed with picnics, children with cocoa-tin spades, fathers with bulging overcoats lined entirely with clinking bottles . . . the postman, having nobody to deliver his letters to, had dumped them and was coming along too.'[24] Part of the appeal of such excursions lay in the absence of the usual control by authority figures: school, church, squire and police. Hence the convivially chaotic proceedings: 'Then the charabancs arrived and everyone clambered aboard, fighting each other for seats . . . The charabancs were high, with broad, open seats and with folded tarpaulins at the rear, upon which, as choirboys, we were privileged to perch and to fall off and break our necks. We all took our places, people wrapped themselves in blankets, horns sounded, and we were ready.'[25] After a day of indulgence in which men, women and children scattered across Weston-super-Mare in pursuit of their own pleasures, the villagers regrouped for 'A long homeward drive through the red twilight, through landscapes already relinquished, the engines humming, the small children sleeping and the young girls gobbling shrimps. At sunset we stopped at a gaslit pub for the men to have one more drink. This lasted till all of them turned bright pink and started embracing their wives.'[26]

In addition to these excursions, village life was enlivened by regular social activities that had not occurred before 1914. In 1919 county councils were permitted to support libraries from the rates, and by 1931 all but three of them did so. As a result, from 1922 onwards mobile libraries reached even the remotest villages. According to Andrew Purves, Roxburgh County Council had established a library in every parish by 1925, usually in the school or village hall where the schoolteacher acted as librarian; the books were changed once a quarter, lists being taken to the outlying farms by schoolchildren for readers to make their selections.[27]

In 1922 the Young Farmers Clubs were established by Lord Northcliffe for anyone aged between 10 and 21; 400 were in operation by 1939. By that time the young farmers' favourite event – dances – had become easy to organise because of the widespread construction of village halls in the aftermath of the war; this was a major innovation for communities in which there had previously been no premises for social gatherings other than the pub and the school. Many of these projects were financed by the Carnegie Trust, but otherwise they relied on local philanthropy. In the village of Slaley, near Hexham in Northumberland, the Slaley Commemoration Hall opened in December 1922. It was built by Charles Hunting, the head of a Tyneside shipping family who lived at Slaley Hall, and his wife Mona, 'in gratitude for the safe return of their children from the war'. The Huntings gave the land in the village street and covered the £5,500 building costs.[28] The building comprised a lobby, a large hall with stage, a small recreation room and a kitchen with sink, cold water, range and store. The village had just been connected to the mains water supply, but it still had no sewage or electricity. As a result those attending hall functions were obliged to go outside to use two earth closets equipped with ash pits to blanket the smell. These were emptied by shovel periodically into a horse-drawn cart and the contents distributed on the fields.[29]

Village halls hosted a wide variety of activities. At Doddington in north Northumberland billiards and dances were regular functions in both the Reading Room and the hall which was built in 1933. Dances were held on Friday from eight to two in the morning and on Saturday until eleven-thirty, presumably so as not to trench upon Sunday. The clientele was well behaved except on occasion when large inebriated parties turned up from the hunt kennels; this led the committee to impose a ban on anyone arriving with alcohol. 'Drinking among girls was virtually unknown in rural areas in those days, and none but the most disreputable females would darken the door of a public house.'[30] In Slaley the hall could be hired for fifteen shillings for private dances, £1 for a dance, whist drive or concert by organisations, twenty-five shillings for trade exhibitions, and seven shillings and sixpence by the Women's Institute. Closing time for dances was two in the morning, though it could be extended for an hour for an extra five shillings and by two hours for ten shillings: 'All dancers must wear dancing shoes'.[31] These halls transformed village social life with their programmes of low-cost events. One such hall in Gloucestershire recorded ten concerts, forty-eight dances, fifty whist drives and four first-aid classes as well as educational lectures, keep-fit demonstrations and air-raid precaution briefings in 1939 alone.

Yet in some ways the most influential single innovation in rural life was the Women's Institute. Throughout the Victorian and Edwardian periods governments had been anxious to find some means of arresting what was seen as the apathy and decay affecting many country communities. They therefore welcomed the pioneering WIs which began on Anglesey in 1915 largely as a way of encouraging women to contribute to the war effort and reduce food shortages by preserving surplus crops, running allotments and providing extra labour for farmers hit by military recruiting. But what had started as a response to a temporary emergency endured because the WIs filled a gap in the lives of countrywomen.

Their origins in wartime initially caused some doubt about the relationship between the movement and the government. As WIs received a state grant the Ministry of Agriculture wanted to turn them into a branch of its Food Department. However, the first president, Lady Denman, dug her heels in and insisted on maintaining their independent character. Aimed at married women or 'homemakers' in the language of the 1920s, WIs were open to anyone for a fee of two shillings. Meetings were intended to offer 'something to see, something to hear, something to do'. They focussed on three types of activity: agricultural and domestic skills including baking, jam, preserving, and the production of poultry, bees, vegetables, rabbits and pigs; music, drama and dancing; and the revival of handicrafts and other rural skills. The regular singing of 'Jerusalem' did not begin until 1924.

Even in these early days some observers professed not to take the WIs too seriously on account of their jam-and-Jerusalem image. E. M. Delafield sharpened her wit with an account of a visit to speak at a WI when she was 'asked if I will judge a Darning Competition' and was advised not to say anything likely to get the secretary overexcited for fear of provoking a heart attack.[32] Inevitably some of the members, who were not accustomed to attending meetings of any kind, found WI talks puzzling. According to the movement's historian some expected 'Current Events' to involve tips about pruning blackcurrant bushes, and others assumed that a speaker on 'Life in the Middle Ages' would explain how to cope after the age of forty.[33] Yet the movement proved a huge success. It took off very quickly in counties such as Cornwall perhaps because the activities fitted easily into an existing pattern of market gardening and smallholdings. It was also seen as a unifying element in a region otherwise divided between Non-conformist and Anglican communities. By 1927 there were already 66 WIs with 5,000 members in the county. 'The result is that there are no "dead" villages in Cornwall today', commented S. L. Bensusan.[34] In the country as a whole the WIs expanded from 760 in 1918 to nearly 4,000 in 1927 and over 5,500 by 1937 when some 318,000 women had enrolled.

Initially WIs had aroused suspicion in some quarters because they introduced a novel element of democracy into rural affairs: the officers and committee had to be elected. In practice, however, there was often a large element of continuity in the choice of personnel. In the case of Slaley's WI, for example, various members of the local Hunting family served as presidents, vice presidents and committee members in every year from 1923 to 1927.[35] On the other hand, war had had some impact in weakening the traditional deference especially among young men serving in the forces and young women who went off to munitions factories and had returned to family homes dissatisfied with the limited opportunities. While the established forms of authority continued to be active in village life, the extent of their influence was conditional upon their promoting social events that offered good value for money. When the doors opened for Slad's Parochial and Church Tea and Annual Entertainment – cost one shilling per head – things quickly got out of hand: 'it was chins and boots and elbows, no queues, we just fought our way in . . . The Tea was an orgy of communal gluttony in which everyone took pains to eat more than his money's worth.'[36]

Other organisations kept better order. Regular hunt balls included a meal, a whist drive, spot prizes and presentations to anyone celebrating a birthday or an anniversary.[37] In well organised rural constituencies the Conservative and Unionist Association organised an annual whist drive and ball which was preceded by a series of qualifying heats held in every village from which the winners went forward to the final. In effect, a dense, and to some extent overlapping, organisational network comprising the Church of England, the YFCs, the WIs, the hunts, the agricultural shows and the Conservative Associations maintained their footing in the community, but largely by tapping into an unsatisfied demand for social functions, notably dances and whist drives. They were obliged to compromise with local tastes, as much as to control, if only because they now found themselves in competition with the cinemas and dances that were only a bus ride away in the nearby towns.

Paradoxically, while the younger country-dwellers looked for ways of escaping to the towns, the urban population increasingly celebrated the countryside as a refuge from town life. 'The English have the ugliest towns and the most beautiful countryside of any nation in the world', claimed C. M. Joad, one of the more dogmatic interwar controversialists.[38] During the nineteenth century the romantic appeal of rural life was associated with writers and pundits, but there are indications that it became a pervasive element in English society after the war. Not only was the countryside regarded as healthy and visually appealing, it was increasingly seen as a key element in English national identity. To some extent a period of political turmoil and prolonged economic uncertainty may have fostered a desire to retreat to a timeless and more secure world. Among the obvious symptoms of this mood was a spate of books including H. V. Morton's *In Search of England* (1927), J. B. Priestley's *English Journey* (1933) and C. Henry Warren's *England is a Village* (1940). Whenever Priestley visited a town he could not help speculating about the delightful green fields and clear streams that had once existed there; even his native Bradford was commended on the basis that 'it has the good fortune to be on the edge of some of the most enchanting country in England'.[39] The success of Agatha Christie's Miss Marple novels, which began with *Murder at the Vicarage* in 1930, and endured for many decades, suggests that they struck a chord by depicting a quintessentially English rural community, albeit one marked by a propensity for bloodshed. Yet the work of serious novelists such as D. H. Lawrence also reflected a preference for rural communities and a bias against towns.

Perhaps the most eloquent exponent of the view that the fundamentals of Englishness resided in her countryside was Stanley Baldwin, three times prime minister between the wars. Baldwin specialised in semi-political eulogies about rural England in general and the delights of his native Worcestershire in particular. 'In London I am but a bird of passage', he told an audience in 1927. 'To us exiles thoughts of Worcestershire in spring pluck at our very heart-strings . . . the verdure of the Evesham gardens, the blossom of the Pershore plum, the cherry orchards from Bewdley to Tenbury.'[40] On another occasion he expressed the hope that 'one might be spared for a few peaceful years . . . to look out once more upon those hills, and ulti-mately to lay one's bones in that red soil from which one was made in the full confidence that whatever may happen to England, whatever defilements of her countryside may take place, whatever disgusting noises may be emitted upon her roads, at any rate in that corner of England the apple blossom will always blow in the spring'.[41]

However, the importance of these effusions is easily exaggerated. Baldwin could not risk this apple-blossom sentimentality when talking to the struggling farmers of his native county. Though he cultivated an image as a relaxed, tweedy, country gentleman, he actually came from a family of ironmasters. Indeed, Baldwin personified the successful evolution of the Conservative Party from its landed origins to its modern role as the party of urban-bourgeois Britain. As prime minister he had no sympathy with the National Farmers Union which he regarded as the mouthpiece of narrow interests.

Yet Baldwin was not untypical of successful middle-class men whose roots lay in the towns but who felt attracted by an idealised version of country life if only because it was associated with a rise in the social scale. Between the wars Britain was not turning into a nation of country-lovers so much as a nation of *suburbanites* who managed to achieve their ambitions by taking advantage of the improvements in road and rail transport; they commuted to their place of employ-ment while living in semi-rural surroundings with large gardens, village greens and adjacent woodlands. However, real country life meant inferior or inconvenient shopping and entertainment, lower temperatures, draughty rooms, muddy boots and wet Labradors; what the suburbanites really wanted was a vicarious sense of the country without sacrificing their urban comforts.

While the commuters settled for the illusion of a rural lifestyle, several vocal and town-based sections of society organised themselves into pressure groups dedicated to preserving the countryside and opening it up to the urban population as a place of leisure. Among them were several late Victorian organisations, notably the Commons Preservation Society (1865), the Society for the Protection of Birds (1889) and the National Trust (1895). But they were joined in 1926 by the Council for the Preservation of Rural England, under Professor Patrick Abercrombie, which had sister organisations in Scotland (1927) and in Wales (1928). In 1930 the cause gained a popular element with the foundation of the Youth Hostels Association which offered accommodation for only one shilling a night, thus putting a cheap holiday within the reach of thousands of walkers. YHA membership grew to 28,000 in 1933 and 50,000 by the end of the decade. The iconic pressure group of this period was the Ramblers Association which was founded in 1935, though its origins went back to 1905. It was strong in the North of England. 'The Central Station at Manchester early on a Sunday morning is an unforgettable sight', wrote Joad, 'with its crowds of ramblers, complete with rucksacks, shorts and hob-nailed boots, waiting for the early train to Edale, Chinley, Hope and the Derbyshire moors.'[42]

Admittedly, these organisations differed in character from the conservative-preservationists at one end of the spectrum to the radical-egalitarians at the other. The former was more characteristic of countryside enthusiasts in the South of England and the latter of those in the Peak District, the Yorkshire Dales, the Lake District and Wales. The nostalgic or backward-looking approach came to be especially associated with the National Trust, although this represented a departure from its Victorian origins. Founded largely by radicals and liberals who put the interests of the community before those of private owners, the National Trust aspired to protect the countryside from development and to allow ordinary people greater access to it. But over time the emphasis changed to reflect different personnel and different policies. By the 1930s its critics believed the trust to be focussed less on obtaining access for the people and more on preserving country houses and even on reinstating their former owners in them.

By contrast the CPRE, whose thinking was influenced more by town planners and architects, adopted a less traditionalist and more interventionist approach towards preserving the countryside; it anticipated achieving its goals through a state planning system rather than by pandering to existing landowners. However, in the prevailing climate of opinion the ideas of the CPRE went against the grain. As the planning legislation enacted in 1919 and 1932 was largely permissive, it was never implemented by the less enterprising councils. A classic failure occurred at Hexham in Northumberland where the authorities permitted the construction of a prominent red-brick cinema in close proximity to the town's abbey, the moot hall and the gaolhouse, thereby ruining for ever a fine medieval townscape. The most notorious example of inadequate planning occurred at Peacehaven, near Brighton in Sussex, where a fine stretch of chalk cliffs at the point where the South Downs met the sea, was turned into an unsightly sprawl of bungalows. Such development was difficult to prevent as most interwar governments disliked planning controls on principle, though they granted limited powers to restrict the spread of petrol stations and roadside advertising; in 1935 ribbon development was restricted, and in 1938 legislation was enacted to preserve London's green belt. But by this time commercial developments had blighted many rural areas.

The gulf between the attitudes of rural- and urban-dwellers was also beginning to manifest itself in the treatment of wildlife. In the Tweed Valley Andrew Lorimer recorded that in the early 1920s local people routinely collected the eggs of peewits (lapwing), curlews and wild ducks for consumption; they packed peewit eggs into special wooden boxes which were collected at railway stations for transport to London.[43] Although traditional rural pursuits such as the hunting of deer, foxes, otters and hares had not yet become a major subject of controversy, the issue was beginning to raise its head within the RSPCA. At the 1926 annual meeting a lively debate took place over whether members of the council should indulge in hunting and shooting. The RSPCA had recently been obliged to decline a £10,000 legacy because a condition had been attached to the effect that all council members should be anti-vivisectionists and opposed to hunting even of birds and fish. Lord Danesfort, admitting that these were his chief hobbies, argued that 'both could certainly be carried out without undue cruelty, at which there was applause and hisses'.[44] Since most of the leading RSPCA figures participated in blood sports at this stage there was no immediate prospect of a change of policy.

However, the chief targets for walkers were not the huntsmen but motorists, developers, landowners and gamekeepers. In a characteristic onslaught in his book, *The Horror of the Countryside* (1931), C. M. Joad complained that motorists did not really enjoy the countryside but actually destroyed what they professed to love by the noise and crowds they generated. Little could be done to stop the weekly flow of motorists, but the immediate aim of the ramblers was to improve access to the wilder districts and to preserve existing footpaths. The roots of this movement lay in the Victorian period when the countryside began to be seen as the best means of providing healthy recreation for the masses; but its aims were frustrated by landowners who had turned the land into a private monopoly through the eighteenth-century enclosures, Highland clearances and the conversion of countryside to deer parks and grouse moors. Walkers found things confusing because maps commonly showed paths but explained in the margin 'the representation on this map of a Road, Track or Footpath is no evidence of the existence of a right of way'. Although the 1925 Law of Property Act forbade the erection of any fence or building that impeded access to a common, about 2,000 complaints about the closure or obstruction of paths were lodged each year. Landowners and keepers erected a variety of notices designed to deter walkers: 'Trespassers will be prosecuted', 'Beware of the Bull', and, as at Glen Einich in the Cairngorms: 'Trespassers Proceed at Own Risk Owing to Shot and Bullets After 12 August. J. P. Grant'. Not that everyone was deterred. In a case at Chester Assizes Mr Justice McKinnon observed: 'People know the notices cannot be enforced. I trespass about once a week.'[45]

The CPRE advocated the creation of national parks for the wilder parts of the country as a way of widening access without provoking confrontations with landowners. But the ramblers' organisations, while supporting the idea, demanded the passage of the Access to Mountains Bill. During the early 1930s, while this measure was being obstructed by the landowners' representatives in Parliament, ramblers in the North of England tried to force the pace. The cockpit of this struggle was the Derbyshire Peak District. Sandwiched between two heavily populated conurbations, Manchester to the north-west and Sheffield to the east, the area was conveniently crossed by a railway line. Consequently every Saturday 15,000 walkers departed from Manchester and a similar number from Sheffield to explore the Peak District.[46] But they found that an area of 215 square miles contained only 12 footpaths more than 2 miles long, and much was closed either by water boards or by landowners for deer and grouse. In 1932 8,000–9,000 ramblers gathered regularly on the hillsides at Winnats Pass near Castleton to hear speeches by Joad and sympathetic MPs and to exchange tips on dealing with aggressive gamekeepers. This culminated one Sunday in April when a group of 500 ramblers organised a mass trespass of Kinder Scout to demonstrate 'for the rights of ordinary people to walk on land stolen from them in earlier times'. The trespass involved a pitched battle with police and keepers in which six walkers were arrested, five of whom received prison sentences of two to six months. Although Kinder Scout stimulated wider public support, opponents continued to obstruct the Access to Mountains Bill until 1939. The only achievement of the ramblers was the Rights of Way Act of 1934 which established that the use of a footpath for a period of twenty years constituted proof that it was a right of way. However, to be effective the Act required energetic action by local authorities in marking public paths on large-scale maps; but as many paths were omitted or simply neglected disputes inevitably arose. All that ramblers could do was to ensure that the paths were regularly walked. During the Second World War the case for improving access to the countryside gained strength largely because the general shift of opinion in favour of egalitarianism and intervention severely marginalised its political opponents. The result was the enactment of the National Parks Act in 1949; this created what came to be called the Countryside Commission, the official body committed to protect areas of outstanding natural beauty for the nation.

14

'Six penn'orth of hope':
Sport and Gambling

'No cricket, no Boat Race, no racing'. Thus the editor of the *Daily Express* complained in his diary twelve months after the start of the First World War. In fact the disruption caused by the war was not quite as universal as he implied. Sport, like so much else in Britain, was strongly influenced by class attitudes, and as a result the sports favoured by the middle and upper classes had been among the first to wind down. Rugby Union, for example, responded promptly to the declaration of war, many clubs enlisting their members en masse for the forces. But the cricketers required more prompting. *The Times* stepped up the pressure by refusing to print the cricket scores and on 27 August W. G. Grace wrote to the *Sportsman* arguing that it was 'not fitting that able-bodied men should be playing day by day and pleasure-seekers look on . . . I should like to see all first-class cricketers of a suitable age set a good example.'[1] Yorkshire stubbornly played seven more matches in the 1914 season, but in January 1915 the County Championship was abandoned for fear of jeopardising cricket's claim to be the national game. Meanwhile the horse-racing community was divided. Some courses closed under local pressure, though supporters argued that racing should continue because of the employment it generated. But pressure was applied through angry letters to the press, by the railway companies who withdrew excursion tickets to the races, and by the government's decision to apply the Defence of the Realm Act to the sport. Even so, the Jockey Club did not capitulate until May 1915. This was only a month after the decision of the reluctant Football Association to abandon the Cup Final at Old Trafford. 'You have played well with one another', Lord Derby told the teams when presenting the Cup, 'play with one another for England now.' In fact the FA had been using club grounds to organise recruiting meetings and an estimated 500,000 men had volunteered through football organisations. But, like racing, football had come under such withering attack for lack of patriotism that it eventually ceased normal activity for the duration of the war.

Despite this, the British troops carried the spirit of sport with them into war, much to the bemusement of allies and enemies alike. Junior officers were reported kicking footballs towards the German lines at the start of Western Front offensives on the assumption that the men's instinctive enthusiasm would drive them forward. In the long intervals between the fighting officers organised games. In June 1915 Robert Graves reported an Officers versus Sergeants game of cricket at Versailles where unhappily 'machine-gun fire broke up the match'.[2] Officers stationed in northern France were delighted to find that the country abounded in foxes, sadly suffering from shell and shrapnel wounds; they wrote home requesting riding crops and hunting horns, and before long several packs of hounds had been shipped across the Channel to keep them occupied now that the fighting had settled into trench warfare.

To other nationalities these activities marked the British as a people almost comically obsessed by sport. Victorian ideas about sport as a means of maintaining manliness and national spirit, and fostering the British qualities of discipline, team spirit, endurance and fair play were still widely endorsed. Certain sports were also seen as important in maintaining the imperial idea and imperial connections not only with British people living abroad but between white settlers and native communities. 'A Test match today is an imperial event', in the words of Sir Pelham 'Plum' Warner, chairman of the selectors. In India the cultivation of cricket, polo and pig-sticking was very reassuring, especially as Indians showed a natural penchant for adopting British values, for example, by routinely appointing maharajas as captains of cricket teams. The foundation of the British Empire Games in 1930 symbolised the importance attached to the connections between sport and empire.

During the interwar period sport continued to be crucial to the British self-image, and the establishment of the National Playing Fields Association in 1926 signified the need to remedy the shortage of open spaces in which boys could play organised games. Boxing and cricket were far more popular sports in the 1920s and 1930s than they are today;

indeed, cricket claimed, with some reason, to be the national sport. Other sports such as golf and tennis had been gaining support before 1914, and continued to do so, though they were conspicuously middle-class games. There were, however, two complications. Although the British took pride in their role in developing the modern forms of most sports and spreading them around the world, after 1918 they faced growing evidence of a decline in British achievements when up against international competition especially at the Olympics. For patriots this was a source of great anguish. Part of the problem lay in Britain's failure to tap the talents of her population, in many sports, because she effectively restricted participation to small minorities. Sports such as cricket still suffered from segregation by social class, others like horse racing, tennis and golf effectively relied on the wealthy as players and used the majority simply as spectators, while football and boxing were treated basically as working-class sports; in athletics and rowing participation actually became narrower as the tradition of working-class participation dwindled. Even angling, one of the most popular participation sports, was deeply divided between rich people who fished for 'game', that is salmon and trout, and the majority who went in for 'coarse fishing' – significant terminology – for perch, roach, pike, rudd and chub.

The status of cricket as Britain's national sport was justified in the sense that it attracted support in all classes, was followed in both North and South, and enjoyed a high level of participation. During the 1930s anything between 200,000 and 400,000 people played the game each week. On the other hand, cricket was plagued by social segregation as indicated by the rigid division into three levels: county, league and recreational cricket. The extent of purely recreational cricket between the wars may be gauged by the fact that in the 1920s the area around Bolton alone boasted no fewer than 70 teams comprising manual workers and lower-middle-class players, rising to 120 by 1939.[3] By contrast county cricket made no concessions to its rank-and-file supporters. Three-day games were played during the working week, thereby putting them beyond the reach of the majority of men. The most flourishing sector of the sport lay in the leagues, based on professional players especially in the North and Midlands. They charged sixpence or eight pence for a seat and sold alcohol to boost their income. Their well-attended matches were timed to start on

Saturday afternoons, allowing workingmen to get home from the morning's work, eat their dinner and reach the ground. The most famous league club was Nelson in Lancashire which signed a leading Australian fast bowler, E. A. MacDonald, at a salary of £700 in 1922, and employed the West Indian, Learie Constantine, at £1,000 from 1929 to 1938. The relatively poor pitches gave an advantage to the bowlers at league games. Nor did the batsmen enjoy the luxury of playing themselves in gradually as in county cricket; they were expected to play attacking cricket and score quickly, failure to do so invariably resulting in their being barracked by the spectators. Consequently, a cricketer like Constantine, who put on 125 runs out of Nelson's 175 in 70 minutes play against Enfield in 1929, became immensely popular.

By comparison county cricket was a dull business, and, though the teams professed to look down on the leagues, they avoided taking on league teams. Throughout the 1920s and 1930s traditionalists determined to preserve the leisurely game rather than attempt 'brighter cricket'. Yet the fifteen first-class teams, augmented by Glamorgan in 1921, were now losing money and struggled to maintain their traditions. Especially in the South of England county matches had become primarily part of the social round that included Ascot, Henley, Wimbledon and the Eton-Harrow match. As a result the county game was an unpleasant, snobbish affair dogged by a stubborn determination to preserve the increasingly anachronistic distinctions between amateur and professional players. Although few amateurs were really good enough to justify their places in the county teams, the cricket authorities continued to pick them and treated the professional players as domestic servants of the clubs. Restricted to separate changing rooms, the professionals used separate entrances on the pitch, stayed in cheaper hotels, received inferior food and wore different dress. The two classes were clearly distinguished in cricketing commentaries as the following example shows: 'Larwood, Tate, Geary and Mr Stevens all bowled well. Larwood, in particular, rendered valuable service by getting rid of Mr Woodfull and Mr Macartney.'[4] Professional men were paid around £300 a year but had to find all their expenses out of this. Yorkshire, the most successful and progressive team of the period, treated its professionals better by giving them higher wages and pensions. But even Yorkshire was unwilling to challenge the prejudice against making a professional their team captain. In 1925 when Jack Hobbs of Surrey, the outstanding batsman of the period, but of working-class origin, was mooted as England captain, Lord Hawke, the Yorshire president, exclaimed: 'Pray heavens no professional should be made captain of the national side'.[5] Hawke simply regarded it as essential to maintain the dominance of upper-class men and keep the workers in their place, even though this increasingly meant that teams were handicapped by the inclusion of amateurs who were inadequate players. Ewart Astill of Leicestershire was thought to be the first professional to be appointed as captain for a brief period in 1935. However, this came about only because Leicestershire had gone through seven captains in ten summers and had failed to persuade an Old Etonian to take the position; they ditched Astill as soon as they found an alternative.[6]

The surprising thing is that by and large the professionals were entirely deferential and made no attempt to challenge the system. Hobbs had no aspiration to the captaincy, though his natural successor as the key England batsman, Wally Hammond, showed what could be achieved by playing the game. Hammond, who played football for Bristol Rovers from 1921 to 1924, made 1,000 runs in May in 1927, the first player to do so since W. G. Grace in 1895. He deliberately distanced himself from his lowly origins and from the other professionals, seeking the company of the amateurs. Eventually Hammond turned amateur in 1938, something that was only possible by getting commercial sponsorship, the vital step to winning the England captaincy to which he aspired. But though Wally Hammond was successful as an upwardly mobile cricketer, he had made himself an anachronism, increasingly outflanked by the emergence of young professionals like Len Hutton and Denis Compton by the end of the 1930s.

In Test cricket the traditionalists suffered acute embarrassment and irritation arising from their dealings with the Australians who refused to recognise the amateur-professional conventions. These feelings were personified by the upper class Douglas Jardine who notoriously captained England in 1932-3. 'He is a queer fellow', admitted Pelham Warner. 'When he sees a cricket ground with an Australian on it he goes mad!'[7] When Jardine walked on to the pitch Australian spectators liked to shout 'Where's your butler to carry your bat?' Despite this the selectors deliberately chose Jardine to recover the Ashes in 1932. To this end he carefully planned what became known as 'bodyline' tactics among the outraged Australians. This involved employing 'leg theory'. Fast bowlers were to deliver short-pitched balls that would bounce at head level on the leg side; meanwhile a semicircle of fielders was set close in to attack the leg stump. This was calculated to contain the brilliant Australian batsman, Don Bradman, whose one weakness was thought to be an inability to play short deliveries on the leg side.

Instrumental in implementing these tactics was Harold Larwood. The son of a Nottingham miner, Larwood had left school at thirteen, gone down the pit and been signed by Nottinghamshire in 1923, aged eighteen, at £2 a week. In the 1932–3 Tests Larwood and the other English bowlers, employing leg theory, hit a number of the Australian batsmen, one of whom was knocked unconscious. This led the Australian Board of Control to protest that bodyline tactics were calculated to injure and intimidate the batsmen and were thus a breach of the gentlemanly conventions hitherto governing the game: 'Unless stopped at once it is likely to upset the friendly relations existing between Australia and England'. They even threatened to cancel the series. However, the MCC, whose members took pride in their gentlemanly standards, took the view that bodyline bowling was not dangerous and that the Australians simply could not play off the leg stump. Larwood took thirty-three wickets in the series and England won 4–1.

But, as 'Plum' Warner had observed, a Test was an imperial event, and political pressure was consequently applied to find a way out of the controversy. Before long the cricketing establishment had backtracked, leading to the abandonment of the notorious leg theory within a year or two. Jardine backed out of the next Test with Australia and retired from cricket at thirty-three, still at his peak but marginalised by the authorities. In 1934 Larwood, who had frankly admitted to the press that the bodyline tactics had been prearranged, was asked by the authorities to apologise. However, Larwood was not a gentleman and he insisted that he had followed his captain's instructions and had nothing to apologise for. In this way the controversy brought an abrupt end to the Test career of the greatest fast bowler of his generation. With some reason Larwood saw himself as the victim of the British class system and the hypocrisy of those who dominated the sport.

The Establishment experienced less resistance in sports such as golf, tennis, athletics and rowing where participation was more socially restricted; golf and tennis especially were seen as central to the leisure and lifestyle of the middle classes rather than as sports as usually understood. Although the Scots, who claimed to have invented golf, argued that it was a game for all classes, this was only true in the sense that it generated jobs for caddies. During the 1890s a new golf club had been founded every fortnight in Britain. As a result 1,224 were in existence by 1914 and a further 373 appeared between the wars, which suggests that the game was reaching its peak by this stage. Modern golf took shape after 1902 with the introduction of the Haskell ball, based on a core of rubber strips that made for greater elasticity; this meant that the ball could be hit further and courses had to become longer.

Golf already enjoyed a reputation as an occupation for affluent men with time on their hands and a propensity for alcohol. During the interwar period it became popular among men employed in sedentary occupations who wanted some undemanding exercise and hoped to make useful business contacts; for suburbanites it was pre-eminently a social sport, combining the amenities and status of a clubhouse with a vaguely rural ambience. In this period golf was predominantly an amateur game and although the amateurs competed with the handful of professionals in open tournaments, they were reluctant to mix with them socially. Many men admitted finding golf preferable to tennis because it was less physically demanding and was free from the presence of women; they claimed that women chattered too much on the course and distracted the men with their shapely feminine swing. This prejudice and the fondness of politicians such as Asquith and Lloyd George for the game explains why the Edwardian suffragettes had often targeted golf courses for acid attacks. As a result women developed separate clubs and nine-hole courses for themselves.

Between the wars golf began to accumulate a number of fashionable accessories. Out went the shabby old Norfolk jackets usually worn before 1914 and in came the baggy plus-four breeches and loudly patterned Argyll socks. Popular novelists including Agatha Christie (*Murder on the Links*) and P. G. Wodehouse (*The Heart of a Goof*) used golf as a suitable setting for the portrayal of middle-class snobbery. In 1936 the *News Chronicle* put up £1,000 prize money for a new tournament and the *Daily Mail* followed with £2,000. However, golf was now reaching its natural limits as a participatory sport. Although a few municipal courses were constructed there was no great demand among the majority of the population. Much to the chagrin of the British, having developed the sport they now found themselves being overtaken by the Americans. In 1921 Americans carried off the British Open at St Andrews and the amateur competition at Hoylake, thus initiating a run of American triumphs. When Henry Cotton, the first British player to take golf seriously as a career, won the British Open in 1934 he was the first to do so for eleven years. But despite further victories in 1937 and 1948 Cotton was a lonely example.

Although tenes, tennys or tennise, as it was originally known, boasted French origins, the modern game had been formulated by the British in the 1870s. Enthusiastically promoted by society magazines, tennis had been quickly adopted as a useful addition to country-house parties in the late Victorian period, before spreading to suburban middle-class society and acquiring its associations with cucumber sandwiches, strawberries and cream and iced claret in the process. To this extent tennis, like golf, was a social activity as much as a sport but with the crucial difference that, far from segregating the sexes, it came to be seen as an ideal means for bringing them together. Tennis was valued by women for providing them with a respectable form of outdoor exercise. Moreover, the interwar concerns about the decline of marriage won the game even more approval as a means of mixing nubile young women and marriageable men in convivial surroundings. As chaperones fell out of favour after the war, middle-class girls were likely to 'come out' by joining tennis clubs. In these circumstances the game was not taken too seriously by most participants, and young men in particular often played tennis as a change from cricket or simply to socialise.

However, by the interwar period tennis had become a well-organised sport run by the Lawn Tennis Association whose highlights were the Wimbledon Championships, founded in 1877, and the Davis Cup, founded in 1900. Radio broadcasting of Wimbledon started in 1927. Some 250 local clubs affiliated to the LTA in 1900, rising to 1,620 by 1925 and 3,230 by 1938. In the 1930s steel-framed rackets were introduced but they were not popular and had to be reintroduced in the 1960s. During the 1920s balls had been tested for their bounce and hardness, but by the 1930s they were required to be harder and faster,

thus permitting serves of around 130 m.p.h. The sport received a boost
in 1919 when King George V, Queen Mary and the Princess Royal
turned up at Wimbledon. Royal patronage turned into participation in
1926 when the Duke of York played in the men's doubles, only to be
eliminated in the first round. However, 1919 also posed a challenge to
the conservative attitudes that dominated the game when the twenty-
year-old French player, Suzanne Lenglen, made her debut. Hitherto,
female players had been encased in long dresses and white stockings,
supposedly because Queen Mary hated to see bare legs. Lenglen
shocked the spectators by appearing in a short, calf-length skirt and
minus the stiff foundation garments usually worn. These steel-boned
corsets were most uncomfortable and, according to one competitor,
'most of them were blood-stained'.[8] The female players used to dry
them off on a rail by the fireplace in the ladies' dressing room. But
Lenglen, happily free from these encumbrances and fortified by small
flasks of cognac, shocked the Wimbledon spectators by defeating the
seven-times ladies' champion, Mrs Chambers, now a venerable forty-
year-old. Next year she delighted the newspapers by appearing in a
brightly coloured silk chiffon scarf, dubbed the 'Lenglen bandeau',
which was widely copied by young women. So many people wanted
to see Lenglen play that the Wimbledon committee abandoned the old
courts at Worple Road for a new stadium at Church Road with a centre
court capable of seating 15,000.

The flaw in British interwar tennis lay in the attitude adopted
towards the minority of players who took the game seriously. It
remained essentially an amateur sport; even those who competed
abroad could expect to receive no more than their travelling expenses.
Yet as there was no clear definition of amateur status tennis was
excluded from the Olympics in 1924 and remained excluded until 1988.
In fact the amateur status of Suzanne Lenglen and other stars was
purely nominal in that they earned fees for writing articles and giving
exclusives in the press and for playing in the United States. By the 1930s
it was regular practice for amateurs to turn professional once they had
reached their peak. But in Britain this limited the recruitment of new
players largely to middle-class people. Britain's one outstanding player,
Fred Perry, came to tennis via table tennis in the early 1920s. Perry
played at Wimbledon in 1929 as an amateur only because his father
subsidised him. He led the British team to victory over France in the

Davis Cup in 1933 and for the next three years; but the cup was never won again. Perry won the Wimbledon championship in 1934, 1935 and 1936, also winning the American and Australian titles at this time. His success was attributable to keeping fit at a time when it was not fashionable in amateur sports in Britain. Unusually confident and driven by a will to win, Perry was seen by tennis snobs as lacking social polish. His attitude and his modest background made him seem an alien figure in sporting circles despite his conspicuous success. Not surprisingly, Perry, who turned professional in 1936 because he needed the money, went to the United States where he acquired an American accent.

Participation in athletics had once been extensive, but since the foundation of the modern sport in the 1860s, largely by men from the universities, the army, the Civil Service and the City, it had become more restrictive; so much so that by 1914 working-class athletes had largely withdrawn. Admittedly, the post-war years saw a rapid expansion of athletics, involving the affiliation of 1,000 athletics clubs to the Amateur Athletics Association by 1930, which made it a little less exclusive. Also, the foundation of the Women's Athletics Association in 1925 posed a challenge to conventional thinking. Before 1914 women had generally been excluded from competitions on the grounds that athletics was unfeminine and on the basis of medical opinion that it damaged women's health. However, women's wartime role in the armed forces had undermined the conventional wisdom. In 1918 a WRAF relay team ran against the men, and in 1919 the Inter-Services Championship included a women's 440 yards relay. By the 1920s medical opinion had revised its earlier prohibition. However, women continued to be barred from the Olympic Games until 1926 – the British men had voted against lifting the ban – and British women did not compete until the 1932 Olympics.

Since the 1890s the AAA, which had devoted its efforts to preventing professionalism and illegal payments in the sport, regularly banned those found guilty. Its only concession was to allow the payment of travelling expenses. No further change was made until 1956 when athletes were permitted pocket money! This policy had the effect of depressing popular interest in athletics in Britain, though enthusiasm was rekindled by international competitions, particularly the 1908 Olympics which were held in Britain. During the 1920s athletics developed into a spectator sport, with 20,000–30,000 attending the major events. However, during the 1930s support dwindled once again, apparently because British competitors were out-performed by those from other countries especially America whose athletes were routinely backed by funds, organisation and personal coaches. The spirit of British athletics between the wars was well captured by the career of Eric Liddell, one of the greatest sporting heroes of the century. The son of Scots missionaries, Liddell was himself dedicated to a life as a Christian missionary in China rather than to sport. In 1924 he was scheduled to compete in the Paris Olympic Games, but refused to run in the 100 and 200 metres because they were held on a Sunday. He subsequently won the 400 metres race. In the following year Liddell took the 100, 200 and 440 yard titles in the Scottish Amateur Athletics Association competition; but this marked the end of his career as an athlete as he departed to work in the Anglo-Chinese College at Tientsin. Despite fleeting successes by men like Liddell, it had become clear by the 1930s that British athletics was still too dominated by a narrow circle of men from Oxford and Cambridge; Britain's poor performance at the 1936 Olympics underlined the point. As a result by 1939 the amateur ethos was increasingly regarded as inadequate and the need to support athletes by tapping the resources of the state was beginning to be accepted.

British rowing was even more socially segregated. Before 1914 its practitioners had been so committed to the languid, amateur, upper-class ideal that leading rowers like Willie Grenfell (Lord Desborough) had made strenuous efforts to have all foreigners banned from competing in regattas on the Thames! Because of doubts about the amateur status of their crews no Americans appeared at Henley until 1914. Nor did rowing aspire to attract spectators. Trapped in a time warp the sport was content to remain an all-British minority interest. Yet despite this, the interwar period came to be regarded as a golden age for rowing. By the time of the 1936 Olympics British competitors had won twelve gold and six silver medals in seven Olympiads. Their success helps to explain the surprising popularity of a sport that otherwise only came to popular attention at Easter each year when the Oxford and Cambridge teams competed in the Boat Race. March 1925 saw the most famous such occasion when the Cambridge crew enjoyed the calmer waters of the Middlesex side of the river while

Oxford hit a stiff breeze on the Surrey side. In this situation Oxford made the mistake of starting at a fast pace, their boat became water-logged, and halfway through the race their cox stood up waving his arms in surrender as the boat was on the verge of sinking.[9] 'TRAGEDY OF THE BOAT RACE: DARK BLUES GIVE UP HALFWAY' reported the newspapers as though recording a major national disaster.

By contrast boxing enjoyed huge support among working-class men both as spectators and as participants throughout this period; but it also benefited from the continuing patronage of upper class and aristocratic men such as Lord David Douglas Hamilton who boxed for Britain at the 1934 Olympics. Boxing was very much a Saturday-night entertain-ment, though in London fights could be seen in small halls on every night of the week including Sundays. In Manchester, another major centre for the sport, there were regular matches at the Free Trade Hall, Belle Vue, the Alhambra and the Adelphi Sports Club. For a ticket costing from one to seven shillings spectators could expect to see three fifteen-round fights – though twenty-round contests still took place – and two six-rounders. Amateur boxing enjoyed its heyday between the wars, the British style being noted for a high level of skill, fast footwork and defensive tactics. Hundreds of amateur clubs flourished all over the country and championship competitions were organised by the Amateur Boxing Association supported by schools, the Boy Scouts and the army. Britain proved very successful especially at light and middleweight divisions. In 1908, when boxing was first included in the Olympic Games, she had carried off all the titles and she continued to do well throughout the period.

Boxing was less troubled by distinctions between amateurs and professionals than other sports. Although the old tradition of prize-fighting had dwindled, there were still plenty of opportunities for young boxers to earn money at boxing booths attached to fairs in a semi-professional capacity. From their ranks a handful of boxers emerged to become national heroes like 'Bombardier' Billy Wells, a heavyweight who usually lost fights against foreign opponents but acquired huge popularity in the process. For talented working-class boys the temptation to see boxing as an escape from a life of poverty had always been strong and it was enhanced by prolonged interwar unemployment, though for most fighters the material gains proved to be modest. Professional boxers endured an enormous number of contests, often over a remarkably long working life. Jackie 'Kid' Berg, for example, had 21 fights in 1925 alone, involving 262 rounds.[10] Len Harvey, who started boxing at the age of sixteen, fought twenty-seven times in London and four times elsewhere during 1924–5; his career lasted twenty years. Tommy Farr, who became British heavyweight champion in 1936, was the son of a South Wales miner who grew up in extreme poverty. At fifteen Farr began in boxing booths where he earned three shillings and sixpence for six rounds during the 1920s; in the 1930s he was paid around £150 a fight, still a modest fee by contemporary standards. In 1937 Farr fought Joe Louis in New York where he boxed brilliantly but lost on points over fifteen rounds. After suffering injuries, or when they had passed their peak, boxers often took employment with anyone who wanted protection including criminals and election candidates in the rougher constituencies. Oswald Mosley used the Jewish boxer Ted 'Kid' Lewis in this capacity. Between the wars Jews formed a high proportion of professional boxers, trainers and promoters, partly because they were concentrated in places such as the East End and Manchester where the sport formed an integral part of local culture and offered a route out of poverty. A colour bar, which was not lifted until 1948, prevented black men boxing for a British title. This excluded one of the best welter-weights of the period, Len Johnson, who was born in Manchester in 1902 to a West Indian seaman. Johnson won 86 of his 116 professional contests, and, as he outpointed Harvey, who later held the title, it seems probable that he would have been a British champion but for the bar.[11]

More than any other sport football had acquired a markedly working-class character by 1914. This was the cause of some concern. The improvers who had tamed the traditional game by imposing a set of rules and organising a competitive system in the late Victorian period had intended to channel working-class energy into respectable forms. But by 1900 football had largely escaped the control of its founding fathers who were dismayed by the boisterous behaviour of the spectators, the dominance of professionalism, the disregard for the rules, the gambling on the results of matches and the large sums of money involved in the game – all characteristics that appeared to be accentuated in the 1920s and 1930s. In this period British football was played on rough pitches under lenient referees who usually turned a blind eye to tackling that was intended to disable or intimidate opponents; kicking star players was widely regarded as a legitimate way of winning.[12] As a good deal of money was at stake the spectators were inclined to become agitated if a game started to go in an unexpected direction and even barracked the team that seemed likely to upset the predicted result, much to the dismay of the FA.

Attitudes towards football had also been soured as a result of the determination of the professional clubs to continue playing for the first eighteen months of the war. Rugby players were considered more patriotic and, as a result, during the early 1920s many public schools and grammar schools abandoned football for rugby; 231 new rugby clubs were founded as a result. Despite these withdrawals football enjoyed a boom between the wars. It was effectively promoted through football pools, cigarette cards, radio broadcasts and cinema newsreels. By the 1930s some 10,000 amateur clubs existed, which meant that at professional matches a high proportion of the spectators felt qualified to criticise the players, the managers and the tactics. Attendances at matches of 60,000–70,000 were routine and 140,000 people were known to turn up at Glasgow's Hampden Park. Entrance usually cost a shilling a head. As money poured into the leading clubs new stadia were constructed notably at Ibrox, Old Trafford and Highbury. In April 1923 Wembley Stadium, built at a cost of £750,000, opened in time for the Cup Final between Bolton Wanderers and West Ham. In addition to the 126,000 fans who bought tickets, thousands climbed over the fences or broke through the turnstiles, filling the pitch until it was cleared by the police.

Another explanation for the popularity of interwar football lay in the expansion of the First and Second Divisions to twenty-two teams, and in the creation of two more divisions for southern and northern teams in 1921. During the 1920s the sport continued to be dominated by the North, so much so that not more than four of the First Division teams came from London and the South. In ten years after the war only Spurs (1921) and Cardiff (1927) took the FA Cup away from the northern and Midland clubs. However, the balance changed in the 1930s with the rise of Arsenal under the management of Sir Henry Norris and Herbert Chapman; Arsenal became First Division champions in 1931, 1933, 1934, 1935 and 1938, and won the Cup in 1930 and 1936.

The prolonged economic depression probably enhanced the appeal of professional football for a generation of sportsmen seeking money and glamour. Soccer scouts travelled the country, especially Scotland and the North of England, spotting talented youths who were lured away to play for well-heeled clubs further south. In 1928 the first £10,000 transfer fee was recorded. However, the FA attempted to limit the role of money by imposing an £8 maximum weekly wage for footballers, though only ten per cent of the players received that much. This low level was justified on the grounds that it kept the professional sport close to amateurism in character, and it prevented the richest clubs simply buying up all the talent. But in this situation some players unashamedly bargained for extras. Frank Barson of Manchester United expected to find a packet filled with money every time he entered the dressing room. 'Where's the doin's?' he would enquire. 'I'm not taking my bloody coat off till I get it.'[13]

Paradoxically, the popularity of interwar football fostered an exaggerated belief in the supremacy of the domestic game and a disregard for the wider world. Having exported football, especially to Europe and South America, the British failed to notice that the English style was beginning to be abandoned by countries like Argentina and Italy in favour of a more flowing, elegant and creative game. Though creative individuals were far from unknown at home they were commonly regarded with suspicion, dismissed as 'stormy petrels' and easily lost their places in the teams.[14] The English professed to regard the foreign style as too delicate and artificial for a primitive, masculine game like football in which strength and endurance were the key qualities for a player.[15] As a result the sport became very insular and nationalistic between the wars. Britain did not even join the International Football League until 1918, but in 1919 she refused to play against Germany and Austria. However, France, Belgium and Italy declined to follow her example and so in the next year Britain withdrew from international competition altogether. British teams did in fact play Germany in Berlin in 1930, drawing 3–3, and again in 1936 in the face of severe criticism from opponents of Nazism; under pressure from the football authorities the British players reluctantly gave the Nazi salute on entering the pitch. These, however, were exceptions. After rejoining the IFL in 1924 Britain became embroiled in a dispute about amateur status and withdrew again in 1928. As this lasted until 1946 it left British football dangerously isolated from wider developments in the game and content to cultivate the domestic game; not until she began to suffer dramatic defeats by Continental teams after the Second World War did she realise how far British football had declined.

For some contemporaries it was a matter of regret that much of the enthusiasm for sport was generated not so much by the spectacle and by the thrill of competition but by the prospect of financial gain. Gambling in its various forms represented a central element in British popular culture involving millions of men who regularly competed for prize money by joining clubs, usually based in pubs, devoted to leek-growing, darts, cards and dominoes, as well as competitive bowls, angling, pigeon-fancying and whippet racing. Above all, the British gambled heavily on horse racing, boxing and football; in fact, sixteen times as many people bet on football as watched it. Moreover, the opportunities for gambling increased considerably during the interwar period largely as a result of the development of greyhound tracks and football pools.

Horse racing was the classic example of a highly exclusive sport whose popular following depended almost entirely on betting rather than on participation or attendance at fixtures. In 1920 Britain had just 317 licensed jockeys. Racing was controlled by a group of self-appointed, wealthy, aristocratic owners in the Jockey Club who set the rules and adjudicated in disputes. One such was the Earl of Derby, whose family had founded the Derby as long ago as 1780; in 1924 he won the race with his horse, Sansovino. But despite its narrow base racing enthusiasts claimed that their sport upheld a vital national interest by maintaining the bloodstock and thus the supply of horses required for hunting and the cavalry. It also created employment for stable boys and blacksmiths and indirectly supported the evening newspapers, who printed the racing results for workingmen, as well as *Sporting Life* and the *Sporting Chronicle*.

Yet as a commercial proposition horse racing had always enjoyed a precarious existence. The expansion of the Victorian railways boosted some courses such as Sandown, only thirteen miles from London's West End, by enabling workingmen to turn up for Saturday afternoon fixtures; with a larger attendance the organisers could charge entrance fees and offer extra prize money. However, the sport was run in a very amateur and conservative way; there was little investment and many of the 113 courses lost money. During the interwar period even the big courses near London met for only twelve to sixteen days each year and elsewhere some of the flat-race courses that met only twice were not viable. Racing obtained a welcome boost, and a measure of respectability, when the BBC overcame its reluctance by broadcasting the Epsom Derby in 1922. In 1927 it went further in appeasing popular tastes by offering live commentary on the Grand National for the first time; the commentators, who were inexperienced in this work, found their task very exacting. But despite this extra publicity, the prize money diminished during the 1920s, and rose around 1930 only to dwindle again for the rest of the decade.

By contrast, the relatively new sport of dog racing, which attracted nineteen million spectators each week during the 1930s, benefited from major investment and entrepreneurial flair – and this despite the fact that it was consistently ignored by the BBC. Britain had a long-standing tradition in the form of hare coursing, made famous by the Waterloo Cup which was held near Liverpool. But modern dog racing was introduced to Britain in 1926 in the form of a circular course using an electronic 'hare', with six dogs decked out in different colours and racing over 400 or 500 yards. This offered 'all the thrills and skill of coursing without cruelty' as a Pathé newsreel put it.[16] Following the opening of the first dogtrack at Manchester's Belle Vue, others were built at Harringay, Hall Green (Birmingham) and Wembley in 1927; by 1932 there were fifty tracks altogether some capable of seating 30,000 people under cover. Champion greyhounds like Mick the Miller, whose 'almost uncanny skill has literally endeared him to thousands', became popular features for the cinema newsreels.[17] This success was partly due to the greater accessibility the dogtracks enjoyed over horse racing. Functions were held after working hours and they were easily reached by public transport. Every Tuesday William Woodruff, then living in the East End, attended the Hackney Wick Greyhound Racing track where he placed a couple of bets: 'Noses pressed against the wire, the dogs scrabbled and whined until the hare flashed by and the gate of the traps flew up. There followed thirty seconds of bedlam while the dogs raced round the track, leaping the hurdles, neck to neck.'[18] While providing excitement, spectacle and the chance to win money, the new tracks were also equipped with bars, smoking lounges, restaurants and even dance floors, everything, in fact, that the working population required in the form of cheap entertainment to liven up dreary winter evenings.

As a result of such innovations gambling in Britain reached its peak between the wars. Most of the nineteen million who attended dog-tracks indulged in a few modest bets. An estimated four million people also bet regularly on horses, though many more had an occasional 'flutter'. In addition the football pools attracted around ten million participants each week in the 1930s. Legal expenditure on gambling increased from £63 million in 1920 to £221 million by 1938, representing five per cent of all consumer spending, though it is, of course, impossible to know the extent of illegal gambling. As a result of legis-lation enacted in 1853 and 1906 cash bets on horse racing were legal only at racecourses, effectively discriminating against working-class gamblers who were less likely to attend meetings or to be acceptable as credit customers. The law, of course, simply forced betting on to the streets, though few gamblers seem to have been troubled by their criminality. In William Woodruff's lodgings one of the residents routinely 'organised the bets with a bookie who had a pitch on the pavement in Bow Road. I never heard of a copper intervening.'[19] For years Parliament had felt reluctant to liberalise the rules for fear of increasing the amount spent on gambling. It intervened in 1926 by imposing a 2.5 per cent tax on course betting and 3.5 per cent on off-course betting, as well as a £10 licence fee on bookmakers which was ignored by cash bookmakers. As a result of the tax the Jockey Club and the National Hunt Committee persuaded the government to find extra money by means of the Tote which was introduced in 1928 with a view to improving racecourses and developing the British thoroughbred.

In effect the authorities were caught between influential upper-class interests, for whom gambling represented a harmless tradition, and vocal middle-class critics who regarded gambling in any form as irrational and as damaging to the living standards of working-class families. However, from a working-class perspective the criticism made little sense. During the 1920s and 1930s few people believed it was practical to save enough money to improve their welfare significantly in later life; consequently, the prospect of an immediate windfall from a bet seemed far more appealing and a more realistic use for spare money. One man indignantly told B. H. Rowntree's social investigators that he would rather have 'six penn'orth of hope than six penn'orth of electricity'.[20] The cultural gulf between the upper- and working-class gamblers on the one hand and the middle- and respectable working-class non-gamblers on the other was unbridgeable. It manifested itself daily in Britain's public libraries where the staff had a habit of pasting out the racing news before allowing the public to enter to read the newspapers!

However, despite the rising level of spending, the critics of gambling probably exaggerated its damaging impact between the wars. Most people laid modest and affordable bets of one or two shillings a week without feeling guilty or disrupting their finances. With their armies of runners and lookouts bookmakers offered welcome jobs to thousands of young boys many of whom were otherwise unemployable. In its survey of Bolton, Mass Observation found one bookie who used no fewer than 170 runners and circulated the pubs buying drinks for everyone; not surprisingly the local community regarded him as an asset.[21] In effect the bookies were an integral part of their local community, helping to pull it together in the face of outside interference by the police and the social investigators. Not that this deterred the critics of gambling. During 1927–8 some 1,600 petitions demanding control over dog racing reached the Home Secretary. But despite some criticism over sharp practice, including allegations that dogs were sedated and overfed before races, the sport offered few targets. Not only did the sport regulate itself, it created a relatively respectable form of gambling appealing to both sexes. Its promoters told the politicians that at a time of unemployment the mass entertainment offered by dog racing should be valued as 'a great antidote to Bolshevism'.[22] This may have been overstating the influence of Mick the Miller, but the authorities took it on board at least to the extent of declining to interfere with betting on greyhound races.

Meanwhile the football pools offered a new but equally difficult target for opponents of betting. Football coupons had flourished in a small way in Lancashire before 1900, but the idea was effectively popularised by John Moores of Liverpool, the founder of Littlewoods. In his work as a telegraphist in Manchester Moores realised the potential of coupons as a form of betting. He launched his new business in 1922 with just £150 of capital, printing 4,000 copies of the first coupon for distribution by hand outside football grounds. For several years Moores's family worked for nothing before the business became profitable. But eventually the punters realised that the odds on winning were better than those offered by the bookies. The only danger lay in the temptation to staff to slip coupons into the checking process after the results were known; if offenders were discovered they were immediately sacked. The football clubs disliked the pools because they feared that players would be tempted to trigger payouts by rigging matches, and they therefore required them to abstain from all coupon betting on penalty of losing their contracts. Sometimes the clubs frustrated the pools companies by withholding publication of the football fixtures until it was too late to print the coupons.[23]

By the late 1930s Littlewoods and Vernons, the biggest pools companies, were taking £800,000 a week, while the Post Office also prospered by selling huge numbers of postal orders. For many people the pools represented their only form of gambling. Risking stakes of two to four shillings, husbands and wives often completed the coupons together at home, attracted by the chance of a big win that would transform their lives. By offering such a respectable, domesticated form of betting the pools came to be regarded more as a national pastime than as gambling. Conscious that even the existing restrictions on betting could not be effectively enforced, Parliament flatly refused all pressures to ban them. In this way football pools completed the marginalisation of the moral critics and reinforced the broader trend towards acceptable forms of leisure in interwar society.

15

'Wings over Everest': The Romance and the Menace of Aviation

The historic success of the Wright brothers in getting airborne in 1903 earned them a magisterial editorial rebuke from *The Times*: 'all attempts at artificial aviation are not only dangerous to human life but foredoomed to failure from an engineering standpoint'. Admittedly these early efforts by the pioneers of aviation did not amount to genuine controlled flight. It was not until 1908 that Wilbur Wright demonstrated that he and his brother had resolved the technical problems when they flew for one minute and forty-five seconds at a height of thirty feet before coming down to land 'like a partridge returning to its nest'. Talk of partridges seems slightly romantic language for machines that were basically powered bicycles with wings, but it reminds us of the idealism aroused among the early aviators and of the aesthetic significance that contemporaries saw in man's new ability to fly. For aviation enthusiasts the aeroplane epitomised the culture of modernism, it opened a new era of dramatic conquests by man over Nature, and it offered an opportunity for youth to make its mark on the world. According to T. E. Lawrence, who later enlisted as an aircraftman in the RAF, the air was 'the only first-class thing that our generation has to do. So everyone should either take to the air themselves or help it forward.'[1] Claude Graham-White, one of the Edwardian pioneers, expressed this sense of youthful exhilaration and masculine pride when he wrote: 'To be in the air! To feel your motor speeding you on! To look below and see the country unfolding itself to your gaze, and to know that you and you alone are the master of the situation – the man who is doing this wonderful thing!'[2] For those who felt constrained and confined by a world increasingly tamed by government, bureaucracy and order, flying offered a return to an independent, buccaneering style, a frontier where men tested themselves against the elements. Britons, Italians, Germans and Frenchmen – who dubbed themselves 'the winged nation' – all sought proof of their heroic qualities by achievements in the air. This helps to explain why fascists found aviation so appealing and why many of the youthful pilots and entrepreneurs ended up espousing fascist ideas during the interwar period. Aviation helped them to express their confidence that the younger generation could demonstrate the superiority of the white race and push aside the timid old men to rejuvenate society along modern, patriotic lines.

In Edwardian Britain the typical pioneer aviationist was a hybrid – inventor, entrepreneur, engineer and sportsman – and, not surprisingly, progress towards developing a viable aviation industry proved distinctly haphazard. Men such as Alliott Verdon-Roe, Geoffrey de Havilland and Frederick Handley-Page, untrained engineers and amateur pilots, were simply keen to build their own aeroplanes and experience the pleasure of flying. In 1908 the Short brothers, Horace, Eustace and Oswald, who had previously made balloons at Battersea, formed a partnership to build six aircraft under licence from the Wright brothers; and in 1909 they moved to the Isle of Sheppey because the land was flat and windy. Meanwhile Harold and Frank Barnwell were experimenting with gliders fitted with motorbike engines at their Causewayhead garage in Scotland. In July 1909 they flew their aeroplane for eighty metres at a height of twelve feet over a field outside Stirling. Most of the early pilots, who were already keen cyclists, balloonists or motorists, brought high spirits, humour and English eccentricity to the business of flying. The first Briton to achieve powered flight was J. T. C. Moore-Brabazon who flew a Voisin at the Isle of Sheppey for 500 yards at a height of 35 feet on 2 May 1909 before crashing. He was awarded the first pilot's certificate, the second going to the Hon. Charles Rolls. Moore-Brabazon won the *Daily Mail* prize of £1,000 as the first Englishman to fly a mile, flew the first circular mile in October 1909, steered an aeroplane under London's Tower Bridge, and even took a pig up for an historic flight.

But amid the enthusiasts and idealists one man took a hard-headed view of the matter: Lord Northcliffe, proprietor of the *Daily Mail* and other newspapers, quickly spotted the commercial and political implications of aviation. As early as 1906 he engaged a full-time aviation correspondent, Harry Harper: 'Make no mistake the future lies in the air', Northcliffe told him. He saw that the successes and failures of the pioneer pilots would generate a succession of the 'splash stories' that sold newspapers. One well tried *Daily Mail* technique was to offer cash prizes for aviation 'firsts'. In 1906 Northcliffe put up £10,000 for the first non-stop flight from London to Manchester, ostensibly to stimulate British aviation, in the confidence that no one could cover the 186 miles. His rivals considered Northcliffe so ridiculous that one, the *Star*, mocked him by offering £10 million to anyone who could fly a mere ten miles from London and back. But within four years an Englishman, Claude Graham-White, and a Frenchman, Louis Paulhan, had accomplished the London-Manchester trip.

Unconcerned, Northcliffe offered a more modest prize of £500 that carried far greater political implications for a flight across the English Channel. On 25 July 1909 Louis Bleriot took off from the cliffs at Sangatte at 4.35 a.m. and crash-landed in a meadow near Dover Castle thirty-six minutes later. Flying in fog, Bleriot, who had lost sight of the destroyer accompanying him, had no idea where he was. But neither the French nor the British had any doubt about the symbolic and strategic significance of his flight. As the *Daily News* put it, a flying machine had 'passed over the sacred silver streak and flitted far above the masts of the greatest battleships'. Even more ominously, in July 1908 the German Count Ferdinand von Zeppelin had flown his gigantic airship or dirigible, LZ4, on a 12-hour journey covering 240 miles, and his government was reportedly considering constructing a fleet of such machines.

These rapid advances by Britain's Continental rivals allowed Northcliffe to combine commerce and patriotism in a satisfying way by starting a campaign which ran throughout the 1920s and 1930s to make the British people 'air-minded'. 'England is no longer an island. There will be no sleeping behind the wooden walls of old England with the Channel our safety moat. It means the aerial chariots of a foe descending on British soil if war comes.' Fears about an attack from the air merely complemented the naval scares he was already running designed to pressurise the government into accelerating the Dreadnought building programme. Before long the *Daily Mail* had produced a report by a retired German official about using a fleet of Zeppelins to convey an army of 350,000 men from Calais to Dover in a single night. Northcliffe commissioned H. G. Wells, whose novel about strategic bombing appeared in 1908, to write three articles on 'the war of the future'. And he published pieces on aerial warfare by Major B. F. S. Baden-Powell and Hiram Maxim, the inventor of the rapid-firing gun, who quaintly suggested that if the enemy dropped 1,000 tons of nitroglycerine on the capital in one night 'it would make London look like a last year's buzzard nest'.[3] The scaremongering resumed in 1909 with the 'Phantom Airship Scare'. In March the police began to receive reports about sightings of dirigibles in the sky over Peterborough. Later the source turned out to be a kite, but meanwhile the 'airship' was reported at Wisbech, Ipswich, Northampton, Clacton, Frinton-on-Sea and Harwich, finally appearing at Cardiff in May. Another panic erupted in February 1913 when the *Daily Mail* reported that strange lights had been seen in the night sky over Hull, Grimsby, Ipswich, Dover, Leeds, Portsmouth and Bristol which were believed to come from an airship. By now many such reports were known to be hoaxes, but by emphatically denying that any of its airships had visited Britain the German government only helped to keep the issue alive; the Admiralty apparently accepted that one airship had flown over Sheerness.

As a result of these developments and scares Britain possessed a hundred aircraft when war broke out in August 1914, but as only forty-three were ready to fly it was widely felt that the air defences were inadequate. During the next four years the industry expanded enormously as private companies were encouraged to tender their designs to the Air Ministry. By 1918 some 122 firms employed 112,000 workers and manufactured 1,250 aeroplanes each month. Initially the aircraft were used for reconnaissance over northern France and for spotting as at Gallipoli where they helped guide the naval bombardment of the Turkish forts. Soon they began to bomb enemy positions. By 1918 the Handley-Page bombers were capable of carrying a 1,650-pound load of bombs as far as Berlin. Many pilots recorded the pleasure they derived from dropping bombs and watching the troops below them scurrying for cover. But they ran terrible risks by going up in flimsy machines that were liable to break down over enemy territory and were easily shot from the ground. By way of compensation wartime pilots revelled in the glamorous, heroic style of warfare offered by their duels with enemy fighters, a stark contrast to the mundane role of the troops bogged down in trenches and even the battleships that remained bottled up in Scapa Flow for much of the war because of their vulnerability to mines and submarines.

Meanwhile among the civilian population the appearance of any aircraft and Zeppelins, including friendly ones, in the sky caused panic, so much so that the authorities printed posters designed to show the difference between British and German machines. One Zeppelin dropped bombs on Dover on Christmas Eve 1914, but the usual tactic was to cross the Channel looking for the River Thames to guide them into London where targets could easily be identified. Altogether the Germans flew 325 sorties between 1915 and 1918 in which they lost 62 aircraft and caused around 3,000 casualties.

Against this background the task of making the British people 'airminded' in the 1920s seemed formidable. Civil aviation was not even permitted until April 1919, under regulation by the Air Ministry, and it was a perilous affair both literally and commercially. In 1910 Charles Rolls had won the dubious distinction of becoming the first Englishman to die in an aviation accident. Rolls, who was participating in a precision-landing competition at Bournemouth, had pulled his elevator lever to gain height at 150 feet; but it cracked and splintered, allowing his Wright Flyer biplane to tilt into an uncontrollable dive to the ground.

However, the enthusiasts quickly identified an immediate way of promoting air-mindedness by offering joy rides at £1 a time; redundant military aircraft could now be bought cheaply and wartime pilots such as Alan Cobham, who purchased an Avro 504-K for £450, were in dire need of employment. By working a ten-hour day these pilots could make forty-two short trips, giving the public a thrill and, in the process, showing them that flying was not as dangerous as they thought. In 1929 Cobham campaigned around Britain under the slogan 'Make the skyways Britain's highways', trying to persuade every town to establish its own aerodrome. By 1932 he had organised 170 'National Air Days' each year at which Cobham's Flying Circus was the main attraction. There customers could enjoy a five-minute trip in an open-cockpit light aircraft, with no seat belts or parachutes, for only five shillings, or a more sedate ride in the comfortable Handley-Page 'Clive' for ten shillings.[4] The spectacle also included air races, aerobatics, 'crazy-flying', wing walking and parachute drops.

Sadly, for many spectators the attraction lay in the prospect of witnessing a disaster. A typical accident occurred in May 1926 at King's Lynn where one of the private aviation companies took joyriders up in pairs. At 2,000 feet the navigator, George Lloyd, walked along the right wing of the aeroplane and performed other feats. Several thousand spectators then watched as the aircraft went into a spiral at about 200 feet, came nose down over a cemetery, struck a tree and crashed in a mass of tangled wreckage among the graves. One passenger jumped out at twenty feet from the ground, Lloyd escaped with a broken jaw, but the pilot, Captain Orde Bigg-Willer, died.[5] In the space of five days during May 1926 the *Daily Graphic* reported no fewer than five air crashes with the loss of three lives at Caterham, Andover, Iver, Bournemouth and Blackley (Manchester), a distribution that reflected the concentration of flying in the southern counties at this time.[6] In these crashes the engine frequently burst into flames and the aircraft went into a nosedive. There were no parachutes, but pilots tried to minimise casualties by aiming for a soft landing in a field; however, the propeller frequently got stuck in the earth leading the machine to turn somersault. More serious were the setbacks suffered by the regular commercial air services. In December 1924, for example, an Imperial Airways aeroplane left Croydon Aerodrome on a flight to Paris and immediately crashed between Croydon and Purley. Eight passengers – 'imprisoned in a furnace' – died in the accident.[7] Aviation enthusiasts made no attempt to play down the dangers. The *Aeroplane*, a weekly journal, meticulously recorded every crash; in 1939, for example, it reported no fewer than forty-one fatal accidents worldwide between January and June alone.

However, aeroplanes appeared safe by comparison with the much larger numbers of deaths suffered in airship disasters. For some years the airships appeared to be more commercially viable than aeroplanes, especially for long-distance travel, because their size enabled them to carry far more passengers and with greater comfort, and their stately progress across the skies seemed more reassuring. But airships were notoriously difficult to control in bad weather. The first major setback occurred on 23 August 1921 to R38, then the largest rigid airship in Britain. While undergoing trials before being sold in the United States, R38 broke into two over the River Humber near Hull and crashed, leaving only five survivors among the forty people on board. The R33 had a narrow escape in April 1925 when a fifty miles per hour gale tore it from its moorings at Pulham in Norfolk. It was blown out into the North Sea but after a flight lasting thirty hours it managed to return with all twenty men on board.[8] Not surprisingly opinion was sharply divided over the viability of airships. 'The truth is that an airship is immensely more dangerous than an aeroplane', commented Oliver Locker-Lampson MP. 'These leviathans are unwieldy and helpless in a wind.' Despite this the Air Ministry was keen to promote them. Lord Thomson of Cardington, who served as minister in 1924 and 1929–30, won approval for an airship programme and was effectively the father of two new petrol-powered machines, R100 and R101. In July 1930 the R100 flew from Cardington to Montreal in seventy-nine hours and returned in fifty-seven hours in August. Thomson was so keen to show his faith in their safety that he joined the twelve passengers and forty-two crew on R101 on 5 October 1930 when it left for India. However, as one of the engines was sluggish the crew had to throw out ballast to make the airship rise.[9] R101 progressed slowly towards the coast but was observed to be ominously low. Over France it flew into a storm, went out of control, hit the ground at Beauvais and exploded in flames. Forty-six of the fifty-four on board died including Thomson himself. The only survivors were below the water ballast tanks which were released by the pilot. This tragedy effectively destroyed the airship programme in Britain.

Even if they had been safe the airships would have found it hard to compete in the pubic imagination with the excitement of flying by aeroplane, the daring exploits of young pilots, their competitiveness and patriotism. The mood was well captured in a speech on the Aerial Navigation Bill in 1919 by one of the wartime pilots, recently elected MP, Oswald Mosley: 'The peculiar genius of our race has always manifested itself in strange new enterprises where the individual stood alone uninspired save by the spirit of adventure.' Throughout the interwar period intrepid pilots made their own bid for public recognition by repeatedly breaking new aviation records, testing themselves and their machines to the limit in the process. A succession of British triumphs was inaugurated in 1919 when Captain John Alcock and Lieutenant Arthur Whitten flew the Atlantic from Newfoundland to Ireland in sixteen hours and twelve minutes, for which they were knighted and won the £10,000 prize offered by the Daily Mail. On 12 November that year Captain Ross Smith left England, becoming the

esidents of Violet Street,
ewcastle-upon-Tyne,
part by charabanc for
rip to the coast.

A family gathers round the 'wireless'
to hear the results of the general
election, December 1923.

Dame Nellie Melba, the first opera
singer to risk a 'wireless' broadcast,
sings from Chelmsford, 1920.

The famous Hammersmith 'Palais de Danse', March 1920.

Bathers, with chests mostly covered, at the Lansbury Lido in Hyde Park, 1930.

Crowds queue to see Harold Davidson, the unfrocked rector of Stiffkey, fasting in a barrel at Blackpool, September 1932.

Spectators invade the pitch at the Bolton Wanderers vs West Ham FA Cup Final, 1923, the first to be played at Wembley.

Social intercourse at Queen's Club, 1918.

Susan Lenglen playing at Wimbledon in July 1923, in her short skirt and trademark bandeau.

In the 1930s cigarette manufacturers attempted to link their products with sport and health.

A Belisha Beacon is erected.

A typical scene of congestion on Blackfriars Bridge as City workers pour in from the suburbs.

The inauguration of the first London–Paris air service in a Handley Page machine, 25 August 1919.

(*Right*) Promoting 'air-mindedness': Alan Cobham (*inset*) at Croydon, 13 March 1926, after his return flight to the Cape; and his sea plane to land on the Thames at Westminster, 1 October 1926, on his return from a 28,000-mile round trip to Australia.

Albert, Duke of York
(King George VI) pictured on
his honeymoon with Lady
Elizabeth Bowes Lyon, 1923.

The Prince of Wales
(King Edward VIII)
visits the home of a
Durham miner in 1929.

The princesses, Elizabeth
and Margaret Rose,
at their model house, 1933.

reet celebrations for King George V's Silver Jubilee at Centre Street, Newcastle-upon-Tyne, 1935.

The scenic railway, amid the peaks of the Canadian Rockies, at the
British Empire Exhibition at Wembley, 1924.

M.K. Gandhi meets cheerful mill workers at Darwen, Lancashire, 1930.

first man to fly to Australia when he arrived at Darwin on 10 December. For aviators eagerly searching for targets nothing was now too small to be overlooked. In 1926 some enthusiasts even managed to land an aeroplane on the grassy summit of Helvellyn, 3,118 feet up in the Lake District, a modest peak but further proof of man's capacity to triumph over Nature.

Meanwhile there were human rivals to beat too. In July 1925 fourteen contestants lined up for the King's Cup, an 804-mile race around the British Isles. The route took the pilots from London to Harrogate, Newcastle, Renfrew, south of Glasgow, then down the West coast to Liverpool, Bristol and finally Croydon. In that year ten of the competitors were obliged to descend in blankets of fog. Captain F. L. Barnard, flying Sir Eric Geddes's Siskin V, was an easy winner, completing his circuit in four hours, one and a half hours ahead of his nearest rival.[10] The following year saw fourteen entries again, only seven of whom remained at the end, the others being forced to give up by engine trouble. This time they faced a more complicated itinerary totalling 1,464 miles including several 166-mile laps from Hendon to Martlesham Heath (Cambridge) and back; one competitor who was reported fifty miles off course was obliged to land at Oxford.[11] Many pilots 'flew by Bradshaw' in the 1920s, that is, when they were unsure where they were they flew very low and tried to read the names of the railway stations!

At this time the Schneider Trophy, the major international competition, provided an opportunity to prove that Britain led the world in aircraft design and engine manufacture. Britain won the trophy twice in the 1920s, but there was outrage in the press in 1930 when Ramsay MacDonald refused to grant government subsidies for the competition again. Lord Semphill asked Lady Lucy Houston, an eccentric but highly patriotic millionaire, to donate the £100,000 required.[12] Always keen to embarrass the government, Houston agreed. Britain subsequently won the Schneider Trophy for the third time in September 1931 when Lieutenant Boothman captured the world air speed record in a 340 m.p.h. monoplane that prefigured the Spitfire of 1936. As a result Lucy Houston gained a reputation as 'the woman who won the war'.

Backing up the efforts of Britain's pilots a series of pressure groups sprang up to promote air-mindedness including the Air League of the British Empire, the British Airline Pilots' Association, the Royal

Aeronautical Society, and two journals, *Flight* and the *Aeroplane*. By 1938 Britain also boasted sixty-six local flying clubs and flying schools, concentrated in southern England and charging between one and three guineas for membership.[13] In 1932 the clubs claimed 6,711 members and had trained 1,554 new pilots. During the mid 1920s aviationists became concerned that the reserve of men who had learned to fly during the Great War was becoming exhausted thereby exposing a new weakness in Britain's security. Mosley argued that if all boys were trained to fly 'we would soon be a nation of potential pilots'. To this end the Air Scouts were formed at RAF Cranwell in 1928 and the RAF Estimates for 1925 included £15.5 million to be used to enrol young civilians in the reserves where they would be trained to fly. But the most effective means of engaging public interest lay in the Hendon Pageant which started in 1920 with 40,000 spectators and was attracting 170,000 by 1932. At Hendon spectators saw formation flying set to popular music, air races, parachute descents, bombing demonstrations, mock battles between fighters and bombers, parades of the latest weaponry and set-piece attacks on mock forts manned by black-faced 'Wottnotts'.

The Air League also cultivated its political allies by forming a Parliamentary Air Committee of backbench enthusiasts including Lt Col Moore-Brabazon, Harold Balfour, Lindsay Everard, the Marquess of Clydesdale and Murray Sueter. After his pre-1914 escapades and war service in the Royal Flying Corps, Moore-Brabazon settled down slightly to become a rebellious right wing Tory MP and was one of the last members to wear a top hat in the Commons. A friend of Mosley, he collaborated with the British Union of Fascists in the 1930s. Most of the interwar air ministers became keen advocates of aviation, notably Winston Churchill, Sir Samuel Hoare, the ill-fated Lord Thomson, Lord Londonderry, who qualified for his pilot's licence in 1934 aged fifty-six, and Sir Philip Sassoon. Churchill had started learning to fly in 1914 but gave up under pressure from his wife, Clemmie, resumed in 1919 and abandoned it after a crash in which he almost killed himself.

At the end of the war Lloyd George appointed Churchill Secretary of State for War *and* Air Minister which air-minded people condemned despite his enthusiasm for aviation. It is usually forgotten that Churchill spent most of his career trying to reduce expenditure on armaments, and after 1918 both he and the government were keen on drastic economies. However, this proved advantageous for air power because Churchill, always up for a novel solution, quickly saw that Britain would be able to police her newly acquired colonial territories by using bombers to intimidate rebellious natives more cheaply than by employing ground troops. As a result Britain relied largely on air-craft against rebel tribesmen in Afghanistan and Egypt in 1919, and in Somaliland, Palestine and the Kurdish areas of Iraq during 1920. British aeroplanes used bombs and machine guns not only against military targets but against demonstrations by civilians especially in Egypt where they also dropped propaganda leaflets. The indiscriminate killing of civilians provoked severe criticism but it impressed the military planners who claimed that bombing had a big moral effect on barbarous tribes. Aviation, according to Sir Samuel Hoare, was 'the key that closes the door on disorder and insecurity'. This was a wild exaggeration; but as Churchill's new policy undoubtedly gave the RAF a very distinct role and an extra appeal among economy-minded politicians, it was largely responsible for saving the Air Ministry from being abolished and the RAF from being merged into the army and the navy.

Beyond the ranks of sympathetic politicians air-mindedness relied on a collection of peers, entrepreneurs and propagandists, many of them characterised by extremism and eccentricity. Lord Rothschild, the Duke of Richmond, Lord Montagu of Beaulieu and the Marquess of Tullibardine were among those willing to risk money to promote experimental designs. Among the manufacturers Geoffrey de Havilland, who had borrowed £500 to start his business in 1905, built the famous Moth in 1925, a simple light aircraft that sold for £650 and in which thousands of men learned to fly. Frederick Handley-Page, who helped to form Imperial Airways in 1924, struggled to make profits as a manufacturer until 1936 when rearmament boosted his business. More successful was Tommy Sopwith whose Sopwith Camel, a single-seater fighter, had been one of Britain's most effective wartime aircraft. In 1923 Sopwith helped form the Hawker Company which, in 1935, produced the Hawker Hurricane fighter, a vital aircraft during the Battle of Britain. Also successful commercially was Alliott Verdon-Roe who built the famous Avro 504-K in 1913, a military biplane that was widely used during the war and copied between the wars. After 1918 he built seaplanes including the Lynx and the Cadet. Like most aviators

Verdon-Roe was very opinionated and hostile towards all governments for what he saw as their lack of support for the industry.

But even Verdon-Roe was comparatively moderate in the strident
world of interwar aviators. The Scottish landowner, Lord Semphill,
was a characteristically buccaneering figure and a bitter critic of
bankers and financiers. After serving in the Royal Flying Corps in 1914
he joined the Royal Naval Air Service in 1916 and the RAF in 1918. An
inveterate competitor in the King's Cup in the 1920s, Semphill chalked
up a string of exploits: he flew a glider all the way to Stockholm,
crashed in the jungle when attempting a solo flight to Australia and
flew a De Havilland Moth to Dublin in a storm in 1926 to prove that
light aircraft could withstand heavy weather.[14] Alienated from his
roots in the British Establishment, Semphill joined the fascist organisations during the 1930s. A similar pattern is evident in the career of
Charles Grey, an engineer and draughtsman who moved into
journalism and founded the *Aeroplane* in 1911. Convinced that aviation
offered the best means of giving expression to the virility and
superiority of the British race, Grey became the centre of a network of
aviators and politicians at his offices in Piccadilly. He used the *Aeroplane*
as an unofficial house journal for the RAF, as a fund of technical
information on aircraft development and as a campaigning platform to
pressurise governments into expanding British air power. Convinced
that the national interest was being undermined by wimpish politicians
and interfering civil servants, he pursued a vendetta against the Royal
Aircraft Factory establishment at Farnborough and attacked the aeronautical inspectors as parasites because they regulated aircraft design
and experimentation but produced nothing themselves.[15] He
complained that it was impossible to get an experimental aeroplane off
the ground unless it had been exhaustively examined by the Air-
worthiness Department of the Air Ministry, which, he argued, deterred
poor but honest entrepreneurs.[16] These grievances left Grey pre-
disposed to a fascist analysis based on conspiracy theories and the
influence of big business. In the 1930s he advocated a dictatorship and
became highly anti-Semitic, commending Hitler's handling of the Jews
as the best way of checking Bolshevik influence.[17] By 1939 Grey's fascist
sympathies had made him so notorious that he was obliged to resign as
editor of the *Aeroplane*.

While only a minority of interwar aviationists were as fascist as Grey and Semphill, many were militantly imperialist and regarded aviation as a means of putting some spine into official policy towards the British Empire. To this end the indefatigable Alan Cobham undertook a series of marathon journeys spanning the most far-flung parts of British territory. In March 1925 he completed a return flight from Croydon to the Cape, followed in June 1926 by a 28,000-mile return trip to Australia, landing his seaplane dramatically on the Thames beside the Houses of Parliament on his return. Cobham was knighted in October. Throughout the period Australia posed the sternest test for British pilots. On 7 February 1928 Bert Hinkler left Croydon in an Avro Avian light aeroplane in an attempt to beat the twenty-eight-day record, landing at Darwin fifteen and a half days later.[18] Wing Commander Kingsford trimmed four days off Hinkler's record in October 1930, and in the following year Jim Mollinson reduced the England–Australia flight time to eight days and twenty hours.[19] In October 1934 a prize of £10,000 was won by T. Campbell Black and C. W. A. Scott, flying a De Havilland Comet, who reached Australia in just two days twenty-three hours.

But what were the implications of these feats? Alan Cobham used his 23,000-mile trip around Africa in a flying boat in 1928 to argue that Britain should develop an 'All-red Air Route' covering the entire continent in order to bind together the scattered British territories and build another British industry in the process.[20] In the minds of contemporaries aviation was intimately associated with the cause of Empire. The peace settlement following the war had brought British territory to its maximum extent by adding several former German colonies. As a result there was no other territory left to colonise. Indeed the upsurge of nationalist movements in Egypt and India in the early 1920s sounded a warning that Britain was now in the early stages of a retreat from Empire. In this situation the development of air routes seemed to offer the possibility of greater economic development of areas that were not immediately threatened by nationalism. At an emotional level flying across these vast territories seemed to contemporaries almost like conquering them all over again; it went some way to restoring British pride at a time when doubts were creeping in, and it offered dramatic proof to native populations of the continuing moral and material superiority of the British people. This was more than a British phenomenon of course. The Italians, for example, were enthusiastic aviator-imperialists in North Africa. When the American, Charles Lindbergh, completed his famous non-stop transatlantic crossing in 1927 he declared aviation to be 'one of those priceless possessions which permit the white race to live at all in a pressing sea of yellow, black and brown'.

For the British the maintenance of a sense of moral superiority was nowhere more pressing than in India. Hence the importance attached to Imperial Airways' announcement of the start of a weekly flight to India at the end of March 1929. The aeroplane was to leave Croydon every Saturday morning, stopping at Genoa, Rome, Bagdhad and Basra en route, and arriving at Karachi in seven days. The fare was set at £130 to Karachi compared with £75–95 by the fast mail steamer which took twenty-one days to Bombay, and £77–99 by the overland route via Marseilles which took fifteen days. This was a service for the elite as, quite apart from the price, only fifteen to eighteen passengers could be carried at a time.[21] Of much wider importance was the introduction at the same time of an air mail service to India for a basic charge of sixpence per letter. In 1930 the first (blue) post box for Empire mail was erected in the Strand.[22] Imperial Airways confessed to being uncertain how to balance mail against passengers; in view of the huge demand for mail, and its greater profitability, the temptation was to restrict the number of passengers carried.[23]

For an Anglo-Indian community feeling a little beleaguered and nervous about the readiness of the authorities at home to make concessions to Indian nationalism, these efforts at bringing them into closer touch with the homeland assumed considerable psychological importance. By the early 1930s the resurgence of Gandhi's massive Civil Disobedience campaign combined with revelations about the expanding military power of Italy and Germany gave many British people a heightened sense of their vulnerability; imperialists felt an urgent need to reassert Britain's will to rule and her capacity to carry out her role. This anxiety was one of the factors behind one of the most remarkable aviation feats of the interwar period: the famous Everest Flight of 1933. The idea of flying an aeroplane over the summit of Mount Everest, which was officially reckoned to be 29,140 feet at that time, was promoted by a self-appointed committee including John Buchan, Lord Semphill, the Marquess of Clydesdale and Lord Burnham of the *Daily Express*, and supported by the Royal

Geographical Society. The motives were partly scientific, in terms of photographing and mapping remote and inaccessible regions. But there were also large elements of romance and politics involved. The Everest Committee spoke expansively of its objective as 'increasing our prestige in India and the East generally and also making a flight in the international interests of British aircraft'.[24]

Before long, however, the committee ran into financial difficulties from which they were rescued by Lady Houston who donated £15,000 to the project. Houston's participation gave the enterprise a sharper political edge for she saw it as another weapon with which to embarrass the National Government over what she regarded as its policy of retreating from Empire. 'The chief aim of the Marquess [of Clydesdale] and myself in this Adventure', she wrote, 'was to show India that we are not the Degenerate Race that its Leaders represent Britain to be.'[25] The thirty-year-old Clydesdale, who was a dashing pilot and amateur middleweight boxer, was an ideal choice as a member of the team; speaking to his constituents at Paisley he argued that a successful mission would have a major psychological effect: 'it will show India that we are still a virile and active race and can overcome difficulties with energy and vigour'.[26] The committee chose two Westland Wapiti biplanes, using Pegasus engines, to make the attempt on Everest, because they functioned well at low temperatures and high altitudes, and shipped them to Karachi where they were reassembled and flown to Purnea in Bihar, fifty miles from the Nepalese border. On 3 April 1933 Clydesdale and his co-pilots took advantage of a drop in the wind to make their attempt. After they climbed through a haze to 20,000 feet Everest became visible. 'The whole panorama produced an almost intoxicating effect', wrote Clydesdale later. But as they flew higher they met violent down-currents caused by the deflection of the winds blowing over the Everest group which forced the aircraft to lose 2,000 feet. The pilots countered the extreme cold by wearing electrically heated flying suits and carried oxygen to combat the rarified atmosphere. One of the pilots trod on his oxygen tube, split it and passed out for a time. But once out of the downcurrent they regained height and eventually cleared the summit by 500 feet.[27] They then flew down the eastern side of the mountain taking photographs before returning to Purnea, a total flying time of three and a quarter hours. A second flight took place on

19 April in order to obtain better photographs. On their triumphant return to Britain the pilots were feted at a banquet organised by *The Times*, and in 1934 Gaumont-British produced a film, *Wings Over Everest*, to record their success. It is doubtful whether the expedition made much impact in India, but it was widely credited with stimulating the establishment of a Scottish aviation industry based at Prestwick.

These achievements by British pilots in setting new aviation records could not obscure the fact that the development of a commercially viable industry proved elusive. Within months of the opening of civil aviation in April 1919 several entrepreneurs began to convert RAF machines for civil purposes. 'Air Transport and Travel' inaugurated a regular London-Paris service on 25 August aimed at businessmen, though several politicians, including Churchill, Lord Milner and Andrew Bonar Law, used it when attending the peace conference at Versailles. Passengers travelled by the District Railway to Hounslow, thence by tram to the aerodrome gates, though later a direct motor service from central London was installed. Journey time to Le Bourget was around two hours and twenty minutes followed by a twenty-five-minute drive into central Paris.

Though Air Transport and Travel did not survive long, other companies including Daimler Airlines and Imperial Airways introduced flights to Paris during 1920-2, while KLM offered a London-Amsterdam service from 1921 onwards. However, the market remained very small and it proved difficult to make money. The initial flight to Paris carried a single passenger but, in any case, the plane contained only four armchairs. By 1920 eight-seat aircraft were in use, and the twelve-seater Handley-Page was introduced in 1921; even in the early 1930s fifteen or eighteen seats was the maximum. However, the main object of the service was to carry mail, parcels and urgent official communications rather than to take passengers who were in fact rather a problem. The weight allowance included the luggage plus the passenger who was subjected to the indignity of being weighed, though the scales were turned to face the clerk so as to minimise embarrassment. Once on board heavy passengers often found themselves being reseated so as to avoid upsetting the balance of the aircraft.

Nor was this embarrassment the only deterrent. At best passengers found these early flights extremely noisy and at worst they were buffeted around by stormy weather over the Channel even to the

extent of bumping their heads on the roof. If the engine failed they had
no parachutes. In fact throughout the war and right up to 1925 pilots
were not issued with parachutes partly because they were associated
with stunts at fairgrounds. According to Harry Ward, who joined the
RAF in 1921, 'Serious aviators didn't want anything to do with them.
They believed that if something went wrong, it would be far better to
stick with the aircraft and try to put it down, rather than jump out of
it.'[28] When an aeroplane came down in the Channel the passengers
simply climbed out, sat on a wing and waited to be rescued. As no
meteorological reports were available until 1921 it was very much up to
individual pilots to use their own judgement about whether to take off.
The fact that they were paid £700 per annum plus ten shillings for every
hour spent in the air gave them an incentive to take the risk. Once in
the air the idea was to follow railway lines to the coast and look for the
shortest sea crossing; if weather conditions deteriorated the pilot tried
to land in a grassy field and waited for things to improve. Any landing
was tricky at this time because aerodromes had no proper runways,
relying on airfields cropped by sheep which were released at the end of
each day's flying and driven off early next morning. Harry Ward
recorded one early morning arrival at Northolt when the sheep were
still contentedly grazing, unnoticed by the pilot who killed two of them
on landing.[29]

During the 1920s conditions became more comfortable, although as
late as 1932 the flight to Paris still took two and a quarter hours. It may
be evidence of national character that the French were the first to
organise in-flight food and wine, while the British pioneered the on-
board lavatory. Stewards, employed by American companies from 1930
onwards, were to be seen on European flights by 1933. Their tasks
included dusting the aircraft, helping to refuel it, screwing down the
seats, and stopping inexperienced passengers opening the exit door
when looking for the lavatory; as late as 1931 Imperial Airways aircraft
carried warning notices: 'It is dangerous to open the door while the
aeroplane is in motion.'

The commercial airlines attempted to boost business by promoting
flying for social climbers. Customers on the Imperial Airways 'Silver
Wing' Flight were reminded that they might find themselves sitting
next to Prince George (the Duke of Kent). In 1927 the airline published
a list of distinguished passengers carried during March alone including

Lord Londonderry, Baron de Rothschild, Viscount Lymington, Prince
and Princess Walkonsky, the Marquess Bonneval and Count Specia,
plus two racing drivers and two boxers. As prime minister, Ramsay
MacDonald occasionally flew to his home at Lossiemouth in Scotland.
But contemporary accounts suggest that he 'didn't go much on flying.
He usually flew in the longer-range Fairey 3-D, muffled up to the
eyebrows and looking thoroughly miserable.'[30] Indeed, many eminent
Britons remained immune to air-mindedness. When Neville
Chamberlain was staying at Balmoral in August 1938 the King tried to
persuade him to stay for an extra day's shooting by offering to fly him
back to London in time for his Cabinet meeting. But the prime
minister firmly declined the offer; he had never flown and disliked the
whole idea. It was therefore a shock when, only a couple of weeks
later, Chamberlain agreed to fly to meet Hitler at Berchtesgaden for
negotiations leading to the Munich Settlement. *In extremis* he had
overcome his objection to flying, and contemporary opinion thought
it brave of a 67-year-old to take to the air.

Eventually the airline companies concluded that any significant
expansion of business would require a more positive attitude towards
flying on the part of well-to-do women who were likely to be deterred
by the prospect of being publicly weighed before taking to the air.
Unfortunately the early proponents of air-mindedness had spent too
much time celebrating aviation as an expression of masculinity and
power; inhabiting a 'Boy's Own' world that was fast disappearing, they
seemed unlikely to welcome any further invasions of the male sphere
by women. Admittedly the Women's Royal Air Force had been
founded in 1918, but three-quarters of the WRAFs had been engaged in
clerical and catering work, though some became drivers, fitters,
welders and carpenters. The WRAFs were known derisively as
'Penguins' because they did not fly. 'As a matter of fact', the *Daily
Express* explained to readers, 'flying is not a woman's job . . . they
always lost their heads in a sudden emergency.'[31]

However, during the 1920s several of the leading pilots realised that
air-mindedness was not going to make much progress unless they
could show that flying was sufficiently civilised for ladies. Accordingly,
the *Daily Graphic* reported that at Whitsun 1926 the Master of Semphill
had taken his wife, Mrs Forbes-Semphill, on a 700-mile trip in a 27 h.p.
Moth with a view to proving that the aircraft was equal to the motor

car for travel and enjoyment.[32] Leaving Hendon on the Saturday morning the couple took lunch at Oxford, proceeding to Cheltenham and then into mid Wales to overfly Cader Idris. After landing at Porth they crossed the Bristol Channel, flew over Devon and Cornwall, landed in the Exe Valley and crossed the River Severn before returning to Hendon. In June 1928 Sir Alan and Lady Cobham returned from a 23,000-mile trip round Africa in a flying boat. Lady Cobham insisted that the journey was very comfortable from a woman's point of view; she had been able to sleep in her bunk and write letters at her desk.[33] At the same time Miss Amelia Earhart, a thirty-year-old Boston social worker, won fame as the first woman passenger to fly the Atlantic in a crossing lasting twenty-two hours. Flying in a Fokker seaplane *Friendship* she had planned a 1,850-mile route to Valentia in southern Ireland, but fog and rain complicated things; after 2,100 miles the aeroplane was running out of fuel and it eventually landed at Bury Port in Carmarthenshire. Although Miss Earhart had taken the controls twice, she admitted that the flight had been 'beastly' and 'there was no fun in it'.[34] She said later she knew the risks involved, but 'women must try to do these things as men have tried. When they fail their failure must be a challenge to others'.[35] Amelia Earhart embarked on her last flight in the summer of 1937 when she vanished while crossing the Pacific Ocean.

Meanwhile several aristocratic ladies had taken the controls into their own hands, notably Lady Heath and Lady Bailey who flew to the Cape in 1930. In the same year the Hon. Mrs Victor Bruce embarked on a round-the-world solo flight only eight weeks after gaining her pilot's licence. En route, Mrs Bruce, who had no parachute, crash-landed in the Arabian desert, and on 11 November, when she found herself over Hong Kong, she apparently stopped her engine in mid-air for two minutes to observe the Armistice. Another renowned pilot, the 'Flying' Duchess of Bedford, commended aviation as an enjoyable experience, but hazardous; as she was deaf she found that the change in atmosphere relieved the buzzing in her ears. When the Duchess took off from Woburn Abbey in March 1937 the servants painted 'Woburn' on the roof in order to help her find her way home; but she failed to return, one of many interwar pilots presumed lost at sea.

But by far the most famous female aviationist of the period was Amy Johnson who worked for the De Havilland company where she received the first engineer's certificate to be awarded to a woman in 1927. Petite and photogenic, Johnson was taken up by Geoffrey de Havilland as an ideal figure to reassure the public that his Moths were so reliable that they could be flown as safely by women as by the buccaneering male pilots. With only fifty hours' flying behind her Amy Johnson left Croydon on 5 May 1930 in *Jason*, a Gipsy Moth biplane, to make a solo flight to Australia in nineteen and a half hours. Unhappily, as her skills did not include navigation, she usually tried to follow coastlines or railway tracks; her epic flight to Australia was hampered by fuel shortages, damage to the aircraft and bad weather which forced her to land in the desert. After her triumph Amy married James Mollison, the self-styled 'Playboy of the Air', who shared her craving for the fame attaching to feats of aviation. In 1932 she flew to the Cape, beating the record set by her husband in the process. When their marriage broke down in 1938 the women's magazines took it as proof that no good could come of tactless attempts by women to pursue equality in roles for which Nature had not designed them. In fact, Amy divorced Mollison for adultery.

Such exploits by a minority of intrepid women may not have helped Imperial Airways in their efforts to convince the public of 'the fascination that flying has for women'. In 1933 they opted for an unapologetic appeal to conventional feminine interests by introducing thirty-minute 'Tea Flights' over London on Friday and Sunday afternoons, for a charge of £1. 10s.: 'a dainty tea will be served to you in your comfortable armchair in the airliner while London unrolls like a map before you'. The aim here was to accustom well-to-do ladies to flying so that they would take advantage of the regular 'Paris Shopping Service'. In their promotional material Imperial Airways took care to assure customers that their pilots were not sportsmen but *family* men, and, by implication, not the sort to indulge in aerial heroics. Advising apprehensive ladies that 'there's absolutely no need for furs, goggles or special gloves', the airline promised: 'Your complexion will not suffer during air travel'. In fact, from 1932 onwards journeys did become more comfortable in the Handley-Page Heracles aeroplanes which boasted two lavatories, inlaid wood panelling, large windows, comfortable armchairs and devices to regulate heating and cool air in the cabins.

Yet despite their best efforts civil aviation was not a commercial success between the wars. By 1930 the two main companies, Imperial

Airways and British Airways, carried 58,000 passengers each year by comparison with 93,000 in Germany and 386,000 in the United States. During the 1920s most companies had found that services to Europe were not economic, though due to the outcry at the prospect of losing them the government introduced a subsidy of £600,000 to be distributed by a committee chaired by Lord Londonderry. But in 1931 the price of a single ticket to Paris was £4, about fifty per cent more than travel by sea and rail, and in 1932 it went up to £5; at a time of general deflation this was a disastrous trend.

Problems dated from the end of the war when aviation, which, like many industries, had expanded to meet military requirements, faced a sudden crisis arising from the cancellation of orders from the ministry. The infant industry had to switch rapidly to civil aviation at a time when the government was unwilling to support it financially. By 1924 the politicians, now alive to the strategic and political importance of cultivating the industry, offered subsidies to Imperial Airways on condition that it used British aeroplanes and developed imperial routes. Subsequently, British Airways developed as a state-owned company. But despite the enthusiasm of aeroplane designers and manufacturers, critics felt that the British aircraft industry was failing to compete effectively with its rivals; in 1924 the *Daily Mail*'s air correspondent complained that the British machines were too slow compared with French and American ones which now flew at 100 m.p.h.[36]

Two main explanations were offered for this backwardness. There was too much concentration on imperial routes where passenger numbers remained low. This also resulted in undue reliance on seaplanes and biplanes, which were fairly safe and comfortable but a dead end technologically and distracted the British industry from developing the superior monoplanes. This bias was accentuated by the RAF which found the seaplanes and biplanes quite satisfactory as it did not require high-performance machines for policing the Empire. As late as 1936 Imperial Airways introduced *Canopus*, the first of twenty-nine new flying boats for Empire routes; they offered lavish meals and a smoking cabin which proved congenial for customers. But what the company really needed was a big commercial airliner.

The other weakness identified by many aviators and journalists was 'the committee method of production' by which they meant the excessive regulation and control exercised by officials of the Air

Ministry and their interference with aircraft design. Yet manufacturers wanted government backing without which most of them would have collapsed. In effect the ministry allocated contracts to 'the ring' or 'family' of companies to keep them afloat and encourage them to specialise. For example, Fairey produced light bombers, Gloster, Bristol and Hawker manufactured fighters, and Shorts, Blackburn and Supermarine concentrated on flying boats. Only De Havilland stayed outside the ring, prospering on the basis of light aircraft notably the famous Moth which was introduced in 1924 using the Gipsy engine. In effect this policy inflated the size of the industry to around fifty-two firms many of which were inefficient but were propped up by the state. None of the British aircraft companies were of a sufficient size to be able to compete commercially, few were capable of mass production, and most lacked adequate research facilities; this had been obvious as early as 1924 when they showed reluctance to switch from wooden to metal aeroplanes because of the production costs involved. As a result of the weaknesses among both the manufacturers and the aviation companies, the whole industry was in the doldrums by the late 1930s, and in 1935 Hawker, Avro, Gloster and Armstrong-Whitworth amalgamated to form the Hawker Siddeley Group. In 1938 the government, concluding that the competition between Imperial Airways and British Airways had been disastrous, amalgamated them to form British Overseas Airways Corporation. At the same time ministers allocated £500,000 for the development of a commercial airliner, but all this was rapidly overtaken by major new investment in rearmament, skewing the industry towards military needs once again.

By the later 1930s some of the early romance of flying had been lost. Even enthusiasts admitted that the air-circuses, record-breaking and long-distance solo flights no longer commanded the popular interest of the 1920s. When De Havilland stopped making the open-cockpit Moths in 1935 the dashing image of the goggled pilot with his scarf streaming in the wind began to fade. Moreover, despite the efforts of the advocates of air-mindedness to arouse patriotism, foster links with the Empire and make air travel safe and fashionable, it was never possible to erase entirely wartime memories of the menace posed by air power. Admittedly, the bombing of civilian targets in British territories during the early 1920s aroused little concern among the general public; in fact, the policy could be presented reassuringly as part of the wider programme of disarmament and thus as promoting peace. The authorities evidently believed it necessary to enlighten the British people about the need for preparedness against future wars in which they would be especially vulnerable to aerial attack because of the concentration of population and industry in comparatively small areas. To this end the government staged 'London's Great Air Battle' in May 1925 which was designed to give the public 'a peep into the future'. A squadron of giant bombers carried out a spectacular night-time raid: 'powerful searchlights . . . stabbed into the path of darkness overhead, sweeping the skies for the menacing machines . . . Guns manned by alert teams rattled away as they spat out their imaginary stream of shells into the heavens, and the invaders circled round and round loosing their cargoes of destruction from the heights'.[37] On the one hand the authorities wanted to satisfy voters by imposing drastic economies on military expenditure which fell from around £600 million annually to under £300 million by 1920 and to £110 million thereafter. On the other hand, as it was unwise to let people assume they would never have to face another great war they found it necessary to make a special case for expanding Britain's air defences. In the context of these overall economies the RAF succeeded in improving its share of the defence estimates by about fifty per cent during 1923–6; whereas in 1922 Britain boasted twenty-three air squadrons (fourteen bombers and nine fighters), the government planned to increase this total to fifty-two squadrons by 1929.

Matters were further complicated by British participation in international efforts to promote peace. In 1928 when the Disarmament Conference began to meet at Geneva the whole idea of aerial warfare came under attack and air power was regarded in many quarters as a major obstacle to peace. In Britain there was support, even within the government, for placing a ban on bombing as a weapon of war and thus for abolishing the manufacture of bombers. Even Churchill changed his opinions and began to condemn the use of aircraft to attack villages in Iraq. At Hendon, where the annual air displays became more restrained, the set-piece bombing of 'Wottnott' forts was abandoned in 1930. Yet, despite making conciliatory noises to its critics at Geneva, the British government insisted on the necessity for retaining bombing for imperial purposes.

However, during the early 1930s the whole question rapidly became engulfed by a well-founded wave of fear and pessimism. In a notorious speech in November 1932 Stanley Baldwin returned to the dangerous business of educating the public: 'I think it is as well for the man in the street to realise that there is no power on earth that can protect him from being bombed. Whatever people may tell him, the bomber will always get through.' Once Hitler came to power in 1933 things began to deteriorate rapidly; Germany withdrew from the Disarmament Conference and the League of Nations and repudiated the military terms of the Treaty of Versailles. It emerged that she had secretly built an air force, leaving Britain merely attempting to achieve parity with Germany in the air. Eventually the National Government adopted a rearmament programme that relied heavily on building a force of bombers as a deterrent to any Continental enemy, but it did not start until 1935. In 1936 Alexander Korda produced an alarming film, *Things to Come*, written by H. G. Wells, depicting the effects of an imaginary aerial onslaught on 'Everytown' in 1940; the film made no attempt to conceal the consequences in terms of immediate death and destruction and the subsequent collapse of civilised society leading to a reversion to the Dark Ages.

Inevitably speculation about the next war was clouded by exaggeration and misinformation. In 1938 the Air Ministry claimed that Germany had 2,909 first-line aircraft by comparison with Britain's 1,550, though in fact the two sides were approximately equal. But by this time fears had been thoroughly aroused by demonstrations of the appalling effects of attack from the air in the Far East, Africa and Spain. The attacks by the Japanese on civilian targets such as Shanghai in 1932 had caused revulsion and shock in the West. But the pioneers of this style of warfare were actually the Italians who had used bombing to suppress native opposition to their rule even before 1914. The Fascist regime had no inhibitions about air power as they demonstrated during Mussolini's invasion of Abyssinia which began in 1935. Initially the Abyssinian troops seemed demoralised by attack from the air and dispersed into the highlands to escape the bombers. But the Italians continued to bomb civilian targets including hospitals and Red Cross establishments, they machine-gunned women and children fleeing from the fighting, and dropped a variety of bombs and chemicals including mustard gas, phosgene and chlorine which were sprayed over wide areas of countryside.

Although the struggle was less unequal in the Spanish Civil War which broke out in 1936, the fact that the casualties were European rather than African made a bigger impression on British thinking. The most notorious episode in the war occurred on 26 April 1937 when the Condor legion of the Luftwaffe bombed the small town of Guernica near Bilbao on a market day when local farmers had gathered to sell their livestock. Initially a single Heinkel dropped its load on the centre of the town after which people emerged from their shelters; but fifteen minutes later the full squadron flew over, bombing, strafing and grenading men, women and children. Yet the main attack was still to come in the shape of two and a half hours of continuous carpet-bombing by relays of Junkers which set the whole town alight, leaving 1,654 dead and 899 injured representing a third of the total population of Guernica.

In Britain the editor of The Times, Geoffrey Dawson, censored his reports on these atrocities in the Basque country because he did not want to upset the Germans. However, reputable newspapers like the News Chronicle gave full coverage to fascist methods in both Spain and Abyssinia. Inevitably the reports fuelled speculation about the consequences for civilians of another war which reached a peak in the summer of 1938 when the deadlock over Hitler's demands for territory in the Sudetenland districts of Czechoslovakia made a war with Germany appear imminent. As preparations were put in hand, Neville Chamberlain stoked up fears with his notorious comment: 'How horrible, fantastic, incredible it is that we should be digging trenches and trying on gas masks here because of a quarrel in a faraway country between people of whom we know nothing.' At this time it was reckoned that every ton of bombs dropped would result in fifty casualties. Extrapolating from this, it was estimated that during the first week of war alone 83,000 people would be killed by bombing in Britain. In fact, only 61,000 British civilians died during the entire six years of the Second World War. In war, as in peace, air power always fell a long way short of the claims made by its proponents; the bombing was invariably wildly inaccurate, and the civilian population proved much better at withstanding the bombardment than the authorities had feared. But in the late 1930s it is hardly surprising that the evidence of Guernica and Abyssinia seemed more compelling.

16

'A talent to amuse':
British Cultural Life

On 15 June 1920 Dame Nellie Melba stood before a microphone, shaped like a huge ear trumpet, clutching her handbag and with her cloche hat wedged firmly on her head, to sing 'Australian Nightingale'. Dame Nellie was the first opera singer willing to take the risk that her voice might be distorted over the airwaves. But the 10,000 listeners who tuned in to the Marconi valve transmitter were reportedly thrilled to hear her voice reaching them from the depths of Chelmsford. As a leading opera singer she was what today would be called a celebrity; she had already given her name to several well-known dishes including Peach Melba, Melba sauce and Melba toast. Her 1920 broadcast is, thus, a partial corrective to the received view that interwar Britain suffered from a deep gulf between 'high' culture and 'popular' culture. Although the 1920s and 1930s were not noted for opera, achievements and innovations in literature, poetry, theatre, ballet, radio and cinema made this a vibrant period in British cultural development. Yet these decades have long enjoyed a reputation as a philistine era. T. S. Eliot's famous description of the 1930s as a 'low, dishonest decade' is typical of the mood among disillusioned intellectuals. Even as progressive a figure as J. B. Priestley disparaged the mass culture that he believed had swamped British society. George Orwell's complaint in *The Lion and the Unicorn* that 'It is a rather restless, cultureless life, centring around tinned food, *Picture Post*, the radio and the combustion engine' serves to remind us that as an observer of contemporary society he was handicapped by both his upper-class origins and his left-wing views. No doubt much of the explanation for the contemporary disparagement of interwar society lies in the fact that nearly all the literary and artistic leaders held anti-Establishment and left-wing opinions, and, as such, they increasingly despaired of the dominance of the National

Governments during the 1930s, the economic depression, appeasement and the apparently inexorable spread of fascism all over Europe.

Many contemporaries detected the advance of popular culture and the retreat of intellect in developments in the world of newspapers. However, this was far from obvious. The British may not have been especially well educated, but they were a literate and politically aware people. As a result sales of national daily newspapers increased from 4.5 million before 1914 to 10.5 million by 1939, a trend accelerated by the adoption of front-page news, larger headlines, more and improved photographs, the 'staggered jigsaw' layout, women's pages, pioneered by the *Daily Mail* in 1919, and crossword puzzles which became a regular feature in the early 1920s. Eighty-two per cent of people also read a Sunday newspaper; the new women's magazines achieved huge circulations, and traditional weeklies such as *John Bull, Titbits* and *My Weekly* flourished. The pessimists were, however, justified in seeing the late Victorian era as the heyday of the sober, provincial press. Provincial towns that had previously supported both a morning and an evening newspaper could no longer do so after the war; even before 1914 much of the provincial press had been subsidised by rich men as a form of support for their party and once this was withdrawn closures and amalgamations inevitably followed. Among the national newspapers, the *Westminster Gazette*, which had survived on a circulation of 12,000, ceased to be viable; the *Daily News* and the *Daily Chronicle* merged to form the *News Chronicle* in 1930; and the *Morning Post* was absorbed by the *Daily Telegraph* in 1937.

Among national newspapers the biggest circulation was achieved by Lord Beaverbrook's *Daily Express*, which sold 2.2 million in 1937, despite the efforts of Lord Rothermere's *Daily Mail* to boost sales by means of a series of scares, including the forged Zinoviev Letter in 1924 and 'Votes-For-Flappers' in 1928, and stunts usually involving extravagant prizes offered to those who broke records in aviation. A circulation war raged among the overcrowded ranks of the middle-market press – the *Express, Mail, News Chronicle, Daily Herald* and *Daily Mirror*. Their proprietors tried to attract new readers by door-to-door campaigns offering free health insurance, and gifts of *Home Doctor* and *Handy Man*, further evidence for the view that Britain was becoming a home-centred society. In 1935 the *Daily Mirror* made the most dramatic and lasting breakthrough by going downmarket and by abandoning its right-wing politics in favour of an anti-Establishment, anti-appeasement line which brought it enormous credit during the Second World War and laid the foundations for its dominance in the 1950s.

However, although mass literacy sustained a popular press, books remained comparatively expensive in Britain, and so most people borrowed from libraries. By the 1930s almost all county councils were using the powers granted to them in 1919 to spend money from the rates to maintain public libraries. Unhappily the staff often treated the reading public as a threat to the maintenance of order. Paul Johnson painted a graphic picture of his local librarian: 'Miss Cartlich, in charge of the desk, was another authoritarian – life was full of tyrants in those days – who regarded boys with particular suspicion. She disliked old men too.'[1] Despite this, readers were not deterred, and public library loans rose from 85 million in 1924 to 247 million in 1939.

However, many people who disliked the books available in public libraries resorted to a multitude of small, commercial lending libraries often run by shopkeepers who acquired stocks from wholesale libraries and charged twopence or threepence to borrowers. In some areas travelling libraries housed in lorries also arrived each month, though 'you had to take what was left after the pushier locals had got the cream'.[2] On a larger scale Boots lending libraries offered 2,000–3,000 novels (45 per cent mysteries, 30 per cent romances and 15 per cent Westerns), as did W.H. Smith (50 per cent romances, 25 per cent adventure stories, 25 per cent crime). With 400 branches and 500,000, mostly female, subscribers, Boots was the largest; it charged ten shillings and sixpence for a year's borrowing. This was a library service aimed at the middle classes. Wealthier people paid to join the exclusive London lending libraries such as Day's and Mudie's. According to Virginia Woolf's jaundiced account, Day's was 'the haunt of fashionable ladies who want to be told what to read. They come in furred like seals and scented like civets, condescend to pull a few novels about the counter, and then demand languidly whether there is *anything* amusing.'[3]

The upper classes may have been philistines, as Woolf believed, but they at least created a market for the expensive volumes marketed by British publishers. At a time when a workingman's weekly wage was around £3. 10s., the typical hardback sold for anything between seven and twelve shillings and enjoyed a small circulation unless reprinted as a cheap edition at 2s. 6d. From time to time attempts were made to publish books at affordable prices, notably by J. M. Dent who published the Everyman series in 1906 at a shilling each. In the early 1930s several newspapers found a new weapon in the circulation wars by offering readers cheap books; the *Daily Herald* sold the collected plays of George Bernard Shaw at 3s. 9d. plus six coupons from the newspaper, and the *Daily Mail* countered with the complete works of Shakespeare for 5s. 9d. and six coupons.[4] Such initiatives posed a threat to the publishers who were too conservative and patronising towards the public to be interested in widening their market; they were especially prejudiced against paperbacks which were simply regarded as incompatible with literary quality.

However, the deadlock was decisively broken in July 1935 when Allen Lane launched Penguin Books, thereby initiating a revolution in British publishing. According to the traditional account, which may be apocryphal, he got the idea in the spring of 1934 when returning by train from a weekend with Agatha Christie and found nothing worth reading at the station bookstall at Exeter. Lane decided that there must be a demand for good literature published in bright, modern-looking paperbacks at a price comparable with a packet of cigarettes. 'People want books, they want good books, and they are willing, even anxious, to buy them if they are presented to them in a straightforward, intelligent manner at a cheap price'. However, W. H. Smith, along with most booksellers, wanted to keep prices as high as possible; and many authors and publishers saw Allen Lane's ideas as a threat to their livelihoods. 'Nobody can live off sixpenny books', pronounced one publisher. 'It is of course a great mistake to imagine that cheap books are good for the book trade', sniffed George Orwell. However, by publishing out-of-print classics at sixpence each Lane hoped to create a new market. Admittedly, scepticism among contemporary authors seems understandable; authors who could earn a twenty per cent royalty on a hardback priced at 7s. 6d. would get around two per cent on a Penguin. Vita Sackville-West sold 64,000 copies of *The Edwardians* but earned a mere £96 in royalties! As late as 1946 Lane offered Walter Elliott £200 to write a Penguin Special on 'The Scots'; even this was a better deal than the usual £2 for 1,000 copies which produced £120 on a 60,000 sale.[5]

Casting around for a suitable name and trademark for his new venture, Lane rejected the phoenix, dolphin and albatross before adopting the Penguin as being 'dignified but flippant'.[6] With some difficulty he secured the right to publish the first ten Penguins, including Ernest Hemingway's *Farewell to Arms*, Agatha Christie's *The Mysterious Affair at Styles* and Compton Mackenzie's *Carnival*. Priced at sixpence and fitting into the pocket of a typical gabardine raincoat, Penguins appeared in colour-coded format, orange for fiction, blue for biography, green for crime, magenta for travel. Lane printed 20,000 copies of each of the initial ten volumes but would break even only when 17,000–18,000 had been sold. Initially the prospects looked poor because many bookshops simply refused to stock his books and they were ignored by the *Times Literary Supplement*. However, Lane's break-through came when Woolworths agreed to sell them. It soon became clear that the time was right for Penguins. By 1935 the country was emerging from the worst of the depression, leaving many people with higher disposable incomes. As Lane correctly saw, 'the book trade have been sitting on a gold mine and not known it'.[7] In four years he sold seventeen million books and became a millionaire. Before long Penguins were being copied and in the process bringing quality literature of all types into millions of British homes.

Hot on the heels of Penguins came a fresh initiative in the shape of the Left Book Club. Founded by the publisher, Victor Gollancz, in March 1936, the LBC also owed its success partly to good timing. It caught the wave of fear generated by the spread of fascism and the Spanish Civil War, and reflected a wide feeling that neither the government nor the official Opposition were doing enough to stop it. Gollancz envisaged the LBC as the engine for a popular front of anti-fascist progressives. Although it failed to achieve this goal, by 1939 it had enrolled 57,000 subscribers and an estimated 500,000 readers. The books, which were priced at 2s. 6d. and had a guaranteed circulation of 50,000, included some of the most influential of the period: Ellen Wilkinson's *The Town That Was Murdered*, George Orwell's *The Road to Wigan Pier*, Wal Hannington's *The Problem of the Distressed Areas*, G. D. H. Cole's *The People's Front*, and John Strachey's *What Are We To Do?*.

'A fierce battle is now raging on the Reading Front' commented the *Evening Standard* following the success of the Left Book Club.[8] By 1939 a series of similar clubs had emerged including the National Book Association, the Labour Book Service, the Right Book Club and the

Liberal Book Club. Of these the most important was the Right Book Club, established in March 1937, by the London bookseller, W. A. Foyle, and his daughter, Christina. Each month it offered 'vital, authoritative' hardbacks at 2s. 6d. designed to counter Communism and left-wing propaganda generally.[9] Typical titles included G. Ward Price's *I Know These Dictators*, Sir Charles Petrie's *Lords of the Inland Sea*, Viscount Lymington's *Famine in England* and Arnold Lunn's *Revolutionary Socialism*. Although the RBC had 25,000 subscribers by 1939 it made less impact than the LBC partly because several of the authors rapidly became discredited as apologists for appeasement and fascism.

Yet despite these symptoms of an appetite for serious books, Britain remained in some ways a society that was uncomfortable about literature. Long-standing prejudice was encapsulated in a pre-1914 advertisement that urged: 'You don't want your boy to be a book-worm. You want him to be a normal, healthy boy.'[10] In the nervous climate of the early 1920s those in authority became increasingly apprehensive that literature could become a vehicle for promoting immorality. Laurie Lee recalled that when the vicar 'caught me reading *Sons and Lovers* [he] took it away and destroyed it', though he also noted that this was not repeated because 'a young apologist succeeded him soon'.[11] In this period the British people were protected from immoral and subversive influences by a series of measures, which, though introduced ad hoc, effectively constituted a system of censorship. The pre-war governments had enacted the Post Office Act (1908) which was designed to curb the movement of indecent and obscene matter, and established the British Board of Film Censors (1912). During the war the public became accustomed to compre-hensive censorship under the Defence of the Realm Act, though because it operated largely through voluntary co-operation between the press and the political-military authorities it felt less oppressive than it might have been. After the war Sir John Reith declared it the BBC's aim to promote public morality by means of programmes on conventional Christianity and by banning all references to atheism, spiritualism, Marxism, family planning, homosexuality, abortion and drugs. Just to make sure, a censor sat in the BBC studio with a finger poised on the cut-off button. During the 1920s publishers of material dealing with topics such as birth control were usually prosecuted for obscenity. As a result, despite her much-vaunted freedoms of speech and press, Britain fell some way short of being the free society she was widely thought to be.

This did not bode well for post-war writers determined to challenge the conventions of British society. In his novel, *Vile Bodies*, Evelyn Waugh depicted the confiscation of his hero's manuscript novel by a sanctimonious customs official who insisted: 'particularly against books is the Home Secretary'. Waugh must have been thinking of the puritanical Sir William Joynson-Hicks, Home Secretary 1924–9, who saw it as his duty to protect the public from depraved literature. In the literary journals he was mocked as being insufficiently intelligent to be capable of recognising literary merit and was accused of trying to establish a dictatorship over morals and literature.

However, Joynson-Hicks, who was popular with the press, probably enjoyed public support for his policy, though the evidence is impressionistic. E. M. Delafield captured the mood in her account of attitudes in provincial Devon: 'old Mrs B observes that much that is published nowadays seems to her unnecessary, and why so much sex in everything?'[12] Certainly Joynson-Hicks encouraged his officials, in collaboration with the police, to pursue anything 'obscene', which in practice meant anything sexually explicit. In 1915 copies of D. H. Lawrence's newly published *The Rainbow* were seized by the police and the book was banned. By 1917 Methuen had bowed to public pressure, suppressed the novel and cancelled their option to publish Lawrence's next three books. The hostility of reviewers and readers towards *The Rainbow* was not solely due to its frank treatment of sexual passion, but to the unpatriotic stance of its heroine. As a result Lawrence delayed the publication of *Women In Love*, which he completed in 1916, until 1921. Meanwhile, during 1917 his mail was opened and his cottage in Penzance was ransacked by the CID who apparently suspected him of espionage because his wife, Frieda, was German by birth and had been seen on the cliffs waving her scarf, presumably signalling to German submarines.[13] Eventually Lawrence found the harassment too much and in 1919 he left Britain to live in Australia, Mexico, America and Italy, returning only for brief periods.

Though a prime target of the moral censors, Lawrence was not alone. E. M. Forster made no attempt to publish his homosexual novel, *Maurice*, written in 1913, during his lifetime. In 1922 James Joyce published *Ulysses* in Paris as it was banned in Britain. In 1926 the Lord Chancellor censored Noel Coward's comedy, *This Was a Man*, in which all the characters were adulterers; as a result the play was performed in New York, Berlin and Paris but not in Britain. Ministers and the police co-ordinated their efforts in 1928 to 'stem the tide of degeneracy' by stopping the circulation of *The Well of Loneliness*, a novel about lesbian love by Radclyffe Hall. Initially they used threats against the publishers who withdrew the book. But when copies were imported from abroad they were seized by the police who launched a prosecution of the author. It was in the same year that *Lady Chatterley's Lover* began its turbulent career. Lawrence, anticipating that the book would make him even more unpopular, and aware that his agent had failed to find a British publisher, had 1,000 copies printed privately and 3,000 more in Paris. The novel was denounced in wild language in the press; *John Bull*, describing it as 'the foulest book in English literature' and 'this fetid masterpiece of this sex-sodden genius', called for it to be banned. This alerted the police who began to seize and destroy copies entering Britain in January 1929.[14] *Lady Chatterley's Lover* remained under the ban until 1960.

However, these ad hoc attempts to suppress undesirable literature paled into insignificance beside the more severe and comprehensive regulation of the cinema by the British Board of Film Censors. The explanation for this may be that the political potential of a medium that now reached millions of people every week was seen to be far greater than that of novels read by comparatively few people. In this spirit the film version of Walter Greenwood's novel, *Love on the Dole*, was rejected by the board in 1936. Further insight into the mentality of the censors may be gleaned from their 1930 report. They had examined 2,275 films, of which 12 were completely rejected and 16 were still under consideration with a view to drastic modification.[15] Exception had also been taken to 191 films for a wide variety of reasons including vulgar noises, swearing and irreverent quotations from the Bible. The censors also objected to 'cruelty', which meant brutal fights, torture, flogging, ill-treatment of animals, 'crime scenes' including hanging, electrocution and anything open to imitation; 'religion', especially blasphemy and portrayals of the hereafter; 'politics', which included the royal family; and 'military scenes' depicting wounded men in pain, uncivilised behaviour in warfare and British officers in equivocal situations. Yet the largest number of objections fell under the heading of 'sexual' and 'social', including 'vamping', habitual immorality, men and women in bed together, intoxicated people, semi-nudity, indecorous dancing, brothels, free love, companionate marriage, birth control and illegal operations (presumably abortion). Despite this intimidating catalogue, a film version of Marie Stopes's birth control classic, *Married Love*, got past the censors as *Masie's Marriage*, largely by depicting the idea of birth control in terms of pruning roses to achieve healthier blooms, an acceptable parable for the horticulturally minded English.

What the censors appreciated were films that fostered optimism and promoted social harmony, a bias that goes some way to justifying the view of interwar cinema as a new form of social control by the upper classes over the masses. Their ideal was realised by Gracie Fields in her relentlessly cheerful songs such as 'Wish Me Luck As You Wave Me Goodbye'. Her classic 1934 film, *Sing As We Go*, centred around the closure of a cotton mill whose unemployed workers, unmoved by a socialist analysis of their condition, cheerfully insisted: 'If we can't spin we can still sing.' In this way the film captured the mood of humour and determination that Britons were expected to display in the face of adversity. But to their critics such productions merely created a dream world in which the workers were beguiled into forgetting their hardships and remaining in mindless ignorance of the political forces responsible for causing them.

As the reaction against work by D. H. Lawrence and Walter Greenwood suggests, many people in authority believed that the promotion of immorality by intellectuals went hand in hand with the spread of politically subversive ideas. The foundation of the Right Book Club reflected a widely felt concern that, although pro-Conservative governments were generally in power, Britain was succumbing to skilful propaganda generated by writers and intellectuals of the liberal Left, by Communist sympathisers and by influences based in the United States. Though exaggerated, these fears had some basis in fact. Among the prominent literary and artistic figures of the period, only T. S. Eliot and Wyndham Lewis held right-wing views. One famous group of poets and novelists of which W. H. Auden was the leading figure, included Stephen Spender, Christopher Isherwood, Cecil Day-Lewis and Louis MacNeice. All were, to some extent, pro-Communist, moved by the Republican cause in the Spanish Civil War and alarmed at the spread of fascism and Nazi influence at home and abroad. Some of the most widely read writers of the period acquired their reputation by articulating popular disillusionment with the First World War. The reaction had been signalled by Siegfried Sassoon in his volume of poetry, *Counter-Attack*, published in 1918. During the following decade the anti-war writers largely kept their heads down, but the years from 1928 to 1933 saw a fresh outpouring of such literature including Sassoon's *Memoirs of a Fox-hunting Man* (1928), Robert Graves's *Goodbye to All That* (1929), Richard Aldington's *Death of a Hero* (1929), R. C. Sheriff's *Journey's End* (1930), Sassoon's *Memoirs of an Infantry Officer* (1930) and Vera Brittain's *Testament of Youth* (1933). The message conveyed by these authors was shocking to some contemporaries because they had played a conventional, patriotic role during the war and appeared to write from personal experience. As Graves admitted, there had been a pecuniary motive: 'the book sold well enough in England and the United States, despite the Depression . . . to pay my debts and leave me free to live and write in Majorca'.[16] But the success of the anti-war books was not an indication that the British had become a nation of pacifists. Novels that took a positive view of war continued to be as popular as ever; but the anxieties aroused by the failure of disarmament and the League of Nations in the early 1930s created renewed fears that Europe was slipping towards another catastrophe and thus led many people to revisit the horrors of the last war once again.

The reputation of British intellectuals as a threat to conventional thinking and behaviour had already been established during the Edwardian period by the most famous literary-artistic coterie: the Bloomsbury Group. The continuing role of Bloomsbury in repudiating all things Victorian was heralded by the publication of Lytton Strachey's *Eminent Victorians* in 1918 in which he questioned the reputation of such national icons as General Gordon, Florence Nightingale and Dr Thomas Arnold. Before the war Bloomsbury had been bohemian but respectable, but after 1918 it was condemned for its sexual perversion, lack of patriotism and Francophilia. Its members included several of the leading writers associated with 'modernism' such as E. M. Forster and Virginia Woolf. The modernists, whose ranks included James Joyce and D. H. Lawrence among others, were in general antagonistic towards all political, social, aesthetic and religious conventions. In literature they criticised the work of leading Edwardian writers such as John Galsworthy and Arnold Bennett, and rejected the Victorian-Edwardian narrative and descriptive approach. The qualities and attitudes of the literary rebels were best encapsulated by Virginia Woolf. Born into an intellectual aristocracy – her father was Sir Leslie Stephen, the founder of the *Dictionary of National Biography* – she achieved fame as a prolific novelist, reviewer, diarist and correspondent; also a feminist and pacifist, she contracted a companionate marriage with Leonard Woolf, engaged in an affair with Vita Sackville-West and refused all offers of honours. Above all Woolf was an experimental novelist, producing a series of books, each different in style and structure, including *To the Lighthouse* (1927), *Mrs Dalloway* (1925), *Orlando* (1928), in which she mocked British social conventions over the previous 360 years, *The Waves* (1930) and *The Years* (1937). Although the previous century had seen some very successful female authors, after the war women became more influential in literary circles than ever before; in addition to Woolf, Rebecca West, Ivy Compton-Burnett, Rosamund Lehmann, E. M. Delafield and Winifred Holtby were leading writers of serious literature.

However, while the intellectuals of the 1920s and 1930s shaped a later generation's perspective on interwar Britain, at the time their influence was much more modest, partly because of their rejection of convention and partly because of their frankly elitist views; they scorned the commercial innovations that were responsible for extending good writing to a wider public and, as literary critics, were inclined to ignore or dismiss 'middlebrow' fiction as largely worthless. Yet the reading public showed far more interest in the work of middlebrow writers such as J. B. Priestley who was catapulted to fame by *The Good Companions* (1929) and *Angel Pavement* (1930), and Daphne du Maurier whose *Jamaica Inn* (1936) and *Rebecca* (1938) were never out of print. Several middlebrow authors who were already popular before 1914 continued to write after 1918, notably Sir Arthur Quiller-Couch and the prolific John Buchan who produced adventure, imperial, historical and Scottish novels. The British brand of humour was also reflected in the work of Evelyn Waugh who wrote *Decline and Fall* (1928), *Vile Bodies* (1930) and *Scoop* (1938), as well as P. G. Wodehouse who, as a young man, wrote desperately in order to earn enough to avoid the fate mapped out for him by his father as a trainee manager at the Hong Kong and Shanghai Bank. Wodehouse managed it without difficulty, publishing *My Man Jeeves* in 1919, the curtain-raiser to a career involving no fewer than ninety-eight novels.

One immensely successful middlebrow genre, the spy novel, was firmly established in British tastes by 1900. Its original popularity was a reflection of the mass literacy achieved during the last thirty years of the nineteenth century, the serialisation of spy stories by the mass circulation newspapers, and the climate of fear created by attempts to subvert the British Isles and the Empire by enemies in Russia and Germany. After 1918 this tradition continued to flourish, not least because conspiracy theories enjoyed wide currency and Russia, in particular, seemed just as dangerous under the Bolsheviks as under the tsars. John Buchan, already famous for *The Thirty-nine Steps*, produced similar stories in *Greenmantle* (1916), *Mr Standfast* (1919) and *Huntingtower* (1922), and he was joined by Compton Mackenzie and Somerset Maugham. Their spy novels gained credibility from the authors' personal experience: Buchan had seen intelligence reports at the Ministry of Information during the war, Mackenzie served with the British Secret Service in Greece, and Maugham had been engaged in a mission to spy on the new Bolshevik regime in Russia in 1918. During the 1930s they were joined by Eric Ambler and Graham Greene whose writing reflected the influence of the ideological battle between Left and Right and the rise of totalitarian regimes across Europe.

The interwar period also proved to be a golden age for the writing of detective stories, a genre in which the British became pre-eminent. Up to the beginning of the century it had been dominated by Sir Arthur Conan Doyle and his Sherlock Holmes stories; but although he continued to write short stories in the 1920s, short-story writing, which had been sustained by magazine sales, was now in long-term decline in British literature. In 1920 Agatha Christie set the tone of British crime writing in *The Mysterious Affair at Styles*, the first of eighty-one novels. For years to come the typical British detective story was set in rural or suburban surroundings and characterised by Christie's ingenious plotting; it underplayed the element of physical violence and reassured readers by largely affirming the existing social order. The majority of these books were written to a regular format: a serious crime, usually a murder, was committed early in the story, the criminal's identity was not revealed until the end, and the author engaged the reader by providing clues pointing to the guilty party and to no one else. The two leading exponents of this genre were Christie, who invented Hercule Poirot and Miss Jane Marple as her sleuths, and Dorothy L. Sayers, who created Harriet Vane and Lord Peter Wimsey. Margery Allingham, Ngaio Marsh, Dornford Yates and Leslie Charteris also wrote widely read crime novels in this period. During the 1930s the genre began to be overtaken by the thrillers written by Graham Greene including *Stamboul Train* (1932) and *Brighton Rock* (1938), in which there was much less emphasis on solving a puzzle and more on the motivation and mentality of the criminal.

The condescension aroused by many of these novels among the literary elite was nothing by comparison with the derision provoked by some of the most successful and widely read authors of romantic fiction including E. M. Hull, Elinor Glyn, Ethel M. Dell, Ruby M. Ayres and Denise Robins. Before the early 1900s writers of romantic literature had usually felt too inhibited to explore female sexuality. For all her pretensions to radical and unconventional ideas, even Virginia Woolf avoided the issue by writing about pre-sexual heroines or keeping their sexuality at a philosophical level; in *Mrs Dalloway* she cast her character in a loveless marriage and made her sleep in a narrow bed in the attic. By contrast, the popular female novelists who cheerfully wrote about women in the throes of sexual passion were roundly abused for their pains. 'They have made the world safe for pornography', thundered the *Daily Express,* referring to Elinor Glyn and Ethel M. Dell. Lord Riddell, the proprietor of the *News of the World*, advised Ruby Ayres that a writer of her type should 'take her heroines as far as the bedroom door and then leave them'.[17] To some extent these authors protected themselves from censorship by setting their scenes of erotic and violent love in exotic locations: by implication this sort of thing did not happen in the British Isles. Also, the very fact that they usually received little or no critical attention may have enabled them to take greater risks in depicting sexuality than the highbrow novelists could do.

As the critics complained, the erotic romances followed a predictable formula. Ethel M. Dell had set a pattern with *The Way of the Eagle* in 1912. In this the heroine escaped from a fort on the North-West Frontier of India, where British troops were besieged, and ended up torn between two lovers, one sensual and masterful, the other tender and kind. Dell relied heavily on her imagination as she was not even married until forty, had never visited India and had no experience of the military. She aroused the scorn of established writers such as Rebecca West and George Orwell, who were no doubt irritated that her book was an instant success, being reprinted twenty-seven times in the first three years: 'No one can write a best-seller by taking thought', sniffed West.[18]

In 1919 Mrs Hull opted for a similarly exotic location for *The Sheik*, a novel in which an English girl was kidnapped in the desert by an Arab sheik and repeatedly raped but grew to enjoy it after five pages: 'Oh you brute, you brute', complained the heroine until his kisses silenced her. But arguably the most notorious writer of romances was Elinor Glyn whose 1907 novel, *Three Weeks*, proved to be very influential in the development of women's fiction. Set in Switzerland, the story centred round a young English aristocrat who was seduced by a Balkan queen who was married to a degenerate and in search of a suitable man to father an heir. Using a tiger skin as the base for operations, the Queen set about teaching her lover everything she could about sexual pleasure and how to satisfy women's masochistic tastes: 'A woman will stand almost anything from a passionate lover. He may beat her and pain her soft flesh.'[19] She even managed to imply that manly practice in the bedroom was a matter of patriotic duty for those who wished to arrest the national trend towards decadence in Britain. The reactions to Glyn's novel were predictable. Rebecca West and Arnold Bennett publicly asked why her work was not banned from the libraries. The explanation may be that unlike some other writers she usually ensured that her female characters paid a price for their passionate pleasure at some stage in the story. Despite the uniform hostility shown by the reviewers towards *Three Weeks*, readers loved it; the book was regularly reprinted during the 1920s, became a film in 1923 and had sold five million copies by the early 1930s.

Elinor Glyn took the view that as it was perfectly normal for women to experience sexual desire she need have no compunction about her work. In any case, she had been denied a formal education and prepared for nothing in life except marriage; she therefore wrote novels from necessity, managing to meet her husband's debts and her own expenses from the proceeds. As a result Glyn turned out a novel almost every year, reaching thirty-eight by 1940. Similar pressures turned the young Barbara Cartland into a prolific and commercially minded writer. Although her novels never approached the levels of eroticism achieved by the other romantic novelists, Cartland claimed that Ethel M. Dell had been her model. Faced with the need to support herself after the war, she started writing for newspaper gossip columns and produced her first novel, *Jigsaw*, in 1923, earning £200 for it. By 1936 Cartland had seventeen books to her credit. They were serialised in the women's magazines but largely ignored by reviewers. Indeed, for the rest of the century the literary establishment generally refused to believe her claims about the enormous readership she acquired in Britain and abroad.

Despite the evidence that native British talent was responsible for the vibrant cultural life of interwar Britain, those who disapproved of contemporary trends took it as axiomatic that all innovations in literature, music and cinema originated in America. Nor were they entirely wrong: 'We children of the 1930s were the first in Britain to grow up with an everyday familiarity with things American', as one boy put it.[20] Young people found American accents appealing, perhaps because they seemed English but classless; they quickly adopted American phrases and accents because, as one contemporary saw, it would have sounded ridiculous to sing the popular songs in an English accent.[21]

For the cinema-going public it was certainly difficult to avoid the influence of American speech. In 1926, for example, only five per cent of the films shown were British. Hollywood's dominance at this stage accentuated a reluctance to recognise the cinema as part of cultural life; it was 'neither art nor smart' as its critics liked to say. But the mass popularity of cinema and the poor performance of the British film industry obliged the government to intervene. In 1927 the Cinematographic Film Act imposed a quota system on cinemas, requiring that British films must comprise a certain proportion of all films shown rising from 7.5 per cent to 20 per cent by 1936. This led to the production of 'quota quickies', but it also stimulated the subsequent development of the industry. As with most infant industries in Britain, the problem was not so much lack of talent but lack of finance. Even so, the success of British film-making was quite narrowly based on a few talented individuals. In 1926 Alfred Hitchcock made his reputation with *The Lodger*, the first of six silent thrillers. He made

Britain's first talkie, *Blackmail*, in 1929, featuring a celebrated chase across the dome of the British Museum. The elaborate chase sequence that became a hallmark of Hitchcock's work also featured in his greatest successes, *The Man Who Knew Too Much* (1934) and *The Thirty-nine Steps* (1935). But after making *The Lady Vanishes* (1938) and *Jamaica Inn* (1939), Hitchcock was lured to America by the offer of greater money and resources. Alexander Korda, an immigrant from Hungary, established his own company, London Film Productions, in 1932. In that year he began his run of historical sagas with *The Private Life of Henry VIII* which cost £60,000. It was premiered in New York and earned £500,000 in a year. This success gave a huge boost to British films, raising the prospect of penetrating the lucrative American market. However, under-finance continued to handicap the industry for many years. Korda himself won backing from the Prudential Assurance Company on the strength of which he built a seven-stage studio at Denham in 1935–6. He went on to make *The Life of Don Juan* (1934), *The Rise of Catherine the Great* (1934), *Sanders of the River* (1935), *The Drum* (1938) and *The Four Feathers* (1939). Yet despite this record the returns on most of Korda's films were modest and they remained largely uneconomic. On the other hand, his work made a significant contribution to the vitality of British theatre by fostering the careers of several talented actors, notably Charles Laughton, Leslie Howard, Laurence Olivier and Vivien Leigh.

Countering what he saw as the insidious influence of America on British culture was one of the chief objectives of Sir John Reith, the first Director General of the BBC from 1922 onwards. A Scots Calvinist of authoritarian inclinations, Reith insisted that most people would happily embrace high culture if it were offered to them; his listeners were to get what was good for them not what they wanted, and the BBC would present 'all that was best in every department of human knowledge, endeavour and achievement'. During the 1920s it broadcast a good deal of classical music and opera, talks by intellectuals, and Sunday programmes dominated by religion and lengthy silences. The announcers wore evening dress and spoke in southern, upper-class accents. Reith also banned jokes about drink, clergymen, illness and Scotsmen – but not Irishmen.

Yet despite his formidable manifesto, Reith felt obliged to compromise in the face of newspaper comment that branded the BBC as elitist, and pressure from the listeners who paid a ten shilling licence fee and enjoyed the option of tuning in to Radio Luxembourg. Before long the BBC was broadcasting light orchestral music and offering less of the high culture originally intended. Admittedly this marked only a limited retreat on Reith's part; it was during the Second World War that broadcasting changed significantly by introducing the Forces Programmes and the post-war Light Programme.

One of the by-products of the foundation of the BBC was a stimulus to the development of orchestras in Britain. Traditionally orchestras had operated on an ad hoc basis, drawing from a pool of players as required. This began to change with the foundation of the Queen's Hall Orchestra in 1895 and the London Symphony Orchestra in 1904. The BBC took over the Queen's Hall Orchestra in 1927, using it as the nucleus for the BBC Symphony Orchestra in 1930 conducted by Adrian Boult. It also formed the BBC Northern Orchestra at Manchester in 1934 and the BBC Scottish Orchestra in 1935. Their players were paid an annual salary, though many orchestras continued to offer a fee for each engagement.

The other great innovative force at this time was Sir Thomas Beecham whose role as conductor and musical entrepreneur made him the most influential single figure in musical life. Beecham had formed his own orchestra in 1909 and an opera company in 1915; he attracted foreign artists, notably the Ballets Russes, to Britain; and he brought composers such as Richard Strauss and Frederick Delius to public attention before they had acquired popular appeal. A blunt and witty man, Beecham was well placed to bridge the gap between high culture and popular culture; he liked to say there were two golden rules for an orchestra: 'Start together and finish together. The public doesn't give a damn what goes on in between.'

This was also true of the leading British composers of the interwar period: Ralph Vaughan Williams, William Walton and Gustav Holst. Both Vaughan Williams and Holst actively promoted amateur music-making and were enthusiasts for English folk music. Vaughan Williams, who collected 800 folk songs, allowed the songs to impart a melodic and nationalistic quality to his work. Holst and Vaughan Williams also wrote pieces for brass bands, several thousand of which flourished especially in the industrial regions of the North and the Midlands.

By contrast, opera was struggling to establish a major national presence in Britain. Pre-war attempts to promote opera at the Royal Opera House, Covent Garden, had ended in failure; and in 1920 Beecham's season of international opera ended in liquidation. However, in 1923 his company became the British National Opera Company, and in 1934 the opera house was opened at Glyndebourne to widen the range of performances. Ballet, on the other hand, had flourished since the early 1900s as the centrepiece of the music-hall variety shows at the Alhambra and the Empire Theatre in London. Up to the war most British ballet dancers performed in commercial theatre, in revues and in pantomime. But the pre-war visits by Sergei Diaghilev's Ballets Russes nurtured the founders of Britain's own ballet companies: Ninette de Valois, Alicia Markova, Anton Dolin and Marie Rambert, all of whom danced for Diaghilev. Ballet schools were opened by Rambert in 1920 and de Valois in 1926. It was in 1926, when the choreographer Frederick Ashton made his debut, that a distinctive British national repertory began to emerge. Together with de Valois, who transferred her school to Sadler's Wells Theatre in 1931 with the support of the producer, Lilian Bayliss, Ashton defined the style of British ballet over the next ten years. From 1935 onwards de Valois used Ashton as her resident choreographer and the young Margot Fonteyn, who had begun her career in 1934 as a snowflake in *The Nutcracker*, as her ballerina. During the 1930s she built a company of international stature based on traditional productions of challenging nineteenth-century classics including *The Sleeping Beauty*, *Swan Lake* and *Giselle*.

After four wartime years in the doldrums British theatre bounced back in the 1920s, largely on the strength of the light musical comedies and revues written by Ivor Novello and Noël Coward, and the emergence of a generation of talented actors and actresses nurtured by Lilian Bayliss at the Old Vic. Ivor Novello had achieved fame in 1914 as the composer of the emotive song, 'Keep the Home Fires Burning', and he was active as an actor-playwright-composer during the 1920s, producing musical comedies and starring in silent films including Hitchcock's *The Lodger*. But his most prolific period was the 1930s when he wrote a series of musical romances and comedies in which he drew upon the tradition of Victorian ballards and the operettas of Franz Lehar, producing many lyrical and emotional songs including 'Rose of England', 'Waltz of My Heart' and 'We'll Gather Lilacs in the Spring'.

Novello also appeared in *The Vortex*, the play that made Noël Coward's name in 1924 and in the subsequent film version.

Noël Coward had spent nine months serving in the Artists' Rifles at Romford during the war, but after suffering a nervous breakdown he was discharged in 1918. Thereafter he spent some time enjoying country-house life, which later informed his work, before visiting New York in 1921 where he was attracted by the sheer pace of delivery of American actors. Coward determined to inject some of the vitality of Broadway into West End theatre, hitherto dominated by staid, drawing-room dramas; the pithy comments with which he littered his writing – 'Very flat, Norfolk', 'A talent to amuse', 'Leave tomorrow behind', 'Certain women should be struck regularly like gongs' – gave his plays a quality not seen on the British stage since Oscar Wilde.

In *The Vortex* Coward neatly caught the atmosphere of hedonism and decadence so typical of smart metropolitan society in the 1920s; his characters frequently appeared in dressing gowns and called each other 'darling'. The story revolved around a middle-aged woman enjoying an affair with a much younger man who took cocaine, a habit often interpreted as a mask for homosexuality at this time. It is not clear how the play escaped the attentions of the Lord Chancellor, and it was noticeable that in the film version all the morally offensive aspects had been toned down, creating a bland reproduction of Coward's original. He followed up his success with *The Vortex* with a succession of memorable productions including *Fallen Angels* and *Hay Fever* in 1925, *Bitter Sweet* in 1929, *Private Lives* in 1930, *Cavalcade* in 1931 and *Design for Living* in 1933.

Coward deliberately cultivated a reputation as an elegant, languid, and slightly camp young man; he took a flippant view of moral and sexual questions and fed the newspapers with provocative observations. 'I am never out of opium dens', he told the *Evening Standard*, 'My mind is a mass of corruption.' Despite this apparent recklessness, his writing betrayed considerable care and shrewdness. He mitigated the impact of his plots with witty dialogue, effectively making his audience laugh before it had time to be outraged; and although he freely included homosexuals in his plays, he did not follow Radclyffe Hall in writing about homosexual love. Coward also reassured the public by demonstrating his patriotism especially in plays like *Cavalcade*; when taking the author's curtain call on the first night he told the audience: 'It is still a pretty exciting thing to be English!' In time patriotism became an increasingly important element in his work. Beyond this, his appeal lay in his simple, melodious songs, many of which entered into the popular culture of the time: 'I'll See You Again', 'Poor Little Rich Girl', 'Mad Dogs and Englishmen', 'The Stately Homes of England', 'Don't Put Your Daughter on the Stage Mrs Worthington'. In these songs Coward faithfully reflected English sentimentality and a capacity for poking fun at the English without forfeiting his claims to patriotism. His work offered English audiences a suggestion of the risqué and the fashionable combined with the reassurance of conventionality. He was the authentic voice of the interwar period.

17

'Brideshead Revisited':
The Decline of the Aristocracy

On 4 May 1939 Edwina Mountbatten flew into Croydon Aerodrome, fresh from a trip to New Guinea, with a pair of wallabies and a boyfriend in tow. As the wallabies clearly fell foul of the regulations, Edwina rang her husband, Dickie, who sent a line, as was usual on these occasions, to the Minister for Agriculture; he ensured that Edwina and her entourage sailed through customs and quarantine with no formalities.[1] But this was an increasingly rare triumph for the deference due to the titled and well connected. For the British aristocracy had spent much of the previous two decades in despair at what appeared to be a spiral of decline in terms of dwindling wealth, lower status and collapsing political power.

To most of their contemporaries this dire picture of decline must have seemed an exaggeration if not a complete fiction. As the British aristocracy had been living in fear of its downfall since the 1880s, whatever decline they did experience was obviously a gradual one. It was also mitigated by the steady recruitment of new recruits bringing fresh, if hardly blue, blood into their order, and, more importantly, injections of extra cash. But many traditional aristocratic families had begun to feel the cold winds of change during the agricultural depression from the 1870s onwards which afflicted much of the South and East of England; in that period profits and rents fell, some farmers went bankrupt and rural land lost some of its value. This, however, was well short of a collapse especially as many peers still owned land that remained very profitable. This was especially true of men like Viscount Ridley and the Duke of Northumberland whose estates held huge coal reserves, or those like the Duke of Westminster and the Duke of Norfolk who owned valuable urban property. Other peers simply sold off unprofitable estates and concentrated on commerce and industry where lucrative company directorships were increasingly available. In 1889, for example, the newly launched British South Africa Company, a dodgy enterprise in need of respectability to reassure shareholders, lured the Duke of Abercorn on to its board. By 1896 167 peers had become company directors, and 232 by 1910. Thus, despite the problems faced by agriculture, many titled men enjoyed huge annual incomes in the late Victorian period: £290,000 for the Duke of Westminster, £225,000 for the Duke of Bedford, £176,000 for the Duke of Northumberland – figures that can be multiplied by about forty to represent present-day values.

However, a more insidious threat seemed to present itself in terms of aristocratic status and influence. In 1880 there were only 580 peers in total, and during the previous fifty years on average only four new titles had been created each year. Contrary to popular belief, the British aristocracy was traditionally a fairly closed circle to which non-aristocrats were only occasionally admitted. However, during the last twenty years of the century the peerage began to be diluted largely because the political parties, anxious to raise large central funds, were willing to bestow titles on anyone who contributed generously to election campaigns or subsidised party newspapers. As a result the rate of creations had risen to nearly ten a year by 1914, but only a quarter of these individuals were connected with existing titled families; one-third went to professionals and one-third to 'plutocrats', that is, wealthy men from commerce and industry. They included mining magnates such as Lords Joicey and Allendale, 'beer barons' from the Alsopp, Bass and Guinness families, and, most controversially, newspaper proprietors. Some of them made no secret of their disrespect for the order they were joining. 'When I want a peerage I'll pay for it like an honest man', declared Alfred Harmsworth, founder of the *Daily Mail* and the *Daily Mirror*, who became a baron in 1905 and was created Viscount Northcliffe in 1918.

Traditionalists detected other symptoms of what looked like a deliberate process of expanding and vulgarising society, often promoted by those who ought to have known better. They noted the inclusion of wealthy Jewish families including Rothschilds and Sassoons. The Prince of Wales, later King Edward VII, attracted private criticism for his friendship with the tea magnate, Sir Thomas Lipton, who loaned him money: 'He's playing golf with his grocer', went the cry. Several cash-strapped peers also resorted to new methods of bolstering failing family fortunes by marrying rich American heiresses, notably Lord Curzon and the Duke of Marlborough. In 1895 'Sunny' Marlborough, heir to the 8th Duke, married Consuelo Vanderbilt. While she gained status and the title he happily spent the Vanderbilt millions. However, the alliance enjoyed only limited success, for Sunny was an arrogant and psychologically damaged man. As an American Consuelo was shocked at the spartan conditions endured by the English aristocracy; she complained about having to live in Blenheim Palace which had 170 rooms but not a single comfortable one, and only a solitary bathroom! As a result they separated, divorced and remarried.

Many peers began to fear that these changes would have the effect of destroying the mystique attaching to titles and thus weaken the deference shown by ordinary British people. This was underlined by unfavourable political trends. Victorian radicals had long aspired to impose taxes on landed wealth and to curb the powers enjoyed by the hereditary peers as members of the House of Lords. As the vote was conceded to workingmen in 1867 and 1885 it seemed likely that the propertyless mass of the population would eventually use its power to vote for the expropriation of private wealth for the benefit of society. One small step in that direction was Sir William Harcourt's Budget of 1894 which introduced a scheme of graduated death duties rising from one per cent on fortunes of £500 to eight per cent on those of £1 million. More disturbing was the collapse of the landed class in Ireland. Under pressure from Irish nationalism successive British governments felt obliged to offer concessions with a view to making the union between the two countries acceptable to the Irish peasantry. As a result even Conservative governments resorted to state intervention designed to buy up the estates of the Anglo-Irish landowners for resale as small farms to former tenants. As much of the land was worth little and rents were hard to collect, this was no great sacrifice, but the loss of eleven million acres of land by 1914 and the retreat of many leading families from Ireland suggested a dangerous precedent for England.

When the Liberals returned to office in 1906, supported by thirty Labour and eighty Irish MPs, the peers became embroiled in a disastrous series of controversies. Choosing to ignore the new government's popular mandate, they mangled much of its legislation, finally overreaching themselves by rejecting the Budget in 1909. This provoked a famous campaign by David Lloyd George who mocked the peers as 'the ennobled indiscretions of kings', alluding to the fact that many Scottish dukes descended from the illegitimate children of Charles II, and questioned the legislative powers exercised by '500 men, ordinary men chosen at random from among the unemployed'. Eventually the 1911 Parliament Act removed the peers' role in financial legislation and curtailed their veto over ordinary legislation. Although the Conservative leaders promised to restore the powers of the House of Lords and to reform its composition, they noticeably failed to do so. The peers correctly sensed that after being dragged into controversy in two unsuccessful elections they were no longer regarded as an asset by leading Conservatives and that their role in the political system had been permanently devalued.

Against this dismal background most peers had responded enthusiastically to the outbreak of war in 1914. War helped restore their pride and sense of purpose. On the other hand, the young men from aristocratic families who flocked into the army and the Royal Air Force suffered very high casualties as junior officers. This in turn exposed their families to punitive death duties especially where two generations happened to die within a short space of time. War also accelerated the existing trend towards higher taxation which was not entirely reversed even after 1918. Governments reduced income tax in the early 1920s, though not to pre-war levels, largely to placate middle-class taxpayers who now loomed larger than the landowners in political calculations. Meanwhile death duties rose to forty per cent by 1919, and had reached fifty per cent in 1930 and sixty per cent in 1939. Wartime also disrupted the wider social life of the upper classes by forcing the closure of country houses and London homes, some of which were put to use as hospitals and convalescent homes. After 1918 it proved difficult to restore them all to their former condition. Experienced staff had been lost, game was neglected and many great gardens had gone into decline. Not all families now had the money or the inclination to maintain all their properties as they had done in Edwardian times. Traditionalists resented the speed with which their role as hostesses was seized by wealthy Americans like Nancy Astor and Lady Maud Cunard. Lady Maud, known as 'Emerald', was the wife of Sir Bache Cunard, head of the famous shipping line. Though obviously not an aristocrat she managed to operate on an equal footing with aristocrats by virtue of her wealth and her energy as a hostess and as a patron for artists, intellectuals, musicians and singers. The Prince of Wales became a regular feature of Emerald Cunard's salon which she later used to promote Mrs Wallis Simpson in society. This American invasion was only part of a range of social changes that irked the traditionalists. In the 1920s cocktails began to be drunk before dinner (instead of whisky) for the first time. The motor car enabled people to live in country houses without really becoming part of county life; and it accelerated the displacement of the long, leisurely country-house party by the shorter 'weekend' visit.

However, several great families made a spirited effort to recreate past glories. On visiting Blenheim Duff Cooper noted that 'the Duke [of Marlborough] keeps high state – wears his Garter for dinner and has a host of powdered footmen'.[2] On 18 November 1919 Edith, the Marchioness of Londonderry, summoned 2,500 guests to a reception of Ruritanian splendour at Londonderry House. 'It was just like old times,' noted Lord Curzon, the Foreign Secretary, 'only three times as many people.' Lady Londonderry stood at the top of her famous staircase to greet the guests, flanked by Lloyd George, now prime minister, and Andrew Bonar Law, the Conservative leader. Festooned in diamonds, she 'looked like a Christmas tree' according to one observer. Clearly the Londonderrys were not giving up without a fight. While lesser families fretted over the servant problem they maintained an army of domestics to service their needs in three main homes: Londonderry House in the West End, Mount Stewart in Northern Ireland and Wynyard in County Durham. As late as the 1930s the staff comprised a comptroller, a groom of the chambers, a butler and an under-butler, three footmen, Lady Londonderry's footman and piper, a nursery footman, an odd-job man, a nightwatchman, the head housekeeper, the housekeeper, cook, head kitchen maid, two kitchen maids, the nursery maid, the schoolroom maid, several daily women to clean the house, a travelling head housemaid to go ahead of the family, a telephonist, a hospital nurse, Lord Londonderry's valet, her ladyship's maid, another maid for her daughters, a governess and four chauffeurs.

Yet this ostentatious expenditure rested on surprisingly insecure foundations. After 1918 those who drew their wealth from mineral royalties and manufacturing suffered reduced profits. Above all it was the problems of agriculture and the consequent collapse of land values during the 1920s that created a sense of crisis by driving agricultural rents down sharply and leading to massive sales of land at knock-down prices. Between 1914 and 1922 alone a quarter of all the land of England came up for sale, as well as a third of that in Scotland and Wales. As the 1920s wore on prices continued to fall, dragging rents down with them and leading to bankruptcies among farmers. This led some landowners to abandon their country seats and retire to the capital. Some 221 country houses were actually demolished between 1920 and 1939 leading to the sale of their paintings, furniture and books. In Cumberland the Earl of Lonsdale simply allowed Lowther Castle to stand empty and disintegrate, leaving a picturesque shell that remains to this day as a monument to hard times. Against the trend, Julius Drewe, the tea baron, finished building Castle Drogo, perched 1,000 feet up on the edge of Dartmoor, in 1931; but it was the last castle to be built in Britain, and was in any case destined for a history as a National Trust property.

It was not until the 1930s that a strategy for saving country houses emerged. In 1930 when Philip Kerr became 11th Marquess of Lothian he inherited more houses than he could possibly manage. He let Ferniehurst Castle to the Scottish Youth Hostels Association and allowed Newbattle Abbey to become an adult education college; he decided to keep Monteviot in Roxburghshire and Melbourne Hall in Derbyshire in the family, but this still left Blickling Hall in Norfolk which was already shut. Lothian concluded that the state ought to intervene in the interests of society as a whole, and in 1934 he suggested that the National Trust offered the best vehicle for tackling the country-house question. With tax concessions from the government he thought the Trust could take over country houses and preserve them as a legacy for the nation. At the time many landowners looked askance at such interference, but in 1937 Lothian presented Blickling Hall to the National Trust and others followed suit. Subsequently these arrangements were regularised so that former owners could continue to live in their houses while transferring ownership to the Trust.

Of course, the financial tribulations suffered by peers between the wars were not an inevitable result of the hostile economic climate. Some families managed to keep their considerable fortunes intact. In

1923 Viscount Allendale died leaving £3.2 million, in 1930 the Duke of Norfolk left £2.5 million and in 1938 Viscount Portman left £4.5 million. The 9th Duke of Devonshire had spent much of the pre-war period detaching himself from agriculture, selling land in Derbyshire and Ireland, and reinvesting in government bonds in Britain, America and the colonies, thereby managing to reduce his debts and pay death duties. As a result, by the 1920s the Duke's investments yielded thirty per cent of his annual income which amounted to £110,000. During 1919–22 land worth £640,000 was sold, as was Devonshire House for £750,000, leading to further investment in equities. All this transformed the Duke's finances so that over two-thirds of his income was now drawn from dividends.[3] Yet he retained Chatsworth and something of his traditional rural lifestyle until his death in 1938, and continued to play a role in public life as Governor General of Canada (1916–21) and Colonial Secretary (1922–3).

On the other hand those families who were unwilling or unable to adjust found themselves dragged down by sheer extravagance or by financial incompetence. The Earl of Derby, for example, who found himself unable to meet his expenditure from his income, resorted to using up his capital instead. By 1939 Lord Londonderry's annual expenditure exceeded his income by £106,000.[4] As the heiress to the immensely wealthy Sir Ernest Cassell, Edwina Mountbatten enjoyed spending lavishly from an early age and never understood the idea of living within one's means; the money simply flowed without interruption. When she arrived at the Paris Ritz in 1922 from a trip to India she found she had run out of cash. She thereupon cashed an IOU with the hotel manager – 'such a divine man, so it doesn't matter' – and promptly headed for the smart shops behind the Champs-Elysées.[5] Dickie Mountbatten, whose family was a good deal less secure than hers, worried that they were 'living at a rate of over £36,000 a year or at least £6,000 above our income'. But Edwina was not easily restrained. In 1930–1 their London home, Brook House, which was part of her inheritance, cost £16,000 to run; when the Mountbattens were in residence they employed twenty-seven indoor and two outdoor staff there, and fourteen indoor and three outdoor when they were away.[6]

In such a situation what was a cash-strapped peer to do? The least stressful and most traditional option for the impecunious aristocrat lay in making a suitable marriage. It was still possible to shore up tottering estates by drawing on wealth amassed through manufacturing and commerce especially among Americans. Lord Curzon was a specialist in this game. In 1895 he had married Mary Leiter the daughter of Chicago millionaire, Levi Leiter, who settled $1 million on his daughter and gave the couple an annual £6,000. Sadly Mary died in 1906. Subsequently Curzon spent eight and a half years with the novelist, Elinor Glyn, who evidently expected him to marry her. But in 1917, after a secret engagement lasting many months, Curzon abruptly ditched her to marry another American, Grace Hinds, the widow of the millionaire, Alfred Duggan. With his financial position thus secured Curzon focussed on his political career, confident of succeeding to the premiership. When his political ambitions were dashed in 1923 his colleague, Arthur Balfour, pointed out the compensations: 'even if he has lost the hope of glory, he still possesses the means of grace'.

Although lucrative marriages were not open to everyone, peers did enjoy other means of capitalising on their standing in the community, notably by seeking dignified employment as governors of far-flung parts of the British Empire, now reaching its territorial maximum in the aftermath of the Great War. In this capacity they earned national honour, generous salaries and expenses, and regular advances up the scale of lordly titles, while also escaping from the uncongenial conditions of domestic British politics. To take one example, Freeman Freeman-Thomas, better known as Lord Willingdon, who sat as an MP from 1900 to 1910, became a baron in that year. He then served as Governor of Bombay 1913–19, and Governor of Madras 1919–24, becoming a viscount in 1924, then as Governor General of Canada 1926–31, becoming an earl in 1931, and finally Viceroy of India from 1931–6 when he was made Marquess of Willingdon. These imperial outlets, which were to dwindle rapidly after 1945, created a comforting illusion of continuity during the interwar period.

On the other hand, for those with insufficient skill and connections even Empire proved an unreliable lifeline. Gerald Strickland, who owned Sizergh Castle in Cumberland and land in Malta, spent his life in a frantic search for a peerage and promotion through the Colonial Service. He advanced by inches from the governorship of the Leeward Islands (1902) to the governorship of Tasmania (1904), the governorship of Western Australia (1909) and the governorship of New South

Wales (1912). But these were mostly low-status posts carrying modest salaries; and at every stage Strickland damaged himself by becoming embroiled in political controversies culminating in his recall from Australia in 1916. Angry and short of money, he spent the 1920s and 1930s partly in Malta, where he rose through the elected assembly to serve briefly as chief minister, and partly as an absentee MP for Lancaster from 1924 to 1927. Though eventually elevated as Baron Strickland of Sizergh in 1928, he was seen as a nuisance by the Conservative and National governments of the period and he became marginalised in his party.[7] An inept politician, Strickland epitomised the landowner-aristocrat who never felt comfortable in an era of mass democracy but who managed to hang on just before the imperial tide finally ran out.

However, many peers felt driven to more drastic expedients. Crippled by his estates, the Earl of Glasgow drew in his horns by moving to Paris, where it was possible to live cheaply, until 1930. Others ventured further afield, notably to the 'White Highlands' of Kenya and to the Rhodesias where they managed to maintain a feudal lifestyle that was increasingly impractical at home. Lord Errol, Lord William Scott, a son of the Duke of Buccleuch, and the Marquess of Graham, heir to the Duke of Montrose, all retreated to Kenya. This, however, was far from a complete solution because plantation farming in the tropics suffered from falling world prices as badly as domestic agriculture. Some of the aristocratic émigrés to Africa were also dismayed at finding themselves caught up in European politics in the 1930s. The British settlers were thrown into a panic every time the government showed interest in conciliating Hitler by returning territories such as Tanganyika that had been acquired as mandates in the peace settlement.

Other attempts at aristocratic enterprise proved even less successful. The Duke of Atholl, who owned extensive but worthless estates in Perthshire, suffered from steadily mounting debts. Casting around for some means of restoring his finances, he invested in a scheme to build 'Atholl Steel Houses' in 1924. A few years later when the country desperately needed the so-called Anderson shelters as a refuge from enemy bombing the Duke might have made a fortune. But in the 1920s only a few steel houses were built and the orders expected from Romania, Italy and France failed to materialise; eventually he lost

£20,000. In 1930 Atholl was persuaded to invest in a large estate in Jamaica with a view to growing sugar and building a refinery for it in Glasgow. But he became another victim of the worldwide deflation and lost another £20,000 on the scheme.[8]

Meanwhile the Duke of Atholl's finances had collapsed in 1926 owing to a large overdraft with the Union Bank of Scotland of which he was a director. The bank informed him that he was losing £20,000 a year and could no longer pay his estate workers. Land and property worth £114,000 was immediately sold to reduce the indebtedness. Atholl's remaining land was now valued at £600,000. But in 1928 it became necessary to dispose of a third of this; the Duke and Duchess also kept Spink, Sotheby's and Christie's busy selling many of their possessions including an emerald tiara which fetched £6,500 and two pearl necklaces for £7,200 and £5,500. As the Duke had no legitimate children his estate would eventually pass to Andrew Murray who had married Angela Pearson, the daughter of Lord Cowdray who had built a business empire based on engineering. Lady Cowdray, who became alarmed at the piecemeal disposal of her grandson's inheritance, initially offered £50,000 to Atholl, but was shocked to discover that in addition to his £47,000 bank overdraft his other debts now reached a crippling £380,000. In 1932 she therefore instructed the lawyers to draw up an agreement under which she would pay off the Duke's debts on condition that all his property and assets were to be owned by a company which would give him £2,000 a year salary and an annuity for the Duchess. Atholl was obliged to sign an undertaking to abstain from all financial speculation and to retire from Blair Castle, which was let, to live at Eastwood House in Dunkeld.[9] Though humiliating for the Duke, this plan relieved him of worry and allowed him to focus on his wife's career as an MP.

For those who were prepared to make their titles work for them it was possible to make ends meet by going downmarket. In 1920 Lady Diana Cooper, daughter of the Duke of Rutland, gladly accepted an offer of £12,000 to act in a film, *The Glorious Adventure*.[10] On the strength of this her husband, Duff Cooper, abandoned his job as a civil servant to enter Parliament. Though a welcome extra this was not quite sufficient for the impecunious Coopers who raised additional funds from journalism. Lunching with Lord Beaverbrook when he was starting the *Sunday Express* they enquired about his terms. 'He said

£200 for four articles. [Diana] said "Done." ' The Duchess was horrified at this until Duff mentioned the money: 'and then she was horrified at the thought of her *not* doing it'.[11] Subsequently Lady Diana wrote for several British and American newspapers on such subjects as the Duke of York's wedding and the length of women's skirts. In fact, as her talents did not run to journalism all the articles were written by her husband!

Meanwhile Viscount Castlerosse, Lord Donegal and Lady Eleanor Smith undertook undignified but regularly paid employment as gossip columnists for newspapers. For this they were roundly condemned by *The Times* as 'sneak-guests' at country-house weekends and were satirised by Evelyn Waugh in *Vile Bodies*. Lord Castlerosse spent thirteen happy years gathering high-class gossip for Lord Beaverbrook's *Daily Express*. When he fell ill over his lunch at Claridge's in the spring of 1939 Beaverbrook spotted an opportunity. He paid for Castlerosse to remain at Claridge's, where he sat in bed imbibing champagne, reading the messages that flooded in from well-wishers, and issuing bulletins on his progress to reassure his anxious readers. There were worse ways for an interwar peer to cope with the decline of his order.

The press assumed considerable importance in the eyes of aristocrats if only because the elevation of newspaper proprietors symbolised the devaluation of their order. Nothing angered them more than the vulgarisation of the peerage under Lloyd George whose premiership from 1916 to 1922 became notorious for the sale of honours. In fact Lloyd George did nothing new; politicians had sold titles since the 1880s when the Marquess of Salisbury, whose heirs complained bitterly about Lloyd George, had been a pioneer in the business. Usually the chief whip drew up lists of appropriate names and passed them to the prime minister who recommended them to the King. However, as Lloyd George lacked a normal party machine, he stood in even greater need of funds than most premiers. Consequently he created more titles than was usual, was less discreet about marketing them, and raised the prices; one of his secretaries, Sir William Sutherland, known derisively as 'Bronco Bill', became notorious for touting titles around the London clubs. By 1918 it had been decided to put the whole thing on a more businesslike footing by employing one Maundy Gregory, an unsavoury character, as, in effect, a broker.

Gregory organised his touts, described by the chief whip, Freddie Guest, as 'grubby little men in brown bowler hats', and took his cut of the proceeds. Knighthoods went for £10,000, baronetcies for £30,000, and peerages for £50,000, though the recipients often bargained for a keener price. In a debate in the Lords in July 1922 the Duke of Northumberland quoted a letter in which one honours tout wrote: 'there are only five knighthoods left for the June list . . . It is not likely the next government will give so many honours, and this is really an exceptional opportunity.'[12] In 1921 to 1922 alone some 26 peerages, 74 baronetcies and 294 knighthoods were created. Some of those ennobled were simply political allies whom Lloyd George wished to keep friendly. When Hildebrand Harmsworth, of the newspaper-owning Harmsworth family, received a baronetcy despite never having done a stroke of work, his relations sent a sarcastic telegram: 'at last a grateful nation has given you your due reward'. But some of the awards were scandalous; peerages were bestowed on Sir William Vestey, a wartime tax-dodger, and on Sir William Robinson, a gold millionaire convicted of fraud, and baronetcies on Rowland Hodge, who was convicted for food-hoarding, and Sir John Drughorn, who had traded with the enemy.

By 1922, when Lloyd George's opponents were using the honours scandal to destabilise his premiership, a Parliamentary Scrutiny Committee had been appointed to vet proposals for honours. In 1925 the Honours (Prevention of Abuses) Act made the traffic in titles a criminal offence. However, sales of honours continued, albeit less blatantly than before. Although many Tories had attacked Lloyd George, what irritated them was that he sold honours to people from whom they themselves wished to raise donations! Even under the 1924 Labour government, Ramsay MacDonald became mired in contro-versy over the baronetcy awarded to Alexander Grant, the proprietor of the Scottish biscuit manufacturers, McVitie and Price. It emerged that the previous year Grant had given MacDonald the use of a Daimler, a loan comprising £30,000-worth of McVitie and Price shares and £10,000 invested in securities to supplement his income while prime minister. Both were returned when he ceased to be premier, but the Westminster wits concluded: 'Every man has his price, but not every man has his McVitie and Price!'

By exposing the peerage to popular derision the post-war honours scandal made the upper classes all the more sensitive about those who appeared to be letting the order down by their embarrassing behaviour. The Lord Chancellor, Lord Birkenhead, for example, enjoyed a deserved reputation for drunkenness. In 1926 when he arrived to speak to a Tory Women's conference in Middlesex, he sat on the platform and leaned heavily on the lady next to him, his dress in disorder and his voice thick with alcohol. These embarrassing performances eventually led Baldwin to deny Birkenhead reappointment as a Cabinet minister. Nancy Cunard, daughter of the hostess, Lady Emerald Cunard, scandalised society in 1920 by rejecting her family in favour of a bohemian lifestyle on the Left Bank in Paris. There she shocked society by embarking on an affair with Henry Crowder, a black American jazz musician. Margot Asquith, who was not known for her tact, greeted Emerald Cunard at a luncheon party: 'Hello Maud, what is it now – drink, drugs or niggers?'[13]

On the whole, however, upper-class women managed to cope more effectively than the men with the changing conditions of the interwar period. While in their teens and twenties upper-class girls continued to be confined to their homes simply waiting for someone to marry them; consequently they were much less likely to emulate their middle-class sisters by pursuing a university education or a career. On the other hand, once they had cleared the hurdle of marriage and produced the required children, life offered them all kinds of opportunities both social and political. In 1932 Violet Milner, wife of Viscount Milner, assumed the editorship of the *National Review* which she held for sixteen years. Stella Isaacs, wife of the Marquess of Reading, undertook several leading roles as chairman of the Personal Service League 1932–8, and the Women's Voluntary Service for Civil Defence (WVS) from 1938 onwards. And although the Conservative Party was unenthusiastic about promoting women as MPs, it acquiesced in the new practice whereby loyal wives stepped in to fill the parliamentary seats previously held by their husbands after death or elevation to the Upper House. Nancy Astor initiated the pattern in a by-election at Plymouth in 1919 following Waldorf Astor's succession to the viscountcy. In 1923 the Duchess of Atholl won West Perth and Kinross, represented by her husband in 1910; and in 1927, when Rupert Guinness, Viscount Elveden, became the Earl of Iveagh, his wife stepped in to what was regarded as the family seat at Southend.

Despite this, the women MPs remained fairly marginal figures in the party. Harold Macmillan believed that Edith, Lady Londonderry, exercised more influence as a conventional political hostess than Nancy Astor could as an MP. Conservatives, who had long relied upon the services of such ladies to the party, recognised Londonderry House as an unofficial centre for the party where connections might be made, deals struck, rebels conciliated and coming men promoted. Before the war Austen Chamberlain claimed he could always gauge his current political standing by the number of fingers – anything from one to four – extended to him by Theresa, Edith's predecessor, when they met at Londonderry House. Although Edith had played a prominent role during the war as colonel-in-chief of the Women's Volunteer Reserve and as Director General of the Women's Legion, as soon as she became Marchioness of Londonderry in 1919 she reverted to the traditional role by resuming the mass receptions at Londonderry House. 'There is still an upper class, its ranks diminished and impoverished by the war, who still wield a certain influence behind the scenes', she wrote in 1938.[14] In fact, the tide was going out for political hostesses. Edith continued to preside at the top of her staircase with a new Tory leader, Stanley Baldwin, beside her; but he privately regarded such functions as 'out of date and at times dubious'. He also resented Edith's attempts to win promotion for her husband, of whom Birkenhead memorably observed: 'he's catering his way to the Cabinet'. Yet Lady Londonderry cultivated a remarkable friendship with the Labour leader, Ramsay MacDonald, which eventually bore fruit when he headed the National Government in 1931. Following the election in October of that year he invited her to Chequers and shortly afterwards it was announced that Lord Londonderry was to become Air Minister. On the other hand Edith had insufficient influence to save her husband in 1935 when Baldwin succeeded as premier and promptly sacked Londonderry. There were no more grand receptions at Londonderry House until 1937 when a new prime minister, Neville Chamberlain, took over! By this time so many families had abandoned their London houses that Lady Londonderry looked increasingly isolated in her role as political hostess. She did not resume her work after the Second World War, and in 1962 Londonderry House was finally demolished.

The awkward relationship between the Londonderrys and Stanley Baldwin epitomised the wider dilemma facing British aristocrats between the wars. Their central role in Conservative politics ought to have been a source of strength and satisfaction to them in a phase of economic and social change; yet although the Conservatives enjoyed office for almost the entire period, albeit often in coalitions, the position of the peers aroused considerable friction and frustration. Young men from aristocratic families were still highly desirable as parliamentary candidates if they could pay their election expenses and appeal to the popular taste like the Marquess of Clydesdale, heir to the Duke of Hamilton, who sat for East Renfrewshire from 1930 to 1940; in Scotland he was a renowned amateur boxer and a glamorous pilot who participated in the Everest flight in 1933. But in politics, as in the law, the army and other professions, the upper classes now faced stiff competition from middle-class men who were often better educated and qualified. As a result of the steady advance of candidates from commercial and professional backgrounds since the 1880s, the composition of the Conservative parliamentary party had changed; by the 1930s only one in ten of the MPs came from a landed background. The success of middle-class men in penetrating the aristocracy can be measured by the 338 Conservatives elected as MPs in 1918 of whom nearly three-quarters subsequently received peerages.

Even at the highest levels the party's character had changed. After 1911 the next three leaders were distinctly bourgeois. Andrew Bonar Law, who came from a family of Scots steelworkers, made no attempt to entertain his colleagues like traditional Tory leaders and, according to one, would not have recognised a pheasant if he saw one. His successor, Stanley Baldwin, who was the son of a Midlands ironmaster, believed the Conservatives must respond to the rise of Labour by freeing themselves from traditionalism and recruiting from a wider social range. In 1937 Neville Chamberlain seemed a more natural party leader but this was partly because he had moved so far from his origins in a family of Birmingham screw-manufacturers.

One striking sign of the decline of the peerage was that all the interwar Tory leaders reneged on the party's promise to reform and restore the House of Lords to its pre-1911 state. This inevitably made the Upper House seem a backwater for the politically ambitious, particularly in 1923 when Lord Curzon, who as a former Viceroy and Foreign Secretary appeared the best-qualified successor to Bonar Law, failed to be chosen as prime minister. In fact Curzon's rejection owed a good deal to his personal unpopularity, but his isolated position in the House of Lords would have been a disadvantage at a time when the chief opponent, the Labour Party, was largely concentrated in the Commons. Even so, it was not impossible for a peer to become prime minister; the Earl of Halifax would almost certainly have done so in 1940 if the Conservative MPs had been able to choose the successor to Chamberlain.

However, by this time there were very few leading candidates in the Upper House. Although peers had been well represented in the Conservative governments of 1922–3 and 1924–9, they were derided as the 'Second Eleven'; not seen as very intelligent or able ministers, they were often appointed to minor or non-departmental posts. The political careers of the representatives of several distinguished families – Lord Robert Cecil, Lord Eustace Percy, Lord Londonderry – faded away, leaving Lord Halifax as the only one whose reputation rose through the 1930s. There was, of course, the interesting case of Winston Churchill who, as the son of Lord Randolph Churchill, a younger son of the Duke of Marlborough, can be included among the aristocratic politicians of the period. But after reluctantly rejoining the Conservatives in 1924 and being appointed Chancellor of the Exchequer, Churchill did his best to alienate himself from his party by rebelling against his leaders over India, rearmament and appeasement; he resigned from the shadow Cabinet in 1930 and was excluded from the National Governments from 1931 until 1940. Widely regarded as an excessively ambitious and even unstable character, Churchill reached the end of the 1930s with virtually no parliamentary following. He was, in fact, the epitome of the flawed aristocrat. He drank too much, scrounged shamelessly and proved unable to manage his finances; the purchase of Chartwell in Kent, which was designed to ape the aristocratic style, proved to be far beyond his means, and by 1938 his debts had reached £18,000. His later triumphs cannot entirely obscure the fact that during the interwar period Churchill was a characteristic example of the failure of the aristocracy to shore up its position in the political system.

Not surprisingly, as titled families became conscious of their political marginalisation, angered by the collapse of agriculture and land values, and fearful of Britain's retreat from Empire, some of their members embroiled themselves in extremist movements. In the immediate aftermath of the war the Duke of Northumberland became obsessed with the idea that Britain was threatened by a vast international Jewish-Bolshevik conspiracy as revealed in a notorious but influential forgery, *The Protocols of the Elders of Zion*. Northumberland interpreted every unwelcome event and every policy of which he disapproved as further proof of this thesis. He completely rejected the system of parliamentary democracy which he blamed for promoting the corrupt and limp-wristed politicians who failed to defend Britain's interests at home and in the Empire. As early as 1923 Britain's first fascist organisation, the National Fascisti, was attracting disaffected aristocrats including the Earl of Glasgow, Lord Ernest Hamilton, Lord Garvagh, the Marquess of Ailesbury, Viscountess Downe and Lady Sydenham of Combe. Mostly obscure figures, they shared Northumberland's alienation from parliamentary democracy. Viscount Lymington, who was heir to the Earl of Portsmouth, promoted the English Mistery, founded in 1930, and went on to found English Array in 1936. These were authentically English and highly reactionary expressions of fascism, aiming to revive the aristocracy, restore the power of the medieval monarchy, abandon liberal democracy, recover the purity of the race by banning miscegenation, revitalise rural life and recreate the stable society Britain had lost as a result of the decline of the feudal system. Not surprisingly, during the abdication crisis of 1936 Lord Lymington emerged as a staunch supporter of Edward VIII who appeared to many British fascists to offer the best prospects for an overthrow of the discredited system of liberal democracy.

Admittedly, many peers, though attracted by the ideas of Sir Oswald Mosley, were embarrassed by the vulgarity of the British Union of Fascists after 1932. It was to attract such people that in 1934 Mosley established the January Club, intending to use it as a front to familiarise members of the political establishment with the idea of the corporate state against the time when the parliamentary system gave way to fascism. Among its titled members were Lymington, Lord Erskine, Earl Jellicoe, the Marquess of Tavistock, the Earl of Glasgow, Lord Midleton and Lord Londonderry. Later in the 1930s other anti-Semitic and pro-Nazi organisations attracted aristocratic support, notably the Anglo-German Fellowship which included Lord Mount Temple, Lord Brocket, the Duke of Wellington, Lords Malcolm and David Douglas-

Hamilton, Lord Nuffield and Londonderry. As Britain seemed to slip towards war with Germany, those who blamed deteriorating Anglo-German relations on Jewish influence joined Captain Ramsay's Right Club including Lord Semphill, Lord Ronald Graham, (a son of the Duke of Montrose), Lord Redesdale and the Duke of Wellington. During the later 1930s peers such as Redesdale, Londonderry, Brocket, and the Duke of Buccleuch visited Nazi Germany and attempted to promote a sympathetic view of Hitler in Britain. In 1937, following two meetings with Hitler, Lady Londonderry wrote ecstatically in the press about Hitler's admiration for England and his yearning for peace. These efforts reached a climax during 1939 and 1940 when Tavistock, Brocket, Buccleuch, Westminster, Graham, the Earl of Mar and the Marquess of Clydesdale undertook a series of missions to Germany to promote peace and pressured the government at home to withdraw from the war. Several of them collaborated with Mosley to achieve this object. However, all this came to an abrupt end in May 1940 when the new Coalition Government suddenly decided to arrest some 747 leading fascists. Remarkably the aristocratic fascists and pro-Nazis escaped detention even though their role in the BUF and the Right Club made them prime targets. The most likely explanation for this is that their arrest would have been too embarrassing for Churchill, whose own position in the Conservative Party was precarious, and it would also have been dangerous in the eyes of the authorities because some of the peers were closely linked to the royal family. Subsequently they kept their heads down and largely managed to cover their tracks as pro-fascists after the end of the war. But the price they paid was a further retreat from the centres of political power in Britain. In working to keep Britain out of the war they acted not simply out of sympathy for Naziism, but because they appreciated that another pro-longed conflict would generate a fresh social and political revolution that would make them and the order they represented even more marginal in British society.

18

'Everybody calls him Bertie':
The Monarchy and the British People

On 13 January 1922 a telegram arrived at Sandringham. It read: 'ALL RIGHT STOP BERTIE'. Though not apparent at the time it heralded what turned out to be a masterstroke for the British monarchy: the engagement of the Duke of York, the King's second son, to Lady Elizabeth Bowes-Lyon. The daughter of a relatively obscure Scottish peer, the Earl of Strathmore, Lady Elizabeth soon showed herself more at ease with British society than any other member of the royal family. When the engagement was announced to the public in January 1923 she promptly granted an interview to a *Daily Star* journalist who presented himself unannounced at the Strathmores' London home at 17 Bruton Street.[1] Though unremarkable by later standards the interview horrified the King who had absolutely no dealings with newspapers and subsequently vetoed the BBC's request to broadcast the Yorks' wedding in April. As one of his private secretaries, Clive Wigram, ruefully admitted, 'there has been a tendency to despise and ignore, if not insult, the Press'.[2]

On the face of it the British monarchy was not well prepared to accommodate a new, democratic era at the end of the Great War. George V had a well-deserved reputation as a dull, charmless, distant and irritable individual. An archetypal conservative, he disliked all forms of change and innovation, notably radio, aeroplanes, jazz, cocktails and women who wore nail varnish and smoked in public. The King was also a shy man who found public appearances a trial, hated entertaining and showed no interest in 'society'. His main source of pleasure was a day spent shooting – his only known skill – at Sandringham or Balmoral. After a frugal dinner, at which he always wore a kilt and the Order of the Thistle if at Balmoral, he spent a happy hour with his stamp collection before retiring early to bed. As post-war

London began to enjoy itself after the privations of wartime the King seemed determined to retire to a quiet family life. Unhappily, his wife, Princess Mary of Teck, did little to mitigate George's limitations. She came from an impoverished family: 'my parents were always in short street so they had to go abroad to economise', she explained.[3] The Queen's poverty left her with a lifelong habit of scrounging gifts from anyone she visited; by expressing her appreciation for some item of furniture, china or a painting she eventually embarrassed the owner into making her a present of it. Originally Mary had been engaged to Prince Eddy, the heir to the throne; but after his death a decent interval was allowed to elapse before George was instructed to propose to her. Thus began a classic arranged royal marriage with a foreign princess. Though livelier than her husband, Queen Mary adopted a strict and conventional view of her role both as Queen and as mother, and her coldness created difficulties for all her children.

Yet despite these unpromising characteristics George V and Queen Mary proved to be a remarkable success. While royal dynasties were being discredited and overthrown by democracy, nationalism and revolution all across Europe, in Britain the King presided serenely over a range of social and political changes of which he fundamentally disapproved, and by the time of his Silver Jubilee in 1935 he had achieved immense popularity. The explanation is partly that George V was widely seen as an old-fashioned patriot doggedly doing his duty. At a time when the country's politicians were immured in corruption and scandal he set an example by leading a dull but unblemished family life. Essentially an ordinary man called to high position by accident, the King was in many ways in tune with his subjects. When he spoke he revealed an accent that was not posh and, unusually for a British monarch, betrayed no trace of German. One of his biographers shrewdly commented that he 'liked a book with a plot, a tune he could hum, and a picture that told a story'.[4] On a rare visit to the Tate Gallery to open a new extension he told the Queen 'Here's something to make you laugh,' as he stood before the French Impressionists. At the National Gallery he shook his stick at a Cézanne and informed the director: 'Tell you what, Turner was *mad*. My grandmother always said so.'[5]

But the survival of George V also owed a good deal to his realistic approach to his role. He had succeeded to the throne in 1910 amid a major political crisis between the Liberal government and the House of Lords. By following the advice of his elected government, despite temptations to the contrary, he avoided the danger of leading the monarchy into partisan controversy and set the pattern that was to see him safely through the interwar period. The idea of a monarch above party politics was still a comparative novelty practised by Edward VII during his short reign; but his predecessor, Queen Victoria, had been a stubborn and unconstitutional partisan. By allowing the Liberals to reduce the powers of the peers in 1910–11 George V indicated that the monarchy was not going to tie its fortunes to the defence of the hereditary element in the political system. Resisting the temptation to make common cause with the aristocracy, the royal family left the peers to go into steady decline while it sailed on to popular acclaim.

This was the more remarkable since the King's views were both conservative and Conservative. During the Edwardian period he and Queen Mary developed a deep fear of socialism and republicanism, routinely referring to Keir Hardie, the Labour MP, as 'that beast'; Hardie's colleague, George Lansbury, described him as 'a short-tempered, narrow-minded, out-of-date Tory'. The royal couple, who went in horror of strikes and trade unions, believed their governments were too conciliatory towards socialism. These fears led them to adopt an energetic policy designed to counter subversive political forces by means of extensive patronage of voluntary and charitable activities and organisations. This was already an established feature by the time George V ascended the throne, but the royal advisers, including Lord Stamfordham and Lord Esher, urged that the growth of an assertive working-class politics made it imperative for them to get out to meet their poorer subjects as much as possible. This involved patronage of and financial contributions to charitable causes and exhaustive visits to hospitals, orphanages, factories, regiments and coal-mining districts especially when mining disasters occurred. In theory this voluntary work was a means of squaring traditional deference towards the country's rulers with the politicisation of working people. Certainly the King and Queen derived comfort from the warmth of their reception on their visits even to the most radical districts of South Wales, Yorkshire, the Potteries and County Durham. 'Keir Hardie would not have liked it', wrote the Queen with satisfaction after a trip to Merthyr Tydfil (his constituency) in 1912.

This role was accentuated by the First World War. Disruption caused by the departure of men for the front and by the subsequent casualties created huge scope for philanthropic work in which all members of the royal family became involved. They doubled their donations and promoted many charities including the King's Fund for Sailors, the Prince of Wales Fund, Queen Mary's Needlework Guild and the Queen's Work for Women Fund. They toured munitions factories, especially where the authorities feared industrial unrest, and food distribution centres, entertained the wounded at Buckingham Palace, and made 300 harrowing visits to hospitals: 'You can't conceive what I suffered going round those hospitals in the war', King George later admitted.

Although he was spared the worst hardships of his people, the King was obliged to have a wire mesh stretched across the palace as a protection against Zeppelin raids. In 1915 he allowed himself to be persuaded by Lloyd George to set an example by abstaining from alcohol for the rest of the war. Rather naively the King expected the politicians to follow up with a general prohibition on alcohol. 'We have been carted', complained Queen Mary when it transpired that everyone else was continuing to drink as before.[6] A more acceptable way of drawing ordinary people into the national effort lay in the extensive distribution of honours in recognition for war service. To this end a new order, the OBE, was created specifically for civilians in 1917, some 22,000 having been awarded by 1919. The OBE incorporated a much wider range of men and women into the honours system, including many in the Labour Movement, some of whom were otherwise sceptical but felt flattered by royal recognition.

Royal efforts to associate themselves with the national cause were not just an optional extra. By provoking a wave of anti-Germanism the war exposed the royal family, which was embarrassingly short of British blood, to the hysteria that drove several prominent men with German-sounding names, or German sympathies, from public life. 'I wonder what my little German friend has got to say', observed Lloyd George on visiting the palace in 1915. When H. G. Wells criticised the monarchy for being alien and uninspiring the King indignantly responded: 'I may be uninspiring but I'm damned if I'm alien.' This was true enough; completely British by upbringing and sentiment, George V showed little enthusiasm for his Continental relatives. But he took the precaution of abandoning his family name – Saxe-Coburg-Gotha, or Guelph or Wettin, it was not certain which – in favour of Windsor. In so doing the royal couple may simply have lost their nerve amid the emotions of wartime, but the change was a shrewd symbolic act.

George V showed how acutely he was attuned to popular attitudes in March 1917 when the suggestion was first mooted that the Russian Tsar and his family, who had been overthrown by revolution, should be offered sanctuary in Britain. While the government seemed willing to co-operate with this, George argued that it 'would be strongly resented by the public and would undoubtedly compromise the position of the King and Queen'.[7] He was right. For years the Tsarist regime had been regarded as a barbarous tyranny by liberal opinion in Britain and the overthrow of such an embarrassing ally had been widely welcomed. Abandoning the Romanovs to their fate was hard but realistic. By 1918 Tsar Nicholas and his family had been shot at Ekaterinburg; the German Kaiser had disappeared into exile in Holland; the Hapsburg Emperor, had seen his territories dismembered and become a fugitive; in the next twenty years the thrones of Spain and Greece were to be overthrown. But in Britain George V succeeded in associating the monarchy firmly with the national-imperial cause and the welfare of the people. Whereas elsewhere war had discredited regimes and rulers, military victory had the effect of enhancing the prestige of Britain's political system and adding to the territories of the Empire; this helped the political establishment to take a calculated risk with the loyalties of the British people in 1918 by undertaking a massive extension of democracy. A few republicans wrote letters to the press about abolishing 'the ancient trappings of throne and sceptre', but no one was listening.

However, in view of events elsewhere in Europe, the royal advisers felt that the King could not afford to be complacent. Wigram warned that 'His Majesty must get out of the habit of hiding his light under a bushell' by enlisting the co-operation of the newspapers even though this went against the grain.[8] Lord Stamfordham argued that 'the monarchy and its cost will have to be justified in the future in the eyes of a war-worn and hungry proletariat endowed with a huge preponderance of voting power'; this meant that the King must be 'a living power for good' not just a remote figurehead. To this end the royal couple determined to enrol their children in their programme of charitable activity, and they became especially anxious for them to make suitable marriages in order to double the personnel available for visits and patronage. Fully conscious that the demise and disgrace of so many royal houses now made the traditional marriage to a foreign prince or princess impractical and undesirable, they agreed that their children could marry members of the English and Scots nobility. In 1922 Princess Mary was the first to adopt the new policy with her engagement to Viscount Lascelles, heir to the Earl of Harewood. The inclusive approach was also underlined by inviting senior Labour politicians to their wedding, which was much appreciated. 'I felt that the vast majority of Labour voters throughout Great Britain would like to be represented at a wedding to which they obviously offered their good wishes', commented J. R. Clynes.[9] As her contribution to the family strategy Princess Mary concentrated on work for the Girl Guides, Great Ormond Street Hospital and visits to unemployment centres.

Her brother, Albert, Duke of York, was also dispatched on trips to factories and docks in Scotland and the North. He became president of the Boys Welfare Association, later the Industrial Welfare Society, for sixteen years, the idea being that his name would enable the organisation to extract donations and attract new members. From 1921 onwards he sponsored the Duke of York's Camp where thousands of public schoolboys met with working-class boys with a view to breaking down social barriers under royal patronage. In 1923 the Duke called at the headquarters of the Amalgamated Engineering Union, the first royal to visit a trade union. Perhaps his most appreciated role was in supporting the National Playing Fields Association which won a royal charter in 1925.

Above all, the royal strategy relied upon the Prince of Wales partly because he was immensely popular and because he was used in an explicitly political way. With his blue eyes, fair hair, easy smile and little-boy-lost look, the heir to the throne reached parts of society other royals could not easily reach. During the 1920s he rapidly became an adored Prince Charming figure; his picture appeared on boxes of chocolates and biscuits, on postcards, on mantlepieces and on bedroom walls all over the country. In August 1919 the Prince embarked on the first of his imperial tours which took him to Canada, the West Indies, New Zealand, Australia, India and South Africa. Advised by Winston Churchill to memorise his speeches if possible but, if not, to read them slowly and deliberately, he proved to be a great success. On his return from Australia in 1920 he received a tumultuous reception when driving through London; his carriage was repeatedly stopped by spectators who called on him for a speech.

The Prince could hardly remain unaware that his popularity carried political implications. At a typical visit to a labour exchange in February 1926, where he met 400 unemployed men, the newspapers presented him as very sympathetic to their plight: 'Prince Rubs Shoulders With Men On The Dole'.[10] The *Daily Graphic* reported him as being depressed at seeing so many men there: 'some of them were in a distressed condition and he was full of sympathy for them'. An impressionable youth, the Prince felt torn by these encounters. After a trip to Glasgow he wrote 'I do feel I've been able to do just a little good propaganda up there and given Communism a knock.'[11] However, on a visit to coal miners in the North-East in 1929 the Prince dropped some off-the-cuff remarks about their 'appalling' and 'perfectly damnable' living conditions, thereby sowing the seed of distrust between himself and the politicians. In time he clearly realised that the politicians were using him for their own purposes. This was blatantly obvious when he was asked to speak on unemployment at the Albert Hall in January 1932 – at the height of the depression and shortly after the re-election of the National Government. The speech, which was written for him, stressed the importance of voluntary work for the unemployed as opposed to state responsibility. In this way the Prince was placed in an awkward position, becoming to some extent a tool for defusing popular discontent with the Cabinet and its policies. Not surprisingly, the more he toured the depressed regions and understood how popular he was with working people, the more he felt tempted to express himself freely. As a result he was disliked by socialists, who regarded royal charity as an attempt to buy loyalty and cultivate deference, but he also attracted right-wing criticism for pandering to popular discontent and undermining deference. To both the Prince appeared as a rival for public affection.

Despite these complications, the royal strategy seemed to pay dividends. At Buckingham Palace the King maintained a special map bedecked with little flags tracing the progress of his family members on their charitable visits around the country; and each Christmas he drew up a chart recording all their work during the previous twelve months. The climax came when he agreed – against his instincts – to make a radio broadcast at Christmas 1932. As early as 1923 the idea had been pressed upon him by Sir John Reith, but he could not be persuaded. The King's script, written by Rudyard Kipling, began by acknowledging that some twenty million people were listening in: 'Through the marvels of modern science I am enabled this Christmas Day to speak to all my peoples throughout the Empire.' Brief and unpretentious, the King's concluding words clearly moved his audience: 'I speak now from my home and from my heart to you all. To men and women so cut off by the snows, the deserts or the sea that only voices out of the air can reach them. To all, to each I wish a happy Christmas. God Bless you.' To his own surprise the King proved to be a natural broadcaster. His slow, clear delivery and sincere, conversational style were an immediate success. Now that 'wireless' was so widely available the majority of the people could feel a direct and personal link to their sovereign for the first time. Yet for George V live Christmas Day broadcasts were a trial: 'This is always an ordeal for me and I don't begin to enjoy Christmas until after it is over', he admitted privately. But he felt obliged to repeat the broadcast each year and it quickly became a central part in the celebration of Christmas for millions of British families.

Despite this, things could so easily have gone wrong on the political front had George V not taken a strict, constitutional view of his role. In common with most royals, he was obsessively fearful about the spread of the Bolshevik Revolution in the early 1920s; the onset of mass unemployment, extensive industrial militancy and the rise of the Labour Party could be – and was in some quarters – interpreted as proof that the contagion had reached Britain. In 1918 Labour became the second largest party in Parliament, and at the elections of 1922 and 1923 it consolidated its position as the King's alternative government. Yet this development never posed the kind of challenge to the system that might have been expected. Few people saw any real inconsistency between a fully-fledged democracy and the retention of a hereditary head of state. Certainly the leading Labour politicians did not regard the monarchy as an obstacle to their advance and on the whole they took little interest in constitutional reform of any sort; once they had won a parliamentary majority the British system appeared to be an effective vehicle for implementing their programme. Their relaxed view was underpinned by the enthusiasm felt for the monarchy among rank and file Labour supporters. According to Jimmy Thomas 'No question of republicanism as a serious proposition ever finds a place in Labour discussions.'[12] When the party conference held a rare debate on the subject in 1923, which lasted about a quarter of an hour, it rejected a pro-republican motion by 3.7 million votes to 380,000. For his part the King, like many upper-class people, had been impressed and reassured by the patriotic response shown by the workers during the war and by their pride in the Empire. The early 1920s saw regular social contacts between Labour politicians and the King and Queen which fostered the confidence expressed by Thomas: 'If Labour came to power tomorrow they would find the King prepared to accept their advice as readily as that of the Liberal and Tory parties.'[13]

The acid test came after the inconclusive general election of December 1923 when the Conservatives lost their majority but remained the largest single party. Led by Ramsay MacDonald, Labour was the next largest party, but, with just 191 MPs could not expect to form a strong or lasting government. Many Conservatives insisted Labour was simply not fit to govern. However, once the Conservatives had been defeated in the House of Commons the King lost no time in inviting MacDonald to become prime minister; he did not even ask him to form a coalition. This show of confidence immediately conferred a measure of legitimacy on Labour and was certainly flattering to its leaders. When the new ministers went to the palace J. R. Clynes noticed how effectively the King put them at their ease: 'I had expected to find him unbending. Instead he was kindness and sympathy itself. Before he gave us leave to go he made an appeal that I have never forgotten: "The immediate future of my people, their whole happiness, is in your hands, gentlemen. They depend on your prudence and sagacity." '[14] Not everyone succumbed to the charm. Beatrice Webb complained: 'This romancing about the royal family is, I fear, only a minor symptom of the softening of the brain of socialists, enervated by affluence, social prestige and political power.'[15] Webb may not have been entirely wrong, but, as usual, she missed the significance of these events. By demonstrating confidence in an untried, minority Labour government in 1923 the King killed what slight stirrings of republicanism there were and helped to integrate Labour and its working-class supporters into the political system. He showed the same skill in charting his way through the General Strike in 1926 when he helped to check the right-wing extremists who wanted to use the power of the state to crush the trade unions. The King intervened with his ministers several times to minimise the use of troops and to deter them from interfering with union funds.

Against this background it is not surprising that the chief criticism of George V came not from the Left but from extreme right-wing peers and politicians who believed that a policy of concessions towards the workers and towards socialism was undermining the British state. In particular they argued that since Queen Victoria's day the parliamentary politicians had gradually turned the monarch into a mere cipher who launched ships, visited hospitals and presided over ceremonial occasions but had been deprived of his power. These critics were not entirely mistaken. Though dogmatic and not afraid to express his opinions privately to prime ministers, George V was politically more marginal than his predecessors; even on matters such as honours, about which he felt strongly, ministers took little notice of him. By contrast the historian, Sir Charles Petrie, pointed to the example of Italy which suggested how a king could effectively replace a failing and corrupt democracy by ushering in a strong, Fascist government; according to Petrie, monarchy had the great advantage of enabling such changes of regime to be accomplished without bloodshed.[16]

Though hardly an accurate description of Mussolini's assumption of power, this view was not as eccentric as it sounds. Many Conservatives who despaired of the leadership of Stanley Baldwin looked to a restoration of royal authority in Britain. Viscount Lymington MP propagated this idea through two fascist organisations, English Mistery and English Array. Regarding modern democracy as a fraud, they frankly aimed to recreate a feudal society based on a hierarchy from peasant to king. Members took a pledge: 'I will strive to restore the King to his rightful position as the mirror of his people's virtues, as their protector from private interests, and as their supreme government. For he alone can guarantee permanence.'[17]

Given his rigid loyalty to his constitutional role George V was unlikely to be tempted by such notions, though the same cannot be said for the Prince of Wales who was enthusiastically welcomed on the far Right for his evident desire to escape from the confines of figurehead monarchy. His ambitions mattered because ordinary British people vaguely assumed that the King already exercised much more influence in the day-to-day running of the country than was really the case; indeed during the war and at times of national crisis they believed he should do so. In any case, although the monarch routinely accepted whatever government commanded a majority in Parliament, he still enjoyed considerable power when no single party held a majority or when an existing administration broke down. The collapse of MacDonald's government in 1931, when the Cabinet was unable to agree on spending cuts to meet the threat to the currency, was such an occasion. Instead of inviting the leader of the Opposition, Baldwin, to form an alternative government – as was his natural constitutional action – the King espoused the idea of a coalition; he took the initiative by inviting the party leaders to join and offered the premiership to MacDonald despite his role as leader of the previous discredited administration. The formation of the National Government, which lasted until 1940, was a striking demonstration of royal authority and a reminder that even George V was more than merely a figurehead in politics.

If there was a flaw in the interwar monarchy it lay in the inability of King George and Queen Mary to handle their six children. The youngest, Prince John, who suffered from epilepsy, was excluded from family life and died in 1919. But the four remaining boys all found family life a trial not least because their parents were so formal and unemotional towards them. The King in particular was notorious for perpetually criticising them for what they saw as trivial reasons involving their clothes. Even Christmas at Sandringham was invariably a dull and formal occasion when each family member collected his or her presents in the ballroom from a section of table demarcated by pink tape. At dinner paper hats were worn by all except the King whose idea of a joke was to play the national anthem on the gramophone when no one was expecting it and see how long it took everyone to realise, stop eating their Christmas dinner and stand up.

During the 1920s the overriding aim of King George and Queen Mary was to make suitable marriages for their five remaining children and involve them in the family programme of compulsory voluntary work. They found their third son, George, Duke of Kent, who was especially well adapted to the 'Roaring Twenties', particularly trying; but to their relief he eventually made a conventional marriage to Princess Marina of Greece in 1934. More tractable but no less problematic was the second son, Albert, Duke of York. A nervous and rather dim youth who spent his early life in the shadow of the Prince of Wales, Albert suffered from an ulcer, which went untreated for years, as well as a bad stutter. His father made things worse by barking 'Get it out' whenever he stammered. In 1909 he had been dispatched to the Royal Naval College on the Isle of Wight where he came bottom in a class of ninety-eight cadets. However, it was there that Albert met the first of the two people who were to transform him from a failure into a success. Louis Greig was a Scots naval surgeon, fourteen years his senior, who took the Prince under his wing and acted as a father figure to him. In 1919 Greig accompanied him when he was allowed to spend a year at Cambridge – the King ruled out taking a degree; there he learned to ride a motorbike and got fined six shillings for smoking in academic dress. Greig introduced him to girls including Madge Saunders, a South African chorus girl, and an Australian, Sheila Chisholm. Inevitably the King objected violently to these friendships and threatened not to make him Duke of York unless he gave up 'poor little Sheilie', which he quickly did.

In effect Louis Greig showed Albert a glimpse of normal life. He taught him to play tennis so well that in 1926 the pair entered the men's doubles at Wimbledon – an amateur competition at that time. Playing against Harold Morris and the Secretary of State for Air, Sir Samuel Hoare, he was too overwhelmed by the occasion to perform well. Spectators shouted out 'Try the other hand, Sir' to the left-handed Prince. But watching from the front row was the other formative influence in Albert's life. He had met Lady Elizabeth Bowes-Lyon in May 1920 at a ball in Grosvenor Square when she was twenty. Described by Chips Channon MP as 'mildly flirtatious in a very proper, romantic, old-fashioned sort of way', the charming, self-assured Elizabeth had spent a happy childhood at Glamis Castle, the Scottish seat of the Earls of Strathmore. Greig quickly saw that she was the sort of strong-minded but motherly woman the Prince needed to lean on. Inevitably Elizabeth had other, more appealing, suitors, and in any case she shrank from exchanging her relaxed life for the cold, formal court of George V. In September 1920 she rejected his first proposal. But

Greig encouraged him to persist; and the redoubtable Queen Mary intervened by repeatedly inviting Elizabeth to royal functions and by ensuring that James Stuart, the man she really loved, was sent away to work in Oklahoma! In January 1922, aged twenty-seven, the Duke tried again: 'It's the third time and it's going to be the last', he confessed.

In January 1923, when she gave her first interview to the *Daily Star*, Lady Elizabeth exchanged obscurity for the celebrity that endured throughout the rest of her life. 'How kind of you to come,' she told the journalist, 'Bertie – you know everybody calls him Bertie – has gone out hunting.'[18] Describing her as 'looking very radiant' and possessing 'a magnetic personality', the delighted journalist set a pattern by recording her dress: 'Lady Elizabeth was wearing a morning frock of greyish blue edged with fur, and round her neck was a double string of pearls.' The undoubted interest in royal dress suggests that the royal family exercised an influence over popular tastes in clothes. However, the royal ladies probably followed the fashion rather than setting it partly because they were handicapped by the unqualified disapproval of King George and Queen Mary for almost anything new. In any case, the new Duchess of York, who wore fox furs and favoured a traditional fringe, was far from being in tune with female dress in the 1920s. She was, however, credited with making the cloche hat popular when she wore it in 1927. As Duchess and later as Queen she helped reintroduce a very feminine and traditional style, favouring long flowing skirts for evening wear and neatly tailored suits for daytime. Her favourite colour, light powder blue, was widely worn with plum-coloured velvet. Even in the 1930s, however, royal officials were known to grumble about her unfashionable taste in clothes. Perhaps as a result the King summoned the young Norman Hartnell in 1937 to help glamorise the Queen's wardrobe for the coronation. Hartnell designed two crinoline evening dresses for state banquets, which were considered well suited to her curvaceous, 'bosomy' figure, and proved a great success. In the following year the Duchess of Kent took the royal line even further by reintroducing Edwardian styles in frocks, hair and wide-brimmed hats with high crowns. However, by this time hardly anyone wore such dress except Christabel Pankhurst, who remained loyal to huge brimmed hats weighed down with fruit and flowers, and the impact of such royal initiatives was negligible.

Members of the royal family may have had a greater impact on men's styles. During the 1920s the soft, coloured homburg hat, which had been introduced by King Edward VII, was replacing both the hard black or brown bowler and the tall silk hat among men. King George popularised single-breasted jackets, though his habit of creasing his trousers down the sides – navy style – rather than front and back failed to catch on. Inevitably it was the Prince of Wales who seemed most in tune with post-war British fashion. He pioneered the cutaway collar and the Windsor knot. Dressed in his Oxford bags, extravagantly coloured Fair Isle pullovers and the classless cloth cap, the Prince was a classic 1920s fashion statement. By the 1930s he went even further towards informality by appearing in slacks and shorts and even going shirtless.

The marriage of the Duke of York and Lady Elizabeth Bowes-Lyon proved to be an immense personal and political success. A million people turned out to see their wedding in 1923 – the first time a commoner had married a royal prince in 300 years. The new Duchess immediately took over the patronage of the National Society for the Prevention of Cruelty to Children and the Young Women's Christian Association from Princess Helena who died in 1923. Although the Duke continued to suffer from outbursts of temper, a symptom of his nerves, his wife exercised a calming effect on him. In 1924 when they visited Northern Ireland he told his father: 'Elizabeth has been marvellous as usual and all the people simply love her already. I am so lucky to have her help as she knows exactly what to do and say to all the people we meet.' In 1925 he agreed to consult Lionel Logue, a speech therapist, about his stutter and embarked on a ten-week course of treatment. He was loyally accompanied by his wife whose wartime experience at Glamis Castle helping shell-shocked and demoralised men enabled her take this in her stride. Logue persuaded the Duke that his stutter was curable, taught him to breathe correctly and introduced daily exercises. He was put to the test during the tour of Australia in January 1927 when he was required to open the new Parliament building in Canberra. Though petrified about this visit, he managed to deliver his speech almost faultlessly. And he continued to rejoice in the support and popularity of his wife. According to the Governor of New South Wales, 'The Duchess leaves us with the responsibility of having a continent in love with her.' All this was immensely reassuring to his father. In June 1929 the King noted that he had 'had several talks with

him and find him very sensible, very different to David [the Prince of
Wales].'[19] This, of course, meant that Albert did not argue with or
rebel against the King's views. In time, as his doubts about the Prince
of Wales deepened, the King realised that Albert would offer
continuity with his own reign. 'I pray to God that my eldest son will
never marry', he wrote in 1935, 'and that nothing will come between
Bertie and Lilibet and the throne.'

'I had a wretched childhood', complained the Prince of Wales,
looking back on an early life suffocated by antiquated court etiquette
and dominated by his father's endless criticism. Though this view is
easily dismissed as the whingeing of a rebellious youth, it was endorsed
by those who were familiar with the royal family. Dickie Mountbatten
commented that 'his father's letters [to the Prince] might be the letters
of a director to his assistant manager'.[20] All his sons found George V's
obsession with punctuality wearying. On one occasion when the Duke
of Gloucester had returned after months spent abroad, just after the
family had sat down to dine, the King's only greeting was: 'Late as
usual, Henry.' He never tired of reprimanding them for petty transgressions of the dress code. 'I hear you were not wearing gloves at the
ball last night. Please see that this does not occur again', was typical.
When the Prince of Wales and Dickie Mountbatten cooled off in a
swimming pool during a visit to the tropics the King complained: 'You
and Dickie in a swimming pool together is hardly dignified . . . you
might as well be photographed naked, no doubt it would please the
public.'[21] This pressure made the princes feel they were constantly
under surveillance and it fostered a desire to rebel, especially in the
Prince of Wales and the Duke of Kent. As he grew older the heir to the
throne increasingly resented the absurd and trivial rules maintained at
court; servants, for example, got into trouble if they referred to 'His
Majesty the King' instead of 'the King', whereas Queen Mary had to be
'Her Majesty the Queen'. Not surprisingly he resolved that he would
be a modern monarch more in tune with his people.

In one respect, however, the Prince misrepresented the oppressive
influence of his parents. They had accepted that their children should
be free to marry British citizens rather than foreigners selected for
them from the dwindling band of Continental princes and princesses.
Despite this, by 1934 the heir to the throne had reached the age of forty
with all his boyish charm intact but still unmarried. He was under

pressure from all sides. 'There is but one wedding to which [the public]
look forward with still deeper interest', pronounced *The Times* in 1923
on the Duke of York's wedding, 'the wedding which will give a wife to
the heir to the throne.' According to *Vanity Fair* he had received 4,187
proposals: 'Hats off to the indestructible Dancing Drinking Tumbling
Kissing Walking Talking and Sleeping – but not Marrying – idol of the
British Empire!' In 1926 he was reportedly amused when the press
circulated rumours that he was to marry Princess Astrid of Sweden.
'But what's to become of the pretty Canadian nurse I danced with, and
all the other "brides" in the Empire they nearly made me marry?' he
asked in mock despair.[22]

Both the royal family and the political establishment found it
frustrating that this prevarication went hand in hand with an energetic
social life. The Prince had been introduced to sex in a conventional,
upper-class way via a French prostitute at Amiens towards the end of
1916. Thereafter he became keen on women, but women of a certain
sort. He fell for a succession of usually older or more mature, married
women including Lady Coke, Freda Dudley Ward, the wife of an MP,
Thelma, Viscountess Furness, and finally Wallis Simpson. His letters to
Mrs Dudley Ward, with whom his relationship lasted sixteen years,
were full of such endearments as 'your very own devoted adoring little
David', 'your little boy is wanting you', and 'my very own darling,
beloved little Mummie', which suggest that, like his brother Albert, the
Prince was in search of a mother figure as much as a wife.[23]

Admittedly these relationships caused no problems provided that
both parties were discreet and a suitable wife was eventually found.
But the Prince grew increasingly unco-operative and independent. In
1929 he acquired the use of Fort Belvedere, an eighteenth-century folly
on the edge of Windsor Great Park, which facilitated his separate social
life and symbolised his intention to pioneer a new style of monarchy.
He met his partner in this enterprise, Bessie Wallis Simpson, in the
autumn of 1930 at a dinner party at the home of the sister of Lady
Furness, his lover at the time. Lively and opinionated, Wallis was not
the sort of American woman who fell in love with English traditions;
on the contrary she thought it absurd for a democratic society to be so
deferential and so obsessed with titles and royalty. But for the Prince of
Wales this was part of her charm. Soon she became his regular dancing
partner. In 1932 he began to invite Wallis along with her long-suffering

second husband, the shipping broker, Ernest Simpson, to stay at Fort Belvedere. They became the best-known threesome in London, attracting jokes about 'the Importance of Being Ernest'. But although she addressed him publicly as 'Sir', in private the Prince was now 'David', and by 1934 Wallis realised that they were both in love. His friend, Walter Monckton, commented that it was a 'mistake to assume that he was merely in love with her in the ordinary physical sense of the term. There was an intellectual companionship, and there is no doubt that his lonely nature found in her a spiritual comradeship'.[24] She delighted in the discovery that the heir to the throne could be so simple, unaffected and unsnobbish a man.

However, the realisation that he was intent on marrying Mrs Simpson, for whom a second divorce would be necessary, horrified upper-class society. 'Personally I cannot but feel that the whole thing has been organised from America with the set purpose of doing him harm', commented Lady Londonderry.[25] Queen Mary, sounding increasingly like Oscar Wilde's Lady Bracknell, declared: 'one divorce could seldom or never be justified, and to divorce twice, on any grounds whatsoever, was [to her] unthinkable'. Although the eventual abdication of Edward VIII in 1936 has usually been seen almost entirely in terms of his determination to marry the unsuitable Mrs Simpson, it was in fact only the symptom of a deeper political problem that rose to the surface in the late 1920s and 1930s as the Prince asserted his independence. Though he complied with the King's wishes by including 776 organisations on his patronage list, the Prince of Wales was a reluctant philanthropist; he gave much less to charities than his father and often failed to turn up at charitable functions.[26] In particular he felt sceptical about the King's dogged support for voluntary hospitals which was seen as a means of staving off state control. The Prince correctly saw that the voluntary sector had become an anachronism and would be better replaced by a comprehensive state system. Then there were his regular visits to areas of unemployment where he seemed to pander to popular sentiment by expressing sympathy for the workers and, by implication, his criticism of the authorities. Despite being in some senses very conservative, his social conscience had been awoken by the war and he was easily roused by progressive ideas through direct contact with ordinary people. The most notorious example came in November 1936, as the crisis over Mrs Simpson reached a climax, when he toured the steelwork at Dowlais and commented: 'Something must be done to meet the situation in South Wales and I will do all I can to assist you.' Coming just after the end of the Jarrow March this touched a sensitive chord. In his diary Ramsay MacDonald noted: 'These escapades should be limited. They are an invasion into the field of politics and should be watched constitutionally.'[27]

Baldwin, who was prime minister by this time, shared MacDonald's concern, not least because by the 1930s the Prince of Wales had acquired a dangerous interest in foreign affairs. He was anti-Communist, hostile to the French and determined to promote Anglo-German friendship. None of these represented a problem in that they reflected the general views held by government ministers. But the Prince repeatedly made it clear that he intended to play a personal role in British foreign policy. He spoke tactlessly to German diplomats expressing sympathy for the Nazis and for dictatorship – 'we might want one in England before long'. He disparaged the government for failing to promote friendship with Germany and advocated an alliance between the two countries. The Cabinet, quite rightly, felt that he should keep his opinions to himself and get his speeches cleared with the Foreign Office first. Meanwhile, the Nazis, who were paranoid about attacks on them in the British press, enthusiastically cultivated the Prince and contributed to an exaggerated impression of his political skills. The Anglo-German Fellowship pandered to the Prince of Wales's sense of own self-importance by quoting one German observer: 'You have a splendid King. Why don't you let him out of his cage?'[28]

By the mid 1930s the politicians felt increasingly apprehensive about his accession to the throne. The approach of the old King's Silver Jubilee in 1935 brought their fears to a head. It was all too clear that he suffered from a congenital inability to endure the essentially dignified role of a constitutional monarch. Right-wing extremists hoped that the new King would be the means of breaking the stranglehold of the National Government and restoring Britain's national pride. In the *Saturday Review* Lady Lucy Houston published a series of articles urging Edward VIII to become a benevolent dictator: 'we look to you, our beloved King, to be our leader, the only leader we can trust to save us'.[29] In this Houston reflected the fashionable notion that each nation

needed its Man of Destiny who would provide the strong government
that Mussolini had given Italy since 1922. The Prince of Wales was not
a fascist, but, like many people of his generation, he was easily
impressed by fascism as a modernising and patriotic force that would
solve unemployment and sweep away the corrupt and temporising
parliamentary politicians. Correspondingly, many fascists regarded
him as one of them, that is, as a member of the younger generation that
was held back by the old men who had dominated government since
the war. Such anti-democratic sentiment extended more widely
through British society than simply the formal fascist organisations.
However, the desire for autocracy failed to achieve real political
influence partly because the sheer popularity of the monarchy acted as
a safety valve for extreme nationalism. In effect the monarchy drew
such emotions out of politics where they would have posed a great
threat, and thereby limited the scope for the emergence of a charis-
matic fascist-type leader to emerge as the national saviour.

The place occupied by King George in British emotions was
underlined by the celebrations held for his Silver Jubilee in May 1935.
Every night for a week the King and Queen appeared on the balcony
of Buckingham Palace. They drove through the East End of London
where streets were decked with flags, bunting and banners and
crammed with long tables bearing food and drink for the street parties;
in one of the worst slum districts the residents hung up their overalls
with the inscription 'LOUSY BUT LOYAL'. When the Jubilee procession
entered Pall Mall the Prince of Wales excited the crowds by waving to
Mrs Simpson watching from an upper window. In a final flowering of
philanthropic enthusiasm King George's Jubilee Trust raised £1 million
within a matter of weeks. However, by the start of 1936 the King's life
was drawing to a close, and just before midnight on 20 January his
doctors put him to sleep with a lethal injection of cocaine and morphia.

Two days later Edward VIII was proclaimed the new King. He lost
no time in demonstrating his determination to be a modern monarch.
He abandoned the wearing of frock coats at court and abolished
'Sandringham Time', the practice instituted by Edward VII whereby all
the clocks were kept half an hour ahead of Greenwich Mean Time in
order to gain extra daylight for shooting game. Meanwhile traditionalists recalled the old King's warning: 'After I am gone the boy will
ruin himself within twelve months'. But for the moment he seemed

intent on enjoying his new-found freedom. He spent the summer with Wallis, Lord Louis Mountbatten, Alfred and Lady Diana Cooper and other friends, on board a yacht, the *Nahlin*, cruising the Dalmatian coast. Though the British newspapers censored themselves, the American and Continental press reported fully on the progress of the lovers and printed pictures of the King sunbathing shirtless on deck. By July the Prince had introduced Mrs Simpson's name into the Court Circular. In September he assembled a large party at Balmoral where the Duke and Duchess of York were miffed at being greeted by Wallis who brazenly acted as hostess; she marched around the house telling the shocked guests 'This tartan's gotta go!' Meanwhile Mrs Simpson's divorce petition was due to be heard at Ipswich on 27 October; six months later when the divorce became absolute, she would be free to remarry. In New York the *Daily Mirror* and other newspapers flourished headlines proclaiming 'KING TO MARRY WALLY: WEDDING NEXT JUNE'.

This alarming prospect led the prime minister to interview the King on 20 October to raise the issue of his marriage and to emphasise the impossibility, as he saw it, of marriage to Wallis Simpson. Stanley Baldwin and his colleagues in both the Conservative and Labour parties flatly refused his request to be granted a morganatic marriage allowing him to marry Wallis without making her Queen. Baldwin simply could not understand why the King would not agree to make a conventional marriage and keep Mrs Simpson as his mistress, which was, after all, routine upper-class practice. Meanwhile the British Establishment convinced itself that apart from her obvious drawbacks as an American, a commoner and a double-divorcee, Mrs Simpson was a pro-Nazi and would leak confidential documents to Germany. During November and December her London home in Cumberland Terrace was kept under surveillance by Special Branch, and the 'intelligence' services surpassed themselves by collecting quantities of salacious gossip about her, notably claims that she controlled the King by means of drink, drugs and the sexual techniques she had acquired in Shanghai! The FBI helpfully informed MI5 that Joachim von Ribbentrop, the German ambassador in London, had sent seventeen carnations to Mrs Simpson, representing one for each time they had slept together.

Stanley Baldwin's account of the abdication crisis, which has until recently been largely accepted by biographers and historians, was that a marriage to Mrs Simpson was totally unacceptable to the British people and to the Empire. We now recognise that this view is essentially contemporary Establishment propaganda. Much of the British Establishment and many upper-class people certainly disapproved of Mrs Simpson as did the handful of colonial premiers and governors consulted by Baldwin. But they scarcely represented public or Empire opinion. Edward VIII had always been more popular among working and middle-class people and there is abundant evidence of their support for him in 1936. In Hoxton Bryan Magee noticed: 'all the people I actually heard express a view were on Edward's side ... why should he not marry the woman he wanted and go on being King was what we wanted to know'.[30] According to Magee's father those in authority were using Mrs Simpson as an excuse to get rid of the King because of his sympathy for the unemployed. As soon as the crisis became public knowledge at the start of December 1936 letters poured into the *Daily Mail*, *Daily Express*, *News Chronicle* and the *Daily Mirror*, newspapers that commanded a substantial majority of national sales, vociferously backing the royal marriage. Readers' letters argued that Edward was an indispensable king and should be allowed to marry for love: 'Snobs are deploring the break with tradition. Some of us, however, can see rather a break with hypocrisy'.[31] They angrily attacked Baldwin for trying to force the King into abdicating and demanded a democratic ballot on the issue. 'It is for the King to say, like every other man, who shall be his partner for life', urged the *News Chronicle*. 'Public opinion nowadays takes a very human view of royalty ... A true love match – and a democratic one at that – would be popular.'[32]

During the first week in December crowds gathered at Buckingham Palace, marched along Whitehall and flocked into Downing Street, which stood unprotected by gates at that time, shouting 'We want Edward', 'God Save the King' and 'Flog Baldwin'. When Cabinet ministers and the Archbishop of Canterbury left meetings at 10 Downing Street they were jostled and booed by angry people as they tried to escape to their waiting cars.[33] Up and down the country members of the British Union of Fascists chalked and painted the slogan 'Stand By The King' in letters three feet tall on roads, pavements, bridges and hoardings.

These outbursts did not mean that a majority of the British people supported the King's marriage with Mrs Simpson, but they certainly meant that the country was far more deeply and evenly divided than the government claimed. The abdication crisis exposed the extent to which society was now split, partly in terms of social class and partly in terms of generations, over moral standards. With their casual acceptance of arranged marriages, discreet adultery and kept mistresses, the moral attitudes of the upper classes now appeared hypocritical to many British people. A generation of men and women had grown up believing in the ideal endlessly propagated in magazines and in romantic fiction about a man falling in love with a girl and then doing the only decent thing by marrying her. Alienated as he was from court circles and the political establishment, Edward was unquestionably in tune with these sentiments; by seeking to marry his 'sweetheart' he conformed to a higher standard of morality than his critics.

Yet despite the groundswell of support in the country and the formation of a 'King's Party' led by Churchill, ready to form a government, Edward's nerve gave way under pressure from Baldwin for a quick decision, and by 8 December he had resigned himself to abdication. 'Our cock won't fight', as Lord Beaverbrook, proprietor of the *Daily Express*, put it. The decision was announced on 10 December and the next day millions of shocked and tearful people gathered around their radios to listen to his broadcast to the nation. 'At long last I am able to say a few words of my own', began the speech, a reminder that until this point the Cabinet had refused to let him broadcast for fear of its effect. For his listeners the most moving passage came when he appealed: 'you must believe me when I tell you that I have found it impossible to carry the heavy burden of responsibility and discharge my duties as King as I would wish to do without the help and support of the woman I love'.

For all the sympathy this aroused, many people condemned the King for running away from his duty. Sir Barry Domvile, for example, took a dim view of 'the King's delinquencies', and after listening to his speech wrote: 'A good riddance. Long live King George VI' in his diary.[34] Meanwhile the prime minister was inundated with letters of congratulation from his political followers on his handling of the crisis by people who felt let down, though others angrily accused him of dethroning the lawful King.[35] Baldwin's judgement had certainly been questionable. It is arguable that more damage was done to the monarchy by forcing the abdication than would have been done by allowing the King to go ahead and marry Mrs Simpson. The crisis left the country very divided for a long time. Many people regarded the new Duke of Windsor as a decent man who had risked all for love, and the Mass Observation surveys suggested that George VI was widely considered to have usurped his brother's throne. Consequently for some years the new King and Queen, who could hardly forget the way the crowds had gathered outside their home shouting 'We want Edward', were understandably paranoid about the Duke and his wife.

Special Branch monitored the Windsors' movements, tapped their telephone calls and examined their mail, ostensibly for their own protection; but in reality they were trying to protect the new King against any campaign for the return of his predecessor from his Continental exile. Both George VI and his government handled the Windsors ineptly. When Edward and Wallis married in May 1937 the newsreel companies agreed to exclude the event from their screens; but the newspapers gave extensive coverage to the wedding, which only highlighted the boycott ungraciously imposed by the royal family. Meanwhile, the royal family and the Home Office became paranoid about an advertising campaign by Bass, the brewers, reminding con-sumers that the company had sold beer under seven monarchs since 1777. In February 1937 Bass succumbed to pressure to drop the latest advertisement featuring Edward VIII even to the extent of destroying the printer's copies and all evidence of the offending material. These attempts to freeze the Windsors out by the British Establishment were unwise if only because they risked provoking the Duchess into retaliating. She and the Duke began to make tours in the United States and Germany much to the embarrassment of the British authorities. In December 1937 the Duke wrote to the prime minister, now Neville Chamberlain: 'When I decided to give up the throne last December . . . I never intended, nor would I ever have agreed, to renounce my native land or any right to return to it, for all time.'[36] But the National Government feared that the Duke would immediately become a focus for opposition to them if he returned. Various fascist and other extremist groups eagerly anticipated this development, and it seemed certain that by organising celebrations for the Duke they would have a divisive effect on the country. As late as January 1939, according to the Gallop polls, sixty-one per cent of the public wanted the Windsors to return against only sixteen per cent opposed. The Duke himself reminded the prime minister, rather pathetically, that he had received 2,000 Christmas cards from sympathisers. But for that very reason Chamberlain prevaricated throughout 1937, 1938 and 1939, continually finding excuses to postpone any visit, until the outbreak of war finally convinced him it was too dangerous to let the Windsors remain on the Continent.

In retrospect the paranoia about the Windsors in royal and government circles seems excessive, especially as sympathy for the ex-King did not necessarily imply hostility towards his successor. Yet the monarchy had suddenly lost its most glamorous and accomplished figurehead for a shy, nervous king with inadequate experience and inferior presentational skills. 'I'm quite unprepared for it', he protested, 'David has been trained for this all his life. I've never even seen a state paper.' This was certainly apparent to his subjects. Bryan Magee's parents, who were 'curious to see what this surprise King looked like', went to St James's Park where the new King and Queen were to ride in an open carriage, but returned disappointed. The King, dressed in a black morning coat and a topper, seemed ordinary: 'He was leaning forward in the carriage with his hat off, tipping it shyly under his nose as if saying goodbye to someone crouching invisibly at his feet. It was a cramped, embarrassed gesture, inward-turned, and I realise now that it betrayed a terrified desire to escape from the crowd . . . I couldn't see what we had come all this way for.'[37] George VI went some way to compensating for his underwhelming presence by holding a spectacular coronation, costing £454,000, two and a half times as much as George V's. It was organised by the Duke of Norfolk who held no fewer than eight rehearsals and introduced microphones into Westminster Abbey so that the ceremony could be heard throughout the country on radio. Norfolk and the Archbishop of Canterbury were empowered to edit all photographs and newsreels of the event. But George VI found the whole thing a great strain. He failed to deliver the Christmas message in December 1936, and in 1938 he left the task to Neville Chamberlain.

In effect, the royal couple reverted to the strategy of George V. This came naturally in as much as the new King, as Baldwin had perceived, was very like his father both in his character and in his idea of his role. By calling him 'King George', rather than 'King Albert' the palace underlined the continuity with his father's reign. George VI took over the patronage of his brother and donated £6,000 to charities each year, a sum comparable with that given by his father. While he continued to feel uncomfortable at public appearances, Queen Elizabeth compensated for his shortcomings. Watching her opening a new building Harold Nicholson thought she possessed 'an astonishing gift for being sincerely interested in dull people and dull occasions'.[38] The Queen managed to be gracious and regal on the one hand while showing humour, informality and the common touch on the other. Above all, the new monarchy was a *partnership* like that of Queen Victoria and Prince Albert, in which the King relied heavily on his wife who was very conscious of the need to gather every scrap of publicity. There was a small but telling illustration of this when she and the King left 10 Downing Street after dining with the Baldwins in June 1937. As the crowd milling around outside could not see them because their car was in darkness Elizabeth promptly ordered the chauffeur to put the lights on.[39]

The country quickly warmed to the idea of a young family on the throne once again, and the unapologetic domesticity of the royal couple and the two little princesses, Elizabeth and Margaret Rose, neatly symbolised the values and aspirations of ordinary British people. After her experience in 1923 the Queen avoided giving interviews, but there was no need to do so as the cinemas and newspapers constantly put the royal family before the public. Gaumont-British, who wrote a script introducing 'King Albert' even before they knew his official name, played a key role in preparing the way for the new monarchy. During the first year of their reign the royal family featured in no fewer than 89 of 101 cinema newsreels. Meanwhile the women's magazines began to rely on the royal family as a major aid to increasing circulation. Their portraits vied with knitting patterns on their front covers, and *Woman's Own* even managed to combine the two by featuring 'Your Coronation Jumpers' in red, white and blue on 1 May 1937. From the coronation issue in May to December – 'Christmas with Princess Margaret Rose' – that year the King and Queen, the two princesses and Queen Mary appeared eight times on the magazine's cover and often on several inside pages too. Commercial interests also seemed especially keen to exploit their popularity, Cow and Gate Milk Foods, for example, claimed that seven royal babies had been fed on their products including princesses Elizabeth and Margaret Rose: 'Nothing but Cow and Gate is good enough for a King's baby and nothing else is good enough for your child.'

As George VI lacked political knowledge and stood in awe of clever people, he adopted a cautious approach towards his ministers. He avoided following his father's advocacy of voluntarism in health, perhaps appreciating that the trend was now in favour of collectivism, and after 1945 he readily accepted the innovations in social policy introduced by his Labour government. As appeasement reached its climax under Chamberlain during 1938-9 and the country reconciled itself to another European war, the royal couple showed themselves, as Baldwin had predicted, much less troublesome to their ministers than Edward VIII. Essentially they were conventionally patriotic, anti-French and anti-Communist, and although Queen Elizabeth held rather reactionary opinions she was good at hiding them. They quickly fell under the spell of Neville Chamberlain, so much so that the King had to be persuaded not to go to Heston Aerodrome to greet him personally on his return from Munich in September 1938. Instead the King and Queen invited Chamberlain to appear with them on the balcony at Buckingham Palace. Privately they were cautioned against committing themselves so blatantly to what shrewder observers now saw as a failing policy and a soon-to-be-discredited leader. In this respect, however, the royals were simply making the same mistake as many of their countrymen, and although they felt very loath to part with Chamberlain in favour of Churchill in 1940, they managed the transition to war very smoothly.

'A Stone's Throw to Australia': Patriotism, Race and Empire

It was Cecil Rhodes who observed that to have been born English was to have won first prize in the lottery of life. Although we associate such sentiments with the more militant nationalism of the Victorian era, they commanded wide approval during the 1920s and 1930s. Indeed, the interwar period, sandwiched as it was between the triumph of one world war and the looming prospect of another one, heightened the embattled sense of patriotism and national unity. Lt Col Alfred Wintle confessed without embarrassment that every night he got down on his knees before going to bed and thanked God for making him an Englishman. 'Never forget', Bryan Magee's uncle told him, 'that an Englishman is worth two foreigners.'[1] As an unemployed Tyneside miner his uncle might well have felt more detached from conventional expressions of patriotism, but he evidently retained a strong sense of national pride in the face of the economic hardships and social conflict of these years. This is more striking if the period is compared with the years from 1880 to 1914 which had been marked by deep political divisions over imperial issues such as Irish Home Rule, the death of General Gordon and the Boer War, to say nothing of the controversies aroused by the taxation of wealth after 1906 and the constitutional crisis over the House of Lords when the Opposition refused to accept the legitimacy of the elected Liberal government. Despite, or perhaps because of, the rise of the Labour Party, the interwar decades were relatively free from such divisive issues partly because the two main political parties fervently endorsed the political system and pursued essentially similar economic and foreign policies. Rising standards of living and the development of a consumerist society also helped to take the edge off social discontent.

Above all the Great War and the subsequent drift towards

authoritarianism on the Continent fostered the sense of Britain as distinct and separate from the rest of Europe. Military victory boosted pride in her political system and institutions, her monarchy, Parliament and Empire, leaving post-war British society much less vulnerable to challenges by extremist movements than in Germany, Italy, France and Russia. There was nothing inevitable about this outcome; but it was accentuated by timely concessions on the part of both politicians and the monarchy who recognised the fundamental loyalty shown by the lower classes during the war by agreeing to incorporate all adults within the pale of the constitution in 1918 and 1928.

The post-war British state also had the advantage of possessing the means of fostering a sense of national community that had not been available in earlier periods in the shape of the BBC. Though relatively free from the propaganda usually associated with official state radio, the BBC was consciously used to promote unity at least to the extent of minimising divisions. This latter aim was in evidence during the General Strike in 1926 and in the later 1930s when Sir Oswald Mosley was excluded from radio. More positively the BBC effectively drew the nation together on the great national occasions: the King's Christmas message, the death of King George V, the abdication broadcast of Edward VIII in 1936, Chamberlain's return from Munich in 1938, and on Empire Day in May each year when it devoted a high proportion of broadcasting time to imperial topics. Sir John Reith was especially alive to the effect of ceremonial in helping the public to experience a sense of participation in otherwise remote events. Each evening they heard the national anthem on the radio and many people stood spontaneously when it was played in cinemas. Commenting on the coronation of George VI in 1937, Mass Observation noted that 'a very high proportion of the people spent the day listening in and thus participating in the central events'.[2]

Naturally, patriotism meant different things to different people. It encompassed loyalty to Empire, monarchy and democracy but it also meant pride in Britain's achievements in sport, manufacturing, seamanship, exploration and aviation. However, as in most societies, national spirit derived much of its force from purely negative forces: prejudice towards foreigners, fear of immigrants, anti-Semitism, and a prevailing assumption of racial superiority towards Africans, Asians and even Mediterranean peoples. It has rightly been noted that in this period British patriotism comprised several distinct strands including monarchism, imperialism and racism. It was possible, in theory, to be a monarchist, for example, without advocating further imperial expansion. On the other hand, in the 1920s and 1930s only an exceptional person would have been pro-monarchy without also being keen on the British Empire; since the late Victorian period the royal family had been seen as the embodiment of Empire and the two continued to go hand in hand after 1918. Ordinary Britons commonly hung portraits of the King and Queen, sometimes simply a page torn from a newspaper, in their homes: 'In this way the King functioned as a buttress to the self-esteem of the ordinary English. It was because he was our King that he governed a third of the world, so his glory was ours.'[3] In effect, then, sentiments like monarchism, imperialism and racism were often mutually reinforcing even though they were notionally distinct.

For the British people negative patriotism expressed itself less obviously in aggression than in a pronounced insularity, symbolised by the famous newspaper headline 'FOG IN CHANNEL: CONTINENT CUT OFF'. However, the insularity was more than geographical. After all, their vast web of commercial and imperial interests involved the British with the rest of the world to an unusual extent. But Empire had the effect of cocooning the British in an alternative community that was 'abroad' but still British, and of making people neurotically suspicious of rivals for imperial territory. British insularity also expressed itself through sport. Indeed, sport may well have been a more significant reinforcement of national identity for many people than political factors. It gave tangible expression to key British characteristics such as fair play and respect for rules which were seen as transferable to non-British people. Since Victorian times British imperialists had regarded active participation in sport as a means of maintaining the virility and competitiveness of the race and, as a result, sporting prowess was often seen as a desirable qualification for men appointed to official positions in the colonies. Hence the importance attached to national sporting occasions including the FA Cup Final, the Grand National and the Oxford and Cambridge Boat Race as well as to international events such as the Olympic Games, Test matches, Wimbledon and aeronautical competitions. The opening of Wembley Stadium in 1923, marked an important expression of this thinking by creating a fitting venue for national sport. The role of sport in national life was also accentuated by BBC radio and by the cinemas whose promotion of sporting fixtures helped to consolidate their own status as national institutions.

At the same time sport undoubtedly fostered the insularity of the British people. Until 1918 Britain had always refused to join the International Football League, and, after joining, she withdrew once again in 1928. As the British considered themselves responsible for developing the modern forms of football, rugby, golf, boxing, tennis, cricket, horse racing, mountaineering and even skiing, they were irritated to find that they were not always successful in competition with foreign rivals. But, as so often, the Empire helped to cushion the decline. Cricket alone created an exclusively British family of sports-men; before 1914 only Australian and South African teams had visited Britain, but they were joined by the West Indies in 1928, New Zealand in 1929 and India in 1932. The foundation of the British Empire Games in 1930 was seen as another means of unifying the disparate collection of overseas territories, but it also accentuated a sense of retreating from an unfriendly world.

To foreigners it often seemed that the British suffered from a superiority complex, a tribute, perhaps, to their long history as a nation state, their success in resisting invasion and the pride they took in their huge Empire. This expressed itself less in hostility than in indifference towards foreign countries and cultures. 'Foreigners, because they were different from us, were funny as well as unfortunate, and were not to be trusted', recalled Bryan Magee. 'Everyone who was not white was inferior to everyone who was; and the definition of "not white" was extreme; it included Latins, who were dagoes.'[4] Despite their service abroad during the war most British soldiers from all walks of life returned with little interest in or sympathy towards other societies. According to Robert Graves the hostility of ex-soldiers towards the French 'amounted almost to an obsession – our natural enemies were the French'.[5] Indeed, the war had the effect of accentuating insularity at all levels of society including the royal family who took much less interest in their Continental relations and regarded the French with distaste. These sentiments resurfaced strongly during the national crisis in the summer of 1940 when the fall of France before the advancing German forces elicited an absurd reaction from the King:

'Personally, I feel happier now that we have no allies to be polite to and pamper'!

In the aftermath of the Great War British hostility towards the 'Huns' was hardly surprising, though in fact the traditional admiration for German culture still flourished and many Britons respected Germans as decent opponents. Far more vitriol was expended on our erstwhile allies, the French, who had made a greater sacrifice for victory than Britain. Throughout society they were routinely condemned for dragging Britain into the war, especially during the later 1930s when another Franco-German conflict loomed. Queen Elizabeth, whose brother, Fergus, had died in the Great War, was typical of those who preferred the appeasement of Germany to further attempts to restrict German territory for the benefit of France. In the eyes of British conservatives France was too democratic, republican and left wing to be an acceptable friend, especially after the election of a Popular Front government in 1936. 'No Englishman ever born really likes the French,' declared Charles Grey, editor of the *Aeroplane*. He quoted one of his RAF friends insisting that he would never fight in another war again: 'Then he paused for a moment and added – "except against the French".'[6]

The British adopted a more ambivalent attitude towards the Americans. Although they had eventually become valuable allies in the war, Britain had good reason to feel let down by the United States during the 1920s and 1930s, partly because of her retreat into isolation and abandonment of the League of Nations, and also because of her failure to use her resources to stimulate the flagging world economy. Nor did the Americans bother to deny that they had no interest in maintaining the British Empire. On the other hand, Americans spoke a similar language, shared many attitudes and provided a prosperous refuge for generations of British emigrants. Above all, America exercised a huge cultural influence on interwar Britain in terms of the cinema, fashion, music and motor cars. However, in some quarters this influence provoked a reaction by those who saw British culture being swamped by vulgar Americanism. At its most extreme this took the form of the fascist critique of the Hollywood-dominated cinema which was assumed to be under Jewish control and was thought to be undermining British imperial values.

In regard to people of non-European stock interwar attitudes reflected a mixture of complacency and superiority. For men and women who had grown to adulthood since the late Victorian era it was almost impossible not to acquire what we would today regard as racist attitudes. The only evidence this generation had to shake its belief in white supremacy was the shocking defeat of Russia by the Japanese in the war of 1905, and they managed, perhaps unwisely, to avoid thinking about its implications. During the 1930s it was considered improper for newspapers to print photographs of dead white people when reporting on wars and disasters, but 'yellow-skinned cadavers were allowed, just as it was permitted to show "native" women bare to the waist'.[7]

For most people the Empire, involving British rule over some 460 million subject peoples, offered incontrovertible evidence of their superiority as a race. Since Victorian times the British had ranked the various races in their Empire in a hierarchy; in India, for example, they traditionally designated Punjabis, both Sikhs and Muslims, as the martial races and Bengalis as 'baboos' or pen-pushers. They admired the Indian princes, however decadent, for their loyalty, the only reservation being their penchant for indulging in liaisons with English women. During the eighteenth and early nineteenth century Englishmen had commonly taken Indian wives and mistresses, whose offspring were known as Eurasians, but the practice had long since ceased to be acceptable. Officials did their best to ignore mixed-race Indians, despite their loyalty, and English officials who persisted in having affairs with native women were transferred to remote, jungly parts of Burma. By contrast the French adopted a relaxed and realistic attitude; even in the twentieth century they encouraged young men stationed in their tropical colonies to marry local women in the belief that this would strengthen French rule. The Indian community in Britain comprised around 7,000–8,000 people, many of them well-educated professionals who spoke good English, adopted Western dress and took a keen interest in cricket. But they remained a very separate community, though some exceptional individuals joined the political mainstream. Two Indians had been elected MPs in the late Victorian period, and in 1922–3 and 1924–9 Shapurji Shaklatava represented Battersea in Parliament. Though his race was not an obstacle, Shaklatava was attacked for his Communist opinions and his support for the General Strike. The other prominent Indian in this period was Krishna Menon who resided in Britain from 1924 onwards in order to campaign for Indian self-government. Strikingly, neither Menon's race nor his frank opposition to the British Empire appeared a major drawback for he was elected as a Labour councillor for St Pancras in 1934 and could have become a Labour MP. However, party members found Menon's views embarrassingly Communistic and thought him too aristocratic and authoritarian for a democratic movement!

Africans, West Indians and Arabs were much less familiar, except in ports like Sunderland and Cardiff where small communities of foreign seamen had settled over a long period. Most British people, however, regarded them as beyond the pale. Nancy Cunard's notorious relationship with a black American jazz musician in the 1930s was acceptable in smart Parisian society but seen as absolutely scandalous in London. In embattled areas of declining industry like William Woodruff's Lancashire, attitudes were apt to be determined primarily by material considerations: 'The other threat posed to Lancashire came from "t' niggers" who were prepared to work for less money. As far as I could discover "t' niggers" were poor people who lived in Asia and Africa . . . they divided most of the world into "us and t' niggers".'8 For a handful of men sport offered a route to popularity. After 1929 when the West Indian, Learie Constantine, arrived in Lancashire his skill as a batsman made him 'the idol of Nelson'. But on the whole the English found it hard to accept black people as human beings on the same level as whites. It was this attitude that so appalled Sylvia Pankhurst in her campaign against the atrocities committed by the Italians in their occupation of Abyssinia in 1935–6 where they bombed and gassed civilians. 'People stood by while Ethiopia was vanquished', she complained. 'This is Africa, this is not a white-man's country, these are primitives, their customs are barbarous'.9 Pankhurst felt that racism, extending across the entire political spectrum, made it easy for politicians, who wanted to keep on the right side of Mussolini, to ignore the deaths of Africans; for a Briton born in the 1880s, like Pankhurst, to be free from racial bias was extremely unusual.

Yet despite their racist attitudes, the British regarded themselves, with some reason, as a tolerant people on account of their long tradition of allowing the immigration of anyone suffering hardship and persecution anywhere in the world. After 1918, however, they imposed more stringent restrictions upon foreigners attempting to obtain British citizenship. To some extent this was a by-product of contemporary paranoia about the supposed infiltration of subversives from Bolshevik Russia, trying to foment class war and industrial chaos at home and promote nationalist agitation in the colonies; this was widely thought to be orchestrated by a worldwide Jewish conspiracy of the sort portrayed in the notorious forgery, *The Protocols of the Elders of Zion*. Although Jews were regarded as aliens and immigrants, the British Jewish community was long-standing and well integrated by the 1920s. Over 41,000 Jews had served in the armed forces during the war. By 1929 seventeen Jews were MPs some of whom had risen to high positions: Herbert Samuel as Home Secretary and Rufus Isaacs as Viceroy of India. Prominent interwar MPs of Jewish origins, including Sir Philip Sassoon (Conservative), Leslie Hore-Belisha (Liberal) and Emmanuel Shinwell (Labour), were notable for their patriotic British attitudes.

Nonetheless, anti-Semitism remained rife at all levels of British society and in all political parties during the 1920s and 1930s. However, this prejudice was largely of a passive sort that did not involve discrimination or political controversy. In his East End community Bryan Magee found that Jews were so numerous that many Yiddish words entered into the local idiom including *spiel* (sales talk), *stumm* (don't say a word), *schmooze* (soft soap) and *schnozzle* (big nose). In retrospect he realised that half his neighbours in the 1930s had been Jewish, 'but at that time it was not a conscious thought . . . I had a rough idea what Jews were, but did not identify somebody as one unless I was told.'[10] He was told in no uncertain terms when Mosley's British Union of Fascists marched round in the later 1930s chanting 'The Yids! The Yids! We gotta get rid of the Yids!' But outside such periods relations were more relaxed especially as Magee's shopkeeping family dealt with Jews on a daily basis: 'My father would shake his head and murmur "typical Yid". It would not have occurred to anyone in his world to think he was being anti-Semitic in saying this, because it was the normal word used by everybody, including Jews themselves.'[11] At the political level expressions of anti-Semitism gained a measure of respectability from the views and policies of Sir William Joynson-Hicks who introduced restrictions designed to obstruct access to naturalisation by Jewish immigrants. The issue resurfaced following Hitler's assumption of power in 1933 and the subsequent persecution that forced Jews to escape to Britain. This led to scaremongering in the press and attacks by some MPs on the 'invasion of undesirable aliens'. At a time of high unemployment it was easy to exploit fears about immigrants taking scarce jobs. In fact, the Jewish refugees included many talented, resourceful and entrepreneurial individuals who created new businesses and extra employment. However, the National Government, now led by the highly anti-Semitic Neville Chamberlain, felt loath to give opportunities to fascist propaganda, and succumbed to *Daily Mail* warnings to the effect that 'the floodgates would be opened and we should be inundated by thousands seeking a home'. As a result Britain admitted only 60,000 Jews from Austria and Germany between 1933 and 1939, a small fraction of those fleeing Nazi persecution; it was barely sufficient to maintain the British reputation for toleration.

For most British people the Empire, in combination with the monarchy, was absolutely central to their notion of national identity between the wars. The Great War had accentuated this by demonstrating the loyalty not only of the white Dominions, who funded battleships and sent troops, but also of the tropical colonies. The Indian princes raised regiments, some 800,000 Indians fought for the Allies in France, East Africa and Mesopotamia, and the Indian revenues contributed £146 million to the war effort. The peace settlement brought the Empire to its maximum territorial extent as Britain acquired new 'mandates' in the shape of former German colonies in Africa and in the Middle East where the Ottoman Empire was carved up. Not surprisingly boyhood recollections of the period reflect this imperial climax: 'It was taken for granted that England was superior to other nations and that the British Empire was the leading force for good in the world because it provided decent government to people who were not yet developed enough to govern themselves, training them for eventual self-government when they would become democracies like us.'[12] Although this particular comment makes the enterprise appear a little philanthropic, perhaps reflecting a later rationale more than the contemporary one, it faithfully reflects one strand of thinking about Britain's imperial role at a time when the government was striving to extend political participation in India.

On the other hand, the triumphal, aggrandising side to popular imperialism was very much to the fore in the 1920s in shape of the official Empire exhibitions, celebrations and royal tours. These great occasions complemented the more routine manifestations of imperial sentiment ranging from the annual Empire Day on 24 May and 'Empire Shopping Weeks' to the mundane but ubiquitous commercial advertising of Empire food products. 'Empire was all around us', recalled John Julius Norwich, 'celebrated on our biscuit tins, chronicled on our cigarette cards, part of the fabric of our lives. We were all imperialists then.'[13] Among cigarette manufacturers Wills offered sets of 'Flags of the Empire' and 'Picturesque People of the Empire' (1926), John Player offered 'Military Uniforms of the British Empire' (1938) and Gallagher 'Scenes from the British Empire' (1936). The cinema also played a major role in bringing the idea of Empire into the lives of millions of people who would never experience it directly. Among the commercial film-makers, London Films at Denham produced *Saunders of the River*, *The Drum* and *The Four Feathers*, Gaumont-British made *Rhodes of Africa* and *King Solomon's Mines*, and even American companies marketed *Clive of India*, *King of the Khyber Rifles* and *Lives of a Bengal Lancer*. There was also a huge output of propagandist films, thinly disguised as documentaries or adventure stories, including *Wildest Africa*, *Senegal to Timbuktu*, *To Lhasa in Disguise*, *Livingstone*, *From Red Sea to Blue Nile*, *Blazing the Airways to India* and *With Cobham to the Cape*, in addition to the Empire Marketing Board's productions such as *Windmill in Barbados* (on sugar) and *Cargo from Jamaica* (on bananas). Finally, the newsreel companies, Gaumont-British, Pathé News and British Movietone News, filled their programmes with features based on royal tours entitled *50,000 Miles With the Prince of Wales* (1920) and *Across India With the Duke of Connaught* (1921).

This material was not always recognised as propagandist because it was complemented by experience at school. In his Blackburn schoolroom William Woodruff recalled seeing: 'A torn map of the world. Most of the map was painted red. "The British Empire, our Empire," Mr Manners assured us'. In Salford Robert Roberts and his schoolmates 'drew Union Jacks, hung classrooms with flags of the Dominions and gazed with pride as [we] pointed out those massed areas of red on the world map'.[14] In the past, efforts to introduce imperial themes into schools had been hampered by the general neglect of history and geography, but by the interwar period the pressure exerted by the

Royal Colonial Institute had borne fruit. Now suitable textbooks were available designed to impress on pupils the sheer extent of British territory and to emphasise the civilising effect of British rule. The message was often conveyed via the lives of heroic individuals, for, as the 1927 HMSO *Handbook for Teachers* warned, children should not be harassed by complicated issues![15] In school textbooks Africans were depicted simplistically as overgrown children, idle and undisciplined and their political systems as backward and barbarous. The books were backed up by boxes comprising samples of raw materials designed to illustrate how far the diet and clothing of British people depended upon supplies from the Empire. And although right-wing politicians, then as now, routinely denounced teachers as socialists, the indications are that they usually followed an orthodox, patriotic line, a reminder that between the wars left-wingers were by no means automatically hostile to the Empire. Robert Roberts thought his Salford teachers, who 'spelt out patriotism among us with a fervour that, with some, edged on the religious', had been influenced by their reading of Rudyard Kipling and Professor Seeley, the author of *Expansion of England*.[16] Mass Observation recorded a 27-year-old teacher who admitted that he was moved almost to tears on seeing cavalry regiments representing several parts of the Empire: 'It affected me to think that England's influence reached so far', he explained.[17]

By far the most striking imperial spectacle of the period was the British Empire Exhibition at Wembley Stadium, opened by King George V and Queen Mary on 4 April 1924. In preparation for the event the Post Office issued a special set of stamps, something rarely done at this time; newspapers published special souvenir supplements; the London and North-East Railway constructed a new station capable of handling 16,000 passengers per hour; and four new roads were built to relieve the congestion. Meanwhile the *Daily Mail* arranged with the Marconi Wireless Telegraph Company to establish wireless receiving stations in a hundred places in time for the opening – the first occasion on which a speech by the King had been broadcast.[18] 'The King's decision to make use of the extraordinary new faculty which the development of wireless has bestowed upon us is characteristic of His Majesty's mental alertness and his sympathy with his people', pronounced the *Mail* in one of its daily puffs for the exhibition.[19]

The opening ceremony was attended by 150,000 people who had

paid anything from 7s. 6d. to three guineas. On normal days a five-shilling ticket bought entry to the 220-acre grounds which included halls for Australia, New Zealand, Canada, South Africa, India, Ceylon, Burma, the West Indies, Bermuda, Sierra Leone, Malta, Hong Kong, British Guiana and Newfoundland, as well as Palaces of Industry, Engineering, Arts and Horticulture. 'It is a stock-taking of the whole resources of Empire', according to the official guide. 'The visitor will be able to inspect the Empire from end to end. From Canada it is but a stone's throw to Australia.' The material and symbolic aspects of Empire were neatly blended by a life-size model of the Prince of Wales sculpted in Canadian butter. In the Indian Pavilion, modelled on the Taj Mahal, visitors could see jungle, snake charmers, jugglers, a display of shikar trophies, a model of the Khyber Pass, silk, carpets, tea and indigo. It was run by Edward Palmer, the founder of E. P. Veeraswamy and Company Indian Food Specialists who imported spices, curry pastes and chutnies. During the summer of 1924 the exhibition arranged torchlight tattoos accompanied by 1,000 military bandsmen, and pageants telling the story of the growth of the Empire with the help of cavalry displays, a script written by Kipling and music composed by Sir Edward Elgar including *Empire March* and *Crown of India*. Among the popular songs designed to promote the Exhibition were 'Let's go to Wembley' and 'Wembling at Wembley with you'. As many imperialists regarded women as susceptible to Empire propaganda special effort was devoted to Women's Weeks when women from the Dominions talked about their lives and depicted the female settler in Australia living in a tent and cooking over a hole in the ground while waiting for her house to be built: 'she has the great outdoors as her kitchen' ventured the commentary rather hopefully. Few non-white women were portrayed except for Queen Salote of the Tonga Islands who appealed to the newspapers as 'a big handsome woman twenty-four years old'.[20]

Altogether some 17.5 million people visited Wembley in 1924, followed by a further 9.75 million in 1925, on the face of it impressive evidence of the centrality of Empire in the lives of British people. Yet on closer inspection the spectacle of Empire created an exaggerated and even misleading impression. It was, after all, largely the work of a handful of keen imperialists who were fearful that the mass of their countrymen had never really signed up for the imperial project.

Empire exhibitions had been staged since the 1850s, and it is arguable that, for all its size and magnificence, Wembley marked the decline of the phenomenon not its climax; in 1938 the Glasgow Empire Exhibition attracted notably fewer visitors than expected. Although people enjoyed the spectacles there are grounds for thinking that they saw them essentially as entertainment or escapism and that their enthusiasm for the imperial cause was rather shallow. 'I had no idea why we had such a big Empire except that it was taken for granted that we were better than anyone else', noted Woodruff. He saw Empire Day in mundane terms: 'The meaning to me was that we got free buns and a half-day off school.'[21] Although the stated objects of Wembley were to stimulate Empire trade and open new markets for home products, it had little commercial impact. Nor was the propaganda of the Empire Marketing Board very effective in persuading shoppers to buy more Empire goods between 1926 and 1932; Empire products only gained ground if the price fell sharply as in the case of butter. The truth is that as *consumers* the British had never been very patriotic or imperially minded. Even in Britain's heyday as a manufacturing power in the nineteenth century she always suffered a deficit on visible trade because foreign imports were irresistible. During the interwar period the reluctance of most Britons to buy home-manufactured motor cars – in marked contrast to the loyalty of French and American consumers to their own products – was already becoming evident.

In any case, the imperial spectacles of the 1920s coincided with the ebbing of the naive Victorian enthusiasm for Empire and the growth of a more critical and sophisticated attitude. *Punch* treated the exhibition as a joke, as did the WGTW (Won't Go To Wembley) Society. Some people complained to the Colonial Office about the portrayal of black Africans at the exhibition, arguing that they were held up to public ridicule. Similar reactions against racist stereotyping were provoked by the 'bombing' of 'Wottnotts' at the Hendon Pageant. In 1926 the Boy Scouts, who had been seen as a means of preparing youth for a military role abroad before 1914, took steps to distance themselves from imperialist organisations. Even the pro-empire films proved to be problematical, often because they were regarded as dated and boring especially among BBC staff who objected to Reith's Empire Day programmes. Films made by the Empire Marketing Board were not in great demand and often cost more to produce than they earned from bookings. In 1938 a projected film about 'The Relief of Lucknow' was scrapped for fear that it would upset relations with Indian nationalists.[22] Films such as *Rhodes of Africa* (1936), intended to promote white emigration to the Rhodesias, were acceptable as entertainment, but, in view of the impact of the slump on African economies, they were pulling against the tide.

Clearly several conflicting pressures were at work in this period; while some people appreciated Empire only in so far as they could see some economic advantage, some remained unmoved by the propaganda, and others objected to the elements of racism. To some extent popular attitudes were all of a piece with the critical reactions towards the extravagant patriotic propaganda issued during the war; now discredited, it had left many people sceptical about all official expressions of patriotism which had rarely been questioned before 1914. Among the many symptoms of irreverence in a period better known for its conventional thinking was the publication in 1930 of *1066 and All That* by W. C. Sellar and R. J. Yeatman. Ostensibly the book represented a light-hearted spoof on English history, but the authors' humour scarcely concealed their dismissal of the supposedly authoritative history textbooks of the time. *1066 and All That* was, in fact, a rather subversive little book that ridiculed Britain's imperial expansion, poked fun at her entry into war in 1914, cast doubt on Britain's self-image as top nation and frankly recognised her decline. Yet, nothing in their background indicated that the authors were unpatriotic or subversive; both had fought in the trenches; both studied at Oriel College, Oxford; and Sellar became a housemaster at Charterhouse. The popularity of such writing does not mean that people had become unpatriotic or anti-imperial, but the humorous approach to what other nations would have taken as serious subjects does underline that the British were always relatively relaxed about and detached from Empire.

On the other hand, it is easy to be too cynical about contemporary attitudes and especially about the evidence to show how apathetic and ignorant British people were about their Empire. For example, in 1925 L. S. Amery, a keen imperialist himself, overheard two ladies on the train from Wembley who were apparently under the impression that Japan was a British colony and that Californian fruit was Empire produce.[23] A 1948 survey of 2,000 people showed that three-quarters of them did not know the difference between a Crown Colony and a Dominion, 48 per cent could not actually name a colony, and a remarkable 3 per cent believed that the United States was still a British possession. However, confusion and ignorance about the details was not inconsistent with enthusiasm for the Empire. Nonetheless, it is tempting to conclude from such evidence that the British Empire was really popular only among minorities of middle- and upper-class people, either because it offered them lucrative employment or because association with it raised their social standing and sense of self-importance, whereas the working-class majority remained largely indifferent or even hostile.[24] Of course, people at different social levels sometimes expressed their imperial or patriotic sentiments in different ways or saw different attractions in Empire. But suggestions that the working class were distinctively hostile are a little perverse – there is much clearer evidence of anti-imperialism higher up the social scale – and flies in the face of contemporary views. Bryan Magee listed his four uncles – one an unemployed miner, one working with a Ceylon tea company, one in the Royal Navy and one serving in the Coldstream Guards: 'I realise now that this collection of occupations says something revealing about the British working class in the age of Empire.'[25] He was right. Between the wars working-class imperialism was volubly expressed by leading Labour politicians such as Jimmy Thomas who served as Colonial Secretary and was closely associated with the Wembley Exhibition and the Empire Marketing Board. As a workingman and trade unionist Thomas suffered no moral inhibitions about Britain's exploitation of her overseas possessions: for him their function was to supply cheap food for consumers, create markets for British exports and boost employment for British workers especially in a period of economic depression. But Thomas also embraced Empire at an emotional level, something that was inseparable from his fervent monarchism and patriotism. He considered it a matter for congratulation that manual workers such as himself and his colleagues in the two Labour governments had risen to high office under a great imperial-democratic monarchy. He expressed his 'gratitude to the constitution that enables the engine cleaner of yesterday to be the minister of today. That constitution, so broad, so wide, so democratic must be preserved, and the Empire which provides it must be maintained.'[26]

These remarks remind us that cross-class imperialism between the wars was underpinned by the political consensus on the subject. In the aftermath of the war Conservative leaders such as Stanley Baldwin felt reassured by the loyalty towards country, Empire and monarchy shown by the workers during the war when the state relied heavily upon them. They concluded that it would be a mistake to revert to the Victorian-Edwardian pattern, a period of bitter controversy between Conservatives and Liberals over imperial and Irish issues. In any case this was unnecessary. For although the Labour Party included some critics of Empire, it was not, as a whole, anti-imperialist. This perception enabled the two parties to pursue a bipartisan approach during the 1920s and 1930s based on the idea of consolidating the Empire in the medium term by making judicious concessions to nationalist demands in Egypt and India, and by refurbishing the imperial mission in Africa by a constructive programme to develop underused resources. This consensus policy reached its climax under the National Government after 1931 when Baldwin and Ramsay MacDonald collaborated to grant a major extension of self-government to India. The passage of that reform underlined that the controversy over Empire was not between the parties but *within* them, notably within the Conservative ranks. Yet this process of gradual reform helps to explain how, despite the superficial enthusiasm engendered by the great imperial celebrations, the country was steadily moving away from the traditional notions of Empire towards the idea of a Commonwealth of self-governing states that we associate more with the post-1945 era. The very use of the term Commonwealth between the wars helped to remove some of the controversy from the whole issue by detaching it from associations with military power and rule over alien peoples. Those Liberals and socialists who felt embarrassed by British imperial rule took the view that Empire was an accomplished fact, that Africans and Asians were better ruled by the British than by the alternative powers, and that this was justified, for the time being, if we prepared them for democratic self-government.

The combination of this political consensus with the spectacular public celebrations of Empire has obscured the extent to which the interwar period marked the start of a gradual *disengagement* from Empire by the British people. Although Britain had possessed extensive territories since the eighteenth century, involvement in imperial expansion had been the concern of a small elite until the late Victorian period. Even then, governments felt loath to accept the risks and financial burdens entailed in acquiring new territories, preferring to leave it to private companies for as long as possible; privately many politicians endorsed Disraeli's famous dismissal of colonies as 'millstones around our neck'. The bottom line was money and taxation. The British Empire had always been run on the cheap, using few British soldiers, relying on cheap native troops instead, and trying to maximise the benefits in terms of trade while minimising the drawbacks in terms of taxation.

After 1918 this traditional calculation was accentuated because governments were anxious to reduce income tax, and to run down the army, hence the reliance on 'policing' rebellious territories by bombing them instead of putting in expensive ground troops. In India governments traditionally paid for all troops, both British and Indian, even when used outside India, from the Indian revenues not from the British Exchequer, but this had ceased to be acceptable to Indian opinion. In 1922 the government of India was exempted from the costs of Indian troops used as garrisons abroad (except in Aden, Colombo and the Malay States). This was a crucial step away from the old imperial system. India was ceasing to be a military asset, indeed, she was about to become a huge liability as the Second World War was to show. Yet India was only part of a wider strategic problem. Before 1914 Britain had dealt with her responsibilities in the Far East by withdrawing battleships and signing an alliance with Japan in 1902 in the hope that a rising Japan would act as a counter to the Russian threat. However, after the war the Anglo-Japanese Alliance was allowed to lapse and nothing effective put in its place. The belated decision to build up the base at Singapore was never properly implemented, leaving the whole Empire vulnerable – with dire consequences in the Second World War. This long-term reluctance to make real sacrifices for Empire was not consistent with the stance adopted by the British as a dedicated imperial people; in effect, they enjoyed having a large Empire but were never prepared to treat it as a priority.

In addition, British policy was inevitably handicapped by lack of co-operation from the colonies themselves. Ever since the late Victorian period enthusiasts had argued that Britain ought to turn her Empire into a more formal federation both for defence and for commercial purposes. However, between the wars it became a looser system largely because of the ambitions of the white Dominions for separation from the mother country. Canada, Australia and New Zealand had no desire to be merely suppliers of food and raw materials for Britain; they wanted to develop their own manufacturing industry not simply buy from Britain. And, despite their loyalty during the war and their acceptance of the King as head of state, they were no longer willing to pool their naval and military resources with Britain; they aspired to be fully self-governing states. They signified this by demanding their own representation at Versailles and in the League of Nations and by refusing to support Britain in 1922 when she appeared to be on the brink of a war with Turkey. War had, in fact, stimulated colonial nationalism especially among Australians, angry about the casualties suffered by their troops through the incompetence of British generals in the Gallipoli campaign. In South Africa, where the pro-British General Smuts was voted out of office, the country moved away from the British sphere. In 1926 Canada, Australia and New Zealand were defined as Dominions, enjoying self-government in external as well as internal affairs, though united by 'a common allegiance to the Crown'; these changes were embodied in the Statute of Westminster in 1931 effectively putting an end to hopes of an imperial federation. In this way Empire was being transformed into a Commonwealth of self-governing states from which the non-white territories could not be excluded in the long run.

Meanwhile the economic rationale for Empire was also being undermined. Admittedly, by 1939 trade with the Empire still formed forty-one per cent of Britain's total as a result of strenuous efforts to strengthen it. But in the crucial case of India the balance of advantage had already shifted. During the war Britain had reduced her output of cotton textiles and the gap had been filled by extra production in Japan, America and India. As India had her own raw cotton, cheap labour and a railway system she could now develop mass production textile mills. During the depression this process continued and spread to other sectors of the economy. For example, imports of jute products from Bengal to Britain increased fourfold between the 1920s and 1930s causing unemployment in the Dundee area. Moreover, during the 1920s the nationalist campaigns to boycott imported cloth made it impossible for the British to suppress the local industry in order to recover lost markets for the manufacturers of Lancashire and

Yorkshire. In effect, India was already on the road to self-sufficiency in several sectors of her economy. The trend was accelerated when Britain gave up her control of tariff policy which had traditionally been used to benefit her own manufacturers. By 1921 India levied an eleven per cent duty on imports, by 1922 fifteen per cent and by 1931 twenty-five per cent. This was complemented by London's loss of control over the exchange rate which began during the war. After a struggle during the 1920s the government of India used the financial crisis of 1931 to devalue the rupee, stimulating exports and pleasing nationalists in the process. As a result of these changes Britain's traditional surplus on visible trade with India had turned into a deficit by the 1930s.

Of course, India remained an important source for British investment; but as the right-wing critics complained, capitalism was not patriotic. Major British companies including ICI, Unilever and Dunlop, were keen to do business in India by investing in subsidiaries. Consequently they shared with Indian manufacturers a common interest in an independent tariff policy and a low exchange rate. They believed that as nationalist leaders like Nehru wanted to develop a sophisticated modern industry, an independent India held no real threat for them.

Some imperialists believed they had an answer to the diminishing economic value of India and the disengagement of the Dominions. L. S. Amery, who served as Colonial Secretary from 1924 to 1929, was an ardent imperialist who felt Britain would be better advised to focus on Africa where she had never exploited the economic potential and where nationalism represented, as yet, only a distant threat. However, lack of communications and a sparse population made for poor markets there until Britain invested in an infrastructure and filled the vast empty spaces. The Colonial Development Act of 1929 was intended to remedy this, but it made little impact partly because the Chancellor, the supposedly imperialist Winston Churchill, was reluctant to divert funds to Africa. The Empire Settlement Act of the same year offered incentives for white emigrants to Kenya, the Rhodesias and Nyasaland. However, during the 1920s and 1930s total emigration from Britain ran well below the pre-1914 levels, despite domestic unemployment, and many emigrants went to America not the Empire. The explanation is partly that the economic depression, and in particular the collapse of agricultural prices, affected the colonies just as badly as Britain, so that those who ventured into Africa to start plantations often made no money or even went bankrupt. As a result, after 1930 more people were *returning* to Britain from the colonies than were leaving for them.

These failures tell us a good deal about British attitudes towards Empire between the wars. At a political level the inability of Conservative governments to rejuvenate the economic rationale meant that no one was likely to do so. Among the population generally it seems that, despite enthusiasm for imperial celebrations, the prolonged depression had the effect of making them turn inwards rather than venturing abroad to seek their fortunes.

In addition to the economic complications there is evidence of a growing detachment between domestic and colonial society. Newcomers to British India, for example, often felt they had been transported back into the Victorian era. They noticed the rather formal lifestyle, dominated by hordes of servants and following strict routines involving riding before breakfast, paying morning calls, resting and letter-writing in the afternoon, and the formal dress at dinner parties where everyone was seated in strict order of precedence. For middle-class women, now acquiring an education and careers, the colonies seemed to have been left behind. Only the landed and aristocratic émigrés, fleeing to the White Highlands of Kenya where they could live cheaply and recreate a feudal lifestyle, felt comfortable.

At the sharp end of imperial change were the men of the Indian Civil Service and the Colonial Service whose livelihoods depended on Empire. The ICS offered prestigious and well-paid employment to around 1,300 men educated at schools such as Winchester and Haileybury who formed the famous 'steel frame' that administered the British Raj. Recruitment of Indians into this elite had been possible since the 1860s, but it was not until the First World War, when a large proportion of British men left for Europe, that the composition changed significantly. During the 1920s and 1930s British applications to the service fell steadily. This was partly because instalments of reform in 1919 and 1935 forced the officers to share power with elected Indian authorities, while the inability of the British to control nationalist agitations steadily undermined their morale. By the later 1930s no one entering the ICS could feel confident of serving out his career in the service. The growing redundancy of the British was obvious in the changing composition of the ICS; whereas in 1919 it included 78 Indians to 1,177 Britons, by 1939 there were 540 Indians to 759 Britons.

Less obvious, but of huge psychological significance, was a gradual shift in the attitudes among those who did serve in India between the wars. Increasingly they were men who recognised the moral challenge posed by the national movement and sympathised with Indian aspirations to self-government. Meanwhile a more subtle challenge to traditional British assumptions was presented by some of the novels of the period, notably E. M. Forster's *A Passage to India* (1924) and George Orwell's *Burmese Days* (1934). Both books focussed on the idea of friendship between Britons and Indians, exposing the insincerity of official British efforts to treat Indians without arrogance and racial prejudice. Today it is difficult to appreciate how subversive *A Passage to India* was in 1924. Ten years later Orwell's novel, coming from a man who had himself served in the Burmese police, was a shocking exposé of the British pretensions as a master race, depicting them as morally flawed, even degenerate, and their whole system as based on a willingness to turn a blind eye to corruption.

This disparagement of imperialism might have been dismissed merely as the work of an intellectual elite had it not been complemented by the first traumatic steps away from imperial control. The ending of the Union with Ireland in 1921, and the grant of virtual self-government to Egypt in 1922 were denounced as evidence that Britain's resolve was weakening and as the first steps to the disintegration of the Empire. In India, where Britain's rule had always rested on a measure of consent, rather than on physical force, it seemed increasingly improbable that she could retain control of such a vast and distant territory; nationalists liked to say that if all Indians made water together the British would be washed into the sea! By 1919 Britain had committed herself to democratic reforms designed to lead the country to self-government, albeit at a distant and unspecified point. In the medium term this policy was calculated to win the continued co-operation of the moderate nationalists. But it was greatly complicated by Gandhi's adoption of the Non-co-operation strategy in the early 1920s which mobilised millions of Indians of all classes and religions, and by the blunder committed by General Dyer in 1919 when his troops fired on a peaceful crowd in Amritsar, killing nearly 400 people in the process. This was not typical of British methods; but although Dyer was relieved of his command his action gave the moral high ground to the nationalists.

In fact, although British politicians liked to dismiss Gandhi as a charlatan, Lord Irwin, who was Viceroy from 1926 to 1931, recognised him as a moral leader, not a mere politician, and appreciated his determination to keep his movement non-violent as far as possible. In this Irwin was correct, for without Gandhi the campaign would surely have been a far bloodier affair. It was in this spirit that the Viceroy offered Gandhi Dominion status in a bid to avoid the civil disobedience campaigns in 1930, conducted negotiations with him while he was in gaol, and finally released him – to the fury of the British community. As a result, Gandhi agreed to suspend civil disobedience and come to London to participate in the Round Table Conference that was trying to settle the next stage of reforms. Although the visit achieved little in a formal sense, it threw interesting light on British attitudes at this crucial stage in the dismantling of the Raj. On arrival Gandhi was besieged by journalists who found it hard to see the fragile and eccentric little man as a leader capable of overthrowing the Raj. 'And what do you think of Western civilisation, Mr Gandhi?' he was asked. 'I think it would be a very good idea,' he replied. In effect Gandhi was now being treated as the real spokesman for India, much to the irritation of British officials. When invited to Buckingham Palace with the other delegates he duly appeared dressed in his usual simple cotton dhoti. Was this an adequate dress for taking tea with the King-Emperor? he was asked. 'The King was wearing enough for both of us,' Gandhi replied.

But the most extraordinary part of his visit was his trip to Lancashire during September 1931. It was characteristic of Gandhi to confront the textile towns including Blackburn, Darwen, Bolton and Clitheroe, where industry was badly affected by the boycotts of British cloth that he had been orchestrating in India. In Blackburn William Woodruff reported people saying: 'that fellow is costing England half a million jobs'; but he admitted that on arrival he was warmly greeted and received by the mayor.[27] Gandhi argued that Indians were boycotting all imports, not just those from Britain, because they wanted to become self-sufficient; he accepted that this contributed to the slump in Britain, though he pointed out that the British industry was suffering from Japanese competition too.[28] According to the secretary of the

Bolton Weavers Association 'a few of our hard-headed folks considered him to be " a bit of a fraud", though [I] felt that a saint had
mingled for a brief moment in time'. At Darwen 20,000 sympathetic
workers gave him a tremendous reception: 'the enthusiasm with
which Mr Gandhi was received whenever he appeared in public is
somewhat extraordinary and bears eloquent testimony to the large-
heartedness of Lancashire workers', observed the *Cotton Factory
Times*.[29] Gandhi praised the workers for putting up with their
economic distress bravely, but frankly reminded them that Indian
workers were much worse off; he admitted that he 'never expected
such courteous treatment'.[30]

While it would be naive to conclude from such accounts that
Gandhi was universally popular, he was received by mayors and
deputations of employers and workers more as though he was a
foreign dignitary than as the leading enemy of the British Empire. This
was hardly the response of a country determined to hang on to Empire
at all costs. Not surprisingly, the National Government pressed ahead
with reforms in the face of bitter resistance led by Churchill. The 1935
Act expanded the Indian electorate from five million to thirty million
voters and gave power into the hands of eleven elected assemblies in
the regions. But for the failure of the princes to ratify the scheme it
would also have created a new all-India central government. Although
Britain had not actually spelt out a timetable for independence, this
was a major step towards it. It meant that during the last years of peace
Indians were to a considerable extent governing and administering
their own country. In this sense the key moral-political battle over the
future of the Empire had already been fought – and lost – before the
outbreak of the Second World War. Although the war helped to
determine the eventual timing of independence, it did not affect the
issue fundamentally. The political will to retain India had gone. After
1945 only a handful of marginal figures in the League of Empire
Loyalists were prepared to try to maintain the Raj. This is not to deny
that many British people continued to derive much of their sense of
national pride and purpose from the Empire during the 1930s; but by
1939 they had effectively been left behind by most of their leaders who
had come to recognise the moral claims of Asians and Africans to
control their own destiny and increasingly looked for ways of
managing Britain's retreat from Empire.

20

'No longer part of England': Regions and Nations in Interwar Britain

On completing their social history, *The Long Weekend*, in 1939, Robert Graves and Alan Hodge confessed that they had given disproportionate attention to London and neglected the rest of the country. 'We have no prejudice in favour of London', they protested, 'but this could not be helped; the tendency was for things either to happen first in London or to be first noted there.'[1] Graves and Hodge were, of course, products of their time. Though well educated and travelled, they were not well informed about the country in which they lived, particularly about the half of the population living north of the River Trent; they used 'England' and 'Britain' casually as interchangeable terms, overlooking England's status as merely one of the four nationalities of which Britain consisted; and, like their contemporaries, they referred to England when they meant London and the Home Counties, disregarding the regions with their different economies, politics, cultures, traditions and accents.

Today it is easier to recognise that Britain, although formally a unitary state, is in reality a multinational country. Yet the explanations for what looks like cultural imperialism are readily apparent. London dominated the country to a much greater extent than the capital cities of other Western countries, and in some ways this imbalance actually increased between the wars. The population of London and the South-East rose sharply, businesses were transferring their headquarters to London and concentrating new factories in the Home Counties, the press was becoming more national than provincial, and the BBC was dominated by a metropolitan mentality that saw little virtue in the provinces. Like Graves and Hodge, most southerners assumed that anything sophisticated, fashionable or interesting was to be found in or around London. 'Must try to remember that Social Success is seldom the portion of those who habitually live in the provinces', wrote E. M. Delafield, a resident of Devon who went in fear of meeting smartly dressed society ladies in London.[2] Not that regional prejudice and condescension was a monopoly of the South. In his famous book, *English Journey* (1934), the professional Yorkshireman, J. B. Priestley, scattered disparaging remarks upon every northern area he visited. On Tyneside he conceded 'the people were not so bad once you got to know them, though even to a Yorkshire lad they appeared uncouth. And I disliked – and I still do – their accent . . . it sounds a most barbarous, monotonous and irritating twang.'[3]

Metropolitan insularity was also the result of history and geography. Britain was such an old-established country that few people were really aware of the Union between England, Wales and Scotland, and even the Union with Ireland, which survived until 1921, began to fade from popular consciousness during the interwar years. The fact that Britain was territorially compact, blessed with good communications and enjoyed a highly centralised system of government seemed to make regional identity implausible or insignificant. In any case, in the absence of formal boundaries many of Britain's regions proved difficult to define on the map. Most of the inhabitants of the 'Home Counties', 'East Anglia', 'Wessex' and the 'Midlands' would have struggled to explain their regional identity. Wessex enjoyed some recognition as the Anglo-Saxon kingdom of Wessex, as Thomas Hardy's Wessex and even as an administrative unit of the gas and electricity boards; but it remained territorially indistinct, possessed no centre or capital and had no obvious common identity or rationale.

On the other hand, the further away from London, the greater the sense of regional identity. Despite being incorporated into the English state for 1,000 years, many Cornish people refused to describe themselves as 'English' during the 1920s and 1930s. Defined by the sea on two sides and the River Tamar on the east, Cornwall had some claim to be part of a group of Celtic nations along with Wales, Ireland and Brittany. Since the early nineteenth century the growth of Wesleyan Methodism had helped to make the region culturally distinct. Economic development, especially copper and tin mining, had generated wealth and pride in being Cornish. On the other hand, while the creation of an elected county council in 1889 gave Cornwall formal political status, it also satisfied what limited desire existed for recognition and devolution.

However, by the 1920s Cornwall had experienced half a century of economic decline and mass emigration which stoked up resentment towards London and the English establishment. The historian, A. L. Rowse, who was very aware of his Cornish accent, always asserted that he was a Celt not an Anglo-Saxon. Cornish anti-metropolitanism manifested itself in a tendency to continue voting for the Liberal Party, which won all the county's seats in 1929, at a time when it was generally in decline. Despite this, most Cornishmen were reluctant to claim parity with Scotland or Wales and between the wars Cornish nationalism expressed itself less in political forms than in cultural activity such as enthusiasm for rugby. However, the period saw a Celtic revival led by the Federation of Old Cornwall Societies which was formed in 1925 with the aim of rejuvenating the Cornish language, publishing a grammar and dictionary, preserving the old Cornish Miracle Plays, saving the county's antiquities and promoting traditional sports such as hurling and wrestling. In 1932 a new pressure group, Land and Language, began to mobilise wider popular support for these causes. But the strength of Liberalism in the county probably delayed the emergence of a nationalist party, Mebyon Kernow, until 1951.[4] Its supporters regarded themselves less as nationalists than as regionalists who sought to devolve more decision-making to Cornwall.

The North of England represented a region equally distinctive in terms of culture, economics, attitudes and territory: the seven counties of Cumberland, Westmorland, Northumberland, Durham, Yorkshire, Lancashire and Cheshire. In the 1920s this area contained half Britain's coal mines, ninety per cent of textile output and seventy-five per cent of steelworkers. However, the North really comprised several distinct regions, notably Yorkshire, Lancashire and the North-East (comprising Northumberland, Tyneside and Durham). Since the Victorian period Yorkshire, with its four million people and extensive territory, had enjoyed a pronounced regional character and its inhabitants took satisfaction in their reputation for being thrifty, blunt, phlegmatic, egalitarian, homely – and superior at cricket. They cheerfully adopted the term 'Tykes', originally a disparaging name for dogs. The

Yorkshire self-image was also promoted by J. B. Priestley, who contrasted his compatriots with neighbouring Lancastrians whom he considered to be addicted to throwing their money around on seaside holidays. This, Priestley insisted, was not a Yorkshire habit: 'we were quieter, less sociable, and less given to pleasure and more self-sufficient and more conceited, I think, than the people at the softer side of the Pennines'.[5]

Geography and history also helped to make North-East England a coherent and distinctive region, defined by the North Sea to the east, the Scottish Border to the north and the sparsely populated, upland areas to the west and south which had effectively isolated it for centuries from the centre of British life. Its population enjoyed a long-standing rivalry with London in sport, originating in rowing competitions in the nineteenth century and football matches in the twentieth. Moreover, the region's role in the Industrial Revolution had fostered pride in its achievements as a producer of coal, ships and engineering, and created an impressive and undisputed regional capital at Newcastle. The region suffered badly in the aftermath of the Great War as its export markets collapsed; by 1932, for example, 37.4 per cent of the North-East labour force was unemployed compared with 22.7 per cent nationally. Between 1921 and 1931 the region experienced an outward migration of 200,000, nearly 8 per cent of its population. The resulting resentment towards London underlined the continuing remoteness and isolation of the region; the marches by unemployed workers for which it became famous were symptomatic of a demand to be heard by the country's decision-makers. Significantly, none of the North-East's eminent public figures gave effective political leadership to the region between the wars. The Duke of Northumberland moved to the extreme right; the coal-owner, Lord Londonderry, had no local influence; Sir Anthony Eden's family sold up their Durham estates. Although Ramsay MacDonald represented a County Durham seat in 1929 his failure to tackle unemployment and his rejection by the voters in 1935 cut him off completely. Dominated by the Labour Party during the 1920s, County Durham developed a highly parochial form of politics. The party's local organisations were focussed on their immediate communities and the distribution of patronage within the county. This, however, made for a rather inward-looking pattern of politics with the result that the region failed to develop the political leadership that might have articulated its distinctive concerns.

The case of the North-East is a reminder of a further element in the explanation for metropolitan attitudes towards the provinces. When the English looked at the regions they recognised them primarily in terms of social class. This perspective coloured several books ostensibly about the English regions written by contemporaries. Katharine Chorley's *Manchester Made Them* (1950) focussed entirely on the role of the upper middle class before and after the Great War. When visiting the North-East Priestley observed: 'There is no escape anywhere in Jarrow from its prevailing misery, for it is entirely a working-class town.' A more recent study, *Geordies: Roots of Regionalism* (1992), also defined the region in terms of its organised working class: 'Even today, a middle-class Geordie sounds wrong', commented one of the authors.[6]

To interwar observers the prevalence of heavy industry in the North made it appear to be dominated by the manual workers. This had further consequences in the shape of a heavily unionised labour force; the proportion of workingmen who belonged to unions was ten times as high in Northumberland and Durham as in South-East England. Conversely, half of all middle-class people in Britain lived in London and the South-East, though the region comprised only a fifth of the population. Consequently regions were seen to develop a pronounced class character, which was often replicated on a very local scale. In his home in the Potteries, for example, Paul Johnson noticed that 'North Staffs despised South Staffs – it was "stuck up". The Potteries despised the rest of North Staffs as "idle". Potteries people especially disliked Newcastle under Lyme, which was older, had no pot-banks and "did nothing" '.[7] Class, however, was far from being a complete explanation for regionalism. In escaping from his Lancashire home to London's East End in 1933 William Woodruff was struck by the cultural differences between the two working-class communities in which he lived. 'I'd been brought up with a strict code of ethics; revival Methodism had drummed into us the difference between right and wrong. In Blackburn the Sabbath was a day of prayer – the trains did not run, and shops and cinemas were closed; even whistling was frowned upon.' He was therefore shocked by the relatively immoral and irreligious attitudes of his neighbours in The Cut in Stratford. The richest resident was Pearly Lilly, 'an attractive blonde, who by plying her profession as a "bride" among the nobs of the West End, earned more in a night than any of us earned in a week'. Surprisingly, Pearly Lilly 'was not ostracised as she would have been in the street where I was born', perhaps because of local respect for money regardless of how it was earned.[8]

Between the wars regional consciousness was certainly affected by the social changes taking place. During the Victorian period the Industrial Revolution had had the effect of enhancing a sense of identity and pride in the provinces, especially in the leading manufacturing centres. One Edwardian cotton manufacturer boasted that Oldham had more spindles than the rest of the world put together: 'If they had the climate and the men and the spindles ... foreigners could never find the brains Lancashire cotton men have for the job. We've been making all the world's cotton cloth that matters for more years than I can tell and we always shall.'[9] In this way the manufacturing regions had acquired a reputation for progress and dynamism which often led them to regard London as backward; the fact that central government had little involvement in social policy, or was simply ineffective, left the major provincial towns to take their own initiatives, to cultivate municipal enterprise and develop civic pride. Surprisingly, in view of the improvements in road and rail communications in the nineteenth and twentieth centuries, most people remained largely ignorant about other parts of the country. On his visits to his mother's relations in Newcastle in the 1930s, Bryan Magee was 'much struck by the way everybody we met quizzed us about London as if that were a strange place'. Priestley noticed that large Victorian towns such as his native Bradford acquired a 'regional self-sufficiency . . . not defying London but genuinely indifferent to it . . . not even thinking of ourselves as being provincial'.[10] Despite its railway connections Bradford remained comparatively isolated and was big enough to generate local traditions and its own social and political life. As a result, during the pre-1914 era Britain had developed a regional pattern comparable to that of France or the United States in which politicians used their local and regional base to promote their ambitions on the national stage. The foremost example was Lancashire where the national political agenda had been changed by a local pressure group, the Anti-Corn Law League, in the 1840s. Throughout the period up to 1914 Manchester regarded itself as the cockpit of British politics, generating both the problems and the solutions to industrial society, and attracting ambitious men to represent its constituencies.

However, by the 1920s this pattern was in decline. Central governments increasingly disliked the results of local democracy and intervened to restrict its activities. Most leading politicians either neglected their local roots or did their best to escape them. Lloyd George was fast losing what influence he had even in North Wales, while Ramsay MacDonald cultivated London and never attempted to represent a Scottish seat. In 1918 Arthur Henderson abandoned his County Durham constituency, hoping to find something more convenient for London. In Birmingham, the Chamberlain family had enjoyed a regional political base since the 1870s, but by 1929 the position of Neville and Austen Chamberlain was being seriously eroded though it was not wholly destroyed until 1945. The only obvious exception to this trend was Herbert Morrison; as the architect of the Labour Party's capture of the London County Council in 1934, Morrison was the one major figure who rose to national prominence on the strength of his local influence and achievements.

But the post-war demise of regional influence was more than political. In her account of Manchester Katharine Chorley painted a compelling picture of a city she believed had suffered from the exodus of prosperous middle-class citizens for the leafy parts of Cheshire, leaving behind a vacuum in the cultural life of the city. Priestley saw something similar in the migration from Bradford to Ilkley and Harrogate.[11] According to Chorley, when Manchester lost its merchant princes it became deprived of the natural leaders and patrons who had founded Owen's College, the Whitworth Art Gallery and the John Rylands Library, and sustained a host of charities, the Chamber of Commerce, three theatres and the City Council.[12] Yet this was an exaggerated view, for Manchester, with its Halle Orchestra and packed concerts at the Free Trade Hall, continued to enjoy a flourishing cultural life.

Perhaps the most significant symptom of regional decline lay in the fluctuating fortunes of the provincial press. In Victorian times many provincial towns boasted their own morning and evening newspapers; the provincial press enjoyed a higher circulation than the national press; and papers like the *Yorkshire Post*, *Manchester Guardian* and *Western Morning News* gave a regional dimension to public debate. But following the foundation of the *Daily Mail* in 1896 the national newspapers began to adopt a common formula based on personalities, stunts, competitions, London society and trivia which gradually absorbed the readership of the older, more sober papers. By 1921 forty-one provincial morning dailies still survived but their number fell to twenty-five by 1939. The *Manchester Guardian* alone made the transition from provincial to national newspaper though it dropped 'Manchester' from its title in 1959.

Admittedly, there were limits to the standardisation imposed by commercial pressures. For many ordinary people their sense of regional identity continued to be reinforced by a multitude of local accents and dialects. 'Anyone who ventures south of the Trent,' observed the Leeds playwright, Alan Bennett, 'is likely to catch an incurable disease of the vowels.' Because a northern accent was widely believed to be a handicap in many walks of life during the 1920s and 1930s it was discarded as soon as possible. The chief perpetrator of linguistic imperialism between the wars was the BBC and its Director General, Sir John Reith (1922–38). Reith appointed a special Committee on Spoken English, partly as a means of checking the Americanisation of the language, and partly with a view to committing his broadcasters to 'Standard English' or the educated speech of southern England. By sticking to this the BBC believed its staff 'may broadcast without fear of adverse intelligent criticism'. In fact, they used the speech of a small minority. 'Standard English is like standard anything else,' snapped J. B. Priestley, 'poor tasteless stuff.'[13] Despite this Priestley was as prejudiced about accents as most Englishmen. Not content with disparaging the Geordie accent, he described Scouse as 'a thick, adenoidy, cold-in-the-head accent, very unpleasant to hear'.[14]

Although the BBC notoriously discriminated against regional accents, the career of Wilfred Pickles suggests that prejudice could be overcome. Born in Halifax, Pickles indulged in amateur dramatics and, significantly, took elocution lessons. He made his broadcasting debut on the BBC's *Children's Hour* in 1927 and became a regional announcer in Manchester in 1938. This, however, was as far as Wilfred Pickles would have advanced but for the Second World War. In 1941 the Minister for Information, Brendan Bracken, summoned him to London to read the news, calculating that Nazi propagandists would find it impossible to impersonate his Yorkshire accent convincingly!

Pickles's cheery 'good neet' to his listeners doubtless confused Berlin as much as it did the London Establishment. However, as a national broadcaster with a northern accent he was very much the exception for years to come.

On the other hand, as the BBC was far from enjoying a monopoly in popular entertainment its influence was limited; and the interwar public was familiar with a range of performers including Harry Lauder, Gracie Fields, Kathleen Ferrier and George Formby for whom Standard English was a foreign language. Gracie Fields, known as the 'Lancashire Britannia', and George Formby, whose catchphrase was 'Turned out nice again', were thought to epitomise the optimism and fatalism of the northern working class in the face of the economic depression. In this sense they managed to blend Lancashire pride with national loyalties. Even Priestley reluctantly admitted that 'Lancashire' had become almost the official accent of music-hall humour, though he professed to regard it as 'something of a mystery'. He even claimed to detect a grimly ironic brand of Lancastrian humour as indicated by the following after-dinner joke: after the death of her husband the wife of a Blackburn weaver refused to have him buried, opting for cremation instead. 'But whatever will yer do wi' th'ashes?' her neighbour enquired. 'Ah'm going to 'ave 'em put into an egg timer,' she explained. 'The 'owd devil wouldn't ever work when 'e were alive, so 'e can start doing a bit now 'e's dead.'[15]

For whatever reason attempts at standardisation by the BBC and by schoolteachers, who often regarded local pronunciation as uncouth, largely failed, leaving provincial accents and local dialects as unmistakable evidence of regional and class distinctions. So much so that they sometimes created barriers to communication. On his visits to Newcastle one young East Ender professed himself unable to understand the locals: 'they spoke with such thick Geordie accents'. And his GP, Dr McCurry, 'sometimes had to repeat himself before I understood. My parents said this was called a Scottish accent.'[16] Moreover, even within a small area localised dialects remained strong. Although southerners labelled all speech from Tyneside, Sunderland and rural Northumberland 'Geordie', the native speakers in these areas used distinct accents. Andrew Purves grew up in Roxburgh in the Scottish Borders but his family came from the adjacent county, East Lothian. As a result he found that 'we came out with words and phrases in the Lothian dialects which our playmates were not slow to notice and ridicule . . . we said *barn, star, haill, hame* whereas our mates said *bern, sterr, hyill* and *hyim*; these and many other examples such as *witter* for *water* and the *pant* for the *pump*, we had perforce to adapt in order to conform.'[17] As Purves suggests, many people modified their original dialect when they moved home, and some tried to accelerate the process in an attempt to win acceptance. As a young working-class northerner Amy Johnson felt a little out of place in the upper-class world of aviation, and, according to one contemporary, 'she tried to disguise that Yorkshire accent but could never quite manage it, poor lass'.[18] A 1930 recording of Amy Johnson certainly suggests that she had recently had elocution lessons, but when she pronounced 'right', 'down' or 'shout' her flat Yorkshire vowels asserted themselves. Not that accents were automatically a handicap. Ramsay MacDonald's soft, musical Highland Scots charmed his aristocratic acquaintances and his audiences. On the whole, however, the accents of experienced public speakers usually merged into a common, neutral tone regardless of their origins. Lloyd George had practically lost his Welsh accent before 1914; Christabel Pankhurst retained only slight traces of Manchester; and Neville Chamberlain betrayed no sign of the Brummagem dialect. Nor did either George V or Edward VIII speak BBC English; in fact, the only variation in the Prince of Wales's speech was his slight but perceptible Cockney twang which he was thought to have picked up from his nurse.

Since late Victorian times the emergence of mass spectator sport had fostered a sense of pride in urban communities and, more generally, promoted the rivalry between North and South; in particular football, cricket and rugby crystallised the cultural differences of the two regions. The rivalry loomed large in professional football which was dominated by the northern and Midland clubs at least up to the 1920s; the seven northern counties produced half of the teams in the Football League and were invariably represented in Cup Finals. On a visit to London in 1910 one Barnsley fan complained: 'They don't know English i' London an' stare at us like we was polecats . . . Why can't they be neighbourly?'[19] Cricket was an especially formative force in the identity of Yorkshire whose team won the championship every year from 1922 to 1925 and seven times during the 1930s. Its popularity seems surprising in that matches were mostly played during working hours before modest crowds of 4,000–5,000 on weekdays, and by 1939 the county club had only 5,500 members. However, the press helped to maintain a sense of involvement among the supporters. In 1938, when Yorkshire's Len Hutton broke the record for the highest Test score by getting 364 runs against Australia, the church bells in his native Pudsey were rung 364 times and the mayor despatched a telegram for every 50 he knotched up.[20] Yet, although cricket sharpened the rivalry between Yorkshire and Lancashire, it also united them against the South. When Yorkshire won the championship in 1924 the Lancashire captain reportedly confessed: 'I'm real glad a rose won it. Red or white, it doesn't matter.'[21] Above all, the North-South divide was reflected in rugby league, known as 'northern union' until 1922. Rugby league originated in a breakaway in 1895 caused by a controversy over whether working-class players should be paid to compensate them for time lost by playing in and travelling to matches. It remained a markedly regional game based in Lancashire, Cumberland, West Yorkshire and Humberside, and a defiant expression of northern rejection of the values of the South.

The clash of cultures proved divisive in cricket because of the control exercised by the sport's governing body, the very southern and upper-class MCC. Yorkshire took pride in recruiting their players from men born in the county, a rule originally adopted by Kent and Nottinghamshire but abandoned. In a sport still dogged by the amateurism of southern upper-class society, Yorkshire filled nine or ten places in its team, though not the captaincy, with professionals during the 1920s; they also invested in a pension fund and made winter payments to the players. Nor did they have any time for the dilettante southern approach to the sport: 'We doan't play cricket in Yorkshire for foon', as Wilfred Rhodes once put it.[22] But to southerners this implied that their rivals were prepared to acquiesce in a certain amount of foul play in order to win.

As a result, emotions always ran high when Yorkshire confronted archetypal southern Establishment teams such as Middlesex and Surrey. In 1924, for example, controversy errupted when some Surrey cricketers accused Yorkshire of intimidating their opponents and roughing up the pitch to assist their own bowlers. But tough tactics were defended as a reflection of the physical, masculine game played by northerners, and complaints were dismissed as typical southern jealousy. It was an article of faith that the London committees who picked the national teams were prejudiced against the North. 'All But Three Players From The South' ran an indignant headline in the *Bradford Daily Telegraph* when the 1924 Test team was announced.[23] During the 1930s regional rivalry grew worse, especially in football, when the traditional northern dominance came under threat from the rise of Arsenal. Its team won the FA Cup in 1930 and 1936 and were League Champions five times between 1931 and 1938. No fewer than seven Arsenal players were picked for the English team that played Italy in 1934.

In this context it is not surprising that the notion of a North-South divide began to take shape between the wars. However, the chief explanation for this lay in the impact of the economic depression which fell very hard on the manufacturing and extractive industries of the West and North of Britain and thereby greatly enhanced perceptions of regional distinction. During the nineteenth century these regions had taken the credit for Britain's wealth and success, leading them to see themselves as morally superior to the South and its idle landowning class. 'Without the textile industries of Lancashire and Yorkshire', wrote William Woodruff, 'there would have been less "Rule Britannia" in the world.'[24] Yet pride in manufacturing often concealed aspirations to emulate the superior cultural achievements of the South. In Stoke-on-Trent Paul Johnson's father liked to point out that the local pot-banks originated in the thirteenth century as farms built around courtyards. 'In fact pot-banks are rather like Oxford and Cambridge colleges', argued Johnson senior. 'They each started with one courtyard of buildings with a porter's lodge opening on to the street. Then, when they expanded, they built another courtyard and so on.'[25]

Inevitably interwar unemployment and the relocation of industry in the South and Midlands severely damaged provincial pride and self-confidence. Northerners became irritated by the habit of upper-class outsiders like George Orwell of portraying their region in terms of poverty and the dole. Yet it was a northerner, Priestley, who continually drew attention to the contrast between southern affluence and northern poverty, and indeed to the awfulness of life outside the Home Counties. Priestley excelled himself in the North-East where he found Durham Castle so grim that it 'makes the city look like some place in a Gothic tale of blood and terror'; as for Gateshead, he commented, 'the whole town appeared to have been carefully planned by an enemy of the human race'.[26] To some extent the value of these literary effusions is limited by the fact that the authors were professional writers striving for effect. William Woodruff, who became an accomplished writer later in life, was born into a family of cotton weavers, grew up in Blackburn, and left school in 1930 when 'half the workers of Blackburn were on the street'. Two years later he watched 'a column of ragged hunger marchers form up to begin the long trek from Blackburn to London'.[27] According to his friends the depression had created two Englands: 'They don't know what we're putting up with, and if they did they wouldn't care. Lancashire's no longer part of England.'[28] But by 1933 Woodruff, now aged sixteen, decided that the prospects were so bleak that he must try his luck in London. He got a ride from Manchester to London in a lorry for five shillings – it would have cost twenty-five shillings by train. At first it seemed an adventure for a youth who had often watched the trains chugging their way south: 'I wondered what the people of the south were really like. Were they like us?'[29] But Woodruff's parting with Blackburn proved to be emotional. 'I took leave of mother the next day without telling her what I was up to. I was afraid that there would be a scene.' Nor did he tell his father who had hoped to see his sons join him as weavers. 'I had felt for him as I watched the cotton industry collapse under his feet. More than any of us, he had believed that it would never die.'[30] Sitting miserably in the lorry Woodruff took comfort from his driver who told him: 'tha mustn't take it badly. If tha falls flat on thi face in London, tha can allus cum 'ome again wi' me.'[31] He swallowed his doubts, reasoning that he had lived through the worst years of Lancashire's history and he had no job to return to. But he considered himself lucky to have been reared there even in poverty: 'Lancashire folk might be rough and ready, but they were never servile.'[32]

If the English Establishment was, as Woodruff argued, dismissive or ignorant of the condition of Lancashire, they were far more aware of the role played by Scotland, Wales and Ireland in the British state. Yet this awareness did not extend far into British society. The majority of English people never visited Scotland, remained ignorant of Anglo-Scottish history, and thought of it largely in terms of Harry Lauder, whisky, kilts and the Loch Ness Monster.

Although reports of a monster in Loch Ness went back hundreds of years, it was in 1933 that the phenomenon burst upon the consciousness of the nation as a result of the construction of a new road and the clearing of scrub along the northern shore of the loch; this made it much easier to observe activity in the water. On 14 April that year Mr and Mrs John Mackay, driving from Inverness to Drumnadrochit, witnessed the surging mass of water caused by 'an enormous animal rolling and plunging' in the loch. This sighting was followed by many reports from sober and responsible observers, thereby triggering the modern monster phenomenon and enabling serious students to build up a reliable picture of the size, appearance and colour of the animals.

Subsequent reactions revealed a good deal about Anglo-Scottish attitudes at this time. Far from trying to publicise the monster, ministers of the Free Church of Scotland condemned visitors for going monster-watching on Sundays. The local MP, Sir Murdoch MacDonald, asked the Scottish Secretary to prevent people interfering with the monster and even contemplated introducing a bill for its preservation.[33] The minister assured him that five police constables had been stationed round Loch Ness although no one had seen it so far. Meanwhile the London media set about trivialising the whole thing. Bertram Mills Circus offered £20,000 for the capture of the monster, and in October the *Daily Mail* and the *Daily Express* dispatched special correspondents to Inverness where they employed a big-game hunter to track it down; this allowed them to run such headlines as 'LOCH NESS MONSTER HUNTED TO ITS WATERY LAIR'.

However, the real mystery was why the scientific experts stubbornly refused to take the authoritative sightings seriously. A succession of authorities from the Natural History Museum in London and elsewhere pronounced the monster to be an otter, a tree trunk and a mass of floating vegetation, and dismissed all sightings as hallucinations on the part of suggestible people. But they made no attempt to see for themselves. Their attitude was partly explicable in terms of the congenital conservatism of the scientific establishment in Britain. But it was also revealing of English attitudes towards Scotland. If the monster had surfaced in, say, the Solent, it would have been properly investigated. The great London institutions eagerly dispatched expeditions to exotic parts of the world to follow up reports about previously unknown animals and birds. But English scientists found it hard to accept that anything significant was to be found north of the border especially in a remote area like Invernesshire whose people were easily dismissed by metropolitan sophisticates as ignorant peasants, or, at best, as people attempting to boost the tourist industry. As a result, over succeeding decades foreigners took more interest in investigating the phenomenon than the British themselves.

Despite the generally dismissive attitude adopted by the English, Scots had generally been content with their subordinate position within the British state. The explanation is partly economic and partly political. Since the Union of England and Scotland in 1707 Scots had prospered by enjoying free trade with the more populous and wealthy areas to the south. They had participated fully in the Industrial Revolution and benefited from imperial expansion, so much so that Glasgow liked to style itself 'The Second City of the Empire' and the West of Scotland 'The Workshop of the British Empire'. During the 150 years before 1914 Scots had, in effect, become an integral part of the British success story. Yet this had not required a sacrifice of Scottish culture or distinctiveness. Scots retained their own legal system and their own Presbyterian Church. They took pride in an educational system that was less class-ridden than England's, traditionally produced a higher level of literacy, offered a broader secondary-school syllabus and employed a much higher proportion of graduates as teachers. Scotland also had four ancient universities that had become leading institutions of learning when their English equivalents were still largely rowing clubs. A higher proportion of Scots attended university, usually by living at home. As a result Scottish attitudes towards education were largely free from the embarrassment and hostility so common in England. When Jimmy Maxton and Jennie Lee stood for election in the 1920s their leaflets proclaimed their achievement as 'MAs', something simply not done by candidates in England at this time.

Scotland was also well integrated, politically, into the British system. Represented by seventy-two MPs and by Scottish representative peers, since 1885 the country had been administered by a minister who usually sat in Cabinet. In 1907 the Liberals had created a standing committee at Westminster to ensure proper consideration for Scottish legislation. British government appeared Anglo-Scottish in character simply because Scots frequently became prime ministers: Lord Rosebery, Campbell-Bannerman, Balfour and Bonar Law, not to mention Ramsay MacDonald who formed three administrations in 1924, 1929–31 and 1931–5. Scots also felt they had their own monarchy. Queen Victoria had worked hard to give the monarchy a Scottish dimension by her regular presence in the country and avowed love of its people. This tradition was enhanced by the marriage of Lady Elizabeth Bowes-Lyon, the daughter of the Earl of Strathmore, to the Duke of York in 1923, an event hailed by the Scottish press as a success for Scotland.

On the other hand, these links led some southern observers to take Scotland for granted. As *The Times* once put it, 'the separate nationalism of Scotland is happily in these days an anachronism'. This was a misreading. Scottish nationalism was alive and well, but closely bound up with Liberalism; it was compatible with the Union provided that Scots' interests were recognised by London. Moreover, the example of the prolonged Irish agitation for a Home Rule Parliament during the nineteenth century inevitably exercised some influence north of the border. A Scots Home Rule Association had been established in 1886, and in the Edwardian period the Young Scots Society campaigned on the issue. Bills for a Scottish Parliament were introduced on seven occasions between 1906 and 1914, winning a majority in 1913.

In the event the war proved to be a turning point in Anglo-Scottish relations. At first Unionist sentiment appeared to be robust as Scots responded enthusiastically to the call for volunteers. However, at the end of the war it transpired that no fewer than twenty-six per cent of those who enlisted had lost their lives – by comparison with only twelve per cent for the rest of the British Army. Dominated by rent strikes and industrial militancy, the war years had a radicalising and unsettling effect on Scottish society. By January 1919 Scots were gripped by the fear that the economic gains made during the war were about to disappear. This provoked a forty-hour strike called to stop the abolition of rent restrictions and wage controls and to reduce unemployment by shortening the working week. The strike culminated in a mass demonstration by 100,000 people in Glasgow's St George's Square, which was absurdly denounced by the Scottish Secretary as 'a Bolshevist rising'. Overreacting to the situation the Coalition Government mobilised 12,000 troops and 6 tanks and set up machine guns on hotel rooftops, making Glasgow feel like a city under

English occupation. Although the authorities became afraid to use the local troops from the Maryhill barracks because their loyalty was uncertain, they allowed the police to draw their batons and charge the crowds, resulting in a riot or 'Bloody Friday' as it became known. As a result, all subsequent Westminster governments, regardless of political complexion, lacked the legitimacy they had usually enjoyed in the pre-1914 era, especially among the working-class population.

Following closely on 'Bloody Friday', the economic collapse of the early 1920s created a mood of disillusionment from which, arguably, the country never really recovered. It was in these years that the traditional Scottish rationale for the Union with England began to unravel, albeit very gradually. The Scots economy proved especially vulnerable during the depression because it was narrowly concentrated on ships, textiles, steel and heavy engineering and was so well integrated into the world economy that it suffered disproportionately from the international climate; this resulted in unemployment of twenty-six per cent in coal and fifty-eight per cent in shipbuilding, for example. Industry also proved vulnerable to imperial competition. For example, exports of jute products from Bengal into Britain increased by 375 per cent between 1928 and 1936 alone, thereby undermining the economy of Dundee; as Westminster was unable to do anything about cheap imports from the Empire, indeed after 1932 it promoted them, London's policies placed a question mark over Scotland's role in the British imperial project.

Unemployment remained consistently higher north of the border throughout the interwar period, and even when recovery began around 1934 it proved to be slower in Scotland. This was partly because manufacturers now found it more attractive to locate industry in the South where incomes were higher and workers thought to be more amenable. The growth industries including motor cars, electrical goods, housing, chemicals and aircraft, were much less developed in Scotland; for example, by 1930 all the pre-1914 Scottish motor-car manufacturers had disappeared. As a result, in contrast to the rest of the country, emigration from Scotland ran at high levels, totalling 393,000 during the 1920s, mostly to Canada and the United States. During the 1930s Scotland suffered an unprecedented net loss of 40,000 people which was especially marked in the Highlands, Grampian, Tayside, Galloway and the Borders regions; among the worst-affected areas the Shetlands lost seventeen per cent and Ross and Cromarty twelve per cent of their population. Admittedly, in 1934 the government allocated £2.5 million to western Scotland under the Special Areas scheme and in 1937 subsidies were offered to reduce rent and rates for new factories; but this did little to check the strategies of businesses that were transferring their headquarters to London, leaving Scotland marginalised within the British economy. In the long run this economic decline, both absolute and relative, made a damaging impact not just on living standards but on Scottish pride and self-confidence, so much so that by the 1930s it was fashionable to regard the decline as terminal.

However, for several decades the disillusionment was slow to translate into political separatism. Hitherto Scottish identity had been reflected in the Liberal Party which went into headlong decline after 1918, leaving the strongly Unionist Conservatives as the largest single party. Initially it appeared that the Labour Party, rapidly gaining votes during the 1920s, had inherited Liberal attitudes. In the post-war years the leading 'Red Clydeside' MPs such as Jimmy Maxton, David Kirkwood and John Wheatley, upheld the Home Rule tradition, being as much anti-English as they were anti-capitalist. However, these ILP rebels soon became marginalized in a party that, under Ramsay MacDonald, aspired to run an orthodox British government rather than to undertake radical reform of the state. Increasingly the Left argued that the answer to Scotland's economic problems lay, not in devolution, but in a socialist policy applied by the experts in London. 'What purpose would there be in our getting a Scottish Parliament in Edinburgh if it has to administer an emigration system, a glorified Poor Law and a desert?' argued Tom Johnson, typical of the new breed of Labour politicians.[34] As a result Labour became as staunchly Unionist as the Conservatives, depriving those who were discontented with Scotland's existing role in Britain of a lead.

Denied a political outlet, many Scots expressed their sense of national identity through sporting achievement, especially against England. Since 1897 there had been a separate Scottish Football Association and Scottish League, and enthusiasm for local teams was enthusiastically cultivated by the Scottish press. The practice of English managers, who toured Scottish clubs to recruit talent, gave some credence to the Scottish belief in their superiority; in 1927 Newcastle

United won the title with seven Scots players while Sunderland took the championship in 1935 with eight. After 1923 an annual England versus Scotland match was played with up to 60,000 Scots invading Wembley equipped with tartan, banners and bagpipes for the game. The fact that the Scots usually lost, whereas before 1900 they had usually won, deepened the mood of gloom but went some way to bolstering the sense of national identity if only by symbolising Anglo-Scottish rivalry. Yet whether sport effectively promoted nationalism is unclear. Clashes with England were only sporadic, whereas Scots teams spent most of their time and energy on internal rivalry rooted in sectarian loyalties towards Protestant teams such as Rangers and Hearts, and to Catholic teams such as Celtic and Hibernians. Sport symbolised the divisions within Scottish society as much as it united them against England.

During the 1920s Scotland settled into a mood of pessimism that was articulated by the MP and novelist, John Buchan, when he told the House of Commons in 1922: 'Something must be done, and done soon, if Scotland is not to lose its historic individuality'. Behind Buchan's comments lurked a series of fears about the depression, the declining population, the dilution of the race by immigrants, and an introspective mood fostered by the erection of memorials to Scotland's war dead. This culminated in the National War Memorial, designed by Sir Robert Lorimer and erected in Edinburgh Castle between 1924 and 1927, which quickly became a place of pilgrimage for Scots. The memorial seemed to commemorate not only those who had recently died but the gradual loss of imperial greatness that had previously underpinned the country's success.[35] 'The first fact about the Scot', wrote George Malcolm Thompson in 1927, 'is that he is a man eclipsed. The Scots are a dying people'. Such comment seems a wild exaggeration, but it reflected contemporary concern about Catholic immigrants. By 1930 Irish immigration had largely ceased and only 124,000 people living in Scotland had been born in Ireland. Yet this did nothing to stop demands for controls on immigration or attacks by the Orange Order and the Presbyterian Church on the 'Scoto-Irish' as an inferior race. Sectarian prejudice was exacerbated by mass unemployment, and it resulted in discrimination against Catholics in jobs and housing by the Protestant-Unionists who held positions of power especially in Clydeside and the West of Scotland.

Eventually the negative mood inspired attempts to revive Scotland's national sentiment in the shape of a literary renaissance led by the poet Hugh MacDiarmid (Murray Grieve), Lewis Grassic Gibbon, Neil Gunn, Compton Mackenzie and others. Yet even in his famous manifesto, *A Drunk Man Looks at the Thistle* (1926), MacDiarmid found it impossible to avoid the same pessimistic tone. He denounced the Scottish political elite as a 'whole gang of high muchy-mucks, famous fatheads . . . and all the touts and toadies and lickspittles of the English ascendancy'. MacDiarmid hoped that new writing and the recovery of the Scots language would help to liberate the people from the cultural dominance of England and promote a new sense of national identity. However, the literary revival proved to be a minority taste that could not compete with the BBC and the commercially promoted popular culture; it made Scots nationalism seem more marginal than it was.

Nonetheless, dissatisfaction over the economy and irritation with the Labour Party for dropping the idea of a Scottish Parliament led to the formation of the National Party of Scotland in 1928. It was a left-wing expression of nationalism aiming to run candidates at by-elections, thereby demonstrating to Labour that Home Rule was more popular than it realised. However, the new party was divided over its objectives; those who damned the English as 'the hereditary enemy' and aspired to eventual independence on the Irish model had the effect of exacerbating the split between nationalism and Labour. Meanwhile London's continuing failure to reverse Scotland's economic decline prompted right-wing nationalists, drawn from the Conservative and Liberal parties to found the Scottish Party in 1932. Eventually in 1935 elements of the two joined to establish the Scottish National Party. It contested seven constituencies but without making a significant impact. The explanation is that despite their dissatisfaction, voters were afraid that things might be even worse if Scotland stood alone to face the depression. Significantly, despite the SNP's lack of impact, the National Government judged it politic to appease nationalist opinion. In 1937 the Scottish Office was moved to St Andrew's House in Edinburgh with a view to making it look like the seat of Scottish government and thus undermining the nationalist appeal. This policy reflected the outlook of conventional Scots politicians, such as John Buchan and Walter Elliott, who combined a sentimental Jacobitism with a hard-headed endorsement of the Union, and thereby managed to fend off the pressures of the nationalist movement for the time being.

Wales appeared to be even more closely assimilated into Britain than Scotland, partly because the country enjoyed a longer period of political integration; an Act of Union with Wales had been passed as long ago as 1536. Administratively Wales was treated like the counties of England; it sent thirty-six MPs to Westminster but had no minister or separate government. However, before 1914 Parliament had recognised the distinctive interests of the Welsh by promoting temperance, land reform, a National University for Wales, the National Library and a Welsh Sunday Closing Act. During the war a special Welsh army division, nicknamed 'Lloyd George's Welsh Army' was created. The culmination of this process came with the disestablishment of the Anglican Church in Wales in 1920 during Lloyd George's premiership. As a result the idea of a Parliament for Wales had never generated much interest.

However, even the traditional relationship with England began to change after 1918. The Welsh economy, which had enjoyed a boom period before 1914 on the basis of coal, steel and shipping, proved extremely vulnerable during the interwar depression. Its previous success was so dependent upon exports that severe disruption became inevitable at a time of international depression. On average Welsh unemployment stood at twenty per cent between 1925 and 1938. But it rose far higher in the industrial districts, reaching thirty-seven per cent in South Wales, and a staggering sixty-two per cent in Merthyr Tydfil in 1932. Some 430,000 people left Wales mostly to seek jobs in the Midlands and South-East England. There were only two mitigating features. During the 1930s new investment was attracted to modern steel plants at Ebbw Vale, Port Talbot and in Flintshire, and after 1936 state investment supported the new Treforest Trading Estate. Also, North and mid Wales suffered less from the depression because of its concentration on livestock and dairy farming.

Yet, as in Scotland, economic distress did not, in the short term at least, destabilise relations with England. The precipitate decline of the Liberal Party, which had effectively integrated Wales into British national politics before 1914, proved unproblematical because Liberal hegemony was largely replaced by Labour dominance between the wars. However, Labour largely lacked the same sympathy with Welsh separate identity. Welsh socialists assumed that the depression could be solved only through intervention from London. The rising young Labour MP, Aneurin Bevan, though ostensibly very Welsh, was typical of the cosmopolitan set and scornful of local nationalism as a divisive force which, he thought, would only isolate the people from the mainstream of British political life.

In any case, Welsh national identity found less need for a political outlet because it expressed itself through cultural forms, its language and literature, its Nonconformity and its love of sport. To some extent these were mutually reinforcing; for example the chapels used Welsh and also maintained the literary and musical festivals or *eisteddfodau*. During the Edwardian period forty-four per cent of people could speak Welsh, though this had declined to thirty-seven per cent by 1931. Admittedly, Welsh-speakers were concentrated in north-western counties such as Anglesey where they numbered eighty-seven per cent, but were very sparse in the South and the counties bordering England. Yet despite the differences between the North and South of the country, Wales was a less divided society than Scotland. The Welsh shared an enthusiasm for football with the rest of Britain, but saved their passion for rugby. It was arguably through rugby that people felt most conscious of their Welshness. The sport united them because it was seen to be classless and democratic, involving migrants from other parts of Britain not just the Welsh-born population. As a small nation the Welsh took pride in defeating the English; but in contrast to Ireland, where sport had been deliberately used to promote separatism via the Gaelic Athletic Association, this did not seem to generate political expressions of nationalism. When the Welsh beat the New Zealand All Blacks at rugby they took pleasure in upholding British honour as much as Welsh. In this way, though sport helped to make Wales distinctive and cohesive, it did not promote separatism.

On the other hand, the decline of Liberalism and the rise of Labour had left a gap, even if not a very large one, in Welsh public life. At a meeting in a temperance hotel in Pwllheli in August 1925 the Welsh National Party, later Plaid Cymru, was formed largely from radical Nonconformists, pacifists, intellectuals and academics. Its immediate aim was to protect the Welsh language and to promote its use in schools and the administration. The party's president from 1926 to 1939 was Saunders Lewis, a poet, essayist and dramatist who, like his

Scottish counterparts, spoke to an intellectual minority. Nationalists argued persuasively that the Welsh language was under threat and might be overwhelmed not only by English, but by the advance of popular American culture via radio, cinema, music and the BBC whose programmes were devised in London; there was no Welsh BBC service until 1937.

Yet by 1939 Plaid Cymru had recruited only 2,000 members. It was symptomatic of the nationalists' dilemma that the best-known Welsh literary figure to emerge in the 1930s, Dylan Thomas, knew no Welsh and was hostile to nationalism. In a way, the party's emergence symbolised the North-South or rural-urban divide within the country. Believing that the deindustrialisation of Wales would have to be accepted, Saunders Lewis sought to promote 'the moral and physical welfare of its population'. But this made the nationalists appear too romantic and nostalgic in the eyes of most Welsh people for whom the link with Britain still seemed likely to offer the most practical means of improving their prosperity.

Welsh nationalists also faced a dilemma over their methods. They contested the Caernarvonshire constituency in 1929, 1931 and 1935, raising their vote from two to seven per cent. Saunders Lewis, reflecting the despair with parliamentary democracy that was becoming fashionable during the 1920s and 1930s, felt tempted by more direct tactics. In 1936 he and twenty colleagues marked the 400th anniversary of the Union with England by setting fire to an RAF bombing school on the Lleyn Peninsula, for which they received nine-month gaol sentences. However, by creating the first martyrs for nationalism their actions attracted widespread sympathy partly from pacifists and partly from resentment at the damage done to local farming by the bombing school. The decision to conduct the trial in English at the Old Bailey provoked outrage even among people who were hostile to Plaid Cymru. Accusing the government of bullying, Lloyd George commented: 'this is the first government that has tried Wales at the Old Bailey'. The controversy gave Plaid Cymru a distinctive profile, but left nationalism a long way from becoming a popular movement.

By contrast with the low-key developments in Wales and Scotland, Anglo-Irish relations were traumatic especially in the immediate post-war years. This was the culmination of a protracted attempt to deny Irish claims to nationhood by the English. In 1800 the Act of Union had abolished the Irish Parliament, and until 1829 Catholics had not even been allowed to sit in the House of Commons. The country was integrated into the British system by means of 103 Irish MPs, an Irish Viceroy in Dublin, and a minister, the chief secretary, who divided his time between London and Dublin. The main bridge between the two countries was the Anglo-Irish landowning class who occupied influential positions in society and in the House of Lords. However, their role had largely disappeared as a result of the rise of a moderate nationalist party committed to winning a Home Rule Parliament and the sale of their Irish estates between the 1890s and 1914.

Meanwhile the majority of the Irish refused to accept that they were primarily British, though their leaders were prepared to accept a compromise that maintained the formal link with Britain in return for their own Parliament in Dublin. The British Liberals wisely recognised the reality of a multinational Britain by allowing Ireland, and, in due course, Scotland and Wales, some form of devolution. But for decades Home Rule legislation designed to give substance to this idea was frustrated by British Unionists and Conservatives entrenched in the House of Lords, and the implementation of the bill was interrupted by the outbreak of war in 1914. This had disastrous consequences. It led frustrated nationalists to launch the Easter Rebellion in 1916 which was bloodily suppressed by the authorities who subsequently executed sixteen of the leaders. The Easter Rebellion had not enjoyed much popular support, but, as Patrick Pearse put it: 'from the graves of patriot men and women spring living nations'. The aftermath of the revolt extinguished the remnants of pro-British sentiment in nationalist Ireland and destroyed the credibility of the Home Rulers who were swept away at the 1918 election by Sinn Fein's candidates. When Sinn Fein refused to attend the Westminster Parliament and set up their own assembly in Dublin a virtual civil war broke out in Ireland, fought between the Irish Republican Army and the notorious Black and Tans, an irregular force raised from former British troops. However, by 1920 the Lloyd George Coalition reluctantly accepted that Ireland could no longer be held by force. The country was partitioned between the six Ulster counties, which remained British, and the Irish Free State which formally came into existence in 1922. For British Unionists the blow was softened by giving the new country the status of a Dominion under the Crown and by creating a new anomaly in the form of 'common citizenship' which permitted citizens of the Free State to vote in British elections.

Although this appeared at the time to have resolved the Irish Question, the new settlement turned out to involve another mistake. It created an unstable situation in Ulster where the large Catholic minority remained reluctant to accept that they were British rather than Irish. It would have been consistent with British resistance to devolution in the rest of the country to absorb the six Ulster counties into the regular administration. Rather perversely the province that had *not* wanted a separate Parliament was given one, housed in a new building at Stormont in the 1930s. Northern Ireland even had a prime minister, Sir James Craig. Unfortunately, following the abolition of proportional representation in 1929, the Protestant-Unionist majority monopolised power and openly discriminated against Catholics in housing and employment. For their part successive British governments turned a blind eye to the situation, thereby storing up enormous problems for themselves later in the century.

Yet despite London's conciliatory stance towards Ulster Unionist rule, the relationship with Britain remained paradoxical. After 1922 the English appeared to want nothing to do with the province they had fought so long to retain. None of the British political parties engaged in constituency politics in Northern Ireland, leaving it to remain sunk in sectarian conflict. For their part the Ulstermen harboured deep resentment towards the British state to which they were ostensibly so loyal. 'I think it is very hard for the English to comprehend the attitude of the Ulster Unionists towards their country', wrote Katharine Chorley, whose mother was an Ulsterwoman; she observed that, though fighting to maintain the Union with England, Ulstermen could still 'express pride in their Irish birth and a kind of contempt for the English way of life'.[36] For people who had long insisted that Ulstermen were British this discovery of their Irishness was a little perverse. In fact, the Northern Ireland people expressed their Britishness largely through their vociferous loyalty to the Crown. Thus the opening of the new Parliament by George V in June 1921 was of great symbolic importance to them; but nothing could hide the Unionists' suspicion that they could not quite rely on the Westminster politicians.

In short, partition did not solve the underlying problem posed by Ulster. Before 1914 the province had seen itself as a dynamic enclave of capitalism and progress trapped in a backward, peasant society, but by separating itself from the rest of Ireland it had thrown away the opportunity to lead the new state in order to become a marginal province of the United Kingdom. Sunk in conservatism and sectarianism, Ulster seemed out of step with the rest of Britain, and, as time passed the cultural and political gap dividing it from the increasingly liberal society on the mainland made it more of an anomaly.

The settlement of Northern Ireland as a province enjoying a unique status had wider implications for interwar Britain. In particular, the unhappy history of Stormont and its administration left many people on the mainland convinced that the experiment with devolution should not be repeated in Scotland or Wales. In view of the limited support for Home Rule in those countries during the 1920s and 1930s this seemed realistic at the time. However, this attitude encouraged the English to ignore the reality of a multinational Britain, and to forget that the Union with Scotland had been a marriage of convenience rather than a permanent arrangement.

21

'Ask Your Father': From War to War

On 3 September 1939 an era that had been announced by the ringing of church bells in 1918 was ushered out by the dismal drone of air-raid sirens. 'Everything that I have worked for, everything that I have hoped for, everything that I have believed in during my public life has crashed into ruins', Neville Chamberlain told the country in a broadcast that announced the declaration of war with Germany. Later that day the King broadcast his message to the nation. 'Because of his stammer, it was as much of an effort for us to listen to him as it was for him to speak', commented one listener. 'That night I heard the wailing of British air-raid sirens for the first time . . . we'd been led to believe that with the declaration of war the bombing would begin, but it was a false alarm.'[1]

These uninspiring rallying cries did nothing to dispel the general dismay, let alone the defeatism, that was widespread, especially in the higher reaches of British society, at the start of the Second World War. Back in 1918 many people had genuinely believed the propaganda designed to persuade them they had fought 'The War to End War', and during the next two decades anti-war sentiment, if not outright pacifism, had been widely articulated. Its core lay among Christian pacifists, notably in the Quaker community, some of whose members had been conscientious objectors in 1914–18. This tradition was reflected in the formation of the Peace Pledge Union in 1936 which had attracted 120,000 signatories by 1937. A wider liberal-left critique of the Great War condemned the pre-1914 arms race, and held that the Treaty of Versailles had been punitive towards Germany and that its terms reflected the aims of the imperialist powers; there was thus no case for fighting to uphold an unjust treaty. Socialists interpreted the new war as proof of the crisis now facing capitalism in its climactic stage, arguing that the failure of the capitalist economy was generating extreme movements, such as fascism, symptoms of a doomed attempt to shore up a failing system. But opposition to war was also common on the Right where many people condemned the new war with Germany and Italy on the grounds that they were simply not the enemy; our real opponent was the Soviet Union. In effect Britain was, for a second time, being dragged to war by the French seeking revenge on the Germans; and if we managed to defeat Germany, which seemed unlikely, we would merely create a dangerous vacuum in central Europe that would be filled by the Soviets. This view overlapped with the ideas of the fascists who argued that war was unnecessary as Germany could safely be left to pursue her interests in central-eastern Europe, Italy in North Africa, and Britain in the Empire, without clashing. They condemned what they saw as a worldwide Jewish conspiracy, orchestrated from the United States, designed to restrict Germany's economy and drive her into a corner. During the summer of 1939 huge numbers of people had turned out to hear – and to applaud – such ideas at meetings held by Oswald Mosley and other fascists.

Yet despite these varied expressions of opposition to another great war, the British had never become a nation of pacifists. Rather, they had placed their hopes, for a time, in alternative ways of managing international conflict by means of disarmament and the League of Nations, but eventually they accepted that these options were not viable. Although it is difficult to be precise, one can say with some certainty that 1935 was the year in which public opinion reluctantly concluded that the League of Nations had become a broken reed, leaving Britain to face the prospect of another war.

It was in 1935 that the League of Nations Union, hoping to remind the government of popular enthusiasm for the League, organised the famous – and misleadingly titled – 'Peace Ballot' in which 11.5 million people participated. On the crucial question, whether voters would support both economic and *military* sanctions against aggressor states, the vote was 6.7 million in favour and only 2.3 million against. This was not merely an abstract question; with Mussolini currently threatening to seize Abyssinia by force, people understood quite well the implications for Britain of trying to check aggression. Abyssinia gave them an example of a just war, helping in the process to dispel the scepticism engendered by the 1914–18 war. At the time the National Government, expecting an election in the autumn, gave the public the impression that it would indeed support the League in resisting Mussolini, only to back away subsequently, arguing that Britain had no interest in Abyssinia and that it would be best to keep on the right side of the Italians.

In several ways the invasion of Abyssinia proved to be a crucial and disastrous step on the road to war. By finally destroying belief in the League it forced the liberal-left to contemplate planning for a war with the dictators. Abroad, it divided Britain from France in her dealings with the fascist powers and forced Italy and Germany into co-operation when they were otherwise divided. It thereby created the opportunity for Hitler to risk marching his troops back into the Rhineland in 1936, effectively violating the peace treaty and revising the strategic situation to the disadvantage of France. This gave Hitler the confidence that he could get away with further territorial revisions in 1938. Meanwhile, public opinion moved further towards reconciling itself to war as a result of the bitter civil war in Spain, which, by highlighting the continued overthrow of elected governments by fascism, seemed to prefigure the next great conflict; as the *News Chronicle* put it: 'Sooner or later the democracies will have to stand.'[2] The National Government crystallised the issue by claiming to be neutral over Spain, which meant refusing arms for the Republicans while the fascist powers supported the Nationalists, a policy designed to provide a respectable cover for the politicians' sympathy for General Franco.

The next stage in popular re-education came in 1938 when Hitler demanded the partition of Czechoslovakia and the transfer of the Sudetenland to Germany. The settlement negotiated by Chamberlain at Munich in September sparked a huge wave of relief. All over the country clergymen of all denominations preached on the text 'Blessed are the peacemakers for they shall be called the Children of God' and effectively told their congregations that God had intervened in the person of Chamberlain to save the world from war.[3] However, in making themselves, not for the first time, the mouthpiece of the state the churches had miscalculated. It was soon realised that the logic of redrawing European boundaries to accommodate German popula-tions was capable of almost indefinite extension. The prime minister's calculation that, as Hitler had a limited list of grievances, the sooner he worked through them the sooner peace would be guaranteed, looked increasingly naive. In October 1938 no less than ninety-three per cent of the public told the pollsters that they did not believe Hitler's claims. By March 1939, when Hitler finally discredited the appeasement strategy by seizing what remained of Czechoslovakia, eighty-four per cent supported the idea that Britain and the Soviet Union should become allies.

Even the government, though working for peace, had gone a long way to preparing the public mind for war. In the aftermath of Munich civilians had been required to present themselves to be issued with gas masks and appeals had been made for people to volunteer to become ARP wardens. In London Herbert Morrison reported in April 1939 that 16,000 women had come forward to fill a quota of only 13,000 ARP posts, though only 2,500 men for 3,000 vacancies. 'I hope this is not a case where men are going to lag behind', he commented.[4] Meanwhile, the authorities stepped up the rearmament programme, reintroduced conscription and recruited 35,000 men into the RAF between March 1938 and April 1939, double the total in the previous year. Preparations for war reached the most unlikely quarters. Golfers were instructed to carry gas masks with them at all times, and their clubs were required to provide slit trenches alongside the greens in case members were caught by an unexpected air raid. At the Duppas Hall recreation ground in Croydon a man lost his dog when it fell into one of the new ten-feet-deep trenches and was unable to get out. The owner leapt into the trench but the dog refused to be rescued and he then realised he could not reach the parapet to escape; he was stuck there for half an hour before passers-by heard the sound of barking.[5]

Against this background of preparation the declaration of war found the British public more resigned than surprised: 'The prevailing atmosphere was one of gloom, hand in hand with a resolution to see it through. No one was under the illusion that it would be a short war, some prophesying that it might even last for ten years'.[6] The first week was devoted to further arrangements against an aerial attack that failed to materialise. At school in London Bryan Magee lined up to receive his gas mask, but, as children were assumed by the authorities to be all the same size, he found nothing to fit him. 'You'll just have to hope the Germans don't use gas', his teacher comforted him.[7] Teacher seemed to be right. 'Not a single German bomb has been dropped on British soil in the first fortnight of the war', the fascist journal, *Action*, triumphantly informed its readers. According to the pro-Nazi MP, Captain Ramsay, 'it soon became apparent that no war was being conducted by Germany against this country'.[8]

To many people it soon began to look as though the reverse was also true. Despite its guarantee to Poland the government had no plans to assist the Poles, and in fact British troops did not take the field until six months after the start of the war. The resulting anticlimax, disparagingly dubbed the 'Phoney War', lasted for nine months. While civilians were required to gather themselves for a great conflict, behind the scenes Chamberlain and several key ministers continued to seek a negotiated peace, employed pro-Nazi emissaries to ascertain the terms of German offers and looked gratefully for evidence that Hitler intended to abstain from attacking Britain; they comforted themselves with the thought that, in any case, Germany was not prepared to fight a long war. Although these efforts were largely unknown among the public at the time, they sensed that the war was not being energetically prosecuted. Eventually the Phoney War was swept aside in May 1940 following a revolt by the government's supporters in a debate over the fiasco of the Norwegian Campaign. The assumption of the premiership by Churchill and the work of the anti-appeasement newspapers who were outing pro-Nazis in high places had the effect of dissipating the mood of fatalism that had kept the National Government in power for so long. Symptomatic of the change of climate was the popular demand for copies of a little book entitled *Guilty Men*, an attack on the leading appeasers that appeared in July 1940 and went through ten editions before the month was out. Meanwhile the popular novelist, J. B. Priestley, had persuaded the BBC to let him make a series of broadcasts at nine on Sunday evenings from June to October 1940. They became compulsive listening. Priestley took pains to warn his audience not to forget the fate of the men who had fought for their country in 1914–18 but returned to experience poverty and unemployment. This message proved so worrying that Brendan Bracken MP, an acolyte of Winston Churchill, demanded that the broadcasts be dropped. It is not clear whether the new prime minister intervened, but the BBC certainly pulled the plug on Priestley even though letters from listeners ran at 300-1 in his favour. He had caught the mood of the country in the early stages of the war.

However, it is significant that, despite his broadly left-wing stance, Priestley recognised that it would be misleading to portray interwar British society simply in terms of poverty and unemployment. He had summed up his view earlier in *English Journey*: 'You need money in this new England, but you do not need much money. It is a large scale, mass-production job, with cut prices. You could almost accept Woolworths as its symbol.' In fact, what made the British people increasingly radical in the early stages of the war was not so much despair over their material hardships as a sense of rising expectations, an anxiety that material improvements were about to be snatched away from them. By 1939, after a period in which people had enjoyed better food, novel leisure opportunities, extra holidays, cheaper motor cars, fashionable clothing and, above all, improved housing, the British were well on the way to becoming a society devoted to the pursuit of consumerism.

They correctly saw that the Second World War would interrupt the progress of consumerism, though, on the positive side, the six-year conflict also helped to accelerate the resolution of issues such as the reform of secondary education and health provision that had been frustrated for many years. Civilians quickly found themselves sub-jected to food rationing, rising prices and the blackout regulations which 'were a real headache at first as folk wrestled nightly with improvised materials such as blankets and tablecloths fixed with drawing pins'.[9] In the unaccustomed darkness Britain's urban motorists returned to their old ways, especially as driving tests were suspended allowing the incompetent back on to the roads. During the first four months of war alone 4,133 people were killed in motoring accidents including 2,657 pedestrians. It was safer to be in the army at this stage. Altogether over 61,000 civilians died in bombing raids, though this was far less than had been predicted. As in 1914–18 the war brought the housing industry to a standstill, and, as four million homes, amounting to a third of the entire housing stock, suffered damage or destruction, by 1945 there was a huge, unsatisfied demand for improved house-building which was to dominate British society for the rest of the century. Meanwhile, holidaymakers endured a graphic symbol of what they had lost when the magnificent new cruise liner, the *Queen Elizabeth*, undertook her maiden voyage, not in Cunard's red, white and black colours but decked out in battleship grey for her role as a troop carrier.

Not surprisingly the authorities became anxious to boost civilian morale, relying heavily on musical entertainments at home and in the army by means of cinema, the BBC and ENSA. Gracie Fields, who was recovering from cancer of the womb when war broke out, promptly offered her services and embarked on a series of concerts for the troops in France. As so often, she caught the mood of cheerful resolution that the government sought to foster with songs such as 'Wish Me Luck As You Wave Me Goodbye'. However, Mass Observation surveys revealed that morale was especially low among women, who often bore the brunt of wartime policies in their daily lives and found the disruption of family and social life hard to bear. They resented the evacuation of 1.5 million children at the start of the war and were instrumental in bringing many home again. Forced to endure prolonged separation from husbands, many pursued wartime affairs which resulted in some hasty marriages and the doubling of the illegitimacy rate to nine per cent of all births by 1945; after the war five times as many people sought divorces and fifty-eight per cent of petitions were lodged by men. However, there was no lasting collapse of moral standards. Marriage and motherhood continued to be the chief goals of most British women. Although the marriage rate fell during 1941 to 1945, thereafter it rapidly increased, exceeded pre-war levels and continued to rise right up to the 1970s. This pattern, again, underlines the point that the interruption caused by war was largely temporary, and that the main social trends of the 1930s continued strongly into the 1950s and 1960s.

In one respect, however, the Second World War marked a sharp, and lasting, discontinuity in the lives of ordinary people. It brought the great depression to an emphatic end and pushed full employment firmly on to the agenda. As in 1914–18 the combination of massive demand for munitions, engineering and shipbuilding with the departure of workers for the forces soon mopped up the remaining ten per cent unemployment that had persisted throughout the 1920s and 1930s. So much so that by 1941, according to the government's Manpower Requirements Committee, the country was short of two million workers. As propaganda and exhortation made little impact, they decided to impose industrial conscription on women, calling them up in age cohorts to register at labour exchanges, so that by 1943 forty-six per cent of all women aged fourteen to fifty-nine were doing paid work for the war effort. This experience reinforced the modest shift in attitudes during the 1930s that had made it more acceptable for women, including married women, to work outside the home.

But for the average worker the question was how long this would last. 'Ask Your Father' proved to be a potent slogan, reminding him of the danger of a return to mass unemployment as had happened after 1918. This fear alone was largely responsible for the radicalising effect of wartime on the civilian population. In the event wartime experience materially helped to undermine the retrenchment philosophy that had hitherto dogged official policy, and the Budget of 1941 came to be regarded as marking the adoption of a Keynesian approach to public finance. The famous White Paper of 1944 committed the government for the first time to maintaining a high and stable level of employment. As a result, during the two decades after 1945 unemployment was rarely more than two per cent, making this a golden age for British workers. During the 1950s full employment fuelled a boom in luxury appliances, housing, motor cars, holidays, fashion and light entertainment. But although the social distribution and the economic impact of this consumerism was unprecedented, it was hardly new, for the society that evolved in Britain in the 1950s and 1960s had largely taken shape during the 1930s.

Notes

1 'Will never really came home'

1   Quoted in Alun Howkins, *Reshaping Rural England: A Social History 1850–1925* (1990), 272.

2   Laurie Lee, *Cider With Rosie* (1959), 23.

3   John Julius Norwich ed., *The Duff Cooper Diaries* (2006), 85, 11 November 1918.

4   Ibid., 86, 17 November 1918.

5   Ibid., 111, 1 November 1919.

6   Ibid., 114, 31 December 1919.

7   Quoted in Mark Connelly, *The Great War, Memory and Ritual* (2002), 29.

8   William Woodruff, *The Road to Nab End: An Extraordinary Northern Childhood* (1993), 32.

9   Norwich, *Duff Cooper*, 14, 3 August 1915.

10 Maurice Jacobs, *Reflections of a General Practitioner* (1965), 81–2.

11 Woodruff, *Nab End*, 33.

12 Connelly, *The Great War*, 27.

13 Woodruff, *Nab End*, 137–8.

14 Quoted in Connelly, *The Great War*, 28.

15 Woodruff, *Nab End*, 22.

16 Andrew Purves, *A Shepherd Remembers* (2001), 40–1.

17 Lee, *Cider With Rosie*, 170–3.

18 Quoted in Stephen Humphries, *Hooligans or Rebels? An Oral History of Working-Class Childhood and Youth 1889–1939* (1981), 187.

19 Woodruff, *Nab End*, 103.

20 *Glasgow Herald*, 7 January 1929.

21 Norwich, *Duff Cooper*, 46, 14 January 1917.

22 Jenny Hazelgrove, *Spiritualism and British Society Between the Wars* (2000), 14–15.

23 Ibid., 18.

24 Ibid., 90.

25 Raphael Samuel ed., *East End Underworld: Chapters in the Life of Arthur Harding* (1981), 237–8.

26 Paul Addison, *Churchill on the Home Front 1900–1951* (1992), 203.

27 Ibid., 204–5.

28 Jean Moorcroft Wilson, *Siegfried Sassoon: The Journey from the Trenches: A Biography 1918–1967* (2003), 35.

29 W. C. Sellar and R. J. Yeatman, *1066 and All That* (1930), 123.

30 Quoted in Connelly, *The Great War*, 142.

2 'A Babylonian touch'

1 As late as 1960 the brown and wholemeal bread consumed in Britain amounted to only a fifteenth of the total.

2 Robert Roberts, *A Ragged Schooling: Growing Up in the Classic Slum* (1971), 199.

3 Paul Johnson, *The Vanished Landscape: A 1930s Childhood in the Potteries* (2004), 135.

4 John Burnett, *Plenty and Want* (1966), 316.

5 H. D. Rennen, *The Origins of Food Habits* (1944), 243.

6 Laurie Lee, *Cider With Rosie* (1959), 14; Andrew Purves, *A Shepherd Remembers* (2001), 45–6.

7 John Walton, *Fish and Chips and the British Working Class 1870–1940* (1992), 13.

8 Bryan Magee, *Clouds of Glory: A Hoxton Childhood* (2003), 26.

9 *Daily Mail*, 16 October 1930.

10 Lee, *Cider With Rosie*, 140.

11 Johnson, *Vanished Landscape*, 105.

12 Magee, *Clouds of Glory*, 273.

13 Johnson, *Vanished Landscape*, 103.

14 Lizzie Collingham, *Curry: A Biography* (2005), 170–1.

15 Magee, *Clouds of Glory*, 17.

16 *Daily Graphic*, 4 February 1926.

17 Johnson, *Vanished Landscape*, 136.

18 E. M. Delafield, *The Diary of a Provincial Lady* (1930), 5.

19 Magee, *Clouds of Glory*, 65.

20 Johnson, *Vanished Landscape*, 130.

21 Magee, *Clouds of Glory*, 29.

22 Martin Pugh, *'Hurrah for the Blackshirts!': Fascists and Fascism in Britain*

Between the Wars (2005), 209–11.

23   Denys Forrest, *Tea for the British* (1973), 213.

24   *News of the World*, 4 January 1925, 1 and 25 February 1925.

25   *Daily Graphic*, 4 February 1926.

26   *News of the World*, 25 January 1925.

3 'Mr Can and Mr Can't'

1   E. M. Delafield, *The Diary of a Provincial Lady* (1930), 28–9; Robert Roberts, *A Ragged Schooling: Growing Up in the Classic Slum* (1971), 134; Jenny Hazelgrove, *Spiritualism and British Society Between the Wars* (2000), 36.

2   Paul Johnson, *The Vanished Landscape: A 1930s Childhood in the Potteries* (2004), 36.

3   E. S. Turner, *Call the Doctor: A Social History of Medical Men* (1958), 290–1.

4   Ibid., 280–1.

5   Laurie Lee, *Cider with Rosie* (1959), 144, 154–5.

6   William Woodruff, *The Road to Nab End: An Extraordinary Northern Childhood* (1993), 300.

7   Ibid.

8   Bryan Magee, *Clouds of Glory: A Hoxton Childhood* (2003), 69.

9   Jonathan Gathorne-Hardy, *Doctors: The Lives and Work of GPs* (1984), 16.

10   Woodruff, *Nab End*, 301.

11   Gathorne-Hardy, *Doctors*, 16.

12   Ibid.

13   Ibid., 14–16.

14   Ibid., 15.

15   John Julius Norwich ed., *The Duff Cooper Diaries* (2006), 96, 10 and 24 April 1918.

16   Ibid., 107, 2 September 1919.

17   Quoted in Roy Porter, *Blood and Guts: A Short History of Medicine* (2002), 42.

18   T. G. H. James, *Howard Carter: The Path to Tutankhamun* (1992), 243.

19   Kenneth Rose, *King George V* (1983), 355–7.

20   Gathorne-Hardy, *Doctors*, 18.

21   Magee, *Clouds of Glory*, 238.

22   *Daily Mail*, 20 October 1930.

23   Norwich, *Duff Cooper*, 129, 9 August 1920.

24   Margery Spring Rice, *Working-Class Wives: Their Health and Conditions* (1939), 28.

25 Ibid., 35.

26 Ibid., 40.

27 Turner, *Call the Doctor*, 273.

28 Woodruff, *Nab End*, 300; Gathorne-Hardy, *Doctors*, 21.

29 Turner, *Call the Doctor*, 276.

4 'Where the air's like wine'

1 William Woodruff, *The Road to Nab End: An Extraordinary Northern Childhood* (1993), 287–9.

2 Ibid., 280.

3 Ibid., 284.

4 *The Labour Woman*, December 1920.

5 William Woodruff, *Beyond Nab End* (2003), 10, 27–8.

6 Bryan Magee, *Clouds of Glory: A Hoxton Childhood* (2003), 15; Woodruff, *Beyond Nab End*, 28.

7 Albert Mansbridge, *Brick Upon Brick: The Co-operative Permanent Building Society* (1934), 80–1.

8 O. R. Hobson, *A Hundred Years of the Halifax* (1953), 91, 100.

9 *National Association of Building Societies Yearbook* (1927), 251.

10 *Evening News*, 3 October 1907.

11 Alan A. Jackson, *Semi-Detached London* (1973), 35, 169.

12 Harold Bellman, *The Building Society Movement* (1927), 50.

13 *Building Societies Yearbook*, 262–3.

14 Bellman, *Movement*, 53.

15 Mansbridge, *Brick Upon Brick*, 96.

16 *Daily Mail*, 5 March 1926; 'Election Notes for Conservative Speakers, 1929', Steel-Maitland Papers (National Archives of Scotland GD 193/284).

17 Martin S. Briggs, *How To Plan Your House* (1937), 6.

18 Magee, *Clouds of Glory*, 15.

19 Paul Johnson, *The Vanished Landscape: A 1930s Childhood in the Potteries* (2004), 68.

20 *Daily Mail*, 16 January 1926.

21 *The Labour Woman*, 1 November 1923.

22 Magee, *Clouds of Glory*, 204.

23 *Daily Mail*, 1 March 1926.

24 Ibid., 3 March 1926.

25 Ibid.

26 Mansbridge, *Brick Upon Brick*, 121.

5 *Wigan Pier Revisited*

1   *Daily Herald*, 1 and 17 October 1922.

2   Wal Hannington, *The Problem of the Distressed Areas* (1937), 66.

3   Quoted in R. I. McKibbin, *Classes and Cultures: England 1918–1951* (1998), 158.

4   Hannington, *Distressed Areas*, 48.

5   Ibid., 47.

6   Ibid., 65.

7   Ibid., 49.

8   William Woodruff, *The Road to Nab End: An Extraordinary Northern Childhood* (1993), 382.

9   Ibid., 383.

10   Matt Perry, *The Jarrow Crusade: Protest and Legend* (2005), 23.

11   *News Chronicle*, 5 October 1936.

12   Ibid., 11 October 1936.

13   Ibid., 31 October 1936.

14   Perry, *Jarrow Crusade*, 33–4.

15   Quoted in Perry, *Jarrow Crusade*, 166.

16   Perry, *Jarrow Crusade*, 46.

17   Austin Harrison, 'The Crushing of the Middle Classes', *The English Review*, 29, 1919, 463–4.

18   R. I. McKibbin, *Classes and Cultures: England 1918–1951* (1998), 61–2.

19   George Orwell, *The Road to Wigan Pier* (1937), 19–21.

20   Woodruff, *Nab End*, 250–1.

21   *Manchester Guardian*, 7 May 1926; PRO HO 144/6902, 9 May 1926.

22   Harold Nicholson, *King George V* (1952), 420.

23   Andrew Purves, *A Shepherd Remembers* (2001), 71.

24   Raphael Samuel ed., *East End Underworld: Chapters in the Life of Arthur Harding* (1981), 268.

25   Bryan Magee, *Clouds of Glory: A Hoxton Childhood* (2003), 107.

26   Woodruff, *Nab End*, 323–4.

27   Clive Emsley, 'The Law, the Police and the Regulation of Motor Traffic in England 1900–1939', *Historical Journal*, 36, 1993, 364.

28   John Walton, *Fish and Chips and the British Working Class 1870–1940* (1992), 27–31.

29   Ibid., 6.

30   Magee, *Clouds of Glory*, 331.

31   Stephen Wagg, 'Time Gentlemen Please': The Decline of Amateur Captaincy in English County Cricket', *Contemporary British History*, 14, 2000, 35–6.

32 Harold Bellman, *The Building Societies Movement* (1927), 56.

33 Hannington, *Distressed Areas*, 14.

34 William Woodruff, *Beyond Nab End* (2003), 16–20, 76.

35 Paul Johnson, *The Vanished Landscape: A 1930s Childhood in the Potteries* (2004), 69.

36 Quoted in McKibbin, *Classes and Cultures*, 152.

37 *News Chronicle*, 21 December 1938.

38 *Action*, 7, 14 and 21 January 1939.

6 Screwneck Webb and Jimmy Spinks

1   *The News of the World*, 11 January 1925.

2   Ibid., 1 March 1925.

3   Ibid., 4 January 1925.

4   Quoted in Clive Emsley, 'The Law, the Police and the Regulation of Motor Traffic in England 1900–1939', *Historical Journal*, 36, 1993, 2, 364.

5   Bryan Magee, *Clouds of Glory: A Hoxton Childhood* (2003), 138–9.

6   George Orwell, *Coming Up For Air* (1939), 52.

7   Clive Emsley, *Hard Men: Violence in England since 1750* (2005), 68.

8   Magee, *Clouds of Glory*, 136–7.

9   Emsley, *Hard Men*, 67.

10 Magee, *Clouds of Glory*, 137–8.

11 See Raphael Samuel ed., *East End Underworld: Chapters in the Life of Arthur Harding* (1981), 182–6; Magee, *Clouds of Glory*, 153–4.

12 William Woodruff, *The Road to Nab End: An Extraordinary Northern Childhood* (1993), 60, 62, 185.

13 Notes on Home Office conference, 23 November 1933, PRO HO 45/25386.

14 Samuel, *East End Underworld*, 176–80.

15 Ibid., 180.

16 Ibid., 266.

17 Martin Pugh, *'Hurrah for the Blackshirts!': Fascists and Fascism in Britain Between the Wars* (2005), 61.

18 Ibid., 58–9.

19 Memorandum, 2 November 1924: National Archives of Scotland – Gilmour Papers GD383/20.

20 Pugh, *'Hurrah for the Blackshirts!'*, 97–100.

21 Samuel, *East End Underworld*, 267.

22 PRO HO 144/6902.

23 Special Branch Report, 25 May 1940, PRO KV 2/884.

24 *The Times*, 8 June 1934.

25 *Hansard*, House of Commons Debates, ccxc, 14 June 1934, c.1984.

26 Ibid., c.2036.

27 Robert Skidelsky, *Oswald Mosley* (1975), 370.

28 Magee, *Clouds of Glory*, 318–20.

7 'The Best Job of All'

1 *Daily Mail*, 18 April 1939.

2 Ibid.

3 Arabella Kenealy, *Feminism and Sex Extinction* (1920), 245–6.

4 Barbara Cartland, *The Isthmus Years* (1942), 157.

5 *My Weekly*, 25 January 1919.

6 *Woman's Own*, 4 March 1933.

7 Ibid., 6 January 1934.

8 Tim Heald, *A Life of Love: The Life of Barbara Cartland* (1994), 59.

9 See A. H. Halsey, *British Social Trends Since 1900* (1988), 74.

10 John R. Gillis, *For Better, For Worse: British Marriages 1600 to the Present* (1985), 263–4.

11. William Woodruff, *The Road to Nab End: An Exraordinary Northern Childhood* (1993), 302–6.

12 *Daily Mail*, 18 April 1939.

13 Ibid.

14 Heald, *Life of Love*, 62.

15 Janet Morgan, *Edwina Mountbatten: A Life of Her Own* (1991), 130–1.

16 *The Star*, 10 November 1923.

17 Anne de Courcy, *Society's Queen: The Life of Edith, Marchioness of Londonderry* (1992), 274.

18 R. R. James, *Bob Boothby: A Portrait* (1991), 113.

19 John Charmley, *Duff Cooper* (1986), 33–4; John Julius Norwich ed., *The Duff Cooper Diaries* (2006), 14, 27 August 1915.

20 de Courcy, *Society's Queen*, 66–7.

21 Ibid., 126.

22 Ibid., 113, 115.

23 Nicholas Mosley, *Rules of the Game* (1983), 247–8.

24 Alistair Horne, *Harold Macmillan 1894–1956* (1988), 87.

25 Ibid., 89.

26 Morgan, *Edwina Mountbatten*, 177, 189.

27 *Hansard*, House of Commons Debates, 160, 2 March 1923, c.2366–7.

28 Norwich, *Duff Cooper*, 110, 23 and 24 October 1919.

29   *Hansard*, House of Commons Debates, 317, 20 November 1936, c.2082–3.

30   *Daily Graphic*, 25 January 1926.

31   de Courcy, *Society's Queen*, 306–7.

32   Nancy Astor Papers (Reading University Library), 14/6/1/1/491–2, and 1302, 1304.

33   *Woman's Own*, 15 and 22 October 1932.

34   Ibid., 3 February 1936.

35   Ibid., 5 January 1935.

36   Ibid., 13 April 1935; Cartland, *Isthmus Years*, 164.

37   *Woman's Own*, 6 January 1934.

38   Ibid., 22 October 1932.

39   David Brett, *Gracie Fields* (1995), 77–8.

40   Heald, *Life of Love*, 67–70.

41   Gillian Gill, *Agatha Christie: The Woman and Her Mysteries* (1990), 17.

42   Ibid., 67.

43   Patricia Hollis, *Jennie Lee: A Life* (1997), 203–7.

44   Ibid., 207, 211.

45   Paul Berry and Mark Bostridge, *Vera Brittain: A Life* (1995), 218–23.

8   'Abnormalities of the brain'

1   *The Church Family News*, 25 May 1915.

2   *Time and Tide*, 4 June 1920; Lady Londonderry, *Retrospect* (1938), 127–8.

3   *Sunday Dispatch*, 10 and 17 March 1929; *Empire News* and *Sunday Chronicle*, 19 February 1956.

4   Arabella Kenealy, *Feminism and Sex Extinction* (1920), 249.

5   Christopher St John, *Ethel Smyth: A Biography* (1959), 9.

6   *Hansard*, House of Commons Debates, 145, 4 August 1921, c.1800–04.

7   Nigel Nicolson, *Portrait of a Marriage* (1973), 196.

8   David Leeming, *Stephen Spender: A Life in Modernism* (1999), 27; Peter Parker, *Isherwood* (2004), 64–5, 79–83; Jean Moorcroft Wilson, *Siegfried Sassoon: The Journey from the Trenches: A Biography 1918–1967* (2003), 28.

9   Oliver Baldwin, *The Questing Beast* (1932), 131.

10   *Oxford Dictionary of National Biography*; A. O. Bell and A. McNeillie eds., *The Diary of Virginia Woolf* (1984), 211.

11   James Lees-Milne, *Prophesying Peace* (1977), 52.

12   John Sutherland, *Stephen Spender* (2004), 109.

13   Matt Houlbrook, *Queer London: Perils and Pleasures in the Sexual Metropolis 1918–1957* (2005), 168.

14   Philip Hoare, *Noël Coward: A Biography* (1995), 122–3.

15   Quoted in Susan A. Williams, *The People's King* (2003), 39.

16   Quoted in Diana Gittens, *Fair Sex: Family Size and Structure* (1982), 77–9.

17   *Hansard*, House of Commons Debates, 15 April 1935, c.1634.

18   Marie Stopes, *Married Love* (1918), 14.

19   Quoted in Ruth Hall, *Marie Stopes: A Life* (1977), 171–2.

20   Naomi Mitchison, *You May Well Ask* (1979), 69–70.

21   Hall, *Stopes*, 89–93.

22   Janet Morgan, *Edwina Mountbatten: A Life of Her Own* (1991), 203.

23   Peter Willmott, *Growing Up in a London Village* (1979), 60.

24   Margery Spring Rice, *Working-Class Wives: Their Health and Conditions* (1939), xi.

25   Marie Stopes, *Wise Parenthood* (1918), 36–8.

26   Edith Summerskill, *A Woman's World* (1967), 50–3.

27   Mary Stocks, *My Commonplace Book* (1970), 160–1.

9 'Keep Young and Beautiful'

1   Anne de Courcy, *Society's Queen: The Life of Edith, Marchioness of Londonderry* (1992), 77–8.

2   Jill Julius Matthews, '"They had Such a Lot of Fun": The Women's League of Health and Beauty Between the Wars', *History Workshop Journal*, 30, 1990, 30.

3   *Beauty*, vol. 1, 2; Mary Bagot Stack, *Building the Body Beautiful* (1931), 3.

4   Matthews, 'The Women's League', 33.

5   *Sunday Chronicle*, 25 September 1938; *Sunday Express*, 16 October 1938.

6   *Woman's Own*, 15 October 1932.

7   Alice Head, *It Could Never Have Happened* (1939), 37.

8   Mary Grieve, *Millions Made My Story* (1964), 80–1.

9   *Woman*, 5 June 1937.

10   Robin Kent, *Aunt Agony Advises: Problem Pages Through the Ages* (1979), 27, 247.

11   Grieve, *Millions Made My Story*, 88.

12   *Good Housekeeping*, March 1922.

13   E. M. Delafield, *The Diary of a Provincial Lady* (1930), 14, 30, 40.

14   Quoted in Deirdrie Beddoe, *Back to Home and Duty: Women Between the Wars* (1989), 62.

15   *Daily Chronicle*, 6 and 7 December 1918.

16   Bryan Magee, *Clouds of Glory: A Hoxton Childhood* (2003), 333.

17   *Good Housekeeping*, March 1922.

18   *Weekly Reports*, Ministry of Labour, 4 January 1919.

19   NUSEC subcommittee minutes, 17 November 1921, The Women's Library, Box 342.

20   Minutes, Women's Employment Committee, Ministry of Reconstruction, Imperial War Museum, EMP 29/2, p.23.

21   Quoted in Elizabeth Roberts, *A Woman's Place: An Oral History of Working-Class Women 1890–1940* (1984), 83, 110–11.

22   Vera Brittain to George Catlin, mid-October 1927, in Paul Berry and Mark Bostridge, *Vera Brittain: A Life* (1995), 220.

23   Ibid., 223.

24   Delafield, *Provincial Lady*, 99–100.

25   Ibid., 57.

26   *The Globe*, April 1921; *Toronto Star Weekly*, 16 October 1926.

27   Quoted in Brian Harrison, *Prudent Revolutionaries: Portraits of British Feminists Between the Wars* (1987), 197.

28   Nigel Nicolson ed., *The Letters of Virginia Woolf, vol. II 1912–1922* (1976), xvii.

29   *Time and Tide*, 31 October 1924.

30   Cicely Hamilton, *Life Errant* (1935), 251.

31   Virginia Woolf, *A Room of One's Own* (1929), 103, 107.

32   Vera Brittain to George Catlin, 8 March 1929, in Berry and Bostridge, *Vera Brittain*, 235.

33   Inez Jenkins, *The History of the Women's Institute Movement in England and Wales* (1953), 142.

34   Ibid., 141, Chapter 12.

10 'The mills were our destiny'

1   Bryan Magee, *Clouds of Glory: A Hoxton Childhood* (2003), 5.

2   Paul Johnson, *The Vanished Landscape: A 1930s Childhood in the Potteries* (2004), 37–8.

3   Janet Morgan, *Edwina Mountbatten: A Life of Her Own* (1991), 167–8.

4   Johnson, *Vanished Landscape*, 75; Magee, *Clouds of Glory*, 225.

5   Johnson, *Vanished Landscape*, 33.

6   Margaret Railton ed., *Andrew Lorimer's Life and Times in the Upper Tweed Valley* (2001), 13.

7   Johnson, *Vanished Landscape*, 134.

8   Quoted in John Springhall, *Sure and Steadfast: A History of the Boys' Brigade 1883–1983* (1983),130.

9   Quoted in Stephen Humphries, *Hooligans or Rebels? An Oral History of Working-Class Childhood and Youth 1889–1939* (1981), 135.

10 William Woodruff, *The Road to Nab End: An Extraordinary Northern Childhood* (1993), 185.

11 Magee, *Clouds of Glory*, 190.

12 Humphries, *Hooligans*, 153.

13 Ibid., 151–5.

14 Andrew Purves, *A Shepherd Remembers* (2001), 74–5.

15 Elizabeth Roberts, *A Woman's Place: An Oral History of Working-Class Women 1890–1940* (1984), 41.

16 Ibid.

17 Ibid., 43.

18 J. B. Priestley, *English Journey* (1934), 183.

19 Roberts, *A Woman's Place*, 71–2.

20 Ibid., 70.

21 Ibid., 71.

22 Ibid., 72–3.

23 Ibid., 73.

24 Laurie Lee, *Cider With Rosie* (1959), 205.

25 Ibid., 206.

26 Railton, *Andrew Lorimer*, 28.

27 Magee, *Clouds of Glory*, 178.

28 Purves, *A Shepherd Remembers*, 53.

29 Railton, *Andrew Lorimer*, 16.

30 Sarah Bradford, *George VI* (1989), 29; Johnson, *Vanished Landscape*, 96.

31 Magee, *Clouds of Glory*, 50.

32 Ibid., 175–9.

33 Lee, *Cider With Rosie*, 48–9.

34 Purves, *A Shepherd Remembers*, 24.

35 Railton, *Andrew Lorimer*, 19.

36 Magee, *Clouds of Glory*, 174–5.

37 Ibid., 75.

38 Lee, *Cider With Rosie*, 44.

39 Railton, *Andrew Lorimer*, 16.

40 Magee, *Clouds of Glory*, 47–8.

41 Purves, *A Shepherd Remembers*, 53.

42 Magee, *Clouds of Glory*, 48.

43 Ibid., 7.

44 Robert Roberts, *A Ragged Schooling: Growing Up in the Classic Slum* (1971), 157.

45 Woodruff, *Nab End*, 133–4.

46 Quoted in Deirdrie Beddoe, *Back to Home and Duty: Women Between the Wars* (1989), 39.

47 Beddoe, *Home and Duty*, 42.

48 A. L. Rowse, *A Cornish Childhood* (1942), 234.

49 Carol Thatcher, *Below the Parapet: The Biography of Denis Thatcher* (1996), 32.

50 Katharine Chorley, *Manchester Made Them* (1950), 251.

51 Ibid., 252.

52 Richard Holt, *Sport and the British* (1989), 291–2

53 Ibid., 207.

II 'Reminiscent of Negro orgies'

1   Janet Morgan, *Edwina Mountbatten: A Life of Her Own* (1991), 153, 187.

2   Matthew Sweet, 'Babylon on Thames', the *Guardian*, 19 May 2006.

3   *News of the World*, 1 February 1925.

4   Ibid., 4 January 1925.

5   *Glasgow Herald*, 29 January 1929.

6   William Woodruff, *The Road to Nab End: An Extraordinary Northern Childhood* (1993), 179.

7   Ibid., 196.

8   Bryan Magee, *Clouds of Glory: A Hoxton Childhood* (2003), 268.

9   Kenneth Rose, *King George V* (1983), 359–60.

10 Magee, *Clouds of Glory*, 268–9.

11 Ibid., 180.

12 Quoted in Matthew Hilton, *Smoking in British Popular Culture 1800–2000* (2000), 99.

13 Quoted in Hilton, *Smoking*, 122.

14 Susan Pedersen, *Eleanor Rathbone and the Politics of Conscience* (2004), 164, 167–8.

15 *Daily Chronicle*, 9 October 1922.

16 Hilton, *Smoking*, 149.

17 Magee, *Clouds of Glory*, 275.

18 Woodruff, *Nab End*, 201–2.

19 Jonathan Gathorne-Hardy, *Doctors: The Lives and Work of GPs* (1984), 12.

20 Magee, *Clouds of Glory*, 22.

21 Peter Haydon, *Beer and Britannia: An Inebriated History of Britain* (2001), 272.

22 Tom Harrison, *The Pub and the People: A Worktown Study by Mass Observation* (1943), 48.

23 Haydon, *Beer and Britannia*, 277.

24 *Daily Mail*, 5 April 1939.

25 Frank Manders, *Cinemas of Newcastle* (2005), 69.

26 David Robinson, *Chaplin: His Life and Art* (1985), 167.

27 Ibid., 161.

28 William Woodruff, *Beyond Nab End* (2003), 38.

29 Magee, *Clouds of Glory*, 219.

30 Ibid., 23.

31 Woodruff, *Nab End*, 166.

32 Ibid., 168.

33 Quoted in James Walvin, *Beside the Seaside: A Social History of the Popular Seaside Holiday* (1978), 125.

34 Laurie Lee, *Cider with Rosie* (1959), 179.

35 *Skegness News*, 1 April 1936.

12 *Yellow Earl and Silver Ghost*

1 David Cannadine, *Aspects of Aristocracy* (1994), 65.

2 Jean Moorcroft, *Siegfried Sassoon: The Journey from the Trenches: A Biography 1918–1967* (2003), 154.

3 Quoted in Martin Adeney, *The Motor Makers: The Turbulent History of Britain's Car Industry* (1988), 37.

4 *The Times*, 1 and 23 January 1919.

5 Quoted in Peter Thorold, *The Motoring Age: The Automobile and Britain 1896–1939* (2003), 129.

6 Bryan Magee, *Clouds of Glory: A Hoxton Childhood* (2003), 35, 329.

7 Carol Thatcher, *Below the Parapet: The Biography of Denis Thatcher* (1996), 34.

8 *Daily Chronicle*, 7 and 28 October 1922.

9 *Daily Mail*, 4 and 25 April 1939.

10 Ibid., 4 April 1939.

11 Stevenson Cook to Sir Arthur Steel-Maitland, 5 December 1918, National Archives of Scotland: Steel-Maitland Papers.

12 Clive Emsley, 'The Law, the Police and the Regulation of Motor Traffic in England 1900–1939', *Historical Journal*, 36, 1993, 369–70.

13 Moorcroft, *Sassoon*, 154.

14 *Daily Mail*, 3 March 1926.

15 *Daily Graphic*, 8 June 1926.

16 *Daily Mail*, 22 April 1939.

17 Ibid., 3 April 1924.

18 Ibid., 8 April 1924, 22 January 1926.

19 Ibid., 24 October 1930.

20 Ibid., 14 January 1926.

21   Ibid.

22   *Daily Mirror,* 19 May 1937.

23   Quoted in Thorold, *The Motoring Age,* 89.

24   Quoted in Thorold, *The Motoring Age,* 135.

25   Quoted in Thorold, *The Motoring Age,* 87.

26   Gillian Gill, *Agatha Christie: The Woman and Her Mysteries* (1990), 71.

27   *The Aeroplane,* 2 May 1934.

28   John Julius Norwich ed., *The Duff Cooper Diaries* (2006), 106, 123.

29   Janet Morgan, *Edwina Mountbatten: A Life of Her Own* (1991), 158.

30   *Daily Mail,* 8 April 1924.

31   *News of the World,* 31 May 1925.

32   Charles Grey to L.T.C. Moore-Brabazon, 13 June 1924, RAF Museum
     Hendon: Moore-Brabazon Papers 71/3/11.

33   *Daily Mail,* 1 October 1930.

34   Ibid.

35   Ibid., 2 October 1930.

36   *The Times,* 11 January 1935.

37   Ibid., 30 May 1935.

38   Joe Moran, 'Crossing the Road in Britain, 1931–1976', *Historical Journal,*
     49, 2006, 480.

39   *The Times,* 7 February 1935.

40   Ibid., 23 February 1935.

41   Quoted in Emsley, 'The Law, the Police and the Regulation of Motor
     Traffic', *Historical Journal,* 36, 365.

42   *The Times,* 11 January 1935.

43   Ibid., 2 March 1935.

44   Ibid., 30 May 1935.

13 *'Cider With Rosie'*

1   *Daily Mail,* 22 October 1930.

2   A. Wainwright, *The Far Eastern Fells* (1957), and *The Central Fells* (1958).

3   William Woodruff, *The Road to Nab End: An Extraordinary Northern
     Childhood* (1993), 399.

4   *Daily Mail,* 15 October 1930.

5   S. L. Bensusan, *Latter-Day Rural England* (1927), 65.

6   Ibid., 51–4.

7   Ibid., 142.

8   *The Dairyman,* March 1925.

9   Ibid., January and February 1925.

10   *The Dairyman*, January 1925.

11   Bensusan, *Latter-Day Rural England*, 58.

12   *The Dairyman*, March 1925.

13   *Daily Mail*, 14 April 1939.

14   Ibid., 17 April 1939.

15   *The Times*, 19 March 1923.

16   Jonathan Brown, 'Agricultural Policy and the National Farmers Union 1908–1939', J. R. Wordie ed., *Agricultural Politics in England 1815–1939* (2000), 179–80.

17   Brown, 'National Farmers Union', 191.

18   Quoted in Carol Twinch, *The Tithe War 1918–1939* (2001), 132.

19   Andrew Purves, *A Shepherd Remembers* (2001), 238.

20   Laurie Lee, *Cider With Rosie* (1959), 8.

21   John Burnett, *Plenty and Want: A Social History of Diet in England from 1815 to the Present Day* (1966), 306.

22   Purves, *A Shepherd Remembers*, 26–7.

23   Ibid., 132–4.

24   Lee, *Cider With Rosie*, 176.

25   Ibid., 178.

26   Ibid., 181.

27   Purves, *A Shepherd Remembers*, 71–2.

28   Patricia Wilson, *Slaley Commemoration Hall: The First Eight Decades* (2002), 5, 19.

29   Ibid., 6.

30   Purves, *A Shepherd Remembers*, 128.

31   Wilson, *Slaley Commemoration Hall*, 21–2.

32   E. M. Delafield, *The Diary of a Provincial Lady* (1930), 39–40.

33   Inez Jenkins, *The History of the Women's Institute Movement in England and Wales* (1953), 146.

34   Bensusan, *Latter-Day Rural England*, 166.

35   Wilson, *Slaley Commemoration Hall*, 29.

36   Lee, *Cider With Rosie*, 182–3.

37   Wilson, *Slaley Commemoration Hall*, 41–2.

38   C. M. Joad, *A Charter for Ramblers or the Future of the Countryside* n.d., 11.

39   J. B. Priestley, *English Journey* (1934), 173.

40   Stanley Baldwin, *Our Inheritance* (1928), 226.

41   Stanley Baldwin, *The Torch of Freedom* (1935), 127–8.

42   Joad, *Charter for Ramblers*, 12.

43   Margaret Railton ed., *Andrew Lorimer's Life and Times in the Upper Tweed Valley* (2001), 135.

44   *Daily Graphic*, 5 June 1926.

45 Quoted in Tom Stephenson ed., *The Countryside Companion*, n.d., 325.
46 Joad, *Charter for Ramblers*, 113.

14 'Six penn'orth of hope'

1   Quoted in Derek Birley, *A Social History of English Cricket* (1999), 207.
2   Birley, *English Cricket*, 208.
3   Jack Williams, 'Recreational cricket in Bolton between the wars', in Richard Holt ed., *Sport and the Working Class in Modern Britain* (1990), 102.
4   Quoted in Birley, *English Cricket*, 233.
5   Birley, *English Cricket*, 222.
6   Stephen Wagg, 'Time Gentlemen Please: The Decline of Amateur Captaincy in English County Cricket', *Contemporary British History*, 14, 2000, 35–7.
7   Birley, *English Cricket*, 249.
8   Helen Walker, 'Lawn Tennis' in Tony Mason ed., *Sport in Britain: A Social History* (1989), 263.
9   *News of the World*, 29 March 1925.
10 Stan Shipley, 'Boxing', in Mason, *Sport in Britain*, 93.
11 Ibid., 97.
12 Richard Holt, *Sport and the British: A Modern History* (1989), 175.
13 Quoted in Holt, *Sport and the British*, 295.
14 David Winner, *Those Feet: An Intimate History of English Football* (2005), 30.
15 Ibid., 31.
16 Quoted in Mike Huggins, 'Going to the Dogs', *History Today*, May 2006, 32.
17 Huggins, 'Going to the Dogs', 33.
18 William Woodruff, *Beyond Nab End* (2003), 81.
19 Ibid., 76.
20 Mike Huggins, *Horse Racing and the British 1919–1939* (2003), 75.
21 Ibid., 80.
22 Quoted in Huggins, 'Going to the Dogs', 35.
23 Mark Clapson, *A Bit of a Flutter: Popular Gambling and English Society 1823–1961* (1992), 170.

15 'Wings over Everest'

1   Robert Wohl, *A Passion for Wings: Aviation and the Western Imagination 1908–1918* (1994), 1.

2   Ibid., 156–7.

3   Ibid., 18.

4   Harry Ward, *The Yorkshire Birdman: Memoirs of a Pioneer Parachutist* (1990), 51–3.

5   *Daily Graphic*, 3 May 1926.

6.   Ibid., 19 September 1926.

7   *News of the World*, 4 January 1925.

8   *Daily Mail*, 6 October 1930.

9   Ibid.

10   *News of the World*, 5 July 1925.

11   *Daily Graphic*, 10 July 1926.

12   J. Wentworth Day, *Lady Houston DBE: The Woman Who Won the War* (1958), 58–70.

13   *The Aeroplane*, 9 March 1938.

14   *Daily Graphic*, 7 January 1926.

15   *The Aeroplane*, 10 January 1934.

16   Ibid., 2 May 1934.

17   Ibid., 31 January 1934.

18   *The Times*, 8 February 1928.

19   *Daily Mail*, 16 October 1930.

20   Ibid., 1 June 1928.

21   *The Times*, 5 and 19 February 1929; 30 March 1929.

22   Ibid., 26 March 1929.

23   Ibid., 19 February 1929.

24   Memorandum, 14 October 1932, National Archives of Scotland: Hamilton Papers 5397.

25   *Saturday Review*, 8 April 1933.

26   Speech, 5 October 1932, National Archives of Scotland: Hamilton Papers 5397.

27   'The Houston-Everest Flight', n.d., by the Marquess of Clydesdale, National Archives of Scotland: Hamilton Papers 5397.

28   Ward, *Yorkshire Birdman*, 21.

29   Ibid., 19.

30   Ibid., 20.

31   *Daily Express*, 10 June 1918.

32   *Daily Graphic*, 27 May 1926.

33   *Daily Mail*, 1 June 1928.

34   Ibid., 19 June 1928.

35   *Daily Herald*, 28 January 1938.

36   *Daily Mail*, 13 May 1924.

37   *News of the World*, 3 May 1925.

16 'A talent to amuse'

1   Paul Johnson, *The Vanished Landscape: A 1930s Childhood in the Potteries* (2004), 69.

2   John Walsh, *Independent*, 29 April 2005.

3   A. O. Bell and A. McNeillie eds., *The Diary of Virginia Woolf*, (1977) vol. 1, 17.

4   Jeremy Lewis, *Penguin Special: The Life and Times of Allen Lane* (2005), 82.

5   W. E. Williams to Walter Elliott, 16 May 1946, Elliott Papers, National Library of Scotland, Acc 6721 Box 3.

6   Lewis, *Penguin Special*, 91.

7   Quoted in Lewis, *Penguin Special*, 88.

8   *Evening Standard*, 13 March 1937.

9   *The English Review*, 64, April 1937, 397–8.

10 Quoted in Lewis, *Penguin Special*, 85.

11 Laurie Lee, *Cider With Rosie* (1959), 206.

12 E. M. Delafield, *The Diary of a Provincial Lady* (1930), 85.

13 Mark Kinkead-Weeks, *D. H. Lawrence: Triumph to Exile 1912–1922* (1996), 348–9, 399–400.

14 David Ellis, *D. H. Lawrence: Dying Game 1922–1930* (1998), 443–4.

15 *Report* (1930), British Board of Film Censors, Steel-Maitland Papers: National Archives of Scotland GD 193/239.

16 Robert Graves, *Goodbye to All That*, Prologue, 1957 edition.

17 Quoted in Nicola Beauman, *A Very Great Profession: The Woman's Novel 1914–1939* (1983), 124.

18 Quoted in Beauman, *The Woman's Novel*, 175.

19 Quoted in Beauman, *The Woman's Novel*, 186.

20 Bryan Magee, *Clouds of Glory: A Hoxton Childhood* (2003), 221.

21 Ibid.

17 'Brideshead Revisited'

1   Janet Morgan, *Edwina Mountbatten: A Life of Her Own* (1991), 269.

2   John Julius Norwich ed., *The Duff Cooper Diaries* (2006), 125, 16 June 1920.

3   David Cannadine, *Aspects of Aristocracy* (1994), 180–1.

4   Anne de Courcy, *Society's Queen: The Life of Edith, Marchioness of Londonderry* (1992), 358.

5   Morgan, *Edwina Mountbatten*, 125.

6   Ibid., 160, 222.

7   Cannadine, *Aspects*, 109–29.

8 S. J. Hetherington, *Katharine Atholl: Against the Tide, 1874–1960* (1989), 125.

9 Ibid., 127–8.

10 Norwich, *Duff Cooper*, 131, 29 August 1920.

11 Ibid., 99, 16 May 1919.

12 *Hansard*, House of Lords Debates, 17 July 1922, c.505.

13 Nancy Cunard, *Black Men and White Ladyship* (1931), 103, in A. Susan Williams, *Ladies of Influence: Women of the Elite in Interwar Britain* (2000), 148.

14 Lady Londonderry, *Retrospect* (1938), 253.

18 'Everybody calls him Bertie'

1 *Daily Star*, 11 January 1923.

2 Kenneth Rose, *King George V* (1983), 226.

3 James Pope-Hennessy, *Queen Mary 1867–1953* (1959), 112.

4 Rose, *George V*, 312.

5 Ibid., 317–18.

6 Ibid., 179.

7 Robert Rhodes James, *A Spirit Undaunted: The Political Role of George VI* (1998), 65.

8 Rose, *George V*, 226.

9 J. R. Clynes, *Memoirs, 1869–1924* (1937), 326.

10 *Daily Graphic*, 18 February 1926.

11 Quoted in Philip Ziegler, *King Edward VIII* (1990), 111.

12 J. H. Thomas, *My Story* (1937), 154.

13 *Daily Telegraph*, 19 March 1923.

14 Clynes, *Memoirs*, 343–4.

15 Norman and Jeanne Mackenzie eds., *The Diary of Beatrice Webb* (1982–5), vol. 4, 194.

16 Sir Charles Petrie, *Monarchy* (1933), 158–9.

17 English Array Memorandum, Lymington Papers F178, Hampshire CRO.

18 *Daily Star*, 11 January 1923.

19 James, *Spirit Undaunted*, 99.

20 Janet Morgan, *Edwina Mountbatten: A Life of Her Own* (1991), 105.

21 Rose, *George V*, 306.

22 *Daily Graphic*, 8 January 1926.

23 Rupert Godfrey ed., *Letters From a Prince* (1998), 157, 169.

24 Lord Birkenhead, *Walter Monckton* (1969), 125–6.

25 Anne de Courcy, *Society's Queen: The Life of Edith, Marchioness of Londonderry* (1992), 325.

26 Frank Prochaska, *Royal Bounty: The Making of a Welfare Monarchy* (1995), 202.

27 MacDonald's Diary, 21 November 1936, PRO 30/691753.

28 *Anglo-German Review*, December 1936.

29 *Saturday Review*, 6 June 1936.

30 Bryan Magee, *Clouds of Glory: A Hoxton Childhood* (2003), 305.

31 See *Daily Mail*, 3, 4, 5 and 7 December 1936; *Daily Express*, 4, 5 and 7 December 1936; *News Chronicle*, 3, 5 and 7 December 1936.

32 *News Chronicle*, 3 December 1936.

33 *Daily Mail*, 7 December 1936.

34 Sir Barry Domvile's Diary, 19 December 1936, Domvile papers 54, National Maritime Museum, Greenwich.

35 See Baldwin Papers, vol. 143, fol. 14, 19, 49, Cambridge University Library; M. Dunne to Walter Elliot, 15 December 1936, Elliot Papers, National Library of Scotland, Acc. 12267/6.

36 Duke of Windsor to Neville Chamberlain, 22 December 1937, PRO PREM 1/465.

37 Magee, *Clouds of Glory*, 160.

38 Nigel Nicholson ed., *Harold Nicholson, Diary and Letters 1945–1962* (1971), 327.

39 *News Review*, 3 June 1937.

19 'A Stone's Throw to Australia'

1 Bryan Magee, *Clouds of Glory: A Hoxton Childhood* (2003), 107.

2 Quoted in Paul Ward, *Britishness Since 1870* (2004), 19.

3 Magee, *Clouds of Glory*, 306.

4 Ibid., 306–7.

5 Robert Graves, *Goodbye to All That* (1928), 240.

6 Charles Grey to J. C. T. Moore-Brabazon, 25 January 1938, Moore-Brabazon Papers AC/71/3/11.

7 Paul Johnson, *The Vanished Landscape: A 1930s Childhood in the Potteries* (2004), 197.

8 William Woodruff, *The Road to Nab End: An Extraordinary Northern Childhood* (1993), 35.

9 *New Times* and *Ethiopia News*, August 1936.

10 Magee, *Clouds of Glory*, 34.

11 Ibid., 64–5.

12 Ibid., 305.

13 Quoted in John M. MacKenzie, *Propaganda and Empire* (1984), 24.

14   Woodruff, *Nab End*, 125.

15   MacKenzie, *Propaganda and Empire*, 178.

16   Robert Roberts, *A Ragged Schooling: Growing Up in the Classic Slum* (1971), 142.

17   Quoted in Ward, *Britishness*, 19.

18   *Daily Mail*, 4 April 1924.

19   Ibid., 5 April 1924.

20   Ibid., 1 April 1924.

21   Woodruff, *Nab End*, 125.

22   MacKenzie, *Propaganda and Empire*, 79.

23   L. S. Amery, *My Political Life* vol. 2 (1953), 340.

24   For a recent, and very extreme, statement of this view see Bernard Porter, *The Absent-Minded Imperialists* (2004).

25   Magee, *Clouds of Glory*, 107.

26   *Financial Times*, 29 January 1924.

27   Woodruff, *Nab End*, 297.

28   *The Cotton Factory Times*, 18 and 25 September 1931; Woodruff, *Nab End*, 375.

29   Quoted in Andrew Thompson, *The Empire Strikes Back* (2005), 78; *The Cotton Factory Times*, 2 October 1931.

30   *Manchester Evening News*, 26 September 1931; *The Cotton Factory Times*, 2 October 1931.

20 'No longer part of England'

1   Robert Graves and Alan Hodge, *The Long Weekend* (1940), 6.

2   E. M. Delafield, *The Diary of a Provincial Lady* (1930), 33.

3   J. B. Priestley, *English Journey* (1934), 290.

4   B. Deacon, D. Cole and G. Tregidga, *Mebyon Kernow and Cornish Nationalism* (2003), 18–19.

5   Priestley, *English Journey*, 254.

6   Ibid., 314 ; R. Colls and B. Lancaster, *Geordies: The Roots of Regionalism* (1992), 22.

7   Paul Johnson, *The Vanished Landscape: A 1930s Childhood in the Potteries* (2004), 87.

8   William Woodruff, *Beyond Nab End*, (2003), 30–1.

9   Quoted in Paul Ward, *Britishness Since 1870* (2004), 68.

10   Bryan Magee, *Clouds of Glory: A Hoxton Childhood* (2003), 109; J. B. Priestley, *Margin Released* (1962), 30–1.

11   Priestley, *English Journey*, 195–6.

12   Katharine Chorley, *Manchester Made Them* (1950), 137–42.

13   Priestley, *English Journey*, 290.

14   Ibid., 253.

15   Ibid., 261.

16   Magee, *Clouds of Glory*, 28, 108.

17   Andrew Purves, *A Shepherd Remembers* (2001), 65.

18   Harry Ward, *The Yorkshire Birdman: Memoirs of a Pioneer Parachutist* (1990), 40.

19   Quoted in Ward, *Britishness*, 80.

20   Dave Russell, 'Sport and Identity: The Case of Yorkshire County Cricket Club 1890–1939', *Twentieth Century British History*, 7, 1996, 215–16.

21   Quoted in Dave Russell, *Looking North: Northern England and the National Imagination* (2004), 257.

22   Quoted in Russell, *Looking North*, 241.

23   Quoted in Russell, *Looking North*, 252.

24   William Woodruff, *The Road to Nab End* (1993), 40.

25   Johnson, *Vanished Landscape*, 111–12.

26   Priestley, *English Journey*, 301, 321.

27   Woodruff, *Nab End*, 381–2.

28   Ibid., 385.

29   Ibid., 398.

30   Ibid., 401.

31   Ibid., 405.

32   Ibid., 406.

33   Nicholas Witchell, *The Loch Ness Story* (1974), 34.

34   T. M. Devine, *The Scottish Nation 1700–2000* (1999), 325.

35   Ibid., 318–19.

36   Chorley, *Manchester Made Them*, 81.

21 'Ask Your Father'

1   William Woodruff, *Beyond Nab End* (2003), 272.

2   *News Chronicle*, 14 August 1936.

3   See *Hexham Courant*, 8 August 1938.

4   *Daily Mail*, 4 April 1939.

5   *Daily Mail*, 3 April 1939.

6   Andrew Purves, *A Shepherd Remembers* (2001), 139.

7   Bryan Magee, *Clouds of Glory: A Hoxton Childhood* (2003), 225–6.

8   *Action*, 23 September 1939; A. H. M. Ramsay, *The Nameless War* (1954), 62.

9   Purves, *A Shepherd Remembers*, 139.

Bibliography

1 'Will never really came home'

J. M. Winter, *Sites of Memory, Sites of Mourning: The Great War in European Cultural History* (1995)

Mark Connelly, *The Great War, Memory and Ritual* (2002)

Arthur Marwick, *The Deluge: British Society and the First World War* (1965)

Jenny Hazelgrove, *Spiritualism and British Society Between the Wars* (2000)

Martin Ceadel, *Pacifism in Britain 1914–1945* (1986)

Callum G. Brown, *Religion and Society in Twentieth-Century Britain* (2006)

D. Englander and J. Osborne, 'Jack, Tommy and Henry Dubb: the Armed Forces and the Working Class', *Historical Journal*, 21, 1978.

William Woodruff, *The Road to Nab End: An Extraordinary Northern Childhood* (1993)

Siegfried Sassoon, *Memoirs of an Infantry Officer* (1930)

John Julius Norwich ed., *The Duff Cooper Diaries* (2006)

2 'A Babylonian touch'

D. J. Oddy, 'Food, Drink and Nutrition' in F. M. L. Thompson ed., *The Cambridge Social History of Britain 1750–1950* vol. 2 (1990)

T. C. Barker ed., *Our Changing Fare: Two Hundred Years of British Food Habits* (1966)

John Burnett, *Plenty and Want: A Social History of Diet in England from 1815 to the Present Day* (1966)

John Burnett, *A History of the Cost of Living* (1969)

John Walton, *Fish and Chips and the British Working Class 1870–1940* (1992)

Maurice Baren, *How It All Began in the Pantry* (2000)

J. Boyd Orr, *Food, Health and Income* (1936)

Paul Johnson, *The Vanished Landscape: A 1930s Childhood in the Potteries* (2004)

David Meredith, 'Imperial Images: the Empire Marketing Board 1926–1932', *History Today*, 37, January 1987

Denys Forrest, *Tea For The British* (1973)

3 'Mr Can and Mr Can't'

Roy Porter, *Blood and Guts: A Short History of Medicine* (2002)

E. S. Turner, *Call the Doctor: A Social History of Medical Men* (1958)

Jonathan Gathorne-Hardy, *Doctors: The Lives and Work of GPs* (1984)

Margery Spring Rice, *Working-Class Wives: Their Health and Conditions* (1939)

Virginia Berridge, 'Health and Medicine' in F. M. L. Thompson ed., *The Cambridge Social History of Britain 1750–1950*, vol.3 (1990)

F. F. Cartwright, *A Social History of Medicine* (1977)

Brian Abel-Smith, *A History of the Nursing Profession* (1960)

Maurice Jacobs, *Reflections of a GP* (1965)

Bernard Harris, *The Origins of the British Welfare State* (2004)

4 'Where the air's like wine'

Harold Bellman, *The Building Society Movement* (1927)

John Burnett, *A Social History of Housing 1815–1970* (1978)

Martin Daunton, 'Housing' in F. M. L. Thompson ed., *The Cambridge Social History of Britain 1750–1950*, vol. 2 (1990)

Martin Daunton, *A Property-Owning Democracy? Housing in Britain* (1987)

Alan A. Jackson, *Semi-Detached London* (1973)

O. R. Hobson, *A Hundred Years of the Halifax* (1953)

Albert Mansbridge, *Brick Upon Brick: The Co-operative Permanent Building Society 1884–1934* (1934)

A. Olechnowicz, *Working-Class Housing in England Between the Wars* (1997)

Colin G. Poole, *Local Authority Housing: Organisation and Development* (1996)

M. Swenarton and A. Hodge, 'The scale and nature of the growth of owner-occupation in Britain between the wars', *Economic History Review*, 38, 1985

William Woodruff, *The Road to Nab End: An Extraordinary Northern Childhood* (1993)

5 *Wigan Pier Revisited*

John Stevenson, 'Myth and Reality: Britain in the 1930s' in A. Sked and C. Cook eds., *Crisis and Controversy* (1976)

John Stevenson, 'The Politics of Violence' in G. Peel and C. Cook eds., *The Politics of Reappraisal* (1975)

R. I. McKibbin, *Classes and Cultures: England 1918–1951* (1998)

R. I. McKibbin, *The Ideologies of Class: Social Relations in Britain 1898–1950* (1990)

Matt Perry, *The Jarrow Crusade: Protest and Legend* (2005)

Peter Kingsford, *The Hunger Marchers in Britain 1920–1940* (1982)

David Vincent, *Poor Citizens: The State and the Poor in Twentieth Century Britain* (1991)

Noreen Branson, *Poplarism 1919–1925: George Lansbury and the Councillors' Revolt* (1985)

G. C. Peden, *British Economic and Social Policy: Lloyd George to Margaret Thatcher* (1991)

B. W. E. Alford, *Depression and Recovery? British Economic Growth 1918–1939* (1972)

Wal Hannington, *The Problem of the Depressed Areas* (1937)

Ellen Wilkinson, *The Town That Was Murdered* (1939)

Walter Greenwood, *Love on the Dole* (1933)

George Orwell, *The Road to Wigan Pier* (1937)

6 Screwneck Webb and Jimmy Spinks

Clive Emsley, *Hard Men: Violence in England since 1750* (2005)

Clive Emsley, *The English Police: A Political and Social History* (1996)

V. A. C. Gatrell, 'Crime, authority and the policeman-state' in F. M. L. Thompson ed., *The Cambridge Social History of Britain 1750–1950*, vol. 3 (1990)

K. D. Ewing and C. A. Gearty, *The Struggle for Civil Liberties: Political Freedom and the Rule of Law in Britain, 1914–1945* (2000)

Raphael Samuel ed., *East End Underworld: Chapters in the Life of Arthur Harding* (1981)

Bryan Magee, *Clouds of Glory: A Hoxton Childhood* (2003)

J. M. Hart, *The British Police* (1951)

Joan Lock, *The British Policewoman: Her Story* (1979)

Jon Lawrence, 'Forging a Peaceable Kingdom: War, Violence and Fear of Brutalisation in Post-First World War Britain', *Journal of Modern History*, 75, 2003

Anne Logan, '"A Suitable Person for Suitable Cases": The Gendering of Juvenile Courts in England, c.1910–39', *Twentieth Century British History*, 16, 2005.

G. R. Searle, *Corruption in British Politics, 1895–1930* (1987)

Tom Cullen, *Maundy Gregory: Purveyor of Honours* (1974)

Alan Hyman, *The Rise and Fall of Horatio Bottomley* (1972)

7 'The Best Job of All'

John R. Gillis, *For Better, For Worse: British Marriages 1660 to the Present* (1985)

Colin S. Gibson, *Dissolving Wedlock* (1994)

O. R. McGregor, *Divorce in England* (1957)

Martin Pugh, *Women and the Women's Movement in Britain 1914–1959* (1992)

Marie Stopes, *Married Love* (1918)

Enid Charles, *The Twilight of Parenthood* (1934)

A. H. Halsey, *British Social Trends Since 1900* (1988)

Arabella Kenealy, *Feminism and Sex Extinction* (1920)

Barbara Cartland, *The Isthmus Years* (1942)

Anne de Courcy, *The Last Season* (1989)

Anne de Courcy, *Society's Queen: The Life of Edith, Marchioness of Londonderry* (1992)

Elizabeth Roberts, *A Woman's Place: An Oral History of Working-Class Women 1890–1940* (1984)

Janet Morgan, *Edwina Mountbatten: A Life of Her Own* (1991)

Paul Berry and Mark Bostridge, *Vera Brittain: A Life* (1995)

Patricia Hollis, *Jennie Lee: A Life* (1997)

Alistair Horne, *Harold Macmillan 1894–1956* (1988)

Gillian Gill, *Agatha Christie: The Woman and Her Mysteries* (1990)

Diana Mosley, *A Life of Contrasts* (2002)

John Charmley, *Duff Cooper* (1986)

R. R. James, *Bob Boothby: A Portrait* (1991)

Tim Heald, *A Life of Love: The Life of Barbara Cartland* (1994)

8 'Abnormalities of the brain'

Jeffery Weeks, *Sex, Politics and Society* (1989)

Matt Houlbrook, *Queer London: Perils and Pleasures in the Sexual Metropolis 1918–1957* (2005)

R. I. McKibbin, *Classes and Cultures: England 1918–1951* (1998)

Paul Ferris, *Sex and the British* (1993)

Sheila Jeffreys, *The Spinster and Her Enemies* (1985)

Radclyffe Hall, *The Well of Loneliness* (1928)

R. A. Soloway, *Birth Control and the Population Question in England 1872–1930* (1982)

Jane Lewis, 'The Ideology and Politics of Birth Control in Interwar England', *Women's Studies International Quarterly*, 2, 1979

Ruth Hall, *Marie Stopes: A Life* (1977)

Marie Stopes, *Wise Parenthood* (1918)

Nigel Nicolson, *Portrait of a Marriage* (1973)

David Leeming, *Stephen Spender: A Life in Modernism* (1999)

John Sutherland, *Stephen Spender* (2004)

Peter Parker, *Isherwood* (2004)

9 'Keep Young and Beautiful'

Deirdrie Beddoe, *Back to Home and Duty: Women Between the Wars* (1989)

Elizabeth Roberts, *A Woman's Place: An Oral History of Working-Class Women 1890–1940* (1984)

Martin Pugh, *Women and the Women's Movement in Britain 1914–1959* (1992)

Brian Harrison, *Prudent Revolutionaries: Portraits of British Feminists Between the Wars* (1987)

Carol Dyhouse, *Feminism and the Family in England 1880–1939* (1989)

Miriam Glucksman, *Women Assemble: Women Workers and the New Industries in Interwar Britain* (1990)

Christina Hardyment, *From Mangle to Microwave: The Mechanisation of Household Work* (1988)

Jill Julius Matthews, '"They had Such a Lot of Fun": The Women's League of Health and Beauty Between the Wars', *History Workshop Journal*, 30, 1990.

Selina Todd, 'Young Women, Work and Leisure in Interwar England', *Historical Journal*, 48, 2005.

Inez Jenkins, *The History of the Women's Institute Movement in England and Wales* (1953)

Maggie Andrews, *The Acceptable Face of Feminism: The Women's Institute as a Social Movement* (1997)

Nicola Beauman, *A Very Great Profession: The Women's Novel 1914–1939* (1983)

E. M. Delafield, *The Diary of a Provincial Lady* (1930)

Susan Pedersen, *Eleanor Rathbone and the Politics of Conscience* (2004)

Virginia Woolf, *A Room of One's Own* (1929)

Paul Berry and Mark Bostridge, *Vera Brittain: A Life* (1995)

10 'The mills were our destiny'

Hugh Cunningham, *Children and Childhood in Western Society since 1500* (1995)

R. I. McKibbin, *Classes and Cultures: England 1918–1951* (1998)

Michael Sanderson, *Educational Opportunity and Social Change in England* (1987)

Elizabeth Roberts, *A Woman's Place: An Oral History of Working-Class Women 1890–1940* (1984)

Stephen Humphries, *Hooligans or Rebels? An Oral History of Working-Class Childhood and Youth 1889–1939* (1981)

Philip Bean and Joy Melville, *Lost Children of the Empire* (1989)

Vyvyen Brendon, *Children of the Raj* (2005)

John Springhall, *Sure and Steadfast: A History of the Boys' Brigade 1883–1983* (1983)

Nicholas Whittaker, *Toys Were Us: A Twentieth-Century History of Toys* (2001)

Deirdrie Beddoe, *Back to Home and Duty: Women Between the Wars* (1989)

A. L. Rowse, *A Cornish Childhood* (1942)

Katharine Chorley, *Manchester Made Them* (1950)

Andrew Purves, *A Shepherd Remembers* (2001)

Paul Johnson, *The Vanished Landscape: A 1930s Childhood in the Potteries* (2004)

Margaret Railton ed., *Andrew Lorimer's Life and Times in the Upper Tweed Valley* (2001)

William Woodruff, *The Road to Nab End: An Extraordinary Northern Childhood* (1993)

Bryan Magee, *Clouds of Glory: A Hoxton Childhood* (2003)

Laurie Lee, *Cider With Rosie* (1959)

11 'Reminiscent of Negro orgies'

Matthew Hilton, *Smoking in British Popular Culture 1800–2000* (2000)

Peter Haydon, *Beer and Britannia: An Inebriated History of Britain* (2001)

John Burnett, *Liquid Pleasures: A Social History of Drinks in Modern Britain* (1999)

James Walvin, *Leisure and Society 1830–1950* (1978)

Frank Manders, *Cinemas of Newcastle* (2005)

J. A. R. Pimlott, *The Englishman's Holiday* (1947)

Steven Briggs and Diane Harris, *Sun, Fun and Crowds: Seaside Holidays Between the Wars* (2000)

James Walvin, *Beside the Seaside: A Social History of the Popular Seaside Holiday* (1978)

Lorraine Coons and Alexander Varias, *Tourist Third Class: Steamship Travel in the Interwar Years* (2003)

Deirdrie Beddoe, *Back to Home and Duty: Women Between the Wars* (1989)

12 Yellow Earl and Silver Ghost

Martin Adeney, *The Motor Makers: The Turbulent History of Britain's Car Industry* (1988)

Peter Thorold, *The Motoring Age: The Automobile and Britain 1896–1939* (2003)

Sean O'Connell, *The Car in British Society: Class, Gender and Motoring 1896–1939* (1998)

Clive Emsley, 'The Law, the Police and the Regulation of Motor Traffic in England 1900–1939', *Historical Journal*, 36, 1993

Lord Brabazon of Tara, *The Brabazon Story* (1956)

R. Church, *Herbert Austin: The British Motor Car Industry to 1941* (1979)

R. J. Overy, *William Morris* (1976)

13 'Cider With Rosie'

Jeremy Burchardt, *Paradise Lost: Rural Idyll and Social Change since 1800* (2002)

W. A. Armstrong, 'The Countryside' in F. M. L. Thompson ed., *The Cambridge Social History of Britain 1750–1950* vol. 1 (1990)

Alun Howkins, *Reshaping Rural England: A Social History 1850–1925* (1991)

Carol Twinch, *The Tithe War 1918–1939* (2001)

Marion Shoard, *This Land Is Our Land: The Struggle for Britain's Countryside* (1987)

S. L. Bensusan, *Latter-Day Rural England* (1927)

Laurie Lee, *Cider With Rosie* (1959)

Tom Stephenson ed., *The Countryside Companion*, n.d.

Andrew Purves, *A Shepherd Remembers* (2001)

C. M. Joad, *A Charter for Ramblers or the Future of the Countryside*, n.d.

14 'Six penn'orth of hope'

Tony Mason ed., *Sport in Britain: A Social History* (1989)

R. I. McKibbin, *Classes and Cultures: England 1918–1951* (1998)

Richard Holt, *Sport and the British: A Modern History* (1989)

James Walvin, *The People's Game* (1994)

David Winner, *Those Feet: An Intimate History of English Football* (2005)

Derek Birley, *A Social History of English Cricket* (1999)

Mike Huggins, *Horse Racing and the British 1919–1939* (2003)

Mike Huggins, 'Going to the Dogs', *History Today*, May 2006

Mike Huggins and Jack Williams, *Sport and the English 1918–1939* (2002)

Mark Clapson, *A Bit of a Flutter: Popular Gambling and English Society 1823–1961* (1992)

R. I. McKibbin, 'Working-Class Gambling in Britain 1880–1939', *Past and Present*, 82, 1979

Richard Holt ed., *Sport and the Working Class in Modern Britain* (1990)

15 'Wings over Everest'

Robert Wohl, *A Passion for Wings: Aviation and the Western Imagination 1908–1918* (1994)

Robert Wohl, *The Spectacle of Flight: Aviation and the Western Imagination, 1920–1950* (2005)

Keith Hayward, *The British Aviation Industry* (1989)

Kenneth Hudson, *Air Travel: A Social History* (1972)

David E. Omissi, *Air Power and Colonial Control: The Royal Air Force 1919–1939* (1990)

Alfred Gollin, *The Impact of Air Power on the British People and Their Government 1909–14* (1989)

Lord Brabazon of Tara, *The Brabazon Story* (1956)

Lord Semphill, *The Air and the Plain Man* (1931)

Harry Ward, *The Yorkshire Birdman: Memoirs of a Pioneer Parachutist* (1990)

A. Verdon-Roe, *The World of Wings and Things* (1939)

L. J. Ludovici, *The Challenging Sky: The Life of Sir Alliott Verdon-Roe* (1956)

P. F. M. Fellowes, *First Over Everest* (1933)

16 'A talent to amuse'

Nicola Beauman, *A Very Great Profession: The Women's Novel 1914–1939* (1983)

S. E. Koss, *The Rise and Fall of the Political Press in Britain* 2 vols. (1981–4)

Jeremy Lewis, *Penguin Special: The Life and Times of Allen Lane* (2005)

John Lewis, *The Left Book Club* (1970)

Quentin Bell, *Virginia Woolf* (1972)

Mark Kinkead-Weeks, *D. H. Lawrence: Triumph to Exile 1912–1922* (1996)

David Ellis, *D. H. Lawrence: Dying Game 1922–1930* (1998)

Andrew Lownie, *John Buchan* (1995)

Gillian Gill, *Agatha Christie: The Woman and Her Mysteries* (1990)

Philip Hoare, *Noël Coward: A Biography* (1995)

Sheridan Morley, *Noël Coward* (2005)

Victoria Glendinning, *Rebecca West* (1987)

17 'Brideshead Revisited'

David Cannadine, *Aspects of Aristocracy* (1994)

David Cannadine, *The Decline and Fall of the British Aristocracy* (1990)

A. Susan Williams, *Ladies of Influence: Women of the Elite in Interwar Britain* (2000)

Peter Mandler, *The Fall and Rise of the Stately Home* (1997)

Ian Kershaw, *The Marquis of Londonderry* (2005)

S. J. Hetherington, *Katharine Atholl: Against the Tide, 1874–1960* (1989)

Janet Morgan, *Edwina Mountbatten: A Life of Her Own* (1991)

Martin Pugh, *'Hurrah for the Blackshirts!': Fascists and Fascism in Britain Between the Wars* (2005)

18 'Everybody calls him Bertie'

Frank Prochaska, *Royal Bounty: The Making of a Welfare Monarchy* (1995)

Kenneth Rose, *King George V* (1983)

Harold Nicholson, *King George V* (1952)

James Pope-Hennessy, *Queen Mary 1867–1953* (1959)

Philip Ziegler, *King Edward VIII* (1990)

Frances Donaldson, *Edward VIII* (1974)

Rupert Godfrey ed., *Letters from a Prince* (1998)

Susan A. Williams, *The People's King* (2003)

Charles Higham, *Mrs Simpson* (1988)

Geordie Greig, *Louis and the Prince* (1999)

Robert Rhodes James, *A Spirit Undaunted: The Political Role of George VI* (1998)

Sarah Bradford, *George VI* (1989)

Ingrid Seward, *The Last Edwardian Lady* (1999)

A. W. Purdue and J. Golby, *The Monarchy and the British People* (1988)

William M. Khun, *Democratic Royalism: The Transformation of the British Monarchy 1861–1914* (1996)

19 'A Stone's Throw to Australia'

Paul Ward, *Britishness Since 1870* (2004)

John M. MacKenzie, *Propaganda and Empire* (1984)

John M. Mackenzie ed., *Imperialism and Popular Culture* (1986)

Bernard Porter, *The Absent-Minded Imperialists* (2004)

Peter Mandler, *The English National Character* (2006)

Andrew Thompson, *The Empire Strikes Back? The Impact of Imperialism on Britain from the Mid-Nineteenth Century* (2005)

Robert Winder, *Bloody Foreigners* (2004)

Jeremy Paxman, *The English* (1998)

P. J. Cain and A. G. Hopkins, *British Imperialism: Crisis and Deconstruction 1914–1990* (1993)

Ronald Hyam, *Empire and Sexuality: The British Experience* (1990)

Colin Holmes, *John Bull's Island: Immigration and British Society 1871–1971* (1988)

J. H. Grainger, *Patriotisms: Britain 1900–1939* (1986)

E. M. Forster, *A Passage to India* (1924)

George Orwell, *Burmese Days* (1938)

W. C. Sellar and R. J. Yeatman, *1066 and All That* (1930)

20 'No longer part of England'

Paul Ward, *Britishness Since 1870* (2004)

Donald Read, *The English Provinces 1760–1960: A Study in Influence* (1964)

Dave Russell, *Looking North: Northern England and the National Imagination* (2004)

D. J. Rowe, 'The North-East' in F. M. L. Thompson ed, *The Cambridge Social History of Britain 1750–1950*, vol.1 (1990)

R. Colls and B. Lancaster, *Geordies: The Roots of Regionalism* (1992)

William Woodruff, *The Road to Nab End: An Extraordinary Northern Childhood* (1993)

Paul Johnson, *The Vanished Landscape: A 1930s Childhood in the Potteries* (2004)

Katharine Chorley, *Manchester Made Them* (1950)

J. B. Priestley, *English Journey* (1934)

B. Deacon, D. Cole and G. Tregidga, *Mebyon Kernow and Cornish Nationalism* (2003)

Bryan Magee, *Clouds of Glory: A Hoxton Childhood* (2003)

Richard Finlay, *Modern Scotland* (2004)

T. M. Devine, *The Scottish Nation 1700–2000* (1999)

T. C. Smout, 'Scotland 1850–1950' in F. M. L. Thompson ed., *The Cambridge Social History of Britain 1750–1950*, vol.1 (1990)

Andrew Purves, *A Shepherd Remembers* (2001)

K. O. Morgan, *Wales: Rebirth of a Nation 1880–1980* (1982)

D. W. Howell and C. Baber, 'Wales' in F. M. L. Thompson ed, *The Cambridge Social History of Britain 1750–1950*, vol.1 (1990)

Index

www.vintage-books.co.uk